Lecture Notes in Computer Science 2951

Edited by G. Goos, J. Hartmanis, and J. van Leeuwen

T0190219

Springer
Berlin
Heidelberg
New York
Hong Kong
London
Milan
Paris
Tokyo

Moni Naor (Ed.)

Theory of Cryptography

First Theory of Cryptography Conference, TCC 2004
Cambridge, MA, USA, February 19-21, 2004
Proceedings

 Springer

Series Editors

Gerhard Goos, Karlsruhe University, Germany
Juris Hartmanis, Cornell University, NY, USA
Jan van Leeuwen, Utrecht University, The Netherlands

Volume Editor

Moni Naor
Weizmann Institute of Science
Department of Computer Science and Applied Mathematics
Rehovot 76100, Israel
E-mail: moni.naor@weizmann.ac.il

Cataloging-in-Publication Data applied for

A catalog record for this book is available from the Library of Congress.

Bibliographic information published by Die Deutsche Bibliothek
Die Deutsche Bibliothek lists this publication in the Deutsche Nationalbibliografie;
detailed bibliographic data is available in the Internet at <http://dnb.ddb.de>.

CR Subject Classification (1998): E.3, F.2.1-2, C.2.0, G, D.4.6, K.4.1, K.4.3, K.6.5

ISSN 0302-9743
ISBN 3-540-21000-8 Springer-Verlag Berlin Heidelberg New York

Springer-Verlag is a part of Springer Science+Business Media

springeronline.com

© Springer-Verlag Berlin Heidelberg 2004
Printed in Germany

Typesetting: Camera-ready by author, data conversion by PTP-Berlin, Protago-TeX-Production GmbH
Printed on acid-free paper   SPIN: 10986196   06/3142   5 4 3 2 1 0

Preface

This volume contains the papers selected for presentation at the 1st Theory of Cryptography Conference (TCC) which was held at the Massachusetts Institute of Technology during February 19–21, 2004. The theory of cryptography deals with the paradigms, approaches and techniques used to conceptualize, define and provide solutions to natural cryptographic problems. The Theory of Cryptography Conference is a new venue dedicated to the dissemination of results in the area. The aim of the conference is to provide a meeting place for researchers and be instrumental in shaping the identity of the theory of cryptography community. A more detailed statement of purpose ('manifesto') is available on the TCC Web site (http://www-cse.ucsd.edu/users/mihir/tcc/).

The TCC 2004 program committee consisted of:

Ran Canetti	IBM T.J. Watson Research Center, USA
Ronald Cramer	Århus University, Denmark
Cynthia Dwork	Microsoft Research, USA
Yuval Ishai	Technion, Israel
Joe Kilian	NEC Research Labs, USA
Phil Mackenzie	Bell Labs, Lucent, USA
Daniele Micciancio	UCSD, USA
Moni Naor (PC Chair)	Weizmann Institute, Israel
Birgit Pfitzmann	IBM Research, Zurich, Switzerland
Omer Reingold	AT&T Research and IAS, USA
Salil Vadhan	Harvard University and Radcliffe Institute, USA

The program committee chose 29 papers out of the 70 submitted to the conference. Two sets of authors decided to merge, so the volume contains 28 papers altogether. In addition, given recent developments in the field, the committee decided to have a panel discussion on *Cryptography and Formal Methods*.

Acknowledgments : First and foremost I wish to thank all the people who submitted papers to the conference. Without them, of course, there would have been no conference. The hard task of reading, commenting on and selecting the papers to be accepted to the conference fell on the program committee members. Given that this is the first conference of its kind the mission was even trickier than usual. I am indebted to the committee members' collective knowledge, wisdom and effort. The committee also used external reviewers to extend the expertise and ease the burden. The names of these reviewers are listed on the pages that follow. My deepest gratitude to them as well.

I thank Joe Kilian for handling (and writing!) the server for submissions and reviews, as well as Omer Reingold and Edna Wigderson for helping out when Joe was away.

I thank Shafi Goldwasser for chairing this conference and making all the necessary arrangements at MIT. Shafi in turn is tremendously grateful to Joanne Talbot who coordinated the conference facilities, hotels, Web page, budgets, and the conference chair relentlessly and without a single complaint. Thank you Joanne. I thank Mihir Bellare for chairing the Steering Committee of TCC and the members of the committee (see the list in the pages that follow) for helping out with many issues concerning the conference, including the proceedings and the TCC Web-site. Finally a big thanks is due to Oded Goldreich who initiated this endeavor and pushed hard for it.

Rehovot, Israel   Moni Naor
December 2003   Program Chair
                                                                          TCC 2004

External Referees

Masayuki Abe	Daniel Gottesman	Jesper Buus Nielsen
Luis van Ahn	Jens Groth	Adriana Palacio
Michael Backes	Shai Halevi	Erez Petrank
Boaz Barak	Danny Harnik	Benny Pinkas
Amos Beimel	Alejandro Hevia	Tal Rabin
Mihir Bellare	Thomas Jakobsen	Oded Regev
Alexandra Boldyreva	Markus Jakobsson	Amit Sahai
Harry Buhrman	Ari Juels	Jean-Pierre Seifert
Christian Cachin	Jonathan Katz	Adam Smith
Jan Camenisch	Hugo Krawczyk	Martijn Stam
Claude Crépeau	Eyal Kushilevitz	Yael Tauman Kalai
Anand Desai	Yehuda Lindell	Michael Waidner
Yan Zong Ding	Anna Lysyanskaya	John Watrous
Yevgeniy Dodis	Tal Malkin	Douglas Wikström
Marc Fischlin	David Meyer	Bogdan Warinschi
Juan Garay	Ashwin Nayak	Stephanie Wehner
Rosario Gennaro	Gregory Neven	Ke Yang

TCC Steering Committee

Mihir Bellare (Chair)	UCSD, USA
Ivan Damgård	Århus University, Denmark
Oded Goldreich	Weizmann Institute, Israel and Radcliffe Institute, USA
Shafi Goldwasser	MIT, USA and Weizmann Institute, Israel
Johan Håstad	Royal Institute of Technology, Sweden
Russell Impagliazzo	UCSD, USA
Ueli Maurer	ETH, Switzerland
Silvio Micali	MIT, USA
Moni Naor	Weizmann Institute, Israel
Tatsuaki Okamoto	NTT, Japan

Sponsoring Institutions

We acknowledge financial support from the following institutions:
CoreStreet Ltd.
IBM Corporation

Table of Contents

Notions of Reducibility between Cryptographic Primitives*

Omer Reingold[1]**, Luca Trevisan[2]***, and Salil Vadhan[3]†

[1] AT&T Labs - Research. Room A201, 180 Park Avenue, Bldg. 103
Florham Park, NJ, 07932. omer@research.att.com
[2] Computer Science Division, U.C. Berkeley, 615 Soda Hall
Berkeley, CA 94720. luca@cs.berkeley.edu
[3] Division of Engineering & Applied Sciences, Harvard University,
33 Oxford Street
Cambridge, MA 02138. salil@eecs.harvard.edu

Abstract. Starting with the seminal paper of Impagliazzo and Rudich [17], there has been a large body of work showing that various cryptographic primitives cannot be reduced to each other via "black-box" reductions. The common interpretation of these results is that there are inherent limitations in using a primitive as a black box, and that these impossibility results can be overcome only by explicitly using the *code of the primitive* in the *construction*.

In this paper we revisit these negative results, give a more careful taxonomy of the ways in which "black-box reductions" can be formalized, strengthen some previous results (in particular giving unconditional impossibility results for reductions that were previously only shown to imply $P \neq NP$), and offer a new interpretation of them: in many cases, there is no limitation in using a primitive as a black box, but there is a limitation in treating *adversaries* as such. In particular, these negative results may be overcome by using the *code of the adversary* in the *analysis*.

1 Introduction

In most of the current body of work in the foundations of cryptography, cryptographic protocols are not shown to be unconditionally secure, but, rather, their security is reduced to the security of seemingly weaker or simpler primitives. We now know that, if one-way functions exist, then there exist private-key encryption and message authentication schemes, as well as (public-key) digital signatures

---

* Research supported in part by US-Israel BSF Grant 2002246.
** Part of this research was performed while visiting the IAS, Princeton, NJ.
*** Supported by NSF grant CCR-9984703, a Sloan Research Fellowship and an Okawa Foundation Grant.
† Supported by NSF Grant CCR-0205423 and a Sloan Research Fellowship. Parts of this research were performed while at the IAS in Princeton and the Radcliffe Institute for Advanced Study at Harvard University.

and zero-knowledge proofs [14,12,24,21,13]. On the other hand, if one-way functions do not exist then most interesting cryptographic problems, including all of the above, have no solution [15,23].

Some cryptographic primitives, however, such as public-key encryption, key agreement, oblivious transfer, collision-resistant hash functions, and non-interactive zero knowledge, are not known to be equivalent to the existence of one-way functions. Furthermore, several of the known constructions based on one-way functions run in polynomial time but are extremely inefficient (e.g. the construction of pseudorandom generators from one-way functions [14], which is a component in several other constructions). Since these are some of the main gaps in our systematization of the foundations of cryptography, it is natural to ask whether additional primitives, such as public-key encryption, can be constructed from one-way functions, and whether known constructions can be made more efficient. One has to be careful in formalizing such questions. It is commonly believed that one-way functions exist and that public-key encryption is possible, which would mean that the existence of one-way functions *implies* the existence of public key encryption in a trivial logical sense. The question is whether *the techniques that we typically use to prove implications of one-way functions in cryptography* have some inherent limitation that prevents us from deriving the existence of public-key encryption from one-way functions.

Impagliazzo and Rudich [17] were the first to give a formal treatment of such issues. They observed that most implications in cryptography are proved using a reduction, where the starting primitive is treated as an oracle, or a "black box," and the analysis shows that if the primitive is secure in a black-box sense then the constructed primitive is also secure. Impagliazzo and Rudich consider various models of black-box reductions (where there are some additional constraints beyond the primitive being treated as a black box) and show that, in one such model, a black-box construction of key agreement based on one-way functions implies a proof that $P \neq NP$. They also show that in a more constrained model such a construction is unconditionally impossible. The formal framework of Impagliazzo and Rudich has subsequently been used to address other "implication" questions, such as one-way functions versus one-way permutations [26,19], one-way functions versus collision-resistant hash functions [27], and between key agreement, oblivious transfer, public-key encryption and trapdoor functions and permutations [9,10]. Variants of the framework have also been used to address the issue of the number of rounds in KA protocols [25], of the efficiency of constructions of universal one-way hash functions based on one-way permutations [20,8], of pseudorandom generators based on one-way permutations [8] and of public-key encryption based on trapdoor permutations [7].

The common interpretation of these results is that there are inherent limitations in using a primitive as a black box, and that these impossibility results can be overcome only by explicitly using the *code of the primitive* in the *construction*.

In this paper we revisit these negative results, give a more careful taxonomy of the ways in which "black-box reductions" can be formalized, strengthen some previous results (in particular giving unconditional impossibility results for reductions that were previously only shown to imply $P \neq NP$), and offer a new interpretation of them: in many cases, there is no limitation in using a primitive as a black box, but there is a limitation in treating *adversaries* as such. In particular, these negative results may be overcome by using the *code of the adversary* in the *analysis*.

1.1 Impossibility Results for Reductions

The starting point of the work of Impagliazzo-Rudich is the observation that most known cryptographic constructions based on one-way functions treat the one-way function as a "black box." (Exceptions are discussed in Section 1.5.) Roughly speaking, a *black-box (BB) reduction* of a primitive Q to one-way functions (OWF) is a construction that uses oracle access to a function f, and guarantees that if f is one-way then the construction is secure. In particular:

- The construction does not use the code of the function f;
- The construction is well defined and efficient even if f is not efficiently computable (as long as it is given as an oracle);
- There is a proof of security that shows that an adversary breaking the protocol yields an adversary that inverts f.

There are various ways to formalize the third condition (which we make precise in Section 2. One possibility considered in [17], which we call *fully-BB*, is that there is an algorithm that converts every adversary that supposedly breaks the construction (according to the definition of security for Q) into a procedure that inverts f. This algorithm is efficient and it is given oracle access to the adversary and to f. In this setting, both the *construction* and the *analysis* are black box. Another way to look at it is that both the *primitive* and the *adversary* are treated as black boxes. Most reductions in the cryptography literature are fully-BB.

Impagliazzo and Rudich [17] prove that there can be no fully-BB reduction of key agreement (KA) to OWF. Since public-key encryption, trapdoor permutations and oblivious transfer all imply KA (by fully-BB reductions), it then follows that there are no fully-BB transformations of OWF into these other primitives as well. It is natural to ask whether the impossibility is due to the fact both the primitive and the adversaries are treated as oracles, or if it is enough that just the primitive is.

Impagliazzo and Rudich also consider a weaker form a BB reduction of KA to OWF, a form that we call *semi-BB* in this paper. In a semi-BB reduction, we have a BB construction of KA based on a function f given as an oracle. The analysis proves that for every *efficient* adversary with oracle to f that breaks the construction, there is an efficient adversary that inverts f if given oracle access to f. This seems to formalize the notion of a BB construction with an arbitrary analysis, but we argue that it does not. If f is a one-way function in the black-box sense,[1] then the construction has to be secure not only against

---

[1] Meaning that no efficient procedure with oracle access to f can invert f on a nonnegligible fraction of inputs.

efficient adversaries, but also against adversaries that have oracle access to f. A proof technique that makes use of the code of the adversary is not BB in this sense.

Impagliazzo and Rudich prove that, if $P = NP$, there is no semi-BB reduction of KA to OWF. This means that, in order to come up with a proof that OWF implies KA, one must either avoid semi-BB reductions or find, along the way, a proof that $P \neq NP$. Impagliazzo and Rudich prove their result by establishing the stronger (and independently interesting) statement that if $P = NP$, then there is no secure KA in the random oracle model. (Note that a random oracle is one-way in the black-box sense even if P=NP.)

1.2   The Limitations of Semi-BB Reductions

In this paper we prove, unconditionally, that there is no semi-BB reduction of OWF to KA. We prove this unconditional result by embedding a PSPACE oracle into a small part of the random oracle used in the Impagliazzo–Rudich result, and use the fact that $P^{PSPACE} = NP^{PSPACE}$. This embedding technique is due to Simon [27].

Following the lead of Impagliazzo and Rudich, several other works explored the limitations of black-box reductions with examples being [25,27,20,8,9,10]. Most results ruled out fully-BB reductions unconditionally, and semi-BB reductions if P=NP. An exception is the work of Gertner et al [10], which involves a model that is slightly different from the one of [17], and which only rules out fully-BB reductions. The embedding technique allows us to prove that semi-BB reductions are unconditionally impossible in all case where semi-BB reductions were previously ruled out conditionally.

More generally, we show that, under mild conditions satisfied by most natural primitives, semi-BB reductions are equivalent to *relativizing reductions* (proofs that the implication holds relative to any oracle). Since the above works rule out relativizing reductions unconditionally, we obtain unconditional impossibility of semi-BB reductions.

1.3   The Power of Mildly-BB Reductions

Semi-BB reductions have typically been considered to be BB constructions with arbitrary proofs, and negative results about semi-BB reductions have typically been interpreted as limitations for constructions that do not use the code of the primitive. In this paper, we present a different perspective.

We first formalize the notion of a BB construction with an arbitrary proof, which we call a mildly-BB reduction. In a mildly-BB reduction of, say, KA to OWF, the construction refers to an oracle function, and it is secure whenever the oracle function is one-way in a black-box sense, but the *analysis* of the construction may be arbitrary. This means that for every oracle f and for every efficient adversary that breaks the KA protocol constructed from f, there is an efficient procedure that inverts f when given oracle access to f. The difference with semi-BB is that we do not consider KA adversaries that require oracle access to f to be efficiently realized.

A first observation is that if we had a provably secure KA scheme, then it would also be a mildly-BB reduction of OWF to KA: just let the parties ignore the oracle, and then the security of the construction in the real world implies that it is also secure as a mildly-BB reduction.

This means that it is unrealistic to look for an unconditional proof that mildly-BB reductions of OWF to KA do not exist; indeed, most likely, such a mildly-BB reduction exists. However one can still wonder whether the only way to come up with a mildly-BB reduction is to "cheat" in this manner, and have the analysis of the construction contain the proof of a strong lower bound (so that the intractability comes not from the primitive used as an oracle but from the proof of correctness of the reduction).

A similar situation arises in the random oracle model studied by Impagliazzo and Rudich [17]: a secure KA protocol in the real world would also be secure in the random oracle model.

However, Impagliazzo and Rudich show that if $P = NP$ then there can be no secure construction of KA in the random oracle model. That is, the only way to construct a secure KA in the random oracle model is to come up with a proof that $P \neq NP$ along the way.

One might expect that, similarly to the Impagliazzo–Rudich result, if $P = NP$ then there is no mildly-BB reduction of KA to OWF. Perhaps surprisingly, we prove that the opposite is true: if $P = NP$ then *there is* a mildly-BB reduction of KA to OWF. Indeed, such a reduction exists even under the weaker assumption that OWFs do not exist.[2]

In other words, if KA is possible, then there is mildly-BB reduction of OWF to ioKA, and if OWF do not exist then there is also a mildly-BB reduction of OWF to KA. That is, if OWF imply KA in the logical sense (i.e., unless OWF exist but KA is impossible) then the implication can be proved using mildly-BB reductions.[3] The significance of this result is that it shows that there is no inherent limitation (at least in KA versus OWF) in ignoring the code of the primitive, although there are limitations in ignoring the code of the adversary as well.

We similarly show that mildly-BB reductions are as powerful as arbitrary reductions in transforming OWF to one-way permutations, to collision-resistant hash functions, to trapdoor permutations, and other primitives.

---

[2] Actually, the reduction only provides "infinitely-often KA" (ioKA) from one-way functions; see Section 4.

[3] To be precise, our result leaves out the case in which ioKA exist but KA do not exist. Even in such a case, it is possible to argue that for every input length, if OWF imply KA in the logical sense for that input length, then the implication can be established with a mildly-BB reduction. See Section 4.3.

1.4   Efficiency of Reductions

We next turn our attention to another line of research about the limitations of black-box reductions, namely, the *efficiency* of reductions. The issue of efficiency was first raised by Rudich [25], who investigated the round complexity of KA schemes. Rudich proved that one cannot use a fully-BB reduction to transform a k-round KA scheme into a $(k-1)$-round one. Later, Kim, Simon and Tetali [20] considered the question of efficiency of constructions of universal one-way hash functions (UOWHFs) based on one-way permutations (OWPs). The known reduction (of [22]) is fully black box and invokes the OWP a number of times that is roughly linear in the compression of the UOWHF. Kim et al. [20] show that every fully-BB construction must invoke the OWP a number of times that is at least (roughly) the square root of the compression.

Gennaro and Trevisan [8] considered again the question of reductions of OWPs to UOWHF, as well as the question of constructions of pseudorandom generators (PRGs) based on OWPs. The Blum-Micali-Yao construction [3,28, 11] invokes the OWP a number of times that is roughly linear in the expansion of the generator. Gennaro and Trevisan proved that if OWF do not exist, then there is no mildly-BB transformation of OWP to PRG and no mildly-BB transformation of OWP to UOWHF where the OWP is invoked a sub-linear number of-times (sub-linear in the expansion and in the compression, respectively). On the other hand, if OWF do exist, then there are zero-query mildly-BB constructions. This means that the only way of improving current constructions, even with a mildly-BB reduction, is to come up with an unconditional construction and disregard the oracle.[4] Gennaro, Gertner and Katz [7] gave similar results for constructions of public-key encryption and signature schemes. [5]

These results by Gennaro et al. [8,7] about the efficiency of reductions are the only ones that rule out even *mildly*-BB reductions.

Regarding the efficiency of known reductions in cryptography, perhaps the most glaring open question is whether the construction of PRG based on OWF by Håstad et al. [14] can be made more efficient. It was conjectured in [8] that black-box transformations of OWF into PRG have to invoke the OWF a super-linear number of times. In this paper, we show that there is a mildly-BB construction of PRG based on OWF that invokes the one-way function *only once*. This sounds like a great improvement over [14] but, unfortunately, we use [14] as part of our construction. The idea is that if OWFs exist, then we can use [14] to obtain a PRG that is secure in the real world, and then it will also be a mildly-BB

---

[4] Gennaro and Trevisan also show unconditionally that there can be no fully-BB sublinear construction and, using our results in Section 3.2, we get an unconditional result for semi-BB constructions.

[5] In the setting of encryption, they show the following: suppose there is a mildly-BB construction of a semantically secure public key cryptosystem based on trapdoor permutations, and such that the trapdoor permutation is used a sublinear number of times in the length of the message; then one-way functions exist unconditionally. Notice that one could imagine a stronger result proving that the unconditional existence of public-key encryption follows from the same assumption.

construction of PRG from OWF (which makes zero oracle queries). On the other hand, if OWFs do not exist, then we describe a mildly-BB construction.[6] How should we interpret such a result? It seems to say that we should not stop looking for more efficient constructions than the one in [14] and that, in this search, we may restrict ourselves to constructions that treat the one-way function as a black box.

1.5 Perspective

It should be stressed that not all reductions in the cryptographic literature are black box. Many of the examples are constructions that make use of the general construction of zero-knowledge proofs (and variants) for arbitrary NP languages [13], as the [13] protocol makes use of the code of the algorithm that verifies witnesses for the NP relation. For example, when using this result to construct identification schemes from any one-way function [5], the identification scheme makes use of the code of the one-way function and thus this is not a black-box reduction. There are a number of other results in cryptography that make non-black-box use of the starting primitive in a similar fashion. Only recently, however, have we seen reductions making non-black-box use of *adversary* in the proof of security, in the exciting works of Barak [1,2].

Given the fact that non-black-box reductions exist in the literature, one might wonder how to interpret black-box reductions and impossibility results. For this, it is useful to consider an analogy with the role of reductions in complexity theory. The first motivation for introducing polynomial-time reducibilities (e.g. Karp reductions and Cook reductions) was to relate the existence of polynomial-time algorithms for various problems: if problem A reduces to problem B, then $B \in P \Rightarrow A \in P$. Note that here the polynomial-time algorithm for B is used in a *black-box* manner. The constructed polynomial-time algorithm for A only uses the B-algorithm as a subroutine and its correctness doesn't make use of the fact that the B-algorithm is efficient.[7] One can envision non-black-box ways of proving implications of the form $B \in P \Rightarrow A \in P$, and there are examples in the literature (one is mentioned below). Still we find reductions to be an extremely useful concept:

- Reductions provide a natural way of comparing the "complexity" of problems (even when we believe neither problem has a polynomial-time algorithm). For example, SAT trivially reduces to QBF_2 (quantified boolean formulae with two alternating quantifiers) and it is known that QBF_2 does not (Cook-)reduce to SAT unless the polynomial-time hierarchy collapses. Nevertheless, the implication SAT $\in P \Rightarrow QBF_2 \in P$ is known to hold, and indeed it (necessarily) makes non-black-box use of the polynomial-time algorithm for

---

[6] There are again some technical issues about infinitely many versus all input lengths.

[7] Note that the black-box use of the B-algorithm is particularly acute when B is a promise problem, since A must work for all oracles that are correct on inputs that satisfy the promise, even undecidable ones.

SAT. Still we interpret the lack of a Cook-reduction from QBF_2 to SAT saying that QBF_2 as a more "complex" problem than SAT.

– Results showing that certain reductions are unlikely to exist provide a guide for attempts to prove the corresponding implication. For example, it is known that for any NP-complete problem L, there is no *nonadaptive* reduction from deciding L in the worst case to deciding L in the average case (with respect to any samplable distribution) unless the polynomial-time hierarchy collapses [6,4]. Thus, in future attempts to establish a worst-case/average-case equivalence for NP, it is natural to start by looking for *adaptive* reductions.

Both of these uses of reductions also seem relevant in cryptography. It is scientifically interesting to have a framework for formalizing the idea that, say, public-key cryptography is a "more complex" primitive than private-key cryptography (even when we believe both to exist). And results on the non-existence of black-box reductions help guide attempts to establish new implications. For example, our results highlight the significance of making non-black-box use of the *adversary*, as in [1,2], and suggest that it may enable us to overcome some previous barriers. We note that when using non-existence of reductions as a guide for future work, it is important to make the notions of reduction precise and carefully interpret their meaning. Indeed, these are some of the goals of the taxonomy and results presented in this paper.

2   Black-Box Constructions and Analyses

2.1   Cryptographic Primitives

In order to define the various notions of reduction between cryptographic primitives we first need to clarify what constitutes a primitive. The definition we use is quite general. Still, for the sake of readability, we do not state our definitions and results in the most general setting possible. In particular, our notion of efficiency will be that of probabilistic polynomial-time (PPT) Turing machines and we assume that all parties involved in the definition of a primitive (including the adversaries) are efficient. Therefore, our results are *stated* in a way that does not apply to non-uniform or information-theoretic notions of security.

Definition 2.1. *A primitive $\mathcal{P}$ is a pair $\langle F_\mathcal{P}, R_\mathcal{P} \rangle$, where $F_\mathcal{P}$ is a set of functions $f : \{0,1\}^* \mapsto \{0,1\}^*$, and $R_\mathcal{P}$ is a relation over pairs $\langle f, M \rangle$ of a function $f \in F_\mathcal{P}$ and a machine M. The set $F_\mathcal{P}$ is required to contain at least one function which is computable by a PPT machine.*

A function $f : \{0,1\}^* \mapsto \{0,1\}^*$ **implements** *$\mathcal{P}$ or is an implementation of $\mathcal{P}$ if $f \in F_\mathcal{P}$. An* **efficient implementation** *of $\mathcal{P}$ is an implementation of $\mathcal{P}$ which is computable by a PPT machine. A machine M $\mathcal{P}$-breaks $f \in F_\mathcal{P}$ if $\langle f, M \rangle \in R_\mathcal{P}$. A* **secure implementation** *of $\mathcal{P}$ is an implementation of $\mathcal{P}$ such that no PPT machine $\mathcal{P}$-breaks f. The primitive $\mathcal{P}$* **exists** *if there exists an efficient and secure implementation of $\mathcal{P}$.*

Let us elaborate on the semantics of the above definition. It is natural that an implementation of a primitive can be represented as a function $f : \{0,1\}^* \mapsto \{0,1\}^*$. For example, in the case of one-way function, f is simply the one-way function itself. In the case of encryption schemes, f represents three functions: the key generation, the encryption and the decryption functions. In the case of key-agreement and protocols in general, f represents the message function (the function that determines the message a party should send given its inputs, its coin tosses, and the previous messages). The set $F_{\mathcal{P}}$ in the definition of a primitive $\mathcal{P}$ captures various structural requirements for an implementation of $\mathcal{P}$. For example, in the case of one-way permutations we require that an implementation f will be a length-preserving permutation. The set $F_{\mathcal{P}}$ also captures correctness requirements (when they are separated from the security of the primitive). For example, for encryption schemes, we require that the decryption of an encryption of a plaintext m will recover m. For key agreement, we require that the two honest parties output the same key. The structural and correctness requirements of a primitive are usually easy to obtain when we do not insist on security. Therefore, it is not very restrictive to require the set $F_{\mathcal{P}}$ to contain at least one efficiently computable function. Finally, the security requirement of a primitive is specified through the definition of breaking an implementation of this primitive. This is captured by the relation $R_{\mathcal{P}}$. For example, for one-way functions, we would define $\langle f, M \rangle \in R_{\mathcal{P}}$ if there is a polynomial p such that $\Pr[M(f(U_n)) \in f^{-1}(f(U_n))] > 1/p(n)$ for infinitely many n. Sometimes, we will need to work with "infinitely often" (io) analogues of primitives, where the security is only required to hold for infinitely many input lengths, i.e. to "break" the primitive, an adversary must succeed on all but finitely many input lengths. For example, if $\mathcal{P}$ is the primitive ioOWF, then we would define $\langle f, M \rangle \in R_{\mathcal{P}}$ if there is a polynomial p such that $\Pr[M(f(U_n)) \in f^{-1}(f(U_n))] > 1/p(n)$ for all but finitely many n.

We will also need to define the existence of a primitive relative to an oracle.

Definition 2.2. *A primitive $\mathcal{P}$ **exists relative to an oracle** Π if there exists an implementation f of $\mathcal{P}$ which is computable by a PPT oracle machine with access to Π and such that no PPT oracle machine with access to Π $\mathcal{P}$-breaks f.*

2.2 Notions of Reducibility

A *reduction* from a primitive $\mathcal{P}$ to a primitive $\mathcal{Q}$ means that the existence of $\mathcal{Q}$ implies the existence of $\mathcal{P}$. In other words, it means that either $\mathcal{P}$ exists or $\mathcal{Q}$ does not exist. Reductions in the literature usually entail much more than that. For example, a reduction from $\mathcal{P}$ to $\mathcal{Q}$ usually gives a constructive way of obtaining a secure and efficient implementation of $\mathcal{P}$ from one of $\mathcal{Q}$. We now define various such types of more restricted and structured reductions. For comparison we refer to an arbitrary reduction as a **free reduction**.

The most restricted form of reduction considered in this paper is what we call a *fully black-box (BB) reduction*, where the construction and analysis (showing that the construction produces a secure implementation of $\mathcal{P}$ given a secure implementation of $\mathcal{Q}$) are both BB. Most, but not all, reductions in the literature are fully BB.

Definition 2.3. *There exists a* **fully-BB** **reduction** *from a primitive* $\mathcal{P} = \langle F_\mathcal{P}, R_\mathcal{P} \rangle$ *to a primitive* $\mathcal{Q} = \langle F_\mathcal{Q}, R_\mathcal{Q} \rangle$, *if there exist PPT oracle machines* G *and* S *such that:*

Correctness. *For every implementation* $f \in F_\mathcal{Q}$ *we have that* $G^f \in F_\mathcal{P}$.
Security. *For every implementation* $f \in F_\mathcal{Q}$ *and every machine* A, *if* A $\mathcal{P}$-*breaks* G^f *then* $S^{A,f}$ $\mathcal{Q}$-*breaks* f.

The next, less restricted, notion of reduction is a reduction that works even if *all parties* get an oracle access to an arbitrary, possibly *inefficient* implementation of $\mathcal{Q}$.

Definition 2.4. *There exists a* **semi-BB** **reduction** *from a primitive* $\mathcal{P} = \langle F_\mathcal{P}, R_\mathcal{P} \rangle$ *to a primitive* $\mathcal{Q} = \langle F_\mathcal{Q}, R_\mathcal{Q} \rangle$ *if there exists a PPT oracle machine* G *such that:*

Correctness. *For every implementation* $f \in F_\mathcal{Q}$ *we have that* $G^f \in F_\mathcal{P}$.
Security. *For every implementation* $f \in F_\mathcal{Q}$, *if there exists a PPT oracle machine* A *such that* A^f $\mathcal{P}$-*breaks* G^f, *then there exists a PPT oracle machine* S *such that* S^f $\mathcal{Q}$-*breaks* f.

It is tempting to view a semi-BB reduction as a BB-construction with an arbitrary analysis, since only f is treated as a black box. However, as we try to argue in Section 3, the analysis in semi-BB reduction is still very much black box. In essence, this is due to the oracle access that A gets to (the computationally unbounded) f. Since f may be the heart of the adversary A^f that breaks $\mathcal{P}$, the access S has to this adversary is in large part black box. Following is our attempt to formalize what we view as a BB construction with arbitrary analysis.

Definition 2.5. *There exists a* **mildly-BB** **reduction** *from a primitive* $\mathcal{P} = \langle F_\mathcal{P}, R_\mathcal{P} \rangle$ *to a primitive* $\mathcal{Q} = \langle F_\mathcal{Q}, R_\mathcal{Q} \rangle$ *if there exists a PPT oracle machine* G *such that:*

Correctness. *For every implementation* $f \in F_\mathcal{Q}$ *we have that* $G^f \in F_\mathcal{P}$.
Security. *For every implementation* $f \in F_\mathcal{Q}$, *if there exists a PPT machine* A *that* $\mathcal{P}$-*breaks* G^f, *then there exists a PPT oracle machine* S *such that* S^f $\mathcal{Q}$-*breaks* f.

Remark 2.6. A definition that might also capture the intuition "a BB construction with arbitrary analysis" is one where S is also denied access to f. For the sake of this discussion, let us refer to such reductions as mildly $'$-BB. One problematic aspect of mildly $'$-BB reductions is that not only such reductions are more restricted that mildly-BB they even seem incomparable to fully-BB reductions. In particular, for many fundamental BB-reductions known in cryptography, it is not clear if the corresponding implications can also be proven via mildly $'$-BB reductions.

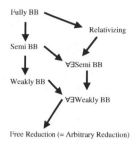

Fig. 1. Simple relations between notions of reduction. An arrow goes from a more restricted form of reduction to a less restricted one.

Related to BB-reductions are relativizing reductions, which turn out very useful in the context of BB separations.

Definition 2.7. *There exists a* **relativizing reduction** *from a primitive* $\mathcal{P} = \langle F_{\mathcal{P}}, R_{\mathcal{P}} \rangle$ *to a primitive* $\mathcal{Q} = \langle F_{\mathcal{Q}}, R_{\mathcal{Q}} \rangle$, *if for every oracle* Π, *if* $\mathcal{Q}$ *exists relative to* Π *then so does* $\mathcal{P}$.

Finally, we consider two additional notions of reductions that are obtained from semi and weak BB reductions by a switch of quantifiers. Previously we asked for a "universal" procedure G that reduces all secure implementations f of $\mathcal{Q}$ to secure implementations G^f of $\mathcal{P}$. But this may not be necessary if we are only trying to show that $\mathcal{P}$ reduces to $\mathcal{Q}$. In the following definitions we are satisfied with the existence of a (possibly different) G for every f (hence the name $\forall \exists$).

Definition 2.8. *There exists a* **$\forall \exists$semi-BB reduction** *from a primitive* $\mathcal{P} = \langle F_{\mathcal{P}}, R_{\mathcal{P}} \rangle$ *to a primitive* $\mathcal{Q} = \langle F_{\mathcal{Q}}, R_{\mathcal{Q}} \rangle$ *if for every implementation* $f \in F_{\mathcal{Q}}$, *there exists a PPT oracle machine* G *such that:*

Correctness. $G^f \in F_{\mathcal{P}}$.
Security. *If there exists a PPT oracle machine* A *such that* A^f $\mathcal{P}$-*breaks* G^f, *then there exists a PPT oracle machines* S *such that* S^f $\mathcal{Q}$-*breaks* f.

Definition 2.9. *There exists a* **$\forall \exists$mildly-BB reduction** *from a primitive* $\mathcal{P} = \langle F_{\mathcal{P}}, R_{\mathcal{P}} \rangle$ *to a primitive* $\mathcal{Q} = \langle F_{\mathcal{Q}}, R_{\mathcal{Q}} \rangle$ *if for every implementation* $f \in F_{\mathcal{Q}}$, *there exists a PPT oracle machine* G *such that:*

Correctness. $G^f \in F_{\mathcal{P}}$.
Security. *If there exists a PPT machine* A *that* $\mathcal{P}$-*breaks* G^f, *then there exists a PPT oracle machine* S *such that* S^f $\mathcal{Q}$-*breaks* f.

Some simple relations between the various notions of reductions are given by the following lemma (and are illustrated in Figure 1).

Lemma 2.10. *For any two primitives* $\mathcal{P}$ *and* $\mathcal{Q}$, *we have the following:*

1. *If there exists a fully-BB reduction from* $\mathcal{P}$ *to* $\mathcal{Q}$ *then there exists a semi-BB reduction from* $\mathcal{P}$ *to* $\mathcal{Q}$ *as well.*
2. *If there exists a semi-BB reduction from* $\mathcal{P}$ *to* $\mathcal{Q}$ *then there exists a mildly-BB reduction from* $\mathcal{P}$ *to* $\mathcal{Q}$ *as well.*
3. *If there exists a semi-BB reduction from* $\mathcal{P}$ *to* $\mathcal{Q}$ *then there exists a* $\forall\exists$*semi-BB reduction from* $\mathcal{P}$ *to* $\mathcal{Q}$ *as well.*
4. *If there exists a mildly-BB reduction from* $\mathcal{P}$ *to* $\mathcal{Q}$ *then there exists a* $\forall\exists$*mildly-BB reduction from* $\mathcal{P}$ *to* $\mathcal{Q}$ *as well.*
5. *If there exists a* $\forall\exists$*semi-BB reduction from* $\mathcal{P}$ *to* $\mathcal{Q}$ *then there exists a* $\forall\exists$*mildly-BB reduction from* $\mathcal{P}$ *to* $\mathcal{Q}$ *as well.*
6. *If there exists a* $\forall\exists$*mildly-BB reduction from* $\mathcal{P}$ *to* $\mathcal{Q}$ *then there exists a free reduction from* $\mathcal{P}$ *to* $\mathcal{Q}$ *as well.*
7. *If there exists a fully-BB reduction from* $\mathcal{P}$ *to* $\mathcal{Q}$ *then there exists a relativizing reduction from* $\mathcal{P}$ *to* $\mathcal{Q}$ *as well.*
8. *If there exists a relativizing reduction from* $\mathcal{P}$ *to* $\mathcal{Q}$ *then there exists a* $\forall\exists$*semi-BB reduction from* $\mathcal{P}$ *to* $\mathcal{Q}$ *as well.*

All relations follows quite easisily from the definitions. We omit a complete proof in this extended abstract.

3   Semi-BB versus Relativization

The study of BB separations in cryptography started with the seminal work of Impagliazzo and Rudich [17]. Previously it was known that the existence of many cryptographic primitives, such as various private-key primitives and digital signatures, reduces to the existence of one-way functions (OWF), which in turn are essentially necessary for all computational aspects of security in Cryptography. Other primitives however such as key-agreement (KA), and thus also various fundamental primitives that imply KA, resisted attempts to be reduced to OWF. Noting that almost all reductions in cryptography are black box, [17] turned to showing that such reductions are simply not sufficiently powerful to reduce KA to OWF or even to one way permutations (OWP).

Theorem 3.1 ([17]). *There is no relativizing reduction from KA to OWP.*

An immediate consequence of Theorem 3.1 is that there is no fully-BB reduction from KA to OWP. At the core of the proof of Theorem 3.1 stands a lemma which states that, relative to a random (permutation) oracle (which is in some sense a "perfect OWP"), there are no KA unless $P \neq NP$. In particular, constructing KA in the random-oracle model is at least as hard as proving $P \neq NP$. In addition, [17] pointed that this lemma "rules out" even less restrictive forms of BB reductions from KA to OWP. Using the taxonomy of this paper, we can state the results of [17] with respect to BB reductions as follows.

Theorem 3.2 ([17]). *There is no fully-BB reduction from key-agreement to one-way permutations. Furthermore, there is no $\forall\exists$semi-BB reduction from KA to OWP unless $P \neq NP$.*

In this section we prove an unconditional version of Theorem 3.2. We generalize this by showing that "usually" $\forall\exists$semi-BB reductions are equivalent to relativizing reductions. This implies unconditional proofs of various results that were previously only known to hold conditionally. Finally, based on the new equivalence between reduction types, we reinterpret the notion of semi-BB reductions.

3.1   Impagliazzo-Rudich Revisited

Based on Theorem 3.1 and using an "embedding technique" due to Simon [27], we are able to strengthen Theorem 3.2 as follows.

Theorem 3.3. *There is no $\forall\exists$semi-BB reduction from KA to OWP.*

Proof. Theorem 3.1 implies that there exists an oracle $\Pi : \{0,1\}^* \mapsto \{0,1\}$ such that relative to Π, OWP exists and KA does not. Let f' be the secure and efficient OWP which exist relative to Π. We define a permutation f such that (1) f is computable by a PPT oracle machine with access to Π, (2) f is one-way relative to Π, and (3) There exists a PPT oracle machine with access to f that evaluates Π. Let us first assume that such an f exist and see how it implies the theorem.

Properties (1) and (2) of f imply that f is one-way relative to itself (since an oracle machine that OWP-breaks f relative to f can be efficiently simulated relative to Π). Properties (1) and (3) of f imply that there is no KA relative to f. This is because an efficient implementation of KA relative to f is also an efficient implementation of KA relative to Π which implies that it can be broken relative to Π and thus also relative to f. Now assume for the sake of contradiction that there exist a $\forall\exists$semi-BB reduction from KA to OWP. Let G be the PPT oracle machine which corresponds to f as guaranteed by the definition of $\forall\exists$semi-BB reduction. From the definition of G, it follows that G^f is a secure KA relative to f. Now, if there exists a $\forall\exists$semi-BB reduction from KA to OWP, then we deduce that there exists a PPT oracle machine S s.t. S^f inverts f. But this contradicts the fact that f is one-way relative to itself.

It remains to define f with the desired properties. Intuitively Π is "embedded" into a small part of f and on the rest of the inputs, f evaluates f'. On a $2n + 1$-bit long input (r, x, σ) where r and x are n-bit long each and σ is a bit, the function f is defined as follows: If r is the all-zero string then $f(r, x, \sigma) = (r, x, \Pi(x) \oplus \sigma)$. Otherwise, $f(r, x, \sigma) = (r, f'(x), \sigma)$. (The definition can be naturally extended to even-length inputs.) That f is a permutation follows trivially from f' being a permutation. Property (2) (the one-wayness of f relative to Π) is also easy as on all but a negligible fraction of its inputs (those with r being the all-zero string), inverting f on a random input is equivalent to inverting f' on a random input. Finally, properties (1) and (3) follows immediately from the definition. □

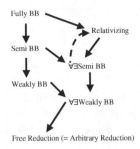

Fig. 2. In addition to the simple relations already shown in Figure 1, the dashed arrow indicates that "usually" relativizing reduction are equivalent to ∀∃semi-BB reduction.

3.2   The General Condition for Equivalence

The equivalence between the existence of a relativizing reduction and a ∀∃semi-BB reduction, is not limited to the reduction from KA to OWP. In fact, essentially the same argument was used by Simon [27] regarding reductions of collision-resistant hash functions to OWP. In general, the two notions of reduction are equivalent for showing a reduction from a primitive $\mathcal{P}$ to a primitive $\mathcal{Q}$, if it is possible to "embed" an arbitrary oracle into $\mathcal{Q}$ as in the proof of Theorem 3.3.

Definition 3.4. *We say that a primitive $\mathcal{Q} = \langle F_\mathcal{Q}, R_\mathcal{Q} \rangle$ allows embedding if for any oracle $\Pi : \{0,1\}^* \mapsto \{0,1\}$ and any $f' \in F_\mathcal{Q}$ that can be computed by a PPT oracle machine with access to Π, there exists $f \in F_\mathcal{Q}$ such that the following hold:*

1. *f is computable by a PPT oracle machine with access to Π,.*
2. *If there exists a PPT oracle machine M^Π that $\mathcal{Q}$-breaks f then there exists a PPT oracle machine N^Π that $\mathcal{Q}$-breaks f'.*
3. *There exists a PPT oracle machine with access to f that evaluates Π.*

The following equivalence is proven in exactly the same way as Theorem 3.3.

Theorem 3.5. *Let $\mathcal{P} = \langle F_\mathcal{P}, R_\mathcal{P} \rangle$ be any primitive and $\mathcal{Q} = \langle F_\mathcal{Q}, R_\mathcal{Q} \rangle$ be any primitive that allows embedding. Then there exist a relativizing reduction from $\mathcal{P}$ to $\mathcal{Q}$ if and only if there exist a ∀∃semi-BB reduction from $\mathcal{P}$ to $\mathcal{Q}$.*

It seems hard to find a natural primitive that does not allow embedding. In fact, the case of OWP is relatively difficult compared to other primitives (because of the need to preserve the permutation property). Therefore, we can informally say that "usually" the above equivalence holds (see Figure 2 for an updated picture which takes this "equivalence" into account). The embedding technique allows us to prove that ∀∃semi-BB reductions are unconditionally impossible in all case where ∀∃semi-BB reductions were previously only conditionally ruled out. Two examples are [25] on reducing the number of rounds in KA and [9] on the relationships among KA, oblivious transfer, public-key encryptions, and trapdoor functions and permutations. In fact, this also holds for the results of [8,7] regarding the *efficiency* of known constructions. In this setting however, it is important to take into account the efficiency of the embedding technique itself. Usually however the embedding is extremely efficient. For example, in the definition of f above evaluating it requires a single oracle query (either to f' or to Π) and similarly evaluating Π requires a single oracle call to f.

3.3   Discussion

It is typical to view semi-BB reductions and certainly $\forall\exists$semi-BB as a BB-construction with arbitrary analysis. However, we feel that the equivalence to relativizing reductions and specifically the embedding technique demonstrate that the analysis in semi-BB reduction is still very much black box. Recall that in a semi-BB reduction from $\mathcal{P}$ to $\mathcal{Q}$, we only consider polynomial time machines A such A^f $\mathcal{P}$-breaks G^f and the requirement is that if such a machine A exists then there also exists an efficient S such that S^f $\mathcal{Q}$-breaks f. This looks less BB than the analysis in fully-BB reductions since S does not get oracle access to A but rather only to f and since we only consider efficient machines A. The reason that this analysis is still very much BB is that the adversary for $\mathcal{P}$ is A^f (which may be very inefficient) rather than A. In particular, the reduction does not have access to a small description of this

adversary (let alone a small circuit that evaluates it). What the embedding technique demonstrates is that often f can be the major part of the adversary A^f, and thus S's access to the adversary is really black box.

4   Mildly-BB versus Arbitrary Reductions

In this section we show various settings for which mildly-BB reductions exist iff free (arbitrary) reductions exist (this is illustrated in Figure 3). In other words, in some settings mildly-BB are as powerful as free reductions. We could therefore concentrate on finding such reductions *which treat the primitive as a black box*. These results also indicate that it is unlikely that we could strengthen some previous BB separations that previously ruled out semi-BB reductions so that they also rule out mildly-BB reductions in the same settings.

4.1   Mildly-BB Reductions from KA to OWF

We now show that if the statement "the existence of OWF implies the existence of ioKA" is true then it can be proved via a mildly-BB construction of KA based on OWF. We note that this means that it is unlikely that we could rule out a mildly-BB reduction from ioKA to OWF whereas [17] and Theorem 3.3 rule out such semi-BB reductions. The equivalence between free reductions and mildly-BB reductions in this context follows from the next two lemmas.

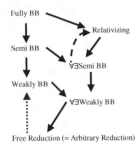

Fig. 3. In addition to the picture given by Figure 2, the dotted arrow indicates that in some interesting cases mildly-BB reductions are equivalent to free (arbitrary) reductions.

Lemma 4.1. *Suppose that ioKA exists. Then there is a mildly-BB reduction from ioKA to OWF.*

Proof. The efficient oracle machine G needed by the definition of mildly-BB reductions simply ignores the oracle f and evaluates from scratch the ioKA which we assume to exist. The reduction is secure as there is no PPTM A that ioKA-breaks G^f. □

Lemma 4.2. *Suppose that OWF do not exist. Then there is a mildly-BB reduction from ioKA to OWF.*

Proof (Sketch). Consider the following construction: given security parameter n and oracle f

- Alice picks at random $x, r \in \{0, 1\}^n$, and sends x, r to Bob.
- Alice and Bob agree on the bit $f(x) \cdot r$.

The protocol does not make much sense in the "real world," but the reader should be reminded that the protocol is only meant to work in case OWFs do not exist, a case in which no KA protocol can exist in the real world.

To prove the Lemma, we will show that if f is a black-box one-way function, then the protocol cannot be broken by an efficient adversary. Intuitively, the reason is that if f is a black-box one-way function, and OWFs do not exist, then f must be a function that cannot be computed efficiently. Using Goldreich-Levin, we can then infer that $f(x) \cdot r$ is hard to predict.

To formalize the above sketch, we need to show that if there is an efficient algorithm that agrees with a function f on an noticeable fraction of inputs, and if one-way functions do not exist, then there is an efficient algorithm that inverts f on a noticeable fraction of inputs. This is somewhat more complicated than it sounds and, in particular, we will need to use a result by Impagliazzo and Luby [16], who show that if one-way functions do not exist and g is an efficiently computable function, then, roughly speaking, given $g(x)$ it is possisble to sample approximately uniformly from the set $\{x' : g(x') = g(x)\}$. We refer the reader to the full version of this paper for the complete proof.   □

From the above two lemmas, we conclude that mildly-BB reductions are as powerful as free reductions for this problem:

Theorem 4.3. *There is mildly-BB reduction from ioKA to OWF if and only if there is a free reduction from ioKA to OWF.*

Next we state a similar result for reducing trapdoor permutations to OWF. We omit the proof in this extended abstract.

Theorem 4.4. *There is a mildly-BB reduction of io-trapdoor permutations to one-way functions if and only if there is a free reduction of io-trapdoor permutations to one-way functions.*

4.2   A Mildly-BB Construction More Efficient than HILL

As mentioned in the introduction, a long-standing open question is to reduce or explain the inefficiency of the construction of pseudorandom generators from general one-way functions [14]. The construction of [14] is a fully black-box reduction that seems to require polynomially many queries to the one-way function even to obtain a pseudorandom generator that stretches by one bit (in contrast to the construction of pseudorandom generators from one-way permutations [3, 28,11], which requires only one query to stretch by one bit).

Theorem 4.5. *There is a mildly-BB construction of ioPRGs from OWFs that makes only one query.*

Thus to show that the inefficiency of [14] is inherent, one must consider more constrained reductions than mildly-BB reductions. In particular, one cannot directly use the approach of [8], which gives lower bounds on the efficiency of mildly-BB reductions. Alternatively, this theorem says that, in attempting to improve the efficiency of [14], there is no loss in treating the OWF as a black box.

Lemma 4.6. *Suppose that OWF exist. Then there is a mildly-BB construction of ioPRG based on OWF, where the construction makes zero oracle queries.*

Lemma 4.7. *Suppose that OWF do not exist. Then there is a mildly-BB construction of ioPRG based on OWF, where the construction makes one oracle query.*

Proof (sketch). The construction is $G^f(x,r) = (x,r,f(x) \cdot r)$, for $|x| = |r|$. The proof that this is a mildly-BB construction is analogous to the proof of Lemma 4.2.

4.3   All Input Lengths versus Infinitely Often

In this section we described various mildly-BB constructions based on OWF, and in each case we are only able to construct the primitive on infinitely many input lengths. We briefly discuss why it is the case, focusing on the construction of KA from OWF for concreteness. We have two cases: if KA is possible in the real world, then we have a trivial mildly-BB construction that ignores the oracle. If OWF do not exist, then we give a construction such that, on each input lenght, the construction is correct provided that every efficient function with related input lenght can be efficiently inverted. Unfortunately, the non-existence of OWF only gives us inverters that work infinitely often. From such an inverter we can only prove that the mildly-BB construction is correct infinitely often.

Note that, however, we are showing something more: roughly speaking, on any input length for which either KA is possible or OWF do not exist (that is, on any input length for which there is a free reduction from OWF to KA) we are able to give a mildly-BB construction of KA based on OWF.

A similar technical problem arises in a paper by Impagliazzo and Levin [18], where the authors prove that a certain strong form of learning (that they call "universal extrapolation") is possible if and only if one-way functions do not exist. Technically, the authors only prove that, on any input length, if OWF do not exist then universal extrapolation is possible, and if OWF exist then universal extrapolation is impossible. As the authors put it, "any given level of technology is capable of either universal extrapolation or cryptography, but not both."

Acknowledgments. We thank Cynthia Dwork, Russell Impagliazzo, Tal Malkin, Moni Naor, and Steven Rudich for helpful discussions, and the anonymous reviewers for useful comments.

References

1. B. Barak. How to go beyond the black-box simulation barrier. In *Proc. of 42nd IEEE Symposium on Foundations of Computer Science (FOCS'01)*, pages 106–115, 2001.
2. Boaz Barak. Constant-round coin-tossing with a man in the middle or realizing the shared random string model. In *Proceedings of the IEEE Symposium on Foundations of Computer Science*, 2002.
3. Manuel Blum and Silvio Micali. How to generate cryptographically strong sequences of pseudorandom bits. *SIAM J. Comput.*, 13(4):850–864, 1984.
4. Andrej Bogdanov and Luca Trevisan. On worst-case to average-case reductions for NP problems. In *Proc. of 44th IEEE Symposium on Foundations of Computer Science (FOCS'03)*, pages 308–317, 2003.
5. Uriel Feige, Amos Fiat, and Adi Shamir. Zero-knowledge proofs of identity. *Journal of Cryptology*, 1(2):77–94, 1988.
6. Joan Feigenbaum and Lance Fortnow. Random-self-reducibility of complete sets. *SIAM J. Comput.*, 22(5):994–1005, 1993.

7. R. Gennaro, Y. Gertner, and J. Katz. Lower bounds on the efficiency of encryption and digital signature schemes. In *STOC 2003*, pages 417–425, 2003.
8. R. Gennaro and L. Trevisan. Lower bounds on the efficiency of generic cryptographic constructions. In *Proceedings of the IEEE Symposium on Foundations of Computer Science*, 2000.
9. Y. Gertner, S. Kannan, T. Malkin, O. Reingold, and M. Viswanathan. The relationship between public key encryption and oblivious transfer. In *Proceedings of the IEEE Symposium on Foundations of Computer Science*, 2000.
10. Yael Gertner, Tal Malkin, and Omer Reingold. Lower bounds on the efficiency of generic cryptographic constructions. In *Proceedings of the IEEE Symposium on Foundations of Computer Science*, pages 126–135, 2001.
11. O. Goldreich and L. Levin. A hard predicate for all one-way functions. In *Proceedings of the ACM Symposium on the Theory of Computing*, 1989.
12. Oded Goldreich, Shafi Goldwasser, and Silvio Micali. How to construct random functions. *Journal of the Association for Computing Machinery*, 33(4):792–807, 1986.
13. Oded Goldreich, Silvio Micali, and Avi Wigderson. Proofs that yield nothing but their validity or all languages in NP have zero-knowledge proof systems. *Journal of the ACM*, 38(3):691–729, July 1991.
14. Johan Håstad, Russell Impagliazzo, Leonid A. Levin, and Michael Luby. A pseudorandom generator from any one-way function. *SIAM Journal on Computing*, 28(4):1364–1396, 1999.
15. R. Impagliazzo and M. Luby. One-way functions are essencial for complexity-based cryptography. In *Proceedings of the 30th Symposium on Foundations of Computer Science, IEEE*, 1989.
16. R. Impagliazzo and M. Luby. One-way functions are essential for complexity based cryptography. In *Proc. of 30th IEEE Symp. on Foun. of Comp. Sci. (FOCS'89)*, pages 230–235, 1989.
17. R. Impagliazzo and S. Rudich. Limits on the provable consequences of one-way permutations. In *Proceedings of the 21st ACM Symposium on the Theory of Computing*, 1989.
18. Russell Impagliazzo and Leonid A. Levin. No better ways to generate hard np instances than picking uniformly at random. In *Proc. of 31st IEEE Symposium on Foundations of Computer Science*, pages 812–821, 1990.
19. Jeff Kahn, Michael Saks, and Cliff Smyth. A dual version of Reimer's inequality and a proof of Rudich's conjecture. In *Proceedings of the 15th Annual IEEE Conference on Computational Complexity*, 2000.
20. Jeong Han Kim, Danial Simon, and Prasad Tetali. Limits on the efficiency of one-way permuation-based hash functions. In *Proc. of the IEEE Symposium on Foundations of Computer Science*, 1999.
21. Moni Naor. Bit commitment using pseudorandomness. *Journal of Cryptology*, 4(2):151–158, 1991.
22. Moni Naor and Moti Yung. Universal one-way hash functions and their cryptographic applications. In *Proceedings of the 21st ACM Symposium on Theory of Computing.*, pages 33–43, 1989.
23. Rafail Ostrovsky and Avi Wigderson. One-way functions are essential for nontrivial zero-knowledge. In *Proc. 2nd Israeli Symp. on Theory of Computing and Systems*, 1993, pp. 3–17.
24. John Rompel. One-way functions are necessary and sufficient for secure signatures. In *Proceedings of the Twenty Second Annual ACM Symposium on Theory of Computing*, pages 387–394, 1990.

25. S. Rudich. The use of interaction in public cryptosysytems. In *Advances in Cryptology – Crypto '91 Proceedings*, pages 242–251, 1991.
26. Steven Rudich. *Limits on the provable consequences of one-way functions*. PhD thesis, U.C. Berkeley, 1988.
27. Dan Simon. Finding collisions on a one-way street: Can secure hash functions be based on general assumptions. In *Proceedings of EUROCRYPT*, 1998.
28. A. Yao. Theory and applications of trapdoor functions. In *Proceedings of the 23rd Symposium on Foundations of Computer Science, IEEE*, 1982.

Indifferentiability, Impossibility Results on Reductions, and Applications to the Random Oracle Methodology[*]

Ueli Maurer, Renato Renner, and Clemens Holenstein

Department of Computer Science,
Swiss Federal Institute of Technology (ETH), Zurich, Switzerland
{maurer,renner,holenste}@inf.ethz.ch

Abstract. The goals of this paper are two-fold. First we introduce and motivate a generalization of the fundamental concept of the indistinguishability of two systems, called indifferentiability. This immediately leads to a generalization of the related notion of reducibility of one system to another. In contrast to the conventional notion of indistinguishability, indifferentiability is applicable in settings where a possible adversary is assumed to have access to additional information about the internal state of the involved systems, for instance the public parameter selecting a member from a family of hash functions.

Second, we state an easily verifiable criterion for a system $\mathcal{U}$ not to be reducible (according to our generalized definition) to another system $\mathcal{V}$ and, as an application, prove that a random oracle is not reducible to a weaker primitive, called asynchronous beacon, and also that an asynchronous beacon is not reducible to a finite-length random string. Each of these irreducibility results alone implies the main theorem of Canetti, Goldreich, and Halevi stating that there exist cryptosystems that are secure in the random oracle model but for which replacing the random oracle by any implementation leads to an insecure cryptosystem.

1 Introduction

1.1 Motivation: Cryptographic Security Proofs

The following generic methodology is often applied in cryptographic security proofs. To prove the security of a cryptosystem $\mathcal{C}(\cdot)$ with access[1] to a (real) component system $\mathcal{S}$, denoted $\mathcal{C}(\mathcal{S})$, one first proves that the system $\mathcal{C}(\mathcal{T})$ is secure for some idealized component system $\mathcal{T}$. Second, one proves the following general relation between $\mathcal{S}$ and $\mathcal{T}$: For *any* cryptosystem $\tilde{\mathcal{C}}(\cdot)$, the security of $\tilde{\mathcal{C}}(\mathcal{T})$ is not affected if $\mathcal{T}$ is replaced by $\mathcal{S}$. Let us consider two examples.

---

[*] This research was supported by SNF Project No. 20-66716.01.
[1] The notation $\mathcal{C}(\cdot)$ means that $\mathcal{C}$ takes as an argument (or is connected to) a system that replies to queries by $\mathcal{C}$.

M. Naor (Ed.): TCC 2004, LNCS 2951, pp. 21–39, 2004.

Example 1. Let $\mathcal{T}$ be a source of truly random bits (secret for two communicating parties A and B) and let $\mathcal{S}$ be a pseudo-random bit generator (with secret key shared by A and B). If $\mathcal{C}(\cdot)$ denotes XOR-based encryption (i.e., $\mathcal{C}(\mathcal{T})$ denotes the one-time pad and $\mathcal{C}(\mathcal{S})$ denotes an additive stream cipher with key-stream generator $\mathcal{S}$), then the security of $\mathcal{C}(\mathcal{S})$ follows from the security of $\mathcal{C}(\mathcal{T})$ and the fact that, for any efficient distinguisher (or adversary), $\mathcal{S}$ behaves essentially like $\mathcal{T}$, i.e., $\mathcal{S}$ and $\mathcal{T}$ are (computationally) indistinguishable.

Example 2. Let $\mathcal{T}$ be a random oracle $\mathcal{R}$, (i.e., a publicly accessible random function) and let $\mathcal{S}$ be a hash function $\mathcal{H}(\mathcal{F})$, where $\mathcal{H}$ is a hash algorithm depending on a public parameter $\mathcal{F}$ (selecting one function from a class of functions). In contrast to pseudo-randomness (where the parameter is secret), no hash function can implement a random oracle in the above sense, as proved by Canetti, Goldreich, and Halevi [6]. In other words, there exists a cryptosystem $\mathcal{C}(\cdot)$ such that $\mathcal{C}(\mathcal{R})$ is secure while $\mathcal{C}(\mathcal{H}(\mathcal{F}))$ is insecure for any hash algorithm $\mathcal{H}$.

It is important to note that the formalization of this second example is more involved than the first. Obviously, a random oracle is easily distinguishable from a hash function if one knows its program and the public parameter, but this fact does not prove the above mentioned claim that a random oracle can generally not be replaced by a hash function. What then is needed to prove this claim and, more generally, similar impossibility results? It is the purpose of this paper to formalize this problem and to provide the answer.

1.2   Random Oracles, Beacons, and Other Systems

In this paper, we will be concerned with the following general question: For given systems $\mathcal{S}$ and $\mathcal{T}$, can $\mathcal{T}$ be replaced by $\mathcal{S}$ in the above sense? A natural extension of this question is whether a system $\mathcal{U}$ can be reduced to a system $\mathcal{V}$, i.e., whether there exists an efficient algorithm $\mathcal{B}$ such that $\mathcal{U}$ can be replaced by $\mathcal{B}(\mathcal{V})$ (in the above sense).

One example of such a system that we will consider more closely is the random oracle. Its importance in cryptography is due to the so called random oracle methodology where the security of a cryptosystem is proven under the assumption that a common randomly chosen function (the *random oracle*) is accessible by each party. This fact is then used as evidence for the security of the corresponding (real) cryptosystem where the random oracle is replaced by a hash function. The methodology was first made explicit by Bellare and Rogaway [2] and has been used in many papers (e.g. [8,9,17,13,2,11,3,16]).

A (binary) random oracle $\mathcal{R}$ can be seen as an infinite sequence $R_1, R_2, \ldots$ of public random bits where any arbitrary bit R_x can be accessed in one computational step. One can also think of weaker primitives where the cost to access the randomness is higher. In particular, we introduce a primitive, called *(binary) asynchronous beacon*[2] $\mathcal{Q}$, defined as a sequence of random bits $R_1, R_2, \ldots$ which

---

[2] The term "beacon", due to Rabin, is used here only in the sense described. In particular, the fact that for Rabin's beacons the randomness is available simultaneously

can only be read sequentially, i.e., the time needed to access R_x is linear in x. A natural question is whether one can implement a random oracle using an asynchronous beacon, i.e., whether there is an efficient algorithm $\mathcal{B}$ such that $\mathcal{B}(\mathcal{Q})$ behaves like $\mathcal{R}$. (Note that for each input, $\mathcal{B}$ could make polynomially many queries to $\mathcal{Q}$ before generating the output.)

An even weaker primitive is a *finite random string* $\mathcal{F}$, i.e., a finite sequence of bits $R_1, \ldots, R_n$ (e.g., accessible in constant time). One could also consider other systems between a finite random string, an asynchronous beacon, and a random oracle, for which the random bits might be accessible faster than sequentially but not in an arbitrary (random access) manner, or where the distribution of the random bits is not uniform. In a sense, a random oracle and a finite random string are two extreme points on a scale, and an asynchronous beacon is somewhere in the middle.

For any two such systems $\mathcal{U}$ and $\mathcal{V}$ one can still ask the question whether $\mathcal{U}$ can be implemented using $\mathcal{V}$. This paper formalizes and solves this problem. We show that, loosely speaking, the answer to this question is characterized by the rates at which entropy can be accessed in the systems $\mathcal{U}$ and $\mathcal{V}$. As special cases one sees that a random oracle cannot be implemented using an asynchronous beacon, and a beacon cannot be implemented using a finite random string. This also proves the main result of [6] as a simple consequence of the fact that a random oracle $\mathcal{R}$ contains substantially more entropy than a finite random string $\mathcal{F}$, in a manner to be made precise.

1.3   Indistinguishability and Indifferentiability

Informally, two systems $\mathcal{S}$ and $\mathcal{T}$ are said to be indistinguishable if no (efficient) algorithm $\mathcal{D}(\cdot)$, connected to either $\mathcal{S}$ or $\mathcal{T}$, is able to decide whether it is interacting with $\mathcal{S}$ or $\mathcal{T}$. As mentioned above, the security of a cryptosystem $\mathcal{C}(\mathcal{S})$ involving a component $\mathcal{S}$ is typically proven by considering the cryptosystem $\mathcal{C}(\mathcal{T})$ obtained from $\mathcal{C}(\mathcal{S})$ where the component $\mathcal{S}$ is replaced by an idealized component $\mathcal{T}$. The original system $\mathcal{C}(\mathcal{S})$ is secure if (a) the system $\mathcal{C}(\mathcal{T})$ is secure, and (b) the component $\mathcal{S}$ is indistinguishable from $\mathcal{T}$ (cf. Example 1).

The notion of reducibility is directly based on indistinguishability. A system $\mathcal{U}$ is said to be reducible to $\mathcal{V}$ if the system $\mathcal{V}$ can be used to construct a new system $\mathcal{B}(\mathcal{V})$ which is indistinguishable from $\mathcal{U}$. Again, reducibility is useful for cryptographic security proofs: If $\mathcal{U}$ is reducible to $\mathcal{V}$, then, for any cryptosystem $\mathcal{C}(\mathcal{U})$ using $\mathcal{U}$ as a component, there is another cryptosystem based on $\mathcal{V}$, namely $\mathcal{C}(\mathcal{B}(\mathcal{V}))$, having the same functionality and, in particular, providing the same security as $\mathcal{C}(\mathcal{U})$.

However, these considerations are all subject to the assumption that the party using such a component has exclusive access to it, i.e., that all other parties, including a possible adversary, are unable to directly influence the component's

---

to all parties, and that future beacon outputs remain secret until released, is not of relevance here.

behavior or obtain any information about its randomness. As described in Example 2, this is not the case for many components. Indeed, while for each party the output of a random oracle $\mathcal{R}$ is indistinguishable from the output of a local random function $\mathcal{R}^{\mathrm{loc}}$, the security of a cryptosystem based on $\mathcal{R}^{\mathrm{loc}}$ (where, e.g., the randomness is used for a randomized encryption) might obviously be lost when replacing this component by $\mathcal{R}$.

In order to extend the definition of indistinguishability such as to include this type of systems, we will propose a new concept of indistinguishability, called *indifferentiability*. Together with its derived notion of reducibility, it will allow for exactly the same general statements about the security of cryptosystems as the conventional definitions. In particular, this means that, first, if a component $\mathcal{S}$ is indifferentiable from $\mathcal{T}$, then the security of any cryptosystem $\mathcal{C}(\mathcal{T})$ based on $\mathcal{T}$ is not affected when replacing $\mathcal{T}$ by $\mathcal{S}$. Second, differentiability of $\mathcal{S}$ from $\mathcal{T}$ implies the existence of a cryptosystem $\mathcal{C}(\cdot)$ for which this replacement of components is not possible, i.e., $\mathcal{C}(\mathcal{T})$ is secure but becomes insecure if $\mathcal{T}$ is substituted by $\mathcal{S}$. Thus, similar to conventional indistinguishability, indifferentiability is the weakest possible property allowing for security proofs of the generic type described above, but it applies to more general settings.

1.4   Organization of the Paper

In Section 2, we give a straightforward proof of the classical separation result in [6] that a random oracle cannot be realized by a (family of) hash functions. While this separation result also follows directly from our general results derived in the subsequent sections, we think that starting with a self-contained proof of this (well-known) example will help the reader to understand the motivation for the definitions and to follow the rest of the paper. Section 4 and Section 5 are concerned with the generalization of the concept of indistinguishability, called indifferentiability, and the corresponding generalization of reducibility, respectively. These notions are then applied in Section 6 to state and prove a general irreducibility criterion, which is used in Section 7 to derive separation results for finite random strings, beacons, and random oracles.

2   A Motivating Example: A Simple Proof of the Impossibility of Implementing a Random Oracle

The following proposition directly implies the separation result as formulated in [6]. Its original proof is quite involved as it is based on techniques like Micali's CS-proofs [11]. Very recently, the same authors [7] showed that their result extends to signature schemes for only short messages. Other similar impossibility results are proposed in [12] and [1].

Proposition 1. *There exists a signature scheme $\mathcal{C}(\cdot)$ (consisting of a key-generating, a signing, and a verification algorithm) with access to either a random oracle $\mathcal{R}$ or an implementation thereof such that the following holds (with respect to some security parameter k):*

- $C(R)$ is secure, i.e., the probability that an attacker against $C(R)$ is successful is negligible in k.[3]
- There is an adversary breaking $C(f)$ for any arbitrary efficiently computable function f. In particular, $C(\mathcal{H}(\mathcal{F}))$ is insecure for any hash function $\mathcal{H}$ with public parameter $\mathcal{F}$.
- $C(\cdot)$ is efficient (i.e., the running time of the algorithms is polynomially bounded in the size of their input and the security parameter k).

Proof. The proof consists of two parts. First, we construct $C(\cdot)$ based on a distinguishing algorithm $\mathcal{D}(\cdot)$ which has the property that the behavior of $\mathcal{D}(R)$ is different from $\mathcal{D}(f)$. Second, we give a construction for $\mathcal{D}(\cdot)$ and prove that it has all the desired properties.

Let us thus assume that $\mathcal{D}(\cdot)$ is an algorithm taking as input a bitstring m (together with a security parameter k) and generating a binary output such that the following holds:

(a) The probability (over the randomness of R) that there exists an input causing $\mathcal{D}(R)$ to output 1 is negligible in k.
(b) For any efficiently computable function f, there exists an input m causing $\mathcal{D}(f)$ to output 1. Moreover, m is easily computable given an algorithm for efficiently computing f.
(c) $\mathcal{D}(\cdot)$ is efficient (i.e., its running time is polynomially bounded by the size of its input m and the security parameter k).

Let $\bar{C}(\cdot)$ be an efficient signature scheme which is secure when accessing a random oracle. The signature scheme $C(\cdot)$ is then constructed by modifying the signing algorithm of $\bar{C}(\cdot)$ as follows: On input m, it first calls $\mathcal{D}(\cdot)$ for input m. If $\mathcal{D}(\cdot)$ outputs 0, m is signed as usual (i.e., by calling the signing algorithm of $\bar{C}(\cdot)$). Otherwise, it behaves completely insecurely (e.g., by revealing a secret key).

It is easy to see that $C(\cdot)$ satisfies the requirements of the proposition: The security of $C(R)$ follows directly from property (a). Furthermore, property (b) implies that there is an input m (efficiently computable by an adversary) causing $C(f)$ to behave completely insecurely. Finally, the efficiency of $C(\cdot)$ follows from the efficiency of $\mathcal{D}(\cdot)$ (property (c)) and the efficiency of $\bar{C}(\cdot)$.

It remains to be proven that an algorithm $\mathcal{D}(\cdot)$ with the desired properties (a) to (c) indeed exists. We give an explicit construction for $\mathcal{D}(\cdot)$ and then show that properties (a) to (c) are satisfied. For the following, assume without loss of generality that the random oracle R is binary, i.e., its outputs are single bits.

Construction of $\mathcal{D}$ $\mathcal{D}(\cdot)$ interprets its input m as a pair (π, t) consisting of an encoding of a program π for a universal Turing machine and a unary encoding of some integer t (i.e., $t \leq |m|$). Let $q = 2|\pi| + k$ (where $|\pi|$ is the length of the encoding of π). For inputs $x = 1, \ldots, q$, $\mathcal{D}(\cdot)$ simulates at most t steps of

---

[3] A function $f : k \mapsto f(k)$ is *negligible* in k if $f(k)$ decreases faster than the inverse of any polynomial in k.

the program π, resulting in outcomes $\pi(1), \ldots, \pi(q)$.[4] Similarly, $\mathcal{D}(\cdot)$ sends the queries $x = 1, \ldots, q$ to the component it is connected to ($\mathcal{R}$ or f), resulting in answers $a(1), \ldots, a(q)$. If $\pi(x) = a(x)$ for all $x = 1, \ldots, q$, $\mathcal{D}(\cdot)$ outputs 1, and 0 otherwise.

$\mathcal{D}$ satisfies property (a). For any fixed program π, let p_π be the probability (over the randomness of $\mathcal{R}$) that for an input m encoding π, $\mathcal{D}(\mathcal{R})$ outputs 1. By construction, this happens if and only if $\pi(x) = a(x)$ for all $x = 1, \ldots, q$. Since, for each x, the random output $a(x)$ (of the binary random oracle $\mathcal{R}$) is equal to the output $\pi(x)$ (of the fixed program π) with probability at most $1/2$, we have $p_\pi \leq 2^{-q} = 2^{-2|\pi|-k}$. Hence, the probability p_l of the event that there exists a program π of length l such that $\mathcal{D}(\mathcal{R})$ outputs 1 is bounded by

$$p_l \leq \sum_{\pi \in \{0,1\}^l} p_\pi \leq 2^l \cdot 2^{-2l-k} = 2^{-l-k} .$$

Finally, the probability p that there exists a program π of arbitrary length causing $\mathcal{D}(\mathcal{R})$ to output 1 is bounded by

$$p \leq \sum_{l=1}^{\infty} p_l \leq \sum_{l=1}^{\infty} 2^{-l} \cdot 2^{-k} \leq 2^{-k} .$$

$\mathcal{D}$ satisfies property (b). Let π be an arbitrary program that efficiently computes f, and let t be the maximum running time of π for all inputs $y \in \{1, \ldots, q\}$ where $q = 2|\pi| + k$. By construction, the values $\pi(x)$ computed by $\mathcal{D}(f)$ on input $m := (\pi, t)$ satisfy $\pi(x) = f(x)$. Consequently, the equalities $\pi(x) = a(x)$ tested by $\mathcal{D}(f)$ hold for all values $x = 1, \ldots, q$, causing $\mathcal{D}(f)$ to output 1. Note that the maximum running time t can be determined efficiently given the program π (since π is efficient). The input m is thus efficiently computable from π.

$\mathcal{D}$ satisfies property (c). The running time of $\mathcal{D}(\mathcal{R})$ is essentially given by the time needed to compute the $q = 2|\pi| + k$ values $\pi(1), \ldots, \pi(q)$. For the computation of each of these values, the program π is executed for at most t steps. Since $|\pi|$ as well as the number t are both bounded by the size of m (recall that t is unary encoded in m), the running time of $\mathcal{D}(\mathcal{R})$ satisfies $O((2|\pi| + k) \cdot t) \leq O((|m| + k)^2)$. $\square$

3   Basic Definitions and Notation

3.1   Interacting Systems

For the representation of (cryptographic) systems, we will basically adapt the terminology introduced in [10]. A $(\mathcal{X}, \mathcal{Y})$-*system* is a sequence of conditional

---

[4] If the program π does not generate an output after t steps, $\pi(i)$ is set to some dummy value.

probability distributions $P_{Y_i|X^iY^{i-1}}$ ($i \in \mathbb{N}$) with $X^i := [X_1, \ldots, X_i]$ and $Y^{i-1} := [Y_1, \ldots, Y_{i-1}]$, where X_i, called the *ith input*, and Y_i, the *ith output*, are random variables with range $\mathcal{X}$ and $\mathcal{Y}$, respectively. Intuitively speaking, a system is defined by the probability distribution of each output Y_i conditioned on all previous inputs X^i and outputs Y^{i-1}. If each output Y_i of $\mathcal{S}$ only depends on the actual input X_i, and possibly some randomness, then $\mathcal{S}$ is called a *random function*. For instance, a system $\mathcal{S}$ might be specified by an algorithm, where, for each input, the output is computed according to a given sequence of instructions. For convenience, we will assume that the systems' inputs and outputs are natural numbers, or, equivalently, their representation as finite bitstrings.

A *configuration of systems* is a set of systems where the systems' interfaces are pairwise connected. Any configuration of systems can be seen as a new system. For instance, let $\mathcal{S}$ be a system with two interfaces and let $\mathcal{T}$ be a system whose interface is connected to the first interface of $\mathcal{S}$. The resulting system, denoted as $\mathcal{S}(\mathcal{T})$, has one interface corresponding to the second (free) interface of $\mathcal{S}$ as shown in Fig. 1(a). In this case, the original system $\mathcal{S}$ is denoted as $\mathcal{S}(\cdot)$, and $\mathcal{T}$ is called *component* of $\mathcal{S}(\mathcal{T})$. More complex constructions are denoted similarly, e.g., $\mathcal{E}(\mathcal{C}^{\mathrm{priv}}, \mathcal{A}(\mathcal{C}^{\mathrm{pub}}))$ and $\mathcal{B}(\mathcal{V}^{\mathrm{priv}})$ for the configuration depicted in Fig. 1(b) and Fig. 1(c), respectively.

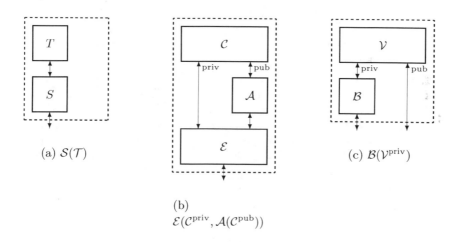

(a) $\mathcal{S}(\mathcal{T})$

(b) $\mathcal{E}(\mathcal{C}^{\mathrm{priv}}, \mathcal{A}(\mathcal{C}^{\mathrm{pub}}))$

(c) $\mathcal{B}(\mathcal{V}^{\mathrm{priv}})$

Fig. 1. Composition of systems.

Many complexity-theoretic and cryptographic properties of systems and particularly of algorithms are defined in terms of their asymptotic behavior with respect to some *security parameter* k. Thus, in the sequel, when speaking of a "system" $\mathcal{S}$, we will rather mean a family $(\mathcal{S}_k)_{k\in\mathbb{N}}$ parameterized by k, where each $\mathcal{S}_k$ is a system in the sense described above.

3.2   A Notion of Efficiency for Systems

An algorithm $\mathcal{B}$ is said to be *computationally efficient* if its running time is bounded by a polynomial in its input size and the security parameter k. Similarly to the computational efficiency of algorithms, we are interested in a certain notion of efficiency for systems $\mathcal{S}$ and constructions based on them. However, since a system $\mathcal{S}$ is not necessarily described by an algorithm, the usual formulation in terms of the number of computational steps is not sufficiently general. A more abstract approach to overcome this problem is to assign to each $(\mathcal{X}, \mathcal{Y})$-system $\mathcal{S}$ a *cost function* c with range $\mathbb{R}^+$ specifying the amount of a certain resource (e.g. time), needed to process an input. For simplicity, we will assume that these costs only depend on the actual input, i.e., c is a function mapping elements from $\mathcal{X}$ to $\mathbb{R}^+$. Additionally, the costs c of a composite system $\mathcal{B}(\mathcal{V})$ must be compatible with the costs $\bar{c}$ of the underlying component $\mathcal{V}$, i.e., for any input x to $\mathcal{B}(\mathcal{V})$, $c(x)$ is at least as large as the sum of the costs $\bar{c}(\bar{x}_i)$ for all queries $\bar{x}_1, \ldots, \bar{x}_n$ sent by $\mathcal{B}$ to $\mathcal{V}$ while processing x.

Similarly to the usual notion of computational efficiency of algorithms, we say that a system $\mathcal{S}$ (or, more precisely, the class $(\mathcal{S}_k)_{k \in \mathbb{N}}$ of systems $\mathcal{S}_k$ with cost functions c_k) is *cost-efficient* if $c_k(x)$ is bounded by a polynomial in the input length $|x|$ and the security parameter k, i.e., $c_k(x) \leq p(|x|, k)$ for some polynomial p. For two systems $\mathcal{U}$ and $\mathcal{V}$, let $\Gamma(\mathcal{V}/\mathcal{U})$ be the set of all deterministic systems[5] $\mathcal{B}(\cdot)$ such that the costs of the system $\mathcal{B}(\mathcal{V})$ are bounded by a polynomial in the costs of the system $\mathcal{U}$ and the security parameter k. This means that, for any $\mathcal{B}(\cdot) \in \Gamma(\mathcal{V}/\mathcal{U})$, the construction $\mathcal{B}(\mathcal{V})$ is as cost-efficient (up to a polynomial factor) as $\mathcal{U}$, and, in particular, if the system $\mathcal{U}$ is cost-efficient, then so is the system $\mathcal{B}(\mathcal{V})$.

We will see in Section 6 that the entropy of the output of a system expressed in terms of the costs to produce this output is a measure allowing for deciding whether a certain reduction is possible. Let the system $\mathcal{S}_k$ be a random function with cost function c_k which is monotonically increasing in its inputs, and let $Y_1, \ldots, Y_{n_t}$ be the sequence of outputs of $\mathcal{S}_k$ on inputs $1, \ldots, n_t$, where n_t is the maximal input x such that $c_k(x) \leq t$. The functions $h_{\mathcal{S}_k}^0$ and $h_{\mathcal{S}_k}^\infty$ are defined, based on two different entropy measures, as

$$h_{\mathcal{S}_k}^0(t) := H_0(Y_1, \ldots, Y_{n_t}) \qquad \text{and} \qquad h_{\mathcal{S}_k}^\infty(t) := H_\infty(Y_1, \ldots, Y_{n_t}),$$

respectively, where $H_0(Z) := \log_2 |\mathcal{Z}|$, and where H_∞ is the min-entropy (defined as $H_\infty(z) := -\log_2 \max_{z \in \mathcal{Z}} P_Z(z)$). That is, for any bound t on the costs c_k determining a maximum input n_t, the quantities $h_{\mathcal{S}_k}^0(t)$ and $h_{\mathcal{S}_k}^\infty(t)$ measure the entropy of the outputs of the system $\mathcal{S}_k$ for inputs $1, \ldots, n_t$ (where the probability is taken over the internal randomness of $\mathcal{S}_k$). Clearly, $h_{\mathcal{S}}^0$ and $h_{\mathcal{S}}^\infty$ are monotonically increasing functions, and $h_{\mathcal{S}}^0(t) \geq h_{\mathcal{S}}^\infty(t)$.

---

[5] The restriction to deterministic systems $\mathcal{B}(\cdot)$ does not restrict the generality of our results. It simply implies that any randomness to be used by $\mathcal{B}(\cdot)$ must be modeled explicitly (by a random system attached to $\mathcal{B}(\cdot)$).

3.3   Cryptosystems and Security

A cryptosystem as well as any cryptographic primitive can generally be modeled as a random system providing interfaces to certain players. Usually, these players are either honest parties or controlled by an adversary. In this paper, we will be concerned with settings where the cryptographic primitives can be accessed by the honest players and the adversary in some predefined way. As an example, consider a publicly accessible resource (e.g., a random oracle or a public random string), where the interfaces to all players are identical. In this case, a possible adversary can access exactly the same information as the honest parties. Another example is a private resource, (e.g., a source of private randomness), to which the adversary is assumed to have no (direct) access at all.

In general, one might want to model situations where the adversary has some partial access to a cryptographic primitive. We thus define a *resource* $\mathcal{S}$ to be a random system with two interfaces, called *private* and *public*, respectively. In the following, we will think of the private and the public interface as being accessible by the honest parties and the adversary, respectively. A resource $\mathcal{S}$ is called *public* if the private and the public interface are identical (i.e., the answers to identical queries are identical).

Let $\mathcal{U}$ and $\mathcal{V}$ be resources. Similarly to the set $\Gamma(\mathcal{V}/\mathcal{U})$, we denote by $\Gamma^{\mathrm{P}}(\mathcal{V}/\mathcal{U})$ the set of deterministic systems $\mathcal{B}(\cdot)$ such that the costs of the system $\mathcal{B}(\mathcal{V}) := \mathcal{B}(\mathcal{V}^{\mathrm{priv}})$ resulting from connecting $\mathcal{B}(\cdot)$ to the private interface of $\mathcal{V}$ (cf. Fig. 1(c)) are polynomially bounded by the costs of $\mathcal{U}$ and a security parameter k.

In the following, we think of a *cryptosystem* $\mathcal{C}$ as being a resource (with a private and a public interface, modeling the access of the honest parties and the adversary, respectively). The security of a cryptosystem $\mathcal{C}$ is characterized relative to an ideal cryptosystem $\mathcal{C}'$ which *by definition* is secure. Obviously, this requires the ability to *compare* the security of cryptosystems, i.e., it needs to be specified what it means for a cryptosystem $\mathcal{C}$ to be *at least as secure* as another cryptosystem $\mathcal{C}'$. The following definition is based on ideas proposed by Canetti [4,5], and by Pfitzmann and Waidner [14,15] (for the case of static adversaries), adapted to our notion of systems.

Let $\mathcal{C}$ and $\mathcal{C}'$ be two cryptosystems, and consider the configuration depicted in Fig. 1(b), where $\mathcal{E}(\cdot, \cdot)$ is a random system with binary output, called *environment*.

Definition 1. $\mathcal{C}$ *is said to be* at least as secure as $\mathcal{C}'$, *denoted* $\mathcal{C} \succ \mathcal{C}'$, *if for all environments* $\mathcal{E}$ *the following holds: For any attacker* $\mathcal{A}$ *accessing* $\mathcal{C}$ *there is another attacker* $\mathcal{A}'$ *accessing* $\mathcal{C}'$ *such that the difference between the probability distributions of the binary outputs of* $\mathcal{E}(\mathcal{C}^{\mathrm{priv}}, \mathcal{A}(\mathcal{C}^{\mathrm{pub}}))$ *and* $\mathcal{E}(\mathcal{C}'^{\mathrm{priv}}, \mathcal{A}'(\mathcal{C}'^{\mathrm{pub}}))$,

$$\left|\mathrm{Prob}[\mathcal{E}(\mathcal{C}^{\mathrm{priv}}, \mathcal{A}(\mathcal{C}^{\mathrm{pub}})) = 1] - \mathrm{Prob}[\mathcal{E}(\mathcal{C}'^{\mathrm{priv}}, \mathcal{A}'(\mathcal{C}'^{\mathrm{pub}})) = 1]\right|,$$

is negligible in the security parameter k.

Similarly, $\mathcal{C}$ *is* computationally at least as secure as $\mathcal{C}'$, *denoted* $\mathcal{C} \succeq \mathcal{C}'$, *if, additionally,* $\mathcal{E}$, $\mathcal{A}$, *and* $\mathcal{A}'$ *are efficient algorithms.*

4   Indifferentiability

4.1   The Conventional Notion of Indistinguishability

Before introducing indifferentiability as a generalization of indistinguishability, we first recall the standard definition of indistinguishability. Let $\mathcal{S} = (\mathcal{S}_k)_{k\in\mathbb{N}}$ and $\mathcal{T} = (\mathcal{T}_k)_{k\in\mathbb{N}}$ be two $(\mathcal{X}, \mathcal{Y})$-systems.

Definition 2. $\mathcal{S}$ and $\mathcal{T}$ are (computationally) indistinguishable *if for any (computationally efficient) algorithm D (called* distinguisher*), interacting with one of these systems and generating a binary output (0 or 1), the advantage*

$$\left|\mathrm{Prob}[D(\mathcal{S}_k) = 1] - \mathrm{Prob}[D(\mathcal{T}_k) = 1]\right|$$

is negligible in the security parameter k.

The relation between indistinguishability and the security of cryptosystems is summarized by the following proposition, which in its generalized form (Theorem 1) will be proven below. Let $\mathcal{S}$ and $\mathcal{T}$ be two resources which have only private interfaces.

Proposition 2. *If and only if $\mathcal{S}$ and $\mathcal{T}$ are indistinguishable, then, for every cryptosystem $\mathcal{C}(\mathcal{T})$ using $\mathcal{T}$ as a component, the cryptosystem $\mathcal{C}(\mathcal{S})$ obtained from $\mathcal{C}(\mathcal{T})$ by replacing the component $\mathcal{T}$ by $\mathcal{S}$ is at least as secure as $\mathcal{C}(\mathcal{T})$.*

The first implication, stating that the security of $\mathcal{C}(\mathcal{S})$ is an immediate consequence of the indistinguishability between $\mathcal{S}$ and $\mathcal{T}$ (and the security of $\mathcal{C}(\mathcal{T})$), is well-known in cryptography. On the other hand, to our knowledge, the (simple) observation that this condition is also necessary in general has not previously been stated explicitly.

It is important to note that Proposition 2 only applies to settings where the resources have no public interfaces, i.e., a possible opponent has no direct access to any additional information correlated with the behavior of the systems.

4.2   Generalization to Indifferentiability

We will now extend the definition of indistinguishability to resources (with private and public interfaces, as defined in Section 3). A first attempt might be to consider a distinguisher $\mathcal{D}$ accessing both the private as well as the public interfaces of the resources. However, it turns out that such an approach leads to a too strong notion of indistinguishability (with respect to Proposition 2). This means, for instance, that there are resources $\mathcal{S}$ and $\mathcal{T}$ which are not indistinguishable (according to such a definition) while, for any cryptosystem $\mathcal{C}(\mathcal{T})$ based on $\mathcal{T}$, replacing $\mathcal{T}$ by $\mathcal{S}$ has no impact on its security, i.e., the second implication of Proposition 2 would not hold.

A notion of indistinguishability overcoming this problem is formalized by the following definition, which, unlike the conventional definition, is not symmetric. Let $\mathcal{S} = (\mathcal{S}_k)_{k\in\mathbb{N}}$ and $\mathcal{T} = (\mathcal{T}_k)_{k\in\mathbb{N}}$ be two resources and let $\mathcal{D}(\mathcal{S}_k^{\mathrm{priv}}, \mathcal{S}_k^{\mathrm{pub}})$ and $\mathcal{D}(\mathcal{T}_k^{\mathrm{priv}}, \mathcal{P}(\mathcal{T}_k^{\mathrm{pub}}))$ denote the configurations of systems as depicted by Fig. 2 (a) and (b), respectively.

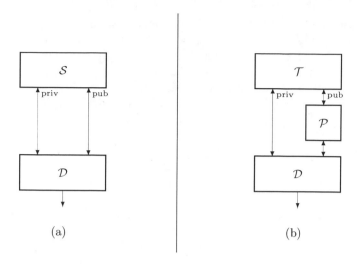

Fig. 2. Indifferentiability: The distinguisher $\mathcal{D}$ for differentiating $\mathcal{S}$ from $\mathcal{T}$ is either connected to the system $\mathcal{S}$ or the system $\mathcal{T}$. In the first case (a), $\mathcal{D}$ has direct access to the private and the public interfaces of $\mathcal{S}$, while in the latter case (b) the access to the public interfaces of $\mathcal{T}$ is replaced by an arbitrary intermediate system $\mathcal{P}$.

Definition 3. $\mathcal{S}$ *is* indifferentiable *from* $\mathcal{T}$, *denoted* $\mathcal{S} \sqsubset \mathcal{T}$, *if for any system* $\mathcal{D}$ *(called* distinguisher*) with binary output (0 or 1) there is a system* $\mathcal{P}$ *such that the advantage*

$$\left| \mathrm{Prob}[\mathcal{D}(\mathcal{S}_k^{\mathrm{priv}}, \mathcal{S}_k^{\mathrm{pub}}) = 1] - \mathrm{Prob}[\mathcal{D}(\mathcal{T}_k^{\mathrm{priv}}, \mathcal{P}(\mathcal{T}_k^{\mathrm{pub}})) = 1] \right|$$

is negligible in the security parameter k. *The indifferentiability is* computational, *denoted* $\mathcal{S} \sqsubseteq \mathcal{T}$, *if only computationally efficient algorithms are considered for* $\mathcal{D}$ *and* $\mathcal{P}$.

Note that indistinguishability is a special (symmetric) case of indifferentiability. Indeed, if the resources have no public interfaces, indifferentiability (Definition 3) is obviously equivalent to indistinguishability (Definition 2).

One important point about our generalization of indistinguishability is that a similar relation between the security of cryptosystems and the indifferentiability of its components as the one stated in Proposition 2 (for indistinguishability) holds. The following theorem shows that indifferentiability is the exact (i.e., necessary and sufficient) criterion needed to make general statements about the security of cryptosystems when substituting their components.

Let $\mathcal{S} = (\mathcal{S}_k)_{k \in \mathbb{N}}$ and $\mathcal{T} = (\mathcal{T}_k)_{k \in \mathbb{N}}$ be two resources.

Theorem 1. *Let* $\mathcal{C}$ *range over the set of all cryptosystems. Then,*

$$\mathcal{S} \sqsubset \mathcal{T} \quad \Longleftrightarrow \quad \forall \mathcal{C} : \mathcal{C}(\mathcal{S}) \succ \mathcal{C}(\mathcal{T}).$$

In the computational case, the same equivalence holds when "$\sqsubset$*" and "*$\succ$*" are replaced by "*$\sqsubseteq$*" and "*$\succeq$*", respectively.*

The theorem implies that if $\mathcal{S}$ is indifferentiable from $\mathcal{T}$ and if a cryptosystem $\mathcal{C}(\mathcal{T})$ based on $\mathcal{T}$ is secure, then so is $\mathcal{C}(\mathcal{S})$, the cryptosystem obtained from $\mathcal{C}(\mathcal{T})$ by replacing the component $\mathcal{T}$ by $\mathcal{S}$. Note that the asymmetry of indifferentiability implies that there is an asymmetry on the right hand side of the equivalence in Theorem 1. In fact, even if security of $\mathcal{C}(\mathcal{S})$ implies security of $\mathcal{C}(\mathcal{T})$, then security of $\mathcal{C}(\mathcal{T})$ does not necessarily imply security of $\mathcal{C}(\mathcal{S})$.

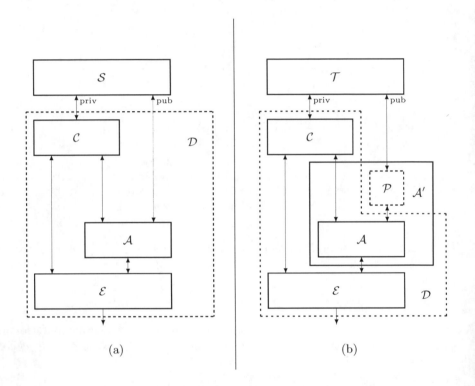

(a)   (b)

Fig. 3. Illustration for proof of Theorem 1 ("$\Longrightarrow$").

Proof. The proof is given for the information-theoretic case, where all systems might be computationally unbounded. It can however easily be adapted to hold for the computational case. To simplify the notation, set

$$d_{\mathcal{D},\mathcal{P}}(k) := \left| \mathrm{Prob}[\mathcal{D}(\mathcal{S}_k^{\mathrm{priv}}, \mathcal{S}_k^{\mathrm{pub}}) = 1] - \mathrm{Prob}[\mathcal{D}(\mathcal{T}_k^{\mathrm{priv}}, \mathcal{P}(\mathcal{T}_k^{\mathrm{pub}})) = 1] \right|$$

where $\mathcal{D}$ is a distinguisher, $\mathcal{P}$ an additional system, and where the configurations of systems are specified by Fig. 2 (as in Definition 3). Similarly, define

$$e_{\mathcal{E},\mathcal{C},\mathcal{A},\mathcal{A}'}(k) := \left| \mathrm{Prob}[\mathcal{E}(\mathcal{C}(\mathcal{S}_k^{\mathrm{priv}}), \mathcal{A}(\mathcal{S}_k^{\mathrm{pub}})) = 1] - \mathrm{Prob}[\mathcal{E}(\mathcal{C}(\mathcal{T}_k^{\mathrm{priv}}), \mathcal{A}'(\mathcal{T}_k^{\mathrm{pub}})) = 1] \right|$$

where $\mathcal{E}$ is an environment, $\mathcal{C}$ a cryptosystem, and where $\mathcal{A}$, $\mathcal{A}'$ are attackers interacting with $\mathcal{S}$ and $\mathcal{T}$, respectively (as shown in Fig. 3). The statement of

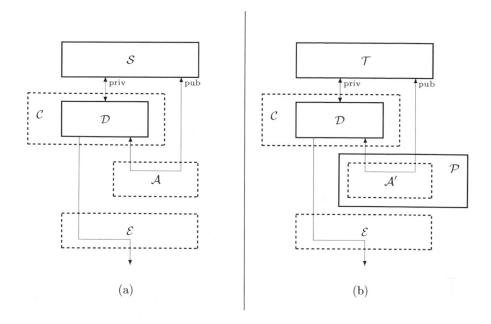

Fig. 4. Illustration for proof of Theorem 1 ("$\Longleftarrow$").

the theorem can then be rewritten as

$$\forall \mathcal{D} : \exists \mathcal{P} : d_{\mathcal{D},\mathcal{P}}(k) \text{ is negl.} \quad \Longleftrightarrow \quad \forall \mathcal{C} : \forall \mathcal{E} : \forall \mathcal{A} : \exists \mathcal{A}' : e_{\mathcal{E},\mathcal{C},\mathcal{A},\mathcal{A}'}(k) \text{ is negl.}$$

The idea for the proof is to relate both sides of this equivalence relation such that $d_{\mathcal{D},\mathcal{P}}(k) = e_{\mathcal{E},\mathcal{C},\mathcal{A},\mathcal{A}'}(k)$ holds.

Let us start with the first implication ("$\Longrightarrow$"). Let $\mathcal{C}$ be any cryptosystem, $\mathcal{E}$ an environment and $\mathcal{A}$ an attacker. Define the distinguisher $\mathcal{D}$ as the system resulting from $\mathcal{C}$, $\mathcal{E}$, and $\mathcal{A}$ being combined as shown in Fig. 3(a), and let $\mathcal{P}$ be the system such that $d_{\mathcal{D},\mathcal{P}}(k)$ is negligible in k. Finally, define the attacker $\mathcal{A}'$ as $\mathcal{A}(\mathcal{P})$ (cf. Fig. 3(b)). The two settings involving the system $\mathcal{S}$ (represented in Fig. 3(a) by solid lines and dashed lines, respectively) as well as the two settings involving the system $\mathcal{T}$ (Fig. 3(b)) are then obviously equivalent, i.e., the probabilities of their outputs are equal. Consequently, $e_{\mathcal{E},\mathcal{C},\mathcal{A},\mathcal{A}'}(k)$ equals $d_{\mathcal{D},\mathcal{P}}(k)$, i.e., $e_{\mathcal{E},\mathcal{C},\mathcal{A},\mathcal{A}'}(k)$ is negligible.

The second implication ("$\Longleftarrow$") is proven similarly. Let $\mathcal{D}$ be any distinguisher. Let the cryptosystem $\mathcal{C}$ be identical to $\mathcal{D}$,[6] and define the environment $\mathcal{E}$ and the attacker $\mathcal{A}$ as a trivial system simply forwarding all queries as shown in Fig. 4(a). Let $\mathcal{A}'$ be an attacker such that $e_{\mathcal{E},\mathcal{C},\mathcal{A},\mathcal{A}'}(k)$ is negligible in k. Finally,

---

[6] Motivated by a construction given in [6], one could also define a more "realistic" cryptosystem containing $\mathcal{D}$ such that, if $\mathcal{D}$ outputs 0, it performs some useful task, while, if $\mathcal{D}$ outputs 1, it behaves completely insecurely by revealing some secret information.

define $\mathcal{P} := \mathcal{A}'$ (cf. Fig. 4(b)). Again, the two settings involving the system $\mathcal{S}$ (Fig. 4(a)) as well as the two settings involving the system $\mathcal{T}$ (Fig. 4(b)) are equivalent, i.e., $d_{\mathcal{D},\mathcal{P}}(k)$ equals $e_{\mathcal{E},\mathcal{C},\mathcal{A},\mathcal{A}'}(k)$ and is thus negligible.   □

5 Reductions and Reducibility

In cryptography one often asks whether a given system $\mathcal{V}$ can be used to construct a (seemingly stronger) system $\mathcal{U}$ which is specified by its functionality. If this is the case, one says that $\mathcal{U}$ is *reducible* to $\mathcal{V}$. The formal definition of reducibility makes clear that this concept is strongly related to the notion of indistinguishability, or, in our generalized setting, to indifferentiability.

Let $\mathcal{U}$ and $\mathcal{V}$ be two resources.

Definition 4. $\mathcal{U}$ *is* information-theoretically securely (computationally securely) reducible *to* $\mathcal{V}$, *denoted* $\mathcal{U} \rightarrow \mathcal{V}$ *(*$\mathcal{U} \rightsquigarrow \mathcal{V}$*), if there exists a (computationally efficient) algorithm* $\mathcal{B} \in \Gamma^{\mathrm{P}}(\mathcal{V}/\mathcal{U})$ *such that* $\mathcal{B}(\mathcal{V}) \sqsubset \mathcal{U}$ *(*$\mathcal{B}(\mathcal{V}) \sqsubset\!\!\!\!\!\cdot\ \mathcal{U}$*).*

Analogously to indistinguishability and indifferentiability, the concept of reducibility is useful for cryptographic security proofs. The following theorem is a direct consequence of Theorem 1 and the above definition of reducibility.

Theorem 2. *Let $\mathcal{C}$ range over the set of all cryptosystems. Then,*

$$\mathcal{U} \rightarrow \mathcal{V} \quad \Longleftrightarrow \quad \exists \mathcal{B} \in \Gamma^{\mathrm{P}}(\mathcal{V}/\mathcal{U}) : \forall \mathcal{C} : \mathcal{C}(\mathcal{B}(\mathcal{V})) \succ \mathcal{C}(\mathcal{U}).$$

In the computational case, the same statement holds when "$\rightarrow$" and "$\succ$" are replaced by "$\rightsquigarrow$" and "$\succ\!\!\!\!\cdot$", respectively.

6 A Sufficient Criterion for Irreducibility

The following theorem gives an easily verifiable sufficient criterion for a public resource $\mathcal{U}$ not to be reducible to another public resource $\mathcal{V}$. This criterion will be formulated in terms of the entropy of the output generated by these resources, as defined in Section 3.

Let $\mathcal{U} = (\mathcal{U}_k)_{k \in \mathbb{N}}$ and $\mathcal{V} = (\mathcal{V}_k)_{k \in \mathbb{N}}$ be two public resources with costs given by $c_{\mathcal{U}_k}$ and $c_{\mathcal{V}_k}$, respectively. For convenience, let us assume that for fixed t, the entropies $h_{\mathcal{U}_k}^{\infty}(t)$ and $h_{\mathcal{V}_k}^{0}(t)$ are monotonically increasing in k. Informally speaking, the theorem states that $\mathcal{U}$ is not reducible to $\mathcal{V}$ if $h_{\mathcal{U}_k}^{\infty}(t)$ grows "sufficiently faster than" $h_{\mathcal{V}_k}^{0}(t)$.

Theorem 3. *If for each $k \in \mathbb{N}$ and any polynomial p the function $h_{\mathcal{U}_k}^{\infty}$ grows asymptotically faster than the function $h_{\mathcal{V}_k}^{0} \circ p$, then $\mathcal{U} \not\rightarrow \mathcal{V}$.*

A similar theorem holds for the computational case. (In the proof given below, the main changes needed to obtain a computational version are indicated.) The proof mainly follows the lines of the proof of Proposition 1 given in Section 2:

It is shown that for any reduction $\mathcal{B}(\cdot)$, there exists a distinguisher for differentiating $\mathcal{B}(\mathcal{V})$ from $\mathcal{U}$. The idea is to let the distinguisher simulate $\mathcal{B}(\mathcal{V})$ and then check whether this simulation corresponds to the behavior of the resource it is connected to ($\mathcal{U}$ or $\mathcal{B}(\mathcal{V})$). By an entropy argument, it can be concluded that this test fails (with high probability) if (and only if) the distinguisher is connected to $\mathcal{U}$.

Proof. It has to be shown that $\mathcal{B}(\mathcal{V}) \not\sqsubseteq \mathcal{U}$ for any $\mathcal{B}(\cdot) \in \Gamma^{\mathrm{p}}(\mathcal{V}/\mathcal{U})$. By the definition of $\Gamma^{\mathrm{p}}(\mathcal{V}/\mathcal{U})$, $\mathcal{B}(\mathcal{V})$'s costs $\bar{c}_k$ are bounded by a polynomial p in the costs $c_{\mathcal{U}_k}$ of $\mathcal{U}_k$ and the security parameter k,

$$\bar{c}_k(x) \le p_k(c_{\mathcal{U}_k}(x)) . \tag{1}$$

Similarly to the proof presented in Section 2, we first give an explicit construction of a distinguisher for differentiating $\mathcal{B}(\mathcal{V})$ from $\mathcal{U}$, and then show that it has all the desired properties.

Construction of $\mathcal{D}$ The distinguisher $\mathcal{D}(\cdot,\cdot)$ for differentiating $\mathcal{B}(\mathcal{V})$ from $\mathcal{U}$ has two interfaces (cf. Fig. 2 where $\mathcal{S} = \mathcal{B}(\mathcal{V})$ and $\mathcal{T} = \mathcal{U}$) which we call $\mathcal{D}^{\mathrm{priv}}$ and $\mathcal{D}^{\mathrm{pub}}$, respectively.

For $r \in \mathbb{N}$, let the min-entropy $H_\infty(Y_1 \cdots Y_r)$ of all outputs Y_i of the system $\mathcal{U}_k$ on inputs $x_i := i$ (for $i = 1, \ldots, r$) be denoted as $\bar{h}_k(r)$, and let l be some positive integer to be determined later. For simplicity, let us assume (without loss of generality) that the functions $\bar{h}_k$ as well as $h_{\mathcal{U}_k}^\infty$ are invertible, and that the outputs of $\mathcal{V}$ are single bits.

$\mathcal{D}$ is constructed as follows: First, $\mathcal{D}$ sends queries $x'_j := j$ for $j = 1, \ldots, l$ to interface $\mathcal{D}^{\mathrm{pub}}$ and stores the received answers $z_1, \ldots, z_l$ (which by assumption are single bits). Then, $\mathcal{D}$ subsequently simulates $\mathcal{B}(\mathcal{V})$ on test inputs $x_i := i$ for $i = 1, \ldots, n$ where $n := (\bar{h}_k)^{-1}(l+k)$, resulting in outcomes $\bar{y}_i$. For the simulation of $\mathcal{B}$, any query $x' \in \{1, \ldots, l\}$ of $\mathcal{B}$ to $\mathcal{V}$ is answered by the corresponding stored value $z_{x'}$. If $x' > l$, $\mathcal{D}$ stops with output 0. The same test inputs x_i are then sent to interface $\mathcal{D}^{\mathrm{priv}}$, resulting in answers y_i. If $y_i = \bar{y}_i$ for all $i = 1, \ldots, n$, $\mathcal{D}$ outputs 1, and 0 otherwise.

The above construction of $\mathcal{D}$ must be modified slightly in order to avoid the following technical problem: The stored values $z_1, \ldots, z_l$ might be arbitrarily chosen by $\mathcal{P}$, in which case they do not necessarily correspond to (potential) outputs of $\mathcal{V}$. The number of queries of the simulated system $\mathcal{B}$ and, in the computational case, the running time of the simulation of $\mathcal{B}$, might thus be unbounded when using $z_1, \ldots, z_l$ as answers for simulating $\mathcal{B}$'s queries. To overcome this problem, $\mathcal{D}$ simply stops the simulation of $\mathcal{B}$ on input x after some maximal number $t_{\max}(x)$ of queries (and, in the computational case, some maximal number $t'_{\max}(x)$ of computational steps) of $\mathcal{B}$, where $t_{\max}(x)$ (and $t'_{\max}(x)$) is the maximal number of queries (computational steps) of $\mathcal{B}$ when receiving correct answers to its queries.

It remains to show that $\mathcal{D}$ satisfies the following properties:

(a) $\mathcal{D}(\mathcal{U}^{\mathrm{priv}}, \mathcal{P}(\mathcal{U}^{\mathrm{pub}}))$ outputs 1 with negligible probability in k.
(b) $\mathcal{D}(\mathcal{B}(\mathcal{V}^{\mathrm{priv}}), \mathcal{V}^{\mathrm{pub}})$ outputs 1 with certainty.

$\mathcal{D}$ **satisfies property (a).** Note that $\mathcal{D}$ can only have output 1 if the n-tuples $y = (y_1, \ldots, y_n)$ and $\bar{y} = (\bar{y}_1, \ldots, \bar{y}_n)$ are equal. It thus suffices to verify that the probability of this event is negligible in k.

Since $\bar{y}$ is fully specified by the bits $z_1, \ldots, z_l$ used for the simulation of $\mathcal{B}(\mathcal{V})$ (note that $\mathcal{B}$ is deterministic) there are at most 2^l possible values for $\bar{y}$. Let $\bar{\mathcal{Y}}$ be the set of these 2^l values. Obviously, y can only be equal to $\bar{Y}$ if $y \in \bar{\mathcal{Y}}$. This happens with probability at most

$$\sum_{y \in \bar{\mathcal{Y}}} P_Y(y) \le |\bar{\mathcal{Y}}| \cdot \max_{y \in \bar{\mathcal{Y}}} P_Y(y) \le 2^l \cdot 2^{-H_\infty(Y)} = 2^l \cdot 2^{-\bar{h}_k(n)} \le 2^{-k} \; ,$$

which concludes the proof of property (a).

$\mathcal{D}$ **satisfies property (b).** We first show that the property holds for l satisfying

$$l \ge h^0_{\mathcal{V}_k}(p_k((h^\infty_{\mathcal{U}_k})^{-1}(l + k))), \tag{2}$$

where $p_k(\cdot)$ is defined as in (1). Second, we prove that condition (2) is always satisfied for l large enough (but polynomially bounded in the computational case).

By the definition of $h^\infty_{\mathcal{U}_k}$, $c_{\mathcal{U}_k}(x) \le (h^\infty_{\mathcal{U}_k})^{-1}(l + k)$ holds for all queries $x = 1, \ldots, n$. By assumption, the costs $c_{\mathcal{U}}$ and $\bar{c}$ (of $\mathcal{U}$ and $\mathcal{B}(\mathcal{V})$, respectively) satisfy condition (1). The costs $c_{\mathcal{V}_k}(x')$ of $\mathcal{V}_k$ for each potential query x' of $\mathcal{B}$ to $\mathcal{V}$ are thus bounded by

$$c_{\mathcal{V}_k}(x') \le p_k((h^\infty_{\mathcal{U}_k})^{-1}(l + k)) \; .$$

Let $x_{\max}$ be the maximal query of $\mathcal{B}$ to $\mathcal{V}$ (i.e., $x' \le x_{\max}$ for all queries of $\mathcal{B}$). It follows from the definition of h^0 that the length l' of the list containing $\mathcal{V}$'s answers to the queries $1, \ldots, x_{\max}$ satisfies

$$l' \le h^0_{\mathcal{V}_k}(p_k((h^\infty_{\mathcal{U}_k})^{-1}(l + k))) \; .$$

By construction, $\mathcal{D}$ outputs 1 if the list of stored values $z_1, \ldots, z_l$ contains the (correct) answers to all queries x' of $\mathcal{B}$ to $\mathcal{V}^{\mathrm{priv}}$ (note that, by assumption, $\mathcal{B}$ is deterministic). Clearly, this is the case if $l' \le l$, which is true if l satisfies inequality (2).

It remains to prove that (2) holds for l large enough: By assumption, for any $k \in \mathbb{N}$, the function $h^0_{\mathcal{V}_k} \circ p_k \circ (h^\infty_{\mathcal{U}_k})^{-1}$ grows slower than the identity function. Hence

$$\lim_{l \to \infty} \frac{l}{h^0_{\mathcal{V}_k}(p_k((h^\infty_{\mathcal{U}_k})^{-1}(l + k)))} \ge 1 \; ,$$

which implies that (for any fixed k) there is a value for l satisfying (2).

7   Applications

7.1   Random Oracles, Asynchronous Beacons, and Finite Random Strings

We will now apply the framework presented in the previous sections to prove separation results for random oracles, beacons, and finite random strings. Each of these cryptographic primitives can be modeled as a public resource $\mathcal{S}$ whose outputs only depend on the previous inputs (i.e., $\mathcal{S}$ is a random function, providing identical private and public interfaces with input set $\mathcal{X} = \mathbb{N}$ and output set $\mathcal{Y} = \{0,1\}$).[7] Each query $x \in \mathcal{X}$ to $\mathcal{S}$ is answered by R_x where $R = R_1 R_2 \cdots$ is a (possibly infinite) bitstring randomly chosen according to some distribution P_R.

Random oracles, beacons, and finite random strings only differ by the length of the string R and the cost function c. For a *random oracle* $\mathcal{R}$, R has infinite length and the costs are $c(x) := 1$, or, alternatively, $c(x) := |x|$, where $|x|$ denotes the length of x. (In the following, we only need an upper bound for the costs of a random oracle, i.e., we will assume that $c(x) \le |x|$.) For an *asynchronous beacon* $\mathcal{Q}$, R is also an infinite bitstring, but the costs for the queries are higher, namely $c(x) := x$. On the other hand, for a *finite random string* $\mathcal{F}$, the length $|R|$ of R is given as a function in the security parameter k which is bounded by a polynomial p, and the costs are $c(x) := C$ for some constant C. Moreover, for any query on input x with $x > |R|$ the output is 0. In the following, we say that a random oracle, beacon, or finite random string is *uniform* if R is uniformly distributed, and denote these objects as $\overline{\mathcal{R}}$, $\overline{\mathcal{Q}}$, and $\overline{\mathcal{F}}$, respectively.

7.2   Impossibility Results

It is obvious that an asynchronous beacon can always be reduced to a random oracle (using an algorithm which merely passes on the inputs and outputs) and that a finite random string can always be reduced to a beacon (using the same trivial algorithm which additionally checks that the input is not larger than some predefined bound). The inverse reductions are, however, not possible.

Theorem 4. *The following irreducibility results hold for both the information-theoretic and the computational case (where "$\not\rightarrow$" is replaced by "$\not\Leftarrow$"):*

$$\overline{\mathcal{R}} \not\rightarrow \mathcal{Q} \qquad and \qquad \overline{\mathcal{Q}} \not\rightarrow \mathcal{F}.$$

Proof. The main task required for the proof of this theorem is the computation of the entropies according to the definitions in Section 3. The assertion then

---

[7] We will assume that the outputs of random oracles, beacons and finite random strings are single bits. This entails no restriction of generality since any of these random functions providing outputs of some length l can efficiently be reduced to a corresponding random function with outputs of length 1 (as long as l grows only polynomially in the security parameter k).

follows directly from Theorem 3. For a random oracle, we obtain

$$h_{\overline{\mathcal{R}}_k}^{\infty}(t) = h_{\mathcal{R}_k}^0(t) \geq \sum_{i=1}^{t} 2^i = 2^{t+1} - 2,$$

and similarly, for an asynchronous beacon,

$$h_{\overline{\mathcal{Q}}_k}^{\infty}(t) = h_{\mathcal{Q}_k}^0(t) = t$$

(independently of $k \in \mathbb{N}$). Since for a finite random string the length of R is given by a function in the security parameter k which is bounded by a polynomial p in k, we have

$$h_{\overline{\mathcal{F}}_k}^{\infty}(t) = h_{\mathcal{F}_k}^0(t) \leq \begin{cases} 0 & \text{if } t < C \\ p(k) & \text{otherwise.} \end{cases}$$

(for all $k \in \mathbb{N}$). Note that the above expressions for $h_{\mathcal{R}_k}^0$, $h_{\mathcal{Q}_k}^0$ and $h_{\mathcal{F}_k}^0$ also hold if the respective systems are not uniform. □

Together with Theorem 2, one can conclude that a random oracle in general can not be replaced by any algorithm interacting with an asynchronous beacon, and similarly, a beacon can not be replaced by any algorithm interacting with a public finite random string without affecting the security of an underlying cryptosystem. The failure of the random oracle methodology can thus be seen as a direct consequence of each of the two irreducibility results of Theorem 4.

8   Conclusions

One crucial motivation for introducing the notion of indifferentiability is that it characterizes exactly when one can replace a subsystem of a cryptosystem by another subsystem without affecting the security. In contrast to indistinguishability, indifferentiability is applicable in the important case of settings where a possible adversary is assumed to have access to additional information about a system. This generality is for instance crucial in the setting of the random oracle methodology, and our abstract framework yields as a simple consequence, actually of each of two different impossibility results, the impossibility result by Canetti, Goldreich and Halevi [6] stating that random oracles can not be implemented. In view of the highly involved arguments of [6] based on CS-proofs, we hope to have presented a more generic approach to arguing about such impossibility results, thus also applicable in other contexts where systems have public parameters or where an adversary can obtain side-information about secret parameters.

References

1. M. Bellare, A. Boldyreva, and A. Palacio. An un-instantiable random-oracle-model scheme for a hybrid-encryption problem. ePrint archive: http://eprint.iacr.org/2003/077/, 2003.

2. M. Bellare and P. Rogaway. Random oracles are practical: a paradigm for designing efficient protocols. In V. Ashby, editor, *1st ACM Conference on Computer and Communications Security*, pages 62–73. ACM Press, 1993.

3. M. Bellare and P. Rogaway. The exact security of digital signatures: How to sign with RSA and Rabin. In *Advances in Cryptology — EUROCRYPT'96*, volume 1070 of *Lecture Notes in Computer Science*, pages 399–416. Springer-Verlag, 1996.

4. R. Canetti. Security and composition of multi-party cryptographic protocols. *Journal of Cryptology*, 13(1):143–202, 2000.

5. R. Canetti. Universally composable security: A new paradigm for cryptographic protocols. In *Proc. 42nd IEEE Symposium on Foundations of Computer Science (FOCS)*, pages 136–145, 2001.

6. R. Canetti, O. Goldreich, and S. Halevi. The random oracle methodology, revisited. In *Proceedings of the 30th Annual ACM Symposium on the Theory of Computing*, pages 209–218. ACM Press, 1998.

7. R. Canetti, O. Goldreich, and S. Halevi. On the random-oracle methodology as applied to length-restricted signature schemes. ePrint archive: http://eprint.iacr.org/2003/150/, 2003.

8. A. Fiat and A. Shamir. How to prove yourself. Practical solutions to identification and signature problems. In *Advances in Cryptology — CRYPTO'86*, volume 263 of *Lecture Notes in Computer Science*, pages 186–189. Springer-Verlag, 1986.

9. L. Guillou and J. Quisquater. A practical zero-knowledge protocol fitted to security microprocessors minimizing both transmission and memory. In *Advances in Cryptology — EUROCRYPT'88*, volume 330 of *Lecture Notes in Computer Science*, pages 123–128. Springer-Verlag, 1988.

10. U. Maurer. Indistinguishability of random systems. In *Advances in Cryptology — EUROCRYPT '02*, volume 2332 of *Lecture Notes in Computer Science*, pages 110–132. Springer-Verlag, 2002.

11. S. Micali. CS proofs. In *Proc. 35th Annual Symposium on Foundations of Computer Science (FOCS)*, pages 436–453. IEEE, 1994.

12. J. B. Nielsen. Separating random oracle proofs from complexity theoretic proofs: the non-committing encryption case. In *Advances in Cryptology - CRYPTO 2002*, volume 2442 of *Lecture Notes in Computer Science*, pages 111–126. Springer-Verlag, 2002.

13. T. Okamoto. Provably secure and practical identification scheme and corresponding signature scheme. In *Advances in Cryptology — CRYPTO'92*, volume 740 of *Lecture Notes in Computer Science*, pages 31–53. Springer-Verlag, 1992.

14. B. Pfitzmann and M. Waidner. Composition and integrity preservation of secure reactive systems. In *7th ACM Conference on Computer and Communications Security*, pages 245–254. ACM Press, 2000.

15. B. Pfitzmann and M. Waidner. A model for asynchronous reactive systems and its application to secure message transmission. In *IEEE Symposium on Security and Privacy*, pages 184–200. IEEE Computer Society Press, 2001.

16. D. Pointcheval and J. Stern. Security proofs for signature schemes. In *Advances in Cryptology — EUROCRYPT'96*, volume 1070 of *Lecture Notes in Computer Science*, pages 387–398. Springer-Verlag, 1996.

17. C. Schnorr. Efficient signature generation by smart cards. *Journal of Cryptology*, 4(3):161–174, 1991.

On the Random-Oracle Methodology as Applied to Length-Restricted Signature Schemes

Ran Canetti[1], Oded Goldreich[2], and Shai Halevi[1]

[1] IBM T.J. Watson Research Center, Hawthorne, NY, USA
{canetti,shaih}@watson.ibm.com
[2] Department of Computer Science, Weizmann Institute of Science, Rehovot, ISRAEL.
oded@wisdom.weizmann.ac.il

Abstract. In earlier work, we described a "pathological" example of a signature scheme that is secure in the Random Oracle Model, but for which no secure implementation exists. For that example, however, it was crucial that the scheme is able to sign "long messages" (i.e., messages whose length is not a-priori bounded). This left open the possibility that the Random Oracle Methodology is sound with respect to signature schemes that sign only "short" messages (i.e., messages of a-priori bounded length, smaller than the length of the keys in use), and are "memoryless" (i.e., the only thing kept between different signature generations is the initial signing-key). In this work, we extend our negative result to address such signature schemes. A key ingredient in our proof is a new type of interactive proof systems, which may be of independent interest.

1 Introduction

A popular methodology for designing cryptographic protocols consists of the following two steps. One first designs an *ideal* system in which all parties (including the adversary) have oracle access to a truly random function, and proves the security of this ideal system. Next, one replaces the random oracle by a "good cryptographic hashing function" such as MD5 or SHA, providing all parties (including the adversary) with a succinct description of this function. Thus, one obtains an *implementation* of the ideal system in a "real-world" where random oracles do not exist. This methodology, explicitly formulated by Bellare and Rogaway [1] and hereafter referred to as the *random oracle methodology*, has been used in many works (see some references in [5]).

In our earlier work [5] we investigated the relationship between the security of cryptographic schemes in the Random Oracle Model, and the security of the schemes that result from implementing the random oracle by so called "cryptographic hash functions". In particular, we demonstrated the existence of "pathological" signature schemes that are secure in the Random Oracle Model, but for which no secure implementation exists. However, one feature of these signature schemes was that they were required to sign "long messages", in particular messages that are longer than the length of the public verification-key.

M. Naor (Ed.): TCC 2004, LNCS 2951, pp. 40–57, 2004.
© Springer-Verlag Berlin Heidelberg 2004

Thus, that work left open the possibility that the Random Oracle Methodology may still be sound with respect to limited schemes that only sign "short messages" (i.e., messages that are significantly shorter than the length of the public verification-key). In this work we extend the negative result of [5] and show that it holds also with respect to signature schemes that are memoryless, and in addition are only required to sign "short messages". That is:

Theorem. 1 (sketch) *There exists a memoryless (i.e., ordinary) signature scheme that is secure in the Random Oracle Model, but has no secure implementations by function ensembles. Furthermore, insecurity is demonstrated by an attack in which the scheme is only applied to messages of poly-logarithmic length (in the security parameter).*

Indeed, the improvement of Theorem 1 over the corresponding result of [5] is only in the "furthermore" clause.

Our proof extends the technique from [5] of constructing these "pathological" signature schemes. Intuitively, in these schemes the signer first checks whether the message to be signed contains a "proof of the non-randomness of the oracle". If the signer is convinced it performs some highly disastrous action, and otherwise it just employs some secure signature scheme. Such a scheme will be secure in the Random Oracle Model, since the the signer is unlikely to be convinced that its oracle is not random. In a "real world implementation" of the scheme, on the other hand, the oracle is completely specified by a portion of the public verification-key. The attacker, who has access to this specification, can use it to convince the signer that this oracle is not random, thus breaking the scheme. The "proof of non-randomness" that was used in [5] was non-interactive, and its length was longer than the verification-key, which is the reason that it is not applicable to "short messages". The crux of our extension is a new type of interactive proof systems, employing a stateless verifier and short messages, which may be of independent interest.

To prove "non-randomness" of a function, we would like to show that there exists a program that can predict the value of this function at "sufficiently many" points. However, it seems that such proof must be at least as long as said program. In our application, the proof needs to predict a function described in a portion of the verification-key, hence it needs to be of length comparable to that portion. But we want a signature scheme that only signs short messages, so the attacker (prover) cannot submit to the signer (verifier) such a long proof in just one message. It follows that we must use many messages to describe the proof, or in other words, we must have a long interaction. But recall that in our application, the proof has to be received and verified by the signing device, which by standard definitions is stateless.[1] Thus, the essence of what we need is an interactive proof with a stateless verifier.

At a first glance, this last notion may not seem interesting. What good is an interaction if the verifier cannot remember any of it? If it didn't accept after

---

[1] Indeed, the statelessness condition is the reason that a non-interactive information transfer seems a natural choice, but in the current work we are unwilling to pay the cost in terms of message length.

the prover's first message, why would it accept after the second? What makes this approach workable is the observation that *the verifier's state can be kept by the prover*, as long as the verifier has some means of authenticating this state. What we do is let the verifier (i.e., signer) emulate a computation of a Turing machine M (which in turn verifies a proof provided by the prover), and do so in an authenticated manner. The messages presented to the verifier will have the form (cc, σ, aux), where cc is a compressed version of an instantaneous configuration of the machine, σ is a "signature on cc", and aux is an auxiliary information to be used in the generation of a compressed version of the next configuration. If the signature is valid then the verifier will respond with the triple (cc', σ', aux'), where cc' is a compressed version of the next configuration, σ' is a "signature on cc'", and aux' is an auxiliary information regarding its update.

Relation to the Adversarial-Memory Model. Our approach of emulating a computation by interaction between a memoryless verifier and an untrusted prover is reminiscent of the interaction between a CPU and an adversarially-controlled memory in the works of Goldreich and Ostrovsky [7] and Blum et al. [2]. Indeed, the technique that we use in this paper to authenticate the state is very close to the "on line checker" of Blum et al. However, our problem still seems quite different than theirs. On the one hand, our verifier cannot maintain state between interactions, whereas the CPUs in both the works from above maintain a small (updatable) state. On the other hand, our authenticity requirement is weaker than in [7,2], in that our solution allows the adversary to "roll back" the memory to a previous state. (Also, a main concern of [7], which is not required in our context, is hiding the "memory-access structure" from the adversary.)

Organization. We first present our interactive proof with stateless verifier while taking advantage of several specific features of our application: We start with an overview (Section 2), and provide the details in Section 3. In Section 4 we then sketch a more general treatment of this kind of interactive proofs.

2   Overview of Our Approach

On a high level, the negative result in our earlier work [5] can be described as starting from a secure signature scheme in the Random Oracle Model, and modifying it as follows: The signer in the original scheme was interacting with some oracle (which was random in the Random Oracle Model, but implemented by some function ensemble in the "real world"). In the modified scheme, the signer examines each message before it signs it, looking for a "proof" that its oracle is not random. If it finds such a convincing "proof" it does some obviously stupid thing, like outputting the secret key. Otherwise, it reverts to the original (secure) scheme. Hence, the crucial step in the construction is to exhibit a "proof" as above. Namely, we have a prover and a verifier, both polynomial-time interactive machines with access to an oracle, such that the following holds:

- When the oracle is a truly random function, the verifier rejects with over-whelming probability, regardless of what the prover does. (The probability is taken also over the choice of the oracle.)
- For any polynomial-time function ensemble,[2] there is a polynomial-time prover that causes the verifier to accept with noticeable probability, when the oracle is implemented by a random member of that ensemble. In this case, the prover receives a full description of the function used in the role of the oracle. (In our application, this description is part of the verification-key in the corresponding implementation of the signature scheme.)

In [5] we used correlation-intractable functions to devise such a proof system.[3] However, simpler constructions can be obtained. For example, when the oracle is implemented by a polynomial-time function ensemble, the prover could essentially just send to the verifier the description of the function that implements the oracle. The verifier can then evaluate that function on several inputs, and compare the outputs to the responses that it gets from the oracle. If the outputs match for sufficiently many inputs (where sufficiently many means more that the length of the description), then the verifier concludes that the oracle cannot be a random function. Indeed, roughly this simplified proof was proposed by Holenstein, Maurer, and Renner [10]. We remark that both our original proof and the simplified proof of Holenstein et al., are *non-interactive* proofs of non-randomness: The prover just sends one string to the verifier, thus convincing it that its oracle is not a random function.

However, implementing the proof in this manner implies that the attacker must send to the verifier a complete description of the function, which in our application may be almost as long as the verification-key. In terms of the resulting "pathological example", this means that the signature scheme that we construct must accept long enough messages.

Clearly, one can do away with the need for long messages, if we allow the signature scheme to "keep history" and pass some evolving state from one signature to the next. In that case the attacker can feed the long proof to the scheme bit by bit, and the scheme would only act on it once its history gets long enough. In particular, this means that the signature scheme will not only maintain a state (between signatures) but rather maintain a state of a-priori unbounded length. Thus, the negative result will refer only to such signature schemes, while we seek to present a negative result that refers also to stateless signature scheme, and in particular to ones that only sign "short messages".

---

[2] A polynomial-time function ensemble is a sequence $\mathcal{F} = \{F_k\}_{k \in N}$ of families of functions, $F_k = \{f_s : \{0,1\}^* \to \{0,1\}^{\ell_{\mathrm{out}}(k)}\}_{s \in \{0,1\}^k}$, such that there exists a polynomial-time algorithm that given s and x returns $f_s(x)$. In the sequel we often call s the description or the seed of the function f_s.

[3] We used (non-interactive) CS-proofs (cf. [13]) to make it possible for the verifier to run in fixed polynomial time, regardless of the polynomial that bounds the running time of the ensemble.

In this work we show how such a result can be obtained. Specifically, we present a signature scheme that operates in the random-oracle model, with the following properties:

- The scheme is *stateless*: the signer only keeps in memory the secret key, and this key does not evolve from one signature to the next.
- The scheme is only required to *sign short messages*: On security parameter k, the scheme can only be applied to messages whose length is less than k. Furthermore, one could even restrict it to messages of length sub-linear in k (e.g., polylog(k)).
- The scheme is *secure in the Random Oracle Model*: When the oracle is implemented by a truly random function, the scheme is existentially unforgeable under an adaptive chosen-message attack.
- The scheme *has no secure implementation*: When the oracle is implemented by any function ensemble (even one with functions having description length that is polynomially longer than k), the scheme is completely breakable under an adaptive chosen-message attack. We remark that in this case the function's description is part of the verification-key.[4]

To construct such a scheme we need to design a "proof system" that only uses very short messages. As opposed to previous examples, we will now have an *interactive* proof system, with the proof taking place during the attack. Each communication-round of the proof is being "implemented" by the attacker (in the role of the prover) sending a message to be signed, and the signer (in the role of the verifier) signing that message.

The ideas that make this work are the following: We start from the aforementioned non-interactive proof (of "non-randomness"), where the verifier is given the description of a function, and compares that function to its own oracle (i.e., compares their values at sufficiently many points). Then, instead of having the verifier execute the entire test on its own, we feed the execution of this test to the verifier "one step at a time" (and, in particular, the input function is fed "one step at a time"). Namely, let M be the oracle Turing machine implementing the aforementioned test. The adversary provides the verifier with the relevant information pertaining to the current step in the test (e.g., the state of the control of M and the character under the head) and the verifier returns the information for the next step. This requires only short messages, since each step of M has a succinct description.

To keep the security of the scheme in the Random Oracle Model, we need to make sure that the adversary can only feed the verifier with "valid states" of the machine M. (Namely, states that can indeed result from the execution of this machine on some input.) To do that, we have the verifier authenticate each step of the computation. That is, together with the "local information" about

---

[4] In contrast, if the function's description is only part of the signing-key then using any pseudorandom function [6] would yield a secure signature scheme. However, this would not be an application of the Random Oracle Methodology, which explicitly refers to making the function's description public.

the current step, the verifier also computes an authentication tag for the "global state" of the machine in this step, which is done using Merkle trees [12]. Such authentication has the property that it can be computed and verified using only the path from the root to the current leaf in the tree, and the authentication tag itself is very short. A little more precisely, the current configuration of the machine M (using some standard encoding) is viewed as the leaves of a Merkle tree, and the verifier provides the prover with an authentication tag for the root of this tree. Then a typical step in the proof proceeds as follows:

1. The attacker sends to the verifier the "relevant leaf" of the tree (i.e., the one containing the head of M), together with the entire path from the root to that leaf (and the siblings for that path), and the authentication tag for the root.
2. The verifier checks the authentication tag of the root and the validity of the root–leaf path (using the siblings). If everything is valid, then the verifier executes the next step of M, and returns to the attacker the updated path to the root, and an authentication tag for the new root.

If the machine M ever enters an accept state, then the verifier accepts. This proof can still be implemented using only short messages, since the root-leaf path has only logarithmic depth. As for security, since it is infeasible for the attacker to "forge a state" of M, then the verifier will accept only if the machine M indeed has an accepting computation.

3   The Details

We now flesh out the description from Section 2. We begin in §3.1 with the basic test that we are going to implement step-by-step. In §3.2 we describe the Merkle-tree authentication mechanism that we use, and in §3.3 we describe the complete "interactive proof system". Finally, we show in §3.4 how this proof system is used to derive our counter-example.

As we did in [5], we avoid making intractability assumptions by using the random oracle itself for various constructs that we need. For example, we implement the Merkle-tree authentication mechanism (which typically requires collision-resistant hash functions) by using the random oracle. We stress that we only rely on the security of this and other constructs in the Random Oracle Model, and do not care whether or not its implementation is secure (because we are going to demonstrate the insecurity of the implementation anyhow). Formally, in the context of the proof system, the security of the constructs only effects the soundness of the proof, which in turn refers to the Random Oracle Model.

In both the basic test and the authentication mechanisms we use access to an oracle (which will be a random function in the Random Oracle Model, and a random member in an arbitrary function ensemble in the "real world"). When we work in the Random Oracle Model, we wish these two oracles to be independent. Thus, we use the single oracle to which we have access to define two oracles that are independent if the original oracle is random (e.g., using the oracle $\mathcal{O}$, we define oracles $\mathcal{O}_i(x) \stackrel{\text{def}}{=} \mathcal{O}(i, x)$).

In the rest of this section, we assume that the reader is familiar with the notion of a polynomial-time function ensemble (as reviewed in Footnote 2).

3.1   The Basic Test

Our starting point is a very simple non-interactive "proof of non-randomness" of an oracle $\mathcal{O}$. (The basic idea for this proof is described by Holenstein et al. in [10].) The verifier is a (non-interactive) oracle Turing machine, denoted M, which is given a candidate proof, denoted π, as input. The input π is supposed to be a program (or a description of a Turing machine) that predicts $\mathcal{O}$. Intuitively, if $\mathcal{O}$ is random then no π may be successful (when we try to use it in order to predict the value of $\mathcal{O}$ on more than $|\pi|$ predetermined inputs). On the other hand, if $\mathcal{O}$ has a short description (as in case where it is taken from some function ensemble) then setting π to be the program that computes $\mathcal{O}$ will do perfectly well. The operation of M, on security parameter k, input π and access to an oracle $\mathcal{O}$, is given below:

Procedure $\mathsf{M}^{\mathcal{O}}(1^k, \pi)$:

1. Let $n = |\pi|$ be the bit length of π.
   (π is viewed as a description of a Turing-machine.)
2. For $i = 1$ to $2n + k$, let $y_i \leftarrow \mathcal{O}(i)$ and $z_i \leftarrow \pi(i)$.
3. If y_i and z_i agree on their first bit for all $i \in [1..2n + k]$, then **accept**.
4. Else **reject**.

Below it will be convenient to think of the machine M as having one *security-parameter tape* (a read-only tape containing 1^k), one "regular" *work tape* that initially contains π, one oracle *query tape* and one oracle *reply tape* (the last having just a single bit, since we only look at the first bit of the answer). A configuration of this machine can therefore be described as a 4-tuple $\mathsf{c} = (q, r, w, sp)$ describing the contents of each tape (i.e., q describes the query, r the reply, w the contents of the work-tape and sp the security-parameter). By convention, we assume that the description of each tape include also the location of the head on this tape, and that the description of the work tape also includes the state of the finite control. Thus, for the above machine M, we always have $|q| = \log(2|\pi| + k) + \log\log(2|\pi| + k)$, $|r| = 1$, $|w| \leq |\pi| + s_k(\pi) + \log(2|\pi| + k) + \log(|\pi| + s(\pi) + \log(2|\pi| + k)) + O(1)$, $|sp| = k$, where $s_k(\pi)$ is the space require for computing $\pi(i)$ for the worst possible $i \in [2|\pi| + k]$. It follows that $|\mathsf{c}| = O(|\pi| + s_k(\pi) + k)$.

Note that M itself is not a "verifier in the usual sense", because its running time may depend arbitrarily on its input. In particular, for some inputs π (describing a non-halting program), the machine M may not halt at all. Nonetheless, we may analyze what happens in the two cases that we care about:

Proposition 2 (Properties of machine M):

1. *Random oracle: For security parameter k, if the oracle $\mathcal{O}$ is chosen uniformly from all the Boolean functions, then*

$$\Pr_{\mathcal{O}} \left[\exists\, \pi \in \{0,1\}^* \text{ s.t. } \mathsf{M}^{\mathcal{O}}(1^k, \pi) \text{ accepts} \right] < 2^{-k}$$

2. Oracle with succinct description: *For every function ensemble* $\{f_s : \{0,1\}^* \to \{0,1\}\}_{s \in \{0,1\}^*}$ *(having a polynomial-time evaluation algorithm), there exists an efficient mapping* $s \mapsto \pi_s$ *such that for every* s *and every* k *it holds that* $\mathsf{M}^{f_s}(1^k, \pi_s)$ *accepts in polynomial-time.*

Proof Sketch. In Item 1, we apply the union bound on all possible (i.e., infinitely many) π's. For each fixed $\pi \in \{0,1\}^*$, it holds that the probability that $\mathsf{M}^{\mathcal{O}}(1^k, \pi)$ accepts is at most $2^{-(2|\pi|+k)}$, where the probability is taken uniformly over all possible choices of $\mathcal{O}$. In Item 2, we use the program π_s obtained by hard-wiring the seed s into the polynomial-time evaluation algorithm associated with the function ensemble.   □

3.2   Authenticating the Configuration

We next describe the specifics of how we use Merkle trees to authenticate the configurations of the machine M. In the description below, we view the configuration $\mathsf{c} = (q, r, w, sp)$ as a binary string (using some standard encoding).

We assume that the authentication mechanism too has access to a random oracle, and this random oracle is independent of the one that is used by the machine M. Below we denote this "authentication oracle" by $\mathcal{A}$. To be concrete, on security parameter k, denote $\ell_{\text{out}} = \ell_{\text{out}}(k) = \lceil \log^2(k) \rceil$,[5] and assume that the oracle is chosen at random, from all the functions $\mathcal{A} : \{0,1\}^* \to \{0,1\}^{\ell_{\text{out}}}$. (Actually, we may consider the functions $\mathcal{A} : \{0,1\}^{3\ell_{\text{out}}} \to \{0,1\}^{\ell_{\text{out}}}$.) We stress again that we do not lose much generality by these assumptions, as they can be easily met in the Random Oracle Model. Also, when the security parameter is k, we use a random ℓ_{out}-bit string for authentication key, which we denote by $\mathsf{ak} \in_R \{0,1\}^{\ell_{\text{out}}}$.

To authenticate a configuration c (on security parameter k, with access to an oracle $\mathcal{A}$, and with key ak), we first pad the binary encoding of c to length $2^d \cdot \ell_{\text{out}}$ (where d is an integer). We then consider a complete binary tree with 2^d leaves, where the i'th leaf contains the i'th ℓ_{out}-bit chunk of the configuration. Each internal node in this tree contains an ℓ_{out}-bit string. For a node at distance i from the root, this ℓ_{out}-bit string equals $\mathcal{A}(i, \texttt{left}, \texttt{right})$, where $\texttt{left}$ and $\texttt{right}$ are the ℓ_{out}-bit strings in the left and right children of that node, respectively. The authentication tag for this configuration equals $\mathcal{A}(d, \mathsf{ak}, \texttt{root})$, where $\texttt{root}$ is the ℓ_{out}-bit string in the root of the tree.

The security property that we need here is slightly stronger than the usual notion for authentication codes. The usual notion would say that for an attacker who does not know the key ak, it is hard to come up with any valid pair (configuration,tag) that was not previously given to him by the party who knows ak. In our application, however, the verifier is only presented with root–leaf paths in

---

[5] The choice of $\ell_{\text{out}}(k) = \lceil \log^2(k) \rceil$ is somewhat arbitrary. For the construction below we need the output length $\ell_{\text{out}}(k)$ to satisfy $\omega(\log k) \leq \ell_{\text{out}}(k) \leq o(k/\log k)$, whereas the input length should be at least $2\ell_{\text{out}}(k) + \omega(\log k)$. (Note that $2\ell_{\text{out}}(k) + \omega(\log k) < 3\ell_{\text{out}}(k)$.)

the tree, never with complete configurations. We therefore require that it is hard even to come up with a single path that "looks like it belongs to a valid configuration", without this path being part of a previously authenticated configuration. We use the following notions:

Definition 3 (valid paths) *Let* $\mathcal{A} : \{0,1\}^* \to \{0,1\}^{\ell_{out}}$ *be an oracle and* $ak \in \{0,1\}^{\ell_{out}}$ *be a string as above. A* valid path with respect to $\mathcal{A}$ *and* ak *is a triple*

$$(\langle \sigma_1 \cdots \sigma_d \rangle, \ \langle (v_{1,0}, v_{1,1}), ..., (v_{d,0}, v_{d,1}) \rangle, \ t)$$

where the σ_i*'s are bits, and the* $v_{i,b}$*'s and* t *are all* ℓ_{out}*-bit strings, satisfying the following conditions:*

1. *For every* $i = 1, ..., d-1$*, it holds that* $v_{i,\sigma_i} = \mathcal{A}(i, v_{i+1,0}, v_{i+1,1})$*.*
2. $t = \mathcal{A}(d, ak, \mathcal{A}(0, v_{1,0}, v_{1,1}))$*.*

This path is said to be consistent with the configuration c *if when placing* c *in the leaves and propagating values described above,*[6] *then for every* $i = 1, ..., d-1$*, the node reached from the root by following the path* $\sigma_1 \cdots \sigma_i$ *is assigned the value* v_{i,σ_i}*, and the sibling of that node is assigned the value* $v_{i,\bar{\sigma}_i}$*.*

In this definition, v_{i,σ_i} is the value claimed for the internal node reached from the root by following the path $\sigma_1 \cdots \sigma_i$. The value claimed for the root is $v_0 \stackrel{\text{def}}{=} \mathcal{A}(0, v_{1,0}, v_{1,1})$, and this value is authenticated by $\mathcal{A}(d, ak, v_0)$, which also authenticates the depth of the tree. Indeed, only the value of the root is directly authenticated, and this indirectly authenticates all the rest.

Fix some $\ell_{out} \in \mathsf{N}$, and let $\mathcal{A}$ be a random function from $\{0,1\}^*$ to $\{0,1\}^{\ell_{out}}$ and ak be a random ℓ_{out}-bit string. Consider a forger, F, that can query the oracle $\mathcal{A}$ on arbitrary strings, and can also issue authentication queries, where the query is a configurations c and the answer is the authentication tag on c corresponding to $\mathcal{A}$ and ak. The forger F is deemed successful if at the end of its run it outputs a path $(\alpha, \bar{v}, t)$ that is valid with respect to $\mathcal{A}$ and ak but is inconsistent with any of the authentication queries. One can easily prove the following:

Proposition 4 *For any* $\ell_{out} \in \mathsf{N}$ *and any forger* F*, the probability that* F *is successful is at most* $q^2/2^{\ell_{out}}$*, where* q *is the total number of queries made by* F *(i.e., both queries to the oracle* $\mathcal{A}$ *and authentication queries). The probability is taken over the choices of* $\mathcal{A}$ *and* ak*, as well as over the coins of the forger* F*.*

Proof Sketch. Intuitively, the authentication of the root's value makes it hard to produce a path that is valid with respect to $\mathcal{A}$ and (the unknown) ak but uses a different value for the root. Similarly for a path of a different length for the same root value. On the other hand, it is hard to form collisions with respect to the values of internal nodes (i.e., obtain two pairs (u, w) and (u', w') such that for some i it holds that $\mathcal{A}(i, u, w) = \mathcal{A}(i, u', w')$). $\square$

---

[6] That is, an internal node at distance i from the root is assigned the value $\mathcal{A}(i, u, w)$, where u and w are the values assigned to its children.

3.3   An Interactive Proof of Non-randomness

We are now ready to describe our interactive proof, where a prover can convince a "stateless" verifier that their common oracle is not random, using only very short messages.

The setting is as follows: We have a prover and a verifier, both work in polynomial time in their input, both sharing a security parameter $k \in \mathsf{N}$ (encoded in unary), and both having access to an oracle, say $\mathcal{O}' : \{0,1\}^* \to \{0,1\}^{\ell_{out}}$. (The parameter ℓ_{out} is quite arbitrary. Below we assume for convenience that this is the same parameter as we use for the authentication scheme, namely $\ell_{out} = \lceil \log^2(k) \rceil$.)[7] In this proof system, the prover is trying to convince the verifier that their common oracle in not random. Specifically, both prover and verifier interpret their oracle as two separate oracles, $\mathcal{A}$ and $\mathcal{O}$ (say, $\mathcal{O}(x) = \mathcal{O}'(0x)$ and $\mathcal{A}(x) = \mathcal{O}'(1x)$), and the honest prover has as input a description of a Turing machine that computes the function $\mathcal{O}$. However, we place some severe limitations on what the verifier can do. Specifically, the verifier has as private input a random string $\mathsf{ak} \in \{0,1\}^{\ell_{out}}$, but other than this fixed string, it is not allowed to maintain any state between steps. That is, when answering a message from the prover, the verifier always begin the computation from a fixed state consisting only of the security parameter k and the string ak. In addition, on security parameter k, the verifier is only allowed to see prover-messages of length strictly smaller than k. (In fact, below we only use messages of size $\mathrm{polylog}(k)$.)

The proof that we describe below consists of two phases. In the first (initialization) phase, the prover uses the verifier to authenticate the initial configuration of the machine $\mathsf{M}^{\mathcal{O}}(1^k, x)$, where k is the security parameter that they both share, and x is some input that the prover chooses. For the honest prover, this input x will be the description of the Turing-machine that implements the oracle $\mathcal{O}$. In the second (computation) phase, the prover takes the verifier step-by-step through the computation of $\mathsf{M}^{\mathcal{O}}(1^k, x)$. For each step, the prover gives to the verifier the relevant part from the current authenticated configuration, and the verifier returns the authentication tag for the next configuration. The verifier is convinced if the machine M ever reaches the accepting state.

For notational convenience, we assume below that on security parameter k, the verifier only agrees to authenticate configurations of M whose length is less than $2^{\ell_{out}(k)}$. Indeed, in our application the honest prover will never need to use larger configuration (for large enough k).

Initialization Phase. This phase consists of two steps. In the first step, the prover will use the verifier in order to authenticate "blank configuration" (lacking a real input) for the computation, whereas in the second step the prover will feed an input into this configuration and obtain (via interaction with the verifier) an initial configuration fitting this input.

---

[7] Note that even a *binary* oracle (i.e., $\ell_{out} = 1$) suffices, since in the Random Oracle Model it is easy to convert one output length to another.

First Step. The *prover begins this phase by sending a message of the form* ('Init', 0, sb) *to the verifier,* where the integer $\mathsf{sb} < 2^{\ell_{\mathrm{out}}(k)}$ is an upper bound on the length of the configurations of M in the computation to come, and it is encoded in binary. In response, the *verifier computes a blank configuration, denoted* c_0, *of length* sb *and sends the authentication tag for this configuration, with respect to oracle* $\mathcal{A}$ *and key* ak. The blank configuration c_0 consists of the security-parameter tape filled with 1^k, all the other tapes being "empty" (e.g., filled with $\star$'s), the heads being at the beginning of each tape, and the finite control being in a special blank state. Specifically, the work-tape consists of sb blanks (i.e., $\star$'s), and the query-tape consists of $\ell_{\mathrm{out}}(k)/2 = \omega(\log k)$ blanks.[8]

We note that authenticating the blank configuration in a straightforward manner (i.e., by writing down the configuration and computing the labels of all nodes in the tree) takes time $O(\mathsf{sb})$, which may be super-polynomial in k. Nonetheless, it is possible to compute the authentication tag in time polynomial in k, because the configuration c_0 is "highly uniform". Specifically, note that the work tape is filled with $\star$'s, and all the other tapes are of size polynomial in k. Thus, in every level of the configuration tree, almost all the nodes have the same value (except, perhaps, a polynomial number of them). Hence, the number of queries to $\mathcal{A}$ and total time that it takes to compute the authentication tag is polynomial in k.

Conventions. For simplicity, we assume that the contents of the query-tape as well as the machine's state are encoded in the first $\ell_{\mathrm{out}}(k)$-bit long block of the configuration. Typically, in all subsequent modifications to the configuration, we will use this block as well as (possibly) some other block (in which the "actual action" takes place). We denote by $\langle i \rangle$ the bit-string describing the path from the root to the leaf that contains the i'th location in the work-tape. Needless to say, we assume that the encoding is simple enough such that $\langle i \rangle$ can be computed efficiently from i.

Second Step. After obtaining the authentication tag for the blank configuration, the prover may fill in the input in this configuration by sending messages of the form ('Init', $i, b, \bar{p}_1, \bar{p}_i, t$) to the verifier. Upon receiving such a message, the verifier checks that $(\langle 1 \rangle, \bar{p}_1, t)$ and $(\langle i \rangle, \bar{p}_i, t)$ are valid paths w.r.t. $\mathcal{A}$ and ak, that path $\bar{p}_1$ shows the heads at the beginning of their tapes and the control in the special "blank state", and that path $\bar{p}_i$ shows the i'th location in the work-tape filled with a $\star$. In case all conditions hold, the verifier replaces the contents of the i'th location in the work-tape with the bit b, recomputes values along the path from that tape location to the root, and returns the new authentication tag to the prover. That is, the values along that path as recorded in $\bar{p}_i$ correspond to a setting of the i'th location to $\star$, and setting this location to b typically yields new values that propagate from this leaf up-to the root.

---

[8] On input $(1^k, x)$, the query tape of M is of size $\log_2(2|x| + k)$. For ensemble F, the honest prover will use $|x| \leq \mathrm{poly}(k) + O(1)$, and so the length of the query tape would be $O(\log k)$.

Thus, using $|x|$ rounds of interaction, the honest prover can obtain (from the verifier) the authentication tag on the initial configuration of $M(1^k, x)$, where x is a string of the prover's choice. Note that a cheating prover may obtain from the prover an authentication tag that does not correspond to such an initial configuration. (In fact, even the honest prover obtains such tags in all but the last iterations of the current step.)

Computation Phase. This phase begin with a message of the form ('Comp', $\bar{p}_1, t$) that the prover sends. The verifier checks that $(\langle 1 \rangle, \bar{p}_1, t)$ is a valid path, and that $\bar{p}_1$ shows the heads at the beginning of their tapes and the control in the special "blank state". If these conditions hold, the verifier changes the state to the initial state of M, recomputes the values on the path $\bar{p}_1$ from the initial tape location to the root, and returns the new authentication tag to the prover. (In fact, one may view this step as belonging to the initialization step.)

Thereafter, upon receiving a message of the form ('Comp', $i, j, \bar{p}_1, \bar{p}_i, \bar{p}_j, t$), where $j \in \{i-1, i, i+1\}$ (and indeed when $j = i$ it holds that $\bar{p}_i = \bar{p}_j$), the verifier checks that $(\langle 1 \rangle, \bar{p}_1, t)$, $(\langle i \rangle, \bar{p}_i, t)$, $(\langle j \rangle, \bar{p}_j, t)$, are all valid paths. Furthermore, it checks that $\bar{p}_i$ contains the head position and $\bar{p}_j$ describes a legal contents of the position that the head will move to after the current step. That is, $\bar{p}_1$ and $\bar{p}_i$ provide sufficient information to determine the single-step modification of the current configuration (which may include a movement of some heads and a change in the contents of a single symbol in some of the tapes). In case all conditions hold, then the verifier executes the current step (making a query to its oracle $\mathcal{O}$ if this step is an oracle query), recomputes the values on the three paths to the root, and returns the new authentication tag to the prover. If after this step the machine M enters its accept state, the verifier accepts.

It can be seen that the honest prover can use these interaction steps to take the verifier step-by-step through the computation of M. It follows that if the input to the honest prover is indeed a polynomial-time machine that computes the function $\mathcal{O}$, then the verifier will halt and accept after polynomially many steps. We conclude this subsection by showing that the above constitutes a proof system for non-randomness (satisfying additional properties that we will need in the next subsection).

Proposition 5 *The above construction constitutes a proof system with the following properties:*

Efficiency. *Each verifier step can be computed in time polynomial in the security parameter k.*

Stateless verifier. *The verifier is stateless in the sense that it begins every step from the same state, consisting only of the security parameter k and its private input $\mathrm{ak} \in \{0, 1\}^{\ell_{\text{out}}}$. Formally, the verifier replies to each incoming message m with $V(1^k, \mathrm{ak}, m)$, where V is a fixed (efficiently computable) function.*[9]

---

[9] We slightly abuse notations here, and use V for both the verifier and the functions that it implements.

Soundness. *If $\mathcal{O}'$ is chosen as a random function $\mathcal{O}' : \{0,1\}^* \to \{0,1\}^{\ell_{out}(k)}$ and ak is chosen at random in $\{0,1\}^{\ell_{out}(k)}$, then for every (possibly cheating) prover P it holds that*

$$\Pr_{\mathcal{O}',\mathrm{ak}} \left[\textit{The verifier } V^{\mathcal{O}'}(1^k, \mathrm{ak}) \textit{ accepts when talking to } P^{\mathcal{O}'} \right]$$
$$\leq (q + \ell_{out}(k) \cdot m)^2 \cdot 2^{-\ell_{out}} + 2^{-k}$$

where q is the total number of queries that P makes to the oracle $\mathcal{A}$ and m is the total number of messages that it sends to the verifier V.

Completeness with short messages. *For every polynomial-time-computable function ensemble $\mathcal{F}$, there exists a polynomial-time prover $P_{\mathcal{F}}$ such that:*

1. *For every choice of $s \in \{0,1\}^{\mathrm{poly}(k)}$ and $\mathrm{ak} \in \{0,1\}^{\ell_{out}(k)}$, the verifier $V^{f_s}(1^k, \mathrm{ak})$ always accepts when talking to $P_{\mathcal{F}}(s)$.*
2. *On security parameter k, the prover $P_{\mathcal{F}}(s)$ only sends to the verifier $\mathrm{poly}(k)$ many messages, each of length $O((\log k) \cdot \ell_{out}(k)) = O(\log^3 k)$.*

Proof Sketch. The only assertions that are not obvious are the soundness bound and the size of the messages. For the soundness bound, recall that (by Proposition 2) when $\mathcal{O}'$ is a random function (and therefore also $\mathcal{O}$ is a random function), the probability that there exists an input x that makes $\mathsf{M}^{\mathcal{O}}(1^k, x)$ accept is at most 2^{-k}. If there is no such input, then the only way to make $V^{\mathcal{O}'}$ accept is "forge" some valid paths, and (by Proposition 4) this can only be done with probability at most $q^2 2^{-\ell_{out}}$. Slightly more formal, consider the transcript of a proof in which $P^{\mathcal{O}'}$ causes $V^{\mathcal{O}'}$ to accept. Considering all the messages that P sent to V in this transcript, one can easily define a "depend-on" relation among then (namely, when one message contains an authentication tag that was obtained in a previous message). This, in turn, allows us to define the complete configurations that were "rightly authenticated" during this transcript (namely, those configurations that correspond to a computation that starts from the initial configuration of M_k on some input x.) Hence, we either find an initial configuration from which $\mathsf{M}(1^k, x)$ accepts (a probability 2^{-k} event), or we find a computation that begins from some non-initial configuration. Since the verifier $V^{\mathcal{O}'}$ never authenticates a non-initial configuration unless it sees a valid path belonging to a configuration that directly precedes it, the valid path belonging to the first non-initial configuration must be a forgery. (By making suitable oracle calls before sending each message to the verifier, we can convert the cheating prover to a forger that makes at most $q + \ell_{out} \cdot m$ queries, and soundness follows.)

As for the size of the messages sent by the honest prover, let $\mathcal{F}$ be any polynomial-time-computable functions ensemble. This means that there is a polynomial $p(\cdot)$ such that on security parameter k, specifying any function $f_s \in \mathcal{F}_k$ can be done using at most $p(k)$ bits, and moreover, computing $f_s(x)$ for any $|x| < k$ takes at most $p(k)$ time. (Below we assume for convenience that $p(k) \geq k$.) For any $f_s \in \mathcal{F}_k$, let π_s be a description of a Turing machine computing f_s. By the above, $|\pi_s| = |s| + O(1) < p(k) + O(1)$. This implies that for any $f_s \in \mathcal{F}_k$, the non-interactive verifier $\mathsf{M}(1^k, \pi_s)$ runs in time at most $O(k + 2p(k)) \cdot p(k) = O(p^2(k))$, and therefore it only has configurations of length at most $O(p^2(k))$.

The honest prover $P_{\mathcal{F}}$, having access to s, can compute the description π_s and take the verifier step-by-step through the execution of $\mathsf{M}^{f_s}(1^k, \pi_s)$, which consists only of $O(p^2(k))$ steps. It begins by sending a message ('Init', 0, sb), with the bound sb being set to $\mathsf{sb} = O(p^2(k))$, and in each step thereafter it only needs to send a constant number of paths in the tree, each of length $\log(\mathsf{sb})$. Since each node in the tree contains a string of length $\ell_{\mathrm{out}}(k)$, it follows that the total length of the prover's queries is $O(\log(\mathsf{sb}) \cdot \ell_{\mathrm{out}}(k)) = O(\ell_{\mathrm{out}}(k) \cdot \log(p^2(k))) = O(\ell_{\mathrm{out}}(k) \cdot \log k)$. $\qquad\square$

3.4   The Signature Scheme

Combining the proof system from the previous section with the ideas outlined in Sections 1 and 2, it is quite straightforward to construct the desired signature scheme (summarized in the next theorem).

Theorem. 6 (Theorem 1, restated) *There exists a signature scheme $\mathcal{S}$ that is existentially unforgeable under a chosen message attack in the Random Oracle Model, but such that when implemented with any efficiently computable function ensemble, the resulting scheme is totally breakable under chosen message attack. Moreover, the signing algorithm of $\mathcal{S}$ is stateless, and on security parameter k, it can only be applied to messages of size poly-logarithmic in k.*

Proof. Let $(P_{\mathrm{pf}}, V_{\mathrm{pf}})$ be the proof system for "non-randomness" described in Section 3.3. Let $\mathcal{S} = (G_{\mathrm{sig}}, S_{\mathrm{sig}}, V_{\mathrm{sig}})$ be any stateless signature scheme that is existentially unforgeable under a chosen message attack in the Random Oracle Model (we know that such schemes exist, e.g., using Naor-Yung [14] with the random oracle used in the role of a universal one-way hash function)). We view all the machines P_{pf}, V_{pf}, G_{sig}, S_{sig}, and V_{sig} as oracle machines (although G_{sig}, S_{sig}, or V_{sig} may not use their oracle). We modify the signature scheme to obtain a different signature scheme $\mathcal{S}' = (G', S', V')$.

– On input 1^k (k being the security parameter), the key generation algorithm G' first runs G_{sig} to obtain a private/public key-pair of the original scheme, $(\mathrm{sk}, \mathrm{vk}) \leftarrow G_{\mathrm{sig}}^{\mathcal{O}}(1^k)$. Then it chooses a random ℓ_{out}-bit "authentication key" $\mathrm{ak} \in_R \{0,1\}^{\ell_{\mathrm{out}}(k)}$ (to be used by V_{pf}). The public verification key is just vk, and the secret signing key is the pair $(\mathrm{sk}, \mathrm{ak})$. (We assume that the security parameter k is implicit in both vk and sk.)
– On message m, signing key $(\mathrm{sk}, \mathrm{ak})$ and access to oracle $\mathcal{O}$, the signature algorithm S' works as follows: If the message m is too long (i.e., $|m| > \log^4 k$) then it outputs an empty signature $\bot$.[10] Otherwise, it invokes both the proof-verifier V_{pf} and the signer S_{sig} on the message m to get $\sigma_{\mathrm{pf}} \leftarrow V_{\mathrm{pf}}^{\mathcal{O}}(\mathrm{ak}, m)$, and $\sigma_{\mathrm{sig}} \leftarrow S_{\mathrm{sig}}^{\mathcal{O}}(\mathrm{sk}, m)$.
If the proof-verifier accepts (i.e., $\sigma_{\mathrm{pf}} = $ "accept") then the signature consists of the secret key $\sigma = (\sigma_{\mathrm{sig}}, (\mathrm{sk}, \mathrm{ak}))$. Otherwise, the signature is the pair $\sigma = (\sigma_{\mathrm{sig}}, \sigma_{\mathrm{pf}})$.

---

[10] Alternatively, S' may return $(S_{\mathrm{sig}}^{\mathcal{O}}(\mathrm{sk}, m), \bot)$, and we should note that in the ("real world") attack described below only short messages are used.

– The verification algorithm V', on message m, alleged signature $\sigma = (\sigma_1, \sigma_2)$, verification key vk and access to oracle $\mathcal{O}$, just invokes the original signature-verifier V_{sig} on the first part of the signature, outputting $V_{\text{sig}}^{\mathcal{O}}(\text{vk}, m, \sigma_1)$.

It is clear from the description that this scheme is stateless, and that it can only be used to sign messages of length at most $\log^4 k$. It is also easy to see that with any implementation via function ensemble, the resulting scheme is totally breakable under adaptive chosen message attack. When implemented using function ensemble $\mathcal{F}$, an attacker uses the prescribed prover $P_{\mathcal{F}}$ (of Proposition 5). Recall that the seed s for the function f_s that is used to implement the oracle is included in the public key, so the attacker can just run $P_{\mathcal{F}}(s)$. The attacker sends the prover's messages to the signer S', and the size of these messages is $O(\log^3 k) < \log^4 k$, where the constant in the O-notation depends on the ensemble $\mathcal{F}$. The second component of the signatures on these messages are the replies from the proof-verifier $V_{\text{pf}}^{f_s}$. From Proposition 5 we conclude that after signing polynomially many such messages, the proof-verifier accepts (with probability one), at which point the signing algorithm will output the secret signing key. Thus, we totally break the scheme's implementation (by any function ensemble).

Next we show that the scheme $\mathcal{S}'$ is existentially unforgeable under a chosen message attack in the Random Oracle Model. Informally, the reason is that in the Random Oracle Model a forger will not be able to cause the proof-verifier to accept, and thus it will be left with the task of forging a signature with respect to the original (secure) signature scheme.

Formally, consider a polynomial-time forger F', attacking the scheme $\mathcal{S}'$, let $\epsilon = \epsilon(k)$ denote the probability that F' issues a forgery, and assume – toward contradiction – that ϵ is non-negligible. Consider the invocations that the signing algorithm makes to the proof-verifier V_{pf} during the attack. Let $\delta = \delta(k)$ be the probability that V_{pf} replies to some query with "accept". Since we can view the combination of F' and the signing algorithm as a (cheating) prover $P^{\mathcal{O}}$, Proposition 5 tells us that $\delta \leq q^2 / 2^{\ell_{\text{out}}} + 2^{-k}$ where q is bounded by the running time of F' (which is polynomial in k). Hence δ is negligible.

Next we show a polynomial-time forger F_{sig} against the original scheme $\mathcal{S}$ that issues a forgery with probability at least $\epsilon - \delta$, contradicting the security of $\mathcal{S}$. The forger F_{sig} is given a public key vk that was generated by $G_{\text{sig}}(1^k)$, it has access to the signing oracle $S_{\text{sig}}^{\mathcal{O}}(\text{sk}, \cdot)$ for the corresponding signing key sk, and also access to the random oracle $\mathcal{O}$. It picks at random an "authentication key" $\text{ak} \in \{0,1\}^{\ell_{\text{out}}(k)}$, and then invokes the forger F' on the same public key vk.

When F' asks for a signature on a message m, the forger F_{sig} behaves much like the signature algorithm S'. Namely, if $|m| > \log^4 k$ it returns $\bot$. Otherwise, it computes $\sigma_{\text{pf}} \leftarrow V_{\text{pf}}^{\mathcal{O}}(\text{ak}, m)$, and it queries its signing oracle on m to get $\sigma_{\text{sig}} \leftarrow S_{\text{sig}}^{\mathcal{O}}(\text{sk}, m)$. If the proof-verifier accepts, $\sigma_{\text{pf}} = $ "accept", then F_{sig} aborts. Else it returns the pair $\sigma = (\sigma_{\text{sig}}, \sigma_{\text{pf}})$. If F' issues a forged message m' with signature (σ_1', σ_2') then F_{sig} issues the same forged message m' and signature σ_1'. It is clear that F_{sig} succeeds in forging a signature if and only if F' forges a signature without causing the proof-verifier V_{pf} to accept, which happens with probability at least $\epsilon - \delta$. □

Remark 7 (Message length)   Tracing through the arguments in this section, it can be seen that the message-length can be decreased from $\log^4 k$ to $\omega(\log^2 k)$: It suffices to use a space-bound $SB = \omega(\log k)$, which yields a (prescribed) proof system with prover message of length $\omega(\log^2 k)$, for any function ensemble. However, achieving poly-logarithmic message length relies heavily on the fact that we use the random oracle for authentication, and on the fact that the random oracle yields authentication with "exponential hardness". In Section 4 below, we instead use standard collision-intractable functions and message-authentication codes, that only enjoy "super-polynomial hardness". In this case, the achievable message length would be $O(k^\epsilon)$ for any desired (fixed) $\epsilon > 0$.

4   A Proof System for Any NP-Language

The description in Section 3 combined the specifics of our application (i.e., proving non-randomness of an oracle) with the general ideas underlying the construction of the new proof system. In this section, we apply the latter ideas in order to derive a new type of proof systems for any language in $\mathcal{NP}$.

The model is similar to ordinary interactive proofs as in GMR [9] (and arguments as in BCC [3]), except that *the verifier is stateless.* That is, the verifier is represented by a randomized process that given the verifier's input and the current in-coming message, determines the verifier's next message. This process is probabilistic polynomial-time, but it cannot effect the verifier's state. In particular, the verifier's decision to accept or reject (or continue in the interaction) will be reflected in its next message. (In a sense, the verifier will not even remember its decision, but merely notify the world of it.)

The above model, per se, allows to prove membership in any NP-set, by merely having the prover send the corresponding NP-witness. However, we are interested in such proof systems in which *the prover only sends short messages.* This rules out the simple solution just suggested. But, as stated, this model does not allow to do much beyond using short NP-witnesses whenever they exist. The reason being that, from the verifier's point of view, there is no "relation" between the various communication rounds, and the only function of the multiple interactions is to provide multiple attempts of the same experiment. The situation changes once we *provide the verifier with an auxiliary secret input.* This input is chosen uniformly from some domain and remains fixed throughout the run of the protocol. The goal of this auxiliary input is to model some very limited form of state that is kept between sending a message and receiving the response.

To summarize, we are interested in proof systems (or arguments) that satisfy the following three conditions:

1. In addition to the common input, denoted x, the verifier receives an auxiliary secret input, denoted s, that is chosen uniformly from some domain. As

usual, we focus on a probabilistic polynomial-time prover that also receives an auxiliary input, denoted y.

2. The verifier employs a stateless strategy. That is, there exists a probabilistic polynomial-time algorithm V such that the verifier answers the current message m with $V(x, s, m)$.

3. The prover can only send short messages. That is, it can only send messages of length $\ell(|x|)$, where $\ell(n) \ll n$ (e.g., $\ell(n) = \sqrt{n}$).

One may think of such proofs as proving statements to a child: The verifier's attention span limits us to sending it only $\ell(n)$ bits at a time, after which its attention is diverted to something else. Moreover, once we again capture the verifier's attention, it has already forgotten everything that had happened before.

Assuming the existence of collision-resistant hash functions, we can show that such a proof system can emulate any proof system (having an efficient prescribed prover strategy).[11] The emulation will only be *computationally-sound* (i.e., it is possible but not feasible to cause the verifier to accept false statements). In fact, we have already shown such a proof system: It is implicit in the description of Section 3, when one replaces the two different roles of $\mathcal{A}$ (see proof of Proposition 4) by a collision-resistant hash function and a message-authentication scheme, respectively. Indeed, the description in Section 3 referred to the emulation of a specific test, but it applies as well to the emulation of any ordinary verifier strategy (i.e., one that does maintain state between communication rounds). Specifically, one may first transform the original interactive proof to one in which the prover sends a single bit in each communication round, and then emulate the interaction of the resulting verifier by following the description in Section 3. Note that what we need to emulate in a non-trivial manner is merely the state maintained by the (resulting) verifier between communication rounds.

Comments: Since anyhow we are obtaining only a computationally-sound interactive proof (i.e., an argument system), we may as well emulate argument systems of low (total) communication complexity (cf. Kilian [11]), rather than interactive proofs or NP-proofs.[12] This way, the resulting proof system will also have low (total) communication complexity (because the length of the state maintained by the original verifier between communication rounds need not exceed the length of the total communication). (We stress that the original argument systems of low communication complexity cannot be executed, per se, in the current model, because its soundness relies on the verifier's memory of a previous message.) We also comment that (like in the description of Section 3),

---

[11] In fact, the existence of one-way functions suffices, but this requires a minor modification of the argument used in Proposition 4. Specifically, instead of using a tree structure to hash configurations into short strings, we use the tree as an authentication tree, where collision-resistant hashing is replaced by (length-decreasing) MACs.

[12] Recall that interactive proof systems are unlikely to have low (total) communication complexity; see the work of Goldreich and Hastad [4]. The interested reader is also referred to a follow-up work by Goldreich, Vadhan and Wigderson [8].

we can handle the case where the actual input (i.e., x) or part of it is sent to the verifier during the proof process (rather than being handed to it at the very start).

References

1. M. Bellare and P. Rogaway. Random oracles are practical: a paradigm for designing efficient protocols. In *1st Conference on Computer and Communications Security*, pages 62–73. ACM, 1993.
2. M. Blum, W. S. Evans, P. Gemmell, S. Kannan and M. Naor, Checking the Correctness of Memories, *Algorithmica*, 12(2/3), pages 225–244, 1994. Preliminary version in *32nd FOCS*, 1991.
3. G. Brassard, D. Chaum and C. Crépeau. Minimum Disclosure Proofs of Knowledge. *JCSS*, Vol. 37, No. 2, pages 156–189, 1988. Preliminary version by Brassard and Crépeau in *27th FOCS*, 1986.
4. O. Goldreich and J. Håstad. On the complexity of interactive proofs with bounded communication. *Information Processing Letters*, 67(4):205–214, 1998.
5. R. Canetti, O. Goldreich and S. Halevi. The Random Oracle Methodology, Revisited. Preliminary version in *Proceedings of the 30th Annual ACM Symposium on the Theory of Computing*, Dallas, TX, May 1998. ACM. TR version(s) available on-line from `http://eprint.iacr.org/1998/011` and `http://xxx.lanl.gov/abs/cs.CR/0010019`.
6. O. Goldreich, S. Goldwasser, and S. Micali. How to construct random functions. *Journal of the ACM*, 33(4):210–217, 1986.
7. O. Goldreich and R. Ostrovsky. Software Protection and Simulation on Oblivious RAMs. *JACM*, Vol. 43, 1996, pages 431–473.
8. O. Goldreich, S. Vadhan and A. Wigderson. On interactive proofs with a laconic provers. In *Proc. of the 28th ICALP*, Springer's LNCS 2076, pages 334–345, 2001.
9. S. Goldwasser, S. Micali and C. Rackoff. The Knowledge Complexity of Interactive Proof Systems. *SICOMP*, Vol. 18, pages 186–208, 1989. Preliminary version in *17th STOC*, 1985.
10. C. Holenstein, U. Maurer, and R. Renner. Indifferentiability, Impossibility Results on Reductions, and Applications to the Random Oracle Methodology. Appears in these proceedings. Also available at `http://eprint.iacr.org/2003/161/`
11. J. Kilian. A Note on Efficient Zero-Knowledge Proofs and Arguments. In *24th STOC*, pages 723–732, 1992.
12. R.C. Merkle. A certified digital signature. Advances in cryptology—CRYPTO '89, Vol. 435 of Lecture Notes in Computer Science, pages 218–238, Springer, New York, 1990.
13. S. Micali. Computationally Sound Proofs. *SICOMP*, Vol. 30 (4), pages 1253–1298, 2000. Preliminary version in *35th FOCS*, 1994.
14. M. Naor and M. Yung. Universal one-way hash functions and their cryptographic applications. In *Proceedings of the 21st Annual ACM Symposium on Theory of Computing*, pages 33–43, 1989.

Universally Composable Commitments Using Random Oracles

Dennis Hofheinz and Jörn Müller-Quade

IAKS, Arbeitsgruppe Systemsicherheit,
Prof. Dr.Th. Beth, Fakultät für Informatik,
Universität Karlsruhe, Germany.
{hofheinz,muellerq}@ira.uka.de

Abstract. In the setting of universal composability [Can01], commitments cannot be implemented without additional assumptions such as that of a publicly available *common reference string* [CF01]. Here, as an alternative to the commitments in the common reference string model, the use of *random oracles* to achieve universal composability of commitment protocols is motivated. Special emphasis is put on the security in the situation when the additional "helper functionality" is replaced by a realizable primitive. This contribution gives two constructions which allow to turn a given non-interactive commitment scheme into a non-interactive universally composable commitment scheme in the random oracle model. For both constructions the binding and the hiding property remain valid when *collision-free hash functions* are used instead of random oracles. Moreover the second construction in this case even preserves the property of perfect binding.

Keywords: cryptographic protocols, universal composition, commitment, random oracle.

1 Introduction

The framework [Can01] for multi-party computations allows to formulate the security and, in particular, the composition of multi-party protocols in a very general way. It is possible to treat security notions for rather different multi-party tasks in a common way. For this, protocols are compared to idealized versions of the respective protocol task. If a protocol "behaves" exactly like this idealization with respect to any attacker and in any environment, it is considered a secure realization of the protocol task in question. In the setting of [Can01] an arbitrary environment surrounding the protocol execution is mimicked by an *environment machine* $\mathcal{Z}$. Furthermore the environment machine $\mathcal{Z}$ serves as a distinguisher between a real protocol and the idealized version. A protocol is securely realizing an ideal functionality if no environment $\mathcal{Z}$ can distinguish between an execution of the real protocol with a real adversary and a run of the ideal functionality together with a simulator trying to mimic the effect of the real attack. For the purpose of distinguishing the environment machine may choose the inputs for all

M. Naor (Ed.): TCC 2004, LNCS 2951, pp. 58–76, 2004.

parties, may see the outputs of all parties, and may interact with the adversary at any time during the protocol.

This notion of security, which implies *universal composability* [Can01], is very strict and it was shown in [CF01], that an idealization of a *commitment* task cannot be securely realized in this sense *without additional assumptions.* (With additional assumptions, we mean special facilities protocol participants may use and which itself may not be securely realizable; as an example, consider public information ideally chosen from some predefined distribution. See below for details.)

However, in [CF01,DN02,CLOS02], several protocols for securely realizing an idealization of a commitment functionality are presented; all of them are formulated in the *common reference string model*, i. e., all of them expect access to public information ideally drawn from some predefined distribution.

The selection of this common reference string is crucial for the security of the commitment protocol. In particular, "imperfect" selections possibly influenced by an adversary may affect the security of the commitment protocol in a very severe way, as will be discussed in Section 3.1. The common reference string in [CF01] serves as a public key to which the corresponding secret key is unknown by assumption. If, in the worst case, the adversary were allowed to choose the common reference string by himself then the binding property as well as the hiding property of a commitment scheme built on this common reference string would be compromised (an analogous statement holds for the constructions in [DN02,CLOS02]). This is especially dangerous as this security leak cannot be "detected", because the public key is chosen with the appropriate distribution. As a different approach, we consider the use of *random oracles* for building bit commitment protocols. Of course, like the common reference string, random oracles are not realizable and the property of universal composability is lost when concrete functions replace the random oracle calls. This is in accordance with other results like [CGH98,Nie02,GTK03,BBP03]. These contributions show explicitly that there are protocols which can be proven secure in the random oracle model, yet lose this security completely when instantiating the random oracles. In contrast to that, we show that there is a construction which turns a given bit commitment protocol into a protocol which is universally composable in the random oracle model and which *remains* binding and hiding when substituting the random oracles with a special class of functions (namely, collision-free hash functions).

As a first solution one might think of using random oracles to derive a common reference string with which universally composable bit commitment can be obtained. But if a random oracle would be replaced by any real hash function no general guarantee for the derived common reference string could be given and all protocols on its basis would be critical. To ensure the common reference string to be chosen at random one could think of deriving it by an interactive protocol which still ensures randomness of the common reference string when random oracles are replaced by real hash functions. But this is not the approach chosen here as this additional interactive protocol reduces the efficiency.

In this contribution we use random oracles in a different way to obtain universal composability which ensures the properties binding and hiding even if the random oracles are replaced by arbitrary collision free hash functions. A random oracle will be used as a function which can be evaluated by every participant of the protocol, but which is not accessible to the environment machine. The equivocabiltiy of a bit commitment, which is important for simulatability, can then easily be obtained as in the ideal protocol no random oracle exists and the ideal adversary can determine the outcome of (simulated) evaluations of the random oracle. (Note that in [Nie02], a similar method was used to obtain non-committing encryption in the random oracle model.)

Furthermore this limitation put up on the environment machine will make it impossible for the environment machine to generate commitments to strings unknown to the attacker thereby preventing attacks where the environment machine uses a corrupted party as a *relay* to insert such bit commitments into the protocol. Specifically, we give two constructions to convert a bit commitment scheme into a universally composable bit commitment scheme using random oracles. Both constructions yield bit commitments which remain binding and hiding if the random oracle used is replaced by an arbitrary collision free hash function. The first and more simple construction however does not conserve the property of being perfectly binding, whereas the second construction yields a commitment scheme which is perfectly binding if the original commitment scheme was.

2   Preliminaries

2.1   The General Framework

To start, we shortly outline the framework for multi-party protocols defined in [Can01]. First of all, *parties* (denoted by P_1 through P_n) are modeled as *interactive Turing machines (ITMs)* (cf. [Can01]) and are supposed to run some (fixed) protocol π. There also is an *adversary* (denoted $\mathcal{A}$ and modeled as an ITM as well) carrying out attacks on protocol π. Therefore, $\mathcal{A}$ may corrupt parties (in which case it learns the party's current state and the contents of all its tapes, and controls its future actions), and intercept or, when assuming unauthenticated message transfer, also fake messages sent between parties. If $\mathcal{A}$ corrupts parties only *before* the actual protocol run of π takes place, $\mathcal{A}$ is called *non-adaptive*, otherwise $\mathcal{A}$ is said to be *adaptive*. The respective local inputs for protocol π are supplied by an *environment machine* (modeled as an ITM and denoted $\mathcal{Z}$), which may also read all outputs locally made by the parties and communicate with the adversary. Here we will only deal with environments guaranteeing a polynomial (in the security parameter) number of total steps all participating ITMs run. For more discussion on this issue, cf. [HMQS03b].

The model we have just described is called the *real* model of computation. In contrast to this, the *ideal* model of computation is defined just like the real model, with the following exceptions: we have an additional ITM called the *ideal functionality* $\mathcal{F}$ and being able to send messages to and receive messages from the parties privately (i.e., without the adversary being able to even intercept these messages). The ideal functionality may not be corrupted by the adversary, yet may send messages to and receive messages from it. Furthermore, the parties $P_1, \ldots, P_n$ are replaced by *dummy parties* $\tilde{P}_1, \ldots, \tilde{P}_n$ which simply forward their respective inputs to $\mathcal{F}$ and take messages received from $\mathcal{F}$ as output. Finally, the adversary in the ideal model is called the *simulator* and denoted $\mathcal{S}$. The only means of attack the simulator has in the ideal model are those of corrupting parties (which has the same effect as in the real model), delaying or even suppressing messages sent from $\mathcal{F}$ to a party, and all actions that are explicitly specified in $\mathcal{F}$. However, $\mathcal{S}$ has no access to the contents of the messages sent from $\mathcal{F}$ to the dummy parties (except in the case the receiving party is corrupted) nor are there any messages actually sent between (uncorrupted) parties $\mathcal{S}$ could intercept. Intuitively, the ideal model of computation (or, more precisely, the ideal functionality $\mathcal{F}$ itself) should represent what we ideally expect a protocol to do. In fact, for a number of standard tasks, there are formulations as such ideal functionalities (see, e. g., [Can01]).

To decide whether or not a given protocol π does what we would ideally expect some ideal functionality $\mathcal{F}$ to do, the framework of [Can01] uses a *simulatability*-based approach: at a time of its choice, $\mathcal{Z}$ may enter its halt state and leave output on its output tape. The random variable describing the first bit of $\mathcal{Z}$'s output will be denoted by $\mathrm{REAL}_{\pi,\mathcal{A},\mathcal{Z}}(k,z)$ when $\mathcal{Z}$ is run on *security parameter* $k \in \mathbb{N}$ and initial input $z \in \{0,1\}^*$ (which may, in case of a non-uniform $\mathcal{Z}$, depend on k) in the real model of computation, and $\mathrm{IDEAL}_{\mathcal{F},\mathcal{S},\mathcal{Z}}(k,z)$ when $\mathcal{Z}$ is run in the ideal model. Now if for any adversary $\mathcal{A}$ in the real model, there exists a simulator $\mathcal{S}$ in the ideal model such that for *any* environment $\mathcal{Z}$ and *any* initial input z, we have that

$$|\mathbf{P}(\mathrm{REAL}_{\pi,\mathcal{A},\mathcal{Z}}(k,z) = 1) - \mathbf{P}(\mathrm{IDEAL}_{\mathcal{F},\mathcal{S},\mathcal{Z}}(k,z) = 1)| \qquad (1)$$

is a negligible[1] function in k, then protocol π is said to *securely realize* functionality $\mathcal{F}$.[2] Intuitively, this means that any attack carried out by adversary $\mathcal{A}$ in the real model can also be carried out in the idealized modeling with an ideal functionality by the simulator $\mathcal{S}$ (hence the name), such that no environment is able to tell the difference. By definition, the trivial protocol which does not generate output realizes *any* ideal functionality securely. (The corresponding simulator just has to suppress delivery of messages from the ideal functionality to the parties.) To avoid such trivial realizations, we will only consider *terminating* protocols, which eventually generate output when all protocol messages in the real model are delivered.

To allow for a modular protocol design, in [Can01] also the $\mathcal{F}$-*hybrid model of computation* (for an arbitrary ideal functionality $\mathcal{F}$) is introduced. Briefly, this model is identical to the real model of computation, but the parties have access to an unbounded number of instances of $\mathcal{F}$, each one identified via a

---

[1] A function $f : \mathbb{N} \to \mathbb{R}$ is called *negligible*, if for any $c \in \mathbb{N}$, there is a $k_0 \in \mathbb{N}$ such that $|f(k)| < k^{-c}$ for all $k > k_0$.

[2] The formulation in [Can01] is slightly different, but equivalent to the one chosen here which allows to simplify our presentation.

session identifier (SID). The modularity of the hybrid model is legitimated by the fundamental *composition theorem* of [Can01]. Summarizing, it states that once protocol τ securely realizes functionality $\mathcal{F}$, in any protocol π running in the $\mathcal{F}$-hybrid model, a polynomial number of instances of $\mathcal{F}$ can be substituted by invocations of τ *without losing security*. Specifically, for every real-life adversary $\mathcal{A}$, there is a hybrid-model adversary $\mathcal{H}$ such that no environment can tell whether it is interacting with $\mathcal{A}$ and π (with $\mathcal{F}$-instances substituted by invocations of τ) in the real model, or with $\mathcal{H}$ and π in the $\mathcal{F}$-hybrid model.

2.2   The Common Reference String Model

To catch the notion of information publicly known to all protocol participants, the modeling of [Can01] can be extended to give any participant (including the adversary) access to a *common reference string*, initially chosen from some distribution D. This can be cast as the $\mathcal{F}_{\text{CRS}}$-hybrid model, where $\mathcal{F}_{\text{CRS}}$ denotes the ideal functionality that in its first activation chooses a value d from a distribution D (the latter over which $\mathcal{F}_{\text{CRS}}$ is parameterized). From this point on, it replies to any request from a party P_i or from the adversary with this value d.

2.3   Collision-Free Hash Functions

A family $\mathcal{H} = \{H_k\}_{k \in \mathbb{N}}$ of functions $H_k : \{0,1\}^* \to \{0,1\}^k$ is called a *family of collision-free hash functions*, if the following requirements are met:

- There is a probabilistic algorithm A computing H_k in time polynomial in both k and input length.
- There is *no* probabilistic algorithm B being able to find $x, y \in \{0,1\}^*$ sufficing $x \neq y$ and $H_k(x) = H_k(y)$ in polynomial time with non-negligible probability.

Using the argument in the proof of [Dam90, Lemma 2.1], one can derive a certain *one-way* property: for a family of collision-free hash functions $\mathcal{H} = \{H_k\}$ as above, there can be *no* probabilistic algorithm C which, on input $y = H_k(x) \in \{0,1\}^k$ for uniformly selected $x \in \{0,1\}^{k+1}$, succeeds with non-negligible probability to find $x' \in \{0,1\}^{k+1}$ sufficing $H(x') = y$ in polynomial time.

2.4   The Random Oracle Model

The *random oracle model* (see, e.g., [BR93]) captures an idealization of a hash function. In particular, the idealized version allows only black-box access and cannot be "predicted" without explicitly evaluating it. Moreover, the function values are uniformly selected random k-bit strings. Using the terminology just described, the random oracle model can be modeled in the setting of [Can01] as the $\mathcal{F}_{\text{RO}}$-hybrid model for the ideal functionality $\mathcal{F}_{\text{RO}}$ given in Figure 1. In the presence of more than one party, $\mathcal{F}_{\text{RO}}$ cannot be realized securely *without* inter-party communication. (In this case, its very definition forces any protocol aimed

---

Functionality $\mathcal{F}_{\mathrm{RO}}$

$\mathcal{F}_{\mathrm{RO}}$ proceeds as follows, running on security parameter k, with parties $P_1, \ldots, P_n$ and an adversary $\mathcal{S}$.

1. $\mathcal{F}_{\mathrm{RO}}$ keeps a list L (which is initially empty) of pairs of bitstrings.
2. Upon receiving a value (sid, m) (with $m \in \{0,1\}^*$) from some party P_i or from $\mathcal{S}$, do:
   - If there is a pair $(m, \tilde{h})$ for some $\tilde{h} \in \{0,1\}^k$ in the list L, set $h := \tilde{h}$.
   - If there is no such pair, choose uniformly $h \in \{0,1\}^k$ and store the pair (m, h) in L.
   Once h is set, reply to the activating machine (i.e., either P_i or $\mathcal{S}$) with (sid, h).

Fig. 1. Functionality $\mathcal{F}_{\mathrm{RO}}$

at realizing $\mathcal{F}_{\mathrm{RO}}$ to behave like an "almost" deterministic function evaluation; yet such a—by construction easily computable and explicitly given—function can be distinguished easily from $\mathcal{F}_{\mathrm{RO}}$, which chooses its return values completely at random in each run.) In particular, one cannot hope to securely realize $\mathcal{F}_{\mathrm{RO}}$ by, e. g., a family of collision-free hash functions. Below we will investigate possible consequences of such "imperfect" realizations of $\mathcal{F}_{\mathrm{RO}}$.

2.5   Security Notions for Commitments

First a general remark: for any probabilistic algorithm A we write $A(x; r)$ to indicate execution of A on input $x \in \{0,1\}^*$ and with explicitly supplied random coins $r \in \{0,1\}^*$. Now a *non-interactive string commitment scheme* $C = \{C_k, V_k\}$, indexed by a security parameter $k \in \mathbb{N}$, is a family of polynomial-time (in both k and input length) algorithms C_k and V_k, where the C_k may be probabilistic. We mandate that C_k outputs a tuple (com, dec) of bitstrings com and dec on input $m \in \{0,1\}^*$, while V_k generates output $m \in \{0,1\}^* \cup \{\bot\}$ on input (com, dec). Furthermore, we require:

1. (Meaningfulness.) $V_k(C_k(m)) = m$ for all $k \in \mathbb{N}$ and $m \in \{0,1\}^*$.
2. (Hiding property.) For any $m \in \{0,1\}^*$, let $\{com(m)\}$ denote the distribution $\{com; (com, dec) \leftarrow C_k(m)\}$. We require that for arbitrary $m_1, m_2 \in \{0,1\}^*$ with $|m_1| = |m_2|$, the distributions $\{com(m_1)\}$ and $\{com(m_2)\}$ are computationally indistinguishable. If any two such distributions are also indistinguishable for computationally *unbounded* algorithms, we say that the scheme is *unconditionally hiding*.
3. (Binding property.) There is *no* probabilistic, polynomial-time (in k) algorithm B which is able to produce with non-negligible probability (in k) a tuple (com, dec_1, dec_2) such that $\bot \neq V_k(com, dec_1) \neq V_k(com, dec_2) \neq \bot$. If this holds even for computationally unbounded B, then the scheme is said to be *unconditionally binding*.

It will be convenient to denote by $com_k^C(m)$ (resp. $dec_k^C(m)$) the first (resp., the second) component of C_k's output when run on input m; in particular, com_k^C and dec_k^C can be viewed as probabilistic algorithms.

3   Commitment in the Random Oracle Model

3.1   Motivation

The common reference string model proved extremely useful for realizing general ideal functionalities: in [CLOS02], it is shown that almost any two-party ideal functionality $\mathcal{F}$ can be realized in the $\mathcal{F}_{CRS}$-hybrid model, under the assumption that trapdoor permutations and augmented two-party non-committing encryption protocols exist. It is also shown there that this result can be extended to the multi-party case when we additionally assume a broadcast channel available (which can also be modeled as an ideal functionality). A key point in the constructions of [CLOS02] is the realization of the commitment functionality $\mathcal{F}_{MCOM}$ (see also Appendix A) in the $\mathcal{F}_{CRS}$-hybrid model. Since $\mathcal{F}_{MCOM}$ cannot be securely realized as a two-party computation in the real model (see [CF01]), one must assume some "helper functionality" such as $\mathcal{F}_{CRS}$ available. Indeed, in [CF01,DN02,CLOS02], several realizations of different commitment functionalities are described in the common reference string model.

Let's shortly recall which additional features the common reference string is to give us, when having in mind securely realizing, e. g., $\mathcal{F}_{MCOM}$ (cf. also the discussion in [CLOS02, Section 5]). First, note that at a time one party initiates a commitment in the ideal model, the simulator $\mathcal{S}$ must be able to supply the environment $\mathcal{Z}$ with a valid commitment *without* knowing to which value P_i is actually committed. Furthermore, in case of a corrupted committer, $\mathcal{S}$ must be able to *extract* the committed bit out of a valid commitment. Since alone *choosing* the common reference string must enable the simulator do to so, the whole security of a commitment protocol formulated in the common reference string model relies on the fact that $\mathcal{F}_{CRS}$ chooses the common reference string *ideally* and in a trusted manner.

Moreover, once we assume "imperfect" implementations of the ideal functionality $\mathcal{F}_{CRS}$ (i. e., publicly available random strings whose choice may somehow be influenced by an adversary), any protocol which realizes $\mathcal{F}_{MCOM}$ in the $\mathcal{F}_{CRS}$-hybrid model may get insecure in a fatal way: in the extreme case in which an adversary may freely *choose* the common reference string, it can generate "fake" commitments which it can later open as 0 *or* 1, as well as "look into" legitimately generated commitments at wish. Specifically, such imperfect common reference strings can damage the security of the general constructions in [CLOS02] in a serious way. That is, a protocol which is to realize some ideal functionality $\mathcal{F}$ using commitments loses not only its universal composability property, but also may lose security in a very "intuitive" way, since the underlying commitment scheme does so.

One way to avoid this is to use another "helper functionality". In this contribution we will present two constructions in the $\mathcal{F}_{RO}$-hybrid model where a random oracle $\mathcal{F}_{RO}$ is available. The constructions of this work allow to turn a given non-interactive string commitment scheme into a non-interactive string commitment scheme in the $\mathcal{F}_{RO}$-hybrid model which is universally composable. Moreover the constructions ensure the hiding and binding proprties even when the random oracles are replaced by arbitrary collision free hash functions. The second construction even preserves the property of perfect binding. In fact, when implementing the ideal commitment functionality via a hiding and unconditionally binding commitment scheme, the construction in [CLOS02] (formulated in the framework of [Can01]) for realizing general ideal functionalities is essentially the one presented in [GMW87,Gol02] in the special case of a *secure function evaluation*.

3.2   A Universally Composable Commitment Scheme

First, let's have a look at the abovementioned functionality $\mathcal{F}_{SCOM}$, which is derived from the functionality $\mathcal{F}_{MCOM}$ of [CLOS02] (the latter which is also given in Appendix A). A description of $\mathcal{F}_{SCOM}$ is given in Figure 2. The commitment phase described is different than that of $\mathcal{F}_{MCOM}$. This is to take into account the following attack, which is described for the case of key exchange in [HMQS03a], and goes back to an argument of Damgård for the case of bit commitment. For this attack, one party P_i is invoked with input b by the environment. Then, before any messages are delivered, the environment instructs the adversary to corrupt P_i and to let it perform the protocol from the start, but using input $b' \neq b$. In the ideal model, P_i's input b is already forwarded to $\mathcal{F}_{MCOM}$ and can *not* be changed anymore, although P_i gets corrupted later on. On the other hand, in the real model, the bit committed to will be $b' \neq b$, as P_i is "reset" when corrupted and no messages were delivered before. This allows for a "trivial" distinction of real and ideal model for *any* protocol aimed at realizing $\mathcal{F}_{MCOM}$; we solved this situation by a modified functionality $\mathcal{F}_{SCOM}$ which lets the adversary decide on the point in time when a commit input is accepted. An alternative to our formulation would be to change the framework to let the adversary also delay messages sent from parties *to* the ideal functionality. This approach was taken in [CLOS02, revision dated July 14th].

Notice that different commitments are handled via different subsession identifiers, each one of them handling at most one commitment per committer–receiver pair. Furthermore, $\mathcal{F}_{SCOM}$ allows committing to a string of bits rather than only to a single bit. It is worthwhile to point out that *no* information (not even length information) about the string m committed to is given to the adversary.

Now assume that $C = \{C_k, V_k\}$ is a non-interactive string commitment scheme as described in Section 2.5. Consider protocol HC$_C$ given in Figure 3. This protocol is formulated in the $\mathcal{F}_{RO}$-hybrid model and aimed at realizing the ideal functionality $\mathcal{F}_{SCOM}$.

Proposition 1. *Assuming authenticated links, protocol* HC$_C$ *securely realizes* $\mathcal{F}_{SCOM}$ *with respect to adaptive adversaries as soon as* $C = \{C_k, V_k\}$ *is a non-interactive string commitment scheme.*

Functionality $\mathcal{F}_{\mathrm{SCOM}}$

$\mathcal{F}_{\mathrm{SCOM}}$ proceeds as follows, running with parties $P_1, \dots, P_n$ and an adversary $\mathcal{S}$:

- **Commit Phase**:
    1. When receiving a message (commit, $sid, ssid, P_i, P_j, m$) from P_i, where $m \in \{0,1\}^*$, first send the message (request, $sid, ssid, P_i, P_j$) to the adversary $\mathcal{S}$ and, if $\mathcal{S}$ then issues a corresponding ready message (see below), proceed to the third step.
    2. When receiving (ready, $sid, ssid, P_i, P_j, \ell$) from the adversary, and at least ℓ messages (commit, $sid, ssid, P_i, P_j, m$) (possibly with different m's) have been received from P_i, perform the third step described below with the message m contained in the ℓth of these messages.
    3. Record the tuple ($ssid, P_i, P_j, m$) and send (receipt, $sid, ssid, P_i, P_j$) to P_j. Ignore any future commit messages with the same $ssid$ from P_i to P_j.
- **Reveal Phase**: Upon receiving a message (reveal, $sid, ssid, P_j$) from P_i: If a tuple ($ssid, P_i, P_j, m$) was previously recorded, then send the message (reveal, $sid, ssid, P_i, P_j, m$) to P_j and $\mathcal{S}$. Otherwise, ignore.

Fig. 2. Functionality $\mathcal{F}_{\mathrm{SCOM}}$

Proof. For any adversary $\mathcal{H}$ mounting attacks on protocol HC$_C$ in the $\mathcal{F}_{\mathrm{RO}}$-hybrid model, we describe a simulator $\mathcal{S} = \mathcal{S}_{\mathcal{H}}$ emulating such attacks in the ideal model. $\mathcal{S}$ internally keeps a *complete* simulation of a run of $\mathcal{H}$ in the $\mathcal{F}_{\mathrm{RO}}$-hybrid model. That is, $\mathcal{S}$ keeps a simulation of parties $P_1^{(s)}$ through $P_n^{(s)}$ running protocol HC$_C$, a simulation of $\mathcal{H}$ interacting with these parties, and (as needed) simulated instances of the ideal functionality $\mathcal{F}_{\mathrm{RO}}$. Communication of $\mathcal{H}$ with the environment is forwarded to the (non-simulated) environment $\mathcal{Z}$ with which $\mathcal{S}$ is to interact. Similarly, messages from $\mathcal{Z}$ to $\mathcal{S}$ are forwarded to the adversary $\mathcal{H}$ in the simulation.

Of course, $\mathcal{S}$ still needs to keep its simulation consistent with all inputs the dummy parties receive from $\mathcal{Z}$; similarly, the output behaviour of the dummy parties has to be the same as that of the simulated parties. (Note that generally, $\mathcal{S}$ has no information about inputs and only existence information about outputs of the dummy parties, unless the ideal functionality explicitly informs $\mathcal{S}$ about incoming input, or about output sent to the parties.) Therefore, $\mathcal{S}$ acts as follows:

- When the simulated $\mathcal{H}$ corrupts a simulated party $P_i^{(s)}$, $\mathcal{S}$ first corrupts the corresponding dummy party P_i and modifies $P_i^{(s)}$'s state to account for ignored inputs possibly handed from $\mathcal{Z}$ to P_i. (Upon corruption of P_i, $\mathcal{S}$ gets to know about such messages when receiving the state of P_i.)
- Upon receiving (receipt, $sid, ssid, P_i, P_j$) from $\mathcal{F}_{\mathrm{SCOM}}$ (in which case P_i and thus $P_i^{(s)}$ must be uncorrupted), $\mathcal{S}$ picks $s \in \{0,1\}^k$ uniformly and computes $com_1 \leftarrow com_k^C(s; r_2)$ and $com_2 \leftarrow com_k^C(\mathcal{O}_{sid}(r_2); r_3)$ for a uniformly chosen r_3 (here the simulated random oracle $\mathcal{F}_{\mathrm{RO}}$ is queried). Then, $\mathcal{S}$ sim-

---

Protocol HC$_C$

These are instructions for parties P_1 through P_n to carry out commitments. The parties expect to be run in the $\mathcal{F}_{\mathrm{RO}}$-hybrid model. For ease of notation, here $\mathcal{O}_{sid}(x)$ denotes the reply of the $\mathcal{F}_{\mathrm{RO}}$-instance with session ID sid to the query x.

- When activated with input (commit, $sid, ssid, P_i, P_j, m$), where $m \in \{0, 1\}^*$, P_i computes $(com_1, dec_1) \leftarrow C_k(\mathcal{O}_{sid}(ssid, i, j, m, r_1); r_2)$ for a uniformly chosen k-bit string r_1. Note that by $r_2 \in \{0, 1\}^*$, we denote the random coins used by C_k during this process. Then, P_i computes $(com_2, dec_2) \leftarrow C_k(\mathcal{O}_{sid}(r_2))$ and sends the message $(sid, ssid, com_1, com_2)$ to P_j while storing $(ssid, j, m, r_1, r_2, dec_2)$. Further (commit, $sid, ssid, P_i, P_j, \cdot$) inputs are ignored.
- When receiving $(sid, ssid, com_1, com_2)$ from P_i, where $com_1, com_2 \in \{0, 1\}^*$ and $ssid$ is a subsession ID under which P_j did not yet get such a message from any party, P_j stores the pair $(ssid, i, com_1, com_2)$ and locally outputs (receipt, $sid, ssid, P_i, P_j$). Any future messages $(sid, ssid, com_1', com_2')$ with the same subsession ID $ssid$ from P_i are ignored.
- When activated on input (reveal, $sid, ssid, P_j$), party P_i checks if it has a tuple $(ssid, j, m, r_1, dec_2)$ (for any m, r_1, dec_2) stored. If so, P_i sends the tuple $(sid, ssid, m, r_1, r_2, dec_2)$ to P_j. Further inputs (reveal, $sid, ssid, P_j$) are ignored.
- When receiving $(sid, ssid, m, r_1, r_2, dec_2)$ with $m, dec_2, r_1, r_2 \in \{0, 1\}^*$ from P_i while already having received a value $(sid, ssid, com_1, com_2)$ also from P_i, P_j first computes $o_2 \leftarrow V_k(com_2, dec_2)$. Then, if $o_2 = \mathcal{O}_{sid}(r_2)$, P_j checks if $com_k^C(\mathcal{O}_{sid}(ssid, i, j, m, r_1); r_2)$ equals com_1. If so, P_j locally outputs (reveal, $sid, ssid, P_i, P_j, m$) and ignores all further $(sid, ssid, \ldots)$ messages. In any other case, P_j does nothing.

Fig. 3. Protocol HC$_C$

ulates a message $(sid, ssid, com_1, com_2)$ from $P_i^{(s)}$ to $P_j^{(s)}$ and stores this message together with r_2, r_3, and s.

- When $\mathcal{H}$ delivers a message $(sid, ssid, com_1, com_2)$ from $P_i^{(s)}$ to $P_j^{(s)}$, and $P_j^{(s)}$ did not yet get such a message with subsession ID $ssid$ from P_i, $\mathcal{S}$ proceeds as follows: if $P_i^{(s)}$ (and hence P_i as well) is uncorrupted, $\mathcal{S}$ sends (ready, $sid, ssid, P_i, P_j, 1$) to $\mathcal{F}_{\mathrm{SCOM}}$, and delivers the receipt message then sent from $\mathcal{F}_{\mathrm{SCOM}}$ to P_j as soon as $P_j^{(s)}$ outputs such a receipt message (i. e., immediately afterwards).

If, on the other hand, $P_i^{(s)}$ (and thus P_i) is corrupted, then first the message m committed to may have to be extracted from com_1 and com_2 which could have been supplied by $\mathcal{Z}$ without appropriate commit input. By looking up all queries to the simulated $\mathcal{F}_{\mathrm{RO}}$-instance with session ID sid, we can reduce to a polynomial number of possible m-r_1-r_2-combinations. Hence by verifying whether com_1 equals $com_k^C(\mathcal{O}_{sid}(ssid, i, j, m, r_1); r_2)$, $\mathcal{S}$ can extract

m alone from com_1, provided that the commitment can be unveiled according to HC and $\mathcal{F}_{\mathrm{RO}}$ did never output the same value twice. (Note that here we use the binding property of C.) In these latter cases, it suffices to set m to 0 (or any other value), since $\mathcal{F}_{\mathrm{RO}}$ produces collisions only in a negligible fraction of runs and commitments generated without explicitly querying the random oracle can be unveiled only with negligible probability. (Here it is important that since the subsession identifier sid and the party identities i and j are hashed together with m, hash values cannot be "re-used" in a different subsession.)

Once m is determined, $\mathcal{S}$ sends (commit, $sid, ssid, P_i, P_j, m$) in the name of the corrupted relay P_i to functionality $\mathcal{F}_{\mathrm{SCOM}}$, followed by a corresponding (ready, $sid, ssid, P_i, P_j, \ell$) signal. Here ℓ denotes the number of already received request notifications plus 1, and thus indicates that the message m just sent is to be committed to. This causes the ideal functionality to send a receipt message to P_j, which then can be delivered by $\mathcal{S}$ as soon as $P_j^{(s)}$ generates output in the simulation.

– Upon receiving (reveal, $sid, ssid, P_i, P_j, m$) from $\mathcal{F}_{\mathrm{SCOM}}$ (which means that P_i is still uncorrupted), $\mathcal{S}$ lets $P_i^{(s)}$ compute a commitment to m at P_j (under session ID sid and subsession ID $ssid$), but forces
  • the simulated $\mathcal{F}_{\mathrm{RO}}$ with session ID sid to output s when queried by $P_i^{(s)}$ with $(ssid, i, j, m, r_1)$ (this is not possible when $\mathcal{F}_{\mathrm{RO}}$ was queried on $(ssid, i, j, m, r_1)$ before; yet, since r_1 is chosen uniformly from $\{0,1\}^k$ by $P_i^{(s)}$, this only occurs with negligible probability)
  • $P_i^{(s)}$ to use the values r_2 and r_3 which $\mathcal{S}$ stored together with the message $(sid, ssid, j, com_1, com_2)$.

  Now $\mathcal{S}$ dismisses the actual commitment message sent from $P_i^{(s)}$ to $P_j^{(s)}$ (note that by construction, this message is exactly the message simulated by $\mathcal{S}$) and modifies $P_i^{(s)}$'s internal state so as to look as if this commitment had been performed exactly at the time the corresponding message $(sid, ssid, com_1, com_2)$ was simulated from $P_i^{(s)}$ to $P_j^{(s)}$.

  Finally, P_i is fed with input (reveal, $sid, ssid, P_i, P_j, m$) to reflect in the simulation the actual decommitment operation $\mathcal{S}$ was informed about. The reveal message sent from $\mathcal{F}_{\mathrm{SCOM}}$ to P_j is delivered as soon as $P_j^{(s)}$ generates as output the corresponding reveal message.

– The same procedure is applied to all commitments P_i has not yet opened when $P_i^{(s)}$ gets corrupted. (Note that then, $\mathcal{S}$ gets to know the corresponding messages committed to by receiving P_i's state.)

– Finally, if $P_j^{(s)}$ generates reveal output while uncorrupted, the corresponding dummy party P_j has to generate output as well. The steps above take care that this output is the same in the ideal model as in the simulation, except in a negligible fraction of runs. Particularly, $\mathcal{S}$ only needs to deliver the corresponding reveal message from $\mathcal{F}_{\mathrm{SCOM}}$ to P_j when the corresponding committer P_i was uncorrupted at the time it got its reveal input. If, on the other hand, P_i was corrupted at that time, $\mathcal{S}$ must first supply $\mathcal{F}_{\mathrm{SCOM}}$ with the corresponding `reveal` input via the corrupted relay P_i. In this case, $\mathcal{S}$ has already extracted the message m needed for this `reveal` input either from P_i's state (when P_i's corruption took place *after* the delivery of the commitment), or, otherwise, from the actual commitment message delivered to $P_j^{(s)}$. (Here we use that except with negligible probability, there is no efficient way to unveil a commitment in more than one way; by construction of protocol HC_C, this follows from the "collision-freeness" of $\mathcal{F}_{\text{RO}}$.)

By construction, $\mathcal{S}$ provides $\mathcal{Z}$ with a view *identical* to one of a run in the hybrid model, until a `reveal` output of a party P_j differs from that of the respective simulated party $P_j^{(s)}$. However, this can only happen when $\mathcal{S}$ is unable to extract a message out of a commitment sent from a corrupted committer $P_i^{(s)}$ to an uncorrupted receiver $P_j^{(s)}$, or when $\mathcal{S}$ cannot unveil a commitment generated by $\mathcal{S}$ itself. As reasoned above, the probability for any of these is only negligible, henceforth we are done. Note that we did *not* use the hiding property of C.   □

For achieving universal composability, we had to incorporate subsession identifiers and the identities of committer and receiver into the message actually committed to. To allow for statements independent of such protocol-inherent information, we drop that requirement on the format of the message and, to be able to formally view the protocol HC_C as a non-interactive string commitment scheme, we set $\text{HC}_C = \{\mathcal{C}_k, \mathcal{V}_k\}$. Here algorithm $\mathcal{C}_k$ computes $com \leftarrow (com_k^C(\mathcal{O}(m, r_1); r_2), com_k^C(\mathcal{O}(r_2); r_3))$ for uniformly chosen $r_1 \in \{0,1\}^k$ and random coins $r_2, r_3 \in \{0,1\}^*$, then $dec \leftarrow (m, r_1, r_2, dec_k^C(\mathcal{O}(r_2); r_3))$ and returns (com, dec). On input (com, dec) of the form $com = (com_1, com_2)$ and $dec = (m, r_1, r_2, dec_2)$, algorithm $\mathcal{V}_k$ computes $o_2 \leftarrow \mathcal{V}_k(com_2, dec_2)$ and, if $o_2 = \mathcal{O}(r_2)$, checks whether com_1 equals $C_k(\mathcal{O}(m, r_1); r_2)$. Only in this case $\mathcal{V}_k$ returns m, otherwise it returns $\perp$.

As mentioned above, we would like to be able to deduce security properties of the scheme HC_C even when having substituted all random oracles $\mathcal{O}$ by suitable hash functions. Let therefore $\text{HC}_{C,\mathcal{H}}$ denote the scheme which is identical to HC_C, except that all $\mathcal{O}$-queries are replaced by evaluations of H_k, where $\mathcal{H} = \{H_k\}$ is a family of collision-free hash functions as defined in the preliminaries.

Proposition 2. *Once $\mathcal{H} = \{H_k\}$ is a family of collision-free hash functions and $C = \{C_k, V_k\}$ is a non-interactive string commitment scheme, the scheme $\text{HC}_{C,\mathcal{H}} = \{\mathcal{C}_k, \mathcal{V}_k\}$ (as described above) is also a non-interactive string commitment scheme. Furthermore, if C is unconditionally hiding, then so is $\text{HC}_{C,\mathcal{H}}$.*

Proof. Meaningfulness, binding and hiding properties of $\text{HC} = \text{HC}_{C,\mathcal{H}}$ need to be checked. The meaningfulness of HC follows directly from that of C. Furthermore, every algorithm B which supplies a HC-commitment together with two decommitments yielding different messages has to supply in particular a C-commitment together with two C-decommitments yielding messages $H_k(m, r_1)$, resp. $H_k(m', r_1')$. If both are equal, B has found a H_k-collision (since $m \neq m'$ by assumption); if the hash values are different, then B breaks the binding property of C. In either case, we have shown the binding property of HC.

Now for the hiding property, consider the scheme $\text{HC}' = \{\mathcal{C}'_k, \mathcal{V}'_k\}$, which is identical to HC, except that the C-commitment to $H_k(r_2)$ (where r_2 denotes the random coins used in the C-commitment to $H_k(m, r_1)$) is replaced by a C-commitment to 0^k. More formally, $\mathcal{C}'_k(m)$ computes to (com', dec') with $com' \leftarrow (com_k^C(H_k(m, r_1); r_2), com_k^C(0^k))$ and $dec' \leftarrow (m, r_1, r_2)$; the definition of $\mathcal{V}'_k$ is obvious.

Let A be a probabilistic, polynomial-time algorithm which breaks the computational hiding property of HC. More specifically, say that there are messages $m_1, m_2 \in \{0, 1\}^*$, such that the difference

$$\mathbf{Adv}(A, \text{HC}, m_1, m_2) := \mathbf{P}(A(com_k^{\text{HC}}(m_1)) \to 1) - \mathbf{P}(A(com_k^{\text{HC}}(m_2)) \to 1)$$

is a non-negligible function in k. Assume first that

$$\mathbf{Adv}(A, \text{HC}', m_1, m_2) := \mathbf{P}(A(com_k^{\text{HC}'}(m_1)) \to 1) - \mathbf{P}(A(com_k^{\text{HC}'}(m_2)) \to 1)$$

is non-negligible in k as well. Since by construction, a C-commitment to a message $H_k(m, r_1)$ can be extended to an HC'-commitment to the message m *without* knowledge of m or r_1, it follows that from A, we can build a probabilistic, polynomial-time algorithm A_1 with

$$\mathbf{P}(A_1(com_k^C(H_k(m_1, r_1)) \to 1)) - \mathbf{P}(A_1(com_k^C(H_k(m_2, r_1)) \to 1)$$

non-negligible in k for a certain, *fixed* $r_1 \in \{0, 1\}^k$. Such an A_1 would break the hiding property of C, thereby yielding a contradiction.

On the other hand, suppose that $\mathbf{Adv}(A, \text{HC}', m_1, m_2)$ is negligible in k. As then,

$$\mathbf{Adv}(A, \text{HC}, m_1, m_2) - \mathbf{Adv}(A, \text{HC}', m_1, m_2)$$
$$= \left(\mathbf{P}(A(com_k^{\text{HC}}(m_1)) \to 1) - \mathbf{P}(A(com_k^{\text{HC}'}(m_1)) \to 1) \right)$$
$$- \left(\mathbf{P}(A(com_k^{\text{HC}}(m_2)) \to 1) - \mathbf{P}(A(com_k^{\text{HC}'}(m_2)) \to 1) \right)$$

is non-negligible, at least one of the addends on the right-hand side of the equation must be as well. So say that $\mathbf{P}(A(com_k^{\text{HC}}(m_i)) \to 1) - \mathbf{P}(A(com_k^{\text{HC}'}(m_i)) \to 1)$ is non-negligible (with fixed $i \in \{1, 2\}$). Then there have to be certain, *fixed* r_1, r_2 for which A can distinguish tuples $(com_k^C(H_k(m_i, r_1); r_2), com_k^C(H_k(r_2)))$ from tuples $(com_k^C(H_k(m_i, r_1); r_2), com_k^C(0^k))$. Hence from A we can construct a probabilistic, polynomial-time algorithm A_2 with

$$\mathbf{P}(A_2(com_k^C(H_k(r_2)) \to 1)) - \mathbf{P}(A_2(com_k^C(0^k)) \to 1)$$

non-negligible in k, thereby breaking the hiding property of C. So in either case, we have a contradiction and there can be no such algorithm A; consequently, HC must be computationally hiding. As this reduction also applies to computationally unbounded algorithms A, a possible unconditional hiding property of C is preserved. $\qquad\square$

3.3   Preserving Unconditional Binding

Although we have shown that the construction $\text{HC}_{C,\mathcal{H}}$ preserves hiding and computational binding properties of C, this is *not* true for a potential *unconditional* binding property: Any algorithm breaking the collision-freeness of $\mathcal{H}$ can be used to generate HC-commitments together with multiple decommitments to different messages. (Note that with HC, we are actually committed only to the hash value of a message.)

An unconditionally binding string commitment scheme cannot completely hide the length of the message committed to; to reflect this in an idealization, we define the ideal functionality $\mathcal{F}_{\text{BSCOM}}$ to be identical to $\mathcal{F}_{\text{SCOM}}$ (cf. Figure 2), *except* that $\mathcal{F}_{\text{BSCOM}}$ supplies the simulator $\mathcal{S}$ upon a commitment to a message m with the bit length $|m|$ of this message. This length information is included in the respective **request** message sent to the simulator.

Let $F_{\mathcal{H}}$ be the following probabilistic, polynomial-time (in both the security parameter k and its input length) algorithm, where $\mathcal{H} = \{H_k\}_k$ is a family of functions $H_k : \{0,1\}^* \to \{0,1\}^k$ which in turn are computable in polynomial time. Upon input $m = m_1 \cdots m_n \in \{0,1\}^n$, $F_{\mathcal{H}}$ uniformly selects $s_1, \ldots, s_n \in \{0,1\}^k$ with each s_i satisfying $s_i H_k(s_i) \neq H_k(s_i) s_i$ and outputs

$$F_{\mathcal{H}}(m) = \pi(m_1, s_1, H_k(s_1)) \cdots \pi(m_n, s_n, H_k(s_n)),$$

where $\pi(0, s, t) = (s, t)$ and $\pi(1, s, t) = (t, s)$ for arbitrary $s, t \in \{0,1\}^*$. Algorithm $F_{\mathcal{H}}$ will be used to encode a message in a (for the simulator) equivocable yet (for parties) binding way. To extract the encoded message, we will use the following polynomial-time computable function $F_{\mathcal{H}}^{-1}$. We set

$$F_{\mathcal{H}}^{-1}(m) = \begin{cases} 0 & \text{if } r = H_k(l) \text{ and } l \neq H_k(r) \\ 1 & \text{if } r \neq H_k(l) \text{ and } l = H_k(r) \\ \bot & \text{else} \end{cases}$$

for $m = lr$ with $l, r \in \{0,1\}^k$. For $m = m_1 \cdots m_\ell$ with $\ell > 1$ and all $m_i \in \{0,1\}^{2k}$, we define $F_{\mathcal{H}}^{-1}(m) = F_{\mathcal{H}}^{-1}(m_1) \cdots F_{\mathcal{H}}^{-1}(m_\ell)$. In all other cases, we set $F_{\mathcal{H}}^{-1}(m) = \bot$.

Given a non-interactive string commitment scheme C, consider a protocol BHC_C, whose "infrastructure" is identical to that of protocol HC_C, but the commitment and decommitment messages differ slightly, as does the verification procedure. Protocol BHC_C is described in Figure 4.

Proposition 3. *Assuming authenticated links, protocol* BHC_C *securely realizes* $\mathcal{F}_{\text{BSCOM}}$ *with respect to adaptive adversaries as soon as* $C = \{C_k, V_k\}$ *is a non-interactive string commitment scheme.*

Proof. The proof is very similar to the one of Proposition 1, and we will only describe the necessary modifications to the simulator $\mathcal{S}$. For generating an equivocable commitment to a message of length ℓ (here we use the length information with which $\mathcal{F}_{\text{BSCOM}}$ supplies $\mathcal{S}$ upon commitment requests), $\mathcal{S}$ picks $s \in \{0,1\}^k$, $f \in \{0,1\}^{2\ell k}$, then generates C-commitments $C_k(s, f; r_2)$ and $C_k(\mathcal{O}_{sid}(r_2))$ and

---

Protocol BHC$_C$

These are instructions for parties P_1 through P_n to carry out commitments in the $\mathcal{F}_{\mathrm{RO}}$-hybrid model.

- When activated with input (commit, $sid, ssid, P_i, P_j, m$), where $m \in \{0,1\}^*$, P_i computes $f \leftarrow F_{\mathcal{O}_{sid}}(m)$ and $(com_1, dec_1) \leftarrow C_k(\mathcal{O}_{sid}(ssid, i, j, f), f; r_2)$. Then, P_i computes $(com_2, dec_2) \leftarrow C_k(\mathcal{O}_{sid}(r_2))$ and sends the message $(sid, ssid, com_1, com_2)$ to P_j while storing $(ssid, j, f, r_2, dec_2)$. Any further (commit, $sid, ssid, P_i, P_j, \cdot$) inputs are ignored.
- When receiving $(sid, ssid, com_1, com_2)$ from P_i, where $com_1, com_2 \in \{0,1\}^*$ and $ssid$ is a subsession ID under which P_j did not yet get such a message from any party, P_j stores the pair $(ssid, i, com_1, com_2)$ and locally outputs (receipt, $sid, ssid, P_i, P_j$). Any future messages $(sid, ssid, com_1', com_2')$ from P_i (with the same sid and $ssid$) are ignored.
- When activated on input (reveal, $sid, ssid, P_j$), P_i checks if it has stored a tuple $(ssid, j, f, r_2, dec_2)$ (for any f, dec_2). If so, P_i sends $(sid, ssid, f, dec_2)$ to P_j. Any future inputs (reveal, $sid, ssid, P_j$) are ignored.
- When receiving $(sid, ssid, f, r_2, dec_2)$ with $f, r_2, dec_2 \in \{0,1\}^*$ from P_i while already having received a value $(sid, ssid, com_1, com_2)$ also from P_i, party P_j first computes $o_2 \leftarrow V_k(com_2, dec_2)$. Then, if $o_2 = \mathcal{O}_{sid}(r_2)$, P_j checks if $com_k^C(\mathcal{O}_{sid}(ssid, i, j, m, f), f; r_2)$ equals com_1 and if $m \neq \perp$ for $m \leftarrow F_{\mathcal{H}}^{-1}(f)$. If so, P_j locally outputs (reveal, $sid, ssid, P_i, P_j, m$) and ignores further $(sid, ssid, \ldots)$ messages. In any other case, P_j does nothing.

Fig. 4. Protocol BHC$_C$

with these simulates a commitment as before. Later, when being forced to unveil this commitment as a commitment to $m \in \{0,1\}^\ell$, $\mathcal{S}$ lets the simulated committer $P_i^{(s)}$ perform a commitment to m as before, *but* forces

- $P_i^{(s)}$ to compute $F_{\mathcal{O}_{sid}}(m)$ as the given f by altering $P_i^{(s)}$'s random tape, resp. the random tape of $\mathcal{F}_{\mathrm{RO}}$
- the simulated $\mathcal{F}_{\mathrm{RO}}$ to output s when queried by $P_i^{(s)}$ on $(ssid, i, j, f)$.

Again, this "tampering" with $\mathcal{F}_{\mathrm{RO}}$ is possible only if $\mathcal{F}_{\mathrm{RO}}$ was not queried on any of these values before. By the hiding property of C and the randomization of $F_{\mathcal{O}_{sid}}$, this is guaranteed to occur only negligibly often. Note here also that both hash values s and f are valid for only one subsession (i. e., for one single commitment).

The extraction of the message committed to from a commitment that was generated according to BHC$_C$ is straightforward; again, if a commitment was *not* generated as specified by BHC$_C$, it can only be unveiled with negligible probability. With these changes, the proof of Proposition 1 applies.   □

Once again, by dropping protocol-inherent information, protocol BHC$_C$ may formally be regarded as a non-interactive commitment scheme. Therefore, we set BHC$_C = \{\mathcal{C}_k, \mathcal{V}_k\}$, where algorithm $\mathcal{C}_k$ computes $f \leftarrow F_{\mathcal{O}}(m)$, then $com \leftarrow (com_k^C(\mathcal{O}(f), f; r_2), com_k^C(\mathcal{O}(r_2); r_3))$ and $dec \leftarrow (f, r_2, dec_k^C(\mathcal{O}(r_2); r_3))$ for random coins $r_2, r_3 \in \{0,1\}^*$, and finally returns (com, dec). On input (com, dec)

of the form $com = (com_1, com_2)$ and $dec = (f, r_2, dec_2)$, algorithm $\mathcal{V}_k$ computes $o_2 \leftarrow V_k(com_2, dec_2)$ and, if $o_2 = \mathcal{O}(r_2)$, checks whether com_1 equals $C_k(\mathcal{O}(f), f; r_2))$. Only in this case $\mathcal{V}_k$ returns $F_{\mathcal{O}}^{-1}(f)$, otherwise it returns $\perp$.

As will be shown, BHC_C preserves not only hiding properties of C, but also a possible unconditional binding property, albeit for the price of being less efficient than HC_C and leaking information about the length $|m|$ of the message being committed to.

Proposition 4. *Once $\mathcal{H} = \{H_k\}$ is a family of collision-free hash functions for which $F_{\mathcal{H}}$ is efficiently computable and $C = \{C_k, V_k\}$ is a non-interactive string commitment scheme, the scheme $\text{BHC}_{C,\mathcal{H}} = \{\mathcal{C}_k, \mathcal{V}_k\}$ (as described above) is also a non-interactive string commitment scheme. If C is unconditionally hiding, then so is $\text{BHC}_{C,\mathcal{H}}$. If C is unconditionally binding, then so is $\text{BHC}_{C,\mathcal{H}}$.*

Proof. The meaningfulness of $\text{BHC}_{C,\mathcal{H}} = \text{BHC}$ follows from that of C. The computational binding property of BHC follows as in the proof of Proposition 2; furthermore, as $F_{\mathcal{H}}^{-1}(F_{\mathcal{H}}(m)) = m$ for any $\mathcal{H}, m$, the same argument shows that BHC is unconditionally binding if C is. Also for the hiding properties of BHC, the argument of the proof of Proposition 2 applies when we set $\text{BHC}' = \{\mathcal{C}_k', \mathcal{V}_k'\}$. When being run on input m, algorithm $\mathcal{C}_k'$ computes the tuple (com', dec') with $com' \leftarrow (com_k^C(H_k(f), f; r_2), com_k^C(0^k; r_3))$ and $dec' \leftarrow (f, r_2)$ for $f \leftarrow F_{\mathcal{H}}(m)$. The definition of $\mathcal{V}_k'$ is obvious. $\square$

4   Conclusions

In the model of [Can01] bit commitment cannot be securely realized without additional assumptions, e.g. the availability of an additional functionality like a common reference string or, as proposed in this work, a random oracle. As a motivation for the use of random oracles we discussed difficulties which may arise when a common reference string functionality is replaced by a cryptographic primitive which is realizable from scratch.

This contribution gave two constructions which allow to turn a given non-interactive bit commitment into a universally composable commitment scheme in the random oracle model. The resulting commitment schemes remain binding and hiding even if the random oracles are replaced by collision resistant hash functions. The second construction even preserves the property of perfect binding.

One referee pointed out that a separation of the random oracle model and the CRS model is a consequence of our result. Namely, [DG03] showed that from the existence of a universally composable bit commitment in a CRS model, a secure key exchange protocol can be derived. However, in the random oracle model, we proved that a binding and concealing bit commitment can be transformed into a universally composable one. So if a random oracle could be implemented using a common reference string (drawn from a suitable distribution), the existence of a binding and concealing bit commitment alone would imply a secure key exchange protocol. (In fact, it seems that a universally composable bit commitment can be implemented in the random oracle model without any further assumptions, thus yielding a stronger separation.) On the other hand, implementing a common reference string in the random oracle model can be—depending on the distribution of the reference string—non-trivial.

It is an interesting open question how the constructions given here affect the *non-malleability* of a given commitment scheme. To the best of our knowledge it is not clear how relations among committed values behave with respect to the use of hash functions in the given constructions.

Acknowledgements. The authors would like to thank Rainer Steinwandt and Dominique Unruh for interesting and valuable discussions, and the anonymous referees for helpful comments.

References

[BBP03]   Mihir Bellare, Alexandra Boldyreva, and Adriana Palacio. An uninstantiable random-oracle-model scheme for a hybrid-encryption problem. IACR ePrint Archive, August 2003. Online available at http://eprint.iacr.org/2003/077.ps.

[BR93]   Mihir Bellare and Phillip Rogaway. Random oracles are practical: A paradigm for designing efficient protocols. In *1st ACM Conference on Computer and Communications Security, Proceedings of CCS 1993*, pages 62–73. ACM Press, 1993. Full version online available at http://www.cs.ucsd.edu/users/mihir/papers/ro.ps.

[Can01]   Ran Canetti. Universally composable security: A new paradigm for cryptographic protocols. In *42th Annual Symposium on Foundations of Computer Science, Proceedings of FOCS 2001*, pages 136–145. IEEE Computer Society, 2001. Full version online available at http://eprint.iacr.org/2000/067.ps.

[CF01]   Ran Canetti and Marc Fischlin. Universally composable commitments. In Joe Kilian, editor, *Advances in Cryptology, Proceedings of CRYPTO 2001*, volume 2139 of *Lecture Notes in Computer Science*, pages 19–40. Springer-Verlag, 2001. Full version online available at http://eprint.iacr.org/2001/055.ps.

[CGH98]   Ran Canetti, Oded Goldreich, and Shai Halevi. The random oracle methodology, revisited. In *Thirtieth Annual ACM Symposium on Theory of Computing, Proceedings of STOC 1998*, pages 209–218. ACM Press, 1998. Preliminary version, extended version online available at http://eprint.iacr.org/1998/011.ps.

[CLOS02]   Ran Canetti, Yehuda Lindell, Rafail Ostrovsky, and Amit Sahai. Universally composable two-party and multi-party secure computation. In *34th Annual ACM Symposium on Theory of Computing, Proceedings of STOC 2002*, pages 494–503. ACM Press, 2002. Extended abstract, full version online available at http://eprint.iacr.org/2002/140.ps.

[Dam90]   Ivan Bjerre Damgård.   A design principle for hash functions.   In
            Gilles Brassard, editor, *Advances in Cryptology, Proceedings of CRYPTO
            '89*, volume 435 of *Lecture Notes in Computer Science*, pages 416–427.
            Springer-Verlag, 1990.
[DG03]   Ivan Damgård and Jens Groth.   Non-interactive and reusable non-
            malleable commitment schemes. In *35th Annual ACM Symposium on
            Theory of Computing, Proceedings of STOC 2003*, pages 426–437. ACM
            Press, 2003. Full version online available at
            http://eprint.iacr.org/2003/080.ps.
[DN02]   Ivan Damgård and Jesper Buus Nielsen. Perfect hiding and perfect bind-
            ing universally composable commitment schemes with constant expan-
            sion factor. In Moti Yung, editor, *Advances in Cryptology, Proceedings
            of CRYPTO 2002*, volume 2442 of *Lecture Notes in Computer Science*,
            pages 581–596. Springer-Verlag, 2002. Full version online available at
            http://eprint.iacr.org/2001/091.
[GMW87]   Oded Goldreich, Silvio Micali, and Avi Wigderson. How to play any
            mental game—a completeness theorem for protocols with honest major-
            ity. In *Nineteenth Annual ACM Symposium on Theory of Computing,
            Proceedings of STOC 1987*, pages 218–229. ACM Press, 1987. Extended
            abstract.
[Gol02]   Oded Goldreich. Secure multi-party computation. Online available at
            http://www.wisdom.weizmann.ac.il/~oded/PS/prot.ps,October 2002.
[GTK03]   Shafi Goldwasser and Yael Tauman Kalai.   On the (in)security of
            the Fiat-Shamir paradigm. In *44th Annual Symposium on Founda-
            tions of Computer Science, Proceedings of FOCS 2003*, pages 102–
            113. IEEE Computer Society, 2003. Full version online available at
            http://eprint.iacr.org/2003/034.
[HMQS03a]   Dennis Hofheinz, Jörn Müller-Quade, and Rainer Steinwandt. Initiator-
            resilient universally composable key exchange. In Einar Snekkenes and
            Dieter Gollmann, editors, *Computer Security, Proceedings of ESORICS
            2003*, volume 2808 of *Lecture Notes in Computer Science*, pages 61–84.
            Springer-Verlag, 2003. Online available at
            http://eprint.iacr.org/2003/063.ps.
[HMQS03b]   Dennis Hofheinz, Jörn Müller-Quade, and Rainer Steinwandt. On model-
            ing IND-CCA security in cryptographic protocols. IACR ePrint Archive,
            February 2003. Online available at
            http://eprint.iacr.org/2003/024.ps.
[Nie02]   Jesper B. Nielsen. Separating random oracle proofs from complexity
            theoretic proofs: The non-committing encryption case. In Moti Yung,
            editor, *Advances in Cryptology, Proceedings of CRYPTO 2002*, volume
            2442 of *Lecture Notes in Computer Science*, pages 111–126. Springer-
            Verlag, 2002.

A   The Functionality $\mathcal{F}_{\mathrm{MCOM}}$

For convenience, here we reproduce the description of the ideal functionality $\mathcal{F}_{\mathrm{MCOM}}$ from [CLOS02]:

Functionality $\mathcal{F}_{\mathrm{MCOM}}$

$\mathcal{F}_{\mathrm{MCOM}}$ proceeds as follows, running with parties $P_1, \ldots, P_n$ and an adversary $\mathcal{S}$:

- **Commit Phase:** Upon receiving a message $(\mathtt{commit}, sid, ssid, P_i, P_j, b)$ from P_i, where $b \in \{0, 1\}$, record the tuple $(ssid, P_i, P_j, b)$ and send the message $(\mathtt{receipt}, sid, ssid, P_i, P_j)$ to P_j and $\mathcal{S}$. Ignore any future commit messages with the same $ssid$ from P_i to P_j.
- **Reveal Phase:** Upon receiving a message $(\mathtt{reveal}, sid, ssid)$ from P_i: If a tuple $(ssid, P_i, P_j, b)$ was previously recorded, then send the message $(\mathtt{reveal}, sid, ssid, P_i, P_j, b)$ to P_j and $\mathcal{S}$. Otherwise, ignore.

Transformation of Digital Signature Schemes into Designated Confirmer Signature Schemes

Shafi Goldwasser[1,2] and Erez Waisbard[1]

[1] Department of Computer Science and Applied Mathematics,
Weizmann Institute of Science, Rehovot 76100, Israel.
{shafi,waisbard}@wisdom.weizmann.ac.il
[2] Laboratory for Computer Science, Massachusetts Institute of Technology.
Cambridge, MA 02139.

Abstract. Since designated confirmer signature schemes were introduced by Chaum and formalized by Okamoto, a number of attempts have been made to design designated confirmer signature schemes which are efficient and at the same time provably secure under standard cryptographic assumptions. Yet, there has been a consistent gap in security claims and analysis between all generic theoretical proposals and any concrete implementation proposal one can envision using in practice. In this paper we propose a modification of Okamoto's definition of security which still captures security against chosen message attack, and yet enables the design of concrete and reasonably efficient designated confirmer signature schemes which can be proved secure without resorting to random oracle assumptions as previously done. In particular, we present simple transformations of the digital signature schemes of Cramer-Shoup, Goldwasser-Micali-Rivest and Gennaro-Halevi-Rabin into secure designated confirmer signature schemes. We prove security of the schemes obtained under the same security assumption made by the digital signature scheme transformed and an encryption scheme we use as a tool.

1 Introduction

Digital signatures introduced by Diffie and Hellman [7] are analogous to signatures in the paper world in the sense that a message that is being signed by the *signer* can later be verified by everyone else. Like in the paper world, a signer can not deny signing a document that carries *his* signature. There are real life scenarios, however, in which the signer wishes that the recipient of the signature would not be able to present the signature to other parties at will.

For example, say a potential employer extends a job offer to a candidate employee including a salary figure. On one hand the employer does not want the employee to show the offer letter to a competitor to elicit a higher salary, and on the other hand the future employee wants to be assured that the offer is binding and can be held up in court. For such a setting we would have like to have a signature schemes in which:

M. Naor (Ed.): TCC 2004, LNCS 2951, pp. 77–100, 2004.
© Springer-Verlag Berlin Heidelberg 2004

• A court of law (or some other third party) is able (if called upon) to verify the authenticity of the signature.

• No one, but the court of law, should be able to validate the authenticity of the signature (unless the signer steps in).

• The signer should be able to convince the recipient of the signature that it is indeed authentic and can be validated by the court if necessary.

The first attempt to address the issue of signatures that can not be verified by everyone was *Undeniable Signature* by Chaum [5]. Undeniable signatures can not be verified without the signer's cooperation. The signer can either validate a signature or prove it invalid. The problem with this idea is that in any setting where the signer becomes unavailable (of which there may be many) nothing can be determined.

A different idea called *Designated Verifier Signature schemes* was presented by Jakobsson, Sako and Impagliazzo [17]. A designated verifier signature is a signature that can only be validated by a single user, designated by the signer. Designated verifier signatures can used to authenticate the identity of the signer without having the ability to convince any third party of its validity. Its merit is also its weakness. There is indeed no way to force the signer to honor his signature.

Designated Confirmer Signature scheme (DCS), introduced by Chaum [4], address both of the above problems. The parties in a DCS are the signer, the recipient of the signature (aka the verifier) and a *designated confirmer*. The idea of DCS is that during the process of signing, that involves the signer and recipient (as usual), a designated confirmer signature σ is generated. The recipient of the signature cannot convince anyone else of the validity of σ. Rather, the designated confirmer, given σ, has the ability to verify it on his own as well as to convince anyone of its validity/invalidity. The designated confirmer remains completely passive, unless the signer becomes unavailable. In such case, the designated confirmer can either convert the designated confirmer signature into an ordinary signature that can be validated by anyone, or engage in an interactive protocol with any verifier to confirm the validity of the signature. The confirmer is only semi-trusted in the sense that he can only extract/validate signatures for messages which the signer designated him to. Perhaps the most natural candidate to act as a semi-trusted designated confirmer is a court of law.

Going back to the job offer scenario, the employer would sign his offer using a DCS scheme, making the court of law the designated confirmer. Using DCS ensures that the candidate would not be able to convince other employers of the authenticity of the offer, and yet if the employer changes his mind (or becomes unavailable) the candidate can present a signed offer to the court of law and ask for compensation.

A straightforward way to construct a designated confirmer signature scheme, using standard cryptographic primitives, such as public-key encryption scheme and digital signature schemes would be to first sign a message m using an ordinary signature scheme and then encrypt the signature using the designated confirmer public key[1]. The resulting ciphertext would serve as the designated confirmer signature σ of m. Since the signature is encrypted, only the designated confirmer can be convinced of its validity. Moreover, the designated confirmer can easily extract an ordinary signature from it. One question remains, if the recipient cannot verify the validity of σ on his own, how can he know that he indeed got a valid one? Zero-knowledge naturally comes to the rescue. In order for the recipient to be convinced of the validity of the DCS, the signer and recipient interact in a zero-knowledge proof in which the signer proves to the verifier that what he got is indeed an encryption of a verifiable ordinary signature of m. Since the last assertion is an NP statement, there exist general protocols that achieve this.

The above construction is straight forward and can be easily proved secure. The main problem is that we do not know of *efficient* zero-knowledge proofs for the assertion that the cleartext corresponding to a given ciphertext contains a valid (or invalid) signature of a given document. Proving such statements using general zero-knowledge proofs for NP involve the reduction step to an NP-complete language which makes them unusable in practice. Several works on DCS attempted to remedy the situation and come up with efficient direct DCS constructions. In doing so they either resort to the random oracle assumption for proving security or make no formal claims of security, and thus all trade efficiency with proofs of security in the standard model. We summarize the state of the art in section 1.2.

The **goal of the current paper** is to present DCS schemes with proofs of security in the standard model which do not involve the inefficient step of using general zero-knowledge proofs for proving the validity of signatures.

Our **approach** in achieving this goal is to modify the original definition of security for DCS due to Okamoto [19] to not require zero-knowledge proofs for validity assertions, and then show efficient constructions of DCS schemes which satisfy the new security definition.

We note that an alternative approach toward the same goal would be to construct custom made – tailored to a particular encryption scheme and a particular digital signature scheme – efficient zero-knowledge proofs for the assertion that the cleartext corresponding to a given ciphertext contains a valid (or invalid) signature of a given document. Indeed, utilizing the Cramer-Shoup CCA2 secure public key encryption scheme in some of the confirmation and disavowal protocols proposed in [2] translates to proving statements concerning the equality (and inequality) of discrete logarithms in zero-knowledge. A recent article of Camenisch and Shoup [3] shows ingenious while somewhat complex ways to accomplish this directly without resorting to general zero-knowledge protocols.

---

[1] All that is required from a designated confirmer in the signing stage is to have a known public key. Other than that the designated confirmer does not need to be aware that his key is used.

1.1   New Results

We propose a new definition of DCS, modifying the original definitions of Okamoto [19] and Camernish and Michels [2] in several ways. The most important modification is to remove the requirement that the confirmation protocols between signer and verifier and confirmer and verifier confirming that a designated confirmer signature is valid must be zero-knowledge[2]. We instead only require that the resulting scheme is existentially unforgeable in the presence of chosen message attack. We stress that a forgery in this context is the ability of anyone but the legal signer to convince a verifier of knowledge of a valid signature of any message. This includes also those messages which have already been signed by the legal signer. Naturally, in the latter case of messages which already have been signed, also the designated confirmer can convince a verifier of the knowledge of valid signatures for these messages, but for no other message.

We give a general transformation that takes any standard digital signature scheme and a public key encryption scheme and turns them into a designated confirmer signature scheme. We prove that if the originating signature scheme is existentially unforgeable under chosen message attack and the public key encryption is secure against CCA2, then the resulting designated confirmer signature scheme is provably secure according to the new definition under the same assumptions made by the digital signature scheme and the encryption scheme.

The main tool our general transformation uses is *strong witness hiding proofs of knowledge* (SWHPOK). Witness hiding proofs of knowledge(WHPOK) for polynomial time verifiable relations R as defined originally by [9], only guarantee that on input x all witnesses w s.t. $(x, w) \in R$ remains hidden. SWHOPK require the additional property that on input x the protocol does not reveal witnesses w' for any other inputs $x' \neq x$. Notably, the general WHPOK protocols for polynomial time verifiable relations [14,9] which exist if one way permutations exist, are already SWHPOK.

Having removed the requirement that the signing and confirmation protocols are zero-knowledge enables using SWHPOK protocols for this purpose instead. The witness in question is a standard digital signature of a message in the sense of [16]. We remark that witness hiding proofs (even strong ones) are in general easier to design than zero-knowledge proofs. Moreover, for a large class of concrete digital signature schemes – including Cramer-Shoup signatures [6], Goldwasser-Micali-Rivest signatures [16] and the Gennaro-Halevi-Rabin signatures [15] – we give simple and direct strong witness hiding proofs of knowledge of a signature for the scheme at hand. Thus, for these digital signature schemes, we give concrete designated confirmer signature schemes which are proved secure under the same

---

[2] An important implication of removing the indistinguishability security requirement, is that [19] proved that designated confirmer signature scheme and public-key encryption are equivalent. The way Okamoto proved that designated confirmer signature imply public key encryption was based on the indistinguishability between a designated confirmer signature of a message m and a fake signature. He used a valid signature to encrypt the bit 0 and a fake signature to sign the bit 1. Clearly, after modifying the security requirement, this proof no longer holds.

cryptographic assumption the original signature scheme was based on and the existence of a CCA2 secure public key encryption scheme.

The second tool our transformation uses is to take a strong witness hiding proof of knowledge of a signature and modify it so as in the process of proving this knowledge the signer also "encrypts" the signature in the confirmer public key so that the confirmer can later "decrypt" and extract the signature. We prove that if the verifier accepts the proof of knowledge, then with high probability the confirmer will be able to extract the signature from the transcript between signer and verifier. We call this modification of a strong witness hiding proof of knowledge *encrypted strong witness hiding proof of knowledge*. The designated confirmer signature of a message is defined to be this transcript of encrypted proof of knowledge. We use the ideas of Camenisch and Damgard [1] in their work on *verifiable encryption* to get encrypted witness hiding proofs of knowledge.[3]

Putting the above ideas together it is straight forward to get a DCS construction from an standard digital signature scheme. For a message m, the signer first produces an ordinary signature of m, denoted $\sigma(m)$. Next, the signer and verifier engage in a encrypted strong witness hiding proof of knowledge of $\sigma(m)$. If the verifier accepts, the transcript of the interaction can be stored by the verifier as the designated confirmer signature of m. Presented with the transcript, the confirmer can extract $\sigma(m)$ from it, and prove knowledge of $\sigma(m)$ using a strong witness hiding proof of knowledge thus confirming the validity of the designated confirmer signature.

Lastly, we note that unlike the SWHPOK protocols for signing and confirmation of validity of a designated confirmer signature, we still advocate and use in our general transformation a **zero-knowledge** proof for the invalidity of a designated confirmer signature – a so called *Disavowal* protocol. This is natural, as when σ' is an invalid designated confirmer signature, there is no witness to speak of whose secrecy one needs to protect! We argue this has little effect on the overall efficiency of the scheme as we expect to rarely use *Disavowal*. Whereas in *undeniable signature schemes* proving the invalidity of a signature via a *Disavowal* protocol had a crucial role, since it was up to the signer to either confirm or disavow an alleged signature and refusal to disavow could be interpreted as confirming it, this is no longer the case in DCS schemes. The need for disavowal protocol in a DCS scheme arises only when a cheating verifier claims an invalid designated confirmer signature σ' is indeed valid. Since the verifier cannot convince anyone of the signature's validity without the help of the designated confirmer, it usually suffice that the designated confirmer will say

---

[3] [1] propose an elegant technique of modifying any 3-round honest verifier zero-knowledge proofs for a relation R so that at the end of the protocol the verifier will be guaranteed with high probability to hold a semantically secure encryption of witness w for a given x where $(w, x) \in R$. They showed relevance of this idea to group signatures, signature sharing, and fair exchange of signatures. We note that we apply the [1] transformation to strong witness hiding proofs rather than to zero-knowledge proofs, and thus can not use the claims they prove about the resulting encryption being semantically secure. Still, the resulting protocol can be shown to work in our context as well.

that the verifier is cheating. The need for disavowal protocol may of course arise in the case where the cheating verifier is charged by the law and a proof of his blame needs to be presented. We expect this to rarely occur.

1.2 Related Work

Soon after Chaum introduced the notion of DCS[4], Okamoto presented a formal model and definition of security of DCS and proved (constructively) that secure designated confirmer signature schemes are equivalent to secure public-key encryption [19]. In a nutshell, his definition requires zero-knowledge confirmation protocols of the validity of the signature (or disavowal of its validity) as a way of ensuring non-transferability of the ability to validate a signature. In addition to theoretical results, Okamoto also gives two concrete practical schemes without an argument nor claim of security. Indeed, [18] showed that one of Okamoto's schemes enables the designated confirmer to universally forge signatures.

Michels and Stadler [18] suggest how to use a tool called *designated confirmer commitments* to construct designated confirmer signature scheme starting from any Fiat-Shamir like signature scheme [11] The resulting DCS schemes can be proved secure only in the random oracle model, inheriting this property from the use of the Fiat-Shamir paradigm for constructing signatures. Another DCS scheme suggested in [18] is based on deterministic RSA signatures which are existentially forgeable and thus again, unless one resorts to the use of the "hash then sign" techniques which are provably secure in the random oracle model. [2] point out attacks on previous DCS schemes (including [18]) when several signers share the same confirmer. They strengthen the DCS security requirements of [19] to address these problems, and show the existence of a secure DCS (under the new definition) using general tools of existentially unforgeable digital signatures schemes, CCA2 secure encryption schemes, and general concurrent ZK protocols for NP statements. For this definition [2] propose concrete implementations of DCS based on either deterministic RSA signatures (or Fiat-Shamir like signatures) whose security again is provable in the random oracle model. Some of the confirmation and disavowal protocols proposed in [2] when using the Cramer-Shoup public encryption function as the underlying CCA2 secure encryption amount to proving statements concerning the equality (and inequality) of discrete logarithms in zero-knowledge. A recent article of Camenisch and Shoup [3] shows direct ways to accomplish this.

2   New Definition for a DCS

2.1   Informal Outline of the Definition

The model consists of three players: signer S, verifier V and designated confirmer C. Throughout, *all parties* receive as input the public keys of the signer and of the designated confirmer, denoted by PK_s and PK_c. The signer has an auxiliary secret input, denoted SK_s and the confirmer has an auxiliary secret input, denoted SK_c.

A pair of important algorithms with respect to which validity of a designated confirmer signature is defined are **Extract** and **Verify**. On inputs a message m, a designated confirmer signature σ, PK_s, PK_c, and SK_c, algorithm Extract either outputs $fail$ or a string σ^*, which can be publicly verified as a valid ordinary digital signature of m with respect to PK_s(as defined in [16]) by running the verification algorithm Verify. In essence, Extract turns a designated confirmer signature that can be verified only by a confirmer into an ordinary digital signature that can be validated by anyone.

The definition also calls for the existence of three main interactive protocols:

ConfirmedSign: a *protocol* between the *signer* and a *verifier* on a common input message m, which produces as output either an accept or reject vote by the verifier along with a string σ referred to as the **designated confirmer signature** of m. If the verifier accept then the string σ should be a valid designated confirmer signature, that is one that can be transformed to an ordinary digital signature using the Extract algorithm. Here the verifier is the recipient of the designated confirmer signature that needs to be convinced of its validity.

By combining the signing process along with the confirmation process we deviate from the definition of [19,18,2]. We argue that this is a natural modification, as the recipient of a DCS always needs to be convinced of the validity of the DCS, thus in practice, the two actions are always performed together.

Conf: a *protocol* between the *confirmer* and a *verifier* on common input a message m and a designated confirmer signature σ, at the end of which the verifier either accept or reject σ as a valid designated confirmer signature of m. If σ is a *valid* designated confirmer signature (i.e. one from which the Extract algorithm can output an ordinary valid signature of m) then the confirmer should be able to convince the verifier of its validity. Here the verifier can be *any* party that needs to be convinced of the validity of the DCS.

Disavowal: a *protocol* between the *confirmer* and *verifier* on common input a message m and a designated confirmer signature σ, at the end of which the verifier either accepts or rejects σ as an *invalid* designated confirmer signature of m (where an invalid designated signature σ is one for which **Extract** outputs $fail$). As in $Conf$, the verifier can be *any* party that needs to be convinced of the validity of the DCS.

The **security requirements** we make fall into two categories: security for signers and security for the confirmer,

1. **Security for the signer:** For any message m *not previously signed*, no one, except for the legal signer can

   a) Run $ConfirmedSign(m, \cdots)$ in the role of the prover, successfully with non-negligible probability.

   b) Produce a publicly verifiable ordinary signature σ^* of m with respect to the signer's public signing key (i.e. $Verify(, PK_s, m, \sigma^*) = $ valid).

   c) Produce a designated confirmer signature σ for m which the legal designated confirmer will confirm as valid with non-negligible probability.

For any *previously signed* message m, no one, except for the legal signer and the legal designated confirmer, can do 1a, 1b as above.[4]

2. **Security for the confirmer:** No one but the legal signer S and designated confirmer C, including any coalition of signers $\{S_j\}$ where all $S_j \neq S$ sharing the same confirmer, can confirm a designated confirmer signature for a message previously signed with respect to SK_s.

2.2 Formal Definition

In the coming definition, $negl(k)$ denotes any function which grows slower than $\frac{1}{k^c}$ for all c for all k sufficiently large.

Definition 1 *A secure designated confirmer signature scheme consists of the following components:*

1. **Key Generation Algorithms** (G_s, G_c): *G_c is a probabilistic polynomial time algorithm that on input 1^n (where n is the security parameter), outputs a pair of strings (SK_c, PK_c) (the designated confirmer's private and public key respectively). G_s is a probabilistic polynomial time algorithm that on input 1^n, outputs a pair of strings (SK_s, PK_s) (the signer's private and public key respectively).*

2. **Signature Extraction:** *A pair of polynomial time algorithms $(Extract, Verify)$ such that Extract on inputs m, σ, PK_s, PK_c and SK_c returns a string σ^* and Verify on input PK_s, m and σ^* outputs valid or invalid. If $Verify(PK_s, m, \sigma^*) = valid$, where $\sigma^* = Extract(m, \sigma, PK_s, PK_c, SK_c)$, then we say that the Extract algorithm was successful and σ^* is a valid ordinary signature of m with respect to PK_s.*

3. **ConfirmedSign:** *An interactive protocol referred to as $ConfirmedSign_{(S,V)}$ between interactive probabilistic polynomial time algorithms(ITM) S and V which on common inputs (m, PK_s, PK_c) outputs a pair (b, σ) where $b \in \{accept, reject\}$ and σ is refereed to as the designated confirmer signature of a signer S on message m. The requirements from ConfirmedSign are: $\exists V$ such that*
   a) **completeness:** *$\exists S$ (with auxiliary input SK_s), such that $\forall (PK_s, SK_s) \in G_s$ and $(PK_c, SK_c) \in G_c$, $\forall m$, $ConfirmedSign_{(S,V)}(m, PK_s, PK_c)$ outputs $(accept, \sigma)$ such that $Verify(PK_s, m, Extract(m, \sigma, PK_s, PK_c, SK_c)) = valid$.*
   b) **Soundness:** *$\forall$ probabilistic polynomial time S' with auxiliary input[5] y, $\forall m$ $Pr[ConfirmedSign_{(S',V)}(m, PK_s.PK_c)$ outputs $(accept, \sigma)$*

---

[4] Ordinary signature schemes are secure if a forger cannot produce a signature on a message that has not been signed before. It is not required that a forger would not be able to produce a different signature on previously signed messages. Similarly, for a designated confirmer signature scheme, we do not require (in part 6 of Def 1) that it is infeasible for a forger F to produce *new* valid designated confirmer signatures for messages previously signed.

[5] This y captures the possible history, available to attackers, of interaction with Signers, Confirmers and Verifiers.

such that $Verify(PK_s, m, Extract(m, \sigma, PK_s, PK_c, SK_c)) \neq valid] < negl(n)$

The probability is taken over all possible coins of the key generation algorithms G_s, G_c and algorithms S', V, and $Extract$.

4. **Confirmation** An interactive protocol referred to as $Conf_{(C,V)}$ between interactive probabilistic polynomial time algorithms(ITM) C and V which on common inputs (m, σ, PK_s, PK_c) outputs $b \in \{accept, reject\}$. The requirements from $Conf$ are: $\exists V$ such that

  a) **Completeness:** $\exists C$ (with auxiliary input SK_C), such that
  $\forall (PK_s, SK_s) \in G_s$ and $(PK_c, SK_c) \in G_c$, $\forall m$, if
  $Verify(PK_s, m, Extract(m, \sigma, PK_s, PK_c, SK_c) = valid$
  then $Conf_{(C,V)}(m, \sigma, PK_s, PK_c)$ outputs accept

  b) **Soundness:** $\forall$ probabilistic polynomial time C' (with auxiliary input y)
  if $Verify(PK_s, m, Extract(m, \sigma, PK_s, PK_c, SK_c) \neq valid$
  then $Pr(Confirm_{(C',V)}(m, \sigma, PK_s, PK_c)$ outputs accept$) < negl(n)$
  The probability is taken over all possible coins of C', V, $Extract$ and the
  key generation algorithms G_s and G_c.

5. **Disavowal** An interactive protocol referred to as $Disavowal_{(C,V)}$ between interactive probabilistic polynomial time algorithms(ITM) C and V which on common inputs (m, σ, PK_s, PK_c) outputs $b \in \{accept, reject\}$, The requirements from $Disavowal$ are: $\exists V$ such that

  a) **Completeness:** $\exists C$ (with auxiliary input SK_c), such that
  $\forall (PK_s, SK_s) \in G_s$ and $(PK_c, SK_c) \in G_c$, $\forall m$, if
  $Verify(PK_s, m, Extract(m, \sigma, PK_s, PK_c, SK_c) \neq valid,$
  then $Disavowal_{(C,V)}(m, \sigma, PK_s, PK_c)$ outputs accept

  b) **Soundness:** $\forall$ probabilistic polynomial-time C' (with auxiliary input y),
  if $Verify(PK_s, m, Extract(m, \sigma, PK_s, PK_c, SK_c)) = valid$
  then $Pr(Disavowal_{(C',V)}(m, \sigma, PK_s, PK_c)$ outputs accept$) < negl(n)$
  The probability is taken over all possible coins of C', V, $Extract$ and the
  key generation algorithms G_s and G_c.

6. We say that a designated confirmer signature scheme is secure if it meets the following requirements:

  a) Let F be a probabilistic polynomial time forging algorithm which, on input strings PK_s, PK_c can first request the execution of $ConfirmedSign_{(S,F)}$, $Conf_{(C,F)}$ and $Disavowal_{(C,F)}$ for polynomially many adaptively chosen inputs of its choice; and then attempts to run the $ConfirmedSign$ protocol on m of its choice in the role of the prover. We require that for all such F and m

$$Pr(ConfirmedSign_{(F,V)}(1^n, m, PK_s, PK_c) = (accept, \sigma)) < negl(n)$$

The probability is taken over all possible coins used by F, S, C, V and the key generation algorithms G_s and G_c.

b) *Let F be a probabilistic polynomial time forging algorithm which, on in-put strings 1^n, PK_s, PK_c can first request the execution of $ConfirmedSign_{(S,F)}$, $Conf_{(C,F)}$ and $Disvowal_{(C,F)}$ for polynomially many adaptively chosen inputs of its choice; and then outputs a pair (m, σ^*). We require that for all such F and m,*

$$Pr(Verify(PK_s, m, \sigma^*) = valid) < negl(n)$$

The probability is taken over all possible coins used by F, S, C, V and the key generation algorithms G_s and G_c

c) *Let F be a probabilistic polynomial time forging algorithm which, on input strings 1^n, PK_s, PK_c, and SK_c, can first request the execution of $ConfirmedSign_{(S,F)}$ for polynomially many adaptively chosen messages $\{m_i\}$, as well as request the execution of $Conf_{(C,F)}$ and $Disvowal_{(C,F)}$ for polynomially many adaptively chosen inputs; and then outputs a pair (m, σ'). We require that for all such F and for message $m \notin \{m_i\}$ (i.e not previously signed)*

$$Pr(Conf_{(C,V)}(1^n, m, \sigma', PK_s, PK_c) = accept) < negl(n)$$

The probability is taken over all possible coins used by F, S, C, V and the key generation algorithms G_s and G_c.[6]

d) ***Security for designated confirmers:*** *Let A be a probabilistic polyno-mial time attacking algorithm which, on input strings 1^n, PK_s, PK_c can request the execution of $ConfirmedSign_{(S,A)}$, $Conf_{(C,A)}$ and $Disvowal_{(C,A)}$ for polynomially many inputs of his choice and finally, for a pair $\{m, \sigma\}$ of his choice, A executes $Conf_{(A,V)}(1^n, m, \sigma, PK_s, PK_c)$. For all such A*

$$Pr(Conf_{(A,V)}(1^n, m, \sigma, PK_s, PK_c) = accept) < negl(n)$$

The probability is taken over all possible coins used by A, S, C, V and the key generation algorithms G_s and G_c.
Moreover, this should hold when many signers share the same confirmer. Meaning, when A knows polynomially many SK_{s_j} such that $SK_{s_j} \neq SK_S$.

3   Tools

Our transformation uses several tools, including ordinary digital signatures se-cure against adaptive chosen message attack as defined in [16], public key en-cryption secure against adaptive chosen ciphertext attack(CCA2) as defined in

---

[6] Note that this requirement also implies that with high probability even the desig-nated confirmer C can not run successfully $ConfirmedSign_{(F,V)}$ protocol on mes-sages not previously signed, nor produce a valid ordinary signature of a message not previously signed.

[8], canonical strong witness hiding proofs of knowledge defined in subsection 3.1, and encrypted strong witness hiding proofs of knowledge defined in subsection 3.2.

3.1   Strong Witness Hiding Proofs of Knowledge

Witness Hiding proof of knowledge (WHPOK) were defined by Feige and Shamir in [10] as follows.

Let R be a polynomial time relation. Namely, there exists a polynomial p and a polynomial time computable function f such that

$$R = \{(x, w) \text{ such that } f(x, w) = 1, |w| < p(|x|)\}$$

Let $w(x)$ denote the set of w such that $(x, w) \in R$.

Definition 2 ([10]) : *We say that G is a instance generator for relation R if on input 1^n it produces instances $(x, w) \in R$ of length n. We say that G is a* hard instance generator *if for any polynomial time witness finding F, $P[(x, F(x)) \in R] < negl(n)$, where $x \in G(1^n)$. The probability is taken over the coin tosses of G and F.*

Definition 3 ([10]) : *Let (P, V) be a proof of knowledge (POK) system for relation R and let G be a hard instance generator for R. We say that (P, V) is witness hiding proof of knowledge (WHPOK) on (R, G) if for any probabilistic polynomial time V' there exist an expected polynomial time witness extractor M, $P[(P(w), V')(x) \in w(x)] < P[M(x) \in w(x)] + negl(n)$ where $x \in G(1^n)$. The probability is taken over the distribution of the inputs chosen by G and witnesses as well as the random tosses of P, V' and M.*

In our context, the relation R we shall be interested in will be the pairs of *a message* and *a valid ordinary digital signature of message*, for some given ordinary digital signature scheme which is secure against chosen message attack. As such, we shall need to deviate from the original definition of WHPOK in a few aspects. First, for a secure digital signature scheme as defined by [16] it is impossible to find a single valid (*message, signature*) pair in polynomial time for messages not previously signed. Thus, our proofs of knowledge should be witness hiding for any polynomial time distribution over R. Second, we require the proof of knowledge to remain witness hiding, even the verifier chooses the input message to run the protocol on after it participated in many executions of the protocol on different input messages which were chosen adaptively by the verifier himself. We call the modified definition *strong witness hiding proofs of knowledge* (SWHPOK).

Definition 4 *Let (P, V) be a proof of knowledge (POK) system for relation R. We say that (P, V) is strong witness hiding (SWH) on R if for any probabilistic polynomial time V' who can in a preliminary stage choose (adaptively) polynomially many x_i and run $(P(w_i), V')(x_i)$, and only later choose a challenge $x \neq x_i$,* *there exist a witness extractor M which runs in expected polynomial time such that $P[(P(w), V')(x) \in w(x)] < P[M(x) \in w(x)] + negl(n)$. The probability is taken over the distribution of witnesses as well as random coin tosses of P, V', G and M.*

Finally, in order to be able to apply the technique of Camenisch and Damgard [1] of encrypted witness hiding proofs of knowledge, we require that our protocols will be of canonical form defined as follows.

Definition 5 *A* Canonical witness hiding proof of knowledge *for a boolean relation $R \subseteq \{0,1\}^* \times \{0,1\}^*$ is a three-move SWHPOK for R which is defined by three probabilistic procedures $(P_1, P_3, Verdict)$, satisfying the following conditions:*
1. On common input x and an auxiliary input w, P's first step uses P_1 to compute the first message to be sent t and some side information r. At the second step the verifier sends a random bit string c as a challenge. At the third step the prover uses x, w, r and c as input to P_3 to compute a response s, which he sends to the verifier. In the forth step the verifier uses the predicate Verdict taking x, t, c and s as inputs to check whether s is a valid response. A triple (t, c, s), such that $Verdict(x, t, c, s)$ accepts is called an accepting triple for x.
2. The number of possible challenges that can be sent by the verifier is polynomial in the security parameter.
3. There exist a knowledge extractor that can extract the witness from knowing the answer to all possible challenges.

Note that we have added the requirement of being strong WH into what we call a canonical WHPOK. Also, note that there is no requirement above of having negligible soundness probability. Indeed in all the canonical WHPOK that on which we perform transformations in this paper, the challenge of the verifier is a single bit which yields an overall soundness probability of $\frac{1}{2}$.

3.2 Encrypted Strong Witness Hiding Proofs of Knowledge of a Signature

An important tool used by the construction is called a *encrypted strong witness hiding proof of knowledge*. The idea is as in [1] where they apply the technique to zero-knowledge protocols.

Start with any signature scheme existentially unforgeable under adaptive chosen message attack $\Sigma = (SG, Sign, Verify)$ where SG is the key generation algorithm, and $Sign$ (and $Verify$) are the signing (and verifying) algorithms. Define the relation

$$R_\Sigma = \{((PK_s, m), \sigma) : Verify(PK_s, m, \sigma) = valid, (PK_s, SK_s) \in SG(1^k)\}$$

Assume you are given, for simplicity of exposition, a canonical strong WH-POK for relation R_Σ defined by three probabilistic algorithms $(P_1, P_2, Verdict)$ where the number of possible challenges of the verifier is two and the soundness probability is $\frac{1}{2}$ (in general the construction works for any polynomial number of challenges).

Canonical witness hiding proof of knowledge for R_Σ:
Common input to both prover and verifier is (PK_s, m). Auxiliary input to the prover is σ, such that $((PK_s, m), \sigma) \in R_\Sigma$.

1. The prover computes $(t, r) = P_1((PK_s, m), \sigma)$ and sends t to the verifier.
2. The verifier selects $b \in_R \{0, 1\}$ and send it to the prover.
3. The prover calculates $s = P_3((PK_s, m), \sigma, r, b)$ and sends it to the verifier.
4. The verifier accepts if $Verdict((PK_s, m), t, b, s) = 1$, otherwise he rejects.

Now, let $Enc = (EG, E, D)$ be a given a CCA2 secure public key encryption scheme. In our context, the public encryption key (and corresponding secret decryption key) will be of the designated confirmer C and we denote them by PK_c (and SK_c respectively). The above protocol is turned into an *encrypted witness hiding proof of knowledge for R_Σ* as follows.

Encrypted canonical witness hiding proof of knowledge for R_Σ:
Common input to both prover and verifier is m, PK_s, PK_c. Auxiliary input to the prover is σ such that $((PK_s, m), \sigma) \in R_\Sigma$.

1. The prover computes $(t, r) = P_1((PK_s, m), \sigma)$, $s_0 = P_3((PK_s, m), \sigma, r, 0)$ and $s_1 = P_3((PK_s, m), \sigma, r, 1)$; encrypts s_0 and s_1, using the designated confirmer's public key to obtains $e_0 \in E_{PK_c}(s_0)$ and $e_1 \in E_{PK_c}(s_1)$. Then, the prover sends (t, e_0, e_1) to the verifier.
2. The verifier selects $b \in_R \{0, 1\}$ and sends it to the prover.
3. The prover reveals s_b and the random coins r_b that were used in the encryption.
4. If $E_{PK_c}(s_b, r_b) = e_b$ and $Verdict((PK_s, m), t, b, s_b) = 1$, the verifier accepts, otherwise he rejects.

Essentially, in this protocol at the first round the prover sends an encrypted answer to both possible challenges one of which will be decrypted on the third round.

Running this basic protocol k times in sequence decreases the probability of cheating to $\frac{1}{2^k}$, but costs a possibly prohibitive $3k$ rounds. To reduce the the number of rounds to constant maintaining negligible probability of error, we can employ ideas similar to Goldreich-Kahan[13][7] or utilize a trapdoor commitment scheme as suggested in [1].

---

[7] Recalling, the idea of [13], is to simply add an initial round in which the verifier commits to all his challenges in advance $b_1, \cdots b_k$, followed by k parallel executions of the above 3-round protocol with the modification that the verifier decommits its challenges $b_1, \cdots, b_k$ in step (2) rather than simply sending them in the clear. This transformation maintains the SWH property.

Theorem 6 *The modified protocol remains a canonical (strong) witness hiding proof of knowledge for the relation R_Σ*

4   A General Construction of Designated Confirmer Signature

Let $\Sigma = (SG, Sign, Verify)$ be a signature scheme which is existentially unforgeable under chosen message attack which has a canonical strong WHPOK for the relation $R_\Sigma{}^8$. Let $Enc = (EG, E, D)$ be a CCA2 secure encryption scheme.

In the following we let S denote the signer, V the verifier in the various protocols, and C the designated confirmer. We let $(PK_s, SK_s) \in SG(1^k)$ denote the public verification key and the secret signing key of the signer and $(PK_c, SK_c) \in EG(1^k)$ be the public encryption key and the private decryption key of the designated confirmer.

The Designated Confirmer signature scheme:

Key Generation Algorithms: $(G_s, G_c) = (SG, EG)$. The key generation algorithm consists of the pair of key generation algorithm for the signature and encryption schemes in use.

ConfirmedSign protocol: S computes an ordinary signature σ of m by computing $\sigma \in Sign_{SK_s}(m)$. Then, the encrypted canonical witness hiding proof of knowledge for R_Σ of section 3.2 is run between the signer S in the role of a prover and verifier V on common inputs m, PK_s and PK_c and auxiliary input σ to S.

The triple $\sigma' = (t, e_0, e_1)$ (defined during the protocol) is defined to be the designated confirmer signature of message m with respect to PK_s. When the protocol is repeated k times, the designated confirmer signature of m is $\{(t_i, e_{i0}, e_{i1}), i = 1, \cdots, k\}$.

Signature Extraction: Extracting an ordinary signature σ of message m such that
$Verify(PK_S, m, \sigma) = valid$ from a designated confirmer signature σ' where $(accept, \sigma') \in ConfirmedSign_{S,V}(m, PK_s, PK_c)$ is straightforward for C. C simply decrypts e_0 and e_1 to obtain s_0 and s_1. Knowing both s_0 and s_1 implies extraction of the ordinary signature σ using the knowledge extractor of the witness hiding proof of knowledge protocol for σ.[9]

---

[8] At the moment we are assuming we are given such a WHPOK. We know that such WHPOK exist if one-way permutations exist. Later we will show efficient construction of such protocols for a large family of signature schemes.

[9] Note that the probability that upon decryption it is discovered that s_0, s_1 were not properly encrypted is essentially the same as the soundness probability of the witness hiding protocol. In the full protocol with k repetitions where the designated confirmer signature is (t_i, e_{i_0}, e_{i_1}) for $i = 1, \cdots, k$, the probability that there exist a pair e_{i_0}, e_{i_1} which properly decrypts to a pair s_0 and s_1 from which σ can be decrypted is negligibly close to 1.

Confirmation protocol: On common inputs m, an alleged designated confirmer signature σ', and PK_s, PK_c the following protocol is run between confirmer C and verifier V. C has as an auxiliary input SK_c. First, C extracts an ordinary signature of m, by $\sigma = Extract(m, \sigma', PK_s, PK_c, SK_c)$. If
$Verify(PK_s, m, \sigma) = invalid$, then the confirmation protocol outputs invalid and stops. If $Verify(PK_s, m, \sigma) = valid$, then C (as prover) and V (as verifier) run the canonical strong WHPOK for R_Σ on common input (PK_s, m) and auxiliary input σ to C.

Disavowal protocol $Disavowal_{(C,V)}$: Given m and alleged DCS σ' for which $Verify(PK_s, m, Extract(m, \sigma, PK_s, PK_c, SK_c)) = invalid$ the disavowal protocol is a zero-knowledge proof that
$Verify(PK_s, m, Extract(m, \sigma, PK_s, PK_c, SK_c)) = invalid.$
The latter is obviously an NP statement.

Theorem 7 *The above system constitutes a secure* Designated Confirmer Signature scheme, *given that Sign is existentially unforgeable under chosen message attack and Enc is a CCA2 secure public key encryption scheme*

Proof. For brevity, let us include only a sketch of the proof.

First, we need to show that any polynomial time adversary A, participating in $ConfirmedSign_{(S,A)}$, $Conf_{(C,A)}$ and $Disavowal_{(C,A)}$ in the role of the verifier on polynomially many messages $m_1, \ldots, m_k$ of his choice, cannot successfully run $ConfirmedSign_{(A,V)}(m, PK_s, PK_c)$ or compute an ordinary signature σ^* such that $Verify(PK_s, m, \sigma^*) = valid$ for any message m of his choice (regardless whether $m \in \{m_1, \cdots, m_k\}$ or not). Suppose for contradiction that such an A does exist. Since $ConfirmedSign_{(A,V)}(m, PK_s, PK_c)$ is a proof of knowledge, an adversary A that successfully run $ConfirmedSign_{(A,V)}(m, PK_s, PK_c)$, can also extract an ordinary signature σ' of m with high probability. This contradicts the assumption that $ConfirmedSign_{(S,A)}$ and $Conf_{(C,A)}$ are *strong witness hiding* and thus do not reveal an ordinary signature for any message.

Next, we need to show that such F cannot produce a pair (m, σ) where $Conf_{(C,V)}(m, \sigma, PK_s, PK_c)$ will be successful, namely for which $Verify(PK_s, m, Extract(m, \sigma, PK_s, PK_c, SK_c)) = valid$, for a new m not previously signed. Suppose for contradiction that such an A does exist. Then, a success of A would constitute a successful malleability attack on the encryption scheme E_{PK_c} which is impossible as E_{PK_c} was taken to be secure against CCA2.

Finally, we need to show that any coalition of probabilistic polynomial time adversaries $\{A_i\}$ with secret signing keys $\{SK_i\}$, playing $ConfirmedSign_{(S,A_i)}$, $Conf_{(C,A_i)}$ and $Disavowal_{(C,A_i)}$ in the role of the verifier on polynomially many messages $m_1, \ldots, m_k$ of their choice, cannot successfully run $Conf_{(A_i,V)}$ on any pair (m, σ) . Here again, since $Conf_{(A_i,V)}$ is a POK, successfully running $Conf_{(A_i,V)}$, means that A_i can extract an ordinary signature of m with high probability which contradicts the fact that $Conf$ and $SignedConf$ are witness hiding. $\square$

4.1   On the Complexity of the Construction

Unlike the efficient WHPOK *ConfirmedSign* and *Conf*, the *Disavowal* protocol is a less efficient ZKPOK. We claim that due to the rare expected use of *Disavowal* it has very lite effect on the overall efficiency of the scheme. See discussion in 1.1.

One problematic point is that per our description the verifier must store the designated confirmer signature in its entirety, i.e $(t, e_{i_0}, e_{i_1}), 1 \leq i \leq k$, in case it needs to be presented in a later time to the confirmer for confirmation. If the signer was honest, σ can be extracted from any of the triples (t, e_{i_0}, e_{i_1}) and thus saving a single triplet would significantly reduce the storage needed. However, saving a single triplet does not suffice in case of a cheating signer as it may be triple which does not enable extraction and was not detected during the signing protocol with probability $\frac{1}{2}$. By choosing to store only a random subset of the triples (hoping you store at least one proper one), one may tradeoff the probability of being able to eventually extract and storage.[10]

5   Cramer-Shoup Based DCS

In this section we show how to transform the Cramer-Shoup (CS) signature scheme [6] into a designated confirmer signature scheme. Since the CS signature scheme is existentially unforgeable under chosen message attack, using the construction in 4 we can transform it into a DCS scheme. In order to do that we describe a canonical WHPOK of a CS signature.

5.1   The Cramer-Shoup Signature Scheme

The Cramer-Shoup signature scheme [6] is an efficient signature scheme, which is existentially unforgeable under chosen message attack under the strong RSA assumption.

Definition 8 *The* **strong RSA assumption** *is the assumption that given a randomly chosen RSA modulus n and a random $z \in Z_n^*$, it is hard find $r > 1$ and $y \in Z_n^*$, such that $y^r = z$.*

The Cramer-Shoup scheme:
      Key Generation: Two random l'-bit primes p and q are chosen, where $p = 2p' + 1$ and $q = 2q' + 1$, with both p' and q' prime. Let $N = pq$. Also chosen are $h, x \in QR_N$ and a random $(l+1)-$bit prime e'. The private key is (p, q) and the public key is (N, h, x, e') along with a collision resistance hash function H (e.g. SHA-1).
      Signature generation: To sign a message m, a random $(l+1)$ bit prime $e \neq e'$ is chosen and a random $x' \in QR_N$ is chosen The equation $y^e = xh^{H(x')} mod \ N$

---

10 A back of the envelope calculation shows that if one chooses at random l out of k pairs to store, the probability (after having passed the confirmation protocol) that the confirmer will not be able to extract the signature is $\frac{1}{2^l} \frac{1}{(k-l)^l}$.

is solved for y and the equation $(y')^{e'} = x'h^{H(m)} mod\ N$ is solved for y'. The Cramer-Shoup signature is (e, y, y').

Signature verification: To verify a signature (e, y, y') on a message m, e is first checked to be an odd $(l + 1)$-bit number different from e'. Second, $x' = (y')^{e'}h^{-H(m)} mod\ N$ is computed. Third, it is checked that $x = y^e h^{-H(x')} mod\ N$.

5.2   Canonical WHPOK of a CS Signature

Proving knowledge of a CS signature of a message m amounts to proving knowledge of (e, y, y') such that $\exists e, x'$ satisfying the equations $y^e = xh^{H(x')}\ mod\ N$ and $(y')^{e'} = x'h^{H(m)}\ mod\ N$. In order to prove knowledge of a CS signature we use a ZKPOK of the ith root as a tool.

Protocol I: Zero-knowledge proof of knowledge of the ith root:
  On common input w, i, N such that $w = s^i\ mod\ N$, and auxiliary secret input s to the prover.

1. The prover picks $r \in_R Z_n^*$, computes $v = r^i\ mod\ N$ and sends v to the verifier.
2. The verifier picks $b \in_R \{0, 1\}$ and sends b to the prover.
3. The prover sends $t = rs^b\ mod\ N$ to the verifier.
4. The verifier accepts iff $t^i \equiv vw^b\ (mod\ N)$. (To achieve lower soundness probability the protocol may be repeated.)

Theorem 9 *Protocol I is a perfect zero-knowledge proof of knowledge of s.*

Protocol II: Strong WHPOK of Cramer-Shoup signatures. On common input message m, a Cramer-Shoup public key (N, h, x, e') and an auxiliary secret input to the prover (e, y, y') (a Cramer-Shoup signature of m).

1. The prover sends e, x' to the verifier where $x' = (y')^{e'}h^{-H(m)}\ mod\ N$.
2. The prover proves in zero-knowledge (using Protocol I of 3.2) that he knows a y, such that $y^e = xh^{H(x')}\ mod\ N$ and that he knows a y', such that $(y')^{e'} = x'h^{H(m)}\ mod\ N$.

Theorem 10 *Protocol II is a strong WHPOK of a Cramer-Shoup signatures*

Proof. It is easy to see that **completeness** holds - a prover that knows a CS signature of m can always convince a verifier.

Since we are using the ZKPOK of a modular root, there exist a knowledge extractor for y (the eth root of $xh^{H(x')}$) and y'(the e'th root of $x'h^{H(m)}$). These y and y', together with the e given in the first round are a CS signature of m, hence a **witness-extractor** exist.

Soundness holds because a cheating prover, that does not know a CS signature, cannot prove knowledge of either, the eth root of $xh^{H(x')}$, or the e'th root of $x'h^{H(m)}$. Thus, the soundness is guaranteed by the soundness of the POK of the eth root.

The most important thing we need to prove in order to apply the general construction to the above protocol is that it is indeed **strong witness hiding**. It was already proved in [6] that seeing a Cramer-Shoup signature on polynomially many messages does not enable an adversary to sign any **new** message that has not been signed before, let alone seeing only a partial CS signature. It remains to show that executing the above protocol does not reveal the Cramer-Shoup signature of any of the messages on which it was run. Assume toward contradiction that there exist an adversary A that on a Cramer-Shoup public key (N, h, x, e'), executes the above protocol in the role of a verifier with the signer in the role of a prover on polynomially many messages of the verifiers choice $m_1, \ldots, m_t$ and finally outputs, with non-negligible probability, a pair (m, σ), where $m \in \{m_1, \ldots, m_t\}$ and σ is a valid Cramer-Shoup signature of m. We show that such algorithm A can be used to construct the following forging algorithm B for the standard Cramer-Shoup signature scheme. B will utilize A's algorithm for this purpose (i.e B will run A on different inputs and random tapes).

The Forging Algorithm B:

Algorithm B's input: A Cramer-Shoup public key (N, h, x, e') and access to A's program.
Algorithm B's output: A pair (m, σ), where m is a message and $\sigma = (e, y, y')$ is a Cramer-Shoup signature of m.

1. **Query phase**: Initially B interacts with A where B acts in the role of the prover and A the verifier in protocol II above, perfectly simulating A's view of interacting with legitimate signer without ever querying the signer. On message m_i of A's choice, B proves to A that he knows a Cramer-Shoup signature of m_i in the following way:
    a) B picks a random $(l+1)$-bit prime e_i and $x'_i \in_R QR_N$ and sends (e_i, x'_i) to A.
    b) B proves to A in zero-knowledge that he knows y_i, such that $y_i^{e_i} = xh^{H(x'_i)} \bmod N$ and y'_i, such that $(y'_i)^{e'} = x'_i h^{H(m_i)} \bmod N$. Naturally, B does not know such y_i and y'_i. Nevertheless, B can perfectly simulate A's view using the standard rewinding technique for proving zero-knowledge - taking advantage on the ability to rewind A upon a challenge that B was not prepared for[11]
2. **Output phase**: If A outputs a valid Cramer-Shoup signature σ for $m \in \{m_1, \ldots m_t\}$ (or any m for that matter), then B outputs $< m, \sigma >$.

Clearly, B runs in expected polynomial time as so does A. B perfectly simulates A's view as the x'_i and e_i are uniformly distributed (completely independent of the m_i) and thus if A outputs a Cramer-Shoup signature with non-negligible

---

[11] The number of possible challenges in each round of the ZKPOK of the e'th root is 2 and thus running the protocol simultaneously for y and y' brings the number of possible challenges to 4 and can be easily simulated.

probability, so does B, contradicting the fact that the Cramer-Shoup signature scheme is existentially unforgeable under the strong RSA assumption.

$\square$

We remark that one could simplify protocol II further and rather than running step 2 as it is, allow the verifier to choose at random whether to engage in a WHPOK of y such that $y^e = xh^{H(x')} \bmod N$ (step 2(a) in protocol II), or a WHPOK of y', such that $(y')^{e'} = x'h^{H(m)} \bmod N$ (step 2(b) in protocol II) but not both. Since, knowing a legal Cramer-Shoup signature of m means knowing both y and y', a cheating prover who cannot answer both challenges will be caught with probability $\frac{1}{2}$.

Finally, protocol II did not have a canonical form. It can be easily turned canonical 3-round protocol (to be repeated in turn k times), included for completion.

Canonical strong WHPOK of Cramer-Shoup signature m: On common input m, Cramer-Shoup public key (N, h, x, e') and auxiliary secret input to prover (e, y, y').

1. prover calculates $x' = (y')^{e'} h^{-H(m)} \bmod N$, picks $r, r' \in_R Z_n^*$, computes $v = r^e \bmod N$, $v' = r'^{e'} \bmod N$ and sends e, x', v, v' to the verifier.
2. verifier picks $b, b' \in_R \{0, 1\}$ and them to the prover.
3. prover sends $t = ry^b \bmod N$ and $t' = r'y'^{b'} \bmod N$ to the verifier.
4. verifier accepts iff $t^e \equiv v(xh^{H(x')})^b \pmod{N}$ and $t'^{e'} \equiv v'(x'h^{H(m)})^{b'} \pmod{N}$.

6   Goldwasser-Micali-Rivest Based DCS

In this section we show how to transform the Goldwasser-Micali-Rivest (GMR) signature scheme into a designated confirmer signature scheme. Since the GMR signature scheme is existentially unforgeable under chosen message attack, using the construction in 4 we can transform it into a DCS scheme. In order to do that we describe a canonical strong WHPOK of a GMR signature.

6.1   The GMR Signature Scheme

The digital signature scheme of Golwasser Micali and Rivest [16] is existentially unforgeable under chosen message attack under the assumption that claw-free trapdoor permutation (pairs f_0, f_1 for which it is hard to find x, y such that $f_0(x) = f_1(y)$) exist. In [16] it is shown that such family of trapdoor permutation exists if factoring is hard.

Before we describe the scheme we recall the followings notation:

Definition 11 Let $\sigma = \sigma_1 \sigma_2 \ldots \sigma_n$ where $\sigma_i \in \{0, 1\}$. we denote by $f_\sigma(x) = f_{\sigma_1}(f_{\sigma_2}(\cdots f_{\sigma_n}(x) \cdots))$ and $f_\sigma^{-1}(y) = f_{\sigma_n}^{-1}(f_{\sigma_{n-1}}^{-1}(\cdots f_{\sigma_1}^{-1}(y) \cdots))$

The GMR scheme is defined by the following three probabilistic algorithms:

Key Generation: Choose two pairs of claw-free permutations, (f_0, f_1) from a common domain D_f and (g_0, g_1), from a common domain D_g for which you know $f_0^{-1}, f_1^{-1}, g_0^{-1}, g_1^{-1}$. Uniformly choose $X \in D_f$. The public key is: $(D_f, X, f_0, f_1, g_0, g_1)$ and the secret key is $(f_0^{-1}, f_1^{-1}, g_0^{-1}, g_1^{-1})$.

Signing a message: We denote by H the history and we set $H_1 = \phi$. To sign the ith message m_i, uniformly choose $R_i \in D_g$. Set $z_1^i = f_{H_i \circ R_i}^{-1}(X)$ and $z_2^i = g_{m_i}^{-1}(R_i)$. The signature is $\sigma(m_i) = (z_1^i, z_2^i, H_i)$ and the history is updated, setting $H_{i+1} = H_i \circ R_i$.

Verifying a signature (z_1, z_2, H)**:** Accept iff $f_{H \circ R}(z_1) = X$ for $R = g_m(z_2)$.

Theorem 12 ([16]) *: If claw-free permutations exist, the above scheme is existentially unforgeable under chosen message attack.*

6.2   Factoring Based GMR Scheme

An implementation based on intractability assumption of factoring is suggested in [16]. Let $N = pq$ be the product of two primes satisfying $p \equiv q \equiv 3 (mod\ 4)$ and $p \neq q (mod\ 8)$. $f_0 = x^2\ mod\ N$ and $f_1 = 4x^2\ mod\ N$ are permutations over the set of quadratic residues mod N.

Theorem 13 ([16]) *Under the intractability assumption of factoring the* $(f_0, f_1)-$*pair are claw-free trapdoor permutations.*

It was noted by Goldreich [12] that the factoring based implementation of the GMR can be sped up. For the $(f_0, f_1)-$pair described above, a fast way of computing $f_\alpha^{-1}(x)$, where $|\alpha| = k$, is by computing

$$f_\alpha^{-1}(x) = \frac{R_N(2^k, x)}{(R_N(2^k, 4))^{i(\alpha)}}$$

Where $i(\alpha)$ denotes the integer encoding of α and $R_N(2^k, x)$ denotes the 2^kth root of x modulo N.

6.3   Canonical WHPOK of the Factoring Based GMR Signature

Proving knowledge of a GMR signature amounts to proving knowledge of a triple (z_1, z_2, H_i) such that $\exists R_i$, such that $z_2 = g_m^{-1}(R_i)$ and $z_1 = f_{H_i \circ R_i}^{-1}(X)$. The WHPOK of a GMR signature that we present[12] takes advantage on the special structure of the factoring based GMR scheme. Let $f_0(x) = x^2\ mod\ N_1$, $f_1(x) = 4x^2\ mod\ N_1$, $g_0(x) = x^2\ mod\ N_2$ and $g_1(x) = 4x^2\ mod\ N_2$. Our

---

[12] In[16] a tree like structure is imposed on the H_i's, but here, for simplicity, we discuss the simpler and less efficient version in which the H_i's grows linearly in the number of signed messages.

protocol uses the fact that in the factoring based GMR scheme, proving knowledge of $g_m^{-1}(R_i)$ and $f_{H_i \circ R_i}^{-1}(X)$ is done by proving knowledge of modular roots. Thus, we can use the ZKPOK of the ith root from 3.2 as a tool, toward a canonical WHPOK of a GMR signature of m.

Protocol III: Strong WHPOK of a Factoring based GMR signature :
On a common input m and public key $(N_1, N_2, X \in Z_{N_1}^*)$ and an auxiliary input to the prover $\sigma = (z_1, z_2, H_i)$ (a valid GMR-signature of m).

1. The prover computes $R_i = g_m(z_2)$ and sends R_i, H_i to the verifier.
2. The prover proves in zero-knowledge that he knows (z_1, z_2) such that $z_2 = g_m^{-1}(R_i)$ and $z_1 = f_{H_i \circ R_i}^{-1}(X)$. Proving knowledge of $g_m^{-1}(R_i)$ amounts to proving knowledge of the $2^{|m|}$th root of $R_i \pmod{N_2}$ and proving knowledge of the $2^{i(|m|)}$th root of 4 $\pmod{N_2}$. Namely, knowing how to calculate both the nominator and the denominator in $g_m^{-1}(R_i) = \frac{R_N(2^{|m|}, R_i)}{(R_N(2^{|m|}, 4))^{i(m)}}$.
   Similarly, proving knowledge of $f_{H_i \circ R_i}^{-1}(X)$ amounts to proving knowledge of the $2^{|H_i \circ R_i|}$th root of $X \pmod{N_1}$ and proving knowledge of the $2^{i(|H_i \circ R_i|)}$th root of 4 $\pmod{N_1}$

Theorem 14 *Protocol III is a strong WHPOK of a GMR signature of m.*

Proof. The proof is essentially the same as 5.2. We include it for completion. It is easy to see that **completeness** holds - a prover that knows a GMR signature of m can always convince a verifier.

Since we are using the ZKPOK of a modular root, there exist a knowledge extractor for the $2^{|m|}$th root of $R_i \pmod{N_2}$ and the $2^{i(|m|)}$th root of 4, hence there exist a knowledge extractor for $z_2 = g_m^{-1}(R_i)$. Similarly there exist a knowledge extractor for $z_1 = f_{H_i \circ R_i}^{-1}(X)$. These z_1, z_2, together with the H_i given in the first round are a GMR signature of m, hence a **witness-extractor** exist.

Soundness holds because a cheating prover, that does not know a GMR signature, cannot prove knowledge of at least one of the modular roots he is required to in step 2 of the protocol of 6.3. Thus, a cheating prover has a probability at most $\frac{3}{4}$ to fool the verifier. Repeating step 2 k times this probability is reduced to $(\frac{3}{4})^k$.

We now show that the above protocol is **strong witness hiding**. It was already proved in [16] that seeing GMR signatures for $m_1, \ldots m_t$ chosen adaptively by the adversary does not enable an adversary to produce a GMR signature for a new $m \notin \{m_1, \ldots m_t\}$, let alone seeing partial GMR signatures. But, suppose toward contradiction that there exists an adversary A, which after running the above protocol III on message $m_1, \ldots m_t$ adaptively chosen can produce a GMR signature (z_1, z_2, H_i) for an $m \in \{m_1, \ldots m_t\}$. We show that the existence of such A implies that the original GMR scheme is not existentially unforgeable and thus contradicts the existence of claw-free trapdoor permutations assumption (e.g. factoring is hard).

Intuitively, since R_i and H_i are chosen at random, independently from the message m and the public key, they do not allow an adversary to sign a message. Formally, using A as an internal procedure whose inputs and random tape can be set, we describe an algorithm B that on a GMR public key forges GMR signatures.

Algorithm B's input: GMR public verifying key $PK = (N_1, N_2, X \in Z_{N_1}^*)$ and A's program.
Algorithm B's output: pair (m, σ) where σ is a valid GMR-signature of m with respect to PK.

1. Initially, B runs algorithm A on input PK. For each chosen message m_i by A, B proves to A on common inputs (m_i, PK) that he knows a GMR signature of m_i (as in protocol III) as follows .
   a) B chooses $R_i \in_R D_g$ and $H_i \in_R D_g$ and gives R_i, H_i to A.
   b) B proves in zero-knowledge that he knows z_1, z_2 such that $z_2 = g_m^{-1}(R_i)$ and $z_1 = h_{H_i \circ R_i}^{-1}(X)$. Naturally, B does not know such z_1 and z_2, nevertheless, B can perfectly simulate A's view using the standard rewinding technique for proving zero-knowledge - taking advantage on the ability to rewind A upon a challenge that B was not prepared for.
2. If A outputs a valid GMR signature (z_1, z_2, H) for $m \in \{m_1, \ldots m_t\}$, then B outputs $(m, (z_1, z_2, H))$.

Clearly, B runs in probabilistic polynomial time as does A. In step 1(c) B perfectly simulates A's view and thus in step 2, the adversary A would output a GMR signature with the same probability as when running with the true signer.
□

We remark that one could simplify the above protocol III further (as we did in the Cramer-Shoup case) so that the verifier chooses at random whether the prover will prove knowledge of z_1 s.t. $z_1 = h_{H_i \circ R_i}^{-1}(X)$, or knowledge of z_2 s.t. $z_2 = g_m^{-1}(R_i)$, but not both.

7   Gennaro-Halevi-Rabin Based DCS

In this section we show how to transform the Gennaro-Halevi-Rabin digital signature (denoted the GHR scheme) [15] into a designated confirmer signature scheme. The GHR-signature scheme is existentially unforgeable under chosen message attack, assuming the strong RSA assumption.

The idea of GHR-signatures is as follows. Let the public key be a triple (n, h, x) where n is an RSA modulus, $x \in_R Z_n^*$ and $h \in_R H$ where H is family of hash functions which [15] is proved to exists under the strong RSA assumption. On a message m, the signature is defined to be $\sigma_n(m) = x^{\frac{1}{h(m)}} \bmod n$.

7.1   Transforming GHR Signatures into a DCS Scheme

In order to turn the GHR signature scheme into a designated confirmer signature scheme using the type of ideas we have used in this paper, we need to give a canonical WHPOK of $R = \{(m, \sigma_n(m))\}$ to be used as a confirmation protocol between signer and verifier. In fact, we do better than that and can give a 3-round zero-knowledge proof of knowledge of a signature.

ZKPOK of a GHR signature of message m: On common input message m and public-key (n, h, x), and a prover's auxiliary input a signature of m, $x^{\frac{1}{h(m)}} \bmod n$:

1. The prover picks a random $r' \in Z_n^*$ and calculates $r = (r')^{h(m)} \bmod n$ (which makes $r' \equiv r^{\frac{1}{h(m)}} \pmod{n}$) and sends r to the verifier.
2. The verifier picks $b \in_R \{0, 1\}$ and sends it to the signer.
3. The prover sends $c = r'(x^{\frac{1}{h(m)}})^b \bmod n$ to the verifier.
4. The verifier accepts iff $c^{h(m)} \equiv rx^b \pmod{n}$.

The above protocol is repeated k times and the verifier accepts iff he accepts in each of the iterations, dropping the error probability to $\frac{1}{2^k}$. It is easy to verify that the protocol is ZKPOK (with respect to sequential repetitions) with standard methods (similarly to the proof given in 3.2). Using the Goldreich-Kahan [13] methods it can be converted to constant rounds.

7.2   Transforming the Deterministic RSA into a DCS Scheme

Instead of using the GHR-signature scheme and the strong-RSA assumption, we could use an even simpler version of the above protocols to get a DCS scheme starting from the plain RSA scheme itself[20]. Let (n, e) be the RSA public key and d be the RSA secret exponent. A RSA signature of m is $m^d \bmod n$. Thus, proving knowledge of RSA signature of m amounts to proving knowledge of the dth modular root of m. This can be done using the ZKPOK of the ith modular root that we already described in 3.2.

We note that as RSA itself is existentially forgeable, so will be the DCS originating from it. Interestingly, however, whereas the plain RSA scheme is universally forgeable under chosen message attack, this is no longer true for the deterministic RSA based DCS. The reason is that the verifier can no longer request the signer for RSA signatures of messages of his choice, but only to execute $ConfirmedSign_{(S,V)}$ (where the signer proves knowledge of an ordinary RSA signature without revealing it). Thus, in a sense the DCS obtained by transforming the RSA signature scheme into a DCS scheme is more secure than the signature scheme one starts with.

Acknowledgements. We are grateful to O. Goldreich, A. Shamir, M. Naor and A. Kipnis for their useful comments. We also like to thank the anonymous referees for their useful and detailed comments.

References

1. J. Camenisch, Ivan Damgård. Verifiable Encryption, Group Encryption, and Their Applications to Separable Group Signatures and Signature Sharing Schemes. ASIACRYPT 2000 pp. 331–345
2. J. Camenisch, M. Michels. Confirmer Signature Schemes Secure against Adaptive Adversaries. EUROCRYPT 2000 pp. 243–258
3. J. Camenisch, V. Shoup. Practical Verifiable Encryption and Decryption of Discrete Logarithms. Cryptology ePrint Archive (November 2002).
4. D. Chaum. Designated confirmer signatures. In EUROCRYPT '94, vol. 950 of LNCS, pp. 86–91. Springer Verlag, 1994.
5. D. Chaum, H. Van Antwerpen. Undeniable Signatures. In CRYPTO 1989 pp. 212–216
6. R. Cramer, V. Shoup. Signature Schemes Based on the Strong RSA Assumption. ACM Conference on Computer and Communications Security 1999 pp. 46–51
7. W. Diffie and M. Hellman, New directions in cryptography. IEEE Trans. Inform. Theory IT-22, (Nov. 1976), pp. 644–654.
8. D. Dolev, C. Dwork, M. Naor. Non-Malleable Cryptography (Extended Abstract). STOC 1991 pp. 542–552
9. U. Feige, A. Fiat, A. Shamir. Zero-Knowledge Proofs of Identity. Journal of Cryptology 1(2) pp. 77–94 (1988)
10. U. Feige, A. Shamir: Witness Indistinguishable and Witness Hiding Protocols. STOC 1990. pp. 416–426.
11. A. Fiat, A. Shamir. How to Prove Yourself: Practical Solutions to Identification and Signature Problems. CRYPTO 1986. pp. 186–194
12. O. Goldreich. Two Remarks Concerning the Goldwasser-Micali-Rivest Signature Scheme. CRYPTO 1986 pp. 104–110
13. O. Goldreich, A. Kahan. How to Construct Constant-Round Zero-Knowledge Proof Systems for NP, Journal of Cryptology 1995.
14. O. Goldreich, S. Micali, A. Wigderson. How to Prove all NP-Statements in Zero-Knowledge, and a Methodology of Cryptographic Protocol Design. CRYPTO 1986: 171–185
15. R. Gennaro, S. Halevi, T. Rabin. Secure Hash-and-Sign Signatures Without the Random Oracle. EUROCRYPT 1999 pp. 123–139
16. S. Goldwasser, S. Micali, R. L. Rivest. A Digital Signature Scheme Secure Against Adaptive Chosen-Message Attacks. SIAM J. Comput. 17(2): 281–308 (1988)
17. M. Jakobsson, K. Sako, R. Impagliazzo. Designated Verifier Proofs and Their Applications. EUROCRYPT 1996 pp. 143–154
18. M. Michels, M. Stadler. Generic Constructions for Secure and Efficient Confirmer Signature Schemes. EUROCRYPT 1998: 406–421
19. T. Okamoto. Designated confirmer signatures and public-key encryption are equivalent. In CRYPTO '94, vol. 839 of LNCS, pp. 61–74. Springer Verlag, 1994.
20. R. L. Rivest, A. Shamir, L. M. Adleman: A Method for Obtaining Digital Signatures and Public-Key Cryptosystems. CACM 21(2): 120–126 (1978)

List-Decoding of Linear Functions and Analysis of a Two-Round Zero-Knowledge Argument

Cynthia Dwork[1], Ronen Shaltiel[2], Adam Smith[3*], and Luca Trevisan[4**]

[1] Microsoft Research, SVC; 1065 La Avenida Mountain View, CA 94043 USA.
dwork@microsoft.com
[2] Department of Computer Science and Applied Math,
The Weizmann Institute of Science, Rehovot 76100 Israel.
ronens@wisdom.weizmann.ac.il
[3] MIT Computer Science and AI Lab, Cambridge, MA 02139.
adsmith@mit.edu
[4] University of California, Berkeley, CA 94720.
luca@cs.berkeley.edu

Abstract. Dwork and Stockmeyer showed 2-round zero-knowledge proof systems secure against provers which are resource-bounded during the interaction [6]. The resources considered are running time and advice (the amount of precomputed information). We re-cast this construction in the language of list-decoding. This perspective leads to the following improvements:

1. We give a new, simpler analysis of the protocol's unconditional security in the advice-bounded case. Like the original, the new analysis is asymptotically tight.

2. When the prover is bounded in both time and advice, we substantially improve the analysis of [6]: we prove security under a worst-case (instead of average-case) hardness assumption. Specifically, we assume that there exists $g \in DTIME(2^s)$ such that g is hard in the *worst case* for MAM circuits of size $O(2^{s(\frac{1}{2}+\gamma)})$ for some $\gamma > 0$. Here s is the input length and MAM corresponds the class of circuits which are verifiers in a 3-message interactive proof (with constant soundness error) in which the prover sends the first message. In contrast, Dwork and Stockmeyer require a function that is *average-case* hard for "proof auditors," a model of computation which generalizes randomized, non-deterministic circuits.

3. Our analyses rely on new results on list-decodability of codes whose codewords are linear functions from $\{0,1\}^{\ell}$ to $\{0,1\}^{\ell}$. For (1), we show that the set of all linear transformations is a good list-decodable code. For (2), we give a new, non-deterministic list-decoding procedure which runs in time quasi-linear in ℓ.

* Work performed while visiting Microsoft Research, SVC.
** Work supported by NSF grant CCR-9984703, a Sloan Research Fellowship and an Okawa Foundation Grant.

M. Naor (Ed.): TCC 2004, LNCS 2951, pp. 101–120, 2004.

1   Introduction

In this paper we consider 2-round (that is, two-message) zero-knowledge proof systems for NP. Recently, Dwork and Stockmeyer constructed 2-round, black-box, public-coin, zero-knowledge interactive arguments for all of NP, in a model in which the prover is resource-bounded [6].

Two kinds of bounds are considered: on the running time of the prover during the interaction, and on the prover's advice, that is the number of bits of advice the prover may have access to during the interaction.

In a little more detail, the prover is split into a preprocessing part and an interaction part. No resource-boundedness is assumed during preprocessing—only the resources used *during* the protocol are limited. In the advice-bounded case, only a bounded amount of information may be passed from the pre-processing part to the interaction part; in the time-bounded case, the running time of the interaction part is bounded. By "bounded", we mean that the resource bounds are *fixed* polynomials in the security parameter.

The Dwork-Stockmeyer (DS) protocol uses as a primitive a linear function f with a certain hardness property. The hardness of f is used to prove the soundness of the protocol against resource-bounded provers. (The specific hardness property varies according to which resources of the prover are bounded; very roughly, f must be hard to compute on random inputs by a circuit with the interacting prover's resources, plus limited non-determinism.) For the case of advice-bounded provers, they show that for each ℓ, if f_ℓ (f restricted to $\{0,1\}^\ell$) is a random linear function from $\{0,1\}^\ell$ to $\{0,1\}^\ell$, then with high probability the chosen f_ℓ will yield a protocol with soundness error $2^{-\ell^{1/d}}$, for any constant $d > 1$. For provers that are time-bounded (and restricted to polynomial advice, but with no specific polynomial bound on advice) they conjecture that a fixed, efficiently computable function f exists that satisfies the appropriate hardness property, but the conjecture is not shown to be implied by standard complexity or cryptographic assumptions, and no candidate for such an f is given.

The goal of this work is a better understanding of the hardness assumptions behind the protocol's soundness. We show that the standard connection between list-decodable error-correcting codes and average-case hardness (see Related Work) holds in this setting. The challenge in applying this connection is that the DS protocol requires *linear* functions—this limits both the kinds of codes one can use and the running time of the list-decoding algorithms. Nonetheless, the connection allows us to give a simpler proof that a random linear function has the required hardness. We also show that a strong, but plausible, complexity-theoretic assumption implies the existence of a fixed function f satisfying the hardness condition needed to make the Dwork-Stockmeyer protocol sound against simultaneously time- and advice-bounded provers.

In the rest of this section, we discuss, informally, the Dwork-Stockmeyer protocol, the connection with coding theory, and our results.

The Dwork-Stockmeyer Protocol

Here is an informal description of the interaction portion of the Dwork-Stockmeyer protocol. The protocol is based on the existence of a "hard" function f (more on the complexity requirements on f later). Suppose the prover wants to prove that $\tau \in L$, where L is an NP language. Then the verifier sends a random x, and the prover replies with a string β and a witness-indistinguishable proof of (roughly) the statement *"either $\tau \in L$ or β is a valid encryption of $f(x)$."*

Intuitively, the protocol is *complete* because the honest prover will just send a random β and will carry out the non-interactive proof using the witness for $\tau \in L$; the protocol is *simulatable* because the simulator (that is not resource bounded) will give a β that is an encryption of $f(x)$ and will use this as the witness for the zap. The main part of [6] involves an implementation that realizes this informal intuition. The main focus of this paper is the *soundness* proof for the protocol, and readers may skip the details of the protocol itself if they wish.

Regarding soundness, if $\tau \notin L$, then a cheating prover must be able to compute an encryption of $f(x)$ given a random x, but (still intuitively) this is difficult if f is computationally hard and the prover is resource-bounded. A number of technical issues arise in formalizing the intuition above; for example, it is not clear that if f is computationally hard, then producing an encryption of f is also computationally hard. Finally, it remains to find the right complexity measure for f which makes the analysis possible.

To this end, Dwork and Stockmeyer introduce the notion of a *proof auditor*.[1] A proof auditor is an abstract computational model that, roughly speaking, is a randomized and non-uniform version of $NP \cap coNP$. The analysis in [6] shows that a prover that successfully cheats with probability χ can be converted into a proof auditor of similar complexity (that is, advice size and running time) that computes f on roughly a χ fraction of inputs.

Hence, for the protocol to be sound, one must use functions f that are hard on average against proof auditors of bounded complexity. For completeness, there is another requirement: one should be able, in polynomial time, to compute an encryption of $f(x)$ given an encryption of x. This is possible if f is a linear function over $GF(2)$ and if the encryption scheme is *XOR malleable*.[2] The Goldwasser-Micali cryptosystem, based on the quadratic residuosity assumption, is XOR-malleable.

In summary, the function f to be used in the Dwork-Stockmeyer protocol should be a linear function over $GF(2)$ and should be hard on average against resource-bounded proof auditors. If we want the protocol to be sound against advice-bounded provers (with no running time restriction), then f has to be hard against advice-bounded proof auditors (with no running time restriction). If we want the protocol to be sound only against time-bounded provers (with an

---

[1] The proof auditor is an imaginary device used in the *analysis* of the protocol, it is not *part* of the protocol.

[2] A 1-bit encryption scheme is XOR-malleable if one can create an encryption of $a \oplus b$ from encryptions of a and b. The value of malleable encryption schemes was first noted by Rivest, Adleman and Dertouzos [19].

Protocol SDS

for language L, using function $f : \{0,1\}^{\ell} \to \{0,1\}^{\ell}$ which is linear on $GF(2)$, committing encryption scheme $\mathcal{E}$ that is XOR-malleable, a probabilistic public-key cryptosystem generator $\mathcal{G}$, a zap (2-round witness-indistinguishable proof system) $\mathcal{Z}$, and constants a, d, e; with inputs τ and w.

0. Before the protocol starts, P does the following precomputation:
   - (i) Run $\mathcal{G}(k)$ to produce an encryption key E. Let s be the random string used to produce E.
   - (ii) Let $\ell = k^d$ and $x^* \in_R \{0,1\}^{\ell}$, choose $\alpha \in_R E(x^*)$ and set $\beta = \phi_f(E, \alpha)$. Here $\phi_f(E, \alpha)$ is a uniformly distributed encryption of $f(x^*)$. The existence of a function ϕ_f (that takes an encryption key E and ciphertext $\alpha \in E(x)$ and produces ciphertext $\beta \in E(f(x))$) follows from the linearity of f and malleability of $\mathcal{E}$.

   (Note: the length of the precomputed information, E, s, α, β, is $O(\ell k)$.)
1. $V \longrightarrow P$: V chooses $x \in_R \{0,1\}^{\ell}$ and an additional string ρ of random bits that will used in zaps, and sends x and ρ to P.
2. $P \longrightarrow V$:
   - (i) Send to V: τ, E, α, and β.
   - (ii) For using the witness w proving that $\tau \in L$, send the second-round message of a zap that

$$\tau \in L \ \vee \ (E \in \mathcal{G}(k) \wedge \alpha \in E(x)). \tag{1}$$

3. V accepts iff:
   - (i) P responds within time ak^e (time-bounded case only), and
   - (ii) $\beta = \phi_f(E, \alpha)$ and
   - (iii) the verifier for the zap in (1) accepts.

Fig. 1. Protocol SDS (simplification of Dwork-Stockmeyer [6] protocol).

advice bound also implied by the time bound), then f has to be hard against time-bounded proof auditors.

Dwork and Stockmeyer [6] give a complicated proof that a random linear function is hard against advice-bounded proof auditors. They conjecture that there are explicit functions that are hard against time-bounded proof auditors, but they give no such construction based on other complexity assumptions.

Figure 1 gives a more precise description of the DS protocol. The version here is somewhat simplified from the original one, and allows us to assume that the proof auditor coming from the reduction is "single-valued" (see Theorem 2.1). Because the focus of this paper is on the assumptions behind the protocol's soundness, we refer the reader to [6] or to the full version of this paper for more details on the protocol itself.

Our Results

Advice-bounded Proof Auditors. Our first result is a connection between list-decodable codes and hardness against advice-bounded proof auditors (of arbitrary running time). We show that if we fix any error-correcting code with good combinatorial list-decoding properties[3], and we pick a random codeword c from the code and let f be the function whose truth-table is c, then with high probability, f is very hard on average against proof auditors of bounded advice. (This is very similar to Trevisan's proof [24] that a random member of a list-decodable code is average-case hard for small circuits with high probability.)

We also show that the set of all linear functions has reasonably good list-decoding properties, even up to twice the minimum distance of the code. It follows that a random linear function is hard on average against advice-bounded proof auditors, and there exist linear functions f for which the Dwork-Stockmeyer protocol is unconditionally sound.[4] Dwork and Stockmeyer had already proved that random linear functions are hard for advice-bounded proof auditors, but our proof is simpler, and it seems to get to the heart of what makes their protocol sound.

Adding Time-Boundedness. Next, we turn to proof auditors that are simultaneously time- and advice-bounded. We show how to construct an explicit hard function starting from more standard complexity-theoretic assumptions.

Roughly speaking, we start from a function g that is hard *in the worst case* against a certain type of sub-exponential non-deterministic circuit. We view the truth-table of g as a matrix A, and we define f to be the linear mapping $x \mapsto Ax$. We then show that if there is a proof auditor that can compute f well on average, then there is a non-deterministic circuit that can reconstruct A, and therefore g, violating g's hardness assumption. This analysis can be seen as an algorithmic version of our results that linear functions have good combinatorial list-decoding properties: here we do the list-decoding explicitly, using non-uniformity to choose from the list, and using non-determinism to help with the decoding.

Specifically, we prove security under the assumption that there exists $g \in DTIME(2^s)$ such that g is hard in the *worst case* for MAM circuits of size $O(2^{s(\frac{1}{2}+\gamma)})$ for some $\gamma > 0$. Here s is the input length and MAM corresponds the class of circuits which are verifiers in a 3-message IP (with constant soundness error) in which the prover sends the first message.

Challenges of List-Decoding Linear Functions. The use of list-decoding to construct hard-on-average functions is not new (see Related Work). However, the fact that we need hard *linear* functions adds challenges which are the focus of the results described above. First of all, the code itself must be a sub-code of the set of all linear functions. More importantly, there is very little room for play in the hardness assumptions. Any linear function can be computed exactly by a circuit of size and time $O(\ell^2)$ on inputs of length ℓ. This means there is at most a quadratic gap between the resources required to remember a single pair $x, f(x)$ and the resources required to cheat in the [6] protocol. This, in turn, means that the reductions we give (i.e. the list-decoding algorithms) must take much

---

[3] That is, a code such that every sphere of bounded radius contains few codewords.
[4] Alternatively, this non-explicit construction can be replaced by a preprocessing phase in which V (or a trusted party) randomly chooses such a function and announces it.

less than quadratic time. For this reason we cannot use standard list-decoding techniques and complexity reductions, since those typically involve polynomial blow-ups.

Non-linear Functions. It is an open question whether *completely malleable* encryption systems exist. By a completely malleable encryption system we mean that given the encryption of x and a circuit C, one can compute an encryption of $C(x)$ (malleable shemes were originally called *privacy homomorphisms* by Rivest, Adleman and Dertouzos [19]).

If semantically secure, completely malleable encryption is possible, then one does not need f to be linear in the Dwork-Stockmeyer protocol. This avoids the difficulties described above. In particular, one can use Reed-Solomon codes instead of linear functions in the case of advice-bounded proof auditors, and a different (more standard) transformation of a worst-case hard function g into an average case hard function f in the time-bounded case. This leads to a larger (arbitrary polynomial) gap between the resources of an honest prover and those required to cheat. However, the assumption of a completely malleable cryptosystem seems very strong; no candidate is known.

Related Work. The work of Dwork and Stockmeyer followed a long line of work on protocols whose participants have bounded computational power and/or bounded communication; we refer the reader to [6] for a discussion. We focus here on the origins of the techniques we use and on previous uses of derandomization in cryptography.

Derandomization Tools in Cryptography. The mathematical tools used in derandomization, such as error-correcting codes, limited independence, expander graphs, and list-decoding, have been used in cryptography for a long time, a prime example being Goldreich-Levin hard bits [7]. There has been a recent explosion of work in cryptography using these tools more explicitly—see, for example, the work of Lu [14] and later Vadhan [26] improving encryption protocols for Maurer's bounded storage model [16,1] (the work of Lu partly inspired this work). The most closely related work to ours is that of Barak, Ong and Vadhan [2]. By de-randomizing the 2-round zap construction in [5], Barak et al. obtained *uniform* non-interactive witness-indistinguishable proofs and arguments ([5] shows the existence of a non-uniform non-interactive protocol). As in our work on the simultaneously advice- and time-bounded case, [2] base security of a cryptographic protocol on an assumed *worst-case* circuit lower bound.

List-Decoding and Average-Case Hardness. The main technique which we take from the derandomization literature is the connection between list-decoding and average-case hardness. The connection had been part of the oral tradition of the community since the early 1990s, due to the independent observation by Impagliazzo and Sudan that the result of [7] could be interpreted as a list-decoding algorithm for the Hadamard code and that other list-decodable codes could be used to prove similar results.

More specifically, our proof that linear functions form a combinatorially good list-decodable code relies on a lemma of Chor and Goldreich [4] on list-decoding punctured Hadamard codes. In the reduction of Section 4, we need to show that the problem of list-decoding a certain code with certain parameters can be solved in quasi-linear "MAM-time." This result is inspired by a reduction in [25], that also involves very efficient list-decoding algorithms that are sped-up using non-deterministism (actually, in [25], list-decoding is performed by circuits with Σ_i gates, for various i).

Finally, the results on non-linear functions rely on the techniques of Trevisan and Vadhan [25] just mentioned, and also on the techniques of [13,18,20] which gave hardness results for non-deterministic circuits.

2   Resource-Bounded Provers and Proof Auditors

As discussed above, Dwork and Stockmeyer reduced the soundness of their protocol to the existence of linear functions which are hard for *i.o. proof auditors* with bounded resources (recall that completeness and zero-knowledge follow from more standard assumptions). In this section we collect the results we will need from [6]. First, we give a precise definition of proof auditors and state the reduction from [6]; we conclude with the statement of their result on the hardness of linear functions for advice-bounded auditors.

In our discussion, we emphasize that the proof auditors coming from the reduction can be made *single-valued*, a property which we will use in the sequel.

Definition 2.1 (i.o. proof auditors). *An* i.o. proof auditor for function f *is a randomized non-deterministic device. In order to bound the non-uniformity involved, we fix a universal Turing machine UTM which takes an advice string* $p \in \{0,1\}^a$. *Let* $\mathcal{A}$ *denote the circuit corresponding to the behaviour of the universal machine on advice string* p. *That is, for any input* $\omega \in \{0,1\}^*$, *we say* $\mathcal{A}(\omega) = UTM(p, \omega)$.

The circuit $\mathcal{A}$ *takes an input* $x \in \{0,1\}^\ell$, *as well as a random input* $r \in \{0,1\}^R$ *and a non-deterministic input* z, *and outputs a pair* $(b, v) \in \{0,1\} \times \{0,1\}^\ell$. *We say that an* i.o. proof auditor has agreement ϵ with a function f if for infinitely many values $\ell \in \mathbf{N}$:

$$\Pr_{x \in \{0,1\}^\ell, r \in \{0,1\}^R} \left[\forall y \left(\exists z \in \{0,1\}^N (\mathcal{A}(x, r, z) = (1, y)) \iff y = f(x) \right) \right] \geq \epsilon(\ell)$$

The important parameters of an auditor are its advice bound a, *its randomness bound* R, *its non-determinism bound* N, *its success probability* ϵ, *and its running time* T. *Here "i.o." stands for infinitely often (over* $\ell \in \mathbf{N}$).

An i.o. proof auditor $\mathcal{A}$ *is said to be* single-valued everywhere *if for any fixed input* x *and sequence of coin tosses* r, *there is at most one value* $y \overset{\text{def}}{=} \tilde{f}_\mathcal{A}(x, r)$ *for which there exists a string* z *such that* $\mathcal{A}(x, z, z) = (1, y)$.

In other words, an single-valued i.o. proof auditor ϵ-approximates f if there is an ϵ fraction of the (input,coins) pairs (x, r) on which the auditor outputs a unique $y = f(x)$. A given circuit $\mathcal{A}$ can ϵ-approximate several different functions.

Theorem 2.1 (Dwork, Stockmeyer [6]). *Let P^* be a cheating prover which is limited, during the protocol, to advice bound $A^*(k)$, time bound $T^*(k)$, and randomness $R^*(k)$. Let $\epsilon^*(k)$ denote P^*'s probability of cheating successfully. There exist constants c_1, c_2, c_3, e such that there is a single valued i.o. proof auditor for f having the following bounds, where $k = \lfloor \ell^{1/d} \rfloor$ for a constant d appearing in the description of the protocol:*

$$advice\ a(k) \leq A^*(k)$$
$$running\ time\ T(k) \leq T^*(k) + O(k^e + \ell k^{c_1} + k^{c_2})$$
$$non\text{-}determinism\ N(k) \leq O(k^{c_3})$$
$$randomness\ R(k) \leq R^*(k)$$
$$agreement\ probability\ \epsilon(k) \leq \epsilon^*(k) - 2 \cdot 4^{-k}$$

Thus, the DS protocol for f is sound against a certain class of cheating provers if f has no proof auditors from (roughly) the same class with non-negligible agreement.

One of the main results of [6] shows that appropriately "hard" linear functions f exist for the advice bounded case—hence, no special assumptions are necessary beyond the XOR malleable cryptosystem (which can be based on standard number theoretic assumptions), and the existence of trapdoor permutations. [5]

Theorem 2.2 (Random linear functions, [6]). *With probability $1 - \delta$, a random linear function $f : \{0,1\}^\ell \to \{0,1\}^\ell$ has no proof auditor with success rate ϵ and advice bound $a = \ell^2 - 3 \log \frac{1}{\epsilon} + \log \delta$.*

3   Advice-Bounded Proof Auditors

In this section we show that a random codeword from a list-decodable code defines a hard function for advice-bounded proof auditors, and we show that linear functions have good list-decodability properties. These two results imply that random linear functions are hard for advice-bounded proof auditors.

Definition 3.1 (List-decodable code.). *Let Σ be a finite alphabet. An injective mapping $C : \{0,1\}^n \to \Sigma^L$ is an $(\epsilon, t(\epsilon))$ list-decodable code if for all $\epsilon > 0$ and all $u \in \Sigma^L$ (u need not be in the image of C), there are fewer than $t(\epsilon)$ codewords (i.e., elements of the image) at Hamming distance $L(1 - \epsilon)$ or less from u.*

We are interested in codes which support list-decoding when almost all of the positions in a codeword have been corrupted. We think of elements in Σ^L as functions mapping $\{0, 1, \ldots, L - 1\}$ to elements of Σ in the following natural way: for $0 \leq i < L$, i is mapped to the ith element in the L-tuple. Let v be a

---

[5] Although the security of the Goldwasser-Micali cryptosystem implies the existence of trapdoor permutations based on factoring, we have no reason to assume that this will be true of all XOR-malleable systems.

codeword. For all functions $g : \{0, 1, \ldots, L-1\} \to \Sigma$, g has agreement ϵ with v if and only if g is within distance $(1 - \epsilon)L$ of v.

We begin with some intuition.

Suppose that an auditor is a deterministic machine restricted to a bits of advice (think of the advice as a description of the auditor, to be fed to a universal Turing machine). Suppose we also have a code such that in any ball of relative radius $1 - \epsilon$ there are at most $t = t(\epsilon)$ codewords. The number of codewords that have agreement ϵ with some auditor is then at most $t2^a$. If we have 2^n codewords and we pick one of them at random, then the probability that we pick a codeword having agreement ϵ with some auditor is at most $t2^a/2^n$. This intuition does not quite suffice, since we are actually using two different notions of agreement: agreement of a function (g) with a function (defined by a codeword v), and agreement of a proof auditor with a function. In the first case, the notion of agreement is over choices of inputs to the function: two functions f, g have agreement ϵ if the probability over inputs x that $f(x) = g(x)$ is ϵ. In the second case, the probability is also over random coin tosses made by the auditor (see Definition 2.1).

In the proof of the theorem below, we use the list-decoding property, which talks about agreement of the first kind, to bound the number of codewords with which an auditor can have agreement of the second kind.

Theorem 3.1. Let $C : \{0,1\}^n \to \Sigma^L$ be a list-decodable error-correcting code, with $L = 2^d$, $\Sigma = \{0,1\}^m$, and list size $t(\epsilon)$. Let $c \in_R C$, and let $f : \{0,1\}^d \to \{0,1\}^m$ be given by $f(i) = c_i$. With probability $1 - \delta$, there is no single-valued i.o. proof auditor for f with advice bound $a = n - \log t(\epsilon^2/4) - \log(2/\epsilon) - \log(1/\delta)$ and which has agreement ϵ or more with f. [6]

Proof. Recall that we describe an auditor as an input to a universal Turing machine. Consider a particular auditor $\mathcal{A} = UTM(p, \cdot)$, where $|p| = a$. We may define a second auditor, $\mathcal{A}'$, that has no non-deterministic inputs, as follows. On input (x, r), $\mathcal{A}'$ tries all possible values for z to see if there is a unique y such that $\mathcal{A}(x, r, z) = (1, y)$ as z varies. If no such y exists, then $\mathcal{A}'(x, r)$ outputs $(0, \bot)$. If such a y exists, then $\mathcal{A}'(x, r)$ outputs $(1, y)$. Note that, by construction of $\mathcal{A}'$, $\forall f$

$$\Pr_{(x,r)}[\mathcal{A}'(x,r) = (1, f(x))] = \Pr_{(x,r)}[\exists z (\mathcal{A}(x,r,z) = (1,y)) \iff y = f(x)]. \quad (2)$$

Thus, for all ϵ and all functions f, $\mathcal{A}$ is a single valued ϵ-auditor for f if and only if $\mathcal{A}'$ is an ϵ-auditor for f.

At this point, it may be that for any given x, there may exist many r', y' such that $\mathcal{A}'(x, r') = (1, y')$. We wish to restrict our attention to those values y' that occur with sufficient support among the choices for r. To this end, we define a third auditor, $\mathcal{A}''$: On input (x, r), $\mathcal{A}''$ runs $\mathcal{A}'(x, r)$ to obtain (b, y). If

---

[6] The parameter m does not appear explicitly in the proof of Theorem 3.1. In fact, m affects the function $t(\epsilon)$ in the definition of a list-decodable code. The proof never needs specific values for this function.

$b = 0$, then $\mathcal{A}''(x, r)$ outputs $(0, \bot)$. If $b = 1$, then $\mathcal{A}''(x, r)$ tries enough of the possible choices for r necessary to see if, for at least an $\epsilon/2$ fraction of the r's, $\mathcal{A}'(x, r) = (1, y)$. If so, $\mathcal{A}''(x, r)$ outputs $(1, y)$; otherwise it outputs $(0, \bot)$. $\mathcal{A}''$ has the property that, on any particular x, different values of r can give rise to at most $2/\epsilon$ different values of $\mathcal{A}''(x, r)$.

Lemma 3.2 *If $\mathcal{A}'$ is an ϵ-auditor for f, then $\mathcal{A}''$ is an $\epsilon/2$-auditor for f.*

Proof. For a particular function f, let $W_f(x)$ denote the fraction of random inputs r such that $\mathcal{A}'(x, r) = (1, f(x))$. We know that the expected value (over choice of x) of $W_f(x)$ is the probability (over x and r) with which $\mathcal{A}'$ agrees with f. If $\mathbb{E}$ denotes expected value, we have:

$$\mathbb{E}_x[W_f(x)] = \Pr_{x,r}[\mathcal{A}'(x, r) = (1, f(x))] \geq \epsilon. \tag{3}$$

By construction, $\mathcal{A}''(x, r) = (1, f(x))$ precisely when both $\mathcal{A}'(x, r) = (1, f(x))$ and $W_f(x) \geq \epsilon/2$, so that

$$\Pr_{x,r}[\mathcal{A}''(x, r) = (1, f(x))] = \mathbb{E}_x[W_f(x)|W_f(x) \geq \epsilon/2] \cdot \Pr_x[W_f(x) \geq \epsilon/2].$$

Hence we can write:

$$\begin{aligned}
\epsilon &\leq \mathbb{E}_x[W_f(x)] \\
&= \Pr_{x,r}[\mathcal{A}''(x, r) = (1, f(x))] + \mathbb{E}_x[W_f(x)|W_f(x) < \epsilon/2] \cdot \Pr_x[W_f(x) < \epsilon/2] \\
&\leq \Pr_{x,r}[\mathcal{A}''(x, r) = (1, f(x))] + \mathbb{E}_x[W_f(x)|W_f(x) < \epsilon/2]
\end{aligned}$$

The second term in the last sum can be at most $\epsilon/2$, since we condition on the fact that $W_f(x) < \epsilon/2$. Thus, the probability (over x and r) with which $\mathcal{A}''$ agrees with f must be at least $\epsilon/2$.   □

To conclude the proof of Theorem 3.1, we let $J = \lfloor 2/\epsilon \rfloor$, and, for each x, choose values $g_1(x), ..., g_J(x)$ so that $\{g_1(x), ..., g_J(x)\} = \{y : \exists r \; \mathcal{A}''(x, r) = (1, y)\}$. The probability (over x and r) with which $\mathcal{A}$ agrees with f is at most the sum of the agreements of f with the functions $g_1(\cdot), ..., g_J(\cdot)$. Assuming $\mathcal{A}''$ is an $\epsilon/2$ auditor for f, there must be some $i \in [J]$ such that f has agreement $\frac{\epsilon}{2J} = \epsilon^2/4$ with g_i. Thus, the total number of functions f for which the original $\mathcal{A}$ is an ϵ auditor is at most $J \cdot t(\epsilon^2/4) = \frac{2}{\epsilon} t(\epsilon^2/4)$. If describing the auditor requires only a bits of advice, we can describe all the functions which have ϵ-auditors with advice bound a using $a + \log t(\epsilon^2/4) + \log J$ bits. Since there are 2^n codewords, choosing one at random will yield a function with an ϵ-auditor with probability at most $(2^{a + \log t(\epsilon^2/4) + \log(2/\epsilon)})/2^n = \delta$ (when $a = n - \log t(\epsilon^2/4) - \log(2/\epsilon) - \log(1/\delta)$, as in the theorem). Thus, choosing a codeword at random yields a function *not* having an ϵ-auditor with advice bound a with probability at least $1 - \delta$.   □

Now let C be the set of all linear functions mapping ℓ bits to ℓ bits. Each element of C can be described by ℓ^2 bits (as a matrix). Letting $\Sigma = \{0,1\}^\ell$ and $L = 2^\ell$, we can also think of each linear function as a vector in Σ^L by listing its evaluation on all possible inputs. In that view, C is an error-correcting code with dimension ℓ^2 and minimum distance $L/2$

Proposition 3.3 *The code C has list-size $t(\epsilon) = 2^{2.7\ell(\log \frac{1}{\epsilon} + \frac{4}{3})} = (\frac{1}{\epsilon})^{O(\ell)}$.*

Note that the proposition does not follow from the Johnson bound [11,10], which is the usual tool for proving list-decodability of a code. That bound applies when the radius of interest is less than the minimum distance of the code. In our case, the minimum distance is $L/2$, but we're interested in bounding the number of words within distance $L(1 - \epsilon)$.

Proof. (Sketch.) For any $v \in \Sigma^L$ and any $x \in \{0,1\}^\ell$, we write $v(x)$ to denote the value of v applied to x (recall, words in Σ^L are functions). To prove the Proposition, it suffices to demonstrate how to describe any $\ell \times \ell$ matrix A having agreement ϵ with v using only $2.7\ell(\log \frac{1}{\epsilon} + 4/3)$ bits. Let $a_1, ..., a_\ell \in \{0,1\}^\ell$ denote the rows of A, and $v_i(x)$ denote the ith bit of $v(x)$.

Fact 3.4 (Chor, Goldreich [4]) *If $S \subseteq \{0,1\}^\ell$ has at least $\epsilon \cdot 2^\ell$ elements, and $g : S \to \{0,1\}$ is an arbitrary function, then there are at most $9/\epsilon$ vectors $a \in \{0,1\}^\ell$ such that $Pr_{x \in S}[g(x) = a \cdot x] > 2/3$, where $a \cdot x$ denotes the inner product of a and x.*

Let E_i denote the event that Ax and $v(x)$ agree in the ith bit, for $x \in \{0,1\}^\ell$ (that is, $a_i \cdot x = v_i(x)$, where a_i is the ith row of A). We have

$$\epsilon \leq \Pr_x[E_1 \cdots E_\ell] = \Pr_x[E_1] \cdot \Pr_x[E_2|E_1] \cdots \Pr_x[E_\ell|E_1 \cdots E_{\ell-1}].$$

We first note that at most $\log_{3/2}(1/\epsilon) < 1.7 \log(1/\epsilon)$ terms in this product can be smaller than $2/3$. To describe the corresponding "bad" rows of A, we specify a_i explicitly, using a total of at most $1.7\ell \log \frac{1}{\epsilon}$ bits.

Now for each of the remaining "good" rows, we have $\Pr[a_i \cdot x = v_i(x)|E_1 \cdots E_{i-1}] \geq 2/3$. Letting $S_i = \{x \in \{0,1\}^\ell | E_1 \wedge \cdots \wedge E_{i-1}\}$, we can apply Fact 3.4 to see that each such "good" a_i requires only $\log(9/\epsilon) \leq \log(1/\epsilon) + 4$ bits to specify (given the description of the previous ones). Hence, the total number of bits required to describe A is $1.7\ell \log \frac{1}{\epsilon} + \ell(\log \frac{1}{\epsilon} + 4)$.

$\square$

The result of [6] on advice bounded provers is now a corollary to Proposition 3.3 and Theorem 3.1[7]. In the next section, we address the non-constructive nature of these results.

---

[7] The bound in [6] is slightly stronger: the 6 is replaced by 3. Another proof can be obtained using a constructions of sets of $2^{\ell^2 - 2\ell \log \frac{1}{\delta}}$ linear functions which have pairwise relative distance $1 - \delta^2/4$ (Meshulam, Sphilka [17,21]). Yet another possible approach comes from the results of Mansour et al. [15] on universal hash families. Unfortunately, they are too general to yield tight bounds for binary linear maps.

Corollary 3.5 ([6], Theorem 7.8 on advice-bounded provers) *There exists a family of linear functions $\{f_\ell\}_{\ell \in \mathbb{N}}$, such that the Dwork-Stockmeyer proof system has soundness error at most $\epsilon + 2 \cdot 4^{-k}$ against provers who are limited to $\ell^2 - 6\ell \log \frac{1}{\epsilon}$ bits of advice (for all $\epsilon < 1/32$).*

4   Simultaneously Time- and Advice-Bounded Provers

We now turn our attention to the case of provers that are simultaneously time- and advice-bounded during the execution of the protocol. We show how to *construct* efficiently decodable linear functions f that have no simultaneously time- and advice- bounded auditors, based on the rather natural assumption that there exist functions $g : \{0,1\}^s \to \{0,1\}$ computable in time $2^{O(s)}$ with no MAM circuits (defined below) of size $O(2^{s(\frac{1}{2}+\gamma)})$, for some $\gamma > 0$. We create a matrix for the linear function by setting its entries to be the truth table of a suitably hard function, call it g. This hard function may have a very short description. The role of the advice bound is again to prevent a cheating prover from bringing the entire matrix of the linear function into the interaction; however, now the prover may be able to bring in the short description of the hard function g, from which the linear function is constructed. It is the time bound, together with the assumed hardness of g, that prevents a cheating prover from computing the entries in the matrix during the course of the execution of the protocol.

One can view the results of this section as an algorithmic version of the results of the previous section: not only are there few linear functions in any given ball of bounded radius, but given the ball, some extra advice, and non-determinism, each of these linear functions is easy to compute.

The basic schema for our proof comes from the literature on derandomization and hardness amplification.

Let A be an $\ell \times \ell$ matrix for a linear function mapping $\{0,1\}^\ell$ to $\{0,1\}^\ell$. Let $\tilde{f} : \{0,1\}^\ell \to \{0,1\}^\ell$ be any (not necessarily linear) function having agreement ϵ with A. Then, given a description of $\tilde{f}$, we can describe A using only $\log t(\epsilon)$ additional bits. This is because, by Proposition 3.3, the linear functions form a list-decodable code with codewords in $(\{0,1\}^\ell)^{2^\ell}$, and f can be represented as a string in $(\{0,1\}^\ell)^{2^\ell}$.

This means that, given a circuit $\mathcal{C}$ for $\tilde{f}$, we can describe A using at most $|\mathcal{C}| + \log t(\epsilon)$ bits, where $|\mathcal{C}|$ denotes the size of $\mathcal{C}$. We now wish to consider situations in which this short description of A is in fact a circuit for computing the bits of A.

Suppose that we have an extremely efficient decoding procedure. That is, suppose that given

(a) a circuit $\tilde{\mathcal{C}}$ that has agreement ϵ with a codeword given by a matrix A, and
(b) $\ell^{1+o(1)}$ additional bits of advice (say, to specify A completely),

we can construct a circuit $\tilde{\mathcal{C}}$ which, on inputs i, j, outputs $A_{i,j}$ in time $\ell^{1+o(1)}$, and using $O(1)$ calls to $\tilde{\mathcal{C}}$. Then the existence of a "small" circuit $\tilde{\mathcal{C}}$ which correctly computes the linear map $x \mapsto Ax$ with probability ϵ implies the existence of a "small" circuit $\mathcal{C}$ which, on inputs i, j, computes $A_{i,j}$, where "small" means size $O(\ell^{(1+\gamma)})$ for some constant $\gamma > 0$. Thus, if we use the *truth table* of a hard function g — one which can't be computed using "small" circuits — to provide the bits of the matrix A, then we know that no small circuit can have agreement ϵ with the linear map $x \mapsto Ax$.

Theorem 4.1. *Suppose there exists a function $g : \{0,1\}^s \to \{0,1\}$ that is in $E = DTIME(2^{O(s)})$, but which has no MAM verifier circuits of size $2^{s(\frac{1}{2}+\gamma)}$, for some constant $\gamma > 0$. Then, if XOR-malleable cryptosystems exist, for any constant γ' such that $0 < \gamma' < 2\gamma$, there is a uniformly constructible Dwork-Stockmeyer proof system with negligible soundness error against provers with advice and computation time bounded by $O(\ell^{1+\gamma'})$, where ℓ is the input/output length of the public function f, and $k = \ell^{\Theta(1)}$ is the security parameter for the encryptions and zaps.*

In order to prove Theorem 4.1, we first give our result on list-decoding of linear functions, where the list-decoding circuits we construct are in fact verifiers for an MAM proof system. We defer the proof of Theorem 4.1 to the end of this section.

Theorem 4.2. *Let F be a field of size $q = 2^{\lceil \log 10/\epsilon^2 \rceil}$. Let $\mathcal{A}$ be a single-valued i.o. proof auditor with non-uniformity bound a, randomness bound R, time bound T, and non-determinism bound N (see Definition 2.1). Let $\tilde{f}_\mathcal{A} : F^{\ell'} \times \{0,1\}^R \to F$ be the function computed by $\mathcal{A}$, that is $\tilde{f}_\mathcal{A}(x, r)$ is the single value that $\mathcal{A}$ may output on inputs x, r. Suppose that $\tilde{f}_\mathcal{A}$ agrees with a linear function given by vector $v \in F^{\ell'}$ with probability at least ϵ, in the following sense:*

$$\Pr_{x,r}[\tilde{f}_\mathcal{A}(x, r) = v \cdot x] \geq \epsilon.$$

Then we can construct a verifier circuit Arthur for an MAM protocol which computes the row vector $v \in F^{\ell'}$ with probability at least $2/3$. The circuit uses $O(a + \log \ell' \log(1/\epsilon))$ bits of non-uniform advice (some of these are necessary just to have v well-specified), and communication $O(\ell' \log \frac{1}{\epsilon} + R + N)$ (this corresponds to non-deterministic advice from Merlin). The running time of the circuit for Arthur is $\tilde{O}(T + \ell' \log \frac{1}{\epsilon} + R + N)$.

Proof (of Theorem 4.2). There are three phases to the reduction. First, use non-determinism (i.e., the first message from the prover Merlin to verifier Arthur) to guess a candidate vector v'. Next, we use a non-deterministic counting technique, due to Stockmeyer [22], to verify that the candidate v' has agreement close to ϵ (specifically, $\epsilon/2$) with $\tilde{f}$. By Lemma 4.3, there are at most $O(1/\epsilon)$ such vectors. Finally, we provide the verifier a few bits of advice, enabling it to perform a test which, among those close vectors, is passed only by v. The remainder of the advice bits are used as advice in the calls to $\mathcal{A}$. We now describe the details of the agreement test and the selection of v using short advice.

Agreement Test. Let $S \subseteq F^{\ell'} \times \{0,1\}^R$ be the set of pairs (x, r) such that $\tilde{f}_{\mathcal{A}}(x, r) = v' \cdot x$. We wish to verify that $|S| \geq \epsilon q^{\ell'} 2^R$. In fact, we only test that $|S| \geq (\epsilon/2) q^{\ell'} 2^R$.

To do this, the verifier chooses a pairwise-independent random sample U of size M/ϵ from the set $\mathcal{D} = F^{\ell'} \times \{0,1\}^R$, where M is some large constant. Consider the set $U \cap S$. One can choose M appropriately so that when $|S| \leq \epsilon q^{\ell'}/2$, the probability of there being more than $3M/4$ points is at most $1/3$. Conversely, when $|S| \geq \epsilon q^{\ell'}$ that same probability is at least $2/3$. Thus, to allow Arthur to check that each of the points is also in S, the prover need only send the verifier $3M/4$ points (x, r) in U, together with the non-deterministic inputs z used by $\mathcal{A}$ to produce an output on the input pairs (x, r) (a different z for each pair).

For representing the sample U and verifying membership efficiently, view $\mathcal{D}$ as the field $GF(2^{\ell' \log q + R})$. Then to choose U, the verifier need only choose 2 elements $\alpha, \beta \in \mathcal{D}$ at random. To specify an element of U, a string of $\log \frac{1}{\epsilon} + O(1)$ bits suffices, and it only takes time $\tilde{O}(\ell' \log q + R)$ to reconstruct the full representation (this is the time needed for multiplication in $\mathcal{D}$).

Using Short Advice to Select v. It remains to give a short test to determine whether a given v', having agreement at least $\epsilon/2$, is the correct v'. Let $e = \log(10/\epsilon^2)$. We view v' as a string of $\ell' \log 10/\epsilon^2 = \ell'e$ bits, and apply a standard polynomial fingerprinting scheme.

Namely, choose $p = O(\ell' \log(1/\epsilon) \cdot \frac{1}{\epsilon^2})$, such that p is a power of 2, and work in $GF(p)$. For any string $a \in \{0,1\}^{\ell'e}$, write a as a sequence of $\frac{\ell'e}{\log p}$ elements in $GF(p)$, and let $a(\cdot) : GF(p) \to GF(p)$ denote the polynomial corresponding to those coefficients. The degree of $a(\cdot)$ is at most $D = \frac{\ell'e}{\log p}$. Choosing $x \in GF(p)$ at random means that any two distinct strings a, a' will satsify $a(x) = a'(x)$ with probability at most $D/p < \ell'e/p$. Now there are $O(1/\epsilon)$ strings which we want to distinguish (Lemma 4.3), and hence $O(\frac{1}{\epsilon^2})$ pairs. Thus, by the union bound the probability that a random point x fails to distinguish some pair is at most $O(\ell'e/(p\epsilon^2))$. To ensure that there is an x distinguishing all pairs, we choose p so as to make this expression less than one. Thus, by appropriately choosing p, we get that there exists some value x such that all the possible strings v' have different values of $v'(x)$. The needed advice is only $x, v(x)$, which requires $2 \log p = O(\log \ell' + e)$ bits. The running time of this procedure is roughly D field operations in $GF(p)$, which takes no more than $\frac{\ell'e}{\log p} \tilde{O}(\log p) = \tilde{O}(\ell'e)$ steps. (This is less than the computation time necessary in previous phases.)   □

The proof above uses the following technical lemma:

Lemma 4.3 *When $q \geq 10/\epsilon^2$, there are at most $O(1/\epsilon)$ candidate vectors $v' \in F^{\ell'}$ which have agreement $\epsilon/2$ with any fixed function $\tilde{f} : F^{\ell'} \times \{0,1\}^R \to F$.*

Proof. Any two distinct linear functions over F agree on at most a $1/q = \epsilon^2/10$ fraction of the points in the set $F^{\ell'} \times \{0,1\}^R$. By the Johnson bound [11,10], any code with minimum relative distance $1 - \epsilon^2/10$ has list size $t(\epsilon) \leq 3/\epsilon$.   □

Finally, we can prove Theorem 4.1:

Proof (Proof of Theorem 4.1). Fix some soundness target ϵ, and choose q to be the smallest power of two greater than $10/\epsilon^2$. Let $\log(1/\epsilon) = \ell^{\gamma'}$, so that $\ell \log \frac{1}{\epsilon} = O(\ell^{1+\gamma'})$ and ϵ is negligible in ℓ.

Let $\ell' = \ell / \log q$. We will use a truth table for g to specify the bits of the matrix $A \in GF(q)^{\ell' \times \ell'}$ describing the (linear) function f to be used for the proof system. We obtain the truth table by listing the value of g on all strings of length $\log(\ell^2)$. Since $g \in E$, we can compute the truth table in time $poly(\ell)$. Moreover, since f is also linear of $GF(2)$, the protocol will be complete (based on the existence of XOR-malleable cryptosystems).

By choosing a sufficiently small constant α such that $k = \ell^\alpha$, we can ensure that the reduction from prover to proof auditor loses no more than $\ell \cdot k^{c_1} \leq \ell^{1+\gamma'}$ (additively) in both running time and required advice (see Theorem 2.1). Thus a cheating prover which uses time and advice $O(\ell^{1+\gamma'})$, no non-determinism, and success probability $\epsilon + 2 \cdot 4^{-k}$, can be converted to a *single-valued* i.o. proof auditor which has time and advice bounds $\ell^{1+\gamma'}$ and success rate ϵ (the single-valued property comes from the specifics of the Dwork-Stockmeyer reduction).

Now a proof auditor for a linear map $x \mapsto Ax$ is, in particular, a proof auditor (with at least the same success rate) for the linear function given by any row v of A. By Theorem 4.2, we can construct a verifier for an MAM proof system which computes the row vector v, and whose circuit size is $\tilde{O}(T+a+\ell \log \frac{1}{\epsilon}) = O(\ell^{1+2\gamma})$. We can modify this circuit to take an additional input $i \in \{1, ..., \ell'\}$, which tells it which row of A it should be computing, so that essentially the same reduction produces a verifier circuit of size $O(\ell^{1+2\gamma})$ which can be used verify the correctness of any bit of the matrix A.[8] This contradicts the (worst-case) hardness assumption for g, and hence we get that the protocol is secure against provers of time and advice bound $\ell^{1+\gamma'}$. $\square$

5   Assuming Complete Malleability

If we are willing to assume the existence of a completely malleable cryptosystem we are no longer forced to work with functions f which are linear. To guarantee the security of the protocol in this setup we only require that f does not have a proof auditor which is simultaneously time bounded and advice bounded. We have no candidate for arbitrarily malleable cryptosystem. Nonetheless, in this section we give two additional illustrations of the power of such a (hypothetical) cryptosystem.

---

[8] The only difficulty here is that there were $\log \ell' \log \frac{1}{\epsilon}$ bits of advice which were specific to v and hence to the index i. However, including all ℓ' possible advice strings that Arthur might use increases the circuit size by at most $O(\ell' \log \ell' \log \frac{1}{\epsilon})$. This is dominated by other terms in the circuit size.

5.1   Advice-Bounded Provers and Reed-Solomon Codes

Theorem 3.1 allows us to use almost any good list-decodable code, regardless of linearity. (Polynomial-time computability of any particular component of a codeword is still necessary for completeness.) A natural candidate is the Reed-Solomon code. Suppose that we want a power p gap between the advice needed by the honest prover during the proving time and the advice necessary in order to cheat with probabilitty (roughly) ϵ. If we consider polynomials of degree $d = \ell^{p-1}$ over the field $F = GF(2^\ell)$, then we get a class of functions such that (a) any function is describable by ℓ^p bits, and (b) any two distinct functions from the class agree on at most a fraction $d/2^\ell$ of the input values in F. By the Johnson bound [11,10], the corresponding Reed-Solomon code has list size $t(\alpha) \leq 3/\alpha$ for any $\alpha > 4\sqrt{d/2^\ell}$.

Setting $\log \frac{1}{\epsilon} = \ell/5$ for concreteness, we can apply Theorem 3.1. Using $\alpha = \epsilon^2/2$, we see that as long as cheating provers have less than $\ell^p - \log t(\alpha) - \log(1/\epsilon) = \ell^p(1 - o(1))$ bits of advice, then there exists a function f (given by some codeword) for which a cheater has at most a probability of $\epsilon + 2 \cdot 4^{-k}$ chance of breaking the protocol, whereas the honest prover requires advice $\ell \cdot k^c$ for some constant c. This in fact also requires $d/2^\ell < \epsilon^4/32$, but this holds whenever $32\ell^{p-1} < 2^{\ell/5}$, i.e. for all sufficently large ℓ.

5.2   Simultaneously Time- and Advice-Bounded Provers

To guarantee the security of the protocol in this setup we only require that f does not have a proof auditor which is simultaneously time bounded and advice bounded.

In this section we show that such a proof auditor gives rise to variants of non-deterministic circuits which compute f on a non-negligible fraction of the inputs. We can use "hardness amplification" techniques to construct (non-linear) functions f which are hard on average from functions h which are hard on the worst case. This allows us to base the security of the Dwork-Stockmeyer protocol on more standard complexity assumptions in which the time it takes to compute the hard function is an arbitrary polynomial in its hardness: There are functions computable in E which cannot be computed *on the worst case* by small Σ_3-circuits.[9] We remark that analogous assumptions are used in derandomization to obtain that $AM = NP$ [13,18,20] and to construct extractors for samplable distributions [25].

Theorem 5.1. *Suppose there exists a constant γ and a function $h = \{h_s\}$, $h_s : \{0,1\}^s \to \{0,1\}$ computable in time $2^{O(s)}$ such that h cannot be computed by Σ_3-circuits of size $2^{\gamma s}$, and assume the existence of a completely malleable cryptosystem. Then let n denote the length of the statement τ, and $k > n$ denote the security parameter. For every constant $p > 1$ the DS protocol is secure with soundness $\epsilon^*(k) = \Omega(2^{-k})$, dishonest prover bounds: $T^*(k) = a^*(k) = k^p$ and*

---

[9] A Σ_i-circuit is a circuit which can have gates which compute a complete language in Σ_i (the i'th level of the polynomial hierarchy).

honest prover bounds $T(k) = a(k) = k^{O(1)}$ for some fixed constant which does not depend on p.

As the prover is both time bounded and advice bounded we can assume that all the parameters of the single valued proof auditor are bounded by some bound S. More precisely, that $a + R + N + T < S$ where these parameters are taken from Definition 2.1. We call such an auditor S-*bounded*. We can also assume that the proof auditor isn't randomized, that is $R = 0$. This is because the auditor can get the "best" random string r as additional short advice.[10] The auditor is now a circuit $\mathcal{A}(x, w)$ of size S such that:

$$\Pr_{x \in \{0,1\}^\ell} \left[(\exists z \in \{0,1\}^N (\mathcal{A}(x,z) = (1,y)) \iff y = f(x)) \right] \geq \epsilon(\ell)$$

In words, on ϵ fraction of the inputs x, there is a unique answer y such that every "non-deterministic guess" z on which $\mathcal{A}$ answers is labelled with y. We have no guarantee on how $\mathcal{A}$ behaves on the remaining x's. In particular it may be the case that for every z, the first output of $A(x, z)$ is 0, or that there are contradictory answers (different z's lead to different y's such that $\mathcal{A}(x, z) = (1, y)$).

We first observe that we can transform $\mathcal{A}$ into a circuit C (with an NP oracle) such that C *does* have a unique value for every input.

Lemma 5.2 *There is a circuit C with NP-oracle of size $S^{O(1)}$ such that*

$$\Pr_{x \in \{0,1\}^\ell} [C(x) = f(x)] \geq \epsilon(l)$$

Proof. Let $\mathcal{A}_1$ (resp. $\mathcal{A}_2$) denote the first (resp. second) output of $\mathcal{A}$. On input x, C uses its NP-oracle to check if $x \in \{x | \forall z. \mathcal{A}_1(x, z) = 0\}$. In that case x is not one of the good inputs on which $\mathcal{A}$ agrees with f and C answers arbitrarily. If x is good then C uses its NP-oracle to find z such that $\mathcal{A}(x, z) = (1, y)$ and outputs y. $\square$

We can now use a result by Trevisan and Vadhan [25] (see also [23]) which shows that if f is a low-degree multivariate polynomial then C can be transformed into a small circuit C' (with Σ_3-oracle) which computes f correctly on every input.

Theorem 5.3. *[25] Let F be a finite field (with some fixed, efficient representation), and let $f : F^t \to F$ be a polynomial of total degree at most d. If there is a Σ_i-circuit C which computes f correctly on at least an $\epsilon = c(\sqrt{d/|F|})$ fraction of points (for some constant c) then there is a Σ_{i+2}-circuit C' with size $poly(|C|, d)$ which computes f correctly everywhere.*

---

[10] This was *not* possible in previous proofs in this paper. For example, in the advice bounded case R could be much larger than a, making it impossible to store the "best" random tape.

A nice feature of this result is that the size of C' does not depend on ϵ. This will allow us to use very small ϵ which translates into negligible success probability of the cheating prover. We now recall that any function can be extended into a low degree polynomial.

Definition 5.1 (Low-degree extension). *The low degree extension of a function* $h : \{0,1\}^s \to \{0,1\}$ *into a multivariate polynomial* $f : F^t \to F$ *over a field* F *with at leats* $2^{s/t}$ *elements works by taking some subset* $H \subseteq F$ *of size* $2^{s/t}$ *and identifying* H^t *with* $\{0,1\}^s$. *For every* $x \in H^t$ *we define* $f(x) = h(x)$. *We can now interpolate and extend* f *into a polynomial in* t *variables with degree at most* $|H|$ *in every variable. The total degree of such a polynomial is at most* $d = |H|t = 2^{s/t}t$.

It immediately follows that:

- If h is computable in time $2^{O(s)}$ then f is computable in time $poly(2^s, \log|F|)$.
- A circuit which computes f induces a circuit which computes h.

Lemma 5.4 *For every constant* $\gamma > 0$ *there exists constant* $\gamma' > 0$ *such that if there exists a function* $h = \{h_s\}$, $h_s : \{0,1\}^s \to \{0,1\}$ *computable in time* $2^{O(s)}$ *such that* h *cannot be computed by* Σ_3*-circuits of size* $2^{\gamma s}$, *then for every* $2 < a \le 2^s$ *there is a function* $f = \{f_s\}$, $f_s : \{0,1\}^{as} \to \{0,1\}^{as}$ *such that* f *is computable in time* $2^{O(s)}$ *and for every* s *and every* NP*-circuit* C *of size* $2^{\gamma' s}$:

$$Pr_{x \in \{0,1\}^{as}}[C(x) = f_s(x)] < 2^{-\Omega(as)}$$

Proof. We let f_s be the low-degree extension of h_s, taking $t = c's/\gamma$ (where c' is a constant to be determined later), and $|F| = 2^{as/t}$. We note that f is computable in time $poly(2^s, \log|F|) = 2^{O(s)}$. By Theorem 5.3 any NP-circuit C of size $2^{\gamma' s}$ which computes f correctly on $\epsilon = c\sqrt{(2^{s/t}t)/2^{as/t}} < 2^{-\Omega(as)}$ can be transformed into a Σ_3-circuit C' of size $poly(2^{\gamma' s}, 2^{s/t}t)$ which computes f everywhere. We choose γ' small enough and c' large enough so that the size of C' is at most $2^{\gamma s}$.   □

We conclude that the assumption of Lemma 5.4 is sufficient for the security of the Dwork-Stockmeyer protocol.

Proof. (of Theorem 5.1) On inputs of length n and security parameter $k > n$ we choose $s = c \log k$ for some constant $c > 1$ to be determined later. We use Lemma 5.4 with $a = k$ We obtain a function f_s that takes inputs of length $\ell = as = O(ck \log k)$, is computable in time $poly(k)$ and is hard for NP-circuits of size $2^{\gamma' s} = k^{c\gamma'}$. By Lemma 5.2, f_s is hard for $(c\gamma')/c'$-bounded proof auditors where c' is the constant hidden in the $O(\cdot)$ notation in Lemma 5.2. By Theorem 2.1 the DS-protocol is $(2^{-\Omega(as)} + 2 \cdot 4^{-k})$-sound against provers with $T^* = T - \Omega(\ell k^{O(1)})$. It follows that for every constant p we can choose the constant c so that $T^* > k^p$ and $\epsilon^*(k) < O(4^{-k})$. Note that the honest prover runs in time $\ell k^{O(1)} = k^{O(1)}$ for some fixed constant that doesn't depend on c.   □

Acknowledgements. We are grateful for discussions with Oded Goldreich, Moni Naor, Amir Shpilka and Madhu Sudan, as well as for comments from our anonymous referees.

References

1. Y. Aumann, Y.Z. Ding, M. Rabin, Everlasting Security in the Bounded Storage Model. *IEEE Transactions on Information Theory*, **48**(6), pp. 1668–1680, 2002.
2. B. Barak, S. J. Ong, S. Vadhan. Derandomization in Cryptography In *CRYPTO* 2003.
3. G. Brassard, D. Chaum, C. Crépeau. Minimum Disclosure Proofs of Knowledge. *J. Comput. Sys. Sci.*, **37**(2), pp. 156–189, 1988.
4. B. Chor, O. Goldreich. Unbiased bits from sources of weak randomness and probabilistic communication complexity. *SIAM J. Computing*, **17**(2), pp. 230–261, 1988.
5. C. Dwork, M. Naor. Zaps and their applications, *Proc. 41st IEEE Symp. on Foundations of Computer Science*, 2000, pp. 283–293.
6. C. Dwork, L. Stockmeyer. 2-Round Zero Knowledge and Proof Auditors. *Proc. 34th ACM Symp. on Theory of Computing*, 2002.
7. O. Goldreich, L. Levin. A hard-core predicate to any one-way function, *Proc. 21st ACM Symp. on Theory of Computing*, 1989.
8. S. Goldwasser, S. Micali. Probabilistic encryption, *J. Comput. Syst. Sci.* **28**, pp. 270–299, 1984.
9. S. Goldwasser, S. Micali, C. Rackoff. The knowledge complexity of interactive proof systems, *SIAM J. Comput.* **18**(1), pp. 186–208, 1989.
10. V. Guruswami, M. Sudan. Extensions to the Johnson bound. Manuscript, 2001.
11. S. Johnson. A new upper bound for error-correcting codes. *IEEE Transactions on Information Theory*, **9**, pp. 198–205, 1963.
12. J. Kamp, D. Zuckerman. Deterministic Extractors for Bit-Fixing Sources and Exposure-Resilient Cryptography. *Proc. 44th IEEE Symp. on Foundations of Computer Science*, 2003.
13. A. R. Klivans, D. van Melkebeek. Graph nonisomorphism has subexponential size proofs unless the polynomial-time hierarchy collapses. In *Proc. 31st ACM Symp. on Theory of Computing*, 1999, 1999.
14. C. Lu. Hyper-encryption against Space-Bounded Adversaries from On-Line Strong Extractors. In *CRYPTO* 2002, pp. 257–271.
15. Y. Mansour, N. Nisan, P. Tiwari. The computational complexity of universal hashing. In *Proc. 22nd ACM Symp. on Theory of Computing*, 1990.
16. U. Maurer. Conditionally-Perfect Secrecy and a Provably-Secure Randomized Cipher. *J. Cryptology*, **5**(1), pp. 53–66, 1992.
17. R. Meshulam. Spaces of Hankel matrices over finite fields, *Linear Algebra Appl.* **218**, pp. 73–76, 1995.
18. P. B. Miltersen, N. V. Vinodchandran. Derandomizing Arthur-Merlin games using hitting sets. In *Proc. 40th IEEE Symp. on Foundations of Computer Science*, 1999, pp. 71–80.
19. R. Rivest, L. Adleman, M. Dertouzos. On data banks and privacy homomorphisms. In *Foundations of Secure Computation*, R. de Millo et al, eds, 1978.
20. R. Shaltiel, C. Umans. Simple extractors for all min-entropies and a new pseudo-random generator. In *Proc. 42nd IEEE Symp. on Foundations of Computer Science*, 2001.

21. Amir Shpilka. A note on matrix rigidity. Manuscript, 2002.
22. L. Stockmeyer. On approximation algorithms for $\#P$. *SIAM J. Computing* **14**(4), pp. 849–861, 1985.
23. M. Sudan, L. Trevisan, S. Vadhan. Pseudorandom generators without the XOR lemma. In *Proc. 31st ACM Symp. on Theory of Computing*, 1999.
24. L. Trevisan. Extractors and pseudorandom generators. *Journal of the ACM*, **48**(4), pp. 860–879, 2001.
25. L. Trevisan, S. Vadhan. Extracting randomness from samplable distributions. In *Proc. 41st IEEE Symp. on Foundations of Computer Science*, 2001, pp. 32–42.
26. S. Vadhan. On Constructing Locally Computable Extractors and Cryptosystems in the Bounded Storage Model. In *CRYPTO* 2003.

On the Possibility of One-Message Weak Zero-Knowledge

Boaz Barak[1] and Rafael Pass[2]

[1] Institute for Advanced Study, Princeton, NJ [* * *]
boaz@ias.edu
[2] Royal Institute of Technology, Sweden. [†]
rafael@nada.kth.se

Abstract. We investigate whether it is possible to obtain any meaningful type of zero-knowledge proofs using a *one-message* (i.e., *non-interactive*) proof system. We show that, under reasonable (although not standard) assumptions, there exists a one-message proof system for every language in **NP** that satisfies the following relaxed form of zero knowledge:

1. The soundness condition holds only against cheating provers that run in *uniform* (rather than non-uniform) probabilistic polynomial-time.
2. The zero-knowledge condition is obtained using a simulator that runs in *quasi-polynomial* (rather than polynomial) time.

We note that it is *necessary* to introduce both relaxations to obtain a one-message system for a non-trivial language. We stress that our result is in the plain model, and in particular we do *not* assume any setup conditions (such as the existence of a shared random string).

We also discuss the validity of our assumption, and show two conditions that imply it. In addition, we show that an assumption of a similar kind is *necessary* in order to obtain a one-message system that satisfies some sort of meaningful zero-knowledge and soundness conditions.

1 Introduction

The seminal notion of *zero-knowledge proofs*, i.e., proofs that yield no knowledge except the validity of the assertion proved, was introduced by Goldwasser, Micali and Rackoff [15]. An interactive proof is said to be *zero-knowledge* if there exist a simulator that can simulate the behavior of every, possibly malicious, verifier, without having access to the prover, in such a way that its output is indistinguishable from the output of the verifier after having interacted with an honest prover. The idea behind this definition is the following: Assuming that a malicious verifier succeeds in doing something after having interacted with a prover, then by running the simulator, he could have done it himself, without any interaction with a prover.

[* * *] Work done while studying in the Weizmann Institute of Science, Israel.
[†] Work done while visiting the Weizmann Institute of Science, Israel.

M. Naor (Ed.): TCC 2004, LNCS 2951, pp. 121–132, 2004.

It has been shown that both *interaction* and *randomness* are necessary for zero-knowledge [14]. In this work, we investigate the possibility of a meaningful relaxation of zero-knowledge which does not require either interaction or randomness from the verifier. Somewhat surprisingly, we show that it *is* in fact possible to obtain a non-interactive proof system that satisfies a meaningful variant of zero-knowledge. Specifically, under reasonable (although non-standard) assumptions, for every $L \in \mathbf{NP}$, we construct a non-interactive system (P, V) (where V is a deterministic polynomial-time non-interactive algorithm) for proving membership in L that satisfies the following properties:

Perfect completeness. For every $x \in L$ and w which is a witness for x,
$V(x, P(x, w)) = 1$.

Soundness against Uniform Provers. For every (possibly cheating) *uniform* probabilistic polynomial-time P^*, the probability that P^* outputs $x \notin L$ and a proof π such that $V(x, \pi) = 1$ is negligible. (Note that this is a relaxation of the standard soundness property for arguments, that require soundness against *non-uniform* polynomial-sized circuits.)

Quasi-polynomial time simulation. There is a $n^{\mathrm{poly}(\log n)}$-time algorithm S such that for every $x \in L \cap \{0, 1\}^n$, and w which is a witness for x, $S(x)$ is computationally indistinguishable (by polynomial-sized circuits) from $P(x, w)$. (Note that this is a relaxation of the standard zero-knowledge property, that requires simulation by a *polynomial-time* algorithm.)

Notes:

- As observed below, both relaxations are essential in order to obtain a non-interactive proof system for non-trivial languages. There do exist stronger models such as the Common Reference String (CRS) Model [4] where one-message zero-knowledge proofs and arguments can be constructed without these relaxations. However, in this paper we concentrate on the *plain* model, (i.e., without any set-up assumptions or random oracles).
- The quasi-polynomial time condition can be replaced with $T(n)$-time where $T(\cdot)$ can be any super-polynomial function.[1] In this paper, for simplicity, we restrict ourselves to quasi-polynomial time simulation. We note that if one allows larger simulation-time, one can obtain a one-message zero-knowledge argument under quantitatively weaker assumptions than the ones we use. We observe below that to obtain one-message systems, it is essential that the running time of the simulator be longer than the running time allowed to a cheating prover.
- As in the case of uniform (i.e., non-auxiliary input) zero-knowledge, the uniform soundness property is highly problematic when such a proof system is used as a subprotocol of a larger system. Also, the assumptions we use are somewhat non-standard, and so haven't been extensively studied. Therefore,

---

[1] However, note that if $T(n)$ is larger than the time it takes to compute a witness from a statement $x \in L \cap \{0, 1\}^n$ then there is a trivial $T(n)$-time simulator that works as long as the system is witness indistinguishable.

we believe that this result serves more to clarify the boundaries of what can and cannot be done in zero-knowledge, than to provide a new practical proof system.

- As we show in Section 5, the non-standard assumption we use is essentially necessary to obtain a non-interactive zero-knowledge argument, even when allowing the two relaxations that we make.

1.1   Related Works

Several relaxations of zero-knowledge have been suggested in the literature:

Witness Indistinguishability. The notion of *witness indistinguishability* was introduced by Feige and Shamir [12] as a relaxation of zero-knowledge. Intuitively, a witness indistinguishable proof is a proof where the view of the verifier is oblivious to the witness the honest prover uses. Recently the existence of one-message witness indistinguishable proofs with deterministic verifier was shown, under complexity theoretic assumptions [2]. Their result shows that, so called, **NP**-proofs, i.e. one-message proofs with deterministic verifiers, can be used to achieve certain security properties also for the prover.

Zero-knowledge arguments. Brassard, Chaum, and Crépeau [5] introduced the notion of *argument* systems, which is a relaxation of the [15] notion of *proof* systems. In an argument system, it may be possible for a cheating prover to convince the honest verifier of a false statement, but only if it makes use of a strategy that cannot be feasibly computed. The usual definition of "feasible computation" is computation by a *non-uniform* circuit family. We note that for one-message systems, this condition is equivalent to the definition of *proof* systems, since if there *exists* a prover message that can convince the verifier of a false statement, a non-uniform prover strategy can have this message "hard-wired" in to it. In this paper, we define "feasible computation" as computation by a *uniform* probabilistic polynomial-time Turing machine.

Weak Zero-knowledge. Recently *simulation in quasi-polynomial time* was explicitly proposed as a meaningful relaxation of zero-knowledge [19]. The notion of quasi-polynomial time simulatability implies that a malicious verifier will only be able to succeed in tasks that are easy for quasi-polynomial time after having interacted with a prover. Intuitively, quasi-polynomial time simulatable proofs only "leak" information that could be calculated in quasi-polynomial time. Since in most applications, the simulation condition is not the desired end result, but rather the means to prove the security of protocols,[2] it turns out that quasi-polynomial simulation suffices for most applications of zero-knowledge, provided one is willing to make quantitatively stronger hardness assumptions. In the following we call proof systems that are simulatable in quasi-polynomial time *weak zero-knowledge*.[3]

---

[2] An interesting exception to this rule is the case of deniable authentication [18,8].

[3] Note that the notion of weak zero-knowledge used in this paper is different from the notion of weak zero-knowledge previously used in the literature (e.g. [16]).

Zero-knowledge with resource-bounded provers. Dwork and Stockmeyer investigate the possibility of two-round zero-knowledge proofs for provers that are resource-bounded (to, say, running time n^5) during the execution of the protocol [10]. Their relaxation of zero-knowledge proofs is somewhat orthogonal to ours. Whereas their definition considers a weaker form of adversaries (namely adversaries that are resource-bounded during the execution of the protocol), we consider a weaker form of zero-knowledge. Both relaxations have in common that the simulator is given a longer running time than the allowed running time of a cheating prover. We note that, as was observed in [10], one-message zero-knowledge proofs can not be obtained for time-bounded provers.

1.2   Impossibility Results

Goldreich and Oren [14] showed that any auxiliary input zero-knowledge (i.e., a system that is zero-knowledge with respect to non-uniform verifiers) proof or argument system for a non-trivial language must have at least three rounds of interaction. Recently, Barak, Lindell and Vadhan [1] showed that, under certain computational assumptions, even uniform zero-knowledge perfect-completeness *proof* systems for **NP** must have at least three rounds of interactions. It can also be shown that (under reasonable computational assumptions) it is impossible to obtain one-message zero-knowledge proofs even if both the zero-knowledge and the soundness conditions are required to hold only with respect to uniform algorithms.[4] Thus to obtain one-message proof systems, one needs to allow the simulator to run in time which is long enough to break the soundness of the system (which we indeed do). As mentioned above (Section 1.1), this implies that the soundness property cannot hold against polynomial-sized non-uniform provers (since the existence of *any* cheating prover implies the existence of a *polynomial-sized* such prover).

1.3   On the Cryptographic Assumptions Used

Our construction relies on three assumptions:

Assumption 1 *There exists a one-message (i.e., non-interactive) WI proof system for every language $L \in$ **NP**.*

Recently, Barak, Ong and Vadhan [2] showed that such a system exists if there exist trapdoor permutations, and if $\mathbf{E} = \mathbf{Dtime}(2^{O(n)})$ contains a function of non-deterministic circuit complexity $2^{\Omega(n)}$. (See [2] for a discussion on the validity and reasonableness of this second condition). The protocol of [2] is obtained by derandomizing the Zaps construction of Dwork and Naor [9].[5]

---

[4] This can be proven in essentially the same way as the proof of Theorem 3.

[5] As noted in [9], Zaps can, in fact, be seen as a *non-constructive, non-uniform* one-message witness indistinguishable proof (i.e., the honest prover and verifier algorithm are implemented by *non-uniform* circuits). Nevertheless, since we are interested in giving a constructive protocol in the plain model, without a shared random string or non-uniformity, we need to rely on the protocol of [2].

Assumption 2 *There exists a non-interactive perfectly binding and computationally hiding commitment scheme, such that given a commitment $C(x)$, the plaintext x can be computed by a $n^{\log^c n}$-time algorithm, where n is the security parameter and c is some constant.*

Such a commitment can be constructed based on the existence of one-way permutations with subexponential hardness (using the well known commitment scheme of Blum [3] with a scaled-down security parameter, see [19] for more details). Alternatively, such a commitment scheme can be based on the assumption that there exists a subexponentially hard one-way *function*, and that $\mathbf{E} = \mathbf{Dtime}(2^{O(n)})$ contains a function of non-deterministic circuit complexity $2^{\Omega(n)}$, using the commitment scheme constructed by [2].

Assumption 3 *There exists a language $\Delta \in \mathbf{P}$ and constants $c_1 < c_2$ such that*

Δ **is hard to sample in time** $n^{\log^{c_1} n}$**:** *For every probabilistic $n^{\log^{c_1} n}$-time algorithm A, the probability that $A(1^n) \in \Delta \cap \{0,1\}^n$ and is negligible.*

Δ **is easy to sample in time** $n^{\log^{c_2} n}$**:** *There exists a $n^{\log^{c_2} n}$ algorithm S_Δ such that for every $n \in N$, $\Pr[S_\Delta(1^n) \in \Delta \cap \{0,1\}^n] > 1 - \mu(n)$, where $\mu(\cdot)$ is a negligible function (i.e., $\mu(n) = n^{\omega(1)}$).*[6]

As far as we are aware, this assumption is new, and therefore needs to be justified. We discuss its validity in Section 4.

2   Definitions and Preliminaries

Witness relations. Recall that a language L is in **NP** if there exists a polynomially-bounded and polynomial-time decidable relation R_L such that $L = \{x \mid \exists y \text{ s.t. } (x, y) \in R_L\}$. We call R_L the *witness relation* of L. We define $L(x)$ to be 1 if $x \in L$ and 0 otherwise.

Interactive proofs and arguments. We will use the notion of *interactive proofs* [15] (see [13] for the definitions). Interactive *arguments* [5] are defined in analogy with interactive proofs, with the only difference that the soundness condition only needs to hold against provers that can be implemented by a polynomial-sized circuit. A *uniform-soundness argument* is defined in an analogous way, where the soundness condition only needs to hold against provers that can be implemented by a *uniform* probabilistic polynomial-time Turing machine.

Weak Zero-knowledge. Recall the standard notion of *zero-knowledge* proofs [15] (See [13] for exact definitions). We will use the following weaker form of zero-knowledge, following [19]:

---

[6] Because $\Delta \in \mathbf{P}$, the probability of success can be amplified, and so this term can be replaced with anything between $1/\mathrm{poly}(n)$ and $1 - 2^{-\mathrm{poly}(n)}$.

Definition 1 *We say that an interactive proof (or argument) (P, V) for the language $L \in \mathbf{NP}$, with the witness relation R_L, is $T(n)$-simulatable if there for every probabilistic polynomial-time machine V^* exists a probabilistic simulator S with running time bounded by $T(n)^{O(1)}$ such that the following two ensembles are computationally indistinguishable (when the distinguishing gap is a function in $n = |x|$)*

- *$\{((\langle P(y), V^*(z) \rangle(x)))\}_{z \in \{0,1\}^*, x \in L}$ for arbitrary $y \in R_L(x)$*
- *$\{S(x, z)\}_{z \in \{0,1\}^*, x \in L}$*

That is, for every probabilistic algorithm D running in time polynomial in the length of its first input, every polynomial p, all sufficiently long $x \in L$, all $y \in R_L(x)$ and all auxiliary inputs $z \in \{0,1\}^*$ it holds that

$$|Pr[D(x, z, (\langle P(y), V^*(z) \rangle(x))) = 1] - Pr[D(x, z, S(x, z)) = 1]| < \frac{1}{p(|x|)}$$

We say that an interactive proof (or argument) is *weakly zero-knowledge* if it is $n^{\mathrm{polylog}(n)}$-simulatable.

Remark 1. Note that the definition used only requires that the output of the simulator is indistinguishable by *polynomial*-sized circuits (as opposed to the quasi-polynomial running time of the simulator).

Extractable commitment scheme. As mentioned above, we define an *extractable commitment scheme* to be a (perfectly binding and computationally hiding) non-interactive commitment scheme, such that it is possible to extract the plain-text from the commitment scheme, in time $n^{\mathrm{polylog}(n)}$.

Witness indistinguishable proof systems. A *witness indistinguishable* (WI) proof system [12] for a language L with witness relation R_L, is a proof system such that for every $x \in L$ and $w, w' \in R_L$, it is infeasible to distinguish between the view of any polynomial-sized verifier when interacting with the honest prover that gets w as auxiliary input, and between its view when it interacts with the honest prover that gets w' as auxiliary input. As mentioned above, we assume that there exists a one-message WI proof system for every $L \in \mathbf{NP}$.

3   One-Message Weak Zero-Knowledge Argument for NP

In this section we show a construction of a one-message weak zero-knowledge argument for **NP** with uniform soundness.

The protocol which follows the Feige-Lapidot-Shamir paradigm [11], can be viewed as a derandomization of the two-round quasi-polynomial-time simulatable protocol of [19]. In order to do so we rely on the one-message witness indistinguishable protocol of [2].

3.1   The Protocol

Let Δ be a language in **P** that is hard to sample in probabilistic time $n^{\log^{c_1} n}$, but easy to sample in time $n^{\log^{c_2} n}$ (where $c_1 < c_2$). Let Com be a commitment scheme extractable by a time $n^{\log^{c_0} n}$ algorithm, where we scale the parameters in such a way that $c_0 < c_1$. We define the following protocol:

Protocol Π - One-message Weak ZK Argument for NP

Common Input: an instance x of a language L with witness relation R_L, 1^n: security parameter (we assume without loss of generality that both the witness size and the statement size are of length n).

The protocol: P $\rightarrow$ V: $\sigma = Com(0^n)$, a one-message WI argument z showing the statement

   Either $x \in L$ or σ is a commitment to a member of Δ

   More formally, the statement proven is that either $x \in L$ or that there exists y, r such that $\sigma = Com(y; r)$ and $y \in \Delta$.

We have the following theorem:

Theorem 1 *Under Assumptions 1, 2 and 3, Protocol Π is a one-message weak zero-knowledge argument with uniform soundness for* **NP**.

Proof We show that the above protocol in both sound against uniform probabilistic polynomial-time and simulatable in quasi-polynomial time.

Soundness. Let us start by the soundness condition. We prove this using complexity leveraging [6]. Assume, for contradiction, that there exist a uniform probabilistic machine P^* that produces an accepting proof c, z for a statement $x \notin L$. Let y be the plaintext that is committed to by c. By the perfect soundness condition of the WI system, either $x \in L$ or y is a member of Δ. Since the protocol uses extractable commitments, there exist a machine E that can extract y in time $n^{\log^{c_0} n}$. Furthermore, since $x \notin L$, it must hold that $y \in \Lambda$. Combining E with the prover P^*, we obtain a uniform machine that outputs a member of Δ in time less than $n^{\log^{c_1} n}$, contradicting the hard to sample condition of Λ.

Simulation. Now, let us turn to quasi-polynomial time simulation. On input x, the simulator will obtain a member $y \in \Lambda$ in time $n^{\log^{c_2} n}$, compute a commitment σ to y and then prove in the WI system the true statement that either $(x, y) \in R_L$ or $y \in \Lambda$. It remains to show that the output of the simulator is indistinguishable from the output of the honest prover. This is done through a standard hybrid argument. That is, for every $(x, w) \in R_L$, we consider an intermediate hybrid $H = \{Com(y), z\}$ where y is the member of Λ obtained by the simulator, but z is a WI proof computed of the combined statement using the witness w for the fact that $x \in L$. The hybrid H is computationally indistinguishable from the simulator's output by the hiding property of the commitment scheme, and is computationally indistinguishable from the honest prover's output by the WI property of the WI system.   ∎

Remark 2. We note that the output of the simulator is only polynomial-time indistinguishable from a valid transcript. By using quantitatively stronger assumptions, such as the existence of WI proofs, where indistinguishability is guaranteed against quasi-polynomial time, the output of the simulator can be made indistinguishable for time $T'(n) = n^{\log^c n}$, for some constant c. Note, however, that in order to prove soundness, we require that the running time $T'(n)$ of the distinguisher is strictly smaller than the running time of the simulator. It is an interesting open problem to come up with a construction (under standard/reasonable assumptions) that allows running time of the distinguisher to be greater than the running time of the simulator.

4   On the New Complexity Theoretic Assumption

In this section we discuss the new complexity theoretic assumption that we use (Assumption 3). We show that Assumption 3 is implied by two different assumptions. Furthermore, in Section 5 we show that a variant of Assumption 3 is *necessary* to obtain a one-message weak zero-knowledge uniform-soundness argument.

4.1   Basing Assumption 3 on Uniform Hash Functions

In this section, we observe that Assumption 3 is implied by the existence of a hash function that is collision resistant against subexponential-time uniform algorithms. That is, if there exists a function H (computed by a polynomial-time algorithm) and a constant $\epsilon > 0$ such that $|H(x)| = \frac{|x|}{2}$, but for every 2^{k^ϵ} algorithm A, the probability that A outputs a pair $x \neq x' \in \{0,1\}^k$ such that $H(x) = H(x')$, is negligible. Note that H is a single function, and not a collection of functions, and so a non-uniform circuit *will* be able to output such a collision.

Define $\Lambda = \{(1^n, x, x') \mid x \neq x' \in \{0,1\}^{\log^{2/\epsilon} n} \text{ and } H(x) = H(x')\}$, and let $k = \log^{2/\epsilon} n$. We see that if A is an algorithm that runs in time less than $2^{k^\epsilon} = 2^{\log^2 n} = n^{\log n}$, then A will not be able to output a member of Δ. On the other hand, one can output a member of Δ by running the trivial collision finding algorithm that runs in time $2^k = n^{\text{polylog}(n)}$.

We note that one candidate for such a uniform hash function may be obtained from the AES cipher [7], since (unlike DES), it uses algebraic components that can be scaled to arbitrarily large input lengths.

4.2   Basing Assumption 3 on the Hardness of NE ∩ coNE

In this section, we show that Assumption 3 is implied by the existence of a *unary* language L in **NP∩coNP** that is hard for subexponential-time algorithms. Note that we only require *worst-case* hardness.[7] However, we do require that for every subexponential algorithm, the set of input lengths, for which the algorithm fails to decide the language, will be sufficiently "dense" in the sense that for every such algorithm A, and every large enough $n \in \mathbb{N}$, there exists $k \in (2^n, 2^{n+1}]$ such that $A(1^k)$ is different from $L(1^k)$. An equivalent way to formalize this requirement, is that there exists a (binary) language L in **NE ∩ coNE** (where **NE** = **Ntime**$(2^{O(n)})$ is the class of all languages decidable in non-deterministic exponential-time) that is worst-case hard for *doubly exponential-time* algorithms, in the sense that for every such algorithm A, and every large enough $n \in \mathbb{N}$, there exists an input $x \in \{0,1\}^n$ such that $A(x) \neq L(x)$. Thus, this can be looked up as a "scaling up" of the assumption that **NP ∩ coNP** $\not\subseteq$ **SUBEXP** (where **SUBEXP** = $\cap_{\epsilon>0}$**Dtime**(2^{n^ϵ}) is the class of all languages having a subexonential algorithm).[8]

Theorem 2 *Suppose that there exists a unary language $L \in$ **NP ∩ coNP** and $\epsilon > 0$ such that for every 2^{n^ϵ}-time probabilistic algorithm A, and every sufficiently large $i \in \mathbb{N}$, there exists $k \in (2^i, 2^{i+1}]$ such that $A(1^k) \neq L(1^k)$.*
   Then, there exists a hard-to-sample language Λ.

Proof Sketch: Let L be the assumed language, and assume (using padding if necessary) that for every k the witness, that 1^k is a member, or is not a member of L, is of length k. We define the language Λ in the following way: the tuple $\langle 1^m, 1^i, w_{2^i+1}, b_{2^i+1}, w_{2^i+2}, b_{2^i+2} \ldots, w_{2^{i+1}}, b_{2^{i+1}} \rangle$ is in Λ if

1. $i = \log(\log^{3/\epsilon} m)$
2. For every $k \in (2^i, 2^{i+1}]$, w_k is a witness that $L(1^k) = b_k$.

Firstly, note that Λ is indeed in **P**. Also note, that an element of Λ can be obtained by finding each of the 2^i witnesses using exhaustive search (taking at most $2^{2^{i+1}}$ steps which is poly-logarithmic in m.)
   Finally, we claim that every $m^{\log m}$-time algorithm A will fail to output a member of Λ starting with 1^m for all (sufficiently large) m's.[9] Indeed, any such algorithm can be converted into an 2^{n^ϵ}-time decision procedure B for the original language L in the following manner: On input 1^k, Algorithm B will find i such

---

[7] Unfortunately, there is no known complete language for **NP ∩ coNP**, which means that, unlike the case in [17] and [2], we do not know of a fixed language $L_0 \in$ **NP ∩ coNP** that satisfies this condition, as long as *some* language L satisfies it.

[8] Note that we assume hardness with respect to *probabilistic* algorithms. However, under standard complexity assumptions, probabilistic algorithms are equivalent to deterministic algorithms (c.f., [17]).

[9] Note that formally, A's job is to output a member of $\Lambda \cap \{0,1\}^m$. However, since any member of Λ starting with 1^m is of length $m + \text{polylog}(m)$ (and this length is a fixed function of m), these two conditions are equivalent.

that $k \in (2^i, 2^{i+1}]$ and compute m such that $m = 2^{(2^i)^{\epsilon/3}}$. Then, it will run A to obtain a member $\langle 1^m, 1^i, w_{2^i+1}, b_{2^i+1}, \ldots, w_{2^{i+1}}, b_{2^{i+1}} \rangle$ of Λ, and then output b_k. Note that this takes at most $m^{\log m} = 2^{\log^2 m}$ steps which is less than 2^{k^ϵ} steps. ∎

Remark 3. Another condition that implies Assumption 3 is the existence of a language in $\mathbf{NE} = \mathbf{Dtime}(2^{0\,(n)})$ that is hard on the average, in the sense that any doubly-exponential algorithm will succeed on at most a $\frac{1}{2} + \delta$ fraction of the inputs (with $\delta < \frac{1}{6}$). Loosely speaking, given such a language L, one can define a language Λ of witnesses for a $\frac{1}{2} - \delta$-fraction of the inputs of a particular length (note at least $\frac{1}{2} - \delta$-fraction of the inputs of any length must belong to L for it to be hard on the average). An algorithm to sample a member of Λ can be converted into an algorithm that decides L with a better than $\frac{1}{2} + \delta$ advantage. Again, this is equivalent to the existence of a hard on the average *unary* language in $\mathbf{NP}$.

5   On the Necessity of the Assumption

In this section we show that the existence of one-message weak zero-knowledge arguments for $\mathbf{NP}$ implies a slightly weaker variant of Assumption 3.

Theorem 3 *Suppose that there exist one-to-one one-way functions hard against quasi-polynomial-time algorithms and that there exists a one-message weak zero-knowledge argument with uniform soundness for every $L \in \mathbf{NP}$. Then, there exists a language Λ that is hard to sample by polynomial-time algorithms, and that can be sampled by a quasi-polynomial-time algorithm.*

Before proving this theorem, note that its conclusion is only weaker from Assumption 3 in that that the language is hard to sample by polynomial-time algorithms, and not by $n^{\log^{c_1} n}$-time algorithms.

Proof Sketch: Let f be a one-to-one one-way function, and let h be its hard-core bit [20]. We define the following $\mathbf{NP}$ language L: $L = \{(f(x), h(x)) \mid x \in \{0,1\}^*\}$. Under the assumptions of the theorem, there exists a one-message weak zero-knowledge uniform-soundness argument system for L. Let V be the verifier algorithm for this system. We define the language Λ as follows

$$\Lambda = \{(y, b, \pi, x) \mid y = f(x), b \neq h(x), V(y, b, \pi) = 1\}$$

that is, Λ is the language of "false proofs" (i.e. proofs for false statements that pass verification). Clearly, the uniform soundness condition of the zero-knowledge system implies that it is infeasible for uniform probabilistic-time algorithms to sample a member of Λ. However, we claim that there is a $n^{\text{polylog}(n)}$-time algorithm A to sample a member of Λ. On input 1^n, Algorithm A will choose x at random from $\{0,1\}^n$, and b at random from $\{0,1\}$, and output $(f(x), b, \pi, x)$ where π is obtained by applying the simulator of the system to the statement (y, b). We claim that

1. The probability that $V(f(x), b, \pi) = 1$ is very close to 1. Indeed, otherwise, the simulator combined with the verifier will be a distinguisher between the distribution $(f(x), b)$ and the distribution $(f(x), h(x))$.
2. The probability that $b \neq h(x)$ is equal to $\frac{1}{2}$ (since the choice of b is independent from the choice of x).

We see that A outputs a member of Λ with probability very close to $\frac{1}{2}$. Since membership in Λ can be verified, this probability can be amplified to $1 - 2^{\Omega(n)}$. (Actually, under computational assumptions, this can be derandomized and so A can output a member of Λ with probability 1.) ∎

Acknowledgments. We wish to thank Johan Håstad, Oded Goldreich, and Avi Wigderson for helpful discussions.

References

1. B. Barak, Y. Lindell and S. Vadhan. Lower Bounds for Non-Black-Box Zero-Knowledge. In *44th FOCS*, 2003.
2. B. Barak, S.J. Ong and S. Vadhan. Derandomization in Cryptography. In *Crypto2003*, Springer LNCS 2729, pages 299–315, 2003.
3. M. Blum. Coin Flipping by Telephone. In *Crypto81*, ECE Report 82-04, ECE Dept., UCSB, pages 11–15, 1982.
4. M. Blum, P. Feldman and S. Micali. Non-Interactive Zero-Knowledge and Its Applications. In *20th STOC*, pages 103–112, 1988.
5. G. Brassard, D. Chaum and C. Crépeau. Minimum Disclosure Proofs of Knowledge. *JCSS*, Vol. 37, No. 2, pages 156–189, 1988. Preliminary version by Brassard and Crépeau in *27th FOCS*, 1986.
6. R. Canetti, O. Goldreich, S. Goldwasser and S. Micali. Resettable Zero-Knowledge. In *32nd STOC*, pages 235–244, 2000.
7. J. Daemen and V.Rijmen. The Design of Rijndael: AES – The Advanced Encryption Standard Springer, ISBN 3-540-42580-2, 2002.
8. C. Dwork, M. Naor and A. Sahai. Concurrent Zero-Knowledge. In *30th STOC*, pages 409–418, 1998.
9. C. Dwork and M. Naor. Zaps and Their Applications. In *41th FOCS*, pages 283–293, 2000.
10. C. Dwork and L. Stockmeyer. 2-Round Zero Knowledge and Proof Auditors. In *34th STOC*, pages 332–331, 2002.
11. U. Feige, D. Lapidot and A. Shamir. Multiple Noninteractive Zero Knowledge Proofs under General Assumptions. *SIAM Jour. on Computing*, Vol. 29(1), pages 1–28, 1999.
12. U. Feige and A. Shamir. Witness Indistinguishability and Witness Hiding Protocols. In *22nd STOC*, pages 416–426, 1990.
13. O. Goldreich. *Foundations of Cryptography – Basic Tools*. Cambridge University Press, 2001.
14. O. Goldreich and Y. Oren. Definitions and Properties of Zero-Knowledge Proof Systems. *Jour. of Cryptology*, Vol. 7, No. 1, pages 1–32, 1994.
15. S. Goldwasser, S. Micali and C. Rackoff. The Knowledge Complexity of Interactive Proof Systems. *SIAM Jour. on Computing*, Vol. 18(1), pages 186–208, 1989.

16. O. Goldreich, S. Vadhan, A. Sahai. Honest Verifier Statistical Zero-Knowledge Equals General Statistical Zero-Knowledge. In *30th STOC*, pages 3999–408, 1998.
17. R. Impagliazzo, A. Wigderson. **P** = **BPP** if **E** requires exponential circuits: Derandomizing the XOR lemma. In *29th STOC*, pages 220–229, 1997.
18. M. Naor. Deniable Ring Authentication In *Crypto2002*, Springer LNCS 2442, pages 481–498, 2002.
19. R. Pass. Simulation in Quasi-polynomial Time and its Application to Protocol Composition. In *EuroCrypt2003*, Springer LNCS 2656, pages 160–176, 2003.
20. O. Goldreich, L. A. Levin. A Hard-Core Predicate for all One-Way Functions. In *21st STOC*, pages 25–32, 1989.

Soundness of Formal Encryption in the Presence of Active Adversaries*

Daniele Micciancio and Bogdan Warinschi

Dept. of Computer Science & Engineering
University of California at San Diego
{daniele,bogdan}@cs.ucsd.edu

Abstract. We present a general method to prove security properties of cryptographic protocols against active adversaries, when the messages exchanged by the
honest parties are arbitrary expressions built using encryption and concatenation
operations. The method allows to express security properties and carry out proofs
using a simple logic based language, where messages are represented by syntactic
expressions, and does not require dealing with probability distributions or asymptotic notation explicitly. Still, we show that the method is sound, meaning that
logic statements can be naturally interpreted in the computational setting in such
a way that if a statement holds true for any abstract (symbolic) execution of the
protocol in the presence of a Dolev-Yao adversary, then its computational interpretation is also correct in the standard computational model where the adversary
is an arbitrary probabilistic polynomial time program. This is the first paper providing a simple framework for translating security proofs from the logic setting
to the standard computational setting for the case of powerful active adversaries
that have total control of the communication network.

1 Introduction

Cryptographic protocols are a fundamental tool in the design of secure distributed computing systems, but they are also extremely hard to design and validate. The difficulty
of designing valid cryptographic protocols stems mostly from the fact that security
properties should remain valid even when the protocol is executed in an unpredictable
adversarial environment, where some of the parties (or an external entity) are maliciously
attempting to make the protocol deviate from its prescribed behavior.

Two approaches have been developed to formulate and validate security properties:
the logic approach and the cryptographic approach. The logic approach is based on
the definition of an abstract security model, i.e., a set of rules that specify how the
protocol is executed and how an adversarial entity may interfere with the execution of the
protocol. Within this model, one can prove that it is not possible to reach a configuration
that violates the desired security property, using the axioms and inference rules of the
system. So, in the logic approach cryptographic primitives are *axiomatized* and treated as
abstract operations, rather then being explicitly *defined*. A different approach is taken by
(complexity theory based) modern cryptography, where basic cryptographic primitives

---

* Research supported in part by NSF Grants CCR-0093029 and CCR-0313241

M. Naor (Ed.): TCC 2004, LNCS 2951, pp. 133–151, 2004.

are explicitly *constructed*, and proved to satisfy some well defined (computational) security property (possibly under some computational hardness assumption). Then, these primitives are combined to build higher level protocols whose security can be formally *proved* within a general computational model.

The cryptographic approach is widely considered as the most satisfactory from a foundational point of view, as it guarantees security in the presence of arbitrary (probabilistic polynomial time) adversaries. Unfortunately, this powerful adversarial model makes also protocol analysis a very difficult task. Typical cryptographic security proofs involve the definition of complex probability spaces, the use of asymptotic notions like polynomial time computability and reductions, negligible functions, etc., and the accurate accounting of the success probability of all possible attacks. Proving security of a protocol using the logic approach is comparatively much simpler: once the rules governing the execution of the protocol are established, security can be easily obtained using the axioms and inference rules of logic. The advantage of the axiomatic approach is also its main weakness: since security is axiomatized (as opposed as being defined from more basic notions) it is usually hard to assess the significance of a security proof in this framework. Proving security in a certain logic framework only means that a formal statement (expressing the desired security property) follows from a given set of axioms that aim to model the security features of typical cryptographic primitives used in the implementation of the protocol. However, since the security axioms do not typically hold true in realistic models of computation, it is not clear if the formal proofs allow to assert anything about concrete executions of the protocol.

Recently, there has been growing interest in trying to bridge these two approaches, with the ambitious goal of coming up with logic systems together with computational interpretations of logic formulas in the standard computational setting, so that if a certain statement can be proved within the logic, and the cryptographic protocol is implemented using primitives that satisfy standard cryptographic security properties, then the computational interpretation of the security statement is also valid in the computational setting. This allows to prove that a protocol meets strong security properties (as typically considered by the cryptography and complexity theory community), while retaining the simplicity of the logic based approach in defining security and carrying out proofs.

An important step toward bridging the gap between these two approaches, while retaining the simplicity of the logic formulation, has been made by Abadi and Rogaway in [2], where a simple language of encrypted expressions is defined, and it is proved that if two expressions are equivalent according to a (syntactically defined) simple logic formalism, then also their natural computational interpretations are equivalent according to the standard notion of computational indistinguishability. The logic of [2] is now well understood from a computational point of view, with completeness results [18] showing that if a sufficiently strong encryption scheme is used, then the any two expressions are computationally equivalent *if and only if* they can be proved equivalent within the logic, and further refinements [12] exactly characterizing the computational requirements on the encryption scheme under which this equivalence holds true. However, the logic model of [2,18,12] is extremely simple, and allows to describe (see [1]) only the simplest kind of attacks, where a set of parties is communicating over a public network, and an adversary is monitoring their conversations in the attempt of extracting additional information.

Such an adversary, that can observe the transmitted messages, but cannot otherwise alter their content or flow, is called a *passive* adversary and is usually considered inadequate in most applications.

1.1 Our Contribution

In this paper we present a logic framework that allows to model *active* adversaries, that beside eavesdropping all network communications, can also drop, modify, reroute, or inject messages in the network. As in [2], we consider protocols where the parties (attempt to) communicate by exchanging messages that are built from a set of basic elements (like nonces, keys and identifiers) using encryption and concatenation operations, but, differently from [2], we give to the adversary total control over the communication network. Despite the complications introduced by active attacks, we show that it is still possible to carry out cryptographically meaningful proofs within a model that retain the simplicity of the Abadi-Rogaway logic. In particular, we consider two possible execution models for the protocols:

- a concrete model, where the protocols are naturally implemented using any encryption scheme (satisfying the standard cryptographic security notion of indistinguishability under chosen ciphertext attacks) and executed in the presence of an active probabilistic polynomial time adversary, and
- an abstract model, where the protocol is executed symbolically, in the presence of an abstract adversary that may modify or forge messages, but only using a set of abstract rules when decomposing and assembling messages.

The rules that govern the symbolic execution of the protocol and the behavior of abstract adversaries originate in the work of Dolev and Yao [10], and are common to most logic based approaches to protocol analysis.

We remark that although we consider protocols written in an abstract language of symbolic expressions, we are ultimately interested in the security properties of the protocol when implemented using standard (computational) cryptographic algorithms, in the presence of probabilistic adversaries that may toss random coins, and perform different actions based on the bit representation of keys and ciphertexts observed on the network. This concrete execution model, where a probabilistic polynomial time adversary has full control of the communication network and parties communicate by exchanging bit-strings is exactly the execution model used in most computational works about cryptographic protocols, e.g., the treatment of mutual authentication protocols by Bellare et Pointcheval and Rogaway [7,8,6].

Our main technical result shows that there is a close correspondence between abstract executions of the protocol in the presence of a Dolev-Yao adversary, and the execution of the implementation of the protocol in the presence of an arbitrary polynomial time adversary. This correspondence provides a general methodology to design and validate security protocols in a cryptographically meaningful way, but using simple abstract (symbolic) adversarial and execution models. Informally, our main technical result shows that with overwhelming probability (over the random coin tosses of the protocol participants and the probabilistic polynomial time adversary) any state[1] reached by the parties running the protocol can be represented (using an injective mapping function) as an abstract state in the symbolic execution of the protocol in the presence of a Dolev-Yao adversary. This connection is used to establish the computational security of the real protocol as follows:

- Express the security property S as a set of "secure" states in the concrete execution of the protocol, and find a set of abstract states A such that any state represented by elements of A also belongs to S.
- Prove, symbolically (i.e., within the abstract Dolev-Yao model), that no formal adversary can make the honest parties ever reach a state outside A.
- Conclude that no concrete adversary can violate the security property S with non-negligible probability.

Notice that both the protocol design and analysis is performed within a logic framework where probability is not explicitly used. A concrete implementation of the protocol and computational proof of security is automatically obtained using our technical result: since real executions can be mapped to valid symbolic executions with overwhelming probability (say $1 - \epsilon$), if there is a concrete polynomial time adversary that in a real execution brings the system in a state outside S with non-negligible probability (say bigger than ϵ), then there must exists a symbolic execution that brings the system to a state outside A.

1.2   Related Work

Bridging the gap between the computational and logic treatment of cryptography has been the subject of many recent research efforts. The works which are more closely related to our paper are [2,18,1,12], which present a simple logic for reasoning about the security protocols written in a language similar to ours, but only for the case of passive adversaries. In this line of work, our paper is the first one to show how to deal with more general active attacks.

Other approaches to bridging the logic and computational models of cryptography have also been considered in the literature, but they all seem considerably more complex than [2,18,1,12]. In [16] the notions of probability, polynomial bounded computation, and computational indistinguishability are incorporated in a process calculus, and security is defined in terms of observational equivalence on processes. Still a different approach has been considered in [4,3], which essentially provides a cryptographic implementation of Dolev-Yao terms, within a general framework where security is defined using a simulation paradigm similar to the universal composability framework of [9]. Another seemingly related work is [13,14], which tries to give a cryptographic definition of secure encryption that captures the intuitive idea of Dolev-Yao adversaries.

---

[1] By state we mean the collective memory content of the parties executing the protocol. In fact, our result establishes a connection between abstract and concrete executions not only for single states of the system at a given point in time, but for the entire sequence of states the system goes through.

In a recent paper [15] Impagliazzo and Kapron introduce a logic which (similarly to [2,18,1,12]) allows to reason about computational indistinguishability in a cryptographically sound way without the explicit use of asymptotics and probabilities. The logic of [15] is much more powerful than the one of [2,18,1,12], allowing the use of limited forms of recursion. The results in [15] can be viewed as complementary to ours, as they are mostly aimed at analyzing the security of low level cryptographic operations (e.g., pseudorandom generators), whereas in this paper we consider the analysis of higher level protocols based on secure cryptographic primitives.

The formal execution model used in this paper is closely related to the trace based framework of [19], and the strand space model of [11]. Proofs in the latter model have been successfully automated [21]. We view our work as an important step toward giving a solid cryptographic foundation to automated tools like the one described in [21].

2   Preliminaries

For a natural number n we will denote by $[n]$ the set $\{1, 2, ..., n\}$, and by $\overline{[n]}$ the set $\{0\} \cup [n]$. As usual, we will say that a function $\nu(\cdot)$ is negligible if it is smaller than the inverse of any polynomial (provided that the input is large enough).

SECURITY OF ENCRYPTION IN THE MULTI-USER SETTING. As usual, an asymmetric encryption scheme $\mathcal{AE} = (\mathcal{K}g, \mathcal{E}, \mathcal{D})$ is given by algorithms for key generation, encryption and decryption. The key generation function is randomized and takes as input the security parameter η and outputs a pair of public-secret keys (pk, sk). The encryption function is also randomized, and we denote by $\mathcal{E}_{\mathrm{pk}}(m; r)$ the process of computing the encryption of message m using random coins r. The decryption function takes as input a secret key and a ciphertext and returns the underlying plaintext. It is mandated that for any message m and random coin tosses r, $m = \mathcal{D}_{\mathrm{sk}}(\mathcal{E}(m; r))$.

In this paper we use a variant of the standard notion of indistinguishability against chosen-ciphertext attack [20], in short IND-CCA. More precisely, we use the extension of this security notion to the multi-user setting, introduced (and proved equivalent to the standard definition) by Bellare, Boldyreva and Micali in [5]. The definition is as follows.

We first define a *left-right* selector as a function LR defined by $\mathrm{LR}(m_0, m_1, b) = m_b$ for all equal-length strings m_0, m_1 and for any bit b. We measure the "strength" of encryption scheme $\mathcal{AE}$ when simultaneously used by a number of n parties by considering the pair of experiments $\mathbf{Exp}_{\mathcal{AE}, \mathcal{A}}^{\mathrm{n-ind}-b}(\eta)$ for $b = 0, 1$. Each experiment involves an adversary $\mathcal{A}$ and is as follows. First, n pairs of keys $(\mathrm{pk}_i, \mathrm{sk}_i)$ are generated by running the key generation algorithm on input the security parameter η, each time with fresh coins. Then, the adversary is given as input the set of n public keys $\mathrm{pk}_1, ..., \mathrm{pk}_n$, and is provided access to a set of n encryption oracles $\{\mathcal{E}_{pk_i}(\mathrm{LR}(\cdot, \cdot, b))\}_{i \in [n]}$. The adversary is also provided access to a set of n decryption oracles $\{\mathcal{D}_{\mathrm{sk}_i}(\cdot)\}_{i \in [n]}$, where sk_i is the secret key associated to pk_i. The adversary can query any of the encryption oracles with any pair of messages (m_0, m_1) (and obtain as result the ciphertext corresponding to m_b) and also, it is allowed to query the decryption oracles. The adversary is forbidden however to submit to decryption oracle $\mathcal{D}_{\mathrm{sk}_i}(\cdot)$ a ciphertext which was obtained as result of a query to encryption oracle $\mathcal{E}_{\mathrm{pk}_i}(\mathrm{LR}(\cdot, \cdot, b))$. At some point, the adversary has to output a guess bit d. The adversary wins if $d = b$ and looses otherwise. We define the advantage of the adversary in defeating IND-CCA security in an environment with n users as

$$\mathbf{Adv}^{\text{n-cca}}_{\mathcal{AE},\mathcal{A}}(\eta) = \Pr\left[\mathbf{Exp}^{\text{n-cca-1}}_{\mathcal{AE},\mathcal{A}}(\eta) = 1\right] - \Pr\left[\mathbf{Exp}^{\text{n-cca-0}}_{\mathcal{AE},\mathcal{A}}(\eta) = 1\right]$$

and say that the encryption scheme is n-IND-CCA secure if $\mathbf{Adv}^{\text{n-cca}}_{\mathcal{AE},\mathcal{A}}(\cdot)$ is a negligible function for any probabilistic polynomial time adversary $\mathcal{A}_c$. The following theorem proved [5] is useful in deriving our results.

Theorem 1. *If $\mathcal{AE}$ is an IND-CCA encryption scheme, then for any polynomial $n(\cdot)$, $\mathcal{AE}$ is n-IND-CCA secure.*

3   Two-Party Protocols

In this section we describe a simple language for defining multi-party protocols, and how such protocols are executed. For simplicity, we concentrate on two party protocols, where the two parties alternate in the transmission of messages. In Section 6 we explain how to extend this setting to multi-party protocols.

3.1   Protocol Syntax

A simple way to represent a large class of two-party protocols is by a sequence of messages $m_1, \ldots, m_n$, where $m_1, m_3, m_5, \ldots$ are the messages sent by the first player (called the initiator), and $m_2, m_4, m_6, \ldots$ are the messages sent by the second player (called the responder). We consider protocols where the messages are arbitrary expressions built from basic values (like the names of the parties involved in the protocol, randomly generated nonces and cryptographic keys) using concatenation and encryption operations. Formally, each message is represented by a term generated according to the following grammar:

$$\mathbf{Term} ::= \mathbf{Id} \mid \mathbf{Key} \mid \mathbf{Nonce} \mid \mathbf{Pair} \mid \mathbf{Ciphertext}$$
$$\mathbf{Pair} ::= (\mathbf{Term}, \mathbf{Term})$$
$$\mathbf{Ciphertext} ::= \{\mathbf{Term}\}_{\text{Key}}$$

where $\mathbf{Id}, \mathbf{Key}, \mathbf{Nonce}$ are three sets of basic symbols corresponding to the party's names (e.g., $\mathbf{Id} = \{I, R\}$ for two party protocols where I represents the initiator and R the responder), $\mathbf{Key} = \{K_I, K_R\}$ their public keys, and $\mathbf{Nonce} = \{X_1, X_2, \ldots, Y_1, Y_2, \ldots\}$ represent nonces generated at random by the protocol participants. For example, the following sequence of terms

$$\mathsf{NSL} = (\{(I, X_1)\}_{K_R}, \{(R, (X_1, Y_1))\}_{K_I}, \{Y_1\}_{K_R}) \tag{1}$$

represents the well known Needham-Schroeder-Lowe protocol [17]. In this protocol, the initiator first sends its identity I followed by a freshly generated random nonce X_1, encrypted under the responder public key. The responder replies with its identity, followed by nonce X_1 and a freshly generated nonce Y_1, all encrypted under the initiator public key. Finally, the initiator concludes the protocol by re-encrypting nonce Y_1 under the responder public key, and transmitting the corresponding ciphertext.

We remark that protocols are a compact way to represent two distinct programs (the one executed by the initiator, and the one executed by the responder), and the way they interact. For example, the initiator program corresponding to protocol (1) is the following:

1. Generate a random nonce X_1, encrypt the pair (I, X_1) under key K_R, and transmit the ciphertext.
2. After receiving a message m_2, try to decrypt m_2 and parse the plaintext as $(R, (X_1, Y_1))$, i.e., check that the first and second component of the message are the intended recipient and the nonce generated in the first step.
3. Encrypt the value Y_1 received in step 2 under K_R, and send it to the receiver.

Similarly, the responder program waits for a message m_1, and tries to decrypt m_1 and parse the plaintext as (I, X_1). If successful, generate a random nonce Y_1, and send $(R, (X_1, Y_1))$ encrypted under the initiator key K_I.

In the cryptographic setting, where protocols are executed in a malicious environment, it is important to specify what happens if anything goes wrong during the execution of a program. For example, if decryption fails, or the decrypted message does not have the expected pattern. We assume that if at any point a party detects a deviation from the protocol, then the party immediately aborts the execution of its program.

Not every sequence of messages is the description of a valid protocol. For example, $(\{X_1\}_{K_I}, \{X_1\}_{K_R})$ is not a valid protocol because the responder, after receiving $\{X_1\}_{K_I}$, cannot decrypt the message and recover the nonce X_1 to be retransmitted in the second message $\{X_1\}_{K_R}$. In particular, we assume that the messages transmitted by each party can be computed from the previously received messages in the Dolev-Yao model, which will be formally defined when describing the adversary. In order to simplify the presentation we also assume that the initiator (resp. responder) encrypt messages only under the responder (resp. initiator) public key. In particular, this implies that the messages received by a party can be immediately and completely decrypted. We remark that our techniques seem to extended to more complex protocols, where parties generate and transmit new keys on the fly (e.g., in the case session keys to be used in hybrid encryption schemes), provided that some reasonable restrictions are imposed on their use. We give some further discussion in Section 6.

3.2   Programs and Their Execution

Notice that the expressions, typically referred to as "messages", in the description of a protocol are not the actual messages being transmitted during the execution of the protocol, but rather the "instructions" to be executed by a party to compute the corresponding messages. We will refer to this kind of expressions as *abstract message descriptions*. For example, the expression "I" does not mean that the symbol "I" should be transmitted literally, but the identity of the initiator should be transmitted. Similarly, expressions of the form X_1 calls for the generation and transmission of a new nonce, rather than the transition of symbol X_1. Below, we define how messages are computed according to a given protocol. For the sake of readability, we only give an informal description. We consider two different ways to execute a protocol: symbolic execution, and concrete execution.

In a symbolic execution, messages are symbolic expressions, built according to grammar **Term** starting from basic symbols **Id** $= \{A, B, C, \ldots\}$ representing the parties, nonces **Nonce** $= \{N, M, \ldots\}$, and keys **Key** $= K_A, K_B, K_C, \ldots$. Messages are computed in the obvious way: in the case of symbolic executions, symbols I and R are replaced by the identity of the initiator and responder, K_I, K_R with their respective public keys, and nonce identifiers X_i, Y_i are set to new nonces from **Nonce** $= \{N, M, \ldots\}$ the first time they occur in the execution of a protocol, or to some value recovered from previous messages. Formally, at every stage of the execution of a protocol, the local state of a party is represented by a program counter pointing to which message should be received next, and a partial function Φ mapping the identifiers $I, R, X_1, Y_1, \ldots$ occurring in the program executed by that party to corresponding symbolic values from $A, B, C, \ldots, N, M, \ldots$. When a message is to be transmitted, the function Φ is used to evaluate the corresponding expression in the program text. When a new message is received, the function Φ is first used to check the validity of the message, and then extended with additional bindings obtained from unifying the received message with the expression in the program text. Notice that each symbol (e.g., X_1) in the description of a protocol corresponds to two different variables, one stored with the protocol initiator and one with the responder. These two variables are usually bound to the same value. However, when the protocol is executed in the presence of an active adversary that may alter the messages transmitted and received by the parties, this is not necessarily the case. So, it is important to distinguish between the variable identifier X_1 used in the description of a protocol from the two variable instances associated to the parties executing the protocol (as well as variable instances corresponding to different executions of the same protocol by other pairs of parties.)

In a concrete execution, messages are bit-strings, obtained running the key generation, encryption and decryption algorithms used in an actual implementation of the protocol. This time, when a nonce identifier firstly occurs in the execution of a protocol, the corresponding party generates a random bit string (of length equal to some security parameter). Public keys K_i are mapped to bit-strings using the key generation algorithm of some specified encryption scheme, and complex expressions are evaluated running the encryption algorithm, and encoding pairs in some standard way. We always assume that the bit representation of an expression allows to uniquely determine its type, and parse it accordingly. This time, the state of a party is given by a program counter, and a partial function mapping the variable identifiers to corresponding bit strings. As before, these bindings are used both to evaluate the messages to be transmitted, and to parse the received messages, with the main difference that this time parsing received messages involves the execution of the decryption algorithm, and computing the answers involves running the (randomized) encryption algorithm.

3.3   Adversaries, Execution Environments, and State Traces

We consider the concurrent execution of several instances of a given protocol. The execution of each protocol instance is called a "session". We assume that the parties executing a protocol communicate using a network that is under the total control of some adversary $\mathcal{A}$. The adversary can sniff messages off the network, send messages to any session of the protocol run by any party and obtain in return the corresponding answer. We do not assume that the communication is guaranteed, i.e. once the adversary obtains a message from a certain session, it may choose to never deliver the message to the intended destination, or may deliver a different message spoofing the sender identity. We also model the collusion of some parties with the adversary by letting the adversary choose a set C of parties and obtain all their private keys.

We model an adversarially controlled communication network by letting all the parties executing the protocol send and receive messages to and from the adversary. Formally, we let the adversary interact with an oracle that runs the honest parties programs. The adversary may issue the following commands to the oracle:

1. $new(A, B)$: start the execution of a new instance of the protocol, with party A acting as the initiator, and party B acting as the responder. In response to this message, the oracle picks a new session identifier s, starts the execution of a new instance of the protocol run by A and B, and returns the session identifier s together with the first message transmitted by party A to the adversary.
2. $send(s : I, m)$: send message m to the initiator of session s. Update the initiator's state accordingly, and return its response to message m to the adversary.
3. $send(s : R, m)$: send message m to the responder of session s. Update the responder state accordingly, and return its response to message m to the adversary.

As for the protocol execution, we consider two different adversarial models: an abstract adversary that communicates with the parties via symbolic expressions, and a concrete one that uses the bit-strings obtained by running some specific encryption algorithm.

The abstract adversary, usually called a Dolev-Yao adversary, is constrained in the way it can compute new messages from messages it already knows, as to capture the security of the cryptographic operations (in our case asymmetric encryption and generation of random nonces.) We first give the formal definition and then we explain the intuition behind it. Consider a set M representing the messages that the adversary knows at a certain point during its execution. This set includes the messages that the adversary had already received from honest parties, as well as some messages which the adversary is assume to be able to compute (for instance new nonces). In particular, M contains the set of identities $Id = \{A_1, A_2, \ldots\}$, the set of all public keys $Keys = K_1, K_2, \ldots$ and a set $Nonce$ of nonce symbols denoting the nonces produced by the adversary, and (depending on the setting) a set of identities C that model corrupted parties that colluding with the adversary. The set of messages that the adversary can compute from M, denoted $\mathsf{closure}(C, M)$ is defined as the smallest set such that

1. $M \subseteq \mathsf{closure}(C, M)$
2. If $T_1, T_2 \in \mathsf{closure}(C, M)$ then $(T_1, T_2) \in \mathsf{closure}(C, M)$

3. If $(T_1, T_2) \in \mathsf{closure}(C, M)$ then $T_1, T_2 \in \mathsf{closure}(C, M)$
4. If $T \in \mathsf{closure}(C, M)$ then $\{T\}_K \in \mathsf{closure}(C, M)$ for all $K \in Keys$
5. If $\{T\}_{K_i} \in \mathsf{closure}(C, M)$ and $A_i \in C$ then $T \in \mathsf{closure}(C, M)$

Most of the constraints above are rather self-explanatory. The first three, say that the adversary can construct new messages which are messages that it already knows (1), are built by pairing messages it knows (2) splitting a pair that it knows (3) or encrypting a message it knows with a key that it knows (4). The fifth requirement which captures the security of encryption, states that if an adversary knows the decryption key corresponding to the key used to encrypt a certain message, then the adversary can recover that message. Notice that this definition precludes the adversary from recovering the plaintext if it does not know the decryption key.

The real adversary is usually constrained to run in (probabilistic) polynomial time, but can otherwise, perform any kind of operations. This is the standard adversary used in computational treatments of authentication and other cryptographic protocols. The real adversary also issues commands of the form $new(i, j)$, $send(s : I, m)$ and $send(s : R, m)$ to the oracle environment, but this time m can be an arbitrary bit string. Similarly, the oracle replies with bit strings computed by the parties using their keys and the encryption function.

In the sequel we will denote by $\mathcal{F}$ the set of symbolic expression used in a formal execution and by $\mathcal{C}_\eta$ the set of all bit-strings that appear in a concrete execution (parameterized by the security parameter η). So, $\mathcal{F}$ is built up from a set of basic symbols $\mathcal{F}^{const}$ (containing identities, keys and nonces) by using the grammar **Term**. Similarly, $\mathcal{C}_\eta$ is built up from a set of basic bit-strings $\mathcal{C}_\eta^{const}$, by pairing and encryption. Here, pairing is assumed to be done via some standard (invertible) encoding, and encryption is done by running the encryption algorithm of a fixed concrete asymmetric encryption scheme $\mathcal{AE}$. The oracle environments for the formal and for the concrete execution models are denoted by $\mathcal{O}^\mathcal{F}$ and $\mathcal{O}^\mathcal{C}$.

If **Identifiers** is the set of identifiers used in the abstract description of a protocol, and Sld is the set of all possible sessions, then the global states maintained by $\mathcal{O}^\mathcal{F}$ and $\mathcal{O}^\mathcal{C}$ are given by pairs (F, k) respectively (f, l), where

$$F : \mathsf{Sld} \times \{I, R\} \to (\textbf{Identifiers} \to \mathcal{F}^{const}) \qquad k : \mathsf{Sld} \times \{I, R\} \to (\mathbb{N} \cup \{\sqrt{}\})$$

and

$$f : \mathsf{Sld} \times \{I, R\} \to (\textbf{Identifiers} \to \mathcal{C}_\eta^{const}) \qquad l : \mathsf{Sld} \times \{I, R\} \to (\mathbb{N} \cup \{\sqrt{}\})$$

Here $F(s, I)$ gives the local state of the initiator of session s, in the formal execution, $f(s, I)$ the local state of the initiator of session s in the formal execution and so on. Functions k and l return the index of the next message expected by a party, or $\sqrt{}$ if the party finished the execution of the protocol.

In the formal world an adversary $\mathcal{A}_f$ is simply a list of queries of the type $send(s : X, M)$ (for simplicity we assume that all possible sessions have been already initiated). We emphasize that this is without loss of generality since security properties in this setting consider *all* valid adversaries.

We call one such adversary a valid Dolev-Yao adversary, or simply valid, if each of the queries that it sends is in the closure of the set formed by some fixed set of adversarial nonces (disjoint from the nonces used by the honest parties), identities of parties, public keys of parties and the responses that it receives from $\mathcal{O}^{\mathcal{F}}$. The result of the interaction between the adversary and the oracle is the sequence of states through which the oracle $\mathcal{O}^{\mathcal{F}}$ passes. So if (F_0, k_0) is the initial state of $\mathcal{O}^{\mathcal{F}}$, for each $i \geq 1$, state (F_i, k_i) is obtained from state (F_{i-1}, k_{i-1}) as result of the ith query of the adversary. We denote the sequence $((F_0, k_0), (F_1, k_1), ...)$ by $\mathsf{STr}(\mathcal{A}_f, \mathcal{O}^{\mathcal{F}})$ and call it the *formal state trace* of the execution of $\mathcal{A}_f$. The set of *all* formal traces is denoted by $\mathcal{F}Strace$.

In the concrete model the execution is randomized, since generating keys, random nonces and encryptions involves the use of random coins. Nevertheless, for each concrete adversary $\mathcal{A}_c$ we can define a similar state trace once the randomness of the oracle and that of the adversaries are fixed. We will denote by $\mathsf{STr}(\mathcal{A}_c(R_\mathcal{A}), \mathcal{O}^{\mathcal{C}}(R_\mathcal{O}))$ *concrete state trace* $((f_0, l_0), (f_1, l_1), ...)$ triggered by the queries of the adversary to the oracle environment, when the random coins of the adversary and those of the environment are $R_\mathcal{A}$ and $R_\mathcal{O}$ respectively. The set of all possible concrete traces is denoted $\mathcal{C}Strace$. We will give the fully formal definition in the full version of this paper.

4 Faithfulness of the Formal Execution Model

In this section we show that when the encryption scheme used in the concrete implementation is secure, then concrete state traces are tightly related to state traces of *valid* formal adversaries. More precisely, we show that almost always a concrete state trace can be obtained by composing the state trace of a valid formal adversary with a representation function that maps symbols to bit-strings. So, in some sense, the concrete adversary does not have more power than the abstract Dolev-Yao adversaries. We will formally show how this connection allows to translate security results from the abstract to the concrete world in Section 5

Definition 1. *We call a function* $\mathcal{R} : \mathcal{F}^{const} \to \mathcal{C}_\eta^{const}$ *a representation function if it is injective, and* $\mathcal{R}(\mathcal{F}^k) \subseteq \mathcal{C}_\eta^k$, $\mathcal{R}(\mathcal{F}^n) \subseteq \mathcal{C}_\eta^n$ *and* $\mathcal{R}(\mathcal{F}^i) \subseteq \mathcal{C}_\eta^i$.

Definition 2. *Let* $cstr = ((f_0, l_0), (f_1, l_1), ..., (f_n, l_n))$ *be a concrete state trace,* $fstr = ((F_0, k_0), (F_1, k_1), ..., (F_n, k_n))$ *be a formal state trace and* $\mathcal{R} : \mathcal{F} \to \mathcal{C}$ *be a representation function. We say that* $cstr$ *is an implementation of* $fstr$ *via representation function* $\mathcal{R}$, *notation* $fstr \preceq_\mathcal{R} cstr$ *if for each* $1 \leq i \leq n$ *it holds that* $F_i; \mathcal{R} = f_i$ *and also* $k_i = l_i$. *We say that* $cstr$ *is an implementation of* $fstr$, *notation* $fstr \preceq cstr$ *if for some representation function* $\mathcal{R}$ *it holds that* $fstr \preceq_\mathcal{R} cstr$.

The above definition says that a concrete trace is a representation of an abstract trace if it is possible to rename *consistently* all symbols in the abstract trace with bit-strings, as to obtain the concrete trace. Another possible interpretation is that the abstract trace is an abstract representation of the concrete trace (via the inverse of function $\mathcal{R}$).

Informally, the core of our paper says that a concrete state trace obtained by fixing the randomness of the adversary and that of the oracle environment, is a representation of the state trace of an abstract attack *which satisfies the Dolev-Yao restrictions*, with overwhelming probability over the coins of the adversary and those of the oracle environment.

Theorem 2. *Let Π be a protocol. If $\mathcal{AE}$ used in the implementation is IND-CCA secure, then for any concrete adversary $\mathcal{A}_c$*

$$\Pr_{R_{\mathcal{A}}, R_{\mathcal{O}}} \left[\exists \mathcal{A}_f \text{ valid } : \mathsf{STr}(\mathcal{A}_f, \mathcal{O}^{\mathcal{F}}) \preceq \mathsf{STr}(\mathcal{A}_c(R_{\mathcal{A}}), \mathcal{O}^{\mathcal{C}}(R_{\mathcal{O}})) \right] \geq 1 - \nu(\eta)$$

for some negligible function $\nu(\cdot)$.

Proof. Since IND-CCA security implies IND-CCA security in a multi-user setting (Theorem 1) it is sufficient to prove the theorem under the assumption encryption scheme is IND-CCA secure in the multi-user setting.

We split the proof of the theorem in two parts. First we show that for any trace $\mathsf{STr}(\mathcal{A}_c(R_{\mathcal{A}}), \mathcal{O}^{\mathcal{C}}(R_{\mathcal{O}}))$, obtained by fixing the randomness of the oracle environment and that of the adversary, it is *always* possible to find an abstract adversary $\mathcal{A}_f$ (and a representation function $\mathcal{R}$) such that $\mathsf{STr}(\mathcal{A}_f, \mathcal{O}^{\mathcal{F}}) \preceq_{\mathcal{R}} \mathsf{STr}(\mathcal{A}_c(R_{\mathcal{A}}), \mathcal{O}^{\mathcal{C}}(R_{\mathcal{O}}))$. For this we provide a construction of $\mathcal{A}_f$, which essentially extracts a formal attack from the concrete attack. In the second part of the proof we show that the constructed formal attacker $\mathcal{A}_f$ satisfy the Dolev-Yao restrictions with overwhelming probability (over the choice of the coins of the adversary and those of the oracle environment), or otherwise the encryption scheme $\mathcal{AE}$ used in the concrete implementation is not $\mathsf{N_p}$-IND-CCA secure, where by $\mathsf{N_p}$ we denote the number of parties in the system.

STEP I. The intuition behind the construction is the following. Since all coins determining the execution are fixed, all bit-strings represent identities, keys and nonces that appear in the computation are also fixed, and thus can be recovered. Then by canonically labeling all these concrete constants with abstract symbols, one can translate each message $send(s : X, q)$ of the concrete adversary into an abstract message $send(s : X, Q)$ such that q is a representation of Q. The sequence of abstract queries $send(s : X, Q)$ determine the abstract adversary. This is done as follows. The keys and nonces used by honest parties can be directly determined once their coin tosses are fixed. The trickier part is obtain the strings that the adversary uses as nonces, (since these can not be obtained directly from the randomness of the adversary). Nevertheless, we can do this by tracking and parsing the queries of the adversary. Whenever we encounter some bit-string x of type nonce which is not the nonce generated by an honest party, then that string is certainly a nonce produced by the adversary. So, we introduce a new (symbol) adversarial nonce $X_k^{\mathcal{A}}$ and assign it to denote x. We will denote the formal adversary constructed this way by $\mathcal{A}_f$.

STEP II. The second step of the proof is to show that the adversary $\mathcal{A}_f$ obtained as above computes its messages following the Dolev-Yao restrictions. We prove this by constructing an adversary $\mathcal{B}$ against the encryption scheme. Adversary $\mathcal{B}$ runs $\mathcal{A}_c$ as a subroutine and we prove that $\mathcal{B}$ wins in the IND-CCA game precisely when the abstract adversary associated to the run of $\mathcal{A}_c$ is not Dolev-Yao. If this happens with non-negligible probability then $\mathcal{B}$ is an adversary that contradicts the security of $\mathcal{AE}$.

The key observation is the following. Consider the queries $q_1, q_2, \ldots$ made by $\mathcal{A}_c$ while run as a subroutine, and let $\mathcal{A}_f$ be the abstract adversary associated to $\mathcal{A}_c$. Then $\mathcal{A}_f$ makes queries $Q_1, Q_2, \ldots$ which are abstract representations of the queries $q_1, q_2, \ldots$. Assume that one of the queries of $\mathcal{A}_f$, say Q_i, is not Dolev-Yao. In this case it is easy to see that Q_i must contain an occurrence of some nonce X (generated by the honest parties) which does not appear in clear in none of the answers that $\mathcal{A}_f$ obtained, and moreover $\mathcal{A}_f$ can not recover this nonce by standard Dolev-Yao operations. Otherwise, Q can be created by the adversary.

We distinguish two cases. The simpler case is when Q_i contains X unencrypted. In this case, message q_i also contains x unencrypted, i.e. the adversary managed to recover nonce x from ciphertexts he should not have been able to decrypt, i.e. it managed to the break the encryption function.

The second case is when X appears in Q_i encrypted, so Q_i has a subterm of the form $T = \{t[X]\}_K$ form some term $t[X]$ containing X and some key symbol K. In this case, neither T nor $t[X]$ appeared in clear (since otherwise Q_i could have been built by the adversary.) So in the concrete world, $\mathcal{A}_c$ makes query q_i which contains an encryption of x which he had not previously seen, so in this case $\mathcal{A}_c$ also contradicts the security of the encryption scheme.

In this extended abstract we only provide an overview of the construction of an the adversary $\mathcal{B}$. A detailed description will be provided in the full version of this paper.

Since $\mathcal{B}$ is an adversary against N_p-IND-CCA encryption, it has access to N_p left-right encryption oracles, and also to the corresponding decryption oracles. $\mathcal{B}$ will use his access to these oracles to mimic the behavior environment $\mathcal{O}^C$, in which the public keys of the parties are the public keys of the encryption oracles. Just simulating the behavior would be easy for $\mathcal{B}$: it can simply select all random nonces of the honest parties, and then when the adversary makes a query to $\mathcal{O}^C$, $\mathcal{B}$ can parse the query (by using the decryption oracles) compute an appropriate answer by following the program of the honest party, return it to the adversary and so on.

The adversary $\mathcal{B}$ that we construct does something more clever than that. For simplicity of the exposition assume for now that $\mathcal{B}$ "knows" the nonce X and the term Q such that Q is not a valid Dolev-Yao query, and X is the nonce that we described above. For his simulation, $\mathcal{B}$ selects all concrete nonces of the honest parties (except the one corresponding to X.) For this nonce, $\mathcal{B}$ selects *two* possible concrete representations x_0 and x_1. Then $\mathcal{B}$ starts running the attacker $\mathcal{A}_c$ carrying the simulation along the lines we have described above: it parses queries of the adversary by using the decryption oracles to which it has access, and answers the queries by following the programs of the honest parties. There are two important points in which the simulation differs from the trivial simulation that we described above. First, when $\mathcal{B}$ needs to pass to $\mathcal{A}_c$ responses for which the abstract representation contains X, $\mathcal{B}$ computes a concrete representation in which X is replaced by x_b, where b is the selection bit of the left-right encryption oracles. This is possible since X appears only encrypted, so we can create concrete representations using the encryption oracles. Let us explain.

Let x_0 and x_1 be the two possible concrete nonce values that $\mathcal{B}$ associates to X, and say that during his simulation of the environment oracle, $\mathcal{B}$ needs to pass to $\mathcal{A}_c$ the representation of terms $\{X\}_{K_i}$ and $\{XX\}_{K_j}$. To accomplish this, $\mathcal{B}$ prepares messages (x_0, x_1) and (x_0x_0, x_1x_1) and submits them to encryption oracles $\mathcal{E}_{\mathrm{pk}_i}(\mathrm{LR}(\cdot, \cdot, b))$ and $\mathcal{E}_{\mathrm{pk}_j}(\mathrm{LR}(\cdot, \cdot, b))$ respectively. (Here pk_i and pk_j are concrete representations of the keys K_i and K_j). The resulting ciphertexts are then passed to $\mathcal{A}_c$. Notice that it is crucial that

X never needs to be sent in clear, since in this case $\mathcal{B}$ would not know which of the two possible concrete representations to send.

The second important point related to the simulation of $\mathcal{O}^{\mathcal{C}}$, is that when it parses the messages sent by $\mathcal{A}_c$, it must avoid sending to a decryption oracle a ciphertext previously obtained from the corresponding encryption oracle. This would render $\mathcal{B}$ invalid. This however can be easily avoided, since $\mathcal{B}$ knows the underlying plaintext of *all* ciphertexts obtained from the encryption oracles, modulo which of the concrete nonces x_0, x_1 is used (notice that all ciphertexts obtained from the encryption oracles contain one of the two nonces, and always the same). So, $\mathcal{B}$ can compute an appropriate answer (possibly involving the encryption oracles in the case that the answer involves the representation of X).

From the point of view of $\mathcal{A}_c$, the simulation of the environment oracle $\mathcal{O}^{\mathcal{C}}$ is perfect. By now it is probably clear how $\mathcal{B}$ determines the bit b that parameterizes the encryption oracles. When $\mathcal{A}_c$ makes its query q (corresponding to a non Dolev-Yao message), $\mathcal{B}$ intercepts the message, and recovers which of the two values x_0, x_1 was actually used in the simulation. If the concrete nonce appears in clear, then this step is trivial. Otherwise, i.e. the nonce appears encrypted, $\mathcal{B}$ simply "peels off" the encryptions surrounding x_b by using the decryption oracles. This is possible, because none of these encryptions was obtained from an encryption oracle.

The final observation that goes in our construction is that $\mathcal{B}$ does not know a priori which nonce X is the "faulty" nonce, nor does it know which of the messages sent by the adversary corresponds to the invalid Dolev-Yao abstract message. But since the total number of nonces and messages appearing in an execution is polynomial in the security parameter, $\mathcal{B}$ can guess both of them with significant probability. If the adversary guesses wrongly, so he either can not recover a nonce from the position that he guessed, or the nonce he recovers is different from x_0, x_1, then $\mathcal{B}$ simply outputs a random guess.

Let us provide an informal analysis of the advantage of $\mathcal{B}$ (formal details will be given in the full version of the paper). There are two possible events that lead $\mathcal{B}$ to successfully guessing the bit b. First of all, if guessing X or Q fail, then he outputs b with probability half. Otherwise, i.e. the abstract adversary $\mathcal{A}_f$ is not Dolev-Yao, and $\mathcal{B}$ guesses both the nonce X, the message Q which is not Dolev-Yao and the position P in this message on which X occurs then $\mathcal{B}$ correctly guesses b. Each of these probabilities can be bounded as follows. For concreteness assume the following: the total number of parties is $\mathsf{N_p}$, the total number of messages exchanged during a session is $\mathsf{N_r}$, each party uses at most $\mathsf{N_n}$ nonces, and each message has at most $\mathsf{N_o}$ nonce occurrences. Then, if $\mathsf{N_s}$ is the total number of possible sessions, i.e. $|\mathsf{Sid}|$, then $\mathcal{B}$ guesses the "right" nonce X with probability at least $\frac{1}{2 \cdot \mathsf{N_r} \cdot \mathsf{N_n}}$, guesses the "right" message Q with probability at least $\frac{1}{\mathsf{N_s} \cdot \mathsf{N_r}}$ and the "right" occurrence of X with probability at least $\frac{1}{\mathsf{N_o}}$. Putting this together we obtain that

$$\mathsf{N_r} \cdot \mathsf{N_n} \cdot \mathsf{N_o} \cdot \mathsf{N_s} \cdot \mathbf{Adv}_{\mathcal{AE},\mathcal{B}}^{\mathsf{N_p}-\text{ind-cca}}(\eta) \geq \Pr\left[\mathcal{A}_f \text{ invalid}\right]$$

Since we assumed that $\mathcal{AE}$ is IND-CCA secure, hence $\mathsf{N_p}$-IND-CCA secure, the left side of the inequality is a negligible function, hence so is the right side. In other words, the adversary $\mathcal{A}_f$ that we construct is not a valid Dolev-Yao adversary only with negligible probability. $\square$

5   Soundness of Formal Proofs

We now use the result of the previous section to prove our main result. In this section we provide a uniform way to specify general security properties, both in the formal and the concrete setting. Then, we exhibit a condition on formal and concrete security notions P_f and P_c such that proving security of some protocol Π with respect to P_f (in the formal world) entails that the protocol is secure with respect to P_c in the concrete world. Finally we provide concrete examples for the case of mutual authentication protocols.

Definition 3. *Fix a protocol Π.*

1. *A formal security notion is any predicate P_f on formal state traces (or equivalently any subset P_f of $\mathcal{F}Strace$). For each security notion $P_f \subseteq \mathcal{F}Strace$, we say that protocol Π satisfies P_f, notation $\Pi \models_f P_f$ if for all valid formal adversaries $\mathcal{A}_f$, it holds that $STr(\mathcal{A}_f, \mathcal{O}^{\mathcal{F}}) \in P_f$.*

2. *A concrete security notion is any predicate P_c on concrete state traces. For each security notion $P_c \subseteq \mathcal{C}Strace$, we say that protocol Π satisfies P_c, notation $\Pi \models_c P_c$, if for all probabilistic polynomial time adversaries $\mathcal{A}_c$ it holds that*

$$\Pr_{R_{\mathcal{A}}, R_{\mathcal{O}}} \left[STr(\mathcal{A}_c(R_{\mathcal{A}}), \mathcal{O}^{\mathcal{C}}(R_{\mathcal{O}})) \in P_c \right] \geq 1 - \nu(\eta)$$

where $R_{\mathcal{A}}$ and $R_{\mathcal{O}}$ are random strings of appropriate length (i.e. polynomially long in the security parameter η) and $\nu(\cdot)$ is some negligible function.

The definitions of satisfiability provided above are rather standard in the settings that we consider. The one for the formal execution model states that no Dolev-Yao adversary can induce a "faulty" formal execution trace. The definition of satisfiability for the concrete execution model states that no probabilistic polynomial time algorithm can induce a faulty concrete execution trace, except with negligible probability.

We now exhibit a relation between formal security notions P_f and concrete security notions P_c such that proving (formally) security with respect to P_f implies security with respect to P_c (in the concrete execution model). The relation is captured in the following theorem.

Theorem 3. *Let P_f and P_c be respectively formal and a concrete security notion such that*

$$(\forall f str \in \mathcal{F}Strace, \forall cstr \in \mathcal{C}Strace)((f str \in P_f \wedge ftr \preceq cstr) \Rightarrow cstr \in P_c).$$

If $\mathcal{AE}$ is IND-CCA secure,

$$\Pi \models_f P_f \Rightarrow \Pi \models_c P_c$$

holds.

Proof. The intuition behind the proof is the following. Let $cstr$ be the state trace caused by an arbitrary adversary $\mathcal{A}_c$. From Theorem 2, with overwhelming probability there exists a valid formal adversary such that its trace $f str$ satisfies $f str \preceq cstr$, and moreover

$fstr \in \mathsf{P_f}$ (since $\Pi \models_f \mathsf{P}_f$). Then, by the assumption on $\mathsf{P_f}$ and $\mathsf{P_c}$, with overwhelming probability $cstr \in \mathsf{P_c}$, i.e. $\Pi \models_c \mathsf{P_c}$. Formally we have the following:

$$\Pr_{R_A, R_O} \left[\mathsf{STr}(\mathcal{A}(R_A), \mathcal{O}^{\mathcal{C}}(R_O)) \in \mathsf{P_c} \right]$$

$$\geq \Pr_{R_A, R_O} \left[\exists fstr \in \mathsf{P_f}, fstr \preceq \mathsf{STr}(\mathcal{A}(R_A), \mathcal{O}^{\mathcal{C}}(R_O)) \right]$$

$$\geq \Pr_{R_A, R_O} \left[\exists \mathcal{A}_f \text{ valid} : \mathsf{STr}(\mathcal{A}_f, \mathcal{O}^{\mathcal{F}}) \preceq \mathsf{STr}(\mathcal{A}(R_A), \mathcal{O}^{\mathcal{C}}(R_O)) \right]$$

$$\geq 1 - \nu(\eta)$$

i.e. $\Pi \models_c \mathsf{P_c}$.   □

MUTUAL AUTHENTICATION. We now show how to apply the above machinery to the case of mutual authentication protocol. Informally, at the end of a secure execution of a mutual authentication protocol, the initiator and the responder are convinced of each other's identity. Various ways of formalizing this property already appeared in the literature [7,8,6,11]. Our formulation is closest to the one in the latest reference, to which we refer the reader for clarifications and motivations about the definition.

There are two properties that a secure mutual authentication protocol should satisfy. The first property, called "initiator's guarantee", states that if in some session between two parties, the initiator sent his last message, and thus finished its execution, then there exists some session between the same parties in which the responder also finished its execution. The second property, called the responder's guarantee, says that if in some session the responder sent his last message (and hence finished its execution), then there exists some session with the same initiator and responder in which the initiator has either finished his execution, or is expecting to receive the last message of the protocol. Finally, a protocol is a secure mutual authentication protocol if it satisfies both initiator's and responder's guarantees.

We can formalize the above informal descriptions by using the language of state traces as follows.

Definition 4. *Let* $t = ((f_0, k_0), (f_1, k_1), ...)$ *be an (abstract or concrete) state trace of a protocol with* $\mathsf{N_r}$ *rounds.*
(1) We say that t *satisfies the initiator's guarantee, if for any position* p *in the trace, the following condition is satisfied. If for some* $s = (i, j, t) \in \mathsf{SId}$ *it holds that* $k_p(s, I) = \sqrt{}$ *then for some* $s' = (i, j, t') \in \mathsf{SId}$ *it holds that* $k_p(s', R) = \sqrt{}$.
(2) We say that t *satisfies the responder's guarantee, if for any position* p, *the following condition is satisfied. If for some* $s = (i, j, t) \in \mathsf{SId}$ *it holds that* $k_p(s, R) = \sqrt{}$ *then for some* $s' = (i, j, t') \in \mathsf{SId}$ *it holds that* $k_p(s', I) = \mathsf{N_r}$ *or* $k_p(s', I) = \sqrt{}$.
(3) We say that t *satisfies the mutual authentication property if it satisfies both initiator's guarantee and responder's guarantee.*

Let us denote by $\mathsf{MA}^{\mathcal{F}}$ (respectively by $\mathsf{MA}^{\mathcal{C}}$) the mutual authentication property in the formal (respectively in the concrete) execution model. It is a simple exercise to show that $\mathsf{MA}^{\mathcal{C}}$ and $\mathsf{MA}^{\mathcal{F}}$ satisfy the conditions of Theorem 3. As a consequence, for any protocol Π

$$\Pi \models_f \mathsf{MA}^{\mathcal{F}} \quad \text{implies} \quad \Pi \models_c \mathsf{MA}^{\mathcal{C}}$$

6   Extensions and Work in Progress

For simplicity of exposition, the framework that we presented in Sections 4 and 5 concentrates on a setting where parties execute multiple instances of a *a single two-party* protocol. The formal and computational models that we presented can be extended in a number of ways, allowing analysis of an increasingly larger class of protocols. In this section we present and discuss some extensions which we have considered. These extensions include:

- considering multi-party protocols (as opposed to only two-party protocols);
- considering execution models in which parties execute instances not of a single but of a set of protocols;
- extending the protocol specification language with other cryptographic primitives, e.g. symmetric encryption, digital signatures, message authentication codes;
- considering more flexible rules for writing protocol, allowing for instance transmission of encrypted keys, forwarding of ciphertexts (without decrypting);
- developing a more general execution model involving reactive parties;
- generalize our abstract definition of security notions to capture secrecy properties.

Our basic setting easily extends to a more general execution model in which parties execute several multi-party protocols, $\Pi_1, \Pi_2, \ldots, \Pi_p$, simultaneously. In the sequel we sketch some details of this extension. A multi-party protocol can be naturally specified by a sequence of actions of the form $A \to B : M$, where A and B are the sender and the receiver respectively, and M is a representation of the message that A sends to B, constructed from variables in **Identifiers**, using the grammar for **Term**.

Given a protocol specified as a list of actions of the form $A \to B : M$, the program run by some party P is determined by selecting from the list of actions only those actions which involve party P as either sender or receiver. The individual execution of these programs in both the formal and the computational models remains essentially unchanged. Furthermore, our formalization of the global execution of the protocols (for both the formal and the concrete world) can be easily adapted. The following discussion pertaining to the formal model, applies to the concrete model too, with some obvious modifications.

In the formal execution model, the behavior of the honest parties is modeled by oracle $\mathcal{O}^{\mathcal{F}}$ maintaining the global state of the execution. The adversary interacts with the oracle by initializing new instances of the protocols, and passing messages between parties as in the two party-case (the syntax of the queries needs to be adapted to the setting we are discussing.) If we denote by Sld be the set of session ids and by max the maximum number of parties involved in running each particular protocol, in the multi-user, multi-protocol setting, we model the global state by a pair of functions (F, k), where

$$F : \mathsf{Sld} \times [max] \to (\mathbf{Identifiers} \to \mathcal{F}^{const}) \qquad\qquad k : \mathsf{Sld} \times [max] \to \mathbb{N} \cup \{\sqrt{}\}.$$

The intuition behind this formalization is the identical to the two-party case: $F(s, l)$ gives the local view of participant number l in the protocol executed in session s, and $k(s, l)$ gives the index of the next instruction of the protocol which the same participant will execute.

The result of the execution is again the sequence of states determined by the formal adversary. In this case, by modeling security properties as sets of "secure" traces one can capture properties of the whole system (as opposed to properties of a single protocol). So, formal and computational satisfaction of security requirements pertains to the entire system. We write $\Pi_1, \Pi_2, \ldots, \Pi_p \models_f P_f$ to denote the fact that protocols $\Pi_1, \Pi_2, \ldots, \Pi_p$ satisfy property P_f in the formal execution model. Similarly, we write $\Pi_1, \Pi_2, \ldots, \Pi_p \models_c P_c$ to mean that the same protocols satisfy security requirement P_c in the concrete execution model. The formal definition of relations $\models_f$ and $\models_c$ is the obvious generalization of Definition 3. In the full version of the paper we will include a proof of the following generalization of Theorem 2:

Theorem 4. *Let $\Pi_1, \Pi_2, \ldots, \Pi_p$ be multi-party protocols and let P_f and P_c be a formal, respectively a concrete security notion such that*

$$(\forall fstr \in \mathcal{F}Strace, \forall cstr \in \mathcal{C}Strace)((fstr \in P_f \wedge ftr \preceq cstr) \Rightarrow cstr \in P_c)$$

Then, if $\mathcal{AE}$ is IND-CCA secure then

$$\Pi_1, \Pi_2, \ldots, \Pi_p \models_f P_f \Rightarrow \Pi_1, \Pi_2, \ldots, \Pi_p \models_c P_c$$

Another interesting extension is to enrich the protocol specification language with other cryptographic primitives, e.g. symmetric encryption, digital signatures and message authentication codes. It seems that our simple models and results can be immediately extended, if we only consider protocols in which parties *never* send encryption of secret keys. We remark that the problem of encrypted secret keys has also been encountered in the complex framework of [4], where it is pointed out that including such encryptions in their treatment is quite problematic. In contrast, we discovered that by imposing certain restrictions, our results can be extended to protocols in which parties exchange encryption of secret keys. For instance, our results hold in a setting where parties generate and send encryptions of symmetric keys under the public keys of other parties, and later use the symmetric keys to encrypt other messages. We require however that symmetric keys are never used to encrypt other symmetric keys. The restrictions that we consider are quite reasonable from a practical point of view, and currently we are seeking the weakest limitations under which our result still holds.

Yet another extension is to consider protocols with input and output, or even more generally, reactive protocols in which parties accept inputs and produce outputs during the execution. While coming up with models for this kind of protocols does not seem to pose any difficulties, finding appropriate, general definitions for security notions is a more subtle problem. In particular, such general definitions should encompass some formal and computational secrecy notions to which our result can be extended. We note that this would enable analysis of a large class of protocols for which secrecy requirements are crucial, e.g. key exchange protocols, which makes this direction particularly interesting to follow in our future research.

References

1. M. Abadi and J. Jürjens. Formal eavesdropping and its computational interpretation. In *TACS 2001*, volume 2215 of *LNCS*, pages 82–94, Sendai, Japan, Oct. 2001. Springer-Verlag.
2. M. Abadi and P. Rogaway. Reconciling two views of cryptography (the computational soundness of formal encryption). *Journal of Cryptology*, 15(2):103–127, 2002.
3. M. Backes and B. Pfitzmann. A cryptographically sound security proof of the Needham-Schroeder-Lowe public-key protocol. Available as Cryptology ePrint Archive, Report 2003/121.
4. M. Backes, B. Pfitzmann, and M. Waidner. A universally composable cryptographic library. Available as Cryptology ePrint Archive, Report 2003/015.
5. M. Bellare, A. Boldyreva, and S. Micali. Public-key encryption in a multi-user setting. In *Proceedings of EUROCRYPT'00*, number 1807 in LNCS, pages 259–274, 2000.
6. M. Bellare, D. Pointcheval, and P. Rogaway. Authenticated key exchange secure against dictionary attacks. In *Proc. of EUROCRYPT'00*, LNCS, 2000.
7. M. Bellare and P. Rogaway. Entity authentication and key distribution. In *CRYPTO'93*, volume 773 of *LNCS*, 1994.
8. M. Bellare and P. Rogaway. Provably secure session key distribution: the three party case. In *Proc. of 27th Anual Symposium on the Theory of Computing*. ACM, 1995.
9. R. Canetti. Universally composable security: A new paradigm for cryptographic protocols. In *Proceedings of FOCS'01*, pages 136–145, 2001.
10. D. Dolev and A. Yao. On the security of public-key protocols. *IEEE Transactions on Information Theory*, 29:198–208, 1983.
11. F. J. T. Fabrega, J. Hertzog, and J. Guttman. Strand spaces: Proving security protocols correct. *Journal of Computer Security*, 7(2/3):191–230, 1999.
12. V. Gligor and D. O. Horvitz. Weak Key Authenticity and the Computational Completeness of Formal Encryption. In D. Boneh, editor, *CRYPTO 2003*, volume 2729 of *LNCS*, pages 530–547. Springer-Verlag, Aug. 2003.
13. J. Herzog. Computational soundness of formal adversaries. Master Thesis.
14. J. Herzog, M. Liskov, and S. Micali. Plaintext awareness via key registration. In *In Proceedings of CRYPTO'03*, 2003.
15. R. Impagliazzo and B. Kapron. Logics for reasoning about cryptographic constructions. In *STOC'03*, pages 372–383, 2003.
16. P. D. Lincoln, J. C. Mitchell, M. Mitchell, and A. Scedrov. A probabilistic poly-time framework for protocol analysis. In *Computer and Communications Security - CCS '98*, pages 112–121, San Francisco, California, USA, Nov. 1998. ACM.
17. G. Lowe. Breaking and fixing the Needham-Schröeder algorithm. In *Proc. of TACAS'96*, pages 147–166. Springer-Verlag, 1996.
18. D. Micciancio and B. Warinschi. Completeness theorems for the Abadi-Rogaway logic of encrypted expressions. *Journal of Computer Security*, 12(1):99–129, 2004.
19. L. C. Paulson. The inductive approach to verifying cryptographic protocols. *Journal of Computer Security*, 6:85–128, 1998.
20. C. Rackoff and D. Simon. Noninteractive zero-knowledge proofs of knowledfe and chosen ciphertext attack. In *CRYPTO'91*, pages 433–444, 1991.
21. D. Song. An automatic checker for security protocol analysis. In *12th IEEE Computer Security Foundations Workshop*, June 1999.

Rerandomizable and Replayable Adaptive Chosen Ciphertext Attack Secure Cryptosystems

Jens Groth[1,2]

[1] BRICS***, University of Aarhus, Ny Munkegade bd. 540, 8000 Århus C, Denmark
jg@brics.dk
[2] Cryptomathic A/S[†], Jægergårdsgade 118, 8000 Århus C, Denmark

Abstract. Recently Canetti, Krawczyk and Nielsen defined the notion of replayable adaptive chosen ciphertext attack (RCCA) secure encryption. Essentially a cryptosystem that is RCCA secure has full CCA2 security except for the little detail that it may be possible to modify a ciphertext into another ciphertext containing the *same* plaintext.

We investigate the possibility of *perfectly* replayable RCCA secure encryption. By this, we mean that anybody can convert a ciphertext y with plaintext m into a different ciphertext y' that is distributed identically to a fresh encryption of m. We propose such a rerandomizable cryptosystem, which is secure against semi-generic adversaries.

We also define a weak form of RCCA (WRCCA) security. For this notion we provide a construction (inspired by Cramer and Shoup's CCA2 secure cryptosystems) that is both rerandomizable and provably WRCCA secure. We use it as a building block in our conjectured RCCA secure cryptosystem.

1 Introduction

Security against adaptive chosen ciphertext attacks (CCA2) has become the golden security standard for public-key cryptosystems. Dolev, Dwork and Naor gave the first construction based on standard primitives in [1] and subsequent work [2,3,4,5] includes practical constructions based on a variety of assumptions. However, an unfortunate side effect of the strong security definition is the exclusion of certain cryptosystems that intuitively are secure. Consider for instance a cryptosystem that expands a CCA2 secure cryptosystem with a single bit, which is ignored in decryption. By flipping this bit it is easy to create a new encryption of the same plaintext and therefore the new cryptosystem is not CCA2 secure even though the message is protected by the same encryption. A few proposals for redefining CCA2 security to cover such cryptosystems were presented in [6,7], but other natural examples that intuitively are "CCA2" secure but do not satisfy these definitions exist. We believe that Canetti, Krawczyk and Nielsen have

---

*** Basic Research in Computer Science (www.brics.dk), funded by the Danish National Research Foundation.
† www.cryptomathic.com

M. Naor (Ed.): TCC 2004, LNCS 2951, pp. 152–170, 2004.

solved this problem satisfactorily in [8] by defining replayable adaptive chosen ciphertext attack (RCCA) security.[1]

RCCA security essentially is the same as CCA2 security, except no guarantees are given against adversaries that just try to modify a ciphertext into a new ciphertext with the same plaintext. CCA2 security implies RCCA security, but not the other way around. We could hope that a weaker definition might give rise to more efficient constructions but this has so far not been the case. On the other hand, it is a proven fact that given RCCA secure encryption we can construct CCA2 secure cryptosystems. We refer the reader to [8] for several other arguments for being interested in RCCA secure encryption.

The question we seek to answer in this paper is to what extend it may be possible to maul an RCCA secure cryptosystem. We have the ambitious goal of finding a cryptosystem, which is RCCA secure and has perfect rerandomization, i.e., an efficient algorithm for converting an encryption y of plaintext m into a ciphertext y' that is perfectly indistinguishable from a fresh encryption of m.

Besides the theoretical perspective, we believe such cryptosystems may have practical applications. Consider for instance an anonymization protocol where in the end some party receives the encrypted messages and acts upon them, for instance a voting protocol based on mix-nets.[2] Here, we may want the ability to rerandomize ciphertexts in order to anonymize them. On the other hand, we may imagine an adversary that can inject ciphertexts into the anonymization protocol and therefore gets access to an adaptive chosen ciphertext attack. Rerandomizable RCCA secure encryption may be just the tool that gives us the better of two worlds.

Constructing a rerandomizable RCCA secure cryptosystem is a hard problem, and is posed as an interesting open problem in [8]. The construction has to be almost CCA2 secure and at the same time have enough mathematical structure to be rerandomizable. In particular, it seems like popular tools for building CCA2 secure encryption such as random oracles and one-time signatures cannot be used.

In this paper, we start out by defining a weaker notion of replayable security called WRCCA security. This notion is stronger than IND-CCA1 but weaker than RCCA security. It turns out that rerandomizable WRCCA secure cryptosystem can be constructed under well-known intractability assumptions.

By choosing an appropriate group to work in, we get a rerandomizable WRCCA secure cryptosystem that may be extended in a way that gives rise to a new rerandomizable cryptosystem. We believe this new cryptosystem is RCCA secure. Since it is an extension of a WRCCA secure cryptosystem, it is provably WRCCA secure. In itself, WRCCA security does not guarantee RCCA security though. We give an additional security argument by proving that a semi-generic adversary cannot break the scheme, where semi-generic means that it can only perform standard group operations on parts of the ciphertext.

---

[1] Independently we came up with exactly the same definition of RCCA security.

[2] Duplication of votes must be avoided, for instance by inserting a nonce in the plaintext and discarding extra pairs of the same vote and nonce.

2 Notions of Replayable Security

Notation. All algorithms and adversaries are modeled as probabilistic polynomial time (possibly interactive) Turing machines. Our proofs hold for both uniform and non-uniform adversaries.

We assume that all algorithms and adversaries get a security parameter as input. We write $p_1 \approx p_2$ if p_1 and p_2 are functions of the security parameter such that $|p_1 - p_2|$ is a negligible function in the security parameter. A function that is not negligible is said to be noticeable.

Definitions. We define a public-key cryptosystem in the usual way. The decryption function outputs `invalid` when a ciphertext does not decrypt properly to a plaintext.

Definition 1 (RCCA security). *A cryptosystem (K, E, D) is RCCA secure if for any adversary $\mathcal{A}$ it is the case that*

$$P[(pk, sk) \leftarrow K(); (m_0, m_1) \leftarrow \mathcal{A}^{\mathcal{O}_1}(pk); y \leftarrow E_{pk}(m_0) : \mathcal{A}^{\mathcal{O}_2}(y) = 1]$$
$$\approx P[(pk, sk) \leftarrow K(); (m_0, m_1) \leftarrow \mathcal{A}^{\mathcal{O}_1}(pk); y \leftarrow E_{pk}(m_1) : \mathcal{A}^{\mathcal{O}_2}(y) = 1],$$

where

- $\mathcal{O}_1$ *works like D_{sk}.*
- $\mathcal{O}_2$ *works like D_{sk} except when the plaintext is m_0 or m_1. On m_0 or m_1 the oracle outputs* test.

Definition 2 (WRCCA security). *A cryptosystem (K, E, D) is WRCCA secure if for any adversary $\mathcal{A}$ it is the case that*

$$P[(pk, sk) \leftarrow K(); (m_0, m_1) \leftarrow \mathcal{A}^{\mathcal{O}_1}(pk); y \leftarrow E_{pk}(m_0) : \mathcal{A}^{\mathcal{O}_2}(y) = 1]$$
$$\approx P[(pk, sk) \leftarrow K(); (m_0, m_1) \leftarrow \mathcal{A}^{\mathcal{O}_1}(pk); y \leftarrow E_{pk}(m_1) : \mathcal{A}^{\mathcal{O}_2}(y) = 1],$$

where

- $\mathcal{O}_1$ *works like D_{sk}.*
- $\mathcal{O}_2$ *works like D_{sk} except when the plaintext is m_0 or m_1. On m_0 or m_1 the oracle outputs* invalid.

Let us illustrate the two types of security with the following example. We assume that we are operating a Swiss bank, and account holders can send anonymous messages to us containing a password, the banking operation they want to perform and perhaps a counter to prevent replay attacks. We do not reply to these messages, but if the password is valid and the counter has not been used before, we perform the banking operation. Suppose a client of ours sends a ciphertext containing some banking operation he wants to perform and he is being wiretapped by somebody who wants to know which operation he carried out. Now the eavesdroppers may open an account with us, send ciphertexts to us, and see what happens with the money in their account. This means that they do have access to a chosen ciphertext attack. However, since they do not know our client's password they cannot probe the system with banking operations on his account. WRCCA security is therefore sufficient to guarantee that the eavesdroppers do not learn anything about the banking operation he performed.

Suppose we change the protocol to be user-friendlier: we send back one type of error message if a banking operation has already been executed and another type of error message if a ciphertext is invalid. Now the eavesdroppers have access to a stronger attack and we need the cryptosystem to be RCCA secure.

In general WRCCA secure cryptosystems are only appropriate in protocols where the adversary does not learn whether an injected ciphertext is valid or invalid. Often this is not the case, consider for instance Bleichenbacher's attack on the PKCS #1 protocol [9].

Other types of security. Bellare and Sahai prove in [10] that non-malleability is equivalent to indistinguishability under parallel attack. By a parallel attack we mean the adversary has access to an oracle $\mathcal{O}_2$ that decrypts any number of ciphertexts but may be invoked only once. This definition makes sense both without and with access to $\mathcal{O}_1$. They call the security notions IND-PA0 and IND-PA1. By modifying $\mathcal{O}_2$ such that it can decrypt one vector of ciphertexts and will respond with respectively test and invalid on m_0 and m_1 we get four other security notions IND-RPA0, IND-RPA1, IND-WRPA0 and IND-WRPA1.[3]

Relationship between security notions. Figure 1 in Appendix A describes completely the relationship between all the security notions. For our purposes the interesting thing to note is that CCA2 security implies RCCA security, which implies WRCCA security, which in turn implies IND-CCA1 security. On the other hand all these notions are separate; IND-CCA1 does not imply WRCCA, WRCCA does not imply RCCA, and RCCA does not imply CCA2 security.

3 Rerandomizable Weak RCCA Secure Encryption

In this section, we describe a rerandomizable WRCCA secure cryptosystem. The idea bears some resemblance to Cramer-Shoup's DDH based CCA2 secure cryptosystem [3]. In their scheme a ciphertext looks like this $(u_L = g_L^r, u_R = g_R^r, v = h^r m, \alpha = (cd^{\mathrm{hash}(u_L,u_R,v)})^r)$.[4] If we have $h = g_L^{x_L} = g_R^{x_R}$, then α is a designated verifier zero-knowledge proof that both decryption with x_L and x_R will give the same plaintext. In the security proof, they use a hybrid argument where at one point we actually have that x_L and x_R would give different decryptions of the challenge ciphertext. At this point we simulate the designated verifier proof α. Raising d to $\mathrm{hash}(u_1, u_2, v)$ ensures that the simulation only works when we are

---

[3] These forms of non-malleability should not be confused with the NM-RCCA notion in [8].

[4] L = left, R = right.

using the actual challenge ciphertext, i.e., the designated verifier proof is simulation sound. Therefore, the adversary cannot fake proofs in the oracle queries, except if it copies the challenge ciphertext directly.

In our case we wish to allow rerandomization, provided the same plaintext is used. Therefore, we wish to ensure that the adversary in the security proof cannot fake the designated verifier proof unless the same plaintext as in the challenge is used. For this reason we make a designated verifier proof that has the form $(cd^{\mathrm{hash}(m)})^r$. The cryptosystem and the proof do become more involved than standard Cramer-Shoup encryption. One of the reasons for this is that we have to take specifically into account in the hybrid argument how to shift from using $\mathrm{hash}(m_0)$ and $\mathrm{hash}(m_1)$, where in the Cramer-Shoup scheme this is always computed as $\mathrm{hash}(u_L, u_r, v)$.

Another problem with using the Cramer-Shoup cryptosystem is that even with this new type of proof we cannot rerandomize it. To solve this problem we instead encrypt the message one bit at a time as $g_{L,i}^r, g_{R,i}^r, h^{m_i r}$ where $m_i = \pm 1$. Now we can rerandomize by choosing a random exponent and then raise all parts of the ciphertext to this exponent.

Key Generation: Choose a collision-free hash-function $\mathrm{h} : \{-1, 1\}^k \to \{0, 1\}^t$.
Choose a cyclic group G of order n where the DDH problem is hard.[5] The order n may be a prime or a composite. We demand that the smallest prime factor of n is larger than 2^t.
Select at random elements $h_1, \ldots, h_k \in G$.
Choose $x_{L,1}, x_{R,1}, \ldots, x_{L,k}, x_{R,k}$ at random from $\mathbb{Z}_n$.
Set $g_{L,1} = h_1^{x_{L,1}^{-1}}, g_{R,1} = h_1^{x_{R,1}^{-1}}, \ldots, g_{L,k} = h_k^{x_{L,k}^{-1}}, g_{R,k} = h_k^{x_{R,k}^{-1}}$.
Select at random $k_{L,1}, k_{R,1}, \ldots, k_{L,k}, k_{R,k} \in \mathbb{Z}_n$ and $l_{L,1}, l_{R,1}, \ldots, l_{L,k}, l_{R,k} \in \mathbb{Z}_n$.
Set

$$c = \prod_{i=1}^{k} g_{L,i}^{k_{L,i}} g_{R,i}^{k_{R,i}} \quad \text{and} \quad d = \prod_{i=1}^{k} g_{L,i}^{l_{L,i}} g_{R,i}^{l_{R,i}}.$$

$pk = (g_{L,1}, g_{R,1}, h_1, \ldots, g_{L,k}, g_{R,k}, h_k, c, d, \mathrm{h})$.
$sk = (pk, x_{L,1}, \ldots, x_{R,k}, k_{L,1}, \ldots, k_{R,k}, l_{L,1}, \ldots, l_{R,k})$.
Encryption: Given input $m = m_1 \ldots m_k \in \{-1, 1\}^k$.[6]
$E_{pk}(m; r) = (g_{L,1}^r, g_{R,1}^r, h_1^{m_1 r}, \ldots, g_{L,k}^r, g_{R,k}^r, h_k^{m_k r}, (cd^{\mathrm{h}(m)})^r)$.
Decryption: Given ciphertext $y = (u_{L,1}, u_{R,1}, v_1, \ldots, u_{L,k}, u_{R,k}, v_k, \alpha)$.
Check that all elements belong to G.
Compute for all i the $m_i \in \{-1, 1\}$ that satisfies $v_i = u_{L,i}^{m_i x_{L,i}} = u_{R,i}^{m_i x_{R,i}}$.
Set $m = m_1 \ldots m_k$.
Check that

$$\alpha = \prod_{i=1}^{k} u_{L,i}^{k_{L,i} + \mathrm{h}(m) l_{L,i}} u_{R,i}^{k_{R,i} + \mathrm{h}(m) l_{R,i}}.$$

If everything works out return m, otherwise return `invalid`.

---

[5] Membership of G should be easy to check and it should be easy to pick a generator for the group.

[6] Using $\{-1, 1\}$ instead of $\{0, 1\}$ makes notation a little less cumbersome.

Rerandomization: Given ciphertext $(u_{L,1}, u_{R,1}, v_1, \ldots, u_{L,k}, u_{R,k}, v_k, \alpha)$.
Select at random $r' \in \mathbb{Z}_n^*$. Return $(u_{L,1}^{r'}, \ldots, v_k^{r'}, \alpha^{r'})$.

It is easy to see that this is a public key cryptosystem with perfect rerandomization. For security, we have the following theorem.

Theorem 1. *The cryptosystem is* WRCCA *secure provided the* DDH *assumption holds for G and the hash-function is collision-free.*

Proof. Consider the experiments in the definition of WRCCA security. The only difference is in the challenge given to the adversary. We define several probabilities $p_0, \ldots, p_6$ of $\mathcal{A}$ outputting 1 given different challenges. I.e., we set $p_i = \Pr[(pk, sk) \leftarrow K(); (m_0, m_1) \leftarrow \mathcal{A}^{\mathcal{O}_1}(pk); y \leftarrow \text{Chal}_i : \mathcal{A}^{\mathcal{O}_2}(y) = 1]$, where Chal_i for the various probabilities returns the following.

p_0: $(g_{L,1}^r, g_{R,1}^r, h_1^{m_{01}r}, \ldots, g_{L,k}^r, g_{R,k}^r, h_k^{m_{0k}r}, (cd^{\text{h}(m_0)})^r)$.

p_1: $(\ldots, g_{L,i}^r, g_{R,i}^{m_{0i}m_{0i}r}, h_i^{m_{0i}r}, \ldots, \prod_{i=1}^k u_{L,i}^{k_{L,i}+l_{L,i}\text{h}(m_0)} u_{R,i}^{k_{R,i}+l_{R,i}\text{h}(m_0)})$.

p_2: $(\ldots, g_{L,i}^r, g_{R,i}^{m_{0i}m_{1i}r}, h_i^{m_{0i}r}, \ldots, \prod_{i=1}^k u_{L,i}^{k_{L,i}+l_{L,i}\text{h}(m_0)} u_{R,i}^{k_{R,i}+l_{R,i}\text{h}(m_0)})$.

p_3: $(\ldots, g_{L,i}^r, g_{R,i}^{m_{0i}m_{1i}r}, h_i^{m_{0i}r}, \ldots, \prod_{i=1}^k u_{L,i}^{k_{L,i}+l_{L,i}\text{h}(m_1)} u_{R,i}^{k_{R,i}+l_{R,i}\text{h}(m_1)})$.

p_4: $(\ldots, g_{L,i}^{m_{0i}m_{1i}r}, g_{R,i}^r, h_i^{m_{1i}r}, \ldots, \prod_{i=1}^k u_{L,i}^{k_{L,i}+l_{L,i}\text{h}(m_1)} u_{R,i}^{k_{R,i}+l_{R,i}\text{h}(m_1)})$.

p_5: $(\ldots, g_{L,i}^{m_{1i}m_{1i}r}, g_{R,i}^r, h_i^{m_{1i}r}, \ldots, \prod_{i=1}^k u_{L,i}^{k_{L,i}+l_{L,i}\text{h}(m_1)} u_{R,i}^{k_{R,i}+l_{R,i}\text{h}(m_1)})$.

p_6: $(g_{L,1}^r, g_{R,1}^r, h_1^{m_{11}r}, \ldots, g_{L,k}^r, g_{R,k}^r, h_k^{m_{1k}r}, (cd^{\text{h}(m_1)})^r)$.

p_0 and p_6 are the probabilities for the definition of WRCCA security. We must therefore prove that $p_0 \approx p_6$. To accomplish this we prove that $p_0 \approx p_1, \ldots, p_5 \approx p_6$.

The proof goes as follows. It is easy to see that $p_0 = p_1$. In p_1 we simulate the proof α, however, the simulation is perfect. $p_1 \approx p_2$ follows from Claim 11. $p_2 \approx p_3$ follows from Claim 13. $p_3 \approx p_4$ follows from Claim 14. $p_4 \approx p_5$ follows by a completely similar proof as for Claim 11. $p_5 = p_6$ is seen by inspection since again the only difference between them is a perfectly simulated proof α.

Claim 11. $p_1 \approx p_2$.

Proof. Assume for contradiction WLOG that p_1 is noticeably larger than p_2. We transform $\mathcal{A}$ into an adversary $\mathcal{B}$ that can break the following hard problem.

Hard problem. We select at random $h_1, \ldots, h_k$ and $g_{R,1}, \ldots, g_{R,k}$ from G. $\mathcal{B}$ sees these and is allowed to choose $m_0, m_1 \in \{-1, 1\}^k$. Subsequently we choose at random $r \in \mathbb{Z}_n^*$. We give either $(g_{R,1}^{m_{01}m_{01}r}, h_1^{m_{01}r}, \ldots, g_{R,k}^{m_{0k}m_{0k}r}, h_k^{m_{0k}r})$ or $(g_{R,1}^{m_{01}m_{11}r}, h_1^{m_{01}r}, \ldots, g_{R,k}^{m_{0k}m_{1k}r}, h_k^{m_{0k}r})$ to $\mathcal{B}$. $\mathcal{B}$ must now output a bit. We consider $\mathcal{B}$ successful if it can distinguish the two tuples.

The hardness of the problem relies on the DDH assumption. Suppose $\mathcal{B}$ can distinguish the two types of challenge. By a hybrid argument there is an index i and a bit b such that $\mathcal{B}$ can distinguish $(g_{R,1}^{m_{01}m_{01}r}, h_1^{m_{01}r}, \ldots, g_{R,i}^{m_{0i}m_{bi}r}, h_i^{m_{0i}r}, \ldots, g_{R,k}^{m_{0k}m_{1k}r}, h_k^{m_{0k}r})$ and

$(g_{R,1}^{m_{01}m_{01}r}, h_1^{m_{01}r}, \ldots, y, h_i^{m_{0i}r}, \ldots, g_{R,k}^{m_{0k}m_{1k}r}, h_k^{m_{0k}r})$, where y is chosen at random.

Consider now a randomly chosen DDH challenge (g, h, z, h^r) where we must determine whether $z = g^r$ or z is chosen at random from G. We set $h_i = h$ and $g_{R,i} = g$. For all $j \neq i$ we select at random $x_j, x_{R,j}$ and compute $h_j = h^{x_j}$ and $g_{R,j} = h_j^{x_{R,j}^{-1}}$. We give $g_{R,1}, h_1, \ldots, g_{R,k}, h_k$ to $\mathcal{B}$ and get the messages m_0 and m_1. Then we give $\mathcal{B}$ the challenge $(g_{R,1}^{m_{01}m_{01}r}, h_1^{m_{01}r}, \ldots, z^{m_{0i}m_{bi}}, h^{m_{0i}r}, \ldots, g_{R,k}^{m_{0k}m_{1k}r}, h_k^{m_{0k}r})$. We have now converted $\mathcal{B}$ into a DDH distinguisher.

The algorithm $\mathcal{B}$. We describe $\mathcal{B}$. In its first invocation it gets the input $g_{R,1}, \ldots, g_{R,k}, h_1, \ldots, h_k$. It selects at random $x_{L,1}, \ldots, x_{L,k} \in \mathbb{Z}_n$. It sets $g_{L,1} = h_1^{x_{L,1}^{-1}}, \ldots, g_{L,k} = h_k^{x_{L,k}^{-1}}$. After this it selects $k_{L,1}, \ldots, l_{R,k}$ and sets

$$c = \prod_{i=1}^{k} g_{L,i}^{k_{L,i}} g_{R,i}^{k_{R,i}} \quad \text{and} \quad d = \prod_{i=1}^{k} g_{L,i}^{l_{L,i}} g_{R,i}^{l_{R,i}}.$$

$\mathcal{B}$ now has something that looks perfectly like a public key for our cryptosystem. It does not know the full secret key since it does not know the discrete logarithms $x_{R,1}, \ldots, x_{R,k}$.

$\mathcal{B}$ runs the algorithm for $\mathcal{A}$ on the public key given above. Whenever $\mathcal{A}$ queries the oracle $\mathcal{O}_1$ then $\mathcal{B}$ answers the query by extracting a message m using its knowledge of $x_{L,1}, \ldots, x_{L,k}$. It then checks that $\alpha = \prod_{i=1}^{k} u_{L,i}^{k_{L,i}+l_{L,i}\mathrm{h}(m)} u_{R,i}^{k_{R,i}+l_{R,i}\mathrm{h}(m)}$. It returns m if everything works out OK. We can see this as $\mathcal{A}$ getting its oracle queries answered by a left-oracle $\mathcal{O}_1^L$. From Claim 12 we see that with overwhelming probability these answers correspond to the answers the real oracle $\mathcal{O}_1$ would make. $\mathcal{A}$ returns two messages m_0 and m_1. This is the output of $\mathcal{B}$ after its first invocation.

A challenge $(u_{R,1}, v_1, \ldots, u_{R,k}, v_k)$ for the hard problem is now selected and given to $\mathcal{B}$. $\mathcal{B}$ converts this challenge into what looks like a ciphertext by setting $u_{L,1} = v_1^{m_{01}x_{L,1}^{-1}}, \ldots, u_{L,k} = v_k^{m_{0k}x_{L,k}^{-1}}$ and $\alpha = \prod_{i=1}^{k} u_{L,i}^{k_{L,i}+l_{L,i}\mathrm{h}(m_0)} u_{R,i}^{k_{R,i}+l_{R,i}\mathrm{h}(m_0)}$. In case we have $u_{R,1} = g_{R,1}^{m_{01}m_{01}r}, v_1 = h_1^{m_{01}r}, \ldots, u_{R,k} = g_{R,k}^{m_{0k}m_{0k}r}, v_k = h_k^{m_{0k}r}$ then the ciphertext will be as in the challenge in p_1. In case we have $u_{R,1} = g_{R,1}^{m_{01}m_{11}r}, v_1 = h_1^{m_{01}r}, \ldots, u_{R,k} = g_{R,k}^{m_{0k}m_{1k}r}, v_k = h_k^{m_{0k}r}$ then we have a ciphertext on the form of the challenge in p_2.

$\mathcal{B}$ now runs $\mathcal{A}$ on this ciphertext. It answers queries in the same way as before, i.e., using $\mathcal{O}_2^L$ that decrypts using $x_{L,1}, \ldots, x_{L,k}$ and then checks the proof. Again using Claim 12 we get that the oracle queries are answered as the real oracle $\mathcal{O}_2$ with access to the discrete logarithms $x_{R,1}, \ldots, x_{R,k}$ would do. In the end, $\mathcal{A}$ answers with a bit. $\mathcal{B}$ uses this bit as its output.

Depending on the challenge, we have either probability p_1 for $\mathcal{B}$ outputting 1 or probability p_2 for $\mathcal{B}$ outputting 1. If the two probabilities are noticeably different, this means that we have created a distinguisher for the hard problem and thereby broken the DDH assumption.

Claim 12. It is infeasible for $\mathcal{A}$ to find a ciphertext y' with proof α' that gets answered differently by the real oracles $\mathcal{O}_1, \mathcal{O}_2$ and modified oracles $\mathcal{O}_1^L, \mathcal{O}_2^L$ that only left-decrypt, even if $\mathcal{A}$ sees a fake ciphertext y as the challenge in p_2 with simulated proof α.

Proof. Consider the difficult case, namely finding a query that $\mathcal{O}_2$ and $\mathcal{O}_2^L$ answer differently. The information available to $\mathcal{A}$ about $k_{L,1}, \ldots, l_{R,k}$ comes from c, d and the fake ciphertext y. If we compute the discrete logarithms with respect to some base g for these elements, we get the following system of linear equations in $\mathbb{Z}_n$ to be satisfied, where α' is the "proof" in the newly created ciphertext.

$$
\begin{pmatrix}
1 & 1 & \cdots & 0 & 0 & \cdots \\
0 & 0 & \cdots & 1 & 1 & \cdots \\
r & r\delta_1 & \cdots & rh(m_0) & r\delta_1 h(m_0) & \cdots \\
r_{L,1} & r_{R,1} & \cdots & r_{L,1}h(m) & r_{R,1}h(m) & \cdots
\end{pmatrix}
\begin{pmatrix}
\log(g_{L,1})k_{L,1} \\
\log(g_{R,1})k_{R,1} \\
\vdots \\
\log(g_{L,1})l_{L,1} \\
\log(g_{R,1})l_{R,1} \\
\vdots
\end{pmatrix}
=
\begin{pmatrix}
\log(c) \\
\log(d) \\
\log(\alpha) \\
\log(\alpha')
\end{pmatrix},
$$

where we define $\delta_i = m_{0i}m_{1i}$.

Since $k_{L,1}, \ldots, l_{R,k}$ are unknown and randomly chosen the only chance for the proof α' to be correct is if the last row is a linear combination of the first three rows. Already at this point we can therefore see that we must have some r_L such that for all i we have $r_L = r_{L,i}$. Reducing the matrix we get

$$
\begin{pmatrix}
1 & 1 & \cdots 0 & 0 & \cdots \\
0 & 0 & \cdots 1 & 1 & \cdots \\
0 & \delta_i - 1 & \cdots 0 & (\delta_i - 1)h(m_0) & \cdots \\
0 & r_{R,1} - r_L & \cdots 0 & (r_{R,1} - r_L)h(m) & \cdots
\end{pmatrix}.
$$

We see that there must be some μ such that the fourth row is μ times the third row. This means that for all i with $\delta_i = 1$ we have $r_{R,i} = r_L$. Consider from now on the remaining i's where $\delta_i = -1$. We see that for all these i's we have

$$
r_{R,i} - r_L = -2\mu \qquad \text{and} \qquad (r_{R,i} - r_L)h(m) = -2\mu h(m_0).
$$

If $\mu = 0$ then $r_{R,i} = r_L$ for all i and therefore both left-decryption and right-decryption give the same result. In that case, the left-oracle answers correctly.

If $\mu \neq 0$ then we have for these i's that $(r_{R,i} - r_L)(h(m) - h(m_0)) = 0$ and $r_{R,i} - r_L \neq 0$. This implies that $h(m) = h(m_0)$, since the hashes are smaller than the smallest prime factor of n. Collision-freeness of the hash-function now implies that $m = m_0$. But in that case, both $\mathcal{O}_2^L$ and $\mathcal{O}_2$ answer invalid. We therefore see that the left-oracle answers the same as the real oracle.

Claim 13. $p_2 \approx p_3$.

Proof. Let i be an index such that $m_{0i} m_{1i} = -1$. We will argue that even if $\mathcal{A}$ is computationally unbounded and given $k_{L,j}, k_{R,j}, l_{L,j}, l_{R,j}$ for all $j \neq i$ it still cannot distinguish the two challenges.

From the available information $\mathcal{A}$ can use c to compute

$$K_i = \log(g_{L,i}) k_{L,i} + \log(g_{R,i}) k_{R,i} \bmod n$$

and d to compute

$$L_i = \log(g_{L,i}) l_{L,i} + \log(g_{R,i}) l_{R,i} \bmod n$$

as well as α to compute

$$
\begin{aligned}
A_i &= \log(g_{L,i})(k_{L,i} + \mathrm{h}(m_b) l_{L,i}) - \log(g_{R,i})(k_{R,i} + \mathrm{h}(m_b) l_{R,i}) + \mathrm{h}(m_b)\Delta \\
&= K_i - 2\log(g_{R,i}) k_{R,i} + \mathrm{h}(m_b)(L_i - 2\log(g_{R,i}) l_{R,i} + \Delta) \bmod n,
\end{aligned}
$$

where Δ depends on the other k's and l's, but not $k_{L,i}, k_{R,i}, l_{L,i}, l_{R,i}$. However, since $k_{L,i}, l_{R,i}, l_{L,i}, l_{R,i}$ are chosen at random this does not reveal whether $b = 0$ or $b = 1$.

$\mathcal{A}$ cannot use the decryption queries to learn anything. If $\mathcal{A}$ wants to make a decryption query that has noticeable chance of being valid it must be on the form $(g_{L,1}^{r_1}, g_{R,1}^{r_1}, h_1^{m_1 r_1}, \ldots, g_{L,i}^{r_i}, g_{R,i}^{r_i}, h_i^{m_i r_i}, \ldots, g_{L,k}^{r_k}, g_{R,k}^{r_k}, h_k^{m_k r_k}, \prod_{j=1}^k g^{K_j + \mathrm{h}(m) L_j})$. This does not reveal any new information on $k_{L,i}, k_{R,i}, l_{L,i}, l_{R,i}$ and therefore b remains hidden.

Claim 14. $p_3 \approx p_4$.

Proof. By a hybrid argument if $\mathcal{A}$ can distinguish the two challenges then there is an index i such that $\mathcal{A}$ can be used to distinguish challenges on the form $(g_{L,1}^r, g_{R,1}^{m_{01} m_{11} r}, h_1^{m_{01} r}, \ldots, g_{L,i}^r, g_{R,i}^{m_{0i} m_{1i} r}, h_i^{m_{0i} r}, \ldots, g_{L,k}^{m_{0k} m_{1k} r}, g_{R,k}^r, h_k^{m_{1k} r}, \prod_{i=1}^k u_{L,i}^{k_{L,i} + l_{L,i} \mathrm{h}(m_1)} u_{R,i}^{k_{R,i} + l_{R,i} \mathrm{h}(m_1)})$ and $(g_{L,1}^r, g_{R,1}^{m_{01} m_{11} r}, h_1^{m_{01} r}, \ldots, g_{L,i}^{m_{0i} m_{1i} r}, g_{R,i}^r, h_i^{m_{1i} r}, \ldots, g_{L,k}^{m_{0k} m_{1k} r}, g_{R,k}^r, h_k^{m_{1k} r}, \prod_{i=1}^k u_{L,i}^{k_{L,i} + l_{L,i} \mathrm{h}(m_1)} u_{R,i}^{k_{R,i} + l_{R,i} \mathrm{h}(m_1)})$.

According to the DDH assumption it is impossible to tell whether a challenge (g, h, g^r, z) has $z = h^r$ or z chosen at random from G. This implies that it is hard to distinguish (g, h, g^r, h^r) and (g, h, g^r, h^{-r}).

So given a challenge (g, h, g^r, z), where $z = h^r$ or $z = h^{-r}$, we set $h_i = h$ and for all $j \neq i$ we compute $h_j = g^{x_j}$, where we choose x_j at random. We have now selected $h_1, \ldots, h_k$ and carry out the rest of the key generation procedure. This gives us a public key and a secret key. Now we run the first invocation of $\mathcal{A}$ on this challenge. $\mathcal{A}$ produces two challenge messages m_0 and m_1. If $m_{0i} = m_{1i}$ we stop and guess at random a bit b. However, if $m_{0i} \neq m_{1i}$ then we set $v_i = z$. We may now set it up such that $z = h^{m_{0i} r}$ gives us the challenge $(g_{L,1}^r, g_{R,1}^{m_{01} m_{11} r}, h_1^{m_{01} r}, \ldots, g_{L,i}^r, g_{R,i}^{m_{0i} m_{1i} r}, h_i^{m_{0i} r}, \ldots, g_{L,k}^{m_{0k} m_{1k} r}, g_{R,k}^r, h_k^{m_{1k} r}, \prod_{i=1}^k u_{L,i}^{k_{L,i} + l_{L,i} \mathrm{h}(m_1)} u_{R,i}^{k_{R,i} + l_{R,i} \mathrm{h}(m_1)})$, while $z = h^{m_{1i} r}$ gives us the challenge $(g_{L,1}^r, g_{R,1}^{m_{01} m_{11} r}, h_1^{m_{01} r}, \ldots, g_{L,i}^{m_{0i} m_{1i} r}, g_{R,i}^r, h_i^{m_{1i} r}, \ldots, g_{L,k}^{m_{0k} m_{1k} r}, g_{R,k}^r, h_k^{m_{1k} r}, \prod_{i=1}^k u_{L,i}^{k_{L,i} + l_{L,i} \mathrm{h}(m_1)} u_{R,i}^{k_{R,i} + l_{R,i} \mathrm{h}(m_1)})$. Since $\mathcal{A}$ can distinguish these two challenges this means we have broken the DDH assumption. $\square$

4   Rerandomizable RCCA Secure Encryption

The WRCCA secure cryptosystem is not RCCA secure. First, let us argue that the WRCCA secure cryptosystem from the previous section is not RCCA secure. So we are given a ciphertext $(u_{L,1}, u_{R,1}, v_1, \ldots, u_{L,k}, u_{R,k}, v_k, \alpha)$ and want to know whether it encrypts m_0 or m_1. We simply transform it into $(u_{L,1} g_{L,1}, u_{R,1} g_{R,1}, v_1 h_1^{m_{01}}, \ldots, u_{L,k} g_{L,k}, u_{R,k} g_{R,k}, v_k h_k^{m_{0k}}, \alpha c d^{h(m_0)})$. We then submit this modified ciphertext to the oracle $\mathcal{O}_2$. If the encrypted message is m_0 then we have a new encryption of m_0, and $\mathcal{O}_2$ answers `test`. On the other hand, if the encrypted message is m_1, then we have messed things up and $\mathcal{O}_2$ answers `invalid`. This means that we can distinguish between encryptions of the two possible plaintexts.

Improving the cryptosystem to have RCCA security. In the following, we attempt to fix the WRCCA secure cryptosystem. The problem in the attack above is that the adversary can rerandomize the ciphertext in a way such that he depending on the message inside gets either `test` or `invalid` as the answer. To prevent this we wish for a cryptosystem where the adversary is forced to make a correct rerandomization, and if he does not then he has overwhelming probability of getting `invalid` as answer.

To accomplish this we raise α to a random value Z. Rerandomization still works by raising all parts of the ciphertext to some random r'. Assuming the receiver knows this secret Z he can decrypt the ciphertext. On the other hand an adversary that does not know Z can only modify the proof in a meaningful way by raising the proof to some exponent. The adversary is therefore forced to either make correct rerandomizations or make some garbage. In particular he cannot use the previous attack where he with 50% probability creates a rerandomization and with 50% probability makes some garbage.

For this to be a public key cryptosystem we need the sender to choose Z and transmit it to the receiver. Therefore, she encrypts Z and sends it to the receiver. Since we want to have perfect rerandomization we also need to be able to rerandomize Z and the encryption of Z. We therefore use a homomorphic cryptosystem with message space $\mathbb{Z}_n$ to transmit Z to the receiver. This could for instance be Paillier-encryption, Cramer-Shoup Lite encryption based on the decisional composite residuosity assumption or perhaps some elliptic curve based cryptosystem.

Key generation: We set up the same public private keys (pk, sk) as in the previous section. Generate also keys (pk_n, sk_n) for an additively homomorphic cryptosystem with message space $\mathbb{Z}_n$. We demand that it is infeasible to find non-trivial factors of n.

The public key is $PK = (pk, pk_n)$.

The secret key is $SK = (sk, sk_n)$.

Encryption: Input: $m \in \{-1, 1\}^k$.
$$E_{PK}(m; r, R, Z) = (g_{L,1}^r, g_{R,1}^r, h_1^{m_1 r}, \ldots, g_{L,k}^r, g_{R,k}^r, h_k^{m_k r}, (cd^{h(m)})^{rZ}, E_{pk_n}(Z; R)).$$

Decryption: Given a ciphertext $Y = (u_{L,1}, u_{R,1}, v_1, \ldots, u_{L,k}, u_{R,k}, v_k, \beta, y)$.

Compute $Z = D_{sk_n}(y)$. Check that $Z \in \mathbb{Z}_n^*$. Set $\alpha = \beta^{Z^{-1}}$. Finally, compute $m = D_{sk}(u_{L,1}, u_{R,1}, v_1, \ldots, u_{L,k}, u_{R,k}, v_k, \alpha)$.

If all checks and computations work out return m, otherwise return `invalid`.

Rerandomization: Input: PK and a ciphertext Y.

Format Y as $(u_{L,1}, u_{R,1}, v_1, \ldots, u_{L,k}, u_{R,k}, v_k, \beta, y)$. Check that all of these elements belong to appropriate groups.

Select randomizers r', Z', R'.

Return $(u_{L,1}^{r'}, u_{R,1}^{r'}, v_1^{r'}, \ldots, u_{L,k}^{r'}, u_{R,1}^{r'}, v_k^{r'}, \beta^{r'Z'}, E_{pk_n}(0; R')y^{Z'})$.

It is straightforward to verify that the cryptosystem is rerandomizable, and WRCCA security follows from the previous section. Left is the question whether it is RCCA secure.

Speaking against this idea is the fact that the adversary does actually get access to a chosen ciphertext attack on the homomorphic cryptosystem. For instance, given a y, it may form $(g_{L,1}^r, \ldots, h_k^r, (cd^{h(1^k)})^z, y)$. Giving this ciphertext to $\mathcal{O}_2$ it can learn whether y contains z or not. Of course, if the adversary can use queries like this to figure out Z of the challenge encryption, then it may use the attack on the WRCCA scheme to violate the RCCA security of the proposed cryptosystem.

The semi-generic model. We are unable to prove security of the cryptosystem directly and likewise unable to break it. We therefore try to formulate a reasonable security model that says something about the security of the cryptosystem. Since random oracles are no good with respect to rerandomizable encryption we instead turn to the generic model, which has been explored in several papers including [11,12,13]. In other words, we will prove that if a generic homomorphic cryptosystem over $\mathbb{Z}_n$ is used to encrypt Z, then the construction is RCCA secure.

By a generic cryptosystem, we mean the following functionality. On an input (Encrypt, z) we choose y at random and store (z, y). On a query (Add, y, y') we look up whether y, y' have already been stored. In that case we select at random y'' and store $(z + z', y'')$. On input (Decrypt, y) we look up whether (z, y) has been stored for some z, and in that case we return z. Note that both adding a known value to an encrypted message and multiplying an encrypted message by some known number can be built from these two functions. This means that we allow use of the well-known homomorphic properties of cryptosystems such as Paillier encryption, CS-Lite encryption or elliptic curve based encryption. In the following, we use the shorthand $[x]$ to denote a generic encryption of x.

Encryption and decryption work as before, except we now use this generic cryptosystem to encrypt Z. The problem in the WRCCA case was that our oracle that just used left-decryption could not tell when to answer `test` and `invalid`, and indeed we showed with a concrete attack that this difference is important. We will argue that this problem goes away in the semi-generic model.

Recall that in the intuition provided for our conjectured RCCA secure cryptosystem we imagined Z to be completely unknown to the adversary. Since the adversary has access to a chosen ciphertext attack it is not possible to use semantic security of the encryption of Z to argue RCCA security. The semi-generic model intuitively corresponds to a "perfect" encryption of Z, which at the same time has the needed homomorphic property.

Theorem 2. *The cryptosystem described above is RCCA secure against semi-generic adversaries under the DDH assumption and the collision-freeness of the hash-function.*

Proof. Consider the definition of RCCA security. We will replace the oracle $\mathcal{O}_2$ with a different oracle $\mathcal{O}'$. $\mathcal{O}'$ works like $\mathcal{O}_2$ except when seeing a ciphertext Y that left-decrypts to m_0 and right-decrypts to m_1. In this special case it will check whether the proof α is valid with either $h(m_0)$ or $h(m_1)$. In those two cases, $\mathcal{O}'$ returns test, while in all other cases it acts like $\mathcal{O}_2$.

Just as in the proof of Theorem 1 we consider probabilities $p_0, \ldots, p_6$ that we define the following way: $p_i = \Pr[(pk, sk) \leftarrow K(); (m_0, m_1) \leftarrow \mathcal{A}^{\mathcal{O}_1}(pk); y \leftarrow \text{Chal}_i : \mathcal{A}^{\mathcal{O}}(y) = 1]$, where Chal_i for the various probabilities gives the following challenges, and in p_0, p_6 we use $\mathcal{O} = \mathcal{O}_2$, while in p_1, p_2, p_3, p_4 we use $\mathcal{O} = \mathcal{O}'$.

p_0: $(g_{L,1}^r, g_{R,1}^r, h_1^{m_{01}r}, \ldots, g_{L,k}^r, g_{R,k}^r, h_k^{m_{0k}r}, (cd^{h(m_0)})^{rZ}, [Z])$.

p_1: $(\ldots, g_{L,i}^r, g_{R,i}^{m_{0i}m_{0i}r}, h_i^{m_{0i}r}, \ldots, (\prod_{i=1}^k u_{L,i}^{k_{L,i}+l_{L,i}h(m_0)} u_{R,i}^{k_{R,i}+l_{R,i}h(m_0)})^Z, [Z])$.

p_2: $(\ldots, g_{L,i}^r, g_{R,i}^{m_{0i}m_1i r}, h_i^{m_{0i}r}, \ldots, (\prod_{i=1}^k u_{L,i}^{k_{L,i}+l_{L,i}h(m_0)} u_{R,i}^{k_{R,i}+l_{R,i}h(m_0)})^Z, [Z])$.

p_3: $(\ldots, g_{L,i}^r, g_{R,i}^{m_{0i}m_1i r}, h_i^{m_{0i}r}, \ldots, (\prod_{i=1}^k u_{L,i}^{k_{L,i}+l_{L,i}h(m_1)} u_{R,i}^{k_{R,i}+l_{R,i}h(m_1)})^Z, [Z])$.

p_4: $(\ldots, g_{L,i}^{m_{0i}m_1i r}, g_{R,i}^r, h_i^{m_1i r}, \ldots, (\prod_{i=1}^k u_{L,i}^{k_{L,i}+l_{L,i}h(m_1)} u_{R,i}^{k_{R,i}+l_{R,i}h(m_1)})^Z, [Z])$.

p_5: $(\ldots, g_{L,i}^{m_1i m_1i r}, g_{R,i}^r, h_i^{m_1i r}, \ldots, (\prod_{i=1}^k u_{L,i}^{k_{L,i}+l_{L,i}h(m_1)} u_{R,i}^{k_{R,i}+l_{R,i}h(m_1)})^Z, [Z])$.

p_6: $(g_{L,1}^r, g_{R,1}^r, h_1^{m_{11}r}, \ldots, g_{L,k}^r, g_{R,k}^r, h_k^{m_{1k}r}, (cd^{h(m_1)})^{rZ}, [Z])$.

To prove that the cryptosystem is RCCA secure we need to prove that $p_0 \approx p_6$. $p_0 \approx p_1$ according to Claim 21. $p_1 \approx p_2$ according to Claim 22. $p_2 \approx p_3$ according to Claim 22. $p_3 \approx p_4$ follows from a similar argument as we gave for Claim 14 in the proof of Theorem 1. $p_4 \approx p_5$ follows from a quite similar argument as the one given for Claim 22. $p_5 \approx p_6$ likewise follows from the proof of Claim 21.

Claim 21. $p_0 \approx p_1$.

Proof. Both challenges are computed the same way. The difference between the probabilities is the oracles $\mathcal{O}_2$ and $\mathcal{O}'$. However, we will argue that it is infeasible even for a computationally unbounded adversary $\mathcal{A}$ to distinguish between the two oracles as long as it may only make a polynomial number of queries, and even if $\mathcal{A}$ is allowed to freely make decryption queries to the generic cryptosystem.

The information available to $\mathcal{A}$ about $k_{L,1}, \ldots, l_{R,k}$ is what it can tell from c and d and the challenge. Consider a query $(u'_{L,1}, u'_{R,1}, v'_1, \ldots, u'_{L,k}, u'_{R,k}, v'_k, \beta', [Z'])$. Calling the respective discrete logarithms $r_{L,1}, r_{R,1}, r_1, \ldots, r_{L,k}, r_{R,k}, r_k, Z'\log(\alpha')$ we get the following system of linear equations.

$$
\begin{pmatrix}
1 & 1 & \cdots & 0 & 0 & \cdots \\
0 & 0 & \cdots & 1 & 1 & \cdots \\
r & r & \cdots & r\mathrm{h}(m_0) & r\mathrm{h}(m_0) & \cdots \\
r_{L,1} & r_{R,1} & \cdots & r_{L,1}\mathrm{h}(m) & r_{R,1}\mathrm{h}(m) & \cdots
\end{pmatrix}
\begin{pmatrix}
\log(g_{L,1})k_{L,1} \\
\log(g_{R,1})k_{R,1} \\
\vdots \\
\log(g_{L,1})l_{L,1} \\
\log(g_{R,1})l_{R,1} \\
\vdots
\end{pmatrix}
=
\begin{pmatrix}
\log(c) \\
\log(d) \\
\log(\alpha) \\
\log(\alpha')
\end{pmatrix}.
$$

If the query is to return something else than `invalid` with more than negligible probability then $\mathcal{A}$ must use $r_{L,1} = r_{R,1} = \cdots = r_{L,k} = r_{R,k}$. But on such queries $\mathcal{O}_2$ and $\mathcal{O}'$ work the same way.

Claim 22. $p_1 \approx p_2$.

Sketch of proof. Just as in Claim 11 in the proof of Theorem 1 we may argue that we can break the DDH assumption if $\mathcal{A}$ distinguishes between the two challenges. The difference between Claim 11 and Claim 22 is the oracles that are used. However, here we may also argue just as in the proof of that claim that left-decryptions work just as well as right-decryptions. This follows from Claim 23.

Claim 23. The oracles $\mathcal{O}_1^L, \mathcal{O}'^L$ that only left-decrypt ciphertexts give the same answers as $\mathcal{O}_1, \mathcal{O}'$.

Proof. We look at the difficult case, namely whether $\mathcal{O}'$ and $\mathcal{O}'^L$ answer the same. Consider the information available to an adversary regarding $k_{L,1}, \ldots, l_{R,k}$. There is c, d and possibly a fake ciphertext. From this it must create a ciphertext with "proof" β'. Since we are using a generic cryptosystem for storing Z, the adversary must store some value $f(Z)$ in the homomorphic encryption. With the generic cryptosystem $f(Z) = aZ + b \bmod n$ with a, b known to the adversary.

Defining $\delta_i = m_{0i}m_{1i}$ we get the following system of linear equations in $\mathbb{Z}_n$.

$$
\begin{pmatrix}
1 & 1 & \cdots & 0 & 0 & \cdots \\
0 & 0 & \cdots & 1 & 1 & \cdots \\
r & r\delta_1 & \cdots & r\mathrm{h}(m_0) & r\delta_1\mathrm{h}(m_0) & \cdots \\
r_{L,1} & r_{R,1} & \cdots & r_{L,1}\mathrm{h}(m) & r_{R,1}\mathrm{h}(m) & \cdots
\end{pmatrix}
\begin{pmatrix}
\log(g_{L,1})k_{L,1} \\
\log(g_{R,1})k_{R,1} \\
\vdots \\
\log(g_{L,1})l_{L,1} \\
\log(g_{R,1})l_{R,1} \\
\vdots
\end{pmatrix}
=
\begin{pmatrix}
\log(c) \\
\log(d) \\
\frac{\log(\beta)}{Z} \\
\frac{\log(\beta')}{f(Z)}
\end{pmatrix}.
$$

It is immediate that for any query with noticeable chance of being valid we must have some $r_L = r_{L,i}$ for all i. Reducing the matrices we get

$$
\begin{pmatrix}
1 & 1 & \cdots 0 & 0 & \cdots & \log(c) \\
0 & 0 & \cdots 1 & 1 & \cdots & \log(d) \\
0 & \delta_1 - 1 & \cdots 0 & (\delta_1 - 1)\mathrm{h}(m_0) & \cdots & \frac{\log(\beta)}{rZ} - \log(c) - \mathrm{h}(m_0)\log(d) \\
0 & r_{R,1} - r_L & \cdots 0 & (r_{R,1} - r_L)\mathrm{h}(m) & \cdots & \frac{\log(\beta')}{f(Z)} - r_L\log(c) - r_L\mathrm{h}(m)\log(d)
\end{pmatrix}
$$

If we have $r_L = r_{R,i}$ for all i then the left-decryption corresponds to the real decryption and both pairs of oracles answer the same. Assuming we are not in this trivial situation we can argue that for all i with $\delta_i = 1$ we have $r_{R,i} = r_L$. Similarly we have some r_R such that for all the other i's we have $r_R = r_{R,i}$. We also see that $m = m_0$ by the collision-freeness of the hash-function. Adding $\frac{r_R - r_L}{2}$ times row three to row four we get:

$$
\begin{pmatrix}
1 & 1 & \cdots 0 & 0 & \cdots & & \log(c) \\
0 & 0 & \cdots 1 & 1 & \cdots & & \log(d) \\
0 \; \delta_1 - 1 & \cdots 0 \; (\delta_1 - 1)\mathrm{h}(m_0) & \cdots & & \frac{\log(\beta)}{rZ} - \log(c) - \mathrm{h}(m_0)\log(d) \\
0 & 0 & \cdots 0 & 0 & \cdots & & \frac{\log(\beta')}{f(Z)} - r_L \log(c) - r_L \mathrm{h}(m_0)\log(d) \\
& & & & & & -\frac{r_L - r_R}{2}\left(\frac{\log(\beta)}{rZ} - \log(c) - \mathrm{h}(m_0)\log(d)\right)
\end{pmatrix}
$$

We must therefore have

$$
2\frac{\log(\beta')}{f(Z)} - (r_L + r_R)(\log(c) + \mathrm{h}(m_0)\log(d)) + (r_R - r_L)\frac{\log(\beta)}{rZ} = 0 \bmod n.
$$

This implies

$$
2\log(\beta')rZ - (r_L + r_R)(\log(c) + \mathrm{h}(m_0)\log(d))rZf(Z) + (r_R - r_L)\log(\beta)f(Z) = 0 \bmod n.
$$

Since we use a generic cryptosystem the adversary cannot produce anything but $f(Z) = aZ + b$ with a and b known. We then get a degree 2 polynomial on the left side of the equation. Since Z is unknown, the adversary can only have a chance at producing correct proofs by making sure that it is the zero-polynomial on the left side.

So if the left side of the equation is the zero-polynomial then we get $(r_R - r_L)\log(\beta)b = 0 \bmod n$. Since b cannot be a non-trivial factor of n this implies $b = 0$ or $r_R - r_L = 0$. In the latter case both right- and left-decryption is the same and we are done. We therefore continue under the assumption that $b = 0$.

Considering the Z^2-part we get $(r_L + r_R)(\log(c) + \mathrm{h}(m_0)\log(d))ra = 0 \bmod n$. This implies $a = 0$ or $r_R = -r_L$. However, $a = 0$ would mean that y' contains $0Z + 0$ which automatically leads to the response **invalid** by both the real oracles and the left-oracles. On the other hand if we have $r_R = -r_L$ then we have for all i's where $\delta_i = -1$ that $r_R = \delta_i r_L$. Since the left-decryption is m_0 then this implies a right-decryption to m_1. But also in this case we then have the left-oracles give the same answer as the real oracle.

Remark 1. It is worth noting that even if we allow other types of mauling of the generic cryptosystem, we may have security. In particular, if we allow it to be algebraically homomorphic (i.e., both addition and multiplication of plaintexts is possible) this does not break our construction. In that case $f(Z)$ becomes a polynomial in Z with a polynomial number of different roots and we can use arguments similar to the one above to show that the left-oracles works the ame way as the real oracles.

Claim 24. $p_2 \approx p_3$

Proof. Assume WLOG that $\mathcal{A}$ is computationally unbounded (but may only make a polynomial number of queries to the oracles) and knows the secret keys except $k_{L,1}, \ldots, l_{R,k}$. We may argue from Claim 13 in the proof of Theorem 1 that it does not have any information on $\mathrm{h}(m_b)$ from the challenge itself, and therefore cannot distinguish the two experiments without making oracle queries.

Let us consider the oracle queries that it may make. We label the discrete logarithms of a successful query $(u'_{L,1}, u'_{R,1}, v'_1, \ldots, u'_{L,k}, u'_{R,k}, v'_k, (\alpha')^{Z'}, [Z'])$ with $(r_{L,1}, r_{R,1}, r_1, \ldots, r_{L,k}, r_{R,k}, r_k, -, -)$. We then have the following system of equations.

$$
\begin{pmatrix}
1 & 1 & \cdots & 0 & 0 & \cdots \\
0 & 0 & \cdots & 1 & 1 & \cdots \\
r & r\delta_1 & \cdots & rh(m_b) & r\delta_1 h(m_b) & \cdots \\
r_{L,1} & r_{R,1} & \cdots & r_{L,1} h(m) & r_{R,1} h(m) & \cdots
\end{pmatrix}
\begin{pmatrix}
\log(g_{L,1}) k_{L,1} \\
\log(g_{R,1}) k_{R,1} \\
\vdots \\
\log(g_{L,1}) l_{L,1} \\
\log(g_{R,1}) l_{R,1} \\
\vdots
\end{pmatrix}
=
\begin{pmatrix}
\log(c) \\
\log(d) \\
\log(\alpha) \\
\log(\alpha')
\end{pmatrix}.
$$

We see that there is an element r_L such that for all i we have $r_{L,i} = r_L$. Reducing the matrix we get.

$$
\begin{pmatrix}
1 & 1 & \cdots 0 & 0 & \cdots \\
0 & 0 & \cdots 1 & 1 & \cdots \\
0 & \delta_1 - 1 & \cdots 0 & (\delta_1 - 1) h(m_b) & \cdots \\
0 & r_{R,1} - r_L & \cdots 0 & (r_{R,1} - r_L) h(m) & \cdots
\end{pmatrix}.
$$

Unless $r_{R,i} = r_L$ for all i, then $\mathrm{h}(m) = \mathrm{h}(m_b)$ and $r_{R,i} = r_{R,1}$ for all i. Those two options correspond to respectively make a new ciphertext, or rerandomize the challenge. In either case, $\mathcal{A}$ does not learn anything new from $\mathcal{O}'$'s answers. $\square$

Theorem 2 tells us is that the scheme is RCCA secure against semi-generic adversaries that only use standard group operations on the encryption of Z. We can instantiate the cryptosystems with many possible homomorphic cryptosystems, for instance Paillier encryption, CS-Lite encryption or elliptic curve encryption. We could also use a multiplicative homomorphic property instead and use standard RSA to encrypt Z. To break the scheme we would have to come up with some non-standard way of mauling these cryptosystems. We believe such a result would be highly interesting in itself.

5   Discussion

To evaluate our results we find it useful to compare them with the development of standard CCA2 secure public key encryption. In this process, Naor and Yung [14] invented a CCA1 secure encryption scheme. Dolev, Dwork and Naor [1] then suggested a CCA2 secure cryptosystem. Several years after this Cramer and Shoup [3] suggested the first practical CCA2 secure cryptosystem. Furthermore, several schemes have been proposed that are secure in the random oracle model. A proof of security in the random oracle model is not a real proof of security, but it is better than no proof at all.

With respect to rerandomizable encryption our intuition is that WRCCA secure encryption is a step on the way. WRCCA secure encryption may have its uses, however, as CCA2 secure encryption is the standard for public key encryption we think RCCA secure encryption is the right standard for rerandomizable encryption. As stated earlier we believe coming up with a rerandomizable RCCA secure encryption scheme is a very hard task, and certainly an interesting open problem. In lack of such a scheme, we have suggested using another security paradigm, namely RCCA security against semi-generic adversaries. Just as proving CCA2 security in the random oracle model is not the same as proving CCA2 security in the standard model, proving RCCA security in the semi-generic model is not the same as proving RCCA security in the standard model, but it is better than no proof at all.

Acknowledgments. Moni Naor suggested the idea of rerandomizable encryption in a conversation with us and we also appreciate his encouragement during the research. Thanks goes to Alon Rosen and Jesper Buus Nielsen for discussions.

References

1. Dolev, D., Dwork, C., Naor, M.: Non-malleable cryptography. SIAM J. of Computing **30** (2000) 391–437 Earlier version at STOC '91.
2. Sahai, A.: Non-malleable non-interactive zero-knowledge and adaptive chosen-ciphertext security. In: proceedings of FOCS '01. (2001) 543–553
3. Cramer, R., Shoup, V.: Design and analysis of practical public-key encryption schemes secure against adaptive chosen ciphertext attack. In: proceedings of CRYPTO '98, LNCS series, volume 1462. (1998) 13–25
4. Cramer, R., Shoup, V.: Universal hash proofs and a paradigm for adaptive chosen ciphertext secure public-key encryption. In: proceedings of EUROCRYPT '02, LNCS series, volume 2332. (2002) 45–64
5. Lindell, Y.: A simpler construction of cca2-secure public-key encryption under general assumptions. In: proceedings of EUROCRYPT '03, LNCS series, volume 2656. (2003) 241–254
6. Shoup, V.: A proposal for an iso standard for public key encryption. Cryptology ePrint Archive, Report 2001/112 (2001) http://eprint.iacr.org/2001/212.
7. An, J.H., Dodis, Y., Rabin, T.: On the security of joint signature and encryption. In: proceedings of EUROCRYPT '02, LNCS series, volume 2332. (2002) 83–107
8. Canetti, R., Krawczyk, H., Nielsen, J.B.: Relaxing chosen-ciphertext security. In: proceedings of CRYPTO '03, LNCS series, volume 2729. (2003) 565–582
9. Bleichenbacher, D.: Chosen ciphertext attacks against protocols based on the rsa encryption standard pkcs 1. In: proceedings of CRYPTO '98, LNCS series, volume 1462. (1998) 1–12

10. Bellare, M., Sahai, A.: Non-malleable encryption: Equivalence between two notions, and an indistinguishability-based characterization. In: proceedings of CRYPTO '99, LNCS series, volume 1666. (1999) 519–536
11. Boneh, D., Lipton, R.J.: Algorithms for black-box fields and their application to cryptography. In: proceedings of CRYPTO '96, LNCS series, volume 1109. (1996) 283–297
12. Shoup, V.: Lower bounds for discrete logarithms and related problems. In: proceedings of EUROCRYPT '97, LNCS series, volume 1233. (1997) 256–266
13. Damgård, I., Koprowski, M.: Generic lower bounds for root extraction and signature schemes in general groups. In: proceedings of EUROCRYPT '02, LNCS series, volume 2332. (2002) 256–271
14. Naor, M., Yung, M.: Public-key cryptosystems provably secure against chosen ciphertext attacks. In: proceedings of STOC '90. (1990) 427–437
15. Bellare, M., Desai, A., Pointcheval, D., Rogaway, P.: Relations among notions of security for public-key encryption schemes. In: proceedings of CRYPTO '98, LNCS series, volume 1462. (1998) 26–45

A   Appendix

Theorem 3. *The directed graph in Figure 1 describes completely the relations between our security notions. ATT1 security implies ATT2 security if there is a path from ATT1 to ATT2. If there is no path from ATT1 to ATT2, then a cryptosystem with ATT1 security implies the existence of a ATT2 secure cryptosystem, which is not ATT1 secure.*

Sketch of proof. It is trivial to follow each arrow and see that it leads to a weaker security notion.

We list the constructions that can be used to separate the security notions. To show that ATT1 $\nrightarrow$ ATT2 we assume that (K, E, D) is an ATT1 secure cryptosystem and present (K', E', D') that is ATT1 secure but not ATT2 secure. K', E' will be as follows

Key generation: K' runs $(pk, sk) \leftarrow K()$. It also selects at random a seed s for a pseudorandom function PRF and a random nonce r. It returns $(pk' = (pk, r), sk' = (sk, r, s))$.
Encryption: $E'_{pk'}(m; r) = (0, E_{pk}(m))$.

Left is to describe how D' works, which we do in the table of inputs and corresponding outputs in the table below.

RCCA+PA1 $\nrightarrow$ CCA2 :
  $(0, y)$: $D_{sk}(y)$
  $(1, y)$: $\mathrm{PRF}_s(y)$
  $(2, p, y)$: If $p = \mathrm{PRF}_s(y)$ return $D_{sk}(y)$, else return invalid.
WRCCA+ATT $\nrightarrow$ RCCA, where ATT$\in${RPA1,RPA1+PA0,PA1}
  $(0, y)$: $D_{sk}(y)$
  $(1, y)$: $\mathrm{PRF}_s(y)$
  $(2, p, m, y)$: If $p = \mathrm{PRF}_s(y)$ and $m = D_{sk}(y)$ return m, else return invalid.

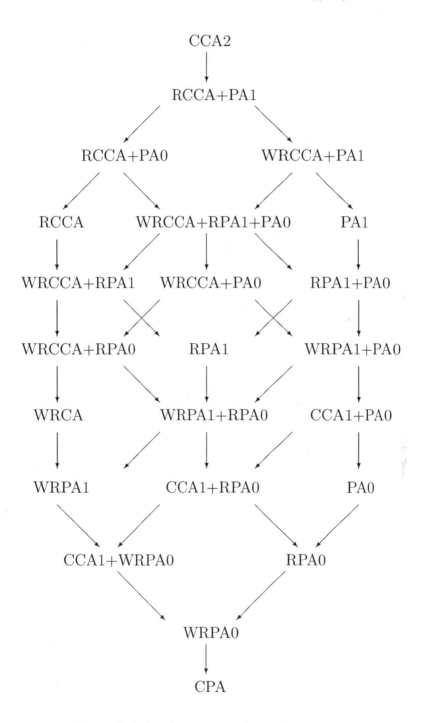

Fig. 1. Relations between security notions.

ATT $\not\to$ WRCCA, ATT$\in$\{PA1,RPA1+PA0,RPA1,WRPA1+RPA0,WRPA1\}

$(0,y) \qquad : D_{sk}(y)$

$(1,y) \qquad : \text{PRF}_s(y)$

$(2,p,m,y) : $ If $p = \text{PRF}_s(y)$ and $m = D_{sk}(y)$ return yes, else return invalid.

CCA1+ATT $\not\to$ WPA1, where ATT$\in$\{PA0,RPA0,WRPA0,nothing\}

$(0,y) \quad : D_{sk}(y)$

$(1,r) \quad : s$

$(2,s,y) : D_{sk}(y).$

ATT $\not\to$ CCA1, where ATT$\in$\{PA0,RPA0,WRPA0,CPA\}

$(0,y) : D_{sk}(y)$

$(1,r) : s$

$(2,s) : sk.$

ATT $\not\to$ WRPA0, where ATT$\in$\{CPA,CCA1\}

$(0,y) \qquad : D_{sk}(y)$

$(1,m,y) : $ If $m = D_{sk}(y)$ then return yes, else return invalid.

ATT $\not\to$ RPA0, where ATT$\in$\{WRPA0,CCA1+WRPA0,WRPA1,WRCCA\}

$(0,y) \qquad : D_{sk}(y)$

$(1,m,y) : $ If $m = D_{sk}(y)$ then return m, else return invalid.

ATT $\not\to$ PA0, where ATT$\in$\{RPA0,CCA1+RPA0,RPA1,WRCCA+RPA0\}

$(0,y) : D_{sk}(y)$

$(1,y) : D_{sk}(y).$

ATT $\not\to$ RPA1, ATT$\in$\{WRCCA,WRCCA+PA0,WRPA1+RPA0,WRPA1+PA0\}

$(0,y) \qquad : D_{sk}(y)$

$(1,r) \qquad : s$

$(2,s,m,y) : $ If $m = D_{sk}(y)$ then return m, else return invalid.

ATT $\not\to$ PA1, ATT$\in$\{WRCCA+RPA1+PA0,RPA1+PA0,RCCA+PA0\}

$(0,y) \qquad : D_{sk}(y)$

$(1,r) \qquad : s$

$(2,s,y) : D_{sk}(y).$

$\square$

It is interesting to note that Theorem 3 implies that a cryptosystem that is both IND-CCA1 secure and NM-CPA secure is not necessarily NM-CCA1 secure. This combination was not considered in [15].

Alternatives to Non-malleability:
Definitions, Constructions, and Applications
(Extended Abstract)

Philip MacKenzie[1], Michael K. Reiter[2], and Ke Yang[2]

[1] Bell Labs, Lucent Technologies, Murray Hill, NJ, USA;
philmac@research.bell-labs.com
[2] Carnegie Mellon University, Pittsburgh, PA, USA;
reiter@cmu.edu,yangke@cs.cmu.edu

Abstract. We explore whether non-malleability is necessary for the applications typically used to motivate it, and propose two alternatives. The first we call weak non-malleability (wnm) and show that it suffices to achieve secure contract bidding (the application for which non-malleability was initially introduced), despite being strictly weaker than non-malleability. The second we call tag-based non-malleability (tnm), and show that it suffices to construct an efficient universally-composable secure message transmission (SMT) protocol, for which the only previous solution was based on a public key encryption functionality whose security is equivalent to non-malleability. We also demonstrate constructions for wnm and tnm encryption schemes that are simpler than known constructions of non-malleable encryption schemes.

1 Introduction

Non-malleability [11] is a security condition for encryption schemes that requires, informally, that an attacker given a challenge ciphertext be unable to produce another, different ciphertext so that the plaintexts underlying the two ciphertexts are "meaningfully related" to each other. Non-malleability is the strongest commonly considered notion of security for encryption, being strictly stronger than indistinguishability [14] under chosen-plaintext or indifferent chosen-ciphertext ("lunchtime") attacks, and being equivalent to indistinguishability under adaptive chosen-ciphertext attacks [1].

In this paper we revisit the definition of non-malleability with an eye toward whether it is *necessary* for applications commonly used to motivate it. Our contributions in this study are twofold. First, we identify alternatives to non-malleability that suffice for applications where previously non-malleability seemed warranted. Second, we identify encryption schemes that implement these variants and that are conceptually simpler than known non-malleable schemes.

The alternative definitions that we propose deviate from non-malleability in different ways. The first notion, which we call *weak non-malleability* (wnm), identifies a point in the space of definitions strictly between non-malleability

M. Naor (Ed.): TCC 2004, LNCS 2951, pp. 171–190, 2004.

and indistinguishability (in those cases where there is room between them, i.e., under chosen-plaintext and lunchtime attacks). Informally, wnm allows mauling of a ciphertext c, but such that this mauling does not benefit the adversary. In particular, a mauling that produces a valid ciphertext c' would imply that the adversary has successfully guessed the plaintext corresponding to c, and thus for many natural applications, this mauling would not be useful. In other words, in such applications, wnm should suffice in place of non-malleability. As an example, we show that a wnm encryption scheme suffices to implement a secure contract bidding auction in the spirit of that originally used to (informally) motivate non-malleability [11]. Still, wnm does allow an adversary to produce a ciphertext c' that has a (very restricted) dependence of a given ciphertext c, and we can in fact show that wnm is a *strictly* weaker property than non-malleability. In addition, we show that this weaker property may be satisfied by very simple encryption schemes similar to those used in Bellare and Rogaway [2] to achieve the (even less stringent) property of indistinguishability under chosen-plaintext attacks [2].[1] These schemes assume p is a prime, H is a hash function (modeled by a random oracle in our security analyses) with range a group X with group operation ".", and f denotes a trapdoor permutation that constitutes the public key (with the trapdoor being the private key):

Mult-Range scheme. The encryption of m is $E(m) = <f(r), H(r) \cdot m>$ where r is chosen randomly (per encryption) from the domain of f, the plaintext space is an integer range $[a, b]$ satisfying $0 < a < b < p$, $a > (b - a)^2$ and $p > 2b^2$, and $X = \mathbb{Z}_p^*$ with $\cdot$ being multiplication in $\mathbb{Z}_p^*$.

Mult-Adjacent scheme. The encryption of m is $E(m) = <f(r), H(r) \cdot (m, m+1)>$ where r is chosen randomly (per encryption) from the domain of f, the plaintext space is $\mathbb{Z}_p^* \setminus \{p-1\}$, and $X = \mathbb{Z}_p^* \times \mathbb{Z}_p^*$ with group operation $\cdot$ being component-wise multiplication in $\mathbb{Z}_p^*$, i.e., $(x_0, x_1) \cdot (y_0, y_1) = (x_0 y_0, x_1 y_1)$.

Add-Square scheme. The encryption of m is $E(m) = <f(r), H(r) \cdot (m, m^2)>$, where the plaintext space is $\mathbb{Z}_p^*$, and $X = \mathbb{Z}_p \times \mathbb{Z}_p$ with group operation $\cdot$ being component-wise addition in $\mathbb{Z}_p$, i.e., $(x_0, x_1) \cdot (y_0, y_1) = (x_0 + y_0, x_1 + y_1)$.

For some intuition behind weak non-malleability, consider the Mult-Range scheme above. Without the range restriction on the plaintext space, this scheme would be completely malleable (similar to the first scheme introduced in [2]). However, simply by restricting the range of plaintexts (as opposed to, e.g., adding an additional hash for verification/redundancy, as is done in [2] to achieve non-malleability) we are able to achieve wnm. Informally, this is because any modification of a ciphertext (v, w) to (v, w') implies a multiplying factor w'/w for which there is only a single plaintext in the range that would be transformed into another plaintext in the range.

---

[1] While there exist efficient encryption systems that implement indistinguishability under adaptive chosen-ciphertext attacks (and thus non-malleability under these attacks, e.g., [2,8]), we are unaware of prior constructions that, like those listed here, so *simply* implement a property strictly stronger than indistinguishability (in this case, weak non-malleability) under chosen-plaintext and lunchtime attacks.

The second alternative to non-malleability that we propose is called *tag-based non-malleability* (tnm). Here, we structurally modify encryption and decryption to take an additional public string argument called a *tag*. Informally, tnm dictates that an adversary be unable to create a (ciphertext,tag) pair with plaintext related to that of the challenge ciphertext and with the tag being different from the challenge tag, even though it is able to obtain decryptions of (ciphertext,tag) pairs with any tag different from the challenge tag. We demonstrate the utility of tnm by using it to implement the "secure message transmission functionality" in the universal composability framework of [5], replacing the use of non-malleable encryption there, and arguably providing a more natural implementation. tnm also admits exceedingly simple implementations, e.g.:

Tag-based scheme. The encryption of m with tag t is $E(m,t) = <f(r), H(r,t)\cdot m>$ where r is chosen randomly (per encryption) from the domain of f. The plaintext space is $\mathbb{Z}_p^*$, and $X = \mathbb{Z}_p^*$ with $\cdot$ being multiplication in $\mathbb{Z}_p^*$.

We also present a tnm construction that is a (simpler) variation of the Cramer-Shoup encryption scheme [8,9]. The change in structure for encryption and decryption (specifically due to the tag) does not permit us to argue that tnm is definitionally weaker than non-malleability. However, given a non-malleable encryption scheme, it is trivial to implement a tnm scheme using it with no additional assumptions or loss in security. We also show how to implement a non-malleable scheme using a tnm scheme and a one-time signature scheme.

2   Preliminaries

Trapdoor Permutations [2,15] A *permutation generator* G_* is a probabilistic polynomial time algorithm that takes as input 1^k and outputs three polynomial-time algorithms (f, f^{-1}, d), the first two being deterministic, and the last being probabilistic. The range of $d(1^k)$ is required to be a subset of $\{0,1\}^k$, and f, f^{-1} are permutations over the range of $d(1^k)$, and are inverses of each other. G_* is a *trapdoor permutation generator* if it is a permutation generator such that for all non-uniform polynomial-time algorithms $\mathcal{A}$, $\Pr[(f, f^{-1}, d) \leftarrow G_*(1^k); x \leftarrow d(1^k); y \leftarrow f(x) : \mathcal{A}(f, d, y) = x]$ is negligible. It is commonly assumed that, for example, RSA is a trapdoor permutation.

Encryption schemes An *encryption scheme* Π is a triple (G, E, D) of algorithms, the first two being probabilistic, and all running in polynomial time. G takes as input 1^k and outputs a public key pair (pk, sk), i.e., $(pk, sk) \leftarrow G(1^k)$. E takes a public key pk and a message m as input and outputs an encryption c for m; we denote this $c \leftarrow E_{pk}(m)$. D takes a private key sk and a ciphertext c as input and returns either a message m such that c is a valid encryption of m, if such an m exists, and otherwise returns $\bot$; we denote this $m \leftarrow D_{sk}(c)$.

As discussed in Section 1, indistinguishability [14] is the most commonly studied goal for encryption. Here we adopt definitions ind-cpa, ind-cca1, and ind-cca2 from [1]. Below we give the definition of non-malleability from Dolev, Dwork and Naor [11], as written explicitly as the simulator-based non-malleable (snm) definition in Bellare and Sahai [4].[2] In this definition and throughout, we use atk to denote one of {cpa, cca1, cca2} and define oracles $\mathcal{O}_1$ and $\mathcal{O}_2$ as follows:

$$\text{atk} = \text{cpa} \Rightarrow \mathcal{O}_1(\cdot) = \epsilon, \mathcal{O}_2(\cdot) = \epsilon$$
$$\text{atk} = \text{cca1} \Rightarrow \mathcal{O}_1(\cdot) = D_{sk}(\cdot), \mathcal{O}_2(\cdot) = \epsilon$$
$$\text{atk} = \text{cca2} \Rightarrow \mathcal{O}_1(\cdot) = D_{sk}(\cdot), \mathcal{O}_2(\cdot) = D_{sk}(\cdot)$$

Definition 1 (snm-cpa, snm-cca1, snm-cca2). *Let* $\Pi = (G, E, D)$ *be an encryption scheme, let* R *be a relation, let* $\mathcal{A} = (\mathcal{A}_1, \mathcal{A}_2)$ *be an adversary, and let* $\mathcal{S} = (\mathcal{S}_1, \mathcal{S}_2)$ *be an algorithm (the "simulator"). For* $k \in \mathbb{N}$ *define* $\text{Adv}^{\text{snm-atk}}_{\mathcal{A},\mathcal{S},\Pi}(R, k) \overset{\text{def}}{=} \Pr[\text{Expt}^{\text{snm-atk}}_{\mathcal{A},\Pi}(R, k) = 1] - \Pr[\text{Expt}^{\text{snm-atk}}_{\mathcal{S},\Pi}(R, k) = 1]$, *where*

$\text{Expt}^{\text{snm-atk}}_{\mathcal{A},\Pi}(R, k):$	$\text{Expt}^{\text{snm-atk}}_{\mathcal{S},\Pi}(R, k):$
$(pk, sk) \leftarrow G(1^k)$	$(pk, sk) \leftarrow G(1^k)$
$(M, s_1, s_2) \leftarrow \mathcal{A}_1^{\mathcal{O}_1}(pk)$	$(M, s_1, s_2) \leftarrow \mathcal{S}_1(pk)$
$x \leftarrow M$	$x \leftarrow M$
$y \leftarrow E_{pk}(x)$	
$\mathbf{y} \leftarrow \mathcal{A}_2^{\mathcal{O}_2}(s_2, y)$	$\mathbf{y} \leftarrow \mathcal{S}_2(s_2)$
$\mathbf{x} \leftarrow D_{sk}(\mathbf{y})$	$\mathbf{x} \leftarrow D_{sk}(\mathbf{y})$
Return 1 iff $y \notin \mathbf{y} \wedge R(x, \mathbf{x}, M, s_1)$	Return 1 iff $R(x, \mathbf{x}, M, s_1)$

We say that Π *is secure in the sense of* snm-atk *for if for every polynomial* $q(k)$, *every* R *computable in time* $q(k)$, *every* $\mathcal{A}$ *that runs in time* $q(k)$ *and outputs a valid message space* M *samplable in time* $q(k)$, *there exists a polynomial-time algorithm* $\mathcal{S}$ *such that* $\text{Adv}^{\text{snm-atk}}_{\mathcal{A},\mathcal{S},\Pi}(R, k)$ *is negligible.*

Technically, for our definitions to hold with respect to random oracles we would need to explicitly include a random oracle in our experiments. However, this can be done in a standard way, and for readability it is not included.

3   Weak Non-malleability

3.1   Definition

Here we propose a definition for weak non-malleable (wnm) encryption schemes. As in Definition 1, a wnm-secure encryption scheme requires the existence of a simulator $\mathcal{S}$ (not given a challenge ciphertext y) that has roughly the same probability as an adversary $\mathcal{A}$ (given y) of generating a vector $\mathbf{y}$ of ciphertexts for which the plaintext vector $\mathbf{x}$ bears some relationship R with the plaintext x

---

[2] Actually we slightly modify the definition of [4] so as to not require that every element of $\mathbf{y}$ decrypt to a valid plaintext. This is needed for the equivalences stated in [4] to hold.

of y. In the wnm definition, the adversary experiment will take exactly the same form as that in Definition 1. The difference lies in the simulator experiment and the form of S. Specifically, S is permitted to make each element y_i of $\mathbf{y}$ contingent upon a "guess" z_i as to the value of x. That is, relation R tests x against a vector $\mathbf{x}$ where each element x_i is the plaintext of the corresponding y_i in $\mathbf{y}$ if either S guessed x or offered no guess (i.e., guessed $\bot$), and where x_i is $\bot$ otherwise.

It is easy to see that any snm-secure encryption scheme is also wnm-secure, since the wnm-simulator is simply given more power. It is perhaps not as easy to see that this power is sufficient to allow a wnm-secure scheme that is not snm-secure, but we will show that in fact this is the case. For example, the wnm-schemes presented in the introduction are not snm-secure in the random oracle model.[3]

The precise definition of wnm security is as follows.

Definition 2 (wnm-cpa, wnm-cca1, wnm-cca2). *Let $\Pi = (G, E, D)$ be an encryption scheme, let R be a relation, let $\mathcal{A} = (\mathcal{A}_1, \mathcal{A}_2)$ be an adversary, and let $S = (\mathcal{S}_1, \mathcal{S}_2)$ be an algorithm ("simulator"). For $k \in \mathbb{N}$ define*
$$\mathsf{Adv}^{\mathsf{wnm\text{-}atk}}_{\mathcal{A},S,\Pi}(R, k) \stackrel{\mathrm{def}}{=} \Pr[\mathsf{Expt}^{\mathsf{wnm\text{-}atk}}_{\mathcal{A},\Pi}(R, k) = 1] - \Pr[\mathsf{Expt}^{\mathsf{wnm\text{-}atk}}_{S,\Pi}(R, k) = 1], \text{ where}$$

$\mathsf{Expt}^{\mathsf{wnm\text{-}atk}}_{\mathcal{A},\Pi}(R, k)$:	$\mathsf{Expt}^{\mathsf{wnm\text{-}atk}}_{S,\Pi}(R, k)$:
$(pk, sk) \leftarrow G(1^k)$	$(pk, sk) \leftarrow G(1^k)$
$(M, s_1, s_2) \leftarrow \mathcal{A}_1^{\mathcal{O}_1}(pk)$	$(M, s_1, s_2) \leftarrow \mathcal{S}_1(pk)$
$x \leftarrow M$	$x \leftarrow M$
$y \leftarrow E_{pk}(x)$	
$\mathbf{y} \leftarrow \mathcal{A}_2^{\mathcal{O}_2}(s_2, y)$	$(\mathbf{y}, \mathbf{z}) \leftarrow \mathcal{S}_2(s_2)$
$\mathbf{x} \leftarrow D_{sk}(\mathbf{y})$	$\mathbf{x} \leftarrow D'_{sk}(\mathbf{y}, \mathbf{z}, x)$
Return 1 iff $(y \notin \mathbf{y}) \wedge R(x, \mathbf{x}, M, s_1)$	Return 1 iff $R(x, \mathbf{x}, M, s_1)$

and $D'_{sk}(\mathbf{y}, \mathbf{z}, x)$ returns the decryption of each $y_i \in \mathbf{y}$ for which $z_i = x$ or $z_i = \bot$, and returns $\bot$ for each other index. We say that Π is wnm-atk-secure if for every polynomial $q(k)$, and every $\mathcal{A}$ that runs in time $q(k)$ and outputs a valid message space M samplable in time $q(k)$, there exists a polynomial-time algorithm S such that for every R computable in time $q(k)$, $\mathsf{Adv}^{\mathsf{wnm\text{-}atk}}_{\mathcal{A},S,\Pi}(R, k)$ is negligible.

The proofs of the following lemmas will appear in the full version of the paper.

Lemma 1. *For any* atk $\in \{\mathsf{cpa}, \mathsf{cca1}, \mathsf{cca2}\}$, snm-atk $\Rightarrow$ wnm-atk $\Rightarrow$ ind-atk.

Lemma 2 (ind-cca1 $\not\Rightarrow$ wnm-cpa). *If there exists an* ind-cca1*-secure encryption scheme, then there exists an* ind-cca1*-secure encryption scheme that is not* wnm-cpa*-secure.*

---

[3] Actually, it is much easier to see that they are not comparison-based non-malleable (cnm) [4], and then use the result in [4] that simulation-based non-malleability implies comparison-based non-malleability. Also, note that our separation result in Lemma 3 holds not just in the random oracle model, but in the standard model.

Lemma 3 (wnm-cca1 $\not\Rightarrow$ snm-cpa). *If there exists an* snm-cca1-*secure encryption scheme, then there exists a* wnm-cca1-*secure encryption system that is not* snm-cpa-*secure.*

3.2 Constructions

In Section 1, we introduced several constructions for wnm-secure encryption, denoted "Mult-Range", "Mult-Adjacent", and "Add-Square". Our goal in this section will be to prove Lemma 4.

Lemma 4. *The Mult-Range, Mult-Adjacent, and Add-Square schemes are all* wnm-atk *secure, for* atk $\in \{$cpa, cca1$\}$.

In fact, we prove a more general result. We show a general construction of weakly non-malleable encryption schemes, of which the three constructions above are special cases. We first introduce a notion called "uniquely identifiable subset," which we will use in our general construction.

We say a sequence of sets $X = \{X_k\}_{k>0}$, $X_k \subseteq \{0,1\}^*$, is *efficient* if there exists a polynomial $p(\cdot)$ such that membership in X_k can be tested in time $p(k)$. For simplicity, we often abuse notation by referring to the sequence $\{X_k\}$ as "the efficient set X" and omitting the subscript k, although it should be understood that X is a sequence of sets. We extend this notation to groups, too, i.e., when we say "X is an efficient finite group," it should be understood that $X = \{X_k\}$ is in fact a sequence of finite groups, whose membership can be efficiently determined. Furthermore, for efficient sets X and S, we use the phrase "S is a subset of X" as shorthand for "for every k, S_k is a subset of X_k."

Definition 3 (Unique Identifiability). *Let X be an efficient finite group with identity element e, and let S be an efficient subset of X. We say S is a* uniquely identifiable subset of X, *if for every $\lambda \in X \backslash \{e\}$, there exists at most one $x_\lambda \in S$, such that $\lambda \cdot x_\lambda \in S$ and for any other $x \in S, x \neq x_\lambda$, $\lambda \cdot x \notin S$. Here "·" is the group operation. We call x_λ the* soft spot *for λ. If no such x_λ exists, we write this as $x_\lambda = \bot$. We denote the soft spot of λ by* ss(λ).

Furthermore, we say S is an efficient uniquely identifiable subset of X, *if there exists a polynomial-time algorithm A that outputs x_λ on input λ.*

Putting the definition in our context, X is the space of all messages and S is the set of all "valid" messages. The group operation "·" is a "mauling" function the converts an encryption of x to an encryption of $\lambda \cdot x$, and we call λ the "mauling factor." The unique identifiability indicates, therefore, for every mauling factor λ, there is at most one valid message x_λ that can be mauled into another valid one (all other valid messages are mapped to invalid ones). For an efficient uniquely identifiable subset, one can in fact find x_λ efficiently.

Next, we give several examples of efficient uniquely identifiable subsets, which are closely related to the Mult-Range, Mult-Adjacent, and the Add-Square schemes.

Example 1 (Mult-Adjacent). Let $X = \mathbb{Z}_p^* \times \mathbb{Z}_p^*$ with the group operation being component-wise multiplication in $\mathbb{Z}_p^*$, i.e., $(x_0, x_1) \cdot (y_0, y_1) = (x_0 \cdot y_0, \ x_1 \cdot y_1)$. Let $S = \{(x, x+1) \mid x \in \mathbb{Z}_p^*\}$.

Example 2 (Add-Square). Let $X = \mathbb{Z}_p \times \mathbb{Z}_p$, with the group operation being component-wise addition in $\mathbb{Z}_p$, i.e., $(x_0, x_1) \cdot (y_0, y_1) = (x_0 + y_0, \ x_1 + y_1)$. Let $S = \{(x, x^2) \mid x \in \mathbb{Z}_p\}$.

Example 3 (Mult-Range). Let $X = \mathbb{Z}_p^*$ with multiplication as the group operation. Let $S = \{a, ..., b\}$, where $a > (b-a)^2$ and $p > 2b^2$.

Lemma 5. *All three examples above are efficient uniquely identifiable systems.*

The proof of Lemma 5 is straightforward for Mult-Adjacent and Add-Square; Mult-Range is not straightforward, however. The proof will be provided in the full version of the paper.

Now we present our general construction of wnm encryption schemes.

Construction 1 *Let X be an efficient finite group. Let S be an efficient uniquely identifiable subset of X, and $H : \{0,1\}^* \to X$ be a hash function. Let G_* be a trapdoor permutation generator. We construct an encryption scheme as follows. G runs G_* to get (f, f^{-1}, d), and sets $pk = <f, d>$, and $sk = f^{-1}$. The plaintext space of E_{pk} is S.[4] To encrypt a message m, $E_{pk}(m)$ generates $r \leftarrow d(1^k)$ and returns $<f(r), H(r) \cdot m>$, where "$\cdot$" is the group operation in X. To decrypt a ciphertext $c = (\alpha, \beta)$, $D_{sk}(c)$ computes $m = \beta \cdot (H(f^{-1}(\alpha))^{-1})$, returns m if $m \in S$, and $\perp$ otherwise.*

Lemma 6. *Following the notation in Construction 1, if $H(\cdot)$ is a random oracle, then Construction 1 is wnm-atk secure, for atk $\in \{\mathsf{cpa}, \mathsf{cca1}\}$.*

The proof of this result is in Appendix A.1.

3.3   Applications

In this section we show that weak non-malleability suffices to implement a secure contract bidding system between two bidders. Intuitively, in an ideal contract bidding system, each of two bidders would submit its bid to a trusted authority through a secure channel (so that the messages are both secret and authenticated). In a real contract bidding system, however, it may be the case that a dishonest bidder may be able to see the encrypted bid from an honest bidder before it submits its own bid. In either case, we assume there is a

---

[4] More precisely, we assume a one-to-one correspondence between plaintexts and elements of S, and efficient encoding and decoding functions to map plaintexts to and from elements of S.

public "award" function over these input bids. Depending on the application, the award function varies. For example, the simplest award function can be Award$((x_0, x_1)) = (y_0, y_1)$, where $y_i = x_i$ if $x_i = \min\{x_0, x_1\}$ and $y_i = 0$ otherwise. This indicates the rule that the lowest bidder wins, with the award being his bid, and the other bidder loses and thus has zero award. (We assume a unique minimum between the bids, otherwise nobody wins.) Other forms of the award function exist.

We specify our contract bidding system as follows:

Setup: A bidding system consisting of two bidders B_0, B_1 and an award function Award. There is also a bidding upper bound $U > 0$, such that the only valid bids are integers between 0 and U. Both bidders are given U and the award function Award.

Award function: The function Award : $\{\bot, 0, 1..., U\}^2 \rightarrow \{0, 1, ..., U\}^2$ takes the bids from the bidders and computes their awards, respectively.[5] We say an award function is *fair*, if for any $\mathbf{x} = (x_0, x_1)$ and any $i \in \{0, 1\}$, Award$(\mathbf{x}|_{\bot \rightarrow [i]})[i] \leq$ Award$(\mathbf{x})[i]$, and Award$(\mathbf{x}|_{x_{1-i} \rightarrow [i]})[i] \leq$ Award$(\mathbf{x})[i]$. Here we use $\mathbf{x}|_{y \rightarrow [i]}$ to indicate the vector obtained by replacing the ith entry of $\mathbf{x}$ by y and we use $\mathbf{x}[i]$ to indicate the ith entry of $\mathbf{x}$. Intuitively, the fairness indicates that B_i would not gain any advantage in profit by changing his bid to $\bot$ or to B_{1-i}'s bid. We note that fairness is a reasonable requirement for bidding systems to be "useful."

Real Adversary: To model security, we consider an adversary $\mathcal{A} = (\mathcal{A}_1, \mathcal{A}_2)$ that corrupts bidder B_1. $\mathcal{A}_1$ receives the public key pk and U, and outputs a polynomial-time samplable distribution M of bids, from which a bid bid_0 is chosen for B_0. $\mathcal{A}_2$ is then given the ciphertext of bid_0 and outputs encrypted bid ebid_1 for B_1. The profit of the adversary is the award of B_1.

Definition 4 (Secure Contract Bidding). *Let* CBS *be a contract bidding system with bidding upper bound U and encryption scheme $\Pi = (G, E, D)$. CBS is secure if for every fair award function* Award, *every polynomial $q(k)$, every adversary $\mathcal{A} = (\mathcal{A}_1, \mathcal{A}_2)$ that runs in time $q(k)$, there exists a polynomial-time simulator $\mathcal{S} = (\mathcal{S}_1, \mathcal{S}_2)$ such that* $\mathsf{Adv}^{\mathrm{profit}}_{\mathcal{A}, \mathcal{S}, \mathsf{CBS}}(k)$ *is negligible,[6] where*

$$\mathsf{Adv}^{\mathrm{profit}}_{\mathcal{A}, \mathcal{S}, \mathsf{CBS}}(k) \stackrel{\mathrm{def}}{=} E[\mathsf{Expt}^{\mathrm{real}}_{\mathcal{A}, \mathsf{CBS}}(k) - \mathsf{Expt}^{\mathrm{ideal}}_{\mathcal{S}, \mathsf{CBS}}(k)], \text{ and}$$

$\mathsf{Expt}^{\mathrm{real}}_{\mathcal{A}, \mathsf{CBS}}(k)$:	$\mathsf{Expt}^{\mathrm{ideal}}_{\mathcal{S}, \mathsf{CBS}}(k)$:
$(pk, sk) \leftarrow G(1^k)$	
$(M, s) \leftarrow \mathcal{A}_1(pk, U)$	$(M, s) \leftarrow \mathcal{S}_1(U)$
$\mathsf{bid}_0 \leftarrow M$	$\mathsf{bid}_0 \leftarrow M$
$\mathsf{ebid}_0 \leftarrow E_{pk}(\mathsf{bid}_0)$	
$\mathsf{ebid}_1 \leftarrow \mathcal{A}_2(\mathsf{ebid}_0, s)$	
$\mathsf{bid}_1 \leftarrow D_{sk}(\mathsf{ebid}_1)$	$\mathsf{bid}_1 \leftarrow \mathcal{S}_2(s)$
return Award$((\mathsf{bid}_0, \mathsf{bid}_1))[1]$	return Award$((\mathsf{bid}_0, \mathsf{bid}_1))[1]$

---

[5] We insist that the award function be a positive function. However, this is entirely arbitrary, since one can always "shift" the award function by a constant without changing its nature.

[6] It may be negative, in which case we also consider it to be negligible.

It is clear that if the encryption scheme Π is malleable, then the system might not be secure. For example, consider the scheme where message m is encrypted as $<f(r), H(r) + m \bmod p>$, where $f(\cdot)$ is a trapdoor permutation and H a random oracle. It is an ind-cpa-secure scheme, but the real bidding system is not secure, since an adversary seeing the bid $<\alpha, \beta>$ from bidder B_0 can submit bid $<\alpha, \beta - 1>$, and underbid B_0 by 1. It is also obvious that if Π is snm-cpa-secure, then the bidding system is secure. The next theorem shows that in fact wnm-cpa-security suffices.

Theorem 1. *Let $\Pi = (G, E, D)$ be a* wnm-*cpa-secure encryption scheme, with a domain that includes the integer range $[0, U]$ where U is polynomially bounded by k. Then a contract bidding system* CBS *with bidding upper bound U and encryption scheme Π is secure.*

The proof of this result is in Appendix A.2. We mention that our result only applies to the case of a single auction, and specifically does not claim that repeated auctions will be secure if they use the same encryption scheme. Obviously, for repeated auctions to be secure, we would need some kind of cca2 security for our encryption scheme.

We also mention that the result does not apply to contract bidding schemes with multiple bidders that may collude. Intuitively, this is because they may each make guesses which cover the possible choices of the honest bidder, and a wrong guess for one party does not reduce the award of the party that guesses correctly. To solve the problem with multiple bidders using a wnm-secure cryptosystem, one could either allow *randomization* in the bids (e.g., each bid would be of the form (bid, r), where $r \leftarrow \{0, 1\}^k$, which would ensure that the adversary has a negligible chance of guessing the full plaintext), or one could change the model to levy *penalties* for invalid bids.

4   Tag-Based Non-malleability

In this section, we introduce tag-based non-malleability as an alternative to standard non-malleability. Informally, in a tag-based encryption system, the encryption and decryption operations take an additional "tag." A tag is simply a binary string of appropriate length (i.e., its length has to be polynomially bounded by the security parameter), and need not have any particular internal structure. We define security for tag-based encryption in manners analogous to security for standard encryption systems. In particular, we define *tag-based non-malleability* (Definition 5) and *tag-based indistinguishability* (Definition 6) with respect to cpa, cca1, and cca2 attacks. The only changes we make to the definitions for standard encryption are: (i) in a cca2 attack, instead of requiring that the adversary $\mathcal{A}$ not query the decryption oracle with the ciphertext y that $\mathcal{A}$ receives as a challenge, we require that $\mathcal{A}$ not query the decryption oracle with a (ciphertext,tag) pair using the same tag with which y was encrypted; (ii) for tag-based non-malleability, instead of requiring that $\mathcal{A}_2$ not output the ciphertext y it receives, we require that $\mathcal{A}_2$ not output any (ciphertext,tag) pair for decryption using the tag with which y was encrypted. Informally, one simply changes the "equality of two ciphertexts" in the standard definitions to "equality of *the tags of* two ciphertexts," and we have a tag-based definition.

4.1 Definition

Tag-based encryption schemes A *tag-based encryption scheme* Π is a triple (G, E, D) of algorithms, the first two being probabilistic, and all running in expected polynomial time. G takes as input 1^k and outputs a public key pair (pk, sk), i.e., $(pk, sk) \leftarrow G(1^k)$. E takes a public key pk, a message m, and a tag t as input and outputs an encryption c for m associated with t; we denote this $c \leftarrow E_{pk}(m, t)$. D takes a private key sk, a ciphertext c, and a tag t as input and returns either a message m such that c is a valid encryption of m associated with t, if such an m exists, and otherwise returns $\bot$; we denote this $m \leftarrow D_{sk}(c, t)$.

Definition 5 (tnm-cpa, tnm-cca1, tnm-cca2). *Let* $\Pi = (G, E, D)$ *be an encryption scheme, let* R *be a relation, let* $\mathcal{A} = (\mathcal{A}_1, \mathcal{A}_2)$ *be an adversary, and let* $\mathcal{S} = (\mathcal{S}_1, \mathcal{S}_2)$ *be an algorithm (the "simulator"). For* $k \in \mathbb{N}$ *define* $\mathsf{Adv}^{\mathsf{tnm\text{-}atk}}_{\mathcal{A}, \mathcal{S}, \Pi}(R, k) \overset{\text{def}}{=} \Pr[\mathsf{Expt}^{\mathsf{tnm\text{-}atk}}_{\mathcal{A}, \Pi}(R, k) = 1] - \Pr[\mathsf{Expt}^{\mathsf{tnm\text{-}atk}}_{\mathcal{S}, \Pi}(R, k) = 1]$, *where*

$\mathsf{Expt}^{\mathsf{tnm\text{-}atk}}_{\mathcal{A}, \Pi}(R, k) :$	$\mathsf{Expt}^{\mathsf{tnm\text{-}atk}}_{\mathcal{S}, \Pi}(R, k) :$
$(pk, sk) \leftarrow G(1^k)$	$(pk, sk) \leftarrow G(1^k)$
$(M, t, s_1, s_2) \leftarrow \mathcal{A}_1^{\mathcal{O}_1}(pk)$	$(M, t, s_1, s_2) \leftarrow \mathcal{S}_1(pk)$
$x \leftarrow M$	$x \leftarrow M$
$y \leftarrow E_{pk}(x, t)$	
$(\mathbf{y}, \mathbf{t}) \leftarrow \mathcal{A}_2^{\mathcal{O}_2}(s_2, y, t)$	$(\mathbf{y}, \mathbf{t}) \leftarrow \mathcal{S}_2(s_2, t)$
$\mathbf{x} \leftarrow D_{sk}(\mathbf{y}, \mathbf{t})$	$\mathbf{x} \leftarrow D_{sk}(\mathbf{y}, \mathbf{t})$
Return 1 iff $(t \notin \mathbf{t}) \wedge R(x, \mathbf{x}, M, s_1)$	Return 1 iff $R(x, \mathbf{x}, M, s_1)$

We require that $\mathcal{O}_2$ *not be queried with the* t *given to* $\mathcal{A}_2$. *We say that* Π *is secure in the sense of* tnm-atk *if for every polynomial* $q(k)$, *every* R *computable in time* $q(k)$, *and every* $\mathcal{A}$ *that runs in time* $q(k)$ *and outputs a valid message space* M *samplable in time* $q(k)$, *there exists a polynomial-time algorithm* $\mathcal{S}$ *such that* $\mathsf{Adv}^{\mathsf{tnm\text{-}atk}}_{\mathcal{A}, \mathcal{S}, \Pi}(R, k)$ *is negligible.*

Definition 6 (tind-cpa,tind-cca1,tind-cca2). *Let* $\Pi = (G, E, D)$ *be a tag-based encryption scheme, and let* $\mathcal{A} = (\mathcal{A}_1, \mathcal{A}_2)$ *be an adversary. For* $k \in \mathbb{N}$ *define* $\mathsf{Adv}^{\mathsf{tind\text{-}atk}}_{\mathcal{A}, \Pi}(k) \overset{\text{def}}{=} 2 \cdot \Pr[\mathsf{Expt}^{\mathsf{tind\text{-}atk}}_{\mathcal{A}, \Pi}(k) = 1] - 1$ *where*

$\mathsf{Expt}^{\mathsf{tind\text{-}atk}}_{\mathcal{A}, \Pi}(k) :$
$(pk, sk) \leftarrow G(1^k)$
$(x_0, x_1, t, s) \leftarrow \mathcal{A}_1^{\mathcal{O}_1}(pk)$
$b \overset{R}{\leftarrow} \{0, 1\}$
$y \leftarrow E_{pk}(x_b, t)$
$b' \leftarrow \mathcal{A}_2^{\mathcal{O}_2}(x_0, x_1, t, s, y)$
Return 1 iff $b = b'$

We require that $|x_0| = |x_1|$, and that $\mathcal{O}_2$ is not queried with tag t. We say that Π is secure in the sense of tind-atk *if for every polynomial $q(k)$ and every adversary $\mathcal{A}$ that runs in time $q(k)$, $\mathsf{Adv}_{\mathcal{A},\Pi}^{\mathsf{tind-atk}}(k)$ is negligible.*

Theorem 2 (tnm-atk $\Rightarrow$ tind-atk). *If an encryption scheme is* tnm-atk-*secure, then it is* tind-atk-*secure, for* atk $\in$ {cpa, cca1, cca2}.

4.2   Constructions

We give two constructions of tag-based encryption schemes, both achieving tnm-cca2-security. The first one is based one-way trapdoor permutations in the random oracle model. It is similar to the semantically secure (ind-cpa) encryption scheme from Bellare and Rogaway [2], but enjoys a higher level of security. The second is a modification of the Cramer-Shoup scheme [8,9], but simpler.

Construction 2 *Let G_* be a trapdoor permutation generator. Let X be a finite group and $H : \{0,1\}^* \to X$ a hash function. We construct an encryption scheme as follows. G runs G_* to get (f, f^{-1}, d), and sets $pk = <f, d>$, and $sk = f^{-1}$. All messages are restricted to be elements in X. To encrypt a message m with tag t, $E_{pk}(m)$ generates $r \leftarrow d(1^k)$ and returns $<f(r), H(r,t) \cdot m>$, where ".". is the group operation in X. To decrypt a ciphertext $c = (\alpha, \beta)$, $D_{sk}(c)$ returns $m = \beta \cdot (H(f^{-1}(\alpha), t)^{-1})$.*

Lemma 7. *Let H be a random oracle. If f is a trapdoor permutation, then the scheme in Construction 2 is* tnm-cca2-*secure.*

The intuition behind the proof of Lemma 7 is that the simulator can simulate the decryption oracles using the knowledge of the random oracle queries, and the fact that the adversary cannot make an $\mathcal{O}_2(\cdot)$ query with the same tag as in the challenge encryption. Details will be given in the full version.

Construction 3 *Let G_q be a finite group in which the DDH assumption holds.[7] We define an encryption scheme as follows.*

$G_{CS}(G_q)$: *Let g be the generator of G_q (included in the description of G_q). Generate $g_2 \xleftarrow{R} G_q$ and $a, b, c, d, e \xleftarrow{R} \mathbb{Z}_q$, and set $U \leftarrow g^a(g_2)^b$, $V \leftarrow g^c(g_2)^d$, and $W \leftarrow g^e$. Let the public key be $<g, g_2, U, V, W>$ and the secret key be $<a, b, c, d, e>$.*

$E_{<g,g_2,U,V,W>}(m,t)$: *Generate $r \xleftarrow{R} \mathbb{Z}_q$ and $x \leftarrow g^r$, $y \leftarrow (g_2)^r$, $w \leftarrow W^r m$, and $v \leftarrow U^r V^{rt}$. Return $<x, y, w, v>$ as the ciphertext.*

$D_{<a,b,c,d,e>}(<x,y,w,v>,t)$: *If $v \neq x^{a+ct}y^{b+dt}$, return $\bot$, else return w/x^e.*

---

[7] Note that one possible group G_q may be found by generating a large prime p such that q divides $p - 1$, and letting G_q be the subgroup of order q in $\mathbb{Z}_p^*$.

Informally, our construction removes the collision-resistant hash function from the original Cramer-Shoup construction, and replaces the hash value $\alpha = H(x, y, w)$ by the tag t.[8]

Lemma 8. *The encryption scheme in Construction 3 is* tnm-cca2-*secure.*

The proof of this lemma almost directly follows the proof of security for the original Cramer-Shoup construction; we omit it here.

4.3   Applications

Intuitively, tag-based encryption schemes (and in particular, tnm schemes) are useful in systems that already have authentication, i.e., in systems where Bob cannot impersonate Alice and send messages using Alice's identity. We stress that even with authentication, we still need non-malleability. For example, in the contract-bidding scenario in both [11] and the previous section, we still need to make sure that Bob cannot underbid Alice by mauling her message. With a tnm system, we can use the sender's identity as the tag to achieve this goal. Suppose Alice sends a encrypted message $c = E_{pk}(m, \mathsf{Alice})$ to Charlie. A malicious Bob may be able to maul c into another ciphertext with the same tag, i.e., Alice — this is allowed in the definition — but this would not be useful for him since he cannot fake Alice's identity. Bob needs to produce some message with the tag Bob, but tnm stipulates that Bob will not have any advantage in doing so. To demonstrate this, we show how to use a tnm-cca2 scheme (in fact, a tind-cca2 scheme) to construct a protocol that realizes the *secure message transmission* functionality in the $\mathcal{F}_{\mathrm{AUTH}}$-hybrid model, in the universal composability framework. Previously, this was done using an ind-cca2 encryption scheme [5].

Universal-composability framework. The universal composability framework was proposed by Canetti [5] for defining the security and composition of protocols. To define security one first specifies an *ideal functionality* using a trusted party that describes the desired behavior of the protocol. Then one proves that a particular protocol operating in a real-life model securely realizes this ideal functionality. Here we briefly summarize the framework.

A (real-life) protocol π is defined as a set of n interactive Turing Machines $P_1, \ldots, P_n$, designating the n parties in the protocol. It operates in the presence of an environment $\mathcal{Z}$ and an adversary $\mathcal{A}$, both of which are also modeled as interactive Turing Machines. The environment $\mathcal{Z}$ provides inputs and receives outputs from honest parties, and may communicate with $\mathcal{A}$. $\mathcal{A}$ controls (and may view) all communication between the parties. (Note that this models asynchronous communication on open point-to-point channels.) We will assume that messages are authenticated, and thus $\mathcal{A}$ may not insert or modify messages between honest parties. (This feature could be added to an unauthenticated model

---

[8] We assume that $t \in \mathbb{Z}_q$. Otherwise, we would need a collision-resistant hash function to hash the tag.

using a message authentication functionality as described in [5].) $\mathcal{A}$ also may corrupt parties, in which case it obtains the internal state of the party.

The ideal process with respect to a functionality $\mathcal{F}$, is defined for n parties $P_1, \ldots, P_n$, an environment $\mathcal{Z}$, and an (ideal-process) adversary $\mathcal{S}$. However, $P_1, \ldots, P_n$ are now dummy parties that simply forward (over secure channels) inputs received from $\mathcal{Z}$ to $\mathcal{F}$, and forward (again over secure channels) outputs received from $\mathcal{F}$ to $\mathcal{Z}$. Thus the ideal process is a trivially secure protocol with the input-output behavior of $\mathcal{F}$.

UC secure message transmission. The functionality $\mathcal{F}_{\mathrm{M-SMT}}$ is given in Figure 1. Intuitively, this functionality allows multiple parties to send messages securely to a single receiver. Both the secrecy and the integrity of the messages are guaranteed. See [5] for more discussions.

$\mathcal{F}_{\mathrm{M-SMT}}$ proceeds as follows, running with parties $P_1, \ldots, P_n$, and an adversary $\mathcal{A}$:

- In the first activation, expect to receive a value (**receiver**, id) from some party P_i. Then send (**receiver**, id, P_i) to the all parties and the adversary. ¿From now on, ignore all (**receiver**, id) values.
- Upon receiving a value (**send**, id, m) from some party P_j, send (id, P_j, m) to P_i and ($id, P_j, |m|$) to the adversary.

Fig. 1. Functionality $\mathcal{F}_{\mathrm{M-SMT}}$

Canetti [5] constructed a protocol that securely realizes this functionality in the $(\mathcal{F}_{\mathrm{AUTH}}, \mathcal{F}_{\mathrm{PKE}})$-hybrid model. He also showed that any ind-cca2 encryption scheme can securely realize the $\mathcal{F}_{\mathrm{PKE}}$ functionality. Therefore, one can construct a protocol using an ind-cca2 encryption scheme to securely realize $\mathcal{F}_{\mathrm{M-SMT}}$ in the $\mathcal{F}_{\mathrm{AUTH}}$-hybrid model. Here, we show that one can instead use a tag-based tind-cca2 encryption scheme.

Given a tind-cca2 encryption scheme $\Pi = (G, E, D)$, the protocol σ runs as follows. In this description, we include the identity of the receiver in the session identifier. (i) When a party P_i receives an input (**receiver**, $id|P_i$), it runs $(pk, sk) \leftarrow G(1^k)$, and sends (key, $id|P_i, pk$) to all other parties using $\mathcal{F}_{\mathrm{AUTH}}$. Any messages of this type with an identifier not in the correct format are ignored. (ii) On receiving the first message $(P_{i'}, P_j, (\text{key}, id|P_{i'}, pk'))$ from $\mathcal{F}_{\mathrm{AUTH}}$, P_j records $(P_{i'}, id, pk')$ and outputs (**receiver**, $id|P_{i'}, P_{i'}$). Any messages of this type with an identifier not in the correct format are ignored. Subsequent messages of this type with identifier $id|P_{i'}$ are ignored. (iii) After this, when P_j receives an input (**send**, $id|P_{i'}, m$), P_j runs $c \leftarrow E_{pk'}(m, P_j)$, and invokes $\mathcal{F}_{\mathrm{AUTH}}$ to send (msg, $id|P_{i'}, c$) to $P_{i'}$. (iv) On receiving a message $(P_j, P_i, (\text{msg}, id|P_i, c))$ from $\mathcal{F}_{\mathrm{AUTH}}$, P_i runs $m \leftarrow D_{sk}(c, P_j)$ and if $m \neq \bot$, outputs $(id|P_i, P_j, m)$. Intuitively, the protocol uses the identity of the senders as the tag for the encryption.

Theorem 3. *The protocol σ securely realizes the SMT functionality in the* $\mathcal{F}_{\text{AUTH}}$ *hybrid model, assuming static corruptions.*

The proof of Theorem 3 is in Appendix A.3.

4.4 Relation to Standard Definitions

We study the relation between the tag-based definitions and the standard ones. First, we note that they are not directly comparable, due to the structural difference in encryption and decryption. However, given a standard encryption scheme $\Pi = (G, E, D)$, it is straightforward to construct a tag-based scheme $\Pi' = (G', E', D')$ with the same security as follows. G' is the same as G; $E'_{pk}(m, t)$ calls $E_{pk}(m \circ t)$, where $x \circ y$ denotes a canonical encoding of the concatenation of two binary strings that can be uniquely parsed; $D'_{sk}(c, t)$ calls $(m, t') \leftarrow D_{sk}(c)$ to and returns m if $t = t'$ and $\perp$ otherwise. It is easy to check that Π' enjoys the same level of security (in the sense of Definition 5) as Π (in the sense of Definition 1).

Interestingly, the other direction also holds: given a tag-based scheme, one can construct a standard scheme, using a strong one-time signature scheme [20].

Construction 4 *Let* $\Pi = (G, E, D)$ *be a tag-based encryption scheme. Let* SIG = (sig_gen, sig_sign, sig_verify) *be a strong one-time signature scheme. We construct a standard scheme* $\Pi' = (G', E', D')$ *as follows.* $G' = G$. *To encrypt massage* m *using* pk, *generate a signing/verification key pair* (sig_vk, sig_sk) ← sig_gen(1^k); *encrypt* m *using* sig_vk *as the tag, i.e.,* $c \leftarrow E_{pk}(m, \text{sig\_vk})$; *sign* c *using* sig_sk, *i.e.,* $s \leftarrow$ sig_sign(sk, c); *and output* (sig_vk, c, s) *as the encryption. To decrypt a ciphertext* (sig_vk, c, s), *verify that* s *is a valid signature of* c *with respect to* sig_vk; *if not, output* $\perp$; *if so, return* $D_{sk}(c, \text{sig\_vk})$.

Theorem 4. *For* atk ∈ {cpa, cca1, cca2}: *if* Π *is* tnm-atk *secure, then* Π' *is* snm-atk *secure; and if* Π *is* tind-atk *secure, then* Π' *is* ind-atk *secure.*

The proof of this result will be given in the full version.

Construction 4 is essentially the construction first shown in [11] and later used in [20,10,17,6] to obtain non-malleable encryption schemes, except that we explicitly separate the underlying tag-based scheme from the "wrapper" that uses the one-time signature scheme. Thus, in each of these papers, there is an implicit tag-based non-malleable encryption scheme.[9] We illustrate this with the scheme of Lindell [17], which we denote as Π_L. In Π_L, an encryption of message m is a tuple $<c_0, c_1, pk_0, pk_1, r, \text{sig\_vk}, \sigma, s>$. Here c_0 and c_1 are two encryptions of m using two ind-cpa systems with public keys pk_0 and pk_1, respectively; sig_vk is a "fresh" verification key of a strong one-time signature

---

[9] In the (independent and concurrent) result of [6], there is actually an explicit *identity-based encryption (IBE) scheme* which corresponds to our tag-based non-malleable encryption scheme. They essentially prove the cca2 case of Theorem 4. (Note: their cpa-secure IBE scheme corresponds to our cca2-secure tnm scheme.)

scheme; r is a random string; σ is an NIZK proof that either c_0 and c_1 are the encryption of the same message, or r is the commitment of sig_vk; s is a signature of the tuple $<c_0, c_1, pk_0, pk_1, \text{sig\_vk}, r, \sigma>$. Then in the underlying tag-based encryption scheme Π, an encryption of message m with tag t is the tuple $<c_0, c_1, pk_0, pk_1, r, t, \sigma>$, where c_0, c_1, pk_0, pk_1, and r are all the same as before, and σ becomes an NIZK proof that either c_0 and c_1 are the encryptions of the same message, or r is the commitment of t. It is easy to verify that Π is tnm-cca2-secure. In fact, one can prove the security for Π almost exactly the same way as for the security proof of Π_L, observing that the use of the strong one-time signature in Π_L is solely for enforcing that an adversary will not make a query to the decryption oracle with a ciphertext having the same verification key. Since in the tag-based system Π, the verification key is replaced by the tag, by definition, the adversary cannot query the decryption oracle with a ciphertext having the same tag. So in fact the proof for the security of Π is even simpler than the proof for for Π_L. Furthermore, Π_L is exactly the transformed version of protocol Π under Construction 4. Therefore, one could obtain an alternative proof of security for Π_L by pluggin Π into Theorem 4.

In the full version of this paper, we will show that many known relations between standard security definitions translate to analogous relations between tag-based definitions.

References

1. M. Bellare, A. Desai, D. Pointcheval, and P. Rogaway. Relations among notions of security for public-key encryption schemes. In *Advances in Cryptology—CRYPTO '98* (Lecture Notes in Computer Science 1462), pp. 26–45, 1998.
2. M. Bellare and P. Rogaway. Random oracles are practical: A paradigm for designing efficient protocols. In 1st *ACM Conf. on Comp. and Comm. Security*, pp. 62–73, 1993.
3. M. Bellare and P. Rogaway. Optimal asymmetric encryption. In *Advances in Cryptology—EUROCRYPT '94* (Lecture Notes in Computer Science 950), pp. 92–111, 1995.
4. M. Bellare and A. Sahai. Non-Malleable Encryption: Equivalence between Two Notions, and an Indistinguishability-Based Characterization. In *Advances in Cryptology—CRYPTO '99* (Lecture Notes in Computer Science 1666), pp. 519–536, 1999.
5. R. Canetti. Universally Composable Security: A new paradigm for cryptographic protocols. http://eprint.iacr.org/2000/067, Extended abstract in 42nd FOCS, 2001.
6. R. Canetti, S. Halevi and J. Katz. Chosen-Ciphertext Security from Identity-Based Encryption. In *ePrint archive*, Report 2003/182.
7. R. Canetti, Y. Lindell, R. Ostrovsky and A. Sahai. Universally composable two-party computation. In *STOC 02*, pp. 494–503, 2002. The full version in *ePrint archive*, Report 2002/140.
8. R. Cramer and V. Shoup. A practical public key cryptosystem provably secure against adaptive chosen ciphertext attack. In *Advances in Cryptology—CRYPTO '98* (Lecture Notes in Computer Science 1462), pp. 13–25, 1998.

9. R. Cramer and V. Shoup. Universal hash proofs and a paradigm for adaptive chosen ciphertext secure public-key encryption. In *Advances in Cryptology—EUROCRYPT 2002* (Lecture Notes in Computer Science 2332), pp. 45–64, 2002.

10. A. De Santis, G. Di Crescenzo, R. Ostrovsky, G. Persiano and A. Sahai. Robust non-interactive zero knowledge. In *Advances in Cryptology – CRYPTO 2001* (LNCS 2139), 566–598, 2001.

11. D. Dolev, C. Dwork and M. Naor. Non-malleable cryptography. *SIAM J. on Comput.*, 30(2):391–437, 2000. An earlier version appeared in *23rd ACM Symp. on Theory of Computing*, pp. 542–552, 1991.

12. T. ElGamal. A public key cryptosystem and a signature scheme based on discrete logarithms. *IEEE Trans. on Info. Theory* 31:469–472, 1985.

13. S. Even, O. Goldreich, and S. Micali. On-line/Off-line digital signatures. *J. Cryptology* 9(1):35-67 (1996).

14. S. Goldwasser and S. Micali. Probabilistic encryption. *Journal of Computer and System Sciences* 28:270–299, 1984.

15. S. Goldwasser, S. Micali, and R. L. Rivest. A digital signature scheme secure against adaptive chosen-message attacks. *SIAM J. on Computing* 17(2):281–308, Apr. 1988.

16. C. Rackoff and D. Simon. Noninteractive zero-knowledge proof of knowledge and chosen ciphertext attack. In *Advances in Cryptology—CRYPTO '91*, (Lecture Notes in Computer Science 576), pp. 433–444, 1991.

17. Y. Lindell. A simpler construction of CCA2-secure public-key encryption under general assumption. In *Advances in Cryptology—EUROCRYPT 2003*, (LNCS 2656), pp. 241–254, 2003.

18. R. L. Rivest, A. Shamir, and L. Adleman. A method for obtaining digital signatures and public-key cryptosystem. *Comm. of the ACM* 21(2):120–126, Feb. 1978.

19. A. M. Rockett and P. Szüsz. Continued Fractions. World Scientific Publishing Co. Pte. Ltd. ISBN 981-02-1047-7, 1992.

20. A. Sahai. Non-malleable non-interactive zero knowledge and adaptive chosen-ciphertext security. In *40th IEEE Symp. on Foundations of Computer Sci.*, pp. 543–553, 1999.

21. V. Shoup and R. Gennaro. Securing threshold cryptosystems against chosen ciphertext attack. In *Advances in Cryptology—EUROCRYPT '98* (Lecture Notes in Computer Science 1403), pp. 1–16, 1998.

A   Proofs

A.1   Proof of Lemma 6

We prove the lemma for $\mathsf{atk} = \mathsf{cca1}$, which will imply the case $\mathsf{atk} = \mathsf{cpa}$. We use the notation of Definition 2 and Construction 1.

For an adversary $\mathcal{A} = (\mathcal{A}_1, \mathcal{A}_2)$, we construct simulators $\mathcal{S} = (\mathcal{S}_1, \mathcal{S}_2)$ as follows. The simulator $\mathcal{S}_1$ runs $\mathcal{A}_1$ and simulates both the random oracle $H(\cdot)$ and the decryption oracle D_{sk} in a quite standard way. More specifically, $\mathcal{S}_1$ maintains a "query list" L consisting of pairs (α, t), such that $H(f^{-1}(\alpha)) = t$. L is initially $\emptyset$. When $\mathcal{A}_1$ makes a query r to H, $\mathcal{S}_1$ checks if $(f(r), t) \in L$ for some t, and replies with t if so; otherwise, $\mathcal{S}_1$ picks a random $t \leftarrow X$, adds $(f(r), t)$ to L, and replies with t. When $\mathcal{A}_1$ makes a query $y = (\alpha, \beta)$ to D_{sk}, $\mathcal{S}_1$ checks if $(\alpha, t) \in L$ for some t, and replies with $\psi(\beta \cdot t^{-1})$ if so; otherwise, $\mathcal{S}_1$ picks a random $t \leftarrow X$, adds (α, t) to L, and replies with $\psi(\beta \cdot t^{-1})$. Finally, when $\mathcal{A}_1$ outputs (M, s_1, s_2), $\mathcal{S}_1$ outputs $(M, s_1, (s_2, L))$.

Upon invocation, the simulator $\mathcal{S}_2$, generates $r \leftarrow d(1^k)$, $\alpha \leftarrow f(r)$, $\beta \leftarrow X$, $y \leftarrow (\alpha, \beta)$. Then $\mathcal{S}_2$ invokes $\mathcal{A}_2$ with parameters (s_2, y), and simulates the random oracle for $\mathcal{A}_2$ in the same way as $\mathcal{S}_1$ does for $\mathcal{A}_1$, using the list L passed from $\mathcal{S}_1$. When $\mathcal{A}_2$ outputs $\mathbf{y} \leftarrow \mathcal{A}_2(s_2, y)$, $\mathcal{S}_2$ aborts if $y \in \mathbf{y}$. Otherwise, we assume that $\mathbf{y} = (y_1, y_2, .., y_\ell)$, where $y_i = (\alpha_i, \beta_i)$ for $i = 1, 2, ..., \ell$. $\mathcal{S}_2$ generates $\mathbf{z}$ as follows. For each i, if $\alpha_i \neq \alpha$, then set $z_i \leftarrow \bot$; otherwise compute $\lambda_i \leftarrow \beta_i \cdot (\beta)^{-1}$, compute its soft spot $x_i \leftarrow \mathsf{ss}(\lambda_i)$, and then set $z_i \leftarrow x_i$. Finally $\mathcal{S}_2$ sets $\mathbf{z} = (z_1, z_1, ..., z_\ell)$, and outputs $(\mathbf{y}, \mathbf{z})$.

Next, we prove that $\mathcal{S}$ is a valid simulator, i.e., that $\Pr[\mathsf{Expt}_{\mathcal{A},\Pi}^{\mathsf{wnm\text{-}atk}}(R, k) = 1] - \Pr[\mathsf{Expt}_{\mathcal{S},\Pi}^{\mathsf{wnm\text{-}atk}}(R, k) = 1]$ is negligible in k. In order to do so, we introduce a new experiment called Mix. Informally, $\mathsf{Mix}_{\mathcal{A},\mathcal{S},\Pi}^{\mathsf{wnm\text{-}atk}}(R, k)$ is the same as $\mathsf{Expt}_{\mathcal{A},\Pi}^{\mathsf{wnm\text{-}atk}}(R, k)$, except using the simulator $\mathcal{S}$ to simulator the random oracle and the decryption. Now let $p_\mathcal{A}$, p_{Mix} and $p_\mathcal{S}$ be the probabilities of success in the real, Mix, and ideal experiments, respectively. We shall prove that both $p_\mathcal{A} - p_{\mathsf{Mix}}$ and $p_{\mathsf{Mix}} - p_\mathcal{S}$ are negligible k, and the lemma will follow directly.

To see that $p_\mathcal{A} - p_{\mathsf{Mix}}$ is negligible, note that the simulation of the random oracle and decryption in Mix will be valid except in the case where $\mathcal{A}_1$ has queried H with r or D_{sk} with (α, β') for some β'. Since r and α are chosen randomly after $\mathcal{A}_1$ is executed, the probability of this is obviously negligible.

To see that $p_{\mathsf{Mix}} - p_\mathcal{S}$ is negligible, note that the two experiments only differ when $\mathcal{A}_2$ queries $H(r)$, and the probability of this is negligible by the security of f. (Using unique identifiability and by viewing random oracle queries, $\mathcal{S}_2$ is able to simulate the decryption exactly.)

Details will be provided in the full version of the paper.

A.2   Proof of Theorem 1

First the intuition. If CBS were not secure, then there would be an adversary $\mathcal{A}$ that breaks it, meaning that for some fair Award, no simulator could achieve an expected award negligibly less than $\mathcal{A}$. But we will construct an adversary $\mathcal{B}$ for Π out of $\mathcal{A}$, and by the wnm-security of Π, there is a simulator $\mathcal{S}'$ that approximates $\mathcal{B}$ for any relation. Then we will use $\mathcal{S}'$ to build a simulator $\mathcal{S}$ for CBS that does achieve an expected award negligibly less than $\mathcal{A}$, which is a contradiction.

Now the details. Assume CBS is not secure. Then for some $q(k)$ there exists an adversary $\mathcal{A}$ that runs in time $q(k)$ and such that for every simulator $\mathcal{S}$, there exists a non-negligible $r(k)$ and an infinite number of k's in which $\mathsf{Adv}_{\mathcal{A},\mathcal{S},\mathsf{CBS}}^{\mathsf{profit}}(k) \geq r(k)$. Let $\mathsf{Edge}_{\mathcal{A},\mathcal{S},\mathsf{CBS}}(k, c) \stackrel{\mathsf{def}}{=} \Pr[\mathsf{Expt}_{\mathcal{A},\mathsf{CBS}}^{\mathsf{real}}(k) \geq c] - \Pr[\mathsf{Expt}_{\mathcal{S},\mathsf{CBS}}^{\mathsf{ideal}}(k) \geq c]$. Then using the definition of expectation, there is a c such that for an infinite number of k's, $\mathsf{Edge}_{\mathcal{A},\mathcal{S},\mathsf{CBS}}(k, c) \geq r(k)/U$. Without loss of generality, we may assume that $\mathcal{A}_2$ never outputs ebid_0, since by the fairness of the Award function, this cannot increase its advantage.

Define relation $R_c(x, \mathbf{x}, M, s_1)$ to return 1 iff $|\mathbf{x}| = 1$ and $\mathsf{Award}(x, \mathbf{x}[0])[1] \geq c$. Consider the following adversary $\mathcal{B}$ for the wnm-cpa-security of Π.

$\mathcal{B}_1(pk):$	$\mathcal{B}_2(s, y):$
$(M, s) \leftarrow \mathcal{A}_1(pk, U)$	$\mathsf{ebid}_1 \leftarrow \mathcal{A}_2(y, s)$
return $(M, \perp, s)$	return ebid_1

Since Π is wnm-cpa-secure, there exists a simulator $\mathcal{S}' = (\mathcal{S}_1', \mathcal{S}_2')$ such that $\mathsf{Adv}_{\mathcal{B}, \mathcal{S}', \Pi}^{\mathsf{wnm\text{-}cpa}}(R_c, k)$ is negligible for all c. Because $R_c(x, \mathbf{x}, M, s_1)$ returns 1 only if $|\mathbf{x}| = 1$, we assume without loss of generality that $\mathcal{S}_2'$ returns one-element vectors $\mathbf{y}$ and $\mathbf{z}$, i.e., values y and z. Now let a simulator $\mathcal{S}'' = (\mathcal{S}_1'', \mathcal{S}_2'')$ for the contract bidding system be defined as follows.

$\mathcal{S}_1''(U):$	$\mathcal{S}_2''(s):$
$(pk, sk) \leftarrow G(1^k)$	
$(M, s_1, s_2) \leftarrow \mathcal{S}_1'(pk)$	$(y, z) \leftarrow \mathcal{S}_2'(s)$
return (M, s_2)	return $D_{sk}(y)$

Note that by the fairness of Award, the award can never decrease when bid_1 is changed from $\perp$ to a valid bid, and so it is easy to see that $\Pr[\mathsf{Expt}_{\mathcal{S}'', \mathsf{CBS}}^{\mathsf{ideal}}(k) \geq c] \geq \Pr[\mathsf{Expt}_{\mathcal{S}', \Pi}^{\mathsf{wnm\text{-}atk}}(R_c, k) = 1]$. Using this fact, one can see that for all c, $\mathsf{Edge}_{\mathcal{A}, \mathcal{S}'', \mathsf{CBS}}(k, c) \leq \mathsf{Adv}_{\mathcal{B}, \mathcal{S}', \Pi}^{\mathsf{wnm\text{-}cpa}}(R_c, k)$, and thus by the discussion above, for all c, $\mathsf{Edge}_{\mathcal{A}, \mathcal{S}'', \mathsf{CBS}}(k, c)$ is negligible. This is a contradiction, so CBS must be secure.

A.3   Proof of Theorem 3

Let $\mathcal{A}$ be an adversary that interacts with parties running σ in the $\mathcal{F}_{\mathrm{AUTH}}$-hybrid model. We will construct an adversary $\mathcal{S}$ in the ideal process for $\mathcal{F}_{\mathrm{M-SMT}}$ such that no environment $\mathcal{Z}$ can distinguish whether it is interacting with $\mathcal{A}$ and σ in the $\mathcal{F}_{\mathrm{AUTH}}$-hybrid model, or with $\mathcal{S}$ and $\mathcal{F}_{\mathrm{M-SMT}}$ in the ideal process. For simplicity, we assume there exists only one instance of $\mathcal{F}_{\mathrm{M-SMT}}$ with identifier $id|P_i$ for some P_i. It is straightforward to extend the behavior of $\mathcal{S}$ to the case of multiple instances. $\mathcal{S}$ runs a simulated copy of $\mathcal{A}$ and maintains a tuple $(pk^*, sk^*, \mathsf{owner})$, where pk^* is the "session public key", sk^* is the corresponding secret key, and owner is the index of the party who "owns" it. [10] The session key pair (pk^*, sk^*) is initialized to $\perp$. Then $\mathcal{S}$ forwards messages from $\mathcal{Z}$ to $\mathcal{A}$, as well as messages from $\mathcal{A}$ to $\mathcal{Z}$. Furthermore, $\mathcal{S}$ also sees the *public part* (also known as "header" [7]) of all the messages from uncorrupted parties to $\mathcal{F}_{\mathrm{M-SMT}}$ and may decide when and if to forward these messages. We refer the readers to [7] for more detailed discussions. In the case of $\mathcal{F}_{\mathrm{M-SMT}}$, all messages to $\mathcal{F}_{\mathrm{M-SMT}}$ are public, except the "payload message" m in $(\mathbf{send}, id, m)$. $\mathcal{S}$ also simulates the ideal functionality $\mathcal{F}_{\mathrm{AUTH}}$.

Next, we describe the behavior of $\mathcal{S}$ in more detail. Note that $\mathcal{S}$ simulates $\mathcal{F}_{\mathrm{AUTH}}$ as normal except as detailed below.

---

[10] Since we assume there is only one instance of $\mathcal{F}_{\mathrm{M-SMT}}$ ideal functionality, there is only one instance of protocol σ, and thus there is only one key. Also, in the case of identifier $id|P_i$, $\mathsf{owner} = i$.

Simulating Communication with $\mathcal{Z}$: $\mathcal{S}$ directly forwards any messages between $\mathcal{Z}$ and $\mathcal{A}$.

Key Generation: If P_i is uncorrupted and $\mathcal{S}$ sees a message (**receiver**, $id|P_i$) from P_i to $\mathcal{F}_{\mathrm{M-SMT}}$, $\mathcal{S}$ forwards this message to $\mathcal{F}_{\mathrm{M-SMT}}$. If $pk^* \neq \perp$ it does nothing else. Otherwise $\mathcal{S}$ generates $(pk, sk) \leftarrow G(1^k)$, sets $(pk^*, sk^*) \leftarrow (pk, sk)$, and owner $\leftarrow i$, and simulates $\mathcal{F}_{\mathrm{AUTH}}$ to send (key, $id|P_i, pk$) to all other parties.

If P_i is corrupted and $\mathcal{S}$ sees P_i send a message (key, $id|P_i, pk$) to $\mathcal{F}_{\mathrm{AUTH}}$, $\mathcal{S}$ simulates $\mathcal{F}_{\mathrm{AUTH}}$. Furthermore, if $pk^* = \perp$ and $pk \neq \perp$, then $\mathcal{S}$ sends message (**receiver**, id) to $\mathcal{F}_{\mathrm{M-SMT}}$ on behalf of P_i and sets owner $\leftarrow i$ and $(pk^*, sk^*) \leftarrow (pk, ?)$. Here "$sk^* =?$" indicates that $\mathcal{S}$ does not know the corresponding secret key.

Delivery of the public key: When $\mathcal{A}$ delivers a message $(P_i, P_j, (\text{key}, id|P_i, pk))$ from $\mathcal{F}_{\mathrm{AUTH}}$ to an uncorrupted party P_j that has not received such a message previously, $\mathcal{S}$ records the tuple $(P_j, (P_i, pk))$ and delivers (**receiver**, $id|P_i, P_i$) from $\mathcal{F}_{\mathrm{M-SMT}}$ to P_j.

Message transfer from an uncorrupted party: If $\mathcal{S}$ sees an uncorrupted party P_j send a message (**send**, $id|P_i, -$) to $\mathcal{F}_{\mathrm{M-SMT}}$, where "$-$" indicates the "private" part of the message that $\mathcal{S}$ does not see, and if $\mathcal{S}$ has stored a tuple $(P_i, (P_j, pk'))$, $\mathcal{S}$ does the following. First $\mathcal{S}$ forwards the **send** message to $\mathcal{F}_{\mathrm{M-SMT}}$, and receives the length ℓ. Next, if P_i is corrupted, then $\mathcal{S}$ receives the message (id, m, P_i) from $\mathcal{F}_{\mathrm{M-SMT}}$ to the ideal P_i, sets $c \leftarrow E_{pk'}(m, P_i)$. If P_i is uncorrupted, then $\mathcal{S}$ sets $c \leftarrow E_{pk^*}(0^\ell, P_i)$. Finally, $\mathcal{S}$ simulates $\mathcal{F}_{\mathrm{AUTH}}$ to send $(id|P_i, c)$ to P_i.

Message transfer from a corrupted party: If $\mathcal{S}$ sees a corrupted party P_j (controlled by $\mathcal{A}$) send message $(id|P_i, c)$ to P_i through $\mathcal{F}_{\mathrm{AUTH}}$, we may assume that P_i is uncorrupted, since otherwise $\mathcal{S}$ does not need to do anything. In this case, $\mathcal{S}$ sets $m \leftarrow D_{sk^*}(c, P_j)$ and if $m \neq \perp$, sends message (**send**, id, m) to $\mathcal{F}_{\mathrm{M-SMT}}$, forwarding the message (id, P_j, m) to the ideal P_i when $\mathcal{A}$ forwards the corresponding message to P_i from $\mathcal{F}_{\mathrm{AUTH}}$.

Now we show that if any $\mathcal{Z}$ can distinguish whether it is interacting with $\mathcal{A}$ and σ in the $\mathcal{F}_{\mathrm{AUTH}}$-hybrid model, or with $\mathcal{S}$ and $\mathcal{F}_{\mathrm{M-SMT}}$ in the ideal process, then this can be used to construct an adversary $\mathcal{B} = (\mathcal{B}_1, \mathcal{B}_2)$ that breaks the tind-cca2-security of Π.

Intuitively, this is true because the only possible difference between the ideal process and the real world is in the case when an uncorrupted party P_j sends a message m to another uncorrupted party P_i. In the real world, an encryption of m is sent through $\mathcal{F}_{\mathrm{AUTH}}$; in the ideal process, $\mathcal{S}$ simulates this message using a encryption of 0^ℓ, since $\mathcal{S}$ does not know m. Notice that the tag for this encryption is always P_j, the identity of an uncorrupted party. $\mathcal{S}$ also performs decryptions, but only for messages from corrupted parties. Therefore, $\mathcal{S}$ only decrypts messages with corrupted parties' identities as tags, and in particular, no ciphertexts with tag P_j are decrypted by $\mathcal{S}$. Then, by the tind-cca2-security of Π, the simulation of $\mathcal{S}$ is indistinguishable from the real world.

We now describe the proof more formally. $\mathcal{B}$ takes a public key pk and decryption oracle, plays the role of $\mathcal{F}_{\mathrm{M-SMT}}$ and runs $\mathcal{S}$ with the following changes. Assume that l messages are sent using $\mathcal{F}_{\mathrm{M-SMT}}$. $\mathcal{B}_1$ choose $h \overset{R}{\leftarrow} \{1, \ldots, l\}$. If an uncorrupted party P_i needs to generate a key pair, pk is used as the public key. Let $id|P_i$ be the associated identifier. Then for the first $h - 1$ messages to P_i with id from uncorrupted parties, $\mathcal{B}$ has $\mathcal{S}$ encrypt the actual messages, instead of the all zeros message. On the hth message to P_i with $id|P_i$, say from an uncorrupted P_j, $\mathcal{B}_1$ outputs the all zeros message, the real message, the tag P_j, and its internal state. Then $\mathcal{B}_2$ uses the challenge ciphertext in the message to P_i, and continues to run $\mathcal{S}$ as normal, encrypting all zeros messages again. $\mathcal{B}_1$ and $\mathcal{B}_2$ both call the decryption oracle on messages to P_i from a corrupted P_j. Note that the tag in this case is always different from the tag returned by $\mathcal{B}_1$. Finally, $\mathcal{B}_2$ outputs whatever $\mathcal{Z}$ outputs. Note that if $h = 0$ and the bit chosen in the tind-cca2 experiment is 0, $\mathcal{B}$ runs like $\mathcal{S}$, and if $h = \ell$ and the bit chosen in the tind-cca2 experiment is 1, $\mathcal{B}$ runs like $\mathcal{A}$ in the real protocol. Then by a standard hybrid argument, if $\mathcal{Z}$ distinguishes whether it is interacting with $\mathcal{A}$ and σ in the $\mathcal{F}_{\mathrm{AUTH}}$-hybrid model, or with $\mathcal{S}$ and $\mathcal{F}_{\mathrm{M-SMT}}$ in the ideal process, $\mathcal{B}$ breaks the tind-cca2-security of Π.

A Note on Constant-Round
Zero-Knowledge Proofs for NP

Alon Rosen

Laboratory for Computer Science.
Massachusetts Institute of Technology.
200 Tech. Square, Cambridge, MA 02139 USA**
alon@lcs.mit.edu

Abstract. We consider the problem of constructing a constant-round zero-knowledge proof system for all languages in $\mathcal{NP}$. This problem has been previously addressed by Goldreich and Kahan (Jour. of Cryptology, 1996). Following recent works on concurrent zero-knowledge, we propose an alternative solution that admits a considerably simpler analysis.

Zero-knowledge ($\mathcal{ZK}$) protocols require no introduction. Since their conceptualization [10], they have become a widely used tool in the design and realization of many cryptographic tasks. The notion of zero-knowledge owes much of its wide applicability to its generality, and specifically, to the fact that every language in $\mathcal{NP}$ can be proved in $\mathcal{ZK}$ [11].

In this paper we consider the basic task of constructing a constant-round zero-knowledge interactive *proof* system for all languages in $\mathcal{NP}$ (with negligible error). Recall that an interactive proof system is required to protect the honest verifier from an all powerful prover that is trying to convince him of the validity of a false assertion. This should be contrasted with the case of an interactive *argument* system (cf. [3]), in which the soundness property is required to hold only w.r.t. computationally bounded provers.

Our goal is to design a "natural" protocol whose zero-knowledge property is demonstrated in as a simple as possible manner. This would be in contrast to previous solutions, which invloved a fairly complicated analysis (cf. Goldreich, Kahan [7]). Our solution is inspired by a new $\mathcal{ZK}$ protocol by Prabhakaran, Rosen and Sahai [18], originally introduced in the context of concurrent Zero-Knowledge. Constant-round, negligible-error, $\mathcal{ZK}$ proofs for $\mathcal{NP}$ are a fundamental and widely used cryptographic tool. Needless to say that a simple construction/analysis of such proofs would be most desirable.

1   Constructing a Constant-Round $\mathcal{ZK}$ Proof for $\mathcal{NP}$

We assume familiarity with the concepts of Interactive Proofs, Zero-Knowledge and Bit Commitment (see Appendix for the actual definitions) [10,11,15,6]. The

---

** Part of this work done while at the Weizmann Institute of Science, Israel.

M. Naor (Ed.): TCC 2004, LNCS 2951, pp. 191–202, 2004.
© Springer-Verlag Berlin Heidelberg 2004

"typical" construction for a constant round interactive proof for any language in $\mathcal{NP}$ would use a protocol of the following sort as a building-block (here we use a protocol for the $\mathcal{NP}$-complete language of Hamiltonicity [2]).[1]

Common Input: A directed graph $G = (V, E)$ with $n \overset{\text{def}}{=} |V|$.

Auxiliary Input to Prover: A directed Hamiltonian Cycle, $C \subset E$, in G.

    $(\widehat{p1})$: Pick a random permutation π of the vertices V and commit (using a perfectly binding commitment) to the adjacency matrix of the resulting permuted graph. That is, send an n-by-n matrix of commitments so that the $(\pi(i), \pi(j))^{\text{th}}$ entry is a commitment to 1 if $(i, j) \in E$, and is a commitment to 0 otherwise.

    $(\widehat{v1})$: Send a randomly chosen bit $\sigma \in \{0, 1\}$.

    $(\widehat{p2})$: If $\sigma = 0$, send π to the verifier along with the revealing (i.e., preimages) of all commitments. Otherwise, reveal only the commitments to entries $(\pi(i), \pi(j))$ with $(i, j) \in C$. In both cases also supply the corresponding decommitments.

    $(\widehat{v2})$: If $\sigma = 0$, check that the revealed graph is indeed isomorphic, via π, to G. Otherwise, just check that all revealed values are 1 and that the corresponding entries form a simple n-cycle. In both cases check that the decommitments are proper (i.e., that they fit the corresponding commitments). Accept if and only if the corresponding condition holds.

Fig. 1. A 3-round interactive proof system for Hamiltonicity.

It can be seen that the above protocol is both complete and sound (with soundness error $1/2$). An additional "useful" property of the protocol (which is also satisfied by many other known protocols) is that if the prover knows the contents of verifier's "challenge" message σ (sent in Step $(\widehat{v1})$) prior to sending its own first message (sent in Step $(\widehat{p1})$), then it is able to convince the verifier that G contains an Hamiltonian cycle even without knowing such a cycle (actually, it will convince the verifier even if G does not contain an Hamiltonian cycle).

Specifically, knowing in advance that $\sigma = 0$, the prover will commit to the entries of the adjacency matrix of the permuted graph (in Step $(\widehat{p1})$), thus being able to reveal a permutation π and the preimages of all commitments in Step $(\widehat{p2})$. On the other hand, knowing in advance that $\sigma = 1$, the prover will commit to the full graph K_n, thus being able to open an arbitrary cycle in the supposedly permuted graph.

The above "useful" property is sufficient in order to prove that the above protocol is black-box zero-knowledge. All that the simulator has to do is to try and "guess" the value of σ prior to determining the value of the prover's first message (and keep trying until it succeeds). Using the computational-hiding property of the prover's commitment in Step $(\widehat{p1})$ we would then have that no

---

[1] The choice of the Hamiltonicity protocol (due to Blum) as a building block is arbitrary (and is made just for clarity of presentation). In fact, any protocol with similar properties (such as the 3-coloring protocol of Goldreich, Micali and Wigderson [11]) could have been used.

matter what an adversary verifier V^* does, the simulator is expected to guess σ's value in a constant number of attempts.

To obtain a useful protocol, however, one must make sure that whenever the statement proved is false, V accepts only with small probability (rather than $1/2$). To achieve this, the protocol described above is repeated many (say, n) times independently. V accepts if and only if it has accepted in all n repetitions. The probability of having V accept a false statement is now reduced to $1/2^n$ (by the independence of the repetitions). To save on the number of rounds, the repetitions are conducted in *parallel* (rather than sequentially).

Unfortunately, repeating the protocol many times in parallel brings up the following difficulty. Whereas in the case of a single execution, the probability that the $\mathcal{ZK}$ simulator "guesses" the value of σ correctly is at least $1/2$, the probability that he does so *simultaneously* for all n repetitions is $1/2^n$. For large n, this probability will be very small and might cause the simulator to run for too long. Thus, it is not clear that the $\mathcal{ZK}$ property of the protocol is preserved. Indeed, the above protocol cannot be proved to be $\mathcal{ZK}$ using black-box simulation (unless $\mathcal{NP} \subseteq \mathcal{BPP}$) [8].[2]

The Goldreich-Kahan Analysis [7]. To overcome the above problem, an additional (V0) message is added at the beginning of the protocol, in which the verifier commits to all n "challenge" bits prior to receiving $\widehat{(\text{p1})}$. The verifier then decommits to all challenge bits in message $\widehat{(\text{v1})}$. The secrecy property of the commitment used in (V0) should then guarantee that the soundness of the protocol is preserved.

At this point, it seems that all that the simulator has to do after obtaining V^*'s commitments in message (V0) is to feed V^* with a "dummy" $\widehat{(\text{p1})}$ and then obtain decommittment to all challenge bits in message $\widehat{(\text{v1})}$. Knowing the challenge bits, the simulator would then "rewind" the interaction with V^* and resend a modified $\widehat{(\text{p1})}$ that would convince the verifier of the validity of the assertion (this is possible due to the "useful" property of the underlying protocol).

Unfortunately, V^* may arbitrarily deviate from the prescribed strategy. In particular, it may be the case that throughout its interaction with the prover (simulator), V^* occasionally sends an ABORT message (that is, V^* may potentially refuse to decommit to any of the previous commitments). Clearly, such an action on behalf of the verifier is considered illegal, and the interaction stops.

Having V^* refuse to decommit may seem as good news (since, once this happens, the simulator does not really need to do anything). The problem is that V^* does not *always* refuse to decommit (but may refuse with some probability $0 \leq p \leq 1$, which is not known in advance by the simulator). Thus, the simulator may find himself in a situation in which the first run is answered with ABORT

---

[2] A recent result by Barak [1] suggests that black-box lower bounds should not be interpreted as impossibility results about $\mathcal{ZK}$, but rather as limitations of the black-box simulation as a technique for proving the $\mathcal{ZK}$ property of protocols. It should be noted, however, that Barak's protocol are only known to apply to certain kinds of *argument* systems (rather than proof systems).

whereas the second run is "properly answered". This means that the simulator has not managed to obtain the "challenge" bits in the first run, and it thus fails to complete its task.

One naïve solution would be to let the simulator always output the run in which V^* has refused to decommit. The problem with this solution is that it "skews" the distribution of transcripts outputted by the simulator towards transcripts that contain ill-formed messages.

Goldreich and Kahan [7] suggested to let the simulator always decide whether to output an aborted run according to the outcome of the first run. Specifically, the simulator will rewind only if "answered properly" in the first run and will continue doing so (i.e., rewinding) until it obtains another "proper answer". Unfortunately, while this simulation strategy guarantees that the simulator's output is correctly distributed, it also introduces technical difficulties. Loosely speaking, these difficulties arise from the fact that probability of V^* refusing to decommit might differ between the case it is fed with a "dummy" commitment (in step $\widehat{(p1)}$) and the case it is fed with a "convincing" commitment. The solution to this problem is somewhat involved and requires having the simulator obtain an estimate on the probability of V^* decommits properly when fed with a "convincing" commitment in step $\widehat{(p1)}$. As we have said before, our goal is to obtain a simpler analysis (even at the cost of analyzing a slightly different protocol).

2   The New Protocol

Consider the following protocol for Hamiltonicity (HC), which is a variant of the $c\mathcal{ZK}$ protocol by Prabhakaran, Rosen and Sahai [18] in which the preamble has only one iteration (rather than a super logarithmic number of iterations as in the PRS proocol).[3]

As shown in [18], the above protocol is both complete and sound (with negligible error). In particular, the construction above is an interactive proof system for HC. The following theorem states that it is also $\mathcal{ZK}$.

Theorem 2.1 (Constant-round $\mathcal{ZK}$ proof for $\mathcal{NP}$) *Assume the existence of perfectly-hiding commitment schemes. Then, the protocol described in Figure 2 is a $\mathcal{ZK}$ proof system for HC.*

2.1   Zero-Knowledge

In order to demonstrate the $\mathcal{ZK}$ property of the protocol, we will show that there exists a "universal" black-box simulator, S, so that for every $G = (V, E) \in HC$ and adversary verifier V^* that runs in polynomial time (in $n = |V|$), $S(G)$ runs in expected time poly(n), and satisfies that the ensemble $\{\text{view}_{V^*}^P(G)\}_{G \in HC}$ is computationally indistinguishable from the ensemble $\{S^{V^*}(G)\}_{G \in HC}$.

---

[3] A related approach has been previously used in order to construct constant-round perfect $\mathcal{ZK}$ *arguments* for $\mathcal{NP}$ (see [5]).

Common Input: A directed graph $G = (V, E)$ with $n \overset{\text{def}}{=} |V|$.
Auxiliary Input to Prover: A directed Hamiltonian Cycle, $C \subset E$, in G.
Additional parameter: A super-logarithmic function $k(n)$.
Stage 1: Commitment to challenge $\sigma \in \{0,1\}^n$ (independent of common input):
    (P1): Send first message for perfectly hiding commitment scheme.
    (V1): Commit to random $\sigma, \{\sigma_i^0\}_{i=1}^k, \{\sigma_i^1\}_{i=1}^k$ s.t. $\sigma_i^0 \oplus \sigma_i^1 = \sigma$ for all i.
    (P2): Send a random k-bit string $r = r_1, \ldots, r_k$.
    (V2): Decommit to $\sigma_1^{r_1}, \ldots, \sigma_k^{r_k}$.
Stage 2: Engage in the 3-round protocol for HC (n parallel repetitions) using $\sigma = \sigma_1, \ldots, \sigma_n$ as challenge:
    (p1): Produce first prover message of HC protocol (as in $(\widehat{\text{p1}})$).
    (v1): Decommit to σ and to $\{\sigma_i^{1-r_i}\}_{i=1}^k$.
    (p2): Answer σ with second prover message of HC protocol (as in $(\widehat{\text{p2}})$).
    (v2): Accept if and only if all corresponding conditions hold (as in $(\widehat{\text{v2}})$).

Fig. 2. A new 7-round, negligible error, $\mathcal{ZK}$ proof for Hamiltonicity.

The Simulator. On input $G = (V, E)$ with $n = |V|$, the simulator S starts by selecting and fixing a random tape $s \in \{0,1\}^{\text{poly}(n)}$ for V^*. It then proceeds by exploring various prefixes of possible interactions between P and V^*. This is done while having only black-box access to V^*. It then acts as follows.

Step (S1): Randomly generate (P1) and obtain $(V1) = V^*(G, (P1); s)$.
Step (S2): Randomly generate (P2) and obtain $(V2) = V^*(G, (P1), (P2); s)$.
    1. If $(V2) \neq \texttt{ABORT}$, proceed to Step (S3).
    2. If $(V2) = \texttt{ABORT}$, output $\langle(P1), (V1), \texttt{ABORT}\rangle$ and stop.
Step (S3): For $j = 1, 2, \ldots$
    1. Randomly generate $(P2)_j$ and obtain $(V2)_j = V^*(G, (P1), (P2)_j; s)$.
    2. If $(V2)_j \neq \texttt{ABORT}$, proceed to Step (S4).
    3. If $(V2)_j = \texttt{ABORT}$ continue.
    end(for)
Step (S4): Let $(P2) = r_1, \ldots, r_k$ be the prover message generated in Step (S2) of the simulation and let $(P2)_j = r'_1 \ldots, r'_k$ be the last prover message generated in Step (S3):
    1. If $(P2) = (P2)_j$, output $\perp$ and stop.
    2. If $(P2) \neq (P2)_j$, there exists $i \in \{1, \ldots, k\}$ so that $r_i \neq r'_i$. Let $\sigma = \sigma_i^{r_i} \oplus \sigma_i^{r'_i}$.
    3. Use σ to produce an accepting transcript (p1), (v1), (p2) for $G \in HC$.
    4. Output $\langle(P1), (V1), (P2), (V2), (p1), (v1), (p2)\rangle$ and stop.

Fig. 3. The black-box simulator S.

Notice that simulator always picks the $(P2)_j$ messages uniformly at random. Since the length of the (P2)'s is super-logarithmic, the probability that *any* two (P1) messages sent during the simulation are equal is negligible (see Section 2.1 for further details). We note that in previous simulators (cf. [7,19,13,14]), the values of the (Pj) messages depended on the values revealed by the verifier in the corresponding (V2) answers, and were *not* chosen uniformly and independently each time. This is the main reason in the complication of previous analysises of the simulator's output distribution.

The simulator's running time. For any $G \in HC$, for any choice of s and of (P1), let $\zeta = \zeta(G, (\text{P1}), s)$ denote the probability that the verifier V^* does not send an ABORT message in message (V2). The probability ζ is taken over the random choices of message (P2). (Or, in other words, over the coin-tosses used by the simulator to generate (P2) during the simulation (both in Steps (S2) and (S3).1).)

Using this notation, the simulator proceeds to Step (S3) with probability ζ and is then expected to reach Step (S4) after repeatedly rewinding in Step (S3).1 for $1/\zeta$ times (since the probability of successfully rewinding in each one of the rewinds is precisely ζ, independently of other rewinds). For $i \in \{1, 2, 3, 4\}$, let $p_i(\cdot)$ be a polynomial bound on the work required in order to perform Step (Si) of the simulation (where in Step (S3), the value $p_3(\cdot)$ represents the work of a single execution of Step (S3).1). The expected running time of the simulator is then:

$$p_1(n) + (1 - \zeta) \cdot p_2(n) + \zeta \cdot \left(p_2(n) + \frac{1}{\zeta} \cdot p_3(n) + p_4(n) \right)$$
$$\leq p_1(n) + p_2(n) + p_3(n) + p_4(n)$$
$$= \text{poly}(n)$$

Since the above holds for any choice of s and (P1), then it is also true for randomly chosen s and (P1) (and offcourse for any $G \in HC$). We thus have,

Proposition 2.2 *The simulator S runs in expected polynomial-time (in $|V|$).*

The simulator's output distribution. We now turn to show that for every $G \in HC$, the simulator's output distribution is computationally indistinguishable from V^*'s view of interactions with the honest prover P. Specifically,

Proposition 2.3 *Suppose that the commitment used in Step (p1) is computationally hiding. Then, the ensemble $\{S^{V^*}(G)\}_{G \in HC}$ is computationally indistinguishable from the ensemble $\{\text{view}_{V^*}^P(G)\}_{G \in HC}$.*

Proof: As a hybrid experiment, consider what happens to the output distribution of the simulator S if we (slightly) modify its simulation strategy in the following way: Suppose that on input $G = (V, E) \in HC$, the simulator S obtains a directed Hamiltonian Cycle $C \subset E$ in G (as auxiliary input) and uses it in order to produce real prover messages whenever it reaches the second stage of the protocol. Specifically, when it reaches the second stage, the hybrid simulator checks whether the original simulator S should output $\bot$ (in which case it also does). If S does not have to output $\bot$, the hybrid simulator follows the prescribed prover strategy and generates prover messages for the corresponding second stage (by using the cycle it possesses rather than its prior knowledge of σ). We claim that the ensemble consisting of the resulting output (which we denote by $\widehat{S}^{V^*}(G,C)$) is computationally indistinguishable from $\{S^{V^*}(G)\}_{G\in HC}$. Namely,

Claim 2.4 *Suppose that the commitment used in Step (p1) is computationally hiding. Then, the ensemble $\{S^{V^*}(G)\}_{G\in HC}$ is computationally indistinguishable from the ensemble $\{\widehat{S}^{V^*}(G,C)\}_{G\in HC}$.*

Proof Sketch: The claim is proved by reducing the proof to the indistinguishability of Blum's simulator's output (that is, if the output of Blum's simulator [2] is computationally indistinguishable from the view of real executions of the basic Hamiltonicity proof system, then $\{S^{V^*}(G)\}_{G\in HC}$ and $\{\widehat{S}^{V^*}(G,C)\}_{G\in HC}$ are indistinguishable as well). The latter is proved to hold based on the computational-hiding property of the commitment scheme that is used by the prover in Step (p1) (see [2,6] for further details). Here we also use the extra property that the output of Blum's simulator is indistinguishable from true interactions even if the distinguisher has a-priori knowledge of a Hamiltonian cycle $C \subset E$.   ∎

We next consider what happens to the output distribution of the hybrid simulator $\widehat{S}$ if we assume that it does not output $\bot$. It turns out that in such a case, the resulting output distribution is *identical* to the distribution of $\{\text{view}_{V^*}^P(G)\}_{G\in HC}$. Namely,

Claim 2.5 *The ensemble $\{\widehat{S}^{V^*}(G,C)\}_{G\in HC}$ conditioned on it not being $\bot$, is identically distributed to the ensemble $\{\text{view}_{V^*}^P(G)\}_{G\in HC}$.*

Proof: Notice that the first stage messages that appear in the output of the "original" simulator (that is, S) are identically distributed to the first stage messages that are produced by an honest prover P (since they are uniformly and independently chosen). Since the first stage messages that appear in the output of the "modified" simulator (that is, $\widehat{S}$) are identical to the ones appearing in the output of S, we infer that they are identically distributed to the first stage messages that are produced by an honest prover P. Using the fact that the second stage messages that appear in the output of the "modified" simulator are (by definition) identically distributed to the second stage messages that are produced by an honest prover P, we infer that the ensemble $\{\widehat{S}^{V^*}(G,C)\}_{G\in HC}$ is identically distributed to $\{\text{view}_{V^*}^P(G)\}_{G\in HC}$.   ∎

As we will show in Proposition 2.7 below, $\widehat{S}$ outputs $\bot$ only with negligible probability. In particular, the ensemble $\{\widehat{S}^{V^*}(G,C)\}_{G\in HC}$ is computationally indistinguishable from (and in fact statistically close to) the ensemble $\{\widehat{S}^{V^*}(G,C)\}_{G\in HC}$, conditioned on it not being $\bot$. Namely,

Claim 2.6 *The ensemble $\{\widehat{S}^{V^*}(G,C)\}_{G\in HC}$ is computationally indistinguishable from the ensemble $\{\widehat{S}^{V^*}(G,C)\}_{G\in HC}$ conditioned on it not being $\bot$.*

As mentioned above, Claim 2.6 follows by establishing the following claim.

Claim 2.7 *For any* $G = (V, E) \in HC$, *the probability that* $\widehat{S}^{V^*}(G, C) = \bot$ *is negligible* (*in* $|V|$).

Proof: Let $G \in HC$ with $n = |V|$. We will show that for any choice of $s \in \{0, 1\}^{\mathrm{poly}(n)}$ and (P1) the probability of $\widehat{S}$ outputting $\bot$ (over random choices of (P2) $= r \in \{0, 1\}^k$) is precisely $1/2^k$. Since k is super-logarithmic it will immediately follow that the probability that $\widehat{S}^{V^*}(G, C) = \bot$ is negligible. Let $\widetilde{V}^* = \widetilde{V}^*((P1), s)$ denote the "residual" strategy of V^* when $\langle (P1), s \rangle$ are fixed (i.e., $\widetilde{V}^*(G, r) \stackrel{\mathrm{def}}{=} V^*(G, (P1), r; s)$), and let ζ be as in Section 2.1. We then have:

$$\Pr_r\left[\widehat{S}^{\widetilde{V}^*}(G, C) = \bot\right]$$

$$= \Pr_r\left[\widehat{S}^{\widetilde{V}^*}(G, C) = \bot \mid \widehat{S} \text{ reaches (S3)}\right] \cdot \Pr_r\left[\widehat{S} \text{ reaches (S3)}\right] \qquad (1)$$

$$= \Pr_r\left[\widehat{S}^{\widetilde{V}^*}(G, C) = \bot \mid \widehat{S} \text{ reaches (S3)}\right] \cdot \zeta$$

$$= \Pr_r\left[(P2) = (P2)_j\right] \cdot \zeta \qquad (2)$$

Now, since (P2) and $(P2)_j$ are uniformly and independently chosen in $\{0, 1\}^k$, and since the number of $r \in \{0, 1\}^k$ for which $\widetilde{V}^*(G, r)$ is not equal to ABORT is precisely $2^k \cdot \zeta$, then it holds that $\Pr[(P2) = (P2)_j] = 1/(2^k \cdot \zeta)$. Using Eq. 2 we infer that:

$$\Pr_r\left[\widehat{S}^{\widetilde{V}^*}(G) = \bot\right] = \frac{1}{2^k \cdot \zeta} \cdot \zeta = \frac{1}{2^k}$$

as required.   ∎

It can be seen that Claims 2.4, 2.5 and 2.6 imply Proposition 2.3.   ∎

Acknowledgements. I would like to thank Oded Goldreich, Yehuda Lindell and Moni Naor for helpful conversations on the subject.

References

1. B. Barak. How to go Beyond the Black-Box Simulation Barrier. In *42nd FOCS*, pages 106–115, 2001.
2. M. Blum. How to prove a Theorem So No One Else Can Claim It. *Proc. of the International Congress of Mathematicians*, Berekeley, California, USA, pages 1444–1451, 1986.
3. G. Brassard, D. Chaum and C. Crépeau. Minimum Disclosure Proofs of Knowledge. *JCSS*, Vol. 37, No. 2, pages 156–189, 1988.
4. I. Damgard, T. Pedersen and B. Pfitzmann. On the Existence of Statistically Hiding Bit Commitment Schemes and Fail-Stop Signatures. In *Crypto93*, Springer LNCS 773, pages 250–265, 1993.

 5. U. Feige. Ph.D. thesis, Alternative Models for Zero Knowledge Interactive Proofs. Weizmann Institute of Science, 1990.
 6. O. Goldreich. *Foundations of Cryptography – Basic Tools*. Cambridge University Press, 2001.
 7. O. Goldreich and A. Kahan. How to Construct Constant-Round Zero-Knowledge Proof Systems for NP. *Jour. of Cryptology*, Vol. 9, No. 2, pages 167–189, 1996.
 8. O. Goldreich and H. Krawczyk. On the Composition of Zero-Knowledge Proof Systems. *SIAM J. Computing*, Vol. 25, No. 1, pages 169–192, 1996.
 9. O. Goldreich and Y. Oren. Definitions and Properties of Zero-Knowledge Proof Systems. *Jour. of Cryptology*, Vol. 7, No. 1, pages 1–32, 1994.
10. S. Goldwasser, S. Micali and C. Rackoff. The Knowledge Complexity of Interactive Proof Systems. *SIAM J. Comput.*, Vol. 18, No. 1, pp. 186–208, 1989.
11. O. Goldreich, S. Micali and A. Wigderson. Proofs that Yield Nothing But Their Validity or All Languages in NP Have Zero-Knowledge Proof Systems. *JACM*, Vol. 38, No. 1, pages 691–729, 1991.
12. J. Hastad, R. Impagliazzo, L.A. Levin and M. Luby. Construction of Pseudorandom Generator from any One-Way Function. *SIAM Jour. on Computing*, Vol. 28 (4), pages 1364–1396, 1999.
13. J. Kilian and E. Petrank. Concurrent and Resettable Zero-Knowledge in Poly-logarithmic Rounds. In *33rd STOC*, pages 560–569, 2001.
14. D. Micciancio and E. Petrank. Simulatable Commitments and Efficient Concurrent Zero-Knowledge. In *EUROCRYPT03*, Springer LNCS 2656, pages 140–159, 2003.
15. M. Naor. Bit Commitment using Pseudorandomness. *Jour. of Cryptology*, Vol. 4, pages 151–158, 1991.
16. M. Naor, R. Ostrovsky, R. Venkatesan and M. Yung. Zero-Knowledge Arguments for NP can be Based on General Assumptions. *Jour. of Cryptology*, Vol. 11, pages 87–108, 1998.
17. M. Naor and M. Yung. Universal One-Way Hash Functions and their Cryptographic Applications. In *21st STOC*, pages 33–43, 1989.
18. M. Prabhakaran and A. Rosen and A. Sahai. Concurrent Zero Knowledge with Logarithmic Round-Complexity. In *43rd FOCS*, pages 366-375, 2002.
19. R. Richardson and J. Kilian. On the Concurrent Composition of Zero-Knowledge Proofs. In *EuroCrypt99*, Springer LNCS 1592, pages 415–431, 1999.

A   Definitions

A.1   Basic Notation

We let N denote the set of all integers. For any integer $k \in N$, denote by $[k]$ the set $\{1, 2, \ldots, k\}$. For any $x \in \{0,1\}^*$, we let $|x|$ denote the size of x (i.e., the number of bits used in order to write it). For two machines M, A, we let $M^A(x)$ denote the output of machine M on input x and given oracle access to A. The term negligible is used for denoting functions that are (asymptotically) smaller than one over any polynomial. More precisely, a function $\nu(\cdot)$ from non-negative integers to reals is called negligible if for every constant $c > 0$ and all sufficiently large n, it holds that $\nu(n) < n^{-c}$.

A.2   Interactive Proofs

We use the standard definitions of interactive proofs (and interactive Turing machines) [10,6] and arguments (a.k.a computationally-sound proofs) [3]. Given a pair of interactive Turing machines, P and V, we denote by $\langle P, V \rangle(x)$ the random variable representing the (local) output of V when interacting with machine P on common input x, when the random input to each machine is uniformly and independently chosen.

Definition A.1 (Interactive Proof System) *A pair of interactive machines* $\langle P, V \rangle$ *is called an* interactive proof system *for a language L if machine V is polynomial-time and the following two conditions hold with respect to some negligible function $\nu(\cdot)$:*

- Completeness: *For every $x \in L$,*

$$\Pr\left[\langle P, V \rangle(x) = 1\right] \geq 1 - \nu(|x|)$$

- Soundness: *For every $x \notin L$, and every interactive machine B,*

$$\Pr\left[\langle B, V \rangle(x) = 1\right] \leq \nu(|x|)$$

In case that the soundness condition is required to hold only with respect to a computationally bounded prover, $\langle P, V \rangle$ is called an interactive argument *system.*

A.3   Zero-Knowledge

Loosely speaking, an interactive proof is said to be *zero-knowledge* ($\mathcal{ZK}$) if it yields nothing beyond the validity of the assertion being proved. This is formalized by requiring that the view of every probabilistic polynomial-time adversary V^* interacting with the honest prover P can be simulated by a probabilistic polynomial-time machine S_{V^*} (a.k.a. the *simulator*). The idea behind this definition is that whatever V^* might have learned from interacting with P, he could have actually learned by himself (by running the simulator S). The transcript of an interaction consists of the common input x, followed by the sequence of prover and verifier messages exchanged during the interaction. We denote by $\mathrm{view}_{V^*}^P(x)$ a random variable describing the content of the random tape of V^* and the transcript of the interaction between P and V^* (that is, all messages that V^* sends and receives during the interaction with P, on common input x).

Definition A.2 (Zero-Knowledge) *Let $\langle P, V \rangle$ be an interactive proof system for a language L. We say that $\langle P, V \rangle$ is* zero-knowledge, *if for every probabilistic polynomial-time interactive machine V^* there exists a probabilistic polynomial-time algorithm S_{V^*} such that the ensembles $\{\mathrm{view}_{V^*}^P(x)\}_{x \in L}$ and $\{S_{V^*}(x)\}_{x \in L}$ are computationally indistinguishable.*

To make Definition A.2 useful in the context of protocol composition, Goldreich and Oren [9] suggested to augment the definition so that the corresponding conditions hold also with respect to all $z \in \{0,1\}^*$, where both V^* and S_{V^*} are allowed to obtain z as auxiliary input. Jumping ahead, we comment that in the context of black-box simulation,, the original definition implies the augmented one (i.e., any black-box $\mathcal{ZK}$ protocol is also $\mathcal{ZK}$ w.r.t. auxiliary inputs). Since in this work we only consider the notion of black-box $\mathcal{ZK}$, we may ignore the issue of auxiliary inputs while being guaranteed that all results hold with repsect to the augmented definition as well.

A.4   Black-Box Zero-Knowledge

Loosely speaking, the definition of black-box zero-knowledge requires that there exists a "universal" simulator, S, so that for every $x \in L$ and every probabilistic polynomial-time adversary V^*, the simulator S produces a distribution that is indistinguishable from $\text{view}_{V^*}^P(x)$ while using V^* as an oracle (i.e., in a "black-box" manner). Essentially, the definition of black-box simulation says that the black-box simulator mimics the interaction of the prover P with any polynomial-time verifier V^* relative to any random input r it might choose. The simulator does so merely by using oracle calls to $V^*(x;r)$ (which specifies the next message that V^* sends on input x and random input r). The simulation is indistinguishable from the true interaction even if the distinguisher (i.e., D) is given access to the oracle $V^*(x;r)$. For more details see Section 4.5.4.2 of [6].

Definition A.3 (Black-Box Zero-Knowledge) *Let $\langle P, V \rangle$ be an interactive proof system for a language L. We say that $\langle P, V \rangle$ is black-box zero-knowledge, if there exists a probabilistic polynomial-time algorithm S, so that for every probabilistic polynomial-time interactive machine V^*, the ensembles $\{\text{view}_{V^*}^P(x)\}_{x \in L}$ and $\{S^{V^*}(x)\}_{x \in L}$ are computationally indistinguishable.*

A.5   Commitment Schemes

Commitment schemes are used to enable a party, known as the *sender*, to commit itself to a value while keeping it secret from the *receiver* (this property is called hiding). Furthermore, the commitment is binding, and thus in a later stage when the commitment is opened, it is guaranteed that the "opening" can yield only a single value determined in the committing phase.

Perfectly-binding commitments. In a perfectly binding commitment scheme, the binding property holds even for an all-powerful sender, while the hiding property is only guaranteed with respect to a polynomial-time bounded receiver.

Non-interactive perfectly-binding commitment schemes can be constructed using any 1–1 one-way function (see Section 4.4.1 of [6]). Allowing interaction (in which the receiver first sends a single message), (almost) perfectly-binding commitment schemes can be obtained from any one-way function [15,12].

Perfectly-hiding commitments. In a perfectly hiding commitment scheme, the binding property is guaranteed to hold only with respect to a probabilistic polynomial-time sender. On the other hand, the hiding property is information-theoretic. That is, the distributions of commitments to 0 and commitments to 1 are identical (statistically-close), and thus even an all-powerful receiver cannot know the value committed to by the sender. (See Section 4.8.2 of [6].)

Perfectly hiding commitment schemes can be constructed from any one-way permutation [16]. However, *constant-round* schemes are only known to exist under stronger assumptions; specifically, assuming the existence of collision-resistant hash functions [17,4] or the existence of a collection of certified clawfree functions [7] (see also [6], Section 4.8.2.3).

Lower Bounds for Concurrent Self Composition*

Yehuda Lindell

IBM T.J.Watson
19 Skyline Drive, Hawthorne,
New York 10532, USA.
lindell@us.ibm.com

Abstract. In the setting of concurrent self composition, a single protocol is executed many times concurrently by a single set of parties. In this paper, we prove that there exist many functionalities that *cannot* be securely computed in this setting. We also prove a *communication complexity lower bound* on protocols that securely compute a large class of functionalities in this setting. Specifically, we show that any protocol that computes a functionality from this class and remains secure for m concurrent executions, must have bandwidth of at least m bits. Our results hold for the plain model (where no trusted setup phase is assumed), and for the case that the parties may choose their inputs adaptively, based on previously obtained outputs. While proving our impossibility result, we also show that for many functionalities, security under concurrent *self* composition (where a single secure protocol is run many times) is actually equivalent to the seemingly more stringent requirement of security under concurrent *general* composition (where a secure protocol is run concurrently with other arbitrary protocols). This observation has significance beyond the impossibility results that are derived by it for concurrent self composition.

1   Introduction

In the setting of two-party computation, two parties with respective private inputs x and y, wish to jointly compute a functionality $f(x,y) = (f_1(x,y), f_2(x,y))$, such that the first party receives $f_1(x,y)$ and the second party receives $f_2(x,y)$. This functionality may be probabilistic, in which case $f(x,y)$ is a random variable. Loosely speaking, the security requirements are that nothing is learned from the protocol other than the output (privacy), and that the output is distributed according to the prescribed functionality (correctness). These security requirements must hold in the face of an adversary who controls one of the parties and can arbitrarily deviate from the protocol instructions (i.e., in this work we consider malicious, static adversaries). Powerful feasibility results have been shown for this problem, demonstrating that *any* two-party probabilistic polynomial-time functionality can be securely computed, assuming the existence of trapdoor permutations [21,11].

---

* A full version of this paper can be found on the Cryptology ePrint Archive.

M. Naor (Ed.): TCC 2004, LNCS 2951, pp. 203–222, 2004.
© Springer-Verlag Berlin Heidelberg 2004

Security under concurrent composition. The feasibility results of [21,11] relate only to the stand-alone setting, where a single pair of parties run a single execution. A more general (and realistic) setting relates to the case that many protocol executions are run concurrently within a network. Unfortunately, the security of a protocol in the stand-alone setting does not necessarily imply its security under concurrent composition. Therefore, it is important to re-establish the feasibility results of the stand-alone setting for the setting of concurrent composition, or alternatively, to demonstrate that this cannot be done.

The notion of protocol composition can be interpreted in many ways. A very important distinction to be made relates to the *context* in which the protocol is executed. This refers to the question of *which protocols* are being run together in the network, or in other words, with which protocols should the protocol in question compose. There are two contexts that have been considered, defining two classes of composition:

1. Self composition: A protocol is said to be secure under *self composition* if it remains secure when it alone is executed many times in a network. We stress that in this setting, there is only one protocol that is being run many times. This is the type of composition considered, for example, in the entire body of work on concurrent zero-knowledge (e.g., [9,20]).

2. General composition: In this type of composition, many different protocols are run together in the network. Furthermore, these protocols may have been designed independently of one another. A protocol is said to maintain security under *general composition* if its security is maintained even when it is run along with other arbitrary protocols. This is the type of composition that was considered, for example, in the framework of universal composability [4].

We stress a crucial difference between self and general composition. In self composition, the protocol designer has control over everything that is being run in the network. However, in general composition, the other protocols being run may even have been designed maliciously after the secure protocol is fixed. We note that this additional adversarial capability has been shown to yield practical attacks against real protocols [13].

Another distinction that we will make relates to the number of times a secure protocol is run. Typically, a protocol is expected to remain secure for any polynomial number of sessions. This is the "default" notion, and we sometimes refer to it as unbounded concurrency. A more restricted notion is that of bounded concurrency. In this case, a fixed bound on the number of concurrent executions is given, and the protocol need only remain secure when the number of concurrent execution does not exceed this bound. (When the bound is m, we call this m-bounded concurrency.) Note that the protocol may depend on this bound.

Feasibility of security under composition. The notion of concurrent general composition was first studied by [19] who considered the case that a secure protocol is executed *once* concurrently with another arbitrary protocol. (A definition and composition theorem were presented in [19], but no general feasibility results were demonstrated.) The unbounded case, where a secure protocol can be run any polynomial number of times in an arbitrary network, was then considered in the framework of universal composability [4]. Informally speaking, a protocol that is proven secure under the definition of universal composability is guaranteed to remain secure when run any polynomial number of times in the setting of concurrent general composition. This setting realistically models the security requirements in modern networks. Therefore, obtaining protocols that are secure by this definition is of great interest. On the positive side, it has been shown that in the case of an honest majority, essentially any functionality can be securely computed in this framework [4]. Furthermore, even when there is no honest majority, it is possible to securely compute any functionality in the *common reference string* (CRS) model [8]. (In the CRS model, all parties have access to a common string that is chosen according to some distribution. Thus, this assumes some trusted setup phase.) However, it is desirable to obtain protocols in a setting where *no* trusted setup phase is assumed. Unfortunately, in the case of no honest majority and no trusted setup, broad impossibility results for universal composability have been demonstrated [5,4,7]. Recently, it was shown in [16] that these impossibility results extend to *any* security definition that guarantees security under concurrent general composition (including the definition of [19]).

Thus, it seems that in order to obtain security without an honest majority or a trusted setup phase, we must turn to *self* composition. Indeed, as a first positive step, it has been shown that any functionality can be securely computed under m-bounded concurrent self composition [14,18]. Unfortunately, however, these protocols are highly inefficient: The protocol of [14] has many rounds of communication and both the protocols of [14] and [18] have high bandwidth. (That is, in order to obtain security for m executions, the protocol of [14] has more than m rounds and communication complexity of at least mn^2. In contrast, the protocol of [18] has only a constant number of rounds, but still suffers from communication complexity of at least mn^2.) In addition to the above positive results, it has also been shown that there exist functionalities so that any protocol that securely computes one of them under m-bounded concurrent self composition, and is proven secure using *black-box simulation,* must have more than m rounds of communication [14]. These works still leave open the following important questions:

1. Is it possible to obtain protocols that remain secure under *unbounded* concurrent self composition, and if yes, for which functionalities?
2. Is it possible to obtain *efficient* protocols that remain secure under unbounded, or even m-bounded, concurrent self composition? (By efficient, we mean that at least, there should be no dependence on the bound m.)

As we have mentioned, these questions are open for the case that no trusted setup phase is assumed and when there is no honest majority, as in the important two party case.

Our results. In this paper, we provide negative answers to the above two questions. More precisely, we show that there exist large classes of functionalities that cannot be securely computed under unbounded concurrent self composition.

We also prove a communication complexity lower bound for protocols that are secure under m-bounded concurrent self composition. This is the first lower bound of this type, connecting the communication complexity of a protocol with the bound on the number of executions for which it remains secure.

Theorem 1 (impossibility for unbounded concurrency – informal): *There exist large classes of two-party functionalities that cannot be securely computed under unbounded concurrent self composition, by any protocol.*

In order to prove this result, we show that for many functionalities, obtaining security under unbounded concurrent *self* composition is actually equivalent to obtaining security under concurrent *general* composition (that is, a protocol is secure under one notion if and only if it is secure under the other). This may seem counter-intuitive, because in the setting of self composition, the protocol designer has full control over the network. Specifically, the only protocol that is run in the network is the specified secure protocol. In contrast, in the setting of general composition, a protocol must remain secure even when run concurrently with arbitrary other protocols. Furthermore, these protocols may be designed maliciously in order to attack the secure protocol. Despite this apparent difference, we show that equivalence actually holds.

The above-described equivalence between concurrent self and general composition is proven for all functionalities that "enable bit transmission". Loosely speaking, such a functionality can be used by each party to send any arbitrary bit to the other party. Essentially, any non-constant functionality that depends on both party's inputs, and where both parties receive output, has this property; see Section 2.3. We note that in a model where the parties can play different roles in the computation (e.g., if zero-knowledge is being computed, then in some executions a party plays the prover and in others it plays the verifier), then *any* functionality with the property that one party's output depends on the other party's input actually enables bit transmission. In Section 3, we prove the following theorem:

Theorem 2 (equivalence of self and general composition – informal): *Let f be a two-party functionality that enables bit transmission. Then, f can be securely computed under unbounded concurrent self composition if and only if it can be securely computed under concurrent general composition.*

The above equivalence holds for any functionality that enables bit transmission. In the full version of this paper, we show that an analogue of Theorem 2 does *not* hold for functionalities that do not enable bit transmission. In the full version, we also show that in the above-mentioned model where the parties can play different roles in the computation, then concurrent self composition is equivalent to concurrent general composition, for *all* functionalities.

Returning back to the proof of Theorem 1, impossibility is derived by combining the equivalence between concurrent self and general composition as stated in Theorem 2 with the impossibility results for concurrent general composition that were demonstrated in [16]. This answers the first question above, at least in that it demonstrates impossibility for large classes of functionalities. (It is still far, however, from a full characterization of feasibility.) Regarding the second question, we prove the following theorem that rules out the possibility of obtaining "efficient" protocols for m-bounded concurrency:

Theorem 3 (communication complexity lower bound – informal): *There exists a large class of two-party functionalities so that any protocol that securely computes a functionality in this class under m-bounded concurrent self composition, must have communication complexity of at least m.*

Theorem 3 is essentially proven by directly combining the proof of Theorem 2 with proofs of impossibility from [16] and [7]; see Section 5.

Remarks. We stress that the above results are unconditional. That is, impossibility holds without any complexity assumptions. Furthermore, we assume nothing about the simulation, and in particular do not assume that it is "black-box". We also note that although Theorems 1 and 3 are stated for two-party functionalities, they immediately imply impossibility results for multi-party functionalities as well. This is because secure protocols for multi-party functionalities can be used to solve two-party tasks as well.

It is important to note that our definition of security under concurrent self composition is such that honest parties may choose their inputs *adaptively,* based on previously obtained outputs. This is a seemingly harder definition to achieve than one where the inputs to all the executions are fixed ahead of time. We stress that allowing the inputs to be chosen adaptively is *crucial* to the proof of our impossibility results. Nevertheless, we believe that this is also the desired definition (since in real settings, outputs from previous executions may indeed influence the inputs of later executions).

Other related work. The focus of this work is the ability to obtain secure protocols for solving general tasks. However, security under concurrent composition has also been studied for specific tasks of interest. Indeed, the study of security under concurrent composition was initiated in the context of concurrent zero knowledge [10,9], where a prover runs many copies of a protocol with many verifiers. Thus, these works consider the question of security under *self* composition. This problem has received much attention; see [20,6,1] for just a few examples. Other specific problems have also been considered, but are not directly related to this paper.

2   Definitions

In this section, we present definitions for security under concurrent self composition and concurrent general composition, and we define the notion of functions that enable bit transmission. We denote the equivalence of distributions by $\equiv$, computational indistinguishability by $\stackrel{c}{\equiv}$, and the security parameter by n. The adversary always runs in time that is polynomial in n.

2.1   Concurrent Self Composition of Two-Party Protocols

We begin by presenting the definition for security under concurrent self composition. The basic description and definition of secure computation follows [12,2,17, 3]. Due to lack of space in this abstract, we present a slightly abridged definition and refer to the full version of this paper and [14] for full definitions. (Note that our definition here actually differs from [14] in that here the honest parties may adaptively choose their input to a session as a function of previously obtained outputs.)

Two-party computation. A two-party protocol problem is cast by specifying a random process that maps pairs of inputs to pairs of outputs (one for each party). We refer to such a process as a functionality and denote it $f : \{0,1\}^* \times \{0,1\}^* \rightarrow \{0,1\}^* \times \{0,1\}^*$, where $f = (f_1, f_2)$. That is, for every pair of inputs (x, y), the output-pair is a random variable $(f_1(x,y), f_2(x,y))$ ranging over pairs of strings. The first party (with input x) wishes to obtain $f_1(x, y)$ and the second party (with input y) wishes to obtain $f_2(x, y)$. We often denote such a functionality by $(x, y) \mapsto (f_1(x, y), f_2(x, y))$. Thus, for example, the zero-knowledge proof of knowledge functionality for a relation R is denoted by $((x, w), \lambda) \mapsto (\lambda, (x, R(x, w)))$. In the context of concurrent composition, each party actually uses many inputs (one for each execution), and these may be chosen adaptively based on previous outputs. We consider both concurrent self composition (where the number of executions is unbounded) and m-bounded concurrent self composition (where the number of concurrent executions is a priori bounded by m and the protocol design can depend on this bound).

Adversarial behavior. In this work we consider a malicious, static adversary that runs in time that is polynomial in the security parameter. Such an adversary controls one of the parties (who is called corrupted) and may then interact with the honest party while arbitrarily deviating from the specified protocol. Our definition does not guarantee any fairness. That is, the adversary always receives its own output and can then decide when (if at all) the honest party will receive its output. The scheduling of message delivery is decided by the adversary.

Security of protocols (informal). The security of a protocol is analyzed by comparing what an adversary can do in the protocol to what it can do in an ideal scenario that is trivially secure. This is formalized by considering an *ideal* computation involving an incorruptible *trusted third party* to whom the parties send their inputs. The trusted party computes the functionality on the inputs and returns to each party its respective output. Unlike in the case of stand-alone computation, here the trusted party computes the functionality many times, each time upon different inputs. Loosely speaking, a protocol is secure if any adversary interacting in the real protocol (where no trusted third party exists) can do no more harm than if it was involved in the above-described ideal computation.

Concurrent executions in the ideal model. In an ideal execution, the parties P_1 and P_2 interact with a trusted third party, sending it inputs and receiving back outputs. Party P_1 and P_2's inputs are determined by polynomial-size input-deciding circuit families $X = \{X_n\}_{n \in \mathbb{N}}$ and $Y = \{Y_n\}_{n \in \mathbb{N}}$, respectively. The circuits X_n and Y_n are polynomial in n and output exactly n bits. These circuits determine the length-n input values to be used, based on the current session number and previous outputs. Note that the number of previous outputs ranges from zero (for the case that no previous outputs have yet been obtained) to some fixed polynomial in n (that depends on the number of session initiated by the adversary).[1] Now, the ideal execution proceeds as follows. Whenever the adversary wishes to initiate a new session, it sends a start-session message to the trusted party. The trusted party then sends (start-session, i) to the honest party, where i is the index of the session (i.e., this is the ith session to be started). Upon receiving (start-session, i) from the trusted party, the honest party applies its input-deciding circuit to (i) and its previous outputs, and obtains a new input v_i for this session. The honest party then sends (i, v_i) to the trusted party.

Whenever it wishes, the adversary can then send a message (i, w_i) to the trusted party, for any $w_i \in \{0,1\}^n$ of its choice. Upon sending this pair, it receives back its output from the trusted party, computed upon inputs (v_i, w_i). Following this, but again whenever it wishes, the adversary can instruct the trusted party to send the honest party its ith output; the adversary does this by sending a (send-output, i) message to the trusted party. Finally, at the conclusion of the execution, the honest party outputs the vector of outputs that it received from the trusted party, and the adversary may output an arbitrary (probabilistic polynomial-time computable) function of its auxiliary input z, the corrupted party's input-deciding circuit and the outputs obtained from the trusted party.

Let $f : \{0,1\}^* \times \{0,1\}^* \mapsto \{0,1\}^* \times \{0,1\}^*$ be a functionality, and let $\mathcal{S}$ be a non-uniform probabilistic polynomial-time machine (representing the ideal-model adversary). Then, the ideal execution of f (on input-deciding circuits (X_n, Y_n) and auxiliary input z to $\mathcal{S}$), denoted $\text{IDEAL}_{f,\mathcal{S}}(X_n, Y_n, z)$, is defined as the output pair of the honest party and $\mathcal{S}$ from the above ideal execution.

(We note that the definition of the ideal model does not differ for the case that unbounded concurrency or m-bounded concurrency is considered. This is because this bound is relevant only to the scheduling allowed to the adversary in the real model; see below.)

Execution in the real model. We next consider the real model in which a real two-party protocol is executed (and there exists no trusted third party). Let f be as above and let ρ be a polynomial-time two-party protocol for computing f. (We say that a protocol is polynomial-time if the running-time of the honest parties in a *single execution* is bound by a fixed polynomial.) In addition, let $\mathcal{A}$ be a non-uniform probabilistic polynomial-time machine that controls either P_1 or P_2. Then, the real concurrent execution of ρ (with input-deciding circuits (X_n, Y_n) and auxiliary input z to $\mathcal{A}$), denoted $\text{REAL}_{\rho,\mathcal{A}}(X_n, Y_n, z)$, is defined as the output pair of the honest party and $\mathcal{A}$, resulting from the following process. The parties run concurrent executions of the protocol, where the ith session is initiated by the adversary by sending a start-session message to the honest party.

---

[1] By convention, if the number of previously obtained outputs is greater than the maximum input length to the circuit, then we define the next input to be $\perp$.

The honest party then applies its input-deciding circuit on (i) and its previous outputs in order to obtain the input for this new session. (As in the ideal model, if the length of all previous outputs is greater than the maximum input length to the input-deciding circuit, then the next input is taken as $\perp$.) The scheduling of all messages throughout the executions is controlled by the adversary. That is, the execution proceeds as follows. The adversary sends a message of the form (i, α) to the honest party. The honest party then adds the message α to the view of its ith execution of ρ and replies according to the instructions of ρ and this view. The adversary continues by sending another message (j, β), and so on. We note that there is no restriction on the scheduling allowed by the adversary. (We sometimes refer to this as unbounded concurrency, in order to distinguish it from m-bounded concurrency that is defined next.)

In addition to the above setting where no restriction is placed on the scheduling, we also consider m-bounded concurrency, where the scheduling by the adversary must fulfill the following condition: for every execution i, from the time that the ith execution begins until the time that it ends, messages from at most m different executions can be sent. (Formally, view the schedule as the ordered series of messages of the form (index, message) that are sent by the adversary. Then, in the interval between the beginning and termination of any given execution, the number of different indices viewed can be at most m.) We note that this definition of concurrency covers the case that m executions are run simultaneously. However, it also includes a more general case where many more than m executions take place, but each execution overlaps with at most m other executions. In this setting, the value m is fixed ahead of time, and the protocol design may depend on the choice of m. We denote the output of the adversary and honest party in the setting of m-bounded concurrency by $\text{REAL}_{\rho,\mathcal{A}}^{m}(X_n, Y_n, z)$.

Security as emulation of a real execution in the ideal model. Having defined the ideal and real models, we can now define security of protocols. Loosely speaking, a protocol is secure if for every real-model adversary $\mathcal{A}$ there exists an ideal model adversary $\mathcal{S}$ such that for all polynomial-size input-deciding circuits, the outcome of an ideal execution with $\mathcal{S}$ is computationally indistinguishable from the outcome of a real protocol execution with $\mathcal{A}$. One important technical issue which arises here is due to the fact that the same $\mathcal{S}$ must work for *all* polynomial-size input-deciding circuits. In particular, this means that the honest parties (who compute their inputs in every execution from these circuits) may run longer than $\mathcal{S}$ can run (specifically, the size of the input-deciding circuits may be greater than $\mathcal{S}$'s running time).[2] This is an "unfair" requirement on $\mathcal{S}$ and we therefore allow a different ideal-model adversary $\mathcal{S}$ for every "size" circuit. That is, we require that for every real adversary $\mathcal{A}$ and polynomial $q(\cdot)$ there exists an ideal adversary $\mathcal{S}$ that works for all input-deciding circuit families $X = \{X_n\}$ and $Y = \{Y_n\}$ of size $O(q(n))$. We stress that any protocol that is secure when $\mathcal{S}$ must work for all polynomial-size input-deciding circuits is also

---

[2] We note that the *number* of executions is not a problem because this is determined by $\mathcal{A}$, and $\mathcal{S}$ comes after $\mathcal{A}$ in the order of quantifiers.

secure under this relaxation. This modification therefore only strengthens our impossibility results.[3] We now present the definition:

Definition 1 (security under concurrent self composition): *Let f and ρ be as above. Protocol ρ is said to* securely compute f under concurrent self composition *if for every real-model non-uniform probabilistic polynomial-time adversary $\mathcal{A}$ controlling party P_i for $i \in \{1, 2\}$ and every polynomial $q(\cdot)$, there exists an ideal-model non-uniform probabilistic polynomial-time adversary $\mathcal{S}$ controlling P_i, such that for all families of input-deciding circuits $X = \{X_n\}_{n \in \mathbb{N}}$ and $Y = \{Y_n\}_{n \in \mathbb{N}}$ of size at most $O(q(n))$, and every auxiliary input $z \in \{0, 1\}^*$,*

$$\left\{ \text{IDEAL}_{f,\mathcal{S}}(X_n, Y_n, z) \right\}_{n \in \mathbb{N}} \overset{\text{c}}{\equiv} \left\{ \text{REAL}_{\rho,\mathcal{A}}(X_n, Y_n, z) \right\}_{n \in \mathbb{N}}$$

Let $m = m(n)$ be a fixed polynomial. Then, we say that ρ securely computes f under m-bounded concurrent self composition *if*

$$\left\{ \text{IDEAL}_{f,\mathcal{S}}(X_n, Y_n, z) \right\}_{n \in \mathbb{N}} \overset{\text{c}}{\equiv} \left\{ \text{REAL}_{\rho,\mathcal{A}}^m(X_n, Y_n, z) \right\}_{n \in \mathbb{N}}$$

Non-trivial protocols. Notice that by the definition of security in the ideal model, the honest party is never guaranteed to receive output. Therefore, the "real" protocol that just hangs and does not provide output to any party is actually secure by definition (and so our impossibility results cannot apply to *all* protocols). We therefore introduce the notion of non-trivial protocols. Such a protocol has the property that if the real-model adversary instructs the corrupted party to act honestly (i.e., follow the protocol specification), then both parties receive output.

2.2   Concurrent General Composition of Two-Party Protocols

Informally speaking, concurrent general composition considers the case that a secure protocol ρ runs concurrently with an arbitrary other protocol π. Furthermore, the inputs to ρ can be influenced (or actually determined) by protocol π. In the formalization of this setting, π is a "controlling protocol" that among other things, contains ideal calls to a trusted party that computes a functionality f. When these calls are replaced by executions of ρ, we denote the composed protocol by π^ρ. We stress that, in addition to representing a "controlling protocol", π can also represent arbitrary protocols that are running concurrently with ρ in the network. Therefore, by requiring that ρ remains secure for every calling protocol π, we derive that ρ remains secure when executed in any network with any set of protocols running. See [16] for more discussion.

---

[3] The reason that we insist on allowing a different $\mathcal{S}$ for every $q(\cdot)$ is due to the fact that, otherwise, it would turn out that concurrent general composition *does not imply* concurrent self composition. This would be absurd. We stress that our proof that concurrent self composition implies concurrent general composition holds in any case.

Let ρ be as above and assume that it computes a functionality f. Then, the security of ρ when composed with π in the real model is formalized by comparing the π^ρ composition to a hybrid execution where π uses ideal calls to a trusted party computing the functionality f. If the results of the hybrid and real executions are indistinguishable, then this means that a real execution of ρ behaves like an ideal call to f, even when run concurrently with π.

The hybrid model. Let π be an arbitrary polynomial-time protocol that utilizes ideal interaction with a trusted party computing a two-party functionality f. This means that π contains two types of messages: standard messages and ideal messages: A standard message is one that is sent between the parties that are participating in the execution of π; an ideal message is one that is sent by a participating party to the trusted third party, or from the trusted third party to a participating party. This trusted party computes f and associates all ideal messages with f. Notice that the computation of π is a "hybrid" between the ideal model (where a trusted party carries out the entire computation) and the real model (where the parties interact with each other only). Specifically, the messages of π are sent directly between the parties, and the trusted party is only used in the ideal calls to f.

The interaction with the trusted party is exactly according to the description of *concurrent executions in the ideal model*, as described in Section 2.1. In contrast, the standard messages are dealt with exactly according to the description of the *real model*, as described in Section 2.1. More formally, computation in the hybrid model proceeds as follows. The computation begins with the adversary receiving the input and random tape of the corrupted party. Throughout the execution, the adversary sends any standard and ideal messages that it wishes in the name of this party (where the format of the ideal messages is as defined in the ideal execution in Section 2.1). The honest party always follows the specification of protocol π. Specifically, upon receiving a message (from the adversary or trusted party), the party reads the message, carries out a local computation as instructed by π, and sends standard and/or ideal messages, as instructed by π. At the end of the computation, the honest party writes the output value prescribed by π on its output tape and the adversary outputs an arbitrary function of its view. Let n be the security parameter, let $\mathcal{S}$ be an adversary for the hybrid model with auxiliary input z, and let $x, y \in \{0,1\}^n$ be the parties' respective inputs to π. Then, the hybrid execution of π with functionality f, denoted $\mathrm{HYBRID}^f_{\pi,\mathcal{S}}(x,y,z)$, is defined as the output of the adversary $\mathcal{S}$ and of the honest party from the above hybrid execution.

The real model – general composition. Let ρ be a polynomial-time two-party protocol for computing the functionality f. Intuitively, the composition of protocol π with ρ is such that ρ takes the place of the interaction with the trusted party that computes f. Formally, each party holds separate probabilistic interactive Turing machines (ITMs) that work according to the specification of protocol ρ for that party. When π instructs a party to send an ideal message α to the trusted party, the party writes α on the input tape of a new ITM for ρ and invokes the machine. Any message that it receives that is marked for this execution of ρ, it forwards to this ITM, and all other messages are answered according to π. (The different executions of ρ are distinguished with indices, as described in Section 2.1. Furthermore, π-messages are distinguished from ρ-messages with a unique index/symbol for π.) Finally, when an execution of ρ concludes and a value β is written on the output tape of an ITM, the party copies β to the incoming communication tape for π, as if β is an ideal message (i.e., output) received from the trusted party. This composition of π with ρ is denoted π^{ρ} and takes place without any trusted help. Let n be the security parameter, let $\mathcal{A}$ be an adversary for the real model with auxiliary input z, and let $x, y \in \{0, 1\}^n$ be the parties' respective inputs to π. Then, the real execution of π with ρ, denoted $\text{REAL}_{\pi^{\rho}, \mathcal{A}}(x, y, z)$, is defined as the output of the adversary $\mathcal{A}$ and of the honest party from the above real execution.

Security as emulation of a real execution in the hybrid model. Having defined the hybrid and real models, we can now define security of protocols. Loosely speaking, the definition asserts that for any context, or calling protocol π, the real execution of π^{ρ} emulates the hybrid execution of π which utilizes ideal calls to f. The fact that the above emulation must hold for *every* protocol π that utilizes ideal calls to f, means that *general composition* is being considered.

Definition 2 (security under concurrent general composition): *Let ρ be a polynomial-time two-party protocol and f a two-party functionality. Then, ρ securely realizes f under concurrent general composition if for every polynomial-time protocol π that utilizes ideal calls to f and every non-uniform probabilistic polynomial-time real-model adversary $\mathcal{A}$ for π^{ρ}, there exists a non-uniform probabilistic polynomial-time hybrid-model adversary $\mathcal{S}$ such that for all inputs $x, y \in \{0, 1\}^n$ and all auxiliary inputs $z \in \{0, 1\}^*$,*

$$\left\{ \text{HYBRID}_{\pi, \mathcal{S}}^{f}(x, y, z) \right\}_{n \in \mathsf{N}} \stackrel{\mathrm{c}}{\equiv} \left\{ \text{REAL}_{\pi^{\rho}, \mathcal{A}}(x, y, z) \right\}_{n \in \mathsf{N}}$$

Note that non-trivial protocols are also defined for general composition. Once again, the requirement is that if $\mathcal{A}$ instructs the corrupted party to act honestly in the execution of ρ, then the honest party receives its output from ρ.

2.3   Functionalities That Enable Bit Transmission

Informally speaking, a functionality enables bit transmission if it can be used by the parties to send bits to each other. For example, the "equality functionality", where both parties receive the output, enables bit transmission as follows. The party who wishes to receive a bit inputs a predetermined value, say 1. Then, if the sending party wishes to send a bit 0, it inputs 0 (in this case, the inputs are not equal and so the output of the computation is 0). On the other hand, if the sending party wishes to send the bit 1, then it inputs 1 (thus, the inputs are equal and the output is 1). Notice that a functionality enables bit transmission only if both parties are able to send bits to each other. Therefore, functionalities like oblivious transfer and zero-knowledge do not enable bit transmission, because only one party receives output. Nevertheless, by considering a more general setting where both parties can play both roles in the functionality (e.g., both parties can prove statements in zero-knowledge and both parties can play the sender in the oblivious transfer), we obtain that *any* functionality with the property that one party's output depends on the other party's input actually enables bit transmission. This generalization is dealt with in the full version of this paper. We now present the formal definition:

Definition 3 (functionalities that enable bit transmission): *A deterministic functionality $f = (f_1, f_2)$* enables bit transmission *from P_1 to P_2 if there exists an input y for P_2 and a pair of inputs x and x' for P_1 such that $f_2(x, y) \neq f_2(x', y)$. Likewise, $f = (f_1, f_2)$* enables bit transmission *from P_2 to P_1 if there exists an input x for P_1 and a pair of inputs y and y' for P_2 such that $f_1(x, y) \neq f_1(x, y')$. We say that a functionality* enables bit transmission *if it enables bit transmission from P_1 to P_2 and from P_2 to P_1.*

We note that the notion of enabling bit transmission can be generalized to probabilistic functionalities in a straightforward way.

3   Self Composition versus General Composition

In this section we show that if a functionality f enables bit transmission, then a protocol ρ securely computes f under (unbounded) concurrent self composition if and only if it securely computes f under concurrent general composition. Thus, the difference between self and general composition no longer holds for such functionalities. We stress that there *is* nevertheless a difference between these notions when *bounded* composition is considered. Specifically, security under bounded-concurrency can be achieved for self composition [14,18], but cannot be achieved for general composition [16]. (By bounded concurrency in the setting of general composition, we mean that the number of executions of the secure protocol is a priori bounded, exactly like in self composition. In contrast, there is no bound on the calling protocol π.)

Theorem 4 *Let f be a two-party functionality that enables bit transmission, and let ρ be a polynomial-time protocol. Then, ρ securely computes f under (unbounded) concurrent self composition if and only if ρ securely computes f under concurrent general composition.*

Intuitively, security under general composition implies security under self composition because in both cases, many copies of the secure protocol are run; the only difference is that in the setting of general composition, other protocols may *also* be run. The other, more interesting direction, is proven as follows. Loosely speaking, the parties use the "bit transmission property" of f in order to emulate an execution of π^ρ, while only running copies of ρ (recall that π^ρ denotes the concurrent general composition of a secure protocol ρ with an arbitrary other protocol π). This can be carried out by sending the messages of π one bit at a time, via executions of the protocol ρ that computes f. Thus, it is possible to emulate the setting of concurrent general composition, within the context of concurrent self composition. The proof of Theorem 4 appears in the full version of this paper. As we have mentioned, we also show that in a model where the parties can play different roles in the computation, *full equivalence* holds between concurrent self composition and concurrent general composition.

In the full version of this paper, we also show a *separation* between concurrent self composition and concurrent general composition, for functions that do *not* enable bit transmission. Specifically, we show that the zero-knowledge proof of knowledge functionality (for an NP-complete language) can be securely computed under concurrent self composition. However, in [16], it has been shown that this cannot be achieved under concurrent general composition.

4   Impossibility for Concurrent Self Composition

An important ramification of Theorem 4 is that known impossibility results for concurrent *general* composition apply also to unbounded concurrent *self* composition, as long as the functionality in question enables bit transmission. As we will see, this rules out the possibility of obtaining security under concurrent self composition for large classes of two-party functionalities. We stress that the impossibility results are *unconditional*. That is, they hold without any complexity assumptions and for any type of simulation (in particular they are not limited to "black-box" simulation).

Impossibility for concurrent general composition. The following impossibility results for concurrent general composition were shown in [16]:

1. Let $f : \{0,1\}^* \times \{0,1\}^* \to \{0,1\}^*$ be a deterministic functionality. If f depends on both parties' inputs,[4] then the functionality $(x, y) \to (f(x, y), f(x, y))$ cannot be securely computed under concurrent general composition by any non-trivial protocol. (Recall that a protocol is non-trivial if it generates output when both parties are honest.)
2. Let $f : \{0,1\}^* \times \{0,1\}^* \to \{0,1\}^* \times \{0,1\}^*$ be a deterministic functionality and denote $f = (f_1, f_2)$. If f is *not completely revealing*,[5] then the functionality $(x, y) \to (f_1(x, y), f_2(x, y))$ cannot be securely computed under concurrent general composition by any non-trivial protocol.

Impossibility results for concurrent self composition. Let Φ be the set of functionalities described above, that cannot be securely realized under concurrent general composition and let Ψ be the set of all two-party functionalities that enable message transmission. Applying Theorem 4 to the results of [16], we obtain the following corollary:

---

[4] Formally, a functionality f depends on both inputs if there exist x_1, x_2, y and x, y_1, y_2 such that $f(x_1, y) \neq f(x_2, y)$ and $f(x, y_1) \neq f(x, y_2)$.

[5] The definition of completely revealing functionalities can be found in Section 5.

Corollary 5 *Let f be a functionality in $\Phi \cap \Psi$. Then, f cannot be securely computed under unbounded concurrent self composition by any non-trivial protocol.*

The set of functionalities $\Phi \cap \Psi$ contains all the functionalities ruled out in [16] that also enable bit transmission. For example, Yao's famous millionaires' problem (i.e., the computation of the "less than" functionality), where both parties receive the output, is included in this set.

5   Communication Complexity Lower Bound

In this section we prove that for a class of functionalities $\mathcal{F}$, if a protocol ρ securely computes a functionality $f \in \mathcal{F}$ under m-bounded concurrent composition, and f enables bit transmission, then ρ must have bandwidth of at least m bits. We prove this for one class of functionalities $\mathcal{F}$, although the proof can be extended to other classes of functionalities that suffer from the impossibility result stated in Corollary 5. The proof of our lower bound combines ideas from [7] and [16], together with the proof of Theorem 4.

Functionalities that are completely revealing. We prove the lower bound for one class of functionalities: those that do not "completely reveal P_1 or P_2's input", and enable bit transmission. In order to state this, we need to formally define what it means for a functionality to be "completely revealing". Loosely speaking, a (deterministic) functionality completely reveals party P_1's input, if party P_2 can choose an input that will enable it to *completely determine* P_1's input (no matter what P_1's input is). That is, a functionality f completely reveals P_1's input if there exists an input y for P_2 so that for every x, it is possible to derive x from $f(x, y)$. For example, let us take the maximum functionality for a given range, say $\{0, \ldots, n\}$. Then, party P_2 can input $y = 0$ and the result is that it will always learn P_1's exact input. In contrast, the less-than functionality is *not* completely revealing because for any input used by P_2, there will always be uncertainty about P_1's input (unless P_1's input is the smallest or largest in the range). For our lower bound here, we will consider functionalities over finite domains only. This significantly simplifies the definition of "completely revealing". However, our proof holds for the general case as well; see the full version of [7] for a complete definition.

We begin by defining what it means for two inputs to be "equivalent": Let $f : X \times Y \to \{0, 1\}^* \times \{0, 1\}^*$ be a two-party functionality and denote $f = (f_1, f_2)$. Let $x, x' \in X$. We say that x and x' are equivalent with respect to f_2 if for every $y \in Y$ it holds that $f_2(x, y) = f_2(x', y)$. Notice that if x and x' are equivalent with respect to f_2, then x can always be used instead of x' (at least regarding P_2's output). We now define completely revealing functionalities:

Definition 6 (completely revealing functionalities over finite domains): *Let $f : X \times Y \to \{0, 1\}^* \times \{0, 1\}^*$ be a deterministic two-party functionality such that the domain $X \times Y$ is finite, and denote $f = (f_1, f_2)$. We say that the functionality*

f_2 completely reveals P_1's input *if there exists a single input $y \in Y$ for P_2, such that for every pair of values $x, x' \in X$ that are not equivalent with respect to f_2, it holds that $f_2(x, y) \neq f_2(x', y)$. Complete revealing for P_2's input is defined analogously. We say that a functionality is* completely revealing *if f_1 completely reveals P_2's input or f_2 completely reveals P_1's input.*

If a functionality completely reveals P_1's input, then party P_2 can set its own input to be y from the definition, and then P_2 will always obtain the exact input used by P_1, or one that is equivalent to it. Specifically, given y and $f_2(x, y)$, it can traverse over all X and find the unique x that must be P_1's input (or one equivalent to it). Thus we see that P_1's input is completely revealed by f_2. In contrast, if a functionality f_2 does *not* completely reveal P_1's input, then there does not exist such an input for P_2 that enables it to completely determine P_1's input. This is because for every y that is input by P_2, there exist two non-equivalent inputs x and x' such that $f_2(x, y) = f_2(x', y)$. Therefore, if P_1's input is x or x', it follows that P_2 is unable to determine which of these inputs were used by P_1. Notice that if a functionality is not completely revealing, P_2 may still learn much of P_1's input (or even the exact input "most of the time"). However, there is a *possibility* that P_2 will not fully obtain P_1's input. As we will see, the existence of this "possibility" suffices for proving the lower bound. Note that we require that x and x' be non-equivalent because in such a case, x and x' are really the same input and so, essentially, both x and x' are P_1's input.

The statement of the theorem below refers to the bandwidth of a protocol ρ. This is defined to be the *total number of bits* sent by *both* parties in a protocol execution. We are now ready to state the lower bound:

Theorem 7 *Let $f = (f_1, f_2)$ be a deterministic two-party functionality over a finite domain that is not completely revealing and enables bit transmission. If a non-trivial protocol ρ securely computes f under m-bounded concurrent self composition, then the* bandwidth *of ρ is greater than or equal to m.*

Proof: As a first step, we note that the proof of Theorem 4 actually proves something stronger than the theorem statement. Before showing this, we first define the bandwidth of a hybrid-model protocol π that utilizes ideal calls to f to equal the total number of bits sent by the parties to *each other*, plus a *single bit* for each call to f.[6] Now, let π be a hybrid-model protocol that utilizes ideal calls to f, and has bandwidth at most m. Then, in the proof of Theorem 4, we actually showed that if f enables bit transmission, then m invocations of ρ suffice for perfectly emulating π^ρ (one invocation for each bit of π and one invocation for replacing each ideal call to f). In other words, for *any protocol π of bandwidth at most m*, an execution of π^ρ can be emulated using m concurrent executions of ρ. Furthermore, this yields a simulator for the hybrid-model execution of π with f. Thus, security under m-bounded concurrent self composition implies security

---

[6] This may seem to be a strange way to count the bandwidth of a hybrid-model protocol. However, what we are really interested in is the bandwidth of a *real* protocol; this is just a tool to reach that aim and defining it in this way simplifies things.

under concurrent general composition for protocols π of bandwidth at most m. We conclude that the following claim holds:

Claim 8 *Let f be a two-party functionality that enables bit transmission, and let ρ be a polynomial-time protocol. If ρ securely computes f under m-bounded concurrent self composition, then for every hybrid-model polynomial-time protocol π of bandwidth at most m that utilizes ideal calls to f and for every non-uniform probabilistic polynomial-time real-model adversary $\mathcal{A}$ for π^ρ, there exists a non-uniform probabilistic polynomial-time hybrid-model adversary $\mathcal{S}$ such that for all $x, y \in \{0,1\}^n$ and all $z \in \{0,1\}^*$,*

$$\{\text{HYBRID}^f_{\pi,\mathcal{S}}(x,y,z)\}_{n\in\mathsf{N}} \stackrel{c}{\equiv} \{\text{REAL}_{\pi^\rho,\mathcal{A}}(x,y,z)\}_{n\in\mathsf{N}} \tag{1}$$

We now proceed with the actual proof of Theorem 7. Let $f = (f_1, f_2)$ be a deterministic two-party functionality over a finite domain, such that f is not completely revealing and enables bit transmission. We prove the theorem for the case that f_2 does not completely reveal P_1's input; the other case is analogously proven. Assume, by contradiction, that there exists a protocol ρ that securely computes f under m-bounded concurrent self composition, and has bandwidth less than m. We then show that in such a case, it is possible to construct a protocol π that utilizes ideal calls to f and has bandwidth at most m, such that π has the following property: There exists a real-model adversary $\mathcal{A}$ for π^ρ such that no hybrid-model adversary/simulator $\mathcal{S}$ can cause Eq. (1) of Claim 8 to hold. This thereby contradicts Claim 8, and we conclude that if ρ securely computes f under m-bounded concurrent self composition, then it must have bandwidth of at least m.

Protocol π of bandwidth m: Protocol π works as follows. Party P_2 receives for input two uniformly chosen values $x \in_R X$ and $y \in_R Y$. (Note that since security must hold for all inputs, it must also hold for uniformly chosen inputs.) Then, P_2 sends the input y to the trusted party for an ideal call to f. In addition, P_2 runs the instructions of P_1 in ρ with input x. At the conclusion, P_2 outputs 1 if and only if the output that it receives from the trusted party is $f_2(x, y)$. This completes the instructions for P_2. Regarding the instructions for Party P_1, it actually makes no difference because this party will always be corrupted in π. Nevertheless, in order for π to make sense, one can define P_1 in an analogous way to P_2. This completes the description of π. Note that by the assumption that ρ has bandwidth of less than m, the protocol π has bandwidth less than or equal to m (if ρ has bandwidth $m-1$, then π will have bandwidth m by adding 1 for the single ideal call to f).

We stress that P_2's instructions in protocol π are *not* equivalent to its instructions in ρ. This is because in π, party P_2 follows the instructions of P_1 in ρ. However, such behaviour may not be in accordance with ρ, because P_1's instructions in ρ may not be symmetric with P_2's instructions (e.g., see the protocols of [15,18] that use asymmetrical instructions in an inherent way). Nevertheless, by Claim 8, protocol ρ must remain secure for *all* protocols π of bandwidth at most m, and in particular, for the protocol π above.

Real-model adversary $\mathcal{A}$ for π^ρ: Let $\mathcal{A}$ be an adversary who controls the corrupted party P_1. Before describing $\mathcal{A}$, notice that the composed protocol π^ρ essentially consists of two executions of ρ: in one of the executions, each party plays its designated role (these are the ρ-messages) and in the other, the parties play reversed roles (these are the π-messages). Adversary $\mathcal{A}$ works as follows. When P_2 sends the first ρ-message to P_1,[7] adversary $\mathcal{A}$ forwards this same message back to P_2 as if it is P_1's first π-message to P_2. Then, when P_2 answers this π-message (according to P_1's instructions in ρ and with input x), $\mathcal{A}$ forwards it back to P_2 as if it is a ρ-message from P_1.

Since party P_2 runs the ρ-instructions of P_1 in π, the execution of π^ρ with adversary $\mathcal{A}$ amounts to P_2 playing both roles in a single execution of ρ, where input x is used for P_1's role and input y is used for P_2's role. Furthermore, P_2 plays both roles honestly and according to the respective instructions of P_1 and P_2. Therefore, the transcript is identical to the case that two honest parties P_1 and P_2 run ρ with respective inputs x and y. By the security of ρ and the fact that it is a non-trivial protocol, we have that except with negligible probability, P_2 receives the P_2-output from this execution of ρ, and that this output must equal $f_2(x, y)$. (This follows from the guaranteed behaviour of such a protocol when two honest parties participate.) Now, since P_2 outputs 1 in π if and only if it receives $f_2(x, y)$ from the trusted party, we have that it outputs 1 in the π^ρ execution with $\mathcal{A}$, except with negligible probability (recall that in π^ρ, the output from ρ is treated by P_2 as if it was received from the trusted party).

Hybrid-model adversary $\mathcal{S}$ for π: By the assumption that ρ is secure under m-bounded concurrent self composition and from Claim 8, we have that there exists a probabilistic polynomial-time hybrid-model adversary $\mathcal{S}$ such that:

$$\{\text{HYBRID}^f_{\pi,\mathcal{S}}(\lambda, (x, y), \lambda)\} \stackrel{c}{\equiv} \{\text{REAL}_{\pi^\rho, \mathcal{A}}(\lambda, (x, y), \lambda)\} \tag{2}$$

Notice here that P_2's input is (x, y) as described above and we can assume that P_1's input and the adversary's auxiliary input are empty strings.

We now make an important observation about the hybrid-model simulator $\mathcal{S}$ from Eq. (2). In the ideal execution, with overwhelming probability, $\mathcal{S}$ must send the trusted party an input $\tilde{x} \in X$ such that for every $\tilde{y} \in Y$, $f_2(\tilde{x}, \tilde{y}) = f_2(x, \tilde{y})$, where x is from P_2's input to π. In other words, $\mathcal{S}$ must send the trusted party a value $\tilde{x}$ that is equivalent to P_2's input x. Otherwise, P_2's output from the hybrid and real executions will be distinguishable. In order to see this, recall that in a real execution with $\mathcal{A}$, party P_2 outputs 1 except with negligible probability. Therefore, the same must be true in the hybrid execution. However, if $\mathcal{S}$ sends an input $\tilde{x}$ for which there exists a $\tilde{y}$ so that $f_2(\tilde{x}, \tilde{y}) \neq f_2(x, \tilde{y})$, then with probability $1/|Y|$ party P_2 will output 0; specifically when P_2's input y equals this $\tilde{y}$ (note that since Y is finite, this is a constant probability). This argument works because P_2 does not use y in any messages sent to $\mathcal{S}$ in the hybrid-model execution of π. Thus, $\mathcal{S}$ works independently of the choice of y.

Until now, we have shown that the hybrid-model adversary $\mathcal{S}$ can "extract" an input $\tilde{x}$ that is equivalent to x. However, notice that $\mathcal{S}$ does this while essen-

---

[7] We assume without loss of generality that the first message in ρ is sent by P_2.

tially running an on-line execution of ρ with party P_1. (Of course, the interaction is actually of π-messages with P_2. Nevertheless, P_2 just plays P_1's role in ρ for this interaction, so this makes no difference.) This means that $\mathcal{S}$ could actually be used by an adversary who has corrupted P_2 and wishes to extract the honest P_1's input, or one equivalent to it. Since f is not completely revealing, this is a contradiction to the security of ρ. We proceed to formally prove this.

A different scenario: We now change scenarios and consider a *single* execution of ρ with an honest party P_1 who has input $x \in_R X$, and a real-model adversary $\mathcal{A}'$ who controls a corrupted P_2. The strategy of $\mathcal{A}'$ is to internally invoke the hybrid-model adversary $\mathcal{S}$, and perfectly emulate for it the hybrid-model execution of π with ideal calls to f. Adversary $\mathcal{A}'$ needs to emulate the trusted party for the ideal call to f that is made by $\mathcal{S}$, as well as the π-messages that $\mathcal{S}$ expects to receive. Notice that in the setting of a hybrid-model execution of π, these π-messages are sent by P_2. However, they are exactly the messages that an honest P_1 would send in a single real-model execution of ρ, with input x. Therefore, $\mathcal{A}'$ forwards $\mathcal{S}$ the messages that it receives from P_1 in its real execution of ρ, as if $\mathcal{S}$ received them from P_2 in a hybrid-model execution of π. Likewise, messages from $\mathcal{S}$ are sent externally to P_1. At some stage of the emulation, $\mathcal{S}$ must send a value $\tilde{x}$ to the trusted party. $\mathcal{A}'$ obtains this $\tilde{x}$, outputs it and halts.

The view of $\mathcal{S}$ in this emulation by $\mathcal{A}'$ (until $\mathcal{A}'$ halts) is *identical* to its view in a hybrid-model execution of π. Therefore, by the above observation regarding $\mathcal{S}$, it holds that $\tilde{x}$ must be such that for every $y \in Y$, $f_2(\tilde{x}, y) = f_2(x, y)$, except with negligible probability. That is, in a single real execution of ρ between an honest P_1 and an adversary $\mathcal{A}'$ controlling P_2, we have that $\mathcal{A}'$ outputs a value $\tilde{x}$ that is equivalent to P_1's input x (except with negligible probability).

It remains to show that in an ideal execution of f, for every ideal-model simulator $\mathcal{S}'$ controlling P_2, the probability that $\mathcal{S}'$ outputs a value $\tilde{x}$ that is equivalent to P_1's input x is less than $1 - 1/p(n)$, for some polynomial $p(\cdot)$. This suffices because the real-model adversary $\mathcal{A}'$ does output such an $\tilde{x}$; this therefore proves that there does not exist a simulator for $\mathcal{A}'$, in contradiction to the (stand-alone) security of ρ. Now, in an ideal execution, $\mathcal{S}'$ sends some input $\tilde{y}$ to the trusted party and receives back $f_2(x, \tilde{y})$. Furthermore, $\mathcal{S}'$ sends $\tilde{y}$ before receiving any information about x. Therefore, we can view the ideal execution as one where $\mathcal{S}'$ first sends some $\tilde{y}$ to the trusted party and then P_1's input $x \in_R X$ is chosen uniformly from X. Now, since f_2 is not completely revealing, we have that for every $\tilde{y} \in Y$, there exist two non-equivalent inputs $x_1, x_2 \in X$ such that $f_2(x_1, \tilde{y}) = f_2(x_2, \tilde{y})$. Since $x \in_R X$, we have that with probability $2/|X|$, party P_1's input x is in the set $\{x_1, x_2\}$. Thus, with probability $2/|X|$, party P_2's output (and so the value received by $\mathcal{S}'$) is $f_2(x_1, \tilde{y}) = f_2(x_2, \tilde{y})$. Given that this event occurred, $\mathcal{S}$ can output a value that is equivalent to x with probability at most $1/2$. (Recall that x_1 and x_2 are not equivalent. Therefore, $\mathcal{S}'$ cannot output a value that is equivalent to both x_1 and x_2. Furthermore, the probability that $x = x_1$ equals the probability that $x = x_2$. In other words, $\mathcal{S}'$ must fail with probability $1/2$ in this case.) We conclude that in the ideal execution, $\mathcal{S}'$ outputs a value that is not equivalent to P_1's input with probability at least $1/|X|$.

Thus, the REAL and IDEAL executions can be distinguished with advantage that is at most negligibly smaller than $1/|X|$. Since X is finite, $1/|X|$ is a constant probability and so this contradicts the security of ρ, completing the proof. ∎

Acknowledgements. I would like to thank Boaz Barak and Jonathan Katz for helpful discussions.

References

1. B. Barak. How to Go Beyond the Black-Box Simulation Barrier. In *42nd FOCS*, pages 106–115, 2001.
2. D. Beaver. Foundations of Secure Interactive Computing. In *CRYPTO'91*, Springer-Verlag (LNCS 576), pages 377–391, 1991.
3. R. Canetti. Security and Composition of Multiparty Cryptographic Protocols. *Journal of Cryptology*, 13(1):143–202, 2000.
4. R. Canetti. Universally Composable Security: A New Paradigm for Cryptographic Protocols. In *42nd FOCS*, pages 136–145, 2001.
5. R. Canetti and M. Fischlin. Universally Composable Commitments. In *CRYPTO'01*, Springer-Verlag (LNCS 2139), pages 19–40, 2001.
6. R. Canetti, J. Kilian, E. Petrank, and A. Rosen. Black-Box Concurrent Zero-Knowledge Requires $\tilde{\Omega}(\log n)$ Rounds. In *33rd STOC*, pages 570–579, 2001.
7. R. Canetti, E. Kushilevitz and Y. Lindell. On the Limitations of Universal Composition Without Set-Up Assumptions. In *EUROCRYPT'03,* Springer-Verlag (LNCS 2656), pages 68–86, 2003.
8. R. Canetti, Y. Lindell, R. Ostrovsky and A. Sahai. Universally Composable Two-Party and Multi-Party Computation. In *34th STOC*, pages 494–503, 2002.
9. C. Dwork, M. Naor, and A. Sahai. Concurrent Zero-Knowledge. In *30th STOC*, pages 409–418, 1998.
10. U. Feige and A. Shamir. Witness Indistinguishability and Witness Hiding Protocols. In *22nd STOC*, pages 416–426, 1990.
11. O. Goldreich, S. Micali and A. Wigderson. How to Play any Mental Game – A Completeness Theorem for Protocols with Honest Majority. In *19th STOC,* pages 218–229, 1987.
12. S. Goldwasser and L. Levin. Fair Computation of General Functions in Presence of Immoral Majority. In *CRYPTO'90,* Springer-Verlag (LNCS 537), 1990.
13. J. Kelsey, B. Schneier and D. Wagner. Protocol Interactions and the Chosen Protocol Attack. In *5th International Workshop on Security Protocols*, Springer-Verlag (LNCS 1361), pages 91–104, 1997.
14. Y. Lindell. Bounded-Concurrent Secure Two-Party Computation Without Setup Assumptions. In *35th STOC*, pages 683–692, 2003. (See [15] for a full version of the upper bound from this paper.)
15. Y. Lindell. Protocols for Bounded-Concurrent Secure Two-Party Computation Without Setup Assumptions. *Cryptology ePrint Archive,* Report #2003/100, http://eprint.iacr.org/2003/100.
16. Y. Lindell. General Composition and Universal Composability in Secure Multi-Party Computation. In *44th FOCS*, pages 394–403, 2003.
17. S. Micali and P. Rogaway. Secure Computation. Unpublished manuscript, 1992. Preliminary version in *CRYPTO'91*, Springer-Verlag (LNCS 576), 1991.

18. R. Pass and A. Rosen Bounded-Concurrent Secure Two-Party Computation in a Constant Number of Rounds. In *44th FOCS*, 2003.
19. B. Pfitzmann and M. Waidner. Composition and Integrity Preservation of Secure Reactive Systems. In *7th CCS*, pages 245–254, 2000.
20. R. Richardson and J. Kilian. On the Concurrent Composition of Zero-Knowledge Proofs. In *EUROCRYPT'99*, Springer-Verlag (LNCS 1592), pp. 415–431, 1999.
21. A. Yao. How to Generate and Exchange Secrets. *27th FOCS*, pp. 162–167, 1986.

Secret-Key Zero-Knowlegde and Non-interactive Verifiable Exponentiation

Ronald Cramer and Ivan Damgård

BRICS*, Aarhus University, Denmark
{cramer,ivan}@brics.dk

Abstract. We consider a new model for non-interactive zero-knowledge where security is not based on a common reference string, but where prover and verifier are assumed to possess appropriately correlated secret keys. We present efficient proofs for equality of discrete logarithms in this model with unconditional soundness and zero-knowledge. This has immediate applications to non-interactive verification of undeniable signatures and pseudorandom function values. Another application is the following: a set of l servers, of which less than $l/2$ are corrupt, hold shares of a secret integer s. A client C specifies g in some finite group G, and the servers want to allow the client to compute g^s non-interactively, i.e., by sending information to C only once. This has immediate applications in threshold cryptography. Using our proof system, the problem can be solved as efficiently as the fastest previous solutions that either required interaction or had to rely on the random oracle model for a proof of security. The price we pay is the need to establish the secret key material once and for all. We present an alternative solution to the problem that is also non-interactive and where clients need no secret keys. This comes at the expense of more communication and the assumption that less than $l/3$ of the servers are corrupt.

1 Introduction

In a zero-knowledge proof system, a prover convinces a verifier via an interactive protocol that some statement is true, i.e., a given word x is in some given language L. The verifier must learn nothing beyond the fact that the assertion is valid. Zero-knowledge is an extremely useful notion and has found innumerable applications. Many variants of the model have been studied, in particular variants where some extra resource is assumed to be available. In some cases, this allows to construct zero-knowledge proofs more efficiently than in the standard model, e.g., in terms of round or communication complexity. For instance, in the well known model of non-interactive zero-knowledge, prover and verifier are assumed to have access to a common random reference string σ. This allows the

* Basic Research in Computer Science (www.brics.dk), funded by the Danish National Research Foundation. Also supported by FICS, Foundations in Cryptography and Security, funded by the Danish Natural Sciences Research Council

prover to prove his statement $x \in L$ simply by computing a single string π and send it to the verifier, who can check it against σ.

In this paper, we propose a new non-interactive variant, where there is no common random string (we do include a public string in our model for convenience, but this is not essential). The new ingredient is that prover and verifier are assumed to have secret keys sk_P, respectively sk_V. These are assumed to be chosen with some appropriate joint distribution depending on the language in question. The prover proves that $x \in L$ by computing a proof π from x, sk_P and some private information related to x. When π is sent to the verifier, he can check it against x and sk_V.

Intuitively, the prover is prevented from cheating because he doesn't know sk_V, and so does not know "how" the verifier will check the proof. On the other hand, although sk_P and sk_V must be correlated in a particular way, sk_V taken by itself has a distribution that is easy to simulate from scratch. Furthermore, we arrange it such that given sk_V and $x \in L$, the proof π that the prover would give is easy to compute, thus allowing the verifier's entire view to be simulated efficiently.

Our motivation for introducing this model is an efficient example we present allowing non-interactive proofs of statements related to discrete logarithms. We give here an informal presentation of the idea, which will be formalized later in the paper.

Let us assume that we have given a finite group G of prime order q, and that P has a secret number $s \in Z_q$. Now, sk_P is a random element $y \in Z_q$, while sk_V is a pair α, β where α is random in Z_q while $\beta = \alpha s + y$. We discuss later how such keys can be set up. Note that sk_V is independent of s. The purpose of the proof system is to allow P to prove that $g, h \in G$ satisfy $g^s = h$, whenever this is the case. To understand how sk_P, sk_V help to do this, think of s as a message, y as an authentication code, and α, β as a verification key. Indeed, if P were to reveal s, y, then V could check that s was in fact the value fixed at key set-up time by verifying $\beta = \alpha s + y$. It is easy to see that to cheat, the prover would have to guess α. Now, since the verification is done by taking a *linear* combination of s, y we can instead do the check "in the exponent" when we are given g^s instead of s. So given $g, h = g^s$, P sends as proof $\pi = g^y$, and V checks that $g^\beta = h^\alpha \pi$. Informally, this is zero-knowledge, since given g, h, sk_V, V can easily compute what π should be.

So the proof consists of sending one group element and requires one exponentiation to compute and at most two for verification. Later, we generalize the idea to arbitrary finite groups, where P, V do not even need to know the order of G. An important fact from a practical point of view is that neither the prover nor the verifier need random coins: security of the proof system relies only on the randomness involved in choosing the keys. Since obtaining random bits securely "on the fly" can be difficult, it is interesting to be able to push the need for randomness to a set-up phase.

We mention that the hash proof systems of Cramer and Shoup [1] are also a special case of our model where sk_P is empty. The most well-known example of hash proof systems also relate to equality of discrete logarithms: given generators g_0, g_1 of prime order group G, the prover can show for given h_0, h_1 that $h_0 = g_0^s, h_1 = g_1^s$. Here, sk_V consists of two random integers a, b, and the prover must know $g_0^a g_1^b$ to compute the proof. Thus, hash proof systems allow proving equality of discrete logs, assuming that the "base elements" g_0, g_1 are fixed.

Our proof system instead fixes the exponent, and allows the base to vary without changing the keys. This dramatically expands the range of possible applications, as we shall see. We emphasize that all our applications must of course assume that correctly chosen secret keys are set up for all would-be provers and verifiers before use. This can always be established by trusted parties, or by secure two-party or multiparty computation. For our main example proof system, we give an efficient key set-up protocol later in the paper. This protocol only involves the prover and verifier, it is constant round and has communication complexity $O(k)$ bits, where k is the security parameter.

An obvious application is to do non-interactive confirmation of undeniable signatures, when using Chaum's original scheme [2], or the convertible scheme of Rabin et al[9]. This is immediate because these schemes produce signatures by computing a group element from the input message and raising this to a fixed secret exponent. A further application is to verify outputs from the pseudo-random functions of Naor and Reingold[11]. A secret key for their construction consists of a set of fixed exponents, and one evaluates the function by raising a fixed element in a prime order group to a sequence of exponenents determined by the input. Using Nielsen's variant of this construction[12], it is safe to reveal the intermediate results. Each of these can be sent along with the function value and verified non-interactively using our proof system. This gives a functionality similar to verifiable pseudorandom functions, but the construction is conceptually simpler and more efficient than known constructions.

A final application is the following: a set of l servers, of which less than $l/2$ are corrupt, hold shares of a secret integer d. A client C specifies g in some finite Abelian group G, and the servers want to allow the client to compute g^d non-interactively, i.e., by sending information to C only once and with no communication between servers. This has immediate connections to threshold cryptography, and can be applied directly to distributed El-Gamal and RSA. Using our proof system, the problem can be solved as efficiently as the fastest previous solutions that either required interaction or had to rely on the random oracle model for a proof of security. The price we pay is, as mentioned, the need to establish the secret key material once and for all. Some variants are possible, however: a client without secret keys can still use the system, at the expense of an extra round of communication. Or he can do a key set-up protocol once and for all with the servers, and then use the system non-interactively.

A different type of "trade-off" is also possible. We present an alternative solution to the problem, which is not directly based on secret-key zero-knowledge, but uses a related technique. It is also non-interactive and needs no secret keys for clients. This comes at the expense of more communication and the assumption that less than $l/3$ of the servers are corrupt.

2   Secret-Key Zero-Knowlegde

Our model involves the following ingredients: interactive Turing Machines $\mathcal{P}, \mathcal{V}$ (Prover and Verifier) and the *Key generator* a PPT algorithm $\mathcal{G}$. In addition a (possibly infinite) set of strings PK.

In the model, we play initially a game where the language in which membership is to be proved is fixed, and where keys are set up: $\mathcal{P}, \mathcal{V}$ get as input $pk \in PK$ and 1^k where k is a security parameter. Then $\mathcal{P}$ outputs strings s, inp_P and $\mathcal{V}$ outputs string inp_v. Then $\mathcal{G}$ is run on input $1^k, pk, s, inp_P, inp_V$, and will output two strings sk_P, sk_V which will later be given to $\mathcal{P}, \mathcal{V}$, respectively.

The meaning of this is as follows: each pair s, pk, where $pk \in PK$, defines a language $L_{s,pk}$, that is, we assume there is a polynomial time algorithm that decides if $x \in L_{s,pk}$, when given s, pk as additional input. One can think of pk as a public key chosen once and for all, and s as a secret piece of information that the prover is committed to after the key set-up phase. Our model captures this by having P give s to G initially. Because the prover is committed to s, the language $L_{s,pk}$ is well defined, even though V gets no information initially on s. For instance, pk might specify a finite group, and s could be a secret discrete logarithm.

$\mathcal{G}$ models a protocol or a trusted party that will set up secret keys for $\mathcal{P}, \mathcal{V}$ which will help $\mathcal{P}$ in convincing $\mathcal{V}$ about membership in $L_{s,pk}$. The strings inp_P, inp_V allow us to model the influence that $\mathcal{P}$ or $\mathcal{V}$ are allowed on the keys produced.

Now, from inputs s, sk_P, pk and $x \in L_{s,pk}$ the prover computes output string $\mathcal{P}(x, s, pk, sk_P)$. This can be thought of as a non-interactive zero-knowledge proof that $x \in L_{s,pk}$. The verifier can from input x, a string pr (supposedly coming from $\mathcal{P}$) and pk, sk_V compute as output 1 for "accept" or 0 for "reject". We now have

Definition 1. *The triple* $(\mathcal{G}, \mathcal{P}, \mathcal{V})$ *is said to be a* secret-key zero-knowledge proof system *for PK with error probability $\epsilon(\cdot, \cdot)$ if the following conditions are satisfied:*

Completeness. *Correct proofs produced and checked using matching keys are always accepted: Fix any $pk \in PK$, and any s, sk_P, sk_V that can be produced by honest $\mathcal{G}, \mathcal{P}, \mathcal{V}$ on input pk. Then for any $x \in L_{s,pk}$, we have $\mathcal{V}(x, \mathcal{P}(x, s, pk, sk_P), pk, sk_V) = 1$ with probability 1.*

Soundness. *Even given the secret prover information, no prover can produce t statements and proofs, and have any false statement accepted with probability better than $\epsilon(pk, t)$: Fix any $pk \in PK$, and for any (possibly unbounded) prover P^*, set $(s, inp_P) = P^*(pk)$. Set $(sk_P, sk_V) = \mathcal{G}(1^k, s, pk, inp_P, \perp)$. Give sk_P as input to P^*. Now do the following for $i = 1...t$: P^* produces a word x_i and a proof pr_i, and recieves $\mathcal{V}$'s output bit $\mathcal{V}(x_i, pr_i, pk, sk_V)$. We require that $\mathcal{V}$ rejects all $x_i \notin L_{s,pk}$ except with probability $\epsilon(pk, t)$.*

Zero-Knowledge. *The verifier's view of the key generation and proof of any true statement(s) can be simulated with the correct distribution. Fix any pair (s, pk) $(pk \in PK)$, and consider any verifier V^*. Set $inp_V = V^*(pk)$,* and $(sk_P, sk_V) = \mathcal{G}(1^k, s, pk, \perp, inp_V)$. *Finally, for any word* $x \in L_{s,pk}$, *run* $\mathcal{P}(x, s, pk, sk_P)$ *to obtain a proof pr. There exists a PPT simulator* $\mathcal{M}_1$ *such that the output distribution* $\mathcal{M}_1(1^k, pk, inp_V)$ *is statistically indistinguishable from that of* sk_V. *Moreover, there exists a PPT simulator* $\mathcal{M}_2$ *such that the output distribution* $\mathcal{M}_2(1^k, pk, sk_V, x)$ *is statistically indistinguishable from that of pr.*

Discussion: In this model, the quality of the simulation is guaranteed by increasing the security parameter k. We do not require that the soundness error vanishes with increasing k, but this can be achieved by generating several independent sets of keys for the same pair s, pk and repeating the proof system in parallel. However, for all the applications we are aware of, this is not necessary, because the application allows us to choose s, pk such that the soundness error is already exponentially small for all polynomial t.

The simulator is given the public string pk and must simulate w.r.t. pk. Thus, unlike standard non-interactive zero-knowledge, the reason why the simulator can work efficiently is not that it gets to choose the public string by itself, but that it knows sk_V and can use this knowledge when simulating the proofs.

Note that the zero-knowledge requirement implies that a cheating verifier's view can be simulated, even in a case where several statements are proved after key generation and where the verifier can decide the order in which they are proved: one simply runs $\mathcal{M}_1$ and then $\mathcal{M}_2$ a number of times using the output of $\mathcal{M}_1$ and the relevant statements to be proved. This works since the honest prover acts independently on each statement, given his secret key.

The definition requires unconditional security for both parties. This is possible since both players possess information that is information theoretically hidden from the other player. However, if $\mathcal{G}$ is realized via a protocol that only offers computational security, this will of course reduce the security of the proof system to computational as well.

Our model may superficially resemble earlier proposals for "zero-knowledge with preprocessing". The essential difference is that we have no restriction on the number of proofs that can be done based on a given key pair, while earlier schemes used the preprocessing phase to build resources that would eventually run out later.

We proceed to present our main example of SKZK. Our set of public keys PK is the set of strings pk that contain (in some fixed format) a specification of a finite Abelian group G and natural numbers k_0, k_1, where the smallest prime factor in the order of G is larger than 2^{k_0}. The language $L_{s,pk}$ consists of pairs of elements $g, h \in G$ such that $h = g^s$, provided that s is an integer in $[0..2^{k_1} - 1]$. Otherwise it is empty.

This specification reflects the fact that a bound on the size of prime factors in the order of G will be needed to estimate the soundness error of our proof system, and that it is only intended to work for values of s up to a certain limit.

The specification of G is a string, such that if it is known, one can decide membership in G and compute the group operation and inverses in G efficiently (poly-time in the size of the specification). For instance, G could be a prime order subgroup of Z_p^* for some prime p, or (a subgroup of) Z_n^* for an appropriately chosen RSA-modulus n.

The key generator is given s, G, k_0, k_1, security parameter k, and two strings inp_P, inp_V that are interpreted as integers in the standard way (recall that these are used to model the allowed influence of (corrupt) P or V on the choice of keys). Test if the following conditions are satisfied: $s \in [0..2^{k_1} - 1]$, $inp_P \in [0..2^{k_0+k_1+k}]$ or inp_P is empty, $inp_V \in]0..2^{k_0}]$ or inp_V is empty.
If the conditions are satisfied, then set $\alpha = inp_V$, or if inp_V is empty, choose α uniformly random in $]0..2^{k_0}]$. Set $y = inp_P$, or if inp_P is empty, choose y uniformly random in $[0..2^{k_0+k_1+k}]$. Set $\beta = \alpha s + y$. Finally, set $sk_P = (s, y)$, $sk_V = (\alpha, \beta)$ and output these values.
If the conditions on s, inp_P, inp_V are violated, output empty strings and stop.

The honest prover and verifier are assumed to always choose empty strings as inp_P, inp_V.

From a practical point of view, this SKZK proof system can be used to allow a prover to get $g \in G$ as input, send g^s to the verifier and non-interactively prove that this was correctly done. The specification of $\mathcal{G}$ allows that a corrupt P can choose s, y (in the correct intervals), but will get no information on α. A corrupt V can choose α as any value in the interval he likes, but he learns no information on s, y other than β. The specification also allows a corrupt party to block the key generation, this models the fact that since we want to implement $\mathcal{G}$ via a two-party protocol, we cannot guarantee successful termination because one player can just stop early.

We proceed to describe the other algorithms:

The prover will on input g, h where $h^s = g$, compute $v = g^y$ as the proof (assuming sk_P is not empty).

The verifier will on input g, h, v check whether $g, h \in G$ and $g^\beta = h^\alpha \cdot v$, and will accept if and only if this is the case.

We have:

Theorem 1. *The above is a SKZK proof system for $\mathcal{L}$ with error probability $t/(2^{k_0} - t)$.*

Proof. Completeness is trivial by simply plugging the values produced by the prover into the equation checked by the verifier. For soundness, assume first that $t = 1$, that G is cyclic, and that we have $h \neq g^s$ and some proof v. Writing everything as a power of a generator a of G, we have $g = a^i, h = a^j, v = a^m$. The assumption $h \neq g^s$ implies $si - j \neq 0 \bmod q^l$ for some prime factor q in the order of G, where q^l is the maximal q-power dividing $|G|$. In order to have the proof accepted, the prover must arrange it such that

$$g^\beta = h^\alpha v$$

which means that $\beta i = \alpha j + m \bmod q^l$. Now, since key generation ensures that $\beta = \alpha s + y$ we find that

$$\alpha(si - j) = (m - iy) \bmod q^l.$$

Let q^b be the maximal q-power dividing both sides of this equation. By choice of α, it is non-zero modulo q, so we have

$$\alpha \frac{si - j}{q^b} = \frac{m - iy}{q^b} \bmod q^{l-b}.$$

The assumption $si - j \neq 0 \bmod q^l$ implies $b < l$. It follows that

$$\alpha = \frac{m - iy}{q^b} \cdot \left(\frac{si - j}{q^b}\right)^{-1} \bmod q^{l-b}.$$

in other words, to have the false g, h accepted, the prover must guess $\alpha \bmod q^{l-b}$. However, α was randomly chosen among $2^{k_0} < q$ possibilities, and by the specification of G, the prover has no a priori information on α. So accept happens with probability at most 2^{-k_0}. If G is not cyclic, we can write G as a direct product of r cyclic components $G_1, ..., G_r$ and g, h as r-tuples $(g_1, ..., g_r), (h_1, ..., h_r)$ in the standard way. If $h \neq g^s$, this means that $h_i \neq g_i^s$ for some i, and we can then use the argument above in the cyclic subgroup G_i.

Finally we consider the case of proving several statements: if a cheating prover sends any correct g, h where $h = g^s$, he can compute from his secret key what the correct proof should be, and since this is the only value the verifier will accept, the prover can predict the verifier's reaction to any proof he might choose to send along with g, h.

Now consider the situation where the prover is about to compute a new proof, assuming that he has not yet made the verifier accept a false statement. By the above, the new information the prover could have learned earlier must come cases where a proof of a false statement was rejected. Assuming that t false proofs were already rejected, the prover can exclude t possible values of α, so the next proof will be accepted with probability at most $1/(2^{k_0} - t)$. This implies the claimed error probability by an easy induction argument.

Zero-knowledge follows since we can simulate the choice of α, β by first choosing $\alpha \in]0..2^{k_0}]$ based on inp_V in the same way as $\mathcal{G}$ would have done it. Then we choose at random $\beta \in [0..2^{k_0+k_1+k}]$. This simulates α perfectly and β with statistically close (in k) distribution, since in real life $\beta = \alpha s + y$ and y is k bits longer than αs. Furthermore, given correctly distributed α, β and $(g, h) \in L$, the (uniquely determined) proof that the honest prover would send is $v = g^\beta h^{-\alpha}$.

2.1   Some Variations

From the proof of the above theorem, it is clear that we do not really need to fix the group G in advance. The same key set-up can be reused for any Abelian group, the only price to pay may be that the soundness error probability can be larger: if the group has a prime factor q in its order smaller than 2^{k_0}, the error probability for one proof will be $\theta(1/q)$.

A variation on this: Suppose G is a direct product $G = H \times K$, where $|H|$ has only primes factors $> 2^{k_0}$. And furthermore for some publically known γ, it holds that $e^\gamma = 1$ for all $e \in K$. Then given an instance (g, h), we can use the original proof system on the pair (g^γ, h^γ), in order to prove that $g^{s\gamma} = h^\gamma$. For some applications, including threshold RSA, this is sufficient.

Finally, we note that some generalizations are possible of the form of statement proved: suppose we have two secrets s, s' and have set up keys y, y' and $(\alpha, \beta), (\alpha', \beta')$ just as above, except that we have designed the key generation such that $\alpha = \alpha'$. It is then possible for the prover to send g, g', h and prove that $h = g^s g'^{s'}$. The proof would be $v = g^y g'^{y'}$ and the verifier would check that $g^\beta g'^{\beta'} = vh^\alpha$.

3   Key Set-Up Protocol

Suppose now that P, V want to agree on a set of keys for the SKZK proof system we have described, assuming that the public string pk has already been generated (i.e., some group has been chosen) and P knows the secret s he will be using. We sketch here an efficient protocol that that securely realizes the $\mathcal{G}$ we specified earlier.

The protocol can be proved secure in Canetti's model for secure function evaluation[14], assuming a static adversary that corrupts P or V. We make no claims here on composability of the protocol, other than the sequential composability that follows from Canetti's definiton. However, we believe that in the common reference string model and using the techniques from [7], a universally composable version could be designed without essential loss of efficiency.

3.1   A First Attempt

We first describe a solution that works if both parties follow the protocol. Suppose V chooses a key pair for a semantically secure and additively homomorphic public-key cryptosystem. As example we will use the one by Paillier[13]. He sends the public key pk_V to P, and also sends the encryption $E_{pk_V}(\alpha)$ where α has been chosen as described in the key generation for the SKZK proof system.

Then (assuming P knows s already) P chooses y as in the key generation for SKZK, uses the homomorphic property to compute an encryption $E_{pk_V}(s\alpha + y)$ and sends this to V. Finally, V decrypts and defines the result to be β. Of course, we want that $\beta = s\alpha + y$ as integers, and the Paillier cryptosystem is only homomorphic w.r.t. addition modulo some RSA modulus - but as long as the modulus is chosen large enough compared to the sizes of α, s and y, no modular reductions will occur, and β will be the correct value.

Clearly, V learns nothing new except β, and a computationally bounded P learns nothing new, assuming he cannot break the semantic security.

3.2   The Real Solution

In order to make a solution secure even against active cheating, we assume that we have available a public key pk_C for an integer commitment scheme such as the one by Damgård and Fujisaki[3], allowing P or V to commit to an integer a of any size and prove efficiently in zero-knowledge that a belongs to some interval using the technique of Baudot[4]. We discuss below where pk_C could come from.

Note that this commitment scheme is homomorphic: from commitments that can be opened to integers a, b it is easy to compute a commitment that can be opened to (only) $a + b$. It is also trapdoor, i.e., knowing a certain piece of side information, it is possible to produce a commitment that can be opened to any desired value. Notation: $Com_{pk_C}(x, r)$ denotes a commitment under public key pk_C to x using random coins r.

A final tool we need is the efficient method outlined in [6] allowing a party to make public a Paillier encryption $E_{pk_V}(\alpha)$ and prove that α belongs to a given interval. This involves making a commitment $Com_{pk_C}(\alpha, r_\alpha)$, proving that it contains the same value as $E_{pk_V}(\alpha)$ and proving that α is in the correct interval using the technique from [4]. For details see [6].

Then we do the following:

1. V sends the key pk_V, the encryption $E_{pk_V}(\alpha)$ and proves in ZK that α is in the correct interval.
2. P chooses s, y as in the key generation for SKZK, makes commitments $S = Com_{pk_C}(s, r_s), Y = Com_{pk_C}(y, r_y)$ and proves that he knows how to open these commitments to integers in the correct intervals. Similarly, he chooses $\bar{s}, \bar{y}$ as random numbers $2k$ bits longer than s respectively y, makes commitments $\bar{S} = Com_{pk_C}(\bar{s}, r_{\bar{s}}), \bar{Y} = Com_{pk_C}(\bar{y}, r_{\bar{y}})$, and proves that $\bar{s}, \bar{y}$ were chosen in the correct intervals.
3. P uses the homomorphic property of the encryption scheme to compute encryptions $E_{pk}(\alpha s + y), E_{pk}(\alpha \bar{s} + \bar{y})$, and sends these to V, who decrypts to get results β, respectively $\bar{\beta}$.
4. V sends a random k-bit challenge e. Both parties use the homomorphic properties of the commitment scheme to compute from $S, Y, \bar{S}, \bar{Y}$ commitments Z_s, Z_y to $z_s = \bar{s} + es, z_y = \bar{y} + ey$. P opens Z_s, Z_y to reveal z_s, z_y to V.
5. V checks that the openings were correct, and that $\bar{\beta} + e\beta = \alpha z_s + z_y$. If so, he accepts using α, β as keys to check proofs from P in the future. Output for P is s, y.

Given an oracle that supplies pk_C, this protocol can be proved to securely realize $\mathcal{G}$ as specified above in Canetti's model for secure function evaluation[14], assuming a static adversary that corrupts P or V. Due to space limitaitons, we only give informally the essential ideas needed for this:

By inspection, it is trivial to check that V always accepts if both parties follow the protocol, and that the outputs generated have the same distribution as $\mathcal{G}$ would have produced.

If a party is corrupt, we need to describe a simulator that interacts one one side with the corrupt player and on the other side with the "ideal function" $\mathcal{G}$

as specified above. It must create a view for the corrupt player that is indistinguishable from the real conversation, and at the same time interact with $\mathcal{G}$ on behalf of the corrupted player. The induced input/output behavior of $\mathcal{G}$ must be consistent with the view generated for the corrupted player. In general, if this game comes to a point where the corrupt player would make the honest player reject and stop, the simulator handles this by sending an illegal value as input to $\mathcal{G}$. This causes $\mathcal{G}$ to stop without generating output, which is consistent with what happens in real life.

Now, assume P is honest and V may actively cheat. The simulator can use rewinding to extract α from the ZK proof of knowledge given in Step 1 and give this to $\mathcal{G}$ as inp_V. Note that it happens with only negligible probability that α is an illegal value simultaneously with the proof being accepted. So we may assume that α is in the correct interval, and and $\mathcal{G}$ will return β to the simulator. From the protocol description, it then follows that $\beta, \bar{\beta}$ have distribution statistically close to that of $y, \bar{y}$, i.e., uniform and independent. In particular, they convey only negligible information on $\bar{s}$. It follows that z_s has distribution statistically close to that of $\bar{s}$, i.e., uniform and independent from $y, \bar{y}$. Finally, z_y always satisfies $\bar{\beta} + e\beta = \alpha z_s + z_y$. It follows that the opened values V sees in the protocol can be simulated with statistically close distribution by choosing $\bar{\beta}, z_s$ uniformly and independently with the same distribution as $y, \bar{y}, \bar{s}$ and setting $z_y = \bar{\beta} + e\beta - \alpha z_s$. So if the simulator knows the trapdoor for pk_C, it can simulate efficiently V's view of the protocol given only pk, pk_C.

Then, assume that V is honest. P's view of Step 1 can be simulated by supplying a random encryption and commitment and simulating the zero-knowledge proof to be given. Step 2 forces P to choose values $s, y, \bar{s}, \bar{y}$ in the correct intervals, and these values can be extracted by a simulator using the ZK proofs of knowledge given in Step 2, and s, y can be given as input to $\mathcal{G}$. Note that in the following steps, P learns no new information, the simulator can just play the game following V's part of the protocol. Hence, the only remaining question is whether the protocol ensures that $\beta = \alpha s + y$. The probability that the protocol completes successfully while this condition is violated must be negligible since otherwise it will not be consistent with what the ideal $\mathcal{G}$ produces. We argue that if $\beta \neq \alpha s + y$, then V accepts with negligible probability. For this, it is sufficient to show that if in Step 4, P can give satisfying answers to a non-negligible fraction of the possible challenges, then $\beta = \alpha s + y$. Under this assumption, by rewinding P, we can efficiently obtain acceptable replies to two distinct values e, e'. Because V accepts in both cases, P has opened values z_s, z_y, z_s', z_y' such that

$$\bar{\beta} + e\beta = \alpha z_s + z_y \quad \bar{\beta} + e'\beta = \alpha z_s' + z_y'$$

from which we conclude that

$$(e - e')\beta = \alpha(z_s - z_s') + z_y - z_y'$$

Now, by the binding property of the commitment scheme, except with negligible probability, it holds that $z_s = \bar{s} + es, z_y = \bar{y} + ey, z_s' = \bar{s} + e's, z_y' = \bar{y} + e'y$. Plugging this in, we immediately obtain $\beta = \alpha s + y$ as desired.

On efficiency, it is straightforward to check by inspection of the above and [4, 6,3] that the protocol requires communicating only a constant number of encryptions and commitments, and can be executed in a constant number of rounds.

Finally, we discuss how to set up the key pk_C. This key consists of an RSA modulus n and two elements $g_0, h_0 \in Z_n^*$ with only "large" prime factors in their order, and such that h_0 is in the group generated by g_0. Fortunately, in our main application, namely threshold RSA, an RSA modulus n is already available. Therefore the key set-up will work, assuming that elements g_0, h_0 have been chosen once and for all. It requires only little effort to do this at the time when n is set up. For instance, if n is a product of safe primes, simply choosing g_0, h_0 as random squares will be correct, except with negligible probability.

Another possibility consists in letting P choose a public key w.r.t. which V can commit, and vice versa. Two-party protocols for setting up a key in this way are described in detail in [3]. Compared to the previous solution, this costs a factor of k in round- and communication complexity, but does not assume any previous key set-up at all.

4   Applications

4.1   Undeniable Signatures

In the original scheme for undeniable signatures by Chaum [2], the public key is a safe prime p, i.e., such that $(p-1)/2 = q$ is also a prime, and elements $g, h \in Z_p^*$, where s, such that $h = g^s \bmod p$ is the private key. A signature on message m is $h(m)^s$, where h is some appropriate hash function that maps into Z_p^*. Signatures seem to hard to forge under the Diffie-Hellman assumption, but furthermore the idea is that it is hard to verify a signature unless the signer is willing to help you, by engaging in a protocol where he proves that the discrete log of h base g equals that of z base $h(m)$ where z is the purported signature. This is called a confirmation protocol.

Clearly, our proof system can be directly used to build a non-interactive confirmation protocol for this scheme, which was not known before, except in the random oracle model. Furthermore, it also applies to the convertible scheme of Rabin et al. [9], since this scheme is essentially the same but where Z_p^* is replaced by Z_n^*, where n is a safe prime product. The idea being that by revealing the "public exponent" corresponding to s, all signatures can be instantly converted to ordinary signtures. Some minor technical problems, related to the fact that the order of Z_n^* contains a small prime factor 2, are handled in [9], and their solutions to this translate easily to our case.

4.2   Pseudorandom Functions

In [11], Naor and Reingold present a pseudorandom function construction based on the DDH assumption. The construction takes place in the same group Z_p^* mentioned above. This has proved a very useful idea for making efficient protocols, for instance, Nielsen [12] describes a variant that can also be computed in a threshold fashion, and shows how this can be used to build efficient asynchronous Byzantine agreement protocols and threshold RSA signatures without random oracles.

The variant from [12] has a private key k consisting of l pairs of random elements from Z_q, $(\alpha_{1,0}, \alpha_{1,1}), ..., (\alpha_{l,0}, \alpha_{l,1})$. Also, a random public $g \in Z_p^*$ of order q is given. The function can take any string $\sigma = (\sigma_1, .., \sigma_m)$ where $m \leq l$ as input, and the output is

$$f_k(\sigma) = g^{\prod_{i=1}^m \alpha_{i,\sigma_i}}$$

Clearly, our proof system can be used to set up key pairs allowing the party who knows the private key k to prove that some element in the subgroup of order q has been raised to powers $\alpha_{j,b}, j = 1..l, b = 0, 1$, respectively.

This leads to a way to non-interactively verify values of f_k when evaluated on strings of length precisely l. Namely, on input $\sigma = (\sigma_1, ..., \sigma_l)$, send

$$g^{\alpha_{1,\sigma_1}}, g^{\alpha_{1,\sigma_1}\alpha_{2,\sigma_2}}, ..., g^{\prod_{i=1}^m \alpha_{i,\sigma_i}} = f_k(\sigma)$$

plus a proof that the j element on the list is the previous one raised to α_{j,σ_j}. Note that the first elements on the list are f_k evaluated on substrings of σ, so it is secure to reveal these by pseudorandomness of $f_k()$. Some applications allow to evaluate the function on consecutive values $0, 1, 00, 01, 10, 11, 000, ..,$ or in general such that we never evaluate the function on an input that is a prefix on a previously calculated value. In this case, is secure to use the domain of all strings of length at most l. With consequtive values, one can exploit the fact that most of the required list of function values needed to verify a new one are already known, so only a single new value and proof needs to be sent.

This gives a functionality similar to that of verifiable pseudorandom functions (VRF), as proposed by Micali, Rabin and Vadhan[10], although of course at the expense of having to set up keys for our proof system first. With a VRF, one can simply publish a public key and then send function values and non-interactive proofs of correctness. However, VRF's are only known to exist under the strong RSA assumption, or under various strong and non-standard variants of the DH/DDH assumptions [5,8]. Moreover, most of these solutions are rather complicated and inefficient – with the exception of [8]. An alternative to the VRF concept would be to commit on the key and use standard non-interactive zero-knowledge to prove that the funcion value is correct, but this would be very inefficient. In contrast, our technique allows us to assume only standard DDH and have a reasonably efficient and conceptually simple solution.

It is easy to adapt our technique also to the threshold pseudorandom function from Nielsen[12]. This gives a non-interactive solution with a smaller communication complexity than the interactive protocol from [12].

5   Non-interactive Verifiable Exponentiation

We consider the following problem: a set of l servers, of which t are corrupt, hold shares of a secret integer d. A client C specifies g in some finite Abelian group

G, and the servers want to allow the client to compute g^d non-interactively, i.e., by sending information to C only once and with no communication between servers. This has immediate connections to threshold cryptography, and can be applied directly to distributed El-Gamal and RSA. Below, we two solutions with different properties.

5.1   Using Secret-Key Zero-Knowledge

To illustrate how we can use secret-key zero-knowledge in this context, the easiest way is to consider Shoups threshold RSA scheme[15], where indeed the purpose is to do non-interactive verifiable exponentiation in the group Z_n^*, where $n = pq$ is a product of safe primes, and where we assume that $t < l/2$. To make this scheme robust (verifiable), each server S_i needs to prove that a given input number was raised to a secret share s_i (of the private RSA exponent) held by S_i. By squaring the inputs, Shoup makes sure that this proof can be done assuming we work in a group with only large prime factors in its order. It is therefore clear that our proof system can be directly plugged in, instead of the random oracle based proofs that were used in [15]. This will even be more efficient by a constant factor.

   Of course, this can only used directly assuming there are keys set up for proofs going from each server to the client. But we can also do something assuming the client has no keys, but we have keys for pairwise interaction between the servers. Namely, the clients requests from each server a signature share $(g^{s_i} \bmod n)$ and proofs of correctness for this share, directed to each of the other servers. Then the client sends these signature shares and proofs back to the severs for approval. He will only keep those signature shares that were approved by a majority of the servers. By soundness of the proofs, this will leave the client with at least $t + 1$ shares, all of which are correct, and this is sufficient to find $g^d \bmod n$.

5.2   An Alternative without Secret Key Zero-Knowledge

The following solution is non-interactive and does not require the client to have any secret keys. This comes at the price of more communication and assuming $t < l/3$. For simplicity, we work over a group G_q of prime order q, and the secret value d is an element of Z_q.

   Consider first a situation where some server S knows a secret value $\hat{d}$, and where the other $l-1$ servers S_r have correct shares $\hat{s}_r$ in $\hat{d}$, according to Shamir's scheme. S also knows the polynomial $F(X) = \hat{d} + d_1X + \cdots + d_tX^t$ according to which $\hat{d}$ was shared. Write $\hat{s}_r = F(r)$.

   Here is a simple protocol where the client C can easily check whether the value h he receives from S is indeed equal to $g^{\hat{d}}$, with $g \in G_q$ specified by the client. There is no interaction between the servers. Each of the servers just sends some information to C, and C performs an off-line check on the total of this information to decide on the correctness of h. The protocol has zero error probability, while C learns only the value $g^{\hat{d}}$.

S sends the value h to C, equal to $g^{\hat{d}}$ if S is honest. Additionally, S sends the values h_j, equal to g^{d_j} if S is honest. Each other server S_r sends the value f_r to C, equal to $g^{\hat{s}_r}$ if S_r is honest.

From the information sent by S and by performing "polynomial evaluation in the exponent," C now computes the values f'_r, equal to $g^{\hat{s}_r}$ if S is honest. Concretely, C computes

$$f'_r = h \cdot \prod h_j^{r^j}. \tag{1}$$

In the case that there are at most t inconsistencies

$$f_r \neq f'_r,$$

C decides that $h = g^{\hat{d}}$ indeed. Otherwise he decides that S is corrupt.

It is easy to see that this works. First, consider the case that S is honest. This implies that h and the h_j are correct. If S_r is honest as well, then clearly $f_r = f'_r$. Up to t of the servers S_r are corrupt, so there are at most t inconsistencies $f_r \neq f'_r$. Thus, C makes the correct decision.

Second, if S is corrupt and $h \neq g^{\hat{d}}$, then there are more than t inconsistencies and C correctly decides that S is corrupt. This is argued as follows. The information sent by S does define, in "the exponents," a polynomial of degree at most t. However, since $\log_g h \neq \hat{d}$ by assumption, it must be a different one from $F(X)$. By Lagrange interpolation and the natural one-to-one correspondence between Z_q and G_q, it follows that at most t of the $l - 1$ values f'_r equal $g^{\hat{s}_r}$. Equivalently, $f'_r \neq g^{\hat{s}_r}$ for at least $(l - 1 - t)$ values of r. However, apart from S, there may be $t - 1$ other corrupt servers S_r. Therefore, $f_r \neq f'_r$ for at least $(l - 1 - t) - (t - 1) = l - 2t$ values of r. But $t < l/3$, so this means that there are more than t inconsistencies, and that C decides that S is corrupt.

Finally, we argue that a static adversary who corrupts C and at most t servers (but not S) will not learn nothing except $g^{\hat{d}}$. We do this by simulating his entire view given this value. From corrupting t servers the adversary will learn $\hat{s}_r$, for t values of r. Suppose without loss of generality that these are $\hat{s}_1, ..., \hat{s}_t$. This can be simulated perfectly by choosing t uniformly random values modulo q. These values together with $\hat{d}$ define a polynomial $F()$ of degree $\leq t$ where $F(0) = \hat{d}, F(1) = \hat{s}_1, ..., F(t) = \hat{s}_t$. Since we have $t + 1$ values of $F()$, it follows that for any coefficient d_j of $F()$, there exists Lagrange interpolation coefficients $\gamma_0, ..., \gamma_t$ such that

$$g^{d_j} = (g^{\hat{d}})^{\gamma_0} \prod_{i=1}^{t} (g^{\hat{s}_i})^{\gamma_i}$$

and this value can easily be computed given $g^{\hat{d}}, \hat{s}_1, ..., \hat{s}_t$, i.e., we can simulate perfectly the extra information sent by S. Finally, we can use these values to simulate the contribution from honest S_r's using (1).

Now we return to the scenario of interest, non-interactive verifiable exponentiation. Each of the l servers S_i has a share s_i of d, according to Shamir's scheme with $t < l/3$. Let $g \in G_q$ be the element specified by the client C.

Additionally we now assume that, for each server S_i, an instance of the above verification protocol has been correctly set up, where S_i plays the role of S, the other servers play the roles of the S_r, and $\hat{d}$ is replaced by s_i.

If we now run the verification protocol above for each server S_i, the client C can easily filter out an incorrect value sent by a corrupt S_i, and remain with at least $l - t > t$ correct values g^{s_i}. By "interpolation in the exponent," i.e., multiplying these correct values g^{s_i} together, raised to appropriate Lagrange interpolation coefficients, C recovers the correct value g^d.

References

1. Ronald Cramer, Victor Shoup: Universal Hash Proofs and a Paradigm for Adaptive Chosen Ciphertext Secure Public-Key Encryption. Proc. of EUROCRYPT 2002: 45–64, Springer Verlag LNCS.
2. David Chaum, Hans Van Antwerpen: Undeniable Signatures. Proc. of CRYPTO 1989, Springer Verlag LNCS. pp.212–217.
3. Ivan Damgård, Eiichiro Fujisaki: A Statistically-Hiding Integer Commitment Scheme Based on Groups with Hidden Order. Proc. of ASIACRYPT 2002: 125–142, Springer Verlag LNCS.
4. Fabrice Boudot: Efficient Proofs that a Committed Number Lies in an Interval. Proc. of EUROCRYPT 2000: 431–444, Springer Verlag LNCS.
5. Anna Lysyanskaya: Unique Signatures and Verifiable Random Functions from the DH-DDH Separation. Proc. of CRYPTO 2002: 597–612, Springer Verlag LNCS.
6. Ivan Damgård, Mads Jurik: Client/Server Tradeoffs for Online Elections. Proc. of Public Key Cryptography 2002: 125–140. Springer Verlag LNCS.
7. Ivan Damgård and Jesper Nielsen: *Efficient Universally Composable Multiparty Computation*, proc. of Crypto 03, Springer Verlag LNCS.
8. Yevgeniy Dodis: *Efficient Construction of (Distributed) Verifiable Random Functions*, Proc. of PKC 2002, Springer Verlag LNCS.
9. Rosario Gennaro, Tal Rabin, Hugo Krawczyk: RSA-Based Undeniable Signatures. Journal of Cryptology 13(4): 397–416 (2000).
10. Silvio Micali, Michael O. Rabin, Salil P. Vadhan: Verifiable Random Functions. Proc. of IEEE FOCS 1999: 120–130.
11. Moni Naor, Omer Reingold: Number-theoretic Constructions of Efficient Pseudo-random Functions. Proc. of IEEE FOCS 1997: 458–467.
12. Jesper Buus Nielsen: A Threshold Pseudorandom Function Construction and Its Applications. Proc. of CRYPTO 2002: 401–416. Springer Verlag LNCS.
13. Pascal Paillier: Public-Key Cryptosystems Based on Composite Degree Residuosity Classes. Proc. of EUROCRYPT 1999: 223–238, Springer Verlag LNCS.
14. Ran Canetti: Security and Composition of Multiparty Cryptographic Protocols. Journal of Cryptology 13(1): 143–202 (2000).
15. Victor Shoup: Practical Threshold Signatures. Proc. of EUROCRYPT 2000: 207–220, Springer Verlag LNCS

A Quantitative Approach to Reductions in Secure Computation

Amos Beimel[1] and Tal Malkin[2]

[1] Department of Computer Science, Ben-Gurion University
beimel@cs.bgu.ac.il
[2] Department of Computer Science, Columbia University
tal@cs.columbia.edu

Abstract. Secure computation is one of the most fundamental cryptographic tasks. It is known that all functions can be computed securely in the information theoretic setting, given access to a black box for some complete function such as AND. However, without such a black box, not all functions can be securely computed. This gives rise to two types of functions, those that can be computed without a black box ("easy") and those that cannot ("hard"). However, no further distinction among the hard functions is made.

In this paper, we take a quantitative approach, associating with each function f the *minimal number* of calls to the black box that are required for securely computing f. Such an approach was taken before, mostly in an ad-hoc manner, for specific functions f of interest. We propose a *systematic* study, towards a general characterization of the hierarchy according to the number of black-box calls. This approach leads to a better understanding of the inherent complexity for securely computing a given function f. Furthermore, minimizing the number of calls to the black box can lead to more efficient protocols when the calls to the black box are replaced by a secure protocol.

We take a first step in this study, by considering the two-party, honest-but-curious, information-theoretic case. For this setting, we provide a complete characterization for deterministic protocols. We explore the hierarchy for randomized protocols as well, giving upper and lower bounds, and comparing it to the deterministic hierarchy. We show that for every Boolean function the largest gap between randomized and deterministic protocols is at most exponential, and there are functions which exhibit such a gap.

1 Introduction

The ability to compute functions securely is one of the most fundamental cryptographic tasks. Very roughly, two-party secure computation (on which we focus in this paper) involves two parties, Alice and Bob, who want to perform some computation on their inputs without leaking any additional information which does not follow from the intended output.

It is known (c.f. [4,9,10,22]) that not all functions can be computed securely in the information-theoretic setting. However, Goldreich and Vainish [16] and

M. Naor (Ed.): TCC 2004, LNCS 2951, pp. 238–257, 2004.
© Springer-Verlag Berlin Heidelberg 2004

Kilian [18] proved that every function can be computed securely in the information theoretic setting, given a black box that computes some *complete* function, such as Oblivious Transfer or the AND function. This type of a reduction is useful, because the security of the protocol is automatically maintained (computationally) when the black box is replaced by any computationally secure implementation of the function (such implementations exist under computational assumptions).[1] Moreover, such reductions provide a qualitative separation between "easy" functions that can be securely computed without calling the black box, and the "hard" functions which are the rest. Indeed, the notion of a reduction plays a central role at the heart of cryptographic foundations research (similarly to its central role in complexity theory). For example, black-box reductions between different cryptographic primitives were given in [6,11,12,19,7, 5,13,21].

A long line of research has focused on studying, in various settings, which functions belong to the "easy" category above, and which are "hard", as well as studying which functions are complete (which in some cases turned out to be the same as all hard functions). In particular, these questions have been answered (with full characterization) for Boolean functions [10], in the two-party model [22,1,3], and completeness results appear in [19,21,3,20]. However, these works do not give rise to a hierarchy of different degrees of hardness, as they do not distinguish among the different functions that can be computed with a specific complete (say AND) black box.

Such a hierarchy exists (for the information-theoretic reduction setting), by a result of Beaver [2], showing that for all k, there are functions that can be securely computed with k executions of the AND black box but cannot be computed with $k - 1$ executions of the black box. We explore the hierarchy in this work.

OUR GOALS. In this paper, we propose to take a *quantitative* approach, classifying functions by *how many* calls to the black box are required to compute them securely. Minimizing the number of calls to the black box is especially desired as it can lead to more efficient protocols when the calls to the black box are replaced by a secure protocol. This problem was previously investigated in an ad-hoc manner, for specific functions of interest (e.g., different forms of OT). In most cases, only upper bounds on the number of calls were given. Two exceptions are Beaver [2] who proved that securely computing n outputs of $\binom{2}{1}$OT with unrelated inputs requires at least n calls to $\binom{2}{1}$OT, and Dodis and Micali [14] who proved that securely computing $\binom{n}{1}$OT requires at least $n - 1$ calls to $\binom{2}{1}$OT (see also [24]).

We propose a systematic study of the quantitative approach to reductions in secure computation, towards a deeper understanding of the inherent complexity of securely computing functions. In particular, focusing for the sake of presentation on the AND black box, we ask the following questions:

- Is there a well-defined rich hierarchy of functions based on how many ANDs are required to securely compute them?

---

[1] In this paper we consider the honest-but-curious model where modular composition is fairly straightforward. In the malicious model modular composition holds as well. See [8] for definitions and results on modular composition in the malicious model.

- Given a function, can we give upper bounds on how many ANDs suffice to securely compute it? Can we give lower bounds?
- Can we give a combinatorial *characterization* of the functions with a certain minimal number of ANDs?

These problems are interesting in several settings. For the first problem, Beaver [2] provided a negative answer (the hierarchy collapses) in the computational setting, and a positive answer in the information theoretic setting, for randomized protocols (and for randomized functions, as well). Recently, Ishai et al. [17] proved that the hierarchy collapses in the random oracle model as well.

We note that by results of [16], lower bounds on the number of ANDs imply circuit lower bounds, meaning that it would be very hard to prove super-linear lower bounds in n for functions of the form $f : \{0,1\}^n \times \{0,1\}^n \to \{0,1\}$. However, it would be very interesting to prove such linear lower bounds and to try to explore tighter connections with circuit complexity and communication complexity[2] of the functions.

OUR RESULTS. We start the investigation by studying the information-theoretic, two-party, honest-but-curious setting, where the output of the AND black box is received only by Alice. Unless otherwise noted, we also consider protocols with perfect correctness and security. For this setting we prove the following results:

DETERMINISTIC PROTOCOLS. For deterministic protocols are we show:

- A complete combinatorial characterization of the minimal number of ANDs required to securely compute f (the characterization is a recursive one, based on the truth-table of f).

For finite functions one can find the optimal protocol using our characterization. However, in general, our characterization does not lead to an efficient algorithm that determines how many ANDs are required to compute a function securely. This motivates the following results:

- A simple, explicit upper bound on the number of ANDs required for f. This upper bound may be exponential in the size of the input.
- For *Boolean* functions f we prove that the above upper bound is tight by showing a matching lower bound. This implies that for some functions, an exponential number of ANDs is necessary.

RANDOMIZED PROTOCOLS. For randomized protocols are we show:

- An exponential gap using randomization: There are functions for which the number of ANDs required in a randomized protocol is exponentially smaller than the number of ANDs required in a deterministic protocol. We further exhibit a tradeoff between the number of random bits used and the number of ANDs required for one such example (Inner Product) where there is an exponential gap.

---

[2] Naor and Nissim [25] give some connections between the communication complexity of a function and the communication complexity for securely computing the function. However, translating them into our model, the number of ANDs is exponential in the communication complexity.

- A lower bound: We prove a lower bound, depending on the function truth-table, on the number of ANDs required by any secure randomized protocol. Using this lower bound, we prove that for Boolean functions the gap cannot be super exponential: For any randomized protocol with q ANDs, there is a deterministic protocol for the same function with at most 2^q ANDs.
- Gap already with 4 ANDS: There is a function that can be securely computed by a randomized protocol with 4 ANDs, however, every deterministic protocol securely computing it requires at least 6 ANDs.
- No gap with 1 AND: The functions that can be securely computed with one call to the AND black box are the same as in the deterministic case with one AND (for which an explicit characterization is given).
- Gap between perfect and non-perfect protocols: There are functions that require at least a linear (in the input length) number of ANDs for any perfect (randomized) protocol, but can be computed with k ANDs (for any k), achieving a protocol with $1/2^k$ probability of error and statistical distance.
- Lower bound for non-perfect protocols: We show that the one-way randomized communication complexity in the shared-randomness model is a lower bound for the number of ANDs required by non-perfect protocols.

EXTENSIONS TO OTHER MODELS AND COMPLETE FUNCTIONS. As explained earlier, we choose the simplest model of secure computation to consider our quantitative approach. Some of our results carry over directly to other models, and some questions still remain open in the other models. We hope that our paper would be a starting point for further research which will clarify the situation in more complex models as multi-party protocols, and the protocols that are secure against malicious parties.

Specifically, only Alice gets the output of the function while Bob should not learn any information on the input of Alice. This one-sided model is the correct model when considering *malicious* two-party secure computation where the first party to get the output can quit the protocol preventing the other party from getting the output. In the honest-but-curious model, the one-sidedness of the output is not the only possibility; we choose it since we want the simplest model. Some results on the two-sided model, where Alice gets an output f^{Alice} and Bob gets an output f^{Bob}, appear in the full version of this paper.

Furthermore, we state all our results counting the number of ANDs needed. However, every finite function (a function with a constant number of inputs) can be computed securely using a constant number of ANDs, and the AND function can be computed with one call to any complete function (this is implied by results of [3]). So, the results of this paper carry to every finite complete function, up to a constant factor. For example, the $\binom{2}{1}\text{OT}$ function can be computed securely with two ANDs. Thus, all lower bounds on the number of ANDs translate into the same lower bounds on the number of $\binom{2}{1}\text{OT}$ up-to a factor of 2.

CIRCUIT COMPLEXITY VS. NUMBER OF ANDS IN SECURE COMPUTATION. As explained above the circuit complexity of a function $f : \{0,1\}^n \times \{0,1\}^n \to \{0,1\}$ provides an upper bound on the number of ANDs required for secure computation of f by a randomized protocol. It might seem tempting to think that the circuit complexity characterizes the number of ANDs. However, this is not true.

There are functions with high circuit complexity which require few or no ANDs. For example, f can be a function only of Alice's input with high circuit complexity which Alice can compute securely without any communication or calls to the AND black box. Furthermore, our results show that circuit complexity does not characterizes the number of ANDs required to securely compute a function by a deterministic protocol (this number of ANDs can be larger or smaller than the circuit complexity).

2   Preliminaries

In this section we define one-sided information-theoretic secure two-party computation in the honest-but-curios model. In our definition we allow the parties to execute a black box to a pre-defined function.

PROTOCOLS. We consider a two-party protocol with a pair of parties (Turing Machines), Alice and Bob. They have an access to a black box BB which computes some function BB : $D_1 \times D_2 \to D_3$. Briefly, on *inputs* (x, y), where x is a private input for Alice and y a private input for Bob, and *random inputs* (r_A, r_B), where r_A is a private random tape for Alice and r_B is a private random tape for Bob, protocol (Alice, Bob) computes its output in a sequence of rounds of three types: Alice's rounds, Bob's rounds, and black-box rounds. In an Alice's round (respectively, Bob's round) only Alice (respectively, only Bob) is active and sends a message (i.e., a string) that will become an available input to Bob (respectively, to Alice) in the next round. In a black-box round Alice puts a value $a \in D_1$ to a register and Bob puts a value $b \in D_2$ to a register. In the end of this round Alice gets the value $BB(a, b)$ in a third register, and Bob gets no information. A computation of Alice and Bob ends in a round in which Alice computes a private *output*. In this paper we focus on an AND black box, where AND: $\{0, 1\} \times \{0, 1\} \to \{0, 1\}$ and $AND(a, b) = a \wedge b$.

TRANSCRIPTS, VIEWS, AND OUTPUTS. Letting E be an execution of protocol (Alice, Bob) on inputs (x, y) and random inputs (r_A, r_B), we make the following definitions:

- The *transcript* of E consists of the sequence of messages exchanged by Alice and Bob, and is denoted by $\text{TRANS}(x, r_A, y, r_B)$;
- The *black-box outputs* of E consists of the outputs of the black box during the execution of the protocol, and is denoted by $\text{BLACK-BOX}(x, r_A, y, r_B)$;
- The *view of Alice* consists of the quadruplet

$$(x, r_A, \text{TRANS}(x, r_A, y, r_B), \text{BLACK-BOX}(x, r_A, y, r_B)),$$

and is denoted by $\text{VIEW}_{\text{Alice}}(x, r_A, y, r_B)$;
- The *view of Bob* consists of $(y, r_B, \text{TRANS}(x, r_A, y, r_B))$, and is denoted by $\text{VIEW}_{\text{Bob}}(x, r_A, y, r_B)$.

We consider the random variables $\text{TRANS}(x, \cdot, y, r_B)$, $\text{TRANS}(x, r_A, y, \cdot)$, and $\text{TRANS}(x, \cdot, y, \cdot)$, respectively obtained by randomly selecting r_A, r_B, or both, and then outputting $\mathrm{TRANS}(x, r_A, y, r_B)$. We also consider the similarly defined random variables for $\mathrm{VIEW}_{\mathrm{Alice}}$ and $\mathrm{VIEW}_{\mathrm{Bob}}$.

In the model we consider, the two-party honest-but-curious model, each party is curious, that is, it may try to deduce as much information possible from its own view of an execution about the other's private input. However, each party is honest, that is, it scrupulously follows the instructions of the protocol. In such conditions, it is easy to enforce the correctness condition (for securely computing a function f), but not necessarily the privacy conditions. Note that, unlike secure computation in the malicious model, in the honest-but-curious model we can separate the security requirement into two separate requirements: correctness and privacy.

In the following definition we consider partial functions $f : A \times B \to C \cup \{*\}$, where A, B and C are some finite sets and $* \notin C$. If $f(x, y) = *$ then we say that f is undefined on x, y. The reason that we consider partial functions is that in Section 3 we use them to characterize the number of ANDs required to securely compute fully-defined functions. To define the privacy in a protocol we consider the *statistical distance* between two distributions Y_0, Y_1 which is defined by $\mathrm{DIST}(Y_0, Y_1) = \frac{1}{2} \sum_y | \Pr[Y_0 = y] - \Pr[Y_1 = y]|$.

Definition 1 (Secure Computation). *Let $f : A \times B \to C \cup \{*\}$ be a function, and $0 \le \epsilon, \delta \le 1$. A protocol (Alice, Bob) (ϵ, δ)-securely computes f, if the following conditions hold:*

Correctness. *For every $x \in A$ and every $y \in B$, if $f(x, y) \neq *$, then the probability that the output of Alice with $\mathrm{VIEW}_{\mathrm{Alice}}(x, \cdot, y, \cdot)$ is $f(x, y)$ is at least $1 - \epsilon$, where the probability is taken over r_A and r_B.*
Bob's Privacy. *$\forall x \in A, \forall y_0, y_1 \in B, \forall r_A$, if $f(x, y_0) = f(x, y_1) \neq *$ then*

$$\mathrm{DIST}(\mathrm{VIEW}_{\mathrm{Alice}}(x, r_A, y_0, \cdot), \mathrm{VIEW}_{\mathrm{Alice}}(x, r_A, y_1, \cdot)) \le \delta.$$

Alice's Privacy. *$\forall x_0, x_1 \in A, \forall y \in B, \forall r_B$, if $f(x_0, y) \neq *$ and $f(x_1, y) \neq *$, then*

$$\mathrm{DIST}(\mathrm{VIEW}_{\mathrm{Bob}}(x_0, \cdot, y, r_B), \mathrm{VIEW}_{\mathrm{Bob}}(x_1, \cdot, y, r_B)) \le \delta.$$

A protocol securely computes f if it $(0, 0)$-securely computes f. In this case, we also say that the protocol computes f with perfect security. A protocol is deterministic if Alice's and Bob's moves in the protocol do not depend on their random inputs.

Notice that the requirements in Alice's privacy and in Bob's privacy are not symmetric. We require that Alice's privacy is protected for all inputs where f is defined. As Alice learns the output of f, we require that Bob's privacy is protected only when $f(x, y_0) = f(x, y_1) \neq *$.

The main measure we consider is the number of calls to the black box during a protocol.

Definition 2 (Number of ANDs). *The number of calls to the AND black box in a protocol is the maximum over the inputs x and y and random inputs r_A and r_B of the number of black-box rounds in the execution with x, y, r_A, and r_B.*

Beimel, Micali, and Malkin [3], following Kushilevitz [22], characterize which functions can be computed securely without any calls to the AND black box. Their characterization uses the following notation and definitions. We represent a function $f : A \times B \to C \cup \{*\}$ by a matrix M_f whose rows are labeled by the elements of A, columns are labeled by the elements of B, and $M_f(x, y) = f(x, y)$.

Definition 3 (Insecure Minor). *A matrix contains an insecure minor if there are x_0, x_1, y_0, y_1 such that $M(x_0, y_0) = M(x_0, y_1) \neq *$, $M(x_1, y_0), M(x_0, y_1) \neq *$, and $M(x_1, y_0) \neq M(x_0, y_1)$.*

The following theorem of [3] states that a function can be computed securely without ANDs iff it does not contain an insecure minor.

Theorem 1 ([3]). *The function f can be computed by a perfectly-secure randomized protocol with 0 ANDs if and only if the function f can be computed by a deterministic protocol with 0 ANDs if and only if M_f does not contain an insecure-minor.*

The next definition is helpful for characterizing the number of required ANDs, by defining a relation on the columns of the matrix M_f.

Definition 4 ([22]). *The relation $\sim_C$ on the columns of a matrix M is defined as follows: $y, y' \in B$ satisfy $y \sim_C y'$ if there exists some $x \in A$ such that $M(x, y) = M(x, y') \neq *$. The equivalence relation $\equiv_C$ on the columns of M is defined as the transitive closure of the relation $\sim_C$. That is, $y \equiv_C y'$, for $y, y' \in B$, if there are $y_1, \ldots, y_\ell$ such that $y \sim_C y_1 \sim_C y_2 \sim_C \cdots \sim_C y_\ell \sim_C y'$.*

In the rest of this section we prove various properties of secure protocols used throughout the paper. We next relate the number of ANDs required to securely compute a function, to the number of ANDs required to securely compute the functions restricted to each equivalence class. The proof of the following lemma appears in the full version of the paper.

Lemma 1. *Let $f : A \times B \to C \cup \{*\}$ be a function, let $B_1, \ldots, B_k$ the equivalence classes of the relation $\equiv_C$, and define $f_i : A \times B_i \to C \cup \{*\}$ as the restriction of f to B_i The function f can be computed securely by a randomized protocol (respectively, deterministic protocol) with q ANDs if and only if each function f_i can be computed securely by a randomized protocol (respectively, deterministic protocol) with q ANDs.*

For the results in this paper, we need the following standard result. Informally, the lemma asserts that if the columns of M_f are equivalent then in perfectly-secure protocols no information is disclosed by the communication, and all the information that Alice needs to compute the function is passed through the outputs of the black box alone.

Lemma 2. *Let $f : A \times B \to C$ be a function s.t. all columns of M_f are equivalent and let c be any communication transcript that can be exchanged between Alice and Bob in a protocol with perfect privacy. Then for every $x, x' \in A$ and every $y, y' \in B$ it holds that $\Pr[c = \mathrm{TRANS}(x, \cdot, y, \cdot)] = \Pr[c = \mathrm{TRANS}(x', \cdot, y', \cdot)]$, where the probability is taken over the random inputs of Alice and Bob.*

The proof of Lemma 2 is omitted. Recall that in any deterministic protocol, for every x, y there is one possible communication transcript. Thus, by Lemma 2, if all the columns of M_f are equivalent, then the same transcript will be exchanged for every pair of inputs. Thus, in deterministic protocols Alice and Bob can discard the communication and only execute the AND black boxes.

Lemma 3. *Let $f : A \times B \to C$ be a function s.t. all columns of M_f are equivalentIn every deterministic secure protocol there is exactly one communication transcript that is exchanged between Alice and Bob for all inputs x, y.*

3   Deterministic Protocols

In this section we examine how many ANDs are needed to compute a function securely by a deterministic protocol. We start by giving an exact characterization of the functions that can be securely computed by deterministic protocols with q ANDs. This characterization proves that there is a complete hierarchy of functions according to the number of ANDs. In particular, we establish that every function can be computed securely by a deterministic protocol provided that enough ANDs are executed. This should be contrasted to the malicious model where it is known that randomization is required [14].

For finite functions one can find the optimal protocol using our characterization. However, in general, our characterization does not lead to an efficient algorithm that determines how many ANDs are required to compute a function securely. Therefore, in Theorem 3 we give a simple and explicit upper bound on the number of ANDs that are required. Finally, we show in Theorem 4 that this upper bound is tight for Boolean functions. We note that our upper bound seems to be impractical since the number of ANDs can be exponential in the length of the input. However, at least for Boolean functions, our lower bound proves that this is unavoidable if we consider deterministic protocols.

To characterize what can be done with q ANDs by a deterministic protocol, we note that first Alice and Bob call the AND black box once, and then execute a protocol with $q - 1$ ANDs to compute a related function described in Figure 1. For the first execution there are sets $A_1 \subseteq A$ and $B_1 \subseteq B$ such that Alice gets output one from the AND black box if and only if $x, y \in A_1 \times B_1$. We have two requirements: (1) Alice does not learn any extra information from the output of the first AND black box, and (2) Alice and Bob can compute the following function f_{A_1,B_1} using $q - 1$ ANDs. Formally, given a function $f : A \times B \to C \cup \{*\}$ and two sets $A_1 \subseteq A$ and $B_1 \subseteq B$ we define a function $f_{A_1,B_1} : (A \cup (A_1 \times \{1\})) \times B \to C \cup \{*\}$, described in Figure 1, as follows:

1. $f_{A_1,B_1}(x, y) = f(x, y)$ for every $x \in A \setminus A_1$ and every $y \in B$.
2. $f_{A_1,B_1}(x, y) = f(x, y)$ for every $x \in A_1$ and every $y \in B \setminus B_1$.
3. $f_{A_1,B_1}(x, y) = *$ for every $x \in A_1$ and every $y \in B_1$.
4. $f_{A_1,B_1}(\langle x, 1 \rangle, y) = *$ for every $x \in A_1$ and every $y \in B \setminus B_1$.
5. $f_{A_1,B_1}(\langle x, 1 \rangle, y) = f(x, y)$ for every $x \in A_1$ and every $y \in B_1$.

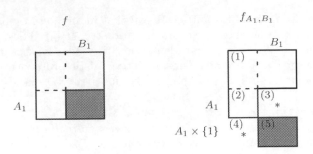

Fig. 1. The matrices of the functions f and f_{A_1,B_1}. The numbers in the description of f_{A_1,B_1} refer to the different cases in its definition.

Theorem 2. *Let $f : A \times B \rightarrow C \cup \{*\}$ be a function such that all columns of M_f are equivalent according to $\equiv_C$. The function f can be computed securely with q calls to the AND black box if and only if there are sets $A_1 \subseteq A$ and $B_1 \subseteq B$ such that the following two requirements hold:*

1. *For every $x \in A_1$, every $y_0 \notin B_1$, and every $y_1 \in B_1$ such that $f(x, y_0), f(x, y_1) \neq *$ it holds that $f(x, y_0) \neq f(x, y_1)$, and*
2. *The function f_{A_1,B_1} can be computed securely with $q - 1$ calls to the AND black box.*

Proof. We first prove that the above conditions are sufficient. Assume the conditions hold. The secure protocol for computing f proceeds as follows:

- Alice and Bob call the AND black box where Alice puts 1 iff $x \in A_1$ and Bob put 1 iff $y \in B_1$.
- Alice and Bob execute the secure protocol for f_{A_1,B_1} with $q - 1$ calls to the AND black box, where Bob's input is y and Alice's input is $\langle x, 1 \rangle$ if the AND output is 1 and x otherwise.
- Alice's output is the output of the protocol for f_{A_1,B_1}.

We first argue that the protocol is correct. On one hand, if the output of the AND black box is 1, then $x \in A_1$ and $y \in B_1$. Thus, by the definition of f_{A_1,B_1} it holds that $f_{A_1,B_1}(\langle x, 1 \rangle, y) = f(x, y)$, and the output of the protocol is correct. On the other hand, if the output of the AND black box is 0, then either $x \notin A_1$ or $y \notin B_1$. Thus, $f_{A_1,B_1}(x, y) = f(x, y)$, and the output of the protocol is correct. Note that the protocol never tries to evaluate f_{A_1,B_1} on inputs where it is not defined.

To argue that the protocol is perfectly-secure, first note that Bob gets no messages during the first step of the protocol, and he does not get any information from the black box. This guarantees Alice's Privacy. To argue about Bob's privacy, note that Alice learns information about y from the first call to the AND black box only if $x \in A_1$. In this case, by Condition 1, Alice learns if $y \in B_1$ from the output of the function f itself. Thus, this step is secure, and Alice is allowed to know the output of the black box and the output of f_{A_1,B_1} which as argued is equal to the desired output of f. Finally, as the protocol for f_{A_1,B_1} is secure, the entire protocol for f is secure.

We next prove that the conditions of the theorem are necessary. Assume that f can be computed securely with q ANDs. By Lemma 3, we can assume w.l.o.g. that Alice and Bob do not exchange any messages, and all information Alice gets is through the outputs of the calls to the AND black boxes. Let A_1 and B_1 be the sets of inputs of Alice and Bob respectively for which they put 1 to the first call to the AND black box. Condition 1 must hold or otherwise Alice learns extra information from the answer of the first AND. As for Condition 2, we can use the following protocol to compute f_{A_1,B_1} securely with $q-1$ ANDs: Alice and Bob execute the protocol for f with the following two changes: (1) If Alice's "real" input is $\langle x, 1 \rangle$ for $x \in A_1$ then she replaces it by the input x, and (2) the first call to the AND black box is not executed. Instead, Alice simulates it by considering its output as 1 if her input is $\langle x, 1 \rangle$ and 0 otherwise. The rest of the protocol is executed without any changes. As the protocol for f uses q ANDs, and Alice and Bob do not use the first AND, the resulting protocol for f_{A_1,B_1} uses $q-1$ ANDs as required. $\square$

Our next theorem gives a simple upper bound on the number of ANDs required to compute a function securely. The proof of this upper-bound gives a simple secure protocol for computing the function.

Theorem 3. *Let $f : A \times B \to C \cup \{*\}$ be a function. The function f can be computed securely by a deterministic protocol with $|A| \lceil \log |C| \rceil$ ANDs.*

Proof. First assume that f is Boolean, i.e., $C = \{0, 1\}$. We next describe a protocol which uses $|A|$ ANDs. Assume the input of Alice is x and the input of Bob is y. For every $z \in A$, Alice and Bob execute the AND black box, where Alice puts 1 to the AND if $x = z$ and 0 otherwise, and Bob puts $f(z, y)$ to the AND. Alice outputs the output of the AND corresponding to x, that is, $\text{AND}(1, f(x, y)) = f(x, y)$ as required. Bob does not gain any information during this protocol (since there is no communication and only Alice gets the output of the black box) and Alice only gains $f(x, y)$.

If $|C| > 2$, then we consider the binary representation of $f(x, y)$ (of length exactly $\lceil \log |C| \rceil$), and execute the above protocol for every bit of $f(x, y)$. $\square$

The following theorem shows that the upper bound of Theorem 3 is tight for every Boolean function. In the theorem we assume that there is some y_0 such that $f(x, y_0) = 0$ for every $x \in A$. This assumption is without loss of generality since Alice learns the output of the protocol and knows x, thus she can use any renaming of the outputs in every row.

Theorem 4. *Let $f : A \times B \to \{0, 1\}$ be a Boolean function such that all the rows of M_f are distinct and non-constant, there is some $y_0 \in B$ such that $f(x, y_0) = 0$ for every $x \in A$, and all of its columns are equivalent according to $\equiv_C$. Then, every deterministic protocol computing f securely must use at least $|A|$ ANDs.*

Proof. Fix any deterministic protocol that computes f securely. By Lemma 3, we can assume, without loss of generality, that Alice and Bob do not exchange any messages and the view of Alice includes her input and the outputs of the black box. Consider any $x \in A$. Since f is Boolean there are exactly two views Alice should see given x: one view for every y such that $f(x,y) = 0$ and another view for every y such that $f(x,y) = 1$. For every x, consider the first black-box call where Alice can get two different answers. As argued above one output corresponds to the case where $f(x,y) = 0$ and the other output corresponds to the case where $f(x,y) = 1$. Thus, Alice can deduce the output of the function $f(x,y)$ from this black-box answer and, therefore, we say that this is the significant call to the AND black box for x.

Assume, towards contradiction, that for two different $x_0, x_1 \in A$ the significant call is the same. Recall that $f(x_0, y_0) = f(x_1, y_0) = 0$, and since the rows corresponding to x_0 and x_1 are not the same, there is some y_1 such that, w.l.o.g., $f(x_0, y_1) = 0$ while $f(x_1, y_1) = 1$. Bob has to put the same value to this significant call when he holds y_0 and y_1 or Alice would learn information when she holds x_0. This means that Alice cannot compute the correct value of $f(x_1, y_0)$ or $f(x_1, y_1)$ since in both cases she gets the same information, contradiction.

To conclude, for every $x \in A$ there is a unique significant call to the AND black box, thus, there are at least $|A|$ calls to the AND black box.   □

In the protocol implied by Theorem 3, Alice is non-adaptive as her inputs to the AND black box depend only on her input and not on the outputs of previous AND black boxes. In Theorem 4 we prove that for Boolean functions this is optimal. However, the protocol implied by Theorem 2 is adaptive, and for non-Boolean functions adaptively does help (namely the bound is not tight), as shown in the following example. Consider the function $f : \{0,1,2\} \times \{0,1,2,3\} \to \{0,1,2\}$ described in Figure 2. We next describe a secure protocol for f which

f	0	1	2	3
0	0	1	0	1
1	0	1	2	2
2	0	0	2	3

The function f

f_{A_1,B_1}	0	1	2	3
0	0	1	0	1
1	0	1	*	*
2	0	0	*	*
$\langle 1,1 \rangle$	*	*	2	2
$\langle 2,1 \rangle$	*	*	2	3

The function f_{A_1,B_1}

Fig. 2. The functions f and f_{A_1,B_1}.

uses two ANDs. For the first AND, Alice puts 1 if $x \in A_1 = \{1,2\}$ and Bob puts 1 if $y \in B_1 = \{2,3\}$. After this AND Alice and Bob need to securely compute the function f_{A_1,B_1} described in Figure 2. Computing f_{A_1,B_1} is done using a second AND where Alice puts 1 if $x \in A_2 = \{0,1,\langle 2,1\rangle\}$ and Bob puts 1 if $y \in B_2 = \{1,3\}$. After this AND, Alice can deduce the output of f from her input and the outputs of the ANDs. In this protocol Alice is adaptive; with input 1, for example, she puts 1 to the second AND if the output of the first AND was 0 and she puts 0 otherwise.

4   Randomized Protocols

In this section we investigate the power of randomization in our setting. We show that, in general, randomization helps: the gap between the number of ANDs required by a randomized protocol and a deterministic one may be exponential. We also quantify *how much* randomization can help, and study its limits. Finally, we show that allowing a statistically secure protocol with some error probability may significantly reduce the number of ANDs compared to the number required by a perfect randomized protocol.

4.1   Randomization Helps

The following theorem, adapted from [16], establishes an upper bound on the number of ANDs needed to securely compute a function, in terms of the number of gates in its circuit. Together with our characterization for deterministic protocols in the previous section, the theorem proves that randomization helps, as we elaborate below.

Theorem 5 ([16]). *If f can be computed by a Boolean circuit with fan-in 2 whose size is s, then there is a perfectly-secure randomized protocol computing f which uses $4s$ AND calls.*

Proof. Theorem 5 is proved in [16] by having each of the parties additively secret-share their inputs, and then processing the shares through each of the gates in the circuit. Depending on the gate, the parties may need to use the primitive of *1-out-of-4 Oblivious Transfer*, which can be implemented using four ANDs.

We next describe the protocol in our context. Alice and Bob compute the function f one gate at a time, such that for each wire in the circuit, Alice and Bob hold two random bits whose exclusive-or is the correct value for that wire in a non-secure computation of the circuit (see Figure 3). For initialization, for every variable x_i held by Alice, the bits held by Alice and Bob respectively are (s_A, s_B) where Alice holds the bit $s_A = x_i$ and Bob holds the bit $s_B = 0$. The variables held by Bob are dealt symmetrically. We next explain how to compute a Boolean gate G where the correct values of its inputs computed by the circuit are $s1$ and $s2$ and the correct value of the output of the gate is $s3 = G(s1, s2)$. Before the computation of the gate Alice holds $(s1_A, s2_A)$ and Bob holds $(s1_B, s2_B)$ such that $s1 = s1_A \oplus s1_B$ and $s2 = s2_A \oplus s2_B$. At the end of the computation Alice and Bob should hold random bits $(s3_A, s3_B)$ such that $s3 = s3_A \oplus s3_B$. To compute the gate, Bob chooses a random bit $s3_B$, and computes the value of $s3_A$ for the 4 possible values $(0,0), (0,1), (1,0),$ and $(1,1)$ of Alice's inputs $(s1_A, s2_A)$. That is, Bob computes for every $a1, a2 \in \{0,1\}$ the value $s3_A = s3_B \oplus G(a1 \oplus s1_B, a2 \oplus s2_B)$. Thereafter, Alice and Bob perform four ANDs, corresponding to the possible values of Alice's inputs, where Alice puts 1 to the AND execution corresponding to her true inputs $(s1_A, s2_A)$, and 0 to the other three, and Bob puts the values of $s3_A$ he computed. For the final gate application, Bob chooses $s3_B = 0$, so that Alice's output for that gate (in the appropriate AND execution) is the output of the function. The correctness and privacy of this protocol are easy to verify.   □

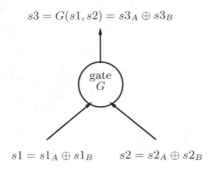

$$s3 = G(s1, s2) = s3_A \oplus s3_B$$

gate
G

$$s1 = s1_A \oplus s1_B \qquad s2 = s2_A \oplus s2_B$$

Fig. 3. A secure evaluation of a gate G.

The above theorem applies for circuits with gates which are arbitrary Boolean functions with fan-in 2. Depending on the circuit, the theorem can be optimized to achieve a smaller number of ANDs, as some of the gates may require only 2 ANDs (when one of the incoming wires is from Bob's initial inputs) or no ANDs (when the gate computes exclusive-or). Such optimizations are used in the following examples to obtain slightly better parameters than guaranteed by a direct application of the theorem as stated.

We conclude that randomization helps for functions where the upper bound promised by Theorem 5 for randomized protocols is smaller than the lower bound established in Theorem 2 for deterministic protocols. We next provide a few concrete examples, which exhibit when and how much randomization helps.

Example 1 (Inner Product IP_n). Let $IP_n : \{0,1\}^n \times \{0,1\}^n \to \{0,1\}$ be the inner-product modulo 2 function, that is, $IP_n(x, y) = \oplus_{i=1}^{n} x_i y_i$. We show that the function IP_n can be computed with $2n$ ANDs using a perfect randomized protocol, but requires at least $2^n - 1$ ANDs in any deterministic protocol.

Lemma 4. *The function IP_n can be securely computed with $2n$ ANDs using a randomized protocol. Any deterministic protocol for securely computing IP_n requires at least $2^n - 1$ ANDs (and there is a deterministic protocol using this number of ANDs).*

Proof. Consider the following protocol on input $x = x_1, \ldots, x_n$ for Alice and $y = y_1, \ldots, y_n$ for Bob. Bob chooses $r_1, \ldots, r_{n-1} \in \{0,1\}^n$ uniformly at random and sets $r_n \leftarrow \oplus_{i=1}^{n-1} r_i$. Then, for each $i = 1, \ldots, n$, Alice and Bob run two ANDs, as follows: $a_i^0 \leftarrow \wedge(1 - x_i, r_i)$ and $a_i^1 \leftarrow \wedge(x_i, y_i \oplus r_i)$. Alice outputs $\oplus_{i=1}^{n} a_i^{x_i} = IP_n(x, y)$. The claims about deterministic protocols for IP_n follow from Theorem 4 and Theorem 3. □

As we will explain in Example 5, the number of ANDs in this protocol is tight up to a constant, since every randomized protocol for IP_n requires at least $n/2$ ANDs even if we allow errors and statistical privacy. We next show a tradeoff between the number of random bits and the number of ANDs.

A randomized protocol for $\mathrm{IP}_3|_{\overline{(1,1,1)}}$ with 4 ANDs

Alice's input: x_1, x_2, x_3 where the number of variables with value 1 is ≤ 2.
Bob's input: y_1, y_2, y_3
Alice's desired output: $x_1 y_1 \oplus x_2 y_2 \oplus x_3 y_3$

Bob chooses r at random from $\{0, 1\}$.
Alice sets $a = 1$ iff exactly one of her inputs has value 1.
Alice and Bob execute the following 4 ANDs:
$$a_1 \leftarrow \wedge(x_1, y_1 \oplus r), \quad a_2 \leftarrow \wedge(x_2, y_2 \oplus r),$$
$$a_3 \leftarrow \wedge(x_3, y_3 \oplus r), \quad a_4 \leftarrow \wedge(a, r).$$
Alice's ouput: $a_1 \oplus a_2 \oplus a_3 \oplus a_4$.

Fig. 4. A randomized protocol with 4 ANDs for a function requiring 6 ANDs in any deterministic protocol.

Lemma 5. *The function IP_n can be securely computed using $R - 1$ random bits and $R2^{\lceil n/R \rceil}$ ANDs, for all $1 \leq R \leq n$.*

Proof. The protocol is a generalization of the protocol described in the proof of Lemma 4. Denote $n' = \lceil n/R \rceil$. Bob chooses $R - 1$ random bits $r_1, \ldots, r_{R-1}$ and sets $r_R \leftarrow \oplus_{i=1}^{R-1} r_i$. Then, for $i = 0$ to $R - 1$ Alice and Bob compute the function $a_i \leftarrow \mathrm{IP}(\langle x_{in'+1}, \ldots, x_{(i+1)n'} \rangle, \langle y_{in'+1}, \ldots, y_{(i+1)n'} \rangle) \oplus r_i$ using the secure deterministic protocol of Theorem 3, which uses $2^{\lceil n/R \rceil}$ ANDs, where Alice's input is $\langle x_{in'+1}, \ldots, x_{(i+1)n'} \rangle$ and Bob's input is $\langle y_{in'+1}, \ldots, y_{(i+1)n'} \rangle, r_i$. Alice outputs the value $\oplus_{i=0}^{R-1} a_i$ which by the properties of IP and the choice of the r_i's is the correct value. Since the first $R - 1$ random bits are chosen independently and the deterministic IP protocol is secure, the protocol we construct is secure. $\square$

Example 2 (Restricted IP_3). Consider the restricted-domain inner product function tion IP_3, where Alice's input cannot be $x = (1, 1, 1)$, and denote it by $\mathrm{IP}_3|_{\overline{(1,1,1)}}$. We show in Figure 4 that this function can be computed with 4 ANDs in a randomized protocol with perfect privacy and correctness, but requires 6 ANDs in any deterministic protocol. We note that 4 is the smallest number of ANDs for which we can prove that randomization helps (in Section 4.3 we will see that for one AND we can prove randomization does not help). We leave as an open problem whether randomization helps or not for the case of 2 or 3 ANDs.

Lemma 6. *The function $\mathrm{IP}_3|_{\overline{(1,1,1)}}$ can be securely computed with 4 ANDs in a randomized protocol, but the minimal number of ANDs required by a deterministic protocol for this function is 6.*

Example 3 (Equality EQ_n). Let $\mathrm{EQ}_n : \{0, 1\}^n \times \{0, 1\}^n \to \{0, 1\}$ be the equality function, that is, $\mathrm{EQ}_n(x, y) = 1$ iff $x = y$. We show below that the number of ANDs required to compute the function EQ_n using a perfect deterministic protocol is exponential in n, while using a perfect randomized protocol this number

---

A randomized (imperfect) protocol with for EQ_n

Alice's input: $x = x_1, \ldots, x_n \in \{0,1\}^n$
Bob's input: $y = y_1, \ldots, y_n \in \{0,1\}^n$
Alice's desired output: $\mathrm{EQ}_n(x,y)$

Bob chooses k vectors $\boldsymbol{r}^1, \ldots, \boldsymbol{r}^k \in \{0,1\}^n$ uniformly at random,
Bob sends $\boldsymbol{r}^1, \ldots, \boldsymbol{r}^k \in \{0,1\}^n$ to Alice
Alice computes $a_j = \mathrm{IP}_n(x, \boldsymbol{r}^j)$ for $j = 1, \ldots, k$, and sets $a = a_1, \ldots, a_k$
Bob computes $b_j = \mathrm{IP}_n(y, \boldsymbol{r}^j)$ for $j = 1, \ldots, k$, and sets $b = b_1, \ldots, b_k$
Alice and Bob use the randomized prot. of Lemma 7 to compute $\mathrm{EQ}_k(a,b)$.
Alice's ouput: the output of the protocol for $\mathrm{EQ}_k(a,b)$.

Fig. 5.   A randomized protocol with $O(k)$ ANDs, $1/2^k$ error and $2/2^k$ distance for EQ_n.

is linear in n, and using a randomized protocol with small error probability and statistical privacy, the number of ANDs is independent of n and depends only on the allowed error and distance (which are exponentially small in the number of ANDs). The specific lemmas are stated below.

Lemma 7. *Any deterministic protocol computing EQ_n must use at least 2^n ANDs, and there is a deterministic protocl with this number of ANDs. Any perfectly-secure randomized protocol computing EQ_n must use at least n ANDs, and there exits such a protocol using $O(n)$ ANDs.*

Proof. Noting that the matrix for EQ_n is the identity matrix, the upper bound for deterministic protocols follows directly from Theorem 3. The lower bound for deterministic protocols follows from Theorem 4, since the matrix satisfies all the conditions of the theorem (including the all-zero column, if we exchange the roles of 0 and 1 outputs in one of the rows). The upper bound for randomized protocols follows from Theorem 5, by noting that there is a Boolean circuit with fan-in 2 and with $O(n)$ gates that computes EQ_n. The lower bound for randomized protocols follows from Theorem 6 below. $\square$

Lemma 8. *For every k, the function EQ_n can be computed with $O(k)$ ANDs by a randimized protocol with $1/2^k$ error and at most $1/2^k$ statistical distance.*

Proof. The protocl securely-computing EQ_n is described in Figure 5. The idea of the protocol is to approximately compare the initial n-bit inputs by (exactly) comparing k inner products of the inputs with random strings, which as we saw can be done using $O(k)$ ANDs. It is clear that if $\mathrm{EQ}_n(x,y) = 1$ (i.e., the inputs are equal) the protocol does not err. On the other hand, $\Pr[a^j \neq b^j | \mathrm{EQ}_n(x,y) = 0] = 1/2$ for every j, and since the vectors r^j are chosen independently at random, $\Pr[\mathrm{EQ}_k(a,b) = 1 | \mathrm{EQ}_n(x,y) = 0] = 1/2^k$, which establishes the error.

We next prove that the protocol has statistical privacy. Intuitively, Alice learns information only when she gets an incorrect output. Formally, fix any $x, y, y' \in \{0,1\}^n$ such that $y \neq y'$ and $\mathrm{EQ}_n(x,y) = \mathrm{EQ}_n(x,y')$, and compute the statistical distance between the view seen by Alice holding input x, when executing the protocol with Bob's input set to y or to y' (we will denote the corresponding vectors computed in the protocol by (a, b) and (a', b') respectively). Observe that if $\text{EQ}_n(x, y) = 1$, y and y' must be identical. Thus, we only need to consider the case where $\text{EQ}_n(x, y) = 0$, namely x, y, y' are three different vectors. The only information that Alice gets in the protocol which depends on Bob's input, is the output of the perfectly secure protocol for $\text{EQ}_k(a, b)$ (or $\text{EQ}_k(a', b')$). This implies that given this output is the same, the views are distributed identically. On the other hand, we can bound the probability that this output is not the same, as follows.

$$\Pr[\text{EQ}_k(a, b) \neq \text{EQ}_k(a', b') | \text{EQ}_n(x, y) = 0]$$
$$\leq \Pr[\text{EQ}_k(a, b) = 1 | \text{EQ}_n(x, y) = 0] + [\text{EQ}_k(a', b') = 1 | \text{EQ}_n(x, y) = 0] = 2/2^k.$$

We may therefore conclude that the statistical distance between Alice's views for input (x, y) vs. (x, y') is at most $1/2^k$. Finally, note that Bob does not receive any messages in this protocol, so Alice's perfect privacy follows immediately. $\quad\square$

The number of ANDs used in the last lemma is independent of n, exhibiting an inherent gap between perfect and imperfect protocols. In order to get exponentially small statistical distance and error in this protocol, the number of ANDs should still be set to be linear in n, though it may be smaller than n. Setting the number of ANDs to be polylogarithmic in n will already give a negligible statistical distance and error. This should be contrasted with the lower bounds of n (or 2^n) ANDs for perfect randomized (or deterministic, resp.) protocols for this function.

4.2   How Much Does Randomization Help?

In the previous section we showed that randomization can help significantly compared to deterministic protocols. In this section we consider the limitations of randomized protocols. We first show lower bounds on the number of ANDs required in randomized protocols. For a function $f : \{0, 1\}^n \times \{0, 1\}^n \to \{0, 1\}^n$ our lower bound is at most n. Notice, that by Theorem 5 we cannot prove super-linear lower-bounds on the number of calls to the AND black box for explicit functions unless we prove super-linear lower-bounds for circuit complexity of explicit functions which is a long-standing open problem. We use our lower bounds to show that for Boolean functions the gap in the number of calls to the AND black box between deterministic protocols and randomized protocols with perfect security can be at most exponential.

We start by giving two lower bounds on the number of ANDs in perfectly-secure protocols. The proofs of these lower bounds is omitted for lack of space.

Theorem 6. *Let* $f : A \times B \to C$ *be a function s.t. all columns of* M_f *are equivalent and no two columns are the same. The number of AND black box calls in any perfectly-secure randomized protocol computing* f *is at least* $\lceil \log |B| \rceil$.

Example 4 (($\binom{n}{1}$OT). Consider the function $\binom{n}{1}$OT : $\{1, \ldots, n\} \times \{0,1\}^n \to \{0,1\}$ defined as $\binom{n}{1}$OT$(i, \langle y_1, \ldots, y_n \rangle) = y_i$. Theorem 6 proves that in any perfectly-secure protocol for $\binom{n}{1}$OT the number of ANDs is at least n.[3] This implies that in any perfectly-secure protocol for $\binom{n}{1}$OT using an $\binom{2}{1}$OT black box the number of $\binom{2}{1}$OT is at least $n/2$. This reproves the result of Dodis and Micali [14] up to a factor of 2 (our proof does not use information theory).

Theorem 7. *Let $f : A \times B \to \{0,1\}$ be a Boolean function s.t. all columns of M_f are equivalent, no two rows of M_f are the same, and there is some $y_0 \in B$ s.t. $f(x, y_0) = 0$ for every $x \in A$. Then, the number of calls to the AND black box in any perfectly-secure randomized protocol computing f is at least $\lceil \log |A| \rceil$.*

The next theorem states that for Boolean functions the gap in the number of AND black-box calls between deterministic protocols and randomized protocols with perfect security is at most exponential. This seems to resemble the simple derandomization of randomized algorithms, however this resemblance is misleading (as executing a secure protocol with all possible random coins might leek information). As an example of the difficulty, the gap can be much larger for non-perfect randomized protocols. Another example is the malicious model where randomization is essential (see, e.g., [14]). We prove the gap between randomized and deterministic protocols by combining the lower bounds we proved on randomized protocols and the upper bounds for deterministic protocols.

Theorem 8. *Let f be a Boolean function. If there exists a perfectly-secure randomized protocol computing f using q ANDs then there is a deterministic protocol computing f with 2^q ANDs.*

Proof. By Lemma 1, the function f can be securely computed with q ANDs if and only if every equivalence class of the columns of M_f can be computed securely with q ANDs. Thus, by Theorem 7, the number of distinct rows in any equivalence class is at most at most 2^q. By Theorem 3, there is a deterministic protocol securely computing every equivalence class of f using 2^q ANDs, and therefore, by Lemma 1, such protocol exists for f.   □

We next generalize Theorem 6 to protocols which might err with some probability. We first recall some definitions from communication complexity (for more information on this subject see [23]). The one-round randomized communication complexity in the public random coin model is defined as follows: Alice and Bob each have a private input and they have a shared random input. Bob sends one message to Alice, and Alice computes the output of the protocol (there are no privacy requirements). The error of the protocol is the probability that Alice outputs a value different than $f(x, y)$. A protocol computes f with error ϵ if for every inputs x, y its error is at most ϵ. Let $R_\epsilon^{\text{pub}, B \to A}(f)$ be the number of communication bits in the best such protocol computing f with error ϵ.

---

[3] Using Theorem 9 below, one can prove that even in statistically-secure protocols for $\binom{n}{1}$OT the number of ANDs is $\Omega(n)$.

Theorem 9. *Let $f : A \times B \to \{0,1\}$ be a Boolean function s.t. all the columns of M_f are equivalent and no two columns are identical. Then, in any randomized (ϵ, δ)-secure protocol computing f, the number of ANDs is at least $R_{\epsilon+7\delta}^{\mathrm{pub}, B \to A}(f)$.*

The proof of Theorem 9 is omitted for lack of space. Theorem 6 is a special case of Theorem 9 since it easy to see that $R_0^{\mathrm{pub}, B \to A}(f) = \lceil \log |B| \rceil$.

Example 5. By [15] it holds that $R_{\epsilon}^{\mathrm{pub}, B \to A}(\mathrm{IP}_n) = n/2$ for every $\epsilon < 1/2$. Thus, unlike EQ_n, for every ϵ, δ where $\epsilon + 7\delta < 1/2$, the inner-product function does not have an (ϵ, δ)-secure protocol which uses less than $n/2$ ANDs.

4.3   One AND: Randomization Does Not Help

We have seen that randomization can significantly reduce (up to an exponential factor) the number of required ANDs, and that already with 4 ANDs, randomized protocols compute a strictly stronger class of functions than deterministic protocols with the same number of ANDs. On the other hand, it is known (see Theorem 1) that for secure computation in our model without any ANDs, randomization does not help. In this section we show that with *one* AND randomization still does not help.

Theorem 10. *Let $f : A \times B \to C$ be a function such that all the columns of M_f are equivalent according to $\equiv_C$. The function f can be computed securely by a randomized protocol using one call to the AND black box if and only if there are $A_1 \subseteq A$ and $B_1 \subseteq B$ such that:*

1. *For every $x \in A_1$, $y_0 \notin B_1$, and $y_1 \in B_1$ it holds that $f(x, y_0) \neq f(x, y_1)$,*
2. *For every $x \in A$ and every $y, y' \in B$ such that either $x \notin A_1$ or $y, y \notin B_1$ it holds that $f(x, y) = f(x, y')$.*
3. *For every $x \in A_1$ and every $y, y' \in B$ it holds that $f(x, y) = f(x, y')$.*

Proof. First, if Conditions (1)-(3) hold then, by Theorem 2, f can be computed by a secure (deterministic) protocol with 1 AND. The function f_{A_1, B_1} can be computed by Alice without any communication since each row of f_{A_1, B_1} is constant.

For the other direction, assume there is a secure protocol that computes f with 1 AND. Fix any communication string c that has positive probability for some fixed inputs; by Lemma 2 c has positive probability given every x, y. Now, define $A_1 = \{x : \Pr[\text{ Alice puts 1 to the black box with } x \text{ and communication } c] > 0\}$, and $B_1 = \{y : \Pr[\text{ Bob puts 1 to the black box with } y \text{ and communication } c] > 0\}$. By the correctness and privacy requirements of the protocol A_1 and B_1 satisfy Conditions (1)-(3). $\square$

The protocol proving the sufficiency of the conditions in Theorem 10 is deterministic. Thus,

Corollary 1. *Randomized protocols with one AND can compute securely exactly the same functions as deterministic protocols with one AND.*

Acknowledgments. We thank Yuval Ishai for helpful discussions and Enav Weinreb for helpful remarks on earlier versions of this paper. We are also grateful to AT&T Labs–Research that hosted us for two weeks and for three years, respectively, during which part of this research was conducted.

References

1. D. Beaver. Perfect privacy for two-party protocols. Technical Report TR-11-89, Computer Science, Harvard University, 1989.
2. D. Beaver. Correlated pseudorandomness and the complexity of private computations. In *the 28th Symp. on the Theory of Computing*, pages 479–488, 1996.
3. A. Beimel, T. Malkin, and S. Micali. The all-or-nothing nature of two-party secure computation. In *CRYPTO '99*, volume 1666 of *LNCS*, pages 80–97. Springer, 1999.
4. M. Ben-Or, S. Goldwasser, and A. Wigderson. Completeness theorems for non-cryptographic fault-tolerant distributed computations. In *the 20th Symp. on the Theory of Computing*, pages 1–10, 1988.
5. G. Brassard and C. Crépeau. Oblivious transfers and privacy amplification. In *EUROCRYPT '97*, volume 1233 of *LNCS*, pages 334–347. Springer, 1997.
6. G. Brassard, C. Crépeau, and J.-M. Robert. Information theoretic reductions among disclosure problems. In *the 27th Symp. on Foundations of Computer Science*, pages 168–173, 1986.
7. G. Brassard, C. Crépeau, and M. Sántha. Oblivious transfers and intersecting codes. *IEEE Trans. on Information Theory*, 42(6):1769–1780, 1996.
8. R. Canetti. Security and composition of multiparty cryptographic protocols. *J. of Cryptology*, 13(1):143–202, 2000.
9. D. Chaum, C. Crépeau, and I. Damgård. Multiparty unconditionally secure protocols. In *the 20th Symp. on the Theory of Computing*, pages 11–19, 1988.
10. B. Chor and E. Kushilevitz. A zero-one law for Boolean privacy. *SIAM J. on Discrete Mathematics*, 4(1):36–47, 1991.
11. C. Crépeau. Equivalence between two flavors of oblivious transfers. In *CRYPTO '87*, volume 293 of *LNCS*, pages 350–354. Springer, 1988.
12. C. Crépeau and J. Kilian. Achieving oblivious transfer using weakened security assumptions. In *29th Symp. on Found. of Computer Science*, pp. 42–52, 1988.
13. I. Damgard, J. Kilian, and L. Salvail. On the (im)possibility of basing oblivious transfer and bit commitment on weakened security assumptions. In *EUROCRYPT '99*, volume 1592 of *LNCS*, pages 56–73. Springer, 1999.
14. Y. Dodis and S. Micali. Lower bounds for oblivious transfer reductions. In *EUROCRYPT '99*, volume 1592 of *LNCS*, pages 42–55, 1999.
15. J. Forster. A linear lower bound on the unbounded error probabilistic communication complexity. In *16th Conf. on Comput. Complexity*, pp. 100–106, 2001.
16. O. Goldreich and R. Vainish. How to solve any protocol problem—an efficiency improvement. In *CRYPTO '87*, vol. 293 of *LNCS*, pages 73–86. Springer, 1988.
17. Y. Ishai, J. Kilian, K. Nissim, and E. Petrank. Extending oblivious transfers efficiently. In *CRYPTO 2003*, volume 2729 of *LNCS*, pages 145–161, Springer, 2003.
18. J. Kilian. Basing cryptography on oblivious transfer. In *Proc. of the 20th Symp. on the Theory of Computing*, pages 20–31, 1988.
19. J. Kilian. A general completeness theorem for two-party games. In *Proc. of the 23th Symp. on the Theory of Computing*, pages 553–560, 1991.
20. J. Kilian. More general completeness theorems for two-party games. In *Proc. of the 32nd Symp. on the Theory of Computing*, pages 316–324, 2000.

21. J. Kilian, E. Kushilevitz, S. Micali, and R. Ostrovsky. Reducibility and completeness in private computations. *SIAM J. on Computing*, 28(4):1189–1208, 2000.
22. E. Kushilevitz. Privacy and communication complexity. *SIAM J. on Discrete Mathematics*, 5(2):273–284, 1992.
23. E. Kushilevitz and N. Nisan. *Communication Complexity*. Cambridge University Press, 1997.
24. U. Maurer. Information-theoretic cryptography. In *CRYPTO '99*, volume 1666 of *LNCS*, pages 47–64. Springer, 1999.
25. M. Naor and K. Nissim. Communication preserving protocols for secure function evaluation. In *Proc. of the 33th Symp. on the Theory of Computing*, 2001.

Algorithmic Tamper-Proof (ATP) Security: Theoretical Foundations for Security Against Hardware Tampering

Rosario Gennaro[1], Anna Lysyanskaya[2], Tal Malkin[3], Silvio Micali[4], and Tal Rabin[1]

[1] IBM T.J. Watson Research Center
{rosario,talr}@watson.ibm.com
[2] Department of Computer Science, Brown University
anna@cs.brown.edu
[3] Department of Computer Science, Columbia University
tal@cs.columbia.edu
[4] M.I.T. Laboratory for Computer Science

Abstract. Traditionally, secure cryptographic algorithms provide security against an adversary who has only *black-box* access to the secret information of honest parties. However, such models are not always adequate. In particular, the security of these algorithms may completely break under (feasible) attacks that tamper with the secret key.

In this paper we propose a theoretical framework to investigate the algorithmic aspects related to tamper-proof security. In particular, we define a model of security against an adversary who is allowed to apply arbitrary feasible functions f to the secret key sk, and obtain the result of the cryptographic algorithms using the new secret key $f(sk)$.

We prove that in the most general setting it is impossible to achieve this strong notion of security. We then show minimal additions to the model, which are needed in order to obtain provable security. We prove that these additions are necessary and also sufficient for most common cryptographic primitives, such as encryption and signature schemes.

We discuss the applications to portable devices protected by PINs and show how to integrate PIN security into the generic security design.

Finally we investigate restrictions of the model in which the tampering powers of the adversary are limited. These restrictions model realistic attacks (like differential fault analysis) that have been demonstrated in practice. In these settings we show security solutions that work even without the additions mentioned above.

1 Introduction

Motivation and Our Main Questions. Traditionally, cryptographic algorithms have been designed to provide security against an adversary who has only *black-box* access to the secret information of honest parties. That is, the adversary can query the cryptographic algorithm on inputs of his choice and analyze the responses, which are always computed according to the correct original

M. Naor (Ed.): TCC 2004, LNCS 2951, pp. 258–277, 2004.
© Springer-Verlag Berlin Heidelberg 2004

secret information. By now, cryptographic design has become so advanced that all the major cryptographic primitives can be proven secure against black-box attacks under very weak complexity assumptions. Proofs of security for such cryptographic algorithms assume (as an abstraction) that there is some secure hardware in which the algorithm and secret key of the honest parties are stored, thus denying the adversary any form of access to this data other than exchanging messages. If this assumption is violated, all guarantees are off.

At a closer analysis, the secure hardware assumption encompasses two different components, informally: (1) *Read-proof hardware;* that is, hardware that prevents an enemy from reading anything about the data stored within it; and (2) *Tamper-proof hardware;* that is, hardware that prevents an enemy from changing anything in the data stored within it.

In particular, traditional cryptographic schemes consist of an algorithm which the adversary knows, but cannot change (i.e., stored in tamper-proof hardware), and a secret key, which the adversary does not know and cannot change (i.e., stored in hardware which is both read-proof and tamper-proof).

It is clear that each of these components is necessary, at least to some extent, in order to achieve security of a cryptographic algorithm. If the adversary can read all information belonging to an honest party, he can also perform all the same functionalities. If the adversary can arbitrarily change the algorithm implemented by the honest party, he can cause the algorithm to output all the secret information. Thus, both read-proofness and tamper-proofness are necessary assumptions. This raises the following natural questions:

> *Is it necessary to have a component which is both read-proof and tamper-proof? Can we decouple these assumptions and achieve security when the adversary has arbitrary tampering powers for any secret information, and complete knowledge of any unchangeable information? What are the minimal physical assumptions necessary for the existence of provably secure implementations of major cryptographic primitives?*

Clearly, if the secret data is only secured via a read-proof hardware then the adversary can destroy the information by overwriting it. Our goal, however, is to prevent the adversary from compromising the security of the card with respect to the original secret data (e.g., by forging a valid digital signature).

In addition to being a natural next step in a line of research aiming to achieve security against ever stronger adversaries, these questions also have direct significance to reducing the gap between cryptographic proofs and practical implementations. The motivation for decoupling is further driven by the current state in secure hardware design. There are two fronts which support the need for decoupling: attacks on, and manufacturing of, the devices.

Known attacks show that it is hard to preserve the security of the cards. Works such as [KJJ99,AARR03] show that a wide variety of "side channels" exist that enable an adversary to read off secret keys. On the other hand, many physical tampering attacks have proved successful, see for example [AK96,SA03]. Boneh, DeMillo, and Lipton [BDL01] show how to use a small number of random faults to break specific, public-key based schemes. Biham and Shamir [BS97] show how to break even unknown secret-key schemes, using a specific kind of random faults. They give these attacks the name *differential fault analysis*.

These types of attacks are of particular concern in light of the way cryptography is used today. For one, many cryptographic applications are carried out by small devices outside the security of a protected environment (e.g., smartcards and PDAs). Such gadgets may fall into the wrong hands with great ease, giving an adversary ample opportunity to apply a battery of *physical attacks*. Moreover, today's widespread use of cryptography, by virtue of its ubiquity, opens the door to increased vulnerabilities, such as opportunities for *insider attacks* by naive or malicious users. Thus it is important to reduce as much as possible the assumptions on the adversary's limitations.

On the manufacturing front, if we wish to store data which is both hardwired and secret this would need to be done at manufacturing time. This implies that the user's secret key should, at some level, be known to the device manufacturer, and this is clearly not desirable. Moreover, producing one-of-a-kind hardware for each of many users, which would be required if a unique key is hardwired in each device, may be totally impractical.

This body of evidence argues that to assume hardware that is both read-proof and tamper-proof is a big leap of faith. From this perspective, granted that both tamper-proof and read-proof security are assumptions, we wish to understand their relative strength. We are asking whether, for a fixed cryptographic algorithm, and a secret key which is stored in a read-proof hardware, the read-proof hardware can be bootstrapped via an algorithm to provide tamper-proofness? We introduce the notion of *Algorithmic Tamper-Proof (ATP) Security* which addresses security in the decoupled environment.

Our Model. We will model devices with two separate components, one being tamper-proof yet readable, and the other being read-proof yet tamperable. These components may be thought of as corresponding to the traditional notions of a hardware (circuitry) and software (memory) components of a given device. We allow only data that is common to all devices (and considered universally known) to be hardwired beyond the tampering reach of the adversary.

We define a very strong *tampering adversary* and the notion of security in our new model. The adversary considers the device's memory, M, as an n-tuple of individual bits, $x_1, \ldots, x_n$, and knows the functionality of each bit-position (e.g., where a given secret key begins and ends). We allow the adversary to specify any polynomial-time computable function $f : \{0,1\}^n \to \{0,1\}^n$ and transform M to $f(M)$. More precisely, we envisage that the adversary may adaptively interact with the device by repeating the following a polynomial number of times:

1. choose a polynomial-time computable function f and replace the current memory content, M, with the new content $f(M)$; and
2. interact with the device with memory content $f(M)$ (e.g., input a message to be signed with the current secret key, enter a PIN. etc.)

We define the notion of *algorithmic tamper-proof security* and require that whatever such an attacker can achieve, could also be achieved by a black-box attack on the system. This definition may be formulated either as a simulation-based definition, or by a direct definition of security for the cryptographic primitive (signature or encryption) with a tampering adversary.

We believe this to make a clear and attractive model for studying our problem. The model unifies and provides a theoretical framework for practical attacks such as differential fault analysis, while at the same time maintaining a more general view of security. The model also provides the next natural step in security against strong adversaries (e.g., for encryption, this is the next step after CCA2 attacks). Further applications may be possible.

Our Answers. We first show that in the model as described above ATP security cannot be achieved. That is having secret data stored in read-proof only hardware does not even preserve the secrecy of the data, let alone provide security for the cryptographic function.

Thus, we consider modifications to the model which still preserve the decoupling property in order to achieve ATP security. The modifications are done in two directions, one to enhance the physical design and the second to limit the tampering capabilities of the adversary.

Enhancing the Physical Design. We show that ATP security in the above model can be achieved iff the device is enhanced with: (1) a self-destructing capability, and (2) some hardwired data (public parameter) which is produced by a separate server that cannot be tampered with.

Specifically, we show that without (1), any cryptographic algorithm can be completely broken by a memory tampering attack, and that without (2), there are signature and encryption schemes that cannot be implemented securely in the face of a tampering attack.

Then we proceed to show that the two enhancements are *sufficient.* We achieve algorithmic tamper-proof security with respect to *arbitrary, feasible functions* f, for fundamental public-key applications such as signing and decryption; but our techniques also apply in the secret-key setting.

One way to interpret these results, is that to achieve general ATP for cryptographic schemes (e.g., signature or decryption), we *do* need a component which is both read-proof and tamper-proof (the memory of the server used for condition 2). However, this component *need not* be part of every device instantiating the scheme, as assumed in traditional models (where the secret key is stored in that component). Rather, it is sufficient to have *one* such component, used *only at setup time*, in order to provide algorithmic tamper-proof security for all instantiations of the scheme on different devices.

Restricting the Power of Tampering. We then initiate a study of tampering attacks under a restricted class of functions. We show that the situation is not hopeless even with a more basic device, that is not enhanced with self-destruct and an external public key. In particular, we show how to achieve ATP security when the adversary is limited to choosing functions f from some restricted, yet useful, classes of functions. The results presented have some practical significance as they address precisely such classes of functions that were successfully used before to attack existing systems [BS97,BDL01]. These include random hardware faults (differential fault analysis), and flipping (or "zapping") specified bits.

PIN-Protected Hardware. The main direct application of our results is in the protection of portable devices such as smartcards or PDAs. Indeed tampering attacks are most likely to be feasible when the device storing the secret key is completely in the hands of the adversary (though one can envision other scenarios). Portable devices are commonly protected by PIN numbers or passwords, to prevent unauthorized access by an adversary. We show how to incorporate PIN numbers in our model and how to make sure that the tampering powers of the adversary are not used to circumvent this extra layer of protection.

Related Work. In addition to the related work mentioned above, there are several works that address the *physical* (as opposed to algorithmic) aspects of tamper-proofing a specific device (typically a smartcard), such as [QS01]. There are many approaches that address security when the *read-proof* (as opposed to tamper-proof) assumption is relaxed in some way. Most relevant in our context, are the recent works of [ISW03], who consider security when the adversary may read part of the inputs going through the circuitry of the device, and of [MR03], who consider a general new model for security against an adversary that can observe arbitrary physical characteristics of a computation ("side channels"). The work of [CGGM00] on resettable zero knowledge can be viewed as a special case of algorithmic tamper-proof security, where the adversary's tampering powers are limited to resetting the randomness.

2   The New Model

2.1   The Device and Adversarial Capabilities

We consider a system with two components: (1) secret content, sc (containing some secret key, sk, randomness, and possibly state information), and (2) a cryptographic algorithm A which uses the secret content (we may think of A as the circuitry component).

We say that the system implements a certain function F, if for any input a, $A(sc, a) = F(a)$. We say that A implements a keyed cryptographic function $F(\cdot, \cdot)$, if for every key sk (from the appropriate domain) there exists a setting sc_{sk} of the secret data, such that the system (A, sc_{sk}) implements the function $F(sk, \cdot)$. An algorithm computing sc_{sk} will be called a *software setup algorithm*. Finally, a device setup protocol implementing $F(\cdot, \cdot)$ is a pair of algorithms. The first generates the algorithm A, possibly with some additional state information to be passed to the second algorithm. The second is a software setup algorithm: given input sk and A, and possibly an additional state information input, the algorithm generates an appropriate sc_{sk}. If the software setup algorithm is stateful, we say that the device uses public parameters. We will consider devices with efficient setup algorithms.

Consider A which implements some $F(\cdot, \cdot)$ (e.g., a signature algorithm). We define a *tampering adversary* who can request three commands to be carried out: Run($\cdot$) and Apply($\cdot$), and Setup.

- The command Run(a), invokes the cryptographic computation A using the software content sc on input a. The output is the output of such computation, i.e., $A(sc, a)$. For example, if the cryptographic algorithm is a signature then the output is a signature on the message a using the secret key stored in sc.

- The command Apply(f) takes as input a function f, and modifies the software content sc to $f(sc)$. From this point on, until a new Apply(f) is requested, all Run(a) operations will use $f(sc)$ as the new software content. f can be a probabilistic function. Note that the next invocation of Apply(f') would change $f(sc)$ to $f'(f(sc))$, i.e. it does not apply f' to the original sc. There is no output for this command.[1]

- The command Setup(sk) invokes the software setup algorithm, outputting sc such that the device (A, sc) implements the function $F(sk, \cdot)$.

The device may also have a *self-destruct* capability, called by the algorithm A. If this happens, every Run command from then on will always output $\perp$.

As mentioned above, security of smartcards and other portable devices is one of the motivations for considering this model. For convenience, throughout this paper we refer to the system interchangeably as a "card" or a "device".

INCORPORATING PIN NUMBERS. Consider the application of the model to smartcards. One goal is to prevent a tampering adversary from learning information about the contents of the card, so that he cannot duplicate and distribute devices with the same functionality (e.g., decryption cards for pay-TV applications). However, it is also often desirable to prevent the adversary from using the functionality of the device *himself*.

Towards this goal, we propose that the card be augmented with a short memorizable PIN, to be entered by the user before any application. That is, a Run query, where it previously took one input, now should take two: the PIN and the input (such as a message m to be signed). The card will only function if the PIN is correct, and, moreover, it will permanently stop functioning (or self-destruct) after a certain (not too big) number of wrong attempts. This requires a counter mechanism.

It is not hard to show that if the adversary cannot tamper with the counter, all our results carry through by considering the PIN as part of the secret key. In Section 5 we show how to achieve ATP security in the setting with PIN, by showing a cryptographic implementation of a counter which is ATP secure, based on one-way permutations or on forward-secure signature schemes. (We thus will not directly deal with the PIN setting in the other parts of the paper.)

---

[1] It is clear that if this command was allowed any output, then it could just output the secret key. Moreover, we cannot even allow f to produce outputs by making calls to Run, or security would be unachievable. Consider the following attack. The adversary chooses two inputs x_0 and x_1. Given that the secret key on the card is $s_1 s_2 ... s_l$, the function f is "for $i = 1$ to l Run(x_{s_i})". Clearly, by executing this function, we extract the whole secret key.

2.2   The Notion of Security

Intuitively, we would like that the extra power given to the adversary to be useless. We present definitions of security for signature and encryption schemes, and discuss the simulation technique that we use to achieve these goals.

Signature Cards. The classical definition of security for signature schemes is *security against adaptive chosen-message attack* introduced by [GMR88]. In our terminology, this corresponds to an adversary who is given a public key pk and the opportunity to issue as many Run commands as he wants on input messages $m_1, \ldots, m_n$, chosen adaptively, and get the corresponding signatures. Then we say that the scheme is *unforgeable* if the adversary is not able to produce a new message $m \neq m_j$ and a valid signature on it.

In our model we augment the power of the adversary by allowing him to also issue Apply commands. That may change the key pair corresponding to the card; namely, instead of the original key pair (pk, sk), the card may now be working relative to various different key pairs (pk', sk'). Yet, we will consider as *relevant* only Run queries for which the adversary gets a valid signature relative to the original public key pk. After interacting with the card, the adversary should not be able to produce a new message m and its valid signature under the public key pk. We count as a forgery a pair (m, s) even if m was asked before, but the card outputs an invalid signature because it had an incorrect secret key stored inside as a consequence of some Apply command.

Formally, let $\mathcal{S} = \langle \mathsf{Gen}, \mathsf{Sig}, \mathsf{Ver} \rangle$ be a signature scheme, where Gen is the key-generation algorithm, Sig is the signature algorithm, and Ver is the verification algorithm. We say that $\mathcal{S}$ is *algorithmically tamper-proof unforgeable* if for every probabilistic polynomial-time adversary $\mathcal{A}$, there exists a negligible function $\mathsf{negl}()$ such that

$$
\Pr \left[
\begin{array}{l}
(pk, sk) \leftarrow \mathsf{Gen}(1^k); \\
H \leftarrow \{\}; \; I \leftarrow \{\}; \; \mathsf{State} \leftarrow \epsilon \\
\text{for } i = 1 \ldots n \\
\quad (\mathsf{State}, \mathsf{Cmd}) \leftarrow \mathcal{A}(\mathsf{State}, pk, H); \\
\quad \text{if } \mathsf{Cmd} = \mathsf{Run}(m_i) \text{ then } s_i \leftarrow \mathsf{Sig}(sk, m_i); \\
\qquad \text{if } \mathsf{Ver}(pk, m_i, s_i) = yes \text{ then } I \leftarrow I \cup \{m_i\}; \\
\quad \text{if } \mathsf{Cmd} = \mathsf{Setup}(sk_i) \text{ then } s_i \leftarrow \mathsf{Setup}(sk_i); \\
\quad \text{if } \mathsf{Cmd} = \mathsf{Apply}(f_i) \text{ then } sk \leftarrow f_i(sk); \\
\quad H \leftarrow H \cup \{(\mathsf{Cmd}, s_i)\}; \\
(m, s) \leftarrow \mathcal{A}(pk, H); \\
m \notin I \; \text{ and } \; \mathsf{Ver}(pk, m, s) = yes
\end{array}
\right] = \mathsf{negl}(k)
$$

Decryption Cards. In the full version of this paper, we give the definition of security for decryption cards. Here, we give an informal sketch of this definition.

Recall that security for encryption schemes comes in at least three different levels: semantic security (security against passive adversary) [GM84], security against lunchtime attacks (security against an adversary who can interact with the decryption oracle during a training stage, before receiving a challenge ciphertext) and security against adaptive chosen ciphertext attacks (CCA-2, where an adversary has a training stage before he receives a challenge ciphertext; once he receives the challenge ciphertext, he can ask the decryption oracle additional queries which must be *distinct* from his challenge ciphertext).

We say that a scheme is *secure against adaptive chosen-ciphertext attack with lunchtime tampering* (or *tamper-proof CCA-2 secure*) if we allow the adversary to issue both Run and Apply commands during the training stage. Then the adversary outputs two messages m_0, m_1 and is given the target ciphertext c, which is the encryption of either m_0 or m_1, chosen at random. Then the adversary can perform *only* Run queries on any ciphertexts other than c. We say that the scheme is secure, if the adversary cannot guess (with probability better than $1/2$) the correct decryption of c.

Note that we do not allow the adversary to modify the secret key after the target ciphertext is released. This is because, for a challenge ciphertext c, and Apply query may be of the form "If c decrypts to 0, self-destruct," and therefore it leaks information about the plaintext.

Proofs by Simulation. The above security goal would follow if we were able to prove that this powerful adversary does not learn any more information about the secret key than an adversary who is simply limited by an input/output relationship with the card (because then, if we start from a card secure in the old model, it is also ATP secure).

We can use the concept of simulation to capture the above idea. Our theorems will be proven according to the following approach. We will construct simulators which have only Run(·) access to the card and Setup(·) access to the issuer, and make them interact with the tampering adversary. The card is resistant to the tampering powers of the adversary (namely Apply commands) if the adversary is not able to distinguish between the case that he interacts with the real card, and the case that he interacts with the simulator.

3   Enhancing the Physical Design

As stated in the Introduction we augment our model with two additions: public parameters and self destruct, and show that these additions are both necessary and sufficient to achieve ATP security.

These results are shown by exhibiting attacks when the enhancements are not available. First, we show an attack that extracts the entire secret key from any cryptographic algorithm, as long as the card never self-destructs. Then, we show that there is a signature scheme for which there is an attack that can extract the entire secret key, for any implementation without public parameters (even with self-destruct). This can be viewed as a very powerful and simple generalization of previous specific attacks such as [BDL01,BS97].

3.1   Self-Destruct Is Necessary

Testing for Malfunctioning. Intuitively, for any meaningful cryptographic functionality, we should be able to determine, perhaps with some degree of error, whether a given device functions properly, i.e., whether the secret content sc stored on the device gives rise to the right functionality.

If no one can tell that a given device is doing its job correctly, then this device can be replaced with another one, based on a secret content sc' that was generated by a separate invocation of the Setup algorithm, and no one will notice the difference. Hence sc is useless, since sc' works just as well, and there is no need to protect it!

For example, suppose that we have a signature device. Provided that we have the corresponding public key, we can test whether the device functions as prescribed by querying the device for a signature on some message, and then checking the validity of the signature. Similarly, for a decryption device in the public-key setting, whether or not it maintains its functionality can be determined by encrypting many messages and checking whether the device decrypted all of them correctly.

Such test may not be perfect. It is possible that, even though the device does not have the correct secret content sc, but some sc' that is close to the correct content, the device will still pass our test with non-negligible probability. It is easy to come up with schemes that still work, even if their secret keys have been altered slightly, but provide the correct output with decreased probability.

Let us assume that for the functionality at hand, we have a testing procedure Test-Dev such that (1) Test-Dev will always accept when given a device whose sc is correct; (2) if Test-Dev accepts a device with secret content sc' with non-negligible probability ϵ, then discovering sc' constitutes a successful attack on the functionality of the device.

The tests described above for signature and decryption functionalities satisfy these two conditions: discovering sc' that allows to generate correct signatures only an ϵ fraction of the time is still an attack on the signature functionality: now the adversary can create an existential forgery. Similarly, being able to decrypt with an ϵ advantage over random guessing constitutes an attack on a cryptosystem. We show the following claim (informally stated):

Claim. No cryptographic device that can be efficiently tested for malfunctioning, can be made tamper-proof without the self-destruct capability.

Sketch of Proof: The Key-Extraction Procedure. Suppose that we are given a procedure Test-Dev as described above. Suppose that the secret content sc of the device consists of n bits. Finally, suppose that the only operation the attacker is allowed to carry out on the secret component of the device is the $Set(i, b)$ operation that sets the i'th bit of sc to b.

Consider the following procedure, that outputs a candidate value $C = C_1...C_n$ for the secret content sc: Initialize $i = 1$. While $i \leq n$: (1) $Set(i, b)$, $b \in \{0, 1\}$ and run Test-Dev. Let b^* be the value such that, when $sc_i = b^*$,

Test-Dev accepted more often than when $sc_i = \bar{b}^*$. (2) $Set(i, b^*)$, $C_i = b^*$. (3) Increment i. Upon completing the while-loop, output C.

The value C outputted at the end is identical to the value sc' stored on the device at the end of the procedure. Note that on each iteration of the loop, this procedure maintains the invariant that, with probability $1 - \nu(n)$ (where $\nu(n)$ is a negligible function), the value currently stored in the secret component sc' of the device is accepted by Test-Dev with non-negligible probability. This can be seen by induction: when $i = 1$, the secret component has not been altered yet, and so we are given that Test-Dev accepts. Suppose that $i > 1$. We know that the current sc is accepted by Test-Dev with non-negligible probability. Let b be the current bit sc_i. Suppose that setting $sc_i = \bar{b}$ results in Test-Dev accepting with only negligible probability ν. Then the probability that $b^* = \bar{b}$ is also negligible. Therefore, the device accepts with non-negligible probability when its secret content is C, thus discovering C constitutes a successful attack.

The above attack relies on the adaptiveness of the adversary, who decides which Apply command to issue next, depending on the result of the previous Run command. In the full version of this paper we show that even a non-adaptive adversary can extract the secret key using a *fixed* list of Run and Apply commands. The functions applied simply exchange pairs of specified bits in the string.   □

3.2 Hardwiring an External Public Key Is Necessary

Let us start with some intuition. For simplicity, consider a card implementing a signature algorithm $F(\cdot, \cdot)$ (the same techniques will work for decryption cards). Having no public parameters means that there is a software setup function g, such that for any sk', $g(sk')$ outputs a corresponding sc' for a card implementing $F(sk', \cdot)$.[2] In particular, for a given card whose software sc corresponds to some sk, the adversary may be able to replace sc by sc' corresponding to another, "adversarial" sk'. Such an sk' might have the property that when the adversary now issues a Run command, the output will include the original sk, which will allow the adversary to completely break the signature scheme. Indeed, we will show below a signature scheme for which this is exactly the case, and thus there is no ATP method which works for this scheme. It follows that for any general ATP method, the software content cannot be computed solely from the information held by the device. Instead, it must make use of some hardwired cryptographic public key Π, such that the corresponding secret key is needed in the setup of sc.[3] Concretely, we prove that for any general algorithmic tamper-proofing method we can view the hardwired content of the device, A, as a public key for a weak signature scheme, secure against universal forgery (i.e., not all messages

---

[2] It may seem that this does not grant the adversary any special powers, since he can always compute this by issuing a Setup(sk') command. However, such a Setup command requires that the adversary knows sk'.

[3] It will be convenient to identify Π as the public key of the card manufacturer, though in reality the corresponding secret key may be held by a third party, or distributed among several parties who participate in the setup stage.

can be forged), in the face of a single known-message attack. We refer the reader to [GMR88] for definitions and discussion of these and other security levels for signature schemes.[4]

Towards making the above intuition formal, for any signature scheme F that has a tamper-proof implementation, consider the following weak signature scheme W_F. The key generation algorithm is the device's setup algorithm for a tamper-proof secure card implementing F. The public key Π is set to the entire content of the card's hardware (the algorithm A), and the secret key is the randomness used to generate the public key. The signing algorithm, upon receiving a message m, checks if m is of the form (pk, sk) which are valid public and secret key pairs for F. If so, output sc as appropriate for a tamper-proof-secure card for a user holding (pk, sk). To verify a signature sc on (pk, sk), the verifier checks if a card containing the hardware Π and the software sc would perform correctly as a signature card for (pk, sk) (this can be done by trying to sign). Accept if the check succeeds.

Claim. There exists a secure signature scheme F such that, if its tamper-proof implementation exists, then W_F (described above) is a weak signature scheme secure against universal forgery in the face of a single known-message attack.

Sketch of Proof. It suffices to show a secure signature scheme F and two messages a and b such that given a valid signature of W_F on a, it is computationally infeasible to compute a valid signature on b.

Consider any secure signature scheme comprised of Gen, Sig, Ver and a security parameter k. We define $F = \mathsf{Gen}', \mathsf{Sig}', \mathsf{Ver}'$ as follows.

- Gen' runs Gen to obtain the key pair pk, sk. Let R be a random string of length k. Let $sk' = sk \circ R$ and $pk' = pk$.
- Sig'(sk', m): for $sk' = sk \circ R$, if $R \neq 0^k$, obtain $\sigma \leftarrow \mathsf{Sig}(sk, m)$. Otherwise, output sk.
- Ver'(pk, m, σ) just runs the algorithm Ver.

The resulting signature scheme F is secure as long as the original one was secure (the probability that $R = 0^k$ happens to be chosen is negligible).

We now turn to W_F, and let $a = (pk, sk \circ R)$ and $b = (pk, sk \circ 0^k)$ for some (pk, sk) generated by Gen and for $R \neq 0^k$. Assume towards contradiction that given a signature $sc = W_F(a)$ one could forge a signature $\hat{sc} = W_F(b)$ by applying some feasible function f. It follows that a card for F containing sc, can be tampered with to produce a forgery. Indeed, the adversary can apply f to the content of the card, thus resulting with $\hat{sc}$ which is valid for the key-pair $(pk, sk \circ 0^k)$. Now the adversary can issue a Run command on any message. The card extracts

---

[4] We note that security against universal forgery with known-message attacks is not a strong enough notion of security for signature schemes (the standard one, which is our default definition for signature security, is security against existential forgery in the face of adaptive chosen-message attacks [GMR88]). Nevertheless, this weak signature scheme already implies that there is *some* cryptographic key Π which *must* be hardwired into the card, and thus in some sense "certifies" sc.

$\hat{sk} = sk \circ 0^k$, runs $F_{\hat{sk}}$ on the selected message, resulting in the output sk. Now the adversary can forge signatures with respect to F (with respect to the original pk). This contradicts the tamper-proof security of the card. (Note that even if the card contains self-destruct capability, it is not useful since there is no way the card can detect any problem, as $\hat{sc}$ encodes a valid $\hat{sk}$). $\qquad\square$

3.3   ATP for Signature and Decryption Schemes

In this section we show how to realize ATP for signature and decryption schemes. Our results meet the definitions of Section 2 in the model enhanced with public parameters and self-destruct (as shown necessary above).

Consider a scheme $\mathcal{F}$ which is either a signature scheme or a public-key encryption scheme, and let sk be a secret signing or decryption key. We would like to store sk in the secret storage of the card, so that an adversary cannot tamper with it in any useful way. A very natural approach is for the card issuer to digitally sign sk and store the signature together with sk in sc, and have the card verify the signature against the issuer's public key before using sk for signing or verifying.

This is indeed the approach that we use, with a few details that need to be taken care of. First, as we already discussed, in order for this to work we must ensure that the card contains the public key of the issuer hardwired into its circuitry, and that the card self-destructs if the check does not succeed. However, it turns out that this is not enough: even if the card issuer uses a signature scheme secure against chosen message attack in the standard sense of [GMR88], we will see an attack that completely recovers sk.

Instead, we will assume that the signature scheme used by the card issuer satisfies a stronger property: not only is it hard to forge a signature on a *new* message, it is hard to forge a *new* signature on an old message. Although this is stronger than the traditional definition, most signature schemes known (c.f., [GMR88,FS87,GQ88,Sch91,CS99,GHR99]) already satisfy it. We call this notion *strong* security against chosen message attack (the formal definition is straight forward and omitted here). The scheme is described in Figure 1.

Theorem 1. *If strong unforgeable signature schemes exist, then there exist ATP unforgeable signature schemes. Specifically, if $\mathcal{I}$ is a strong signature scheme, and $\mathcal{F}$ is a standard signature scheme (unforgeable against adaptive chosen message attack), then the implementation in Figure 1 is an ATP unforgeable signature scheme.*

The proof is given in the full version. Very briefly, the proof proceeds by constructing a simulator that, for any adversary, launches an adaptive chosen message attack on the underlying signature scheme $\mathcal{F}$. The simulator guesses which query of the adversary changes sc, and guesses that this query in fact replaced sc with some pair $(sk', \sigma_{II}(sk'))$ which is one of the queries the adversary issued to the card issuer's signing oracle. For these guesses, the simulator can now an-

Let $\mathcal{I} = (G, \sigma, V)$ be a *strong* signature scheme (used by the card issuer). Let $\mathcal{F}$ be either a signature scheme of the form $\mathcal{F} = (\mathsf{Gen}, \mathsf{Sig}, \mathsf{Ver})$ or an encryption scheme of the form $\mathcal{F} = (\mathsf{Gen}, \mathsf{Enc}, \mathsf{Dec})$, and let F be the algorithm Sig or Dec, respectively. Let $(\Sigma, \Pi) \leftarrow G(1^k)$ be the secret and public signing keys of the card issuer, and let $(sk, pk) \leftarrow \mathsf{Gen}(1^k)$ be secret and public (signing or encryption) keys for $\mathcal{F}$.

During card setup, Π is hardwired into the card's circuitry (as part of the algorithm below), and the pair $(sk, \sigma_\Pi(sk))$ is stored in the protected memory sc (where $\sigma_\Pi(\cdot) = \sigma(\Sigma, \cdot)$ is the issuer's signing algorithm).

Upon receiving a $\mathsf{Run}(a)$ query, the card performs the following algorithm:
(1) Checks that the storage is of the form $(sk, \sigma_\Pi(sk))$ (using the verification algorithm V).
(2) If so, run $F(sk, a)$ (either signature or decryption) and output the result. Otherwise: self-destruct.

Fig. 1. Tamper-Proofing a Signature or Decryption Scheme

swer all of the adversary's queries, as it knows the content of sc.[5] We then prove that either: (1) the simulator succeeds in producing a forgery with probability polynomially related to that of the adversary (thus breaking the underlying signature scheme), or (2) another simulator can be constructed which produces a forgery to the card issuer's signature scheme.

Theorem 2. *If CCA2 (resp., CCA1) secure encryption schemes and strong unforgeable signature schemes exist, then there exist cryptosystems that are ATP CCA2-secure with lunchtime tampering (resp., ATP CCA1-secure). Specifically, if $\mathcal{I}$ is a strong signature scheme, and $\mathcal{F}$ is a CCA2 (resp., CCA1) secure encryption schemes, then the implementation in Figure 1 is secure against CCA2 with lunch time tampering (resp., tamper-proof CCA1 secure).*

The proof of this theorem is slightly more complicated than the proof for the signature scheme, but it follows the same general idea. It also appears in the full version of this paper.

A strong signature scheme is necessary for this construction. The following attack works in the case where the issuer's signature scheme is unforgeable according to the traditional definition. In other words, assume that it is possible, given a valid message/signature pair (m, σ), to construct a new valid pair (m, σ') with $\sigma' \neq \sigma$.

---

[5] Intuitively, the only useful change to sc that the adversary can make is by replacing it with a signed pair. This is where the proof requires that the signature scheme for the issuer is strong: this property guarantees that the only signatures the adversary can get are exactly those directly queried, thus allowing the simulator to answer Apply queries from the adversary.

Assume that the issuer's signature scheme has the following property: a signature σ consists of two parts, σ_1 and σ_2. The second component is ignored by the verification algorithm, which really uses only σ_1 to authenticate messages. Thus, the pair (sk, σ) is stored on the card, where $\sigma(\sigma_1, \sigma_2)$ is the manufacturer's signature on sk.

The adversary does the following: first he obtains, from the issuer via a Setup query, a signature $\sigma' = (\sigma'_1, \sigma'_2)$ on a secret key sk'. Then he replaces the value σ_2 in the card, with the values (sk, σ_1). Note that this will not have any effect on the card's functionality and will not cause the card to self-destruct. Then for each bit sk_i of the secret key he will do the following: if $sk_i = 0$ then do nothing, otherwise replace sk with sk', σ_1 with σ'_1, but do not touch the modified σ_2 (this way a record of the old secret key remains). Now by simply querying the card on a given message m, the adversary will be able to see if sk or sk' is being used, and thus if $sk_i = 0$ or not. The adversary then restores sk and σ_1 and repeats the above process for $i + 1$.

On Private Card Setup. In the above solutions, we need to have the issuer's signature on the secret key sk. It is important to note that this does not imply that the card's issuer must know sk. Indeed, one solution is running generic secure two-party protocols [Yao82,GMW87,Gol98], as a result of which the user obtains $\sigma_{\Pi}(sk)$, and the issuer obtains nothing. The proof of security can be extended to this case as well, by having the simulator *extract* the value sk from the adversary (who no longer sends sk in the clear to the signing oracle). The drawback of this general solution described above is that it may be expensive. Another existing solution is blind signatures. Although providing the desired property that the issuer learns nothing about sk, they are an overkill because neither does the issuer learn σ! A more efficient solution follows.

TIGHT COMMITMENT SCHEME. Recall that a non-interactive commitment scheme Com is (informally) a function such that for all x, for a random r, it is hard to infer any information about x from the value $\text{Com}(x, r)$, and it is infeasible to find (x, r) and (x', r') such that $\text{Com}(x, r) = \text{Com}(x', r')$, and $x \neq x'$. Let Com be a secure non-interactive commitment scheme with a special security property that is similar to the special security scheme of the signature scheme that we use for the device issuer. Namely, not only is it infeasible to open a commitment in two different ways, but it is infeasible to even find a value x and values $r \neq r'$ such that $\text{Com}(x, r) = \text{Com}(x, r')$. Let us call a commitment scheme with this property a *tight* commitment scheme. Pedersen commitment [Ped92] is an example of a tight commitment scheme.

Suppose that we are given a tight commitment scheme with an efficient zero-knowledge proof of knowledge of how to open a commitment. For example, the Pedersen commitment has such a protocol. Then the issuing protocol can be implemented as follows: the user forms a commitment $c = \text{Com}(sk, r)$. He then proves knowledge of the commitment opening. Finally, the issuer sends to the user the value $\sigma = \sigma_{\Pi}(c)$. The secret component sc of the device will consist of (sk, r, σ).

The proof that a tight commitment scheme is necessary for the security of this construction is similar to the proof that a strong signature is necessary, and is omitted here.

4   ATP via Restricted Classes of Functions

In this section, we consider an adversary that is limited to issuing Apply commands from some restricted, yet useful, class of functions. It turns out that in this case, ATP results are possible even without self-destruct and public parameters.

The results presented below have some practical significance, not only because the model they require is more realistic (e.g., without the self-destruct requirement), but also since we address precisely such classes of functions that were successfully used before to attack existing systems [BS97,BDL01]. These include random hardware faults termed *differential fault analysis*, and flipping (or *zapping*) specified bits. Using our solutions, attacks like the above ones can be protected against.

Since our definition of security requires the functionality of the card to remain secure even when the adversary knows the PIN, we concentrate below on protecting the functionality of the card. Adding PIN protection can be done in a similar manner to our above general solutions.

Differential Fault Analysis. The following results holds for cards with any cryptographic functionality, with neither self-destruct nor a hardwired external key.

Suppose the adversary is limited to the following attack: He specifies two values $p_0, p_1 \in [0, 1]$. $f_{p_0,p_1}(x)$ transforms *each* bit x_i of x as follows: if $x_i = b$, leave it that way with probability p_b otherwise flip it. Note that this transformation is exactly the same for each bit. (In information-transmission terms, this transformation can be viewed as sending x through an adversarial memoryless channel.)

Although seemingly benign compared to other attacks we have considered, this is in fact a very powerful attack, invented by Biham and Shamir [BS97] (following Boneh, DeMillo, and Lipton[BDL01]), and known as the *differential fault analysis*. Biham and Shamir use it to recover the entire secret key of a decryption card, such as DES.[6]

Securing a smart-card against such an attack does not require any enhancement to the minimal model. Rather, we can just encode the secret s using an error-detecting code whose distance d is such that $1/2^d$ is negligible. Before running its intended application, the card sees if there are any errors in its storage. If so, it does nothing, otherwise, it works as intended.

It is easy to see that this is sufficient, because if the card's storage changes, it is very unlikely that it will change into a valid encoding; therefore, a simulator that just computes the probability that the card is unusable after a given Apply query and acts accordingly is sufficient for the proof.

---

[6] Their attack uses asymmetric memory, where $p_0 = 1$, and p_1 is relatively large, but less than 1. That is, a bit which is 1 has a small non-negligible probability to flip.

We note that using error-detecting codes follows the approach alluded to by Boneh, DeMillo, and Lipton [BDL01], who suggest that a cryptographic computation needs to be checked before the output is given.

The Flip Function in the Model Without Self-Destruct. Suppose the external public key of the issuer is wired in, but there is no self-destruct.

Consider the function $\mathsf{Flip}(x, i) = x'$ where x' is equal to x in all the bits except the ith one which is complemented. (This generalizes differential fault analysis by giving the adversary control over which bits to flip, and the certainty that the bit has been flipped). If the adversary is limited to issuing commands of the form $\mathsf{Apply}(\mathsf{Flip}(x, i))$, then the self-destruction property is not required.

Suppose sk is the secret that needs to be stored on the card. Each bit sk_i of sk is encoded using two random bits, $e_{i,1}$ and $e_{i,2}$ such that $e_{i,1} \oplus e_{i,2} = sk_i$. The resulting encoding, $e(sk)$, is then signed by the card manufacturer. The values $(e, \sigma(e))$ are stored on the card.

For each Run command, the card first checks that in its storage, (e, σ), σ is a valid signature on e. If so, the card reconstructs the secret key sk from $e(sk)$ and performs whatever operation is required. Otherwise, the card does nothing.

A sketch of the proof that the latter solution provides ATP security against an adversary limited to flipping bits can be found in the full version of this paper.

5   ATP of Devices Using PIN Numbers

We saw that security of portable devices, such as smart-cards, provides strong motivation for considering ATP security. Indeed, one goal is to prevent an adversary capable of tampering with the device from learning information about its contents, so that such an adversary cannot duplicate and distribute devices with the same functionality (e.g., decryption cards for pay-tv applications). However, it is also often desirable to prevent the adversary from using the functionality of the device *himself*.

To address this problem, we propose that the device be augmented with a short memorizable PIN to be entered by the user before any application. That is, a Run query, where it previously took one input, now should take two: the PIN and the input (such as a message m to be signed). The device will only function if the PIN entered is correct, and, moreover, it will permanently stop functioning (or self-destruct) after a certain (not too big) number of wrong attempts. This can be implemented by a counter which is incremented with every failed attempt. We may consider a model where the device self-destructs once the counter has reached a certain number. A better model, but harder to achieve, is one where the number of *consecutive* wrong attempts is also limited (this limit could then be very small, such as 3).

As a starting point, assume that the adversary cannot tamper with the counter implementation. In this case, all the results we saw so far can be extended to the PIN setting, by considering the PIN as part of the secret key. In particular, in the model with public parameters the signature of the card issuer will be on the secret key *together with the PIN*.

We now turn to addressing the implementation of the counter. Clearly, if the counter is kept in regular tamperable memory, the adversary can recover the PIN by trying all possible PIN combinations, zeroing the counter after each failure. In order to avoid this attack, we suggest two types of counter implementations.

Hardware Implementation. In some situations it may be reasonable to assume that the counter is implemented in hardware, in such a way that the adversary cannot tamper with it. Note that this assumption is more reasonable than assuming all of the secret key is in non-tamperable hardware. Indeed, the counter mechanism is the same for all cards, and is not secret, making it easier to mass produce on hardware. However, the counter (unlike our other public parameters) cannot be implemented by a write-once memory, since it needs to be incremented with every failed attempt. This can be addressed by using an asymmetric type of memory, where incrementing (e.g. by zeroing one bit) is easy, while undoing it is very hard. For example, an operation akin to cutting a wire would be very appropriate. We note that [BS97] also use, in a different way, an asymmetric type of memory where flipping a bit from 1 to 0 is much easier than flipping it from 0 to 1.

Counter Implementation in Tamperable Memory. Consider now the case that the counter can only be implemented in regular (tamperable) memory. Below we provide a solution which is tamper-proof secure, based on any one-way permutation. In the full version we generalize the idea to construct a solution based on any forward-secure digital signature scheme. This generalization provides more flexibility in obtaining good trade-offs among the time and space parameters according to the constraints of the given application, and can allow for better performance overall. All our solutions rely on the mechanisms of self-destruct and public parameters, as described in previous sections. We start by assuming that the model requires a limit M on the total number of failed attempts.

Intuitively, our goal is to construct a counter such that even a tampering adversary can only increment it (or destroy it), but not decrease it. Consequently, such an adversary will not be able to try more than the specified number of guesses for the PIN before the device self-destructs. Our solution will use the existence of one-way permutations, namely, informally, permutations which are easy to compute but hard to invert (for formal definitions see, e.g., [Gol01]).

It works as follows: Let f be a one-way permutation, and let M be the total number of failed attempts we are willing to tolerate. Let R_0 be a random string from the domain of f, generated by the Setup algorithm. For $j = 1, \ldots, M$ we define $R_j = f(R_{j-1})$, namely $R_j = f^j(R_0)$. The setup algorithm will output counter value $(R_0, 0)$ as part of the secret component sc, and the value R_M to be stored and signed together with sk and the PIN. Every failed attempt to enter the PIN will result in replacing the current counter value (R_i, i) with $(f(R_i), i + 1)$.

Every time the device is invoked, it checks the validity of the current value in the counter, and in particular whether $f^{M-j}(R_j) = R_M$. This can generally be done by applying f $M - j$ times. Depending on f, this computation may be done much more efficiently. For instance, assume f is the Rabin function, namely squaring modulo a product of two Blum primes, or the RSA function with a small exponent (both are standard candidates for a one-way permutations). In this case, raising a number to a small power T times can be done efficiently, requiring $O(\log T)$ multiplications.

A more detailed description and proof of security are given in the full version, where we also give a more general implementation based on forward-secure signatures.

Limiting the Number of Consecutive Failed Attempts. Limiting the number of *consecutive* failed attempts to some small number m can be done whenever the adversary is restricted to a certain class of functions, which does not include functions allowing to update the counter (e.g., in our solution above, the one-way permutation f or any power of it). In this case, we can change the device algorithm as follows: Before the validity check, check whether the counter value $\bmod m = 0$ and if so self-destruct. Also, after the PIN check step, if the PIN is correct, update the counter to the next value which equals 1 *mod m*.

It is not hard to prove that this implementation is ATP secure against a restricted adversary which cannot apply the update function. We leave it as an open problem to construct general tamper-proof counters which limit number of consecutive failed attempts (or conversely to prove that this is not possible in this strong model).

Acknowledgments. We acknowledge Eric Lehman for suggesting the general solution for the non-adaptive key extraction procedure described in the full version of this paper. We also thank Yevgeniy Dodis for valuable discussions. Finally, we thank Charanjit Jutla, Hugo Krawczyk, and Adi Shamir for participating in the lunch-time conversation where the initial seeds for this work were planted.

References

[AARR03]   Dakshi Agrawal, Bruce Archambeault, Josyula R. Rao, and Pankaj Rohatgi. The EM side-channel(s). In Burton S. Kaliski Jr., Çetin Kaya Koç, and Christof Paar, editors, *Cryptographic Hardware and Embedded Systems - CHES 2002*, volume 2523 of *Lecture Notes in Computer Science*, pages 29–45. Springer, 2003.

[AK96]   Ross Anderson and Markus Kuhn. Tamper Resistance - a Cautionary Note. In *Proceedings of the Second Usenix Workshop on Electronic Commerce*, pages 1–11, November 1996.

[BDL01]   Dan Boneh, Richard A. DeMillo, and Richard J. Lipton. On the importance of eliminating errors in cryptographic computations. *Journal of Cryptology*, 14(2):101–119, 2001.

[BS97]   Eli Biham and Adi Shamir. Differential fault analysis of secret key cryp-
            tosystems. In Burt Kaliski, editor, *Advances in Cryptology — CRYPTO
            '97*, volume 1294 of *Lecture Notes in Computer Science*, pages 513–525.
            Springer Verlag, 1997.

[CGGM00]   Ran Canetti, Oded Goldreich, Shafi Goldwasser, and Silvio Micali. Re-
            settable zero-knowledge (extended abstract). In *Proc. 32nd Annual ACM
            Symposium on Theory of Computing (STOC)*, pages 235–244, 2000.

[CS99]   Ronald Cramer and Victor Shoup. Signature schemes based on the strong
            RSA assumption. In *Proc. 6th ACM Conference on Computer and Com-
            munications Security*, pages 46–52. ACM press, nov 1999.

[FS87]   Amos Fiat and Adi Shamir. How to prove yourself: Practical solution
            to identification and signature problems. In Andrew M. Odlyzko, editor,
            Advances in Cryptology — CRYPTO '86, volume 263 of *Lecture Notes in
            Computer Science*, pages 186–194. Springer Verlag, 1987.

[GHR99]   Rosario Gennaro, Shai Halevi, and Tal Rabin. Secure hash-and-sign sig-
            natures without the random oracle. In Jacques Stern, editor, *Advances in
            Cryptology — EUROCRYPT '99*, volume 1592 of *Lecture Notes in Com-
            puter Science*, pages 123–139. Springer Verlag, 1999.

[GM84]   Shafi Goldwasser and Silvio Micali. Probabilistic encryption. *Journal of
            Computer and System Sciences*, 28(2):270–299, April 1984.

[GMR88]   Shafi Goldwasser, Silvio Micali, and Ronald Rivest. A digital signature
            scheme secure against adaptive chosen-message attacks. *SIAM Journal
            on Computing*, 17(2):281–308, April 1988.

[GMW87]   Oded Goldreich, Silvio Micali, and Avi Wigderson. How to play any men-
            tal game or a completeness theorem for protocols with honest majority.
            In *Proc. 19th Annual ACM Symposium on Theory of Computing (STOC)*,
            pages 218–229, 1987.

[Gol98]   Oded Goldreich. Secure multi-party computation. Manuscript. Available
            from http:www.wisdom.weizmann.ac.il/~oded/pp.html, 1998.

[Gol01]   Oded Goldreich. *Foundations of Cryptography*. Cambridge University
            Press, 2001.

[GQ88]   Louis C. Guillou and Jean-Jacques Quisquater. A "paradoxical" identity-
            based signature scheme resulting from zero-knowledge. In Shafi Gold-
            wasser, editor, *Advances in Cryptology — CRYPTO '88*, volume 403 of
            Lecture Notes in Computer Science, pages 216–231. Springer Verlag, 1988.

[ISW03]   Yuval Ishai, Amit Sahai, and David Wagner. Private circuits: Securing
            hardware against probing attacks. In Dan Boneh, editor, *Advances in
            Cryptology — CRYPTO 2003*, volume 2729 of *Lecture Notes in Computer
            Science*. Springer Verlag, 2003.

[KJJ99]   Paul C. Kocher, Joshua Jaffe, and Benjamin Jun. Differential power anal-
            ysis. In Michael J. Wiener, editor, *Advances in Cryptology — CRYPTO
            '99*, volume 1666 of *Lecture Notes in Computer Science*, pages 388–397.
            Springer Verlag, 1999.

[MR03]   Silvio Micali and Leonid Reyzin. Physically observable cryptography.
            http://eprint.iacr.org/2003/120, 2003.

[Ped92]   Torben Pryds Pedersen. Non-interactive and information-theoretic secure
            verifiable secret sharing. In Joan Feigenbaum, editor, *Advances in Cryp-
            tology – CRYPTO '91*, volume 576 of *Lecture Notes in Computer Science*,
            pages 129–140. Springer Verlag, 1992.

[QS01]   J. J. Quisquater and D. Samyde. Electro magnetic analysis (EMA): Mea-
           sures and countermeasures for smart cards. In *International Conference
           on Research in Smart Cards – Esmart*, volume 435 of *Lecture Notes in
           Computer Science*, pages 200–210, Cannes, France, 2001. Springer Verlag.
[SA03]   Sergei P. Skorobogatov and Ross J. Anderson. Optical fault induction
           attacks. In Burton S. Kaliski Jr., Çetin Kaya Koç, and Christof Paar,
           editors, *Cryptographic Hardware and Embedded Systems - CHES 2002*,
           volume 2523 of *Lecture Notes in Computer Science*, pages 2–12. Springer,
           2003.
[Sch91]   Claus P. Schnorr. Efficient signature generation for smart cards. *Journal
           of Cryptology*, 4(3):239–252, 1991.
[Yao82]   Andrew C. Yao. Protocols for secure computations. In *Proc. 23rd IEEE
           Symposium on Foundations of Computer Science (FOCS)*, pages 160–164,
           1982.

Physically Observable Cryptography

(Extended Abstract)

Silvio Micali[1] and Leonid Reyzin[2]

[1] MIT CSAIL
200 Technology Square
Cambridge MA 02139 USA
[2] Boston University Computer Science
111 Cummington Street
Boston MA 02215 USA
reyzin@cs.bu.edu

Abstract. Complexity-theoretic cryptography considers only abstract notions of computation, and hence cannot protect against attacks that exploit the information leakage (via electromagnetic fields, power consumption, etc.) inherent in the *physical* execution of any cryptographic algorithm. Such "physical observation attacks" *bypass* the impressive barrier of mathematical security erected so far, and successfully *break* mathematically impregnable systems. The great practicality and the inherent availability of physical attacks threaten the very relevance of complexity-theoretic security.

To respond to the present crisis, we put forward *physically observable cryptography*: a powerful, comprehensive, and precise model for defining and delivering cryptographic security against an adversary that has access to information leaked from the physical execution of cryptographic algorithms. Our general model allows for a variety of adversaries. In this

paper, however, we focus on the strongest possible adversary, so as to capture what is cryptographically possible in the worst possible, physically observable setting. In particular, we

- consider an adversary that has full (and indeed adaptive) access to any leaked information;
- show that some of the basic theorems and intuitions of traditional cryptography no longer hold in a physically observable setting; and
- construct pseudorandom generators that are provably secure against *all* physical-observation attacks.

Our model makes it easy to meaningfully restrict the power of our general physically observing adversary. Such restrictions may enable schemes that are more efficient or rely on weaker assumptions, while retaining security against meaningful physical observations attacks.

M. Naor (Ed.): TCC 2004, LNCS 2951, pp. 278–296, 2004.

1   Introduction

"NON-PHYSICAL" ATTACKS.   A *non-physical attack* against a cryptographic algorithm A is one in which the adversary is given some access to (at times even full control over) A's explicit inputs (e.g., messages and plaintexts) and some access to A's outputs (e.g., ciphertexts and digital signatures). The adversary is also given full knowledge of A —except, of course, for the secret key— but absolutely no "window" into A's internal state during a computation: he may know every single line of A's code, but whether A's execution on a given input results in making more multiplications than additions, in using lots of RAM, or in accessing a given subroutine, remains totally unknown to him. In a non-physical attack, A's execution is essentially a *black box*. Inputs and outputs may be visible, but what occurs within the box cannot be observed at all.

For a long time, due to lacking cryptographic theory and the consequent naive design of cryptographic algorithms, adversaries had to search no further than non-physical attacks for their devious deeds. (For instance, an adversary could often ask for and obtain the digital signature of a properly chosen message and then forge digital signatures at will.) More recently, however, the sophisticated reduction techniques of complexity-theoretic cryptography have shut the door to such attacks. For instance, if one-way functions exist, fundamental tools such as pseudorandom generation [17] and digital signatures [27,24] can be implemented so as to be *provably* secure against *all* non-physical attacks.

Unfortunately, other realistic and more powerful attacks exist.

"PHYSICAL-OBSERVATION" ATTACKS.   In reality, a cryptographic algorithm A must be run in a *physical* device P, and, quite outside of our control, the laws of Nature have something to say on whether P is reducible to a black box during an execution of A. Indeed, like for other physical processes, a real algorithmic execution generates all kinds of physical *observables*, which may thus fall into the adversary's hands, and be quite informative at that. For instance, Kocher et al. [20] show that monitoring the electrical power consumed by a smart card running the DES algorithm [25] is enough to retrieve the very secret key! In another example, a series of works [26,2] show that sometimes the electromagnetic radiation emitted by a computation, even measured from a few yards away with a homemade antenna, could suffice to retrieve a secret key.

PHYSICALLY OBSERVABLE CRYPTOGRAPHY.   Typically, physical-observation attacks are soon followed by defensive measures (e.g., [9,19]), giving us hope that at least *some* functions could be securely computed in our physical world. However, no rigorous theory currently exists that identifies *which* elementary functions need to be secure, and to *what extent*, so that we can construct complex cryptographic systems *provably* robust against *all* physical-observation attacks. This paper puts forward such a theory.

Our theory is not about "shielding" hardware (neither perfectly[1] nor partially[2]) but rather about how to *use partially shielded hardware in a provably secure manner*. That is, we aim at providing rigorous answers to questions of the following *relative* type:

(1) *Given a piece of physical hardware $\mathcal{P}$ that is guaranteed to compute a specific, elementary function $f(x)$ so that only some information $L_{\mathcal{P},f}(x)$ leaks to the outside,*

is it possible to construct

(2) *a physical pseudorandom generator, encryption scheme, etc., provably secure against all physically-observing adversaries?*

Notice that the possibility of such reductions is far from guaranteed: hardware $\mathcal{P}$ is assumed "good" only for computing f, while any computation outside $\mathcal{P}$ (i.e., beyond f) is assumed to be fully observable by the adversary.

Providing such reductions is important even with the current, incomplete knowledge about shielding hardware.[3] In fact, physically observable cryptography may properly *focus* the research in hardware protection by identifying which specific and elementary functions need to be protected and how much.

A NEW AND GENERAL MODEL. Physically observable cryptography is a new and fascinating world defying our traditional cryptographic intuition. (For example, as we show, such fundamental results as the equivalence of unpredictability and indistinguishability for pseudorandom generators [30] fail to hold.) Thus, as our first (and indeed main) task, we construct a precise model, so as to be able to reason rigorously.

There are, of course, many possible models for physically observable cryptography, each rigorous and meaningful in its own right. How do we choose? We opted for the most pessimistic model of the world that still leaves room for cryptography. That is, we chose a very general model for the interplay of physical computation, information leakage, and adversarial power, trying to ensure that security in our model implies security in the real world, no matter how unfriendly the latter turns out to be (unless it disallows cryptographic security altogether).

FIRST RESULTS IN THE GENERAL MODEL. A new model is of interest only when non-trivial work can be done within its confines. We demonstrate that this is the case by investigating the fundamental notion of pseudorandom generation. In order to do so, we provide physically-observable variants of the traditional definitions of one-way functions, hardcore bits, unpredictability and indistinguishability. Already in the definitions stage, our traditional intuition is challenged by

---

[1] Perfectly shielded hardware, so that all computation performed in it leaks nothing to the outside, might be impossible to achieve and is much more than needed.

[2] We are after a computational theory here, and constructing totally or partially shielded hardware is not a task for a computational theorist.

[3] Had complexity-theoretic cryptography waited for a proof of existence of one-way functions, we would be waiting still!

the unexpected behavior of these seemingly familiar notions, which is captured by several (generally easy to prove) claims and observations.

We then proceed to the two main theorems of this work. The first theorem shows that *unpredictable* physically observable generators with arbitrary expansion can be constructed from any (properly defined) physically observable one-way permutation. It thus provides a physically observable analogue to the results of [13,7] in the traditional world. Unfortunately, this construction does not result in *indistinguishable* physically observable generators.

Our second main theorem shows that indistinguishable physically observable generators with *arbitrary expansion* can be constructed from such generators with *1-bit expansion*. It is thus the equivalent of the hybrid argument (a.k.a. "statistical walk") of [15].

Both of these theorems require non-trivial proofs that differ in significant ways from their traditional counterparts, showing how different the physically observable world really is.

SPECIALIZED MODELS. The generality of our model comes at a price: results in it require correspondingly strong assumptions. We wish to emphasize, however, that in many settings (e.g., arising from advances in hardware manufacturing) it will be quite meaningful to consider specialized models of physically observable cryptography, where information leakage or adversarial power are in some way restricted. It is our expectation that more efficient results, or results relying on lesser assumptions, will be awaiting in such models.

PASSIVE VS. ACTIVE PHYSICAL ADVERSARIES. Traditional cryptography has benefited from a thorough understanding of computational security against passive adversaries before tackling computational security against active adversaries. We believe similar advantages can be gained for physical security. Hence, for now, we consider *physically observing* adversaries only. Note, however, that our adversary has a traditional computational component and a novel physical one, and we do not start from scratch in its computational component. Indeed, our adversary will be computationally quite active (e.g., it will be able to adaptively choose inputs to the scheme it attacks), but will be passive in its physical component (i.e., it will observe a physical computation without tampering with it). Attacks (e.g., [4,8,6,5,28]), defenses (e.g., [26,23]), and models (e.g., [12]) for physically active adversaries are already under investigation, but their full understanding will ultimately depend on a full understanding of the passive case.

OTHER RELATED WORK. We note that the question of building protected hardware has been addressed before with mathematical rigor. In particular, Chari, Jutla, Rao and Rohatgi [9] consider how to protect a circuit against attackers who receive a noisy function of its state (their motivation is protection against power analysis attacks). Ishai, Sahai and Wagner [18] consider how to guarantee that adversaries who can physically probe a limited number of wires in a circuit will not be able to learn meaningful information from it. This line of research is complementary to ours: we consider reductions among physical computing devices in order to guarantee security against all physical observation attacks under some assumptions, whereas the authors of [9] and [18] consider how to build particular physical computing devices secure against a particular class of physical observations attacks. In a way, this distinction is analogous to the distinction in traditional cryptography between research on cryptographic reductions on the one hand, and research on finding instantiations of secure primitives (one-way functions, etc.) on the other.

2   Intuition for Physically Observable Computation

Our model for physically observable (PO for short) computation is based on the following (overlapping)

Informal Axioms

1. *Computation, and only computation, leaks information*
   Information may leak whenever bits of data are accessed and computed upon. The leaking information actually depends on the particular operation performed, and, more generally, on the configuration of the currently active part of the computer. However, there is no information leakage in the absence of computation: data can be placed in some form of storage where, when not being accessed and computed upon, it is totally secure.
2. *Same computation leaks different information on different computers*
   Traditionally, we think of algorithms as carrying out computation. However, an algorithm is an abstraction: a set of general instructions, whose physical implementation may vary. In one case, an algorithm may be executed in a physical computer with lead shielding hiding the electromagnetic radiation correlated to the machine's internal state. In another case, the same algorithm may be executed in a computer with a sufficiently powerful inner battery hiding the power utilized at each step of the computation. As a result, the same elementary operation on 2 bits of data may leak different information: e.g., (for all we know) their XOR in one case and their AND in the other.
3. *Information leakage depends on the chosen measurement*
   While much may be observable at any given time, not all of it can be observed simultaneously (either for theoretical or practical reasons), and some may be only observed in a probabilistic sense (due to quantum effects, noise, etc.). The specific information leaked depends on the actual measurement made. Different measurements can be chosen (adaptively and adversarially) at each step of the computation.
4. *Information leakage is local*
   The information that may be leaked by a physically observable device is the same in any execution with the same input, independent of the computation that takes place before the device is invoked or after it halts. In particular, therefore, *measurable information dissipates:* though an adversary can choose what information to measure at each step of a computation, information not measured is lost. Information leakage depends on the *past*

computational history only to the extent that the *current* computational configuration depends on such history.

5. *All leaked information is efficiently computable from the computer's internal configuration.*
   Given an algorithm and its physical implementation, the information leakage is a polynomial-time computable function of (1) the algorithm's internal configuration, (2) the chosen measurement, and possibly (3) some randomness (outside anybody's control).

Remarks

As expected, the real meaning of our axioms lies in the precise way we use them in our model and proofs. However, it may be worthwhile to clarify here a few points.

- *Some form of security for unaccessed memory is mandatory.* For instance, if a small amount of information leakage from a stored secret occurs at every unit of time (e.g., if a given bit becomes 51% predictable within a day) then a patient enough adversary will eventually reconstruct the entire secret.
- *Some form of security for unaccessed memory is possible.* One may object to the requirement that only computation leaks information on the grounds that in modern computers, even unaccessed memory is refreshed, moved from cache and back, etc. However, as our formalization below shows, all we need to assume is that there is *some* storage that does not leak information when not accessed. If regular RAM leaks, then such storage can be the hard drive; if that also leaks, use flash memory; etc.
- *Some form of locality for information leakage is mandatory.* The hallmark of modern cryptography has been constructing complex systems out of basic components. If the behavior of these components changed depending on the context, then no general principles for modular design could arise. Indeed, if corporation A produced a properly shielded device used in computers build by corporation B, then corporation B should not damage the shielding on the device when assembling its computers.
- *The restriction of a single adversarial measurement per step should not mis-interpreted.* If two measurements M_1 and M_2 can be "fruitfully" performed one after the other, our model allows the adversary to perform the single measurement $M = (M_1, M_2)$.
- *The polynomial-time computability of leaked information should not be mis-interpreted.* This efficient computability is quite orthogonal to the debate on whether physical (e.g., quantum) computation could break the polynomial-time barrier. Essentially, our model says that *the most* an adversary may obtain from a measurement is the entire current configuration of the cryptographic machine. And such configuration is computable in time linear in the number of steps executed by the crypto algorithm. For instance, if a computer stores a Hamiltonian graph but not its Hamiltonian tour, then

performing a breadth-first search on the graph should not leak its Hamiltonian tour.

(Of course, should an adversary more powerful than polynomial-time be considered, then the power of the leakage function might also be increased "accordingly.")

Of course, we do not know that these axioms are "exactly true", but definitely hope to live in a world that "approximates" them to a sufficient degree: life without cryptography would be rather dull indeed!

3   Models and Goals of Physically Observable Cryptography

Section 3.1 concerns itself with abstract computation, not yet its physical implementation. Section 3.2 describes how we model physical implementations of such abstract computation. Section 3.3 defines what it means, in our model, to build high-level constructions out of low-level primitives.

3.1   Computational Model

MOTIVATION. Axiom 1 guarantees that unaccessed memory leaks no information. Thus we need a computing device that clearly separates memory that is actively being used from memory that is not. The traditional Turing machine, which accesses its tape sequentially, is not a suitable computational device for the goal at hand: if the reading head is on one end of the tape, and the machine needs to read a value on the other end, it must scan the entire tape, thus accessing every single memory value. We thus must augment the usual Turing machine with random access memory, where each bit can be addressed individually and independently of other bits, and enable the resulting machine to copy bits between this random-access memory and the usual tape where it can work on them. (Such individual random access can be realistic implemented.)

Axiom 4 guarantees that the leakage of a given device is the same, independent of the computation that follows or precedes it. Thus we need a model that can properly segregate one portion of a computation from another. The traditional notion of computation as carried out by a *single* Turing machine is inadequate for separating computation into multiple independent components, because the configuration of a Turing machine must incorporate (at a minimum) all future computation. To enable the modularity of physically observable cryptography, our model of computation will actually consist of *multiple* machines, each with its own physical protection, that may call each other as subroutines. In order to provide true independence, each machine must "see" its own memory space, independent of other machines (this is commonly known as virtual memory). Thus our multiple machines must be accompanied by a *virtual memory manager* that would provide for parameter passing while ensuring memory independence that is necessary for modularity. (Such virtual memory management too can be realistically implemented.)

FORMALIZATION WITHOUT LOSS OF GENERALITY. Let us now formalize this model of computation (without yet specifying how information may leak). A detailed formalization is of course necessary for proofs to be meaningful. This is particularly true in the case of a new theory, where no strong intuition has yet been developed. However, the particular choice of these details is not crucial. Our theorems are robust enough to hold also for different reasonable instantiations of this model.

ABSTRACT VIRTUAL-MEMORY COMPUTERS. An *abstract virtual-memory computer*, or *abstract computer* for short, consists of a *collection* of special Turing machines, which invoke each other as subroutines and share a special common memory. We call each member of our collection an *abstract virtual-memory Turing machine* (abstract VTM or simply VTM for short). We write $A = (A_1, \ldots, A_n)$ to mean that an abstract computer A consists of abstract VTMs $A_1, \ldots, A_n$, where A_1 is a distinguished VTM: the one invoked first and whose inputs and outputs coincide with those of A. Note that abstract computers and VTMs are *not* physical devices: they represent logical computation, may have many different physical implementations. We consider physical computers in Section 3.2, after fully describing logical computation.

In addition to the traditional input, output, work and random tapes of a probabilistic Turing machine, a VTM has random access to its own *virtual address space* (VAS): an unbounded array of bits that starts at address 1 and goes on indefinitely.

The salient feature of an abstract virtual memory computer is that, while each VTM "thinks" it has its own individual VAS, in reality all of them, via a proper memory manager, share a single *physical address space (PAS)*.

VIRTUAL-MEMORY MANAGEMENT. As it is common in modern operating systems, a single *virtual-memory manager* (working in polynomial time) supervises the mapping between individual VASes and the unique PAS. The virtual-memory manager also allows for parameter passing among the different VTMs.

When a VTM is invoked, from its point of view every bit in its VAS is initialized to 0, except for those locations where the caller placed the input. The virtual-memory manager ensures that the VAS of the caller is not modified by the callee, except for the callee's output values (that are mapped back into the caller's VAS).

Virtual-memory management is a well studied subject (outside the scope of cryptography), and we shall refrain from discussing it in detail. The only explicit requirement that we impose onto our virtual-memory manager is that it should only *remap* memory addresses, but never *access* their content. (As we shall discuss in later sections, this requirement is crucial to achieving cryptographic security in the *physical world*, where each memory access may result in a leakage of sensitive information to the adversary.)

ACCESSING VIRTUAL MEMORY. If A is a VTM, then we denote by m_A the content of A's VAS, and, for a positive integer j, we denote by $m_A[j]$ the bit value stored at location j. Every VTM has an additional, special *VAS-access tape*. To read the bit $m_A[j]$, A writes down j on the VAS-access tape, and enters a special state. Once A is in that state, the value $m_A[j]$ appears on the VAS-access tape at the current head position (the mechanics of this are the same as for an oracle query). To write a bit b in location j in its VAS, A writes down (j, b) on the VAS-access tape, and enters another special state, at which point $m_A[j]$ gets set to b.

Note that this setup allows each machine to work almost entirely in VAS, and use its work tape for merely computing addresses and evaluating simple gates.

INPUTS AND OUTPUTS OF A VTM. All VTM inputs and outputs are binary strings always residing in virtual memory. Consider a computation of a VTM A with an input i of length ℓ and an output o of length L. Then, at the start of the computation, the input tape of A contains 1^ℓ, the unary representations of the input length. The input i itself is located in the first ℓ bit positions of A's VAS, which will be read-only to A. At the end of the computation, A's output tape will contain a sequence of L addresses, $b_1, \ldots, b_L$, and o itself will be in A's VAS: $o = m_A[b_1] \ldots m_A[b_L]$. (The reason for input length to be expressed in unary is the preservation of the notion of polynomial running time with respect to the length of the *input tape*.)

CALLING VTMs AS SUBROUTINES. Each abstract VTM in the abstract virtual-memory computer has a unique name and a special *subroutine-call tape*. When a VTM A' makes a subroutine call to a VTM A, A' specifies where A' placed the input bits to A and where A' wants the output bits of A, by writing the corresponding addresses on this tape. The memory manager remaps locations in the VAS of A' to the VAS of A and vice versa. Straightforward details are provided in the full version of the paper.

3.2   Physical Security Model

PHYSICAL VIRTUAL-MEMORY COMPUTERS. We now formally define what information about the operation of a machine can be learned by the adversary. Note, however, that an abstract virtual-memory computer is an abstract object that may have different physical implementations. To model information leakage of any particular implementation, we introduce a *physical* virtual-memory computer (physical computer for short) and a *physical* virtual-memory Turing machine (physical VTM for short). A physical VTM $\mathcal{P}$ is a pair (L, A), where A is an abstract VTM and L is the *leakage function* described below. A physical VTM is meant to model a single shielded component that can be combined with others to form a computer. If $\mathcal{A} = (A_1, A_2, \ldots, A_n)$ is an abstract computer and $P_i = (L_i, A_i)$, then we call P_i a *physical implementation* of A_i and $\mathcal{P} = (P_1, P_2, \ldots P_n)$ a *physical implementation* of $\mathcal{A}$.

If a physical computer $\mathcal{P}$ is deterministic (or probabilistic, but Las Vegas), then we denote by $f_{\mathcal{P}}(x)$ the function computed by $\mathcal{P}$ on input x.

THE LEAKAGE FUNCTION. The leakage function L of a physical VTM $P = (L, A)$ is a function of three inputs, $L = L(\cdot, \cdot, \cdot)$.

- The first input is the current internal configuration C of A, which incorporates everything that is in principle measurable. More precisely, C is a binary string encoding (in some canonical fashion) the information of all the tapes of A, the locations of all the heads, and the current state (but *not* the contents of its VAS m_A). We require that only the "touched" portions of the tapes be encoded in C, so that the space taken up by C is polynomially related to the space used by T (not counting the VAS space).

- The second input M is the setting of the measuring apparatus, also encoded as a binary string (in essence, a specification of what the adversary chooses to measure).
- The third input R is a sufficiently long random string to model the randomness of the measurement.

By specifying the setting M of its measuring apparatus, while A is in configuration C, the adversary will receive information $L(C, M, R)$, for a fresh random R (unknown to the adversary).

Because the adversary's computational abilities are restricted to polynomial time, we require the function $L(C, M, R)$ to be computable in time that is polynomial in the lengths of C and M.

THE ADVERSARY. Adversaries for different cryptographic tasks can be quite different (e.g., compare a signature scheme adversary to a pseudorandom generator distinguisher). However, we will augment all of the them in the same way with the ability to observe computation. We formalize this notion below.

Definition 1. *We say that the adversary F observes the computation of a physical computer $\mathcal{P} = (P_1, P_2, \ldots, P_n)$, where $P_i = (L_i, A_i)$ if:*

1. *F is invoked before each step of a physical VTM of $\mathcal{P}$, with configuration of F preserved between invocations.*
2. *F has a special read-only name tape that contains the name of the physical VTM P_i of $\mathcal{P}$ that is currently active.*
3. *At each invocation, upon performing some computation, F writes down a string M on a special observation tape, and then enters a special state. Then the value $L_i(C, M, R)$, where P_i is the currently active physical VTM and R is a sufficiently long fresh random string unknown to F, appears on the observation tape, and $\mathcal{P}$ takes its next step.*
4. *This process repeats until $\mathcal{P}$ halts. At this point F is invoked again, with its name tape containing the index 0 indicating that $\mathcal{P}$ halted.*

Notice that the above adversary is adaptive: while it cannot go back in time, its choice of what to measure in each step can depend on the results of measurements chosen in the past. Moreover, while at each step the adversary can measure only one quantity, to have a strong security model, we give the adversary all the time it needs to obtain the result of the previous measurement, decide what to measure next, and adjust its measuring apparatus appropriately.

Suppose the adversary F running on input x_F observes a physical computer $\mathcal{P}$ running on input $x_\mathcal{P}$, then $\mathcal{P}$ halts and produces output $y_\mathcal{P}$, and then F halts and produces output y_F. We denote this by

$$y_\mathcal{P} \leftarrow \mathcal{P}(x_\mathcal{P}) \rightsquigarrow F(x_F) \rightarrow y_F .$$

Note that F sees neither $x_\mathcal{P}$ nor $y_\mathcal{P}$ (unless it can deduce these values indirectly by observing the computation).

3.3 Assumptions, Reductions, and Goals

In addition to traditional, complexity-theoretic assumptions (e.g., the existence of one-way permutations), physically observable cryptography also has *physical assumptions*. Indeed, the very existence of a machine that "leaks less than complete information" is an assumption about the physical world. Let us be more precise.

Definition 2. *A physical VTMs is* trivial *if its leakage function reveals its entire internal configuration*[4] *and non-trivial* otherwise.

Fundamental Premise. *The very existence of a non-trivial physical VTM is a physical assumption.*

Just like in traditional cryptography, the goal of physically observable cryptography is to rigorously derive desirable objects from simple (physical and computational) assumptions. As usual, we refer to such rigorous derivations as *reductions*. Reductions are expected to use stated assumptions, *but should not themselves consist of assumptions!*

Definition 3. *Let $\mathcal{P}'$ and $\mathcal{P}$ be physical computers. We say that $\mathcal{P}'$ reduces to $\mathcal{P}$ (alternatively, $\mathcal{P}$ implies $\mathcal{P}'$) if every non-trivial physical VTM of $\mathcal{P}'$ is also a physical VTM of $\mathcal{P}$.*

4   Definitions and Observations

Having put forward the rules of physically observable cryptography, we now need to gain some experience in distilling its first assumptions and constructing its first reductions.

We start by quickly recalling basic notions and facts from traditional cryptography that we use in this paper.

4.1   Traditional Building Blocks

We assume familiarity with the traditional GMR notation (recalled in our Appendix A).

We also assume familiarity with the notions of one-way function [10] and permutation; with the notion of of hardcore bits [7]; with the fact that all one-way functions have a Goldreich-Levin hardcore bit [13]; and with the notion of

---

[4] It suffices, in fact, to reveal only the current state and the characters observed by the reading heads—the adversary can infer the rest by observing the leakage at every step.

a *natural* hardcore bit (one that is simply a bit of the input, such as the last bit of the RSA input [3]). Finally, recall the well-known *iterative generator* of Blum and Micali [7], constructed as follows:

> *iterate a one-way permutation on a random seed, outputting the hardcore bit at each iteration.*

(All this traditional material is more thoroughly summarized in the full version of the paper.)

4.2   Physically Observable One-Way Functions and Permutations

AVOIDING A LOGICAL TRAP. In traditional cryptography, the *existence* of a one-way function is currently an assumption, while the *definition* of a one-way function does not depend on any assumption. We wish that the same be true for physically observable one-way functions. Unfortunately, the most obvious attempt to defining physically observable one-way functions does not satisfy this requirement. The attempt consists of replacing the Turing machine T in the one-way function definition with a physical computer $\mathcal{P}$ observed by F. Precisely,

Definition Attempt: A *physically observable (PO) one-way functions* is a function $f : \{0,1\}^* \rightarrow \{0,1\}^*$ such that there exists a polynomial-time physical computer $\mathcal{P}$ that computes f and, for any polynomial-time adversary F, the following probability is negligible as a function of k:

$$\Pr[x \xleftarrow{R} \{0,1\}^k ; y \leftarrow \mathcal{P}(x) \rightsquigarrow F(1^k) \rightarrow state ; z \leftarrow F(state, y) : f(z) = y].$$

Intuitively, physically observable one-way functions should be "harder to come by" than traditional ones: unless no traditional one-way functions exist, we expect that only some of them may also be PO one-way. Recall, however, that *mathematically* a physical computer $\mathcal{P}$ consists of pairs (L, A), where L is a leakage function and A an abstract VTM, in particular a single Turing machine. Thus, by setting L be the constant function 0, and $A = \{T\}$, where T is the Turing machine computing f, we obtain a non-trivial computer $\mathcal{P} = \{(L, A)\}$ that ensures that f is PO one-way as soon as it is traditionally one-way. The relevant question, however, is not whether such a computer can be mathematically defined, but whether it can be *physically* built. As we have said already, the mere existence of a non-trivial physical computer is in itself an assumption, and *we do not want the definition of a physically observable one-way function to rely on an assumption.* Therefore, we do not define what it means for a *function* f to be physically observable one-way. Rather, we define what it means for a particular *physical computer computing* f to be one-way.

We shall actually introduce, in order of strength, three physically observable counterparts of traditional one-way functions and one-way permutations.

MINIMAL ONE-WAY FUNCTIONS AND PERMUTATIONS. Avoiding the logical trap discussed above, the first way of defining one-way functions (or permutations) in the physically observable world is to say that $\mathcal{P}$ is a one-way function if it computes a permutation $f_{\mathcal{P}}$ that is hard to invert despite the leakage from $\mathcal{P}$'s computation. We call such physically observable one-way functions and permutations "minimal" in order to distinguish them from the other two counterparts we are going to discuss later on.

Definition 4. *A polynomial-time deterministic physical computer $\mathcal{P}$ is minimal one-way function if for any polynomial-time adversary F, the following probability is negligible as a function of k:*

$$\Pr[x \stackrel{R}{\leftarrow} \{0,1\}^k \ ; \ y \leftarrow \mathcal{P}(x) \rightsquigarrow F(1^k) \rightarrow state \ ; \ z \leftarrow F(state, y) : f_{\mathcal{P}}(z) = y].$$

Furthermore, if $f_{\mathcal{P}}$ is length-preserving and bijective, we call $\mathcal{P}$ a minimal one-way permutation.

DURABLE FUNCTIONS AND PERMUTATIONS. A salient feature of an abstract permutation is that the output is random for a random input. The following definition captures this feature, even in the presence of computational leakage.

Definition 5. *A durable function (permutation) is a minimal one-way function (permutation) $\mathcal{P}$ such that, for any polynomial-time adversary F, the value $|p_k^P - p_k^R|$ is negligible in k, where*

$$p_k^P = \Pr[x \stackrel{R}{\leftarrow} \{0,1\}^k \ ; \ y \leftarrow \mathcal{P}(x) \rightsquigarrow F(1^k) \rightarrow state : F(state, y) = 1]$$
$$p_k^R = \Pr[x \stackrel{R}{\leftarrow} \{0,1\}^k \ ; \ y \leftarrow \mathcal{P}(x) \rightsquigarrow F(1^k) \rightarrow state \ ; \ z \stackrel{R}{\leftarrow} \{0,1\}^k \ :$$
$$F(state, z) = 1].$$

MAXIMAL ONE-WAY FUNCTIONS AND PERMUTATIONS. We now define physically observable one-way functions that leak nothing at all.

Definition 6. *A maximal one-way function (permutation) is a minimal one-way function (permutation) $\mathcal{P}$ such that the leakage functions of its component physical VTMs are independent of the input x of $\mathcal{P}$ (in other words, x has no effect on the distribution of information that leaks).*

One can also define *statistically maximal* functions and permutations, where for any two inputs x_1 and x_2, the observed leakage from $\mathcal{P}(x_1)$ and $\mathcal{P}(x_2)$ is statistically close; and *computationally maximal* functions and permutations, where for any two inputs x_1 and x_2, what $\mathcal{P}(x_1)$ leaks is indistinguishable from what $\mathcal{P}(x_2)$ leaks. We postpone defining these formally.

4.3   Physically Observable Pseudorandomness

One of our goals in the sequel will be to provide a physically observable analogue to the Blum-Micali [7] construction of pseudorandom generators. To this end, we provide here physically observable analogues of the notions of indistinguisha-bility [30] and unpredictability [7].

UNPREDICTABILITY. The corresponding physically observable notion replaces "unpredictability of bit $i+1$ from the first i bits" with "unpredictability of bit $i+1$ from the first i bits and the leakage from their computation."

Definition 7. *Let p be a polynomially bounded function such that $p(k) > k$ for all positive integers k. Let $\mathcal{G}$ be a polynomial-time deterministic physical computer that, on a k-bit input, produces $p(k)$-bit output, one bit at a time (i.e., it writes down on the output tape the VAS locations of the output bits in left to right, one a time). Let $\mathcal{G}^i$ denote running $\mathcal{G}$ and aborting it after it outputs the i-th bit. We say that $\mathcal{G}$ is a* PO *unpredictable generator with expansion p if for any polynomial-time adversary F, the value $|p_k - 1/2|$ is negligible in k, where*

$$p_k = \Pr[(i, state_1) \leftarrow F(1^k) ; x \xleftarrow{R} \{0,1\}^k ;$$
$$y_1 y_2 \dots y_i \leftarrow \mathcal{G}^i(x) \rightsquigarrow F(state_1) \rightarrow state_2 : F(state_2, y_1 \dots y_i) = y_{i+1}],$$

(where y_j denotes the j-th bit of $y = \mathcal{G}(x)$).

INDISTINGUISHABILITY. The corresponding physically observable notion re-places "indistinguishability" by *"indistinguishability in the presence of leakage."* That is, a polynomial-time adversary F first observes the computation of a pseu-dorandom string, and then receives either that same pseudorandom string or a totally independent random string, and has to distinguish between the two cases.

Definition 8. *Let p be a polynomially bounded function such that $p(k) > k$ for all positive integers k. We say that a polynomial-time deterministic physical computer $\mathcal{G}$ is a* PO *indistinguishable generator with expansion p if for any polynomial-time adversary F, the value $|p_k^G - p_k^R|$ is negligible in k, where*

$$p_k^G = \Pr[x \xleftarrow{R} \{0,1\}^k ; y \leftarrow \mathcal{G}(x) \rightsquigarrow F(1^k) \rightarrow state : F(state, y) = 1]$$
$$p_k^R = \Pr[x \xleftarrow{R} \{0,1\}^k ; y \leftarrow \mathcal{G}(x) \rightsquigarrow F(1^k) \rightarrow state ; z \xleftarrow{R} \{0,1\}^{p(k)} :$$
$$F(state, z) = 1].$$

4.4   First Observations

Reductions in our new environment are substantially more complex than in the traditional setting, and we have chosen a very simple one as our first exam-ple. Namely, we prove that minimal one-way permutations compose just like traditional one-way permutations.

Claim. A minimal one-way permutation $\mathcal{P}$ implies a minimal one-way permuta-tion $\mathcal{P}'$ such that $f_{\mathcal{P}'}(\cdot) = f_{\mathcal{P}}(f_{\mathcal{P}}(\cdot))$.

Proof. To construct $\mathcal{P}'$, build a trivial physical VTM that simply runs $\mathcal{P}$ twice. See full version of the paper for details. We wish to emphasize that, though simple, the details of the proof of Claim 4.4 illustrate exactly how our axioms for physically observable computation (formalized in our model) play out in our proofs.

Despite this good news about our simplest definition, minimal one-way permutations are not suitable for the Blum-Micali construction due to the following observation.

Observation 1 *Minimal one-way permutations do not chain. That is, an adversary observing the computation of $\mathcal{P}'$ from Claim 4.4 and receiving $f_\mathcal{P}(f_\mathcal{P}(x))$ may well be able to compute the intermediate value $f_\mathcal{P}(x)$.*

This is so because $\mathcal{P}$ may leak its entire output while being minimal one-way.

Unlike minimal one-way permutations, maximal one-way permutations do suffice for the Blum-Micali construction.

Claim. A maximal one-way permutation $\mathcal{P}$ implies a PO unpredictable generator.

Proof. The proof of this claim, whose details are omitted here, is fairly straightforward: simply mimic the Blum-Micali construction, computing $x_1 = \mathcal{P}(x_0)$, $x_2 = \mathcal{P}(x_1)$, ..., $x_n = \mathcal{P}(x_{n-1})$ and outputting the Goldreich-Levin bit of x_n, of x_{n-1}, ..., of x_1. Note that the computation of Goldreich-Levin must be done on a trivial physical VTM (because to do otherwise would involve another assumption), which will result in full leakage of x_n, x_{n-1}, ..., x_0. Therefore, for unpredictability, it is crucial that the bits be computed and output one at a time and in reverse order like in the original Blum-Micali construction.

Observation 2 *Using maximal (or durable or minimal) one-way permutations in the Blum-Micali construction does not yield PO indistinguishable generators.*

Indeed, the output from the above construction is easily distinguishable from random in the presence of leakage, because of the eventual leakage of $x_0, x_1, \ldots, x_n$.

The above leads to the following observation.

Observation 3 *A PO unpredictable generator is not necessarily PO indistinguishable.*

However, indistinguishability still implies unpredictability, even in this physically observable world.

If the maximal one-way permutation satisfies an additional property, we can obtain PO indistinguishable generators. Recall that a (traditional) hardcore bit of x is *natural* if it is a bit in some fixed location of x.

Claim. A maximal one-way permutation $\mathcal{P}$ for which $f_{\mathcal{P}}$ has a (traditional) natural hardcore bit implies a PO indistinguishable generator.

Proof. Simply use the previous construction, but output the natural hardcore bit instead of the Goldreich-Levin one. Because all parameters (including inputs and outputs) are passed through memory, this output need not leak anything. Thus, the result is indistinguishable from random in the presence of leakage, because there is no meaningful leakage.

The claims and observations so far have been fairly straightforward. We now come to the two main theorems.

5   Theorems

Our first main theorem demonstrates that the notion of a durable function is in some sense the "right" analogue of the traditional one-way permutation: when used in the Blum-Micali construction, with Goldreich-Levin hardcore bits, it produces a PO unpredictable generator; moreover, the proof seems to need all of the properties of durable functions. (Identifying the *minimal* physically observable assumption for pseudorandom generation is a much harder problem, not addressed here.)

Theorem 1. *A durable function implies a PO unpredictable generator (with any polynomial expansion).*

Proof. Utilize the Blum-Micali construction, outputting (in reverse order) the Goldreich-Levin bit of each x_i, just like in Claim 4.4. The hard part is to show that this is unpredictable. Durable functions, in principle, could leak their own hardcore bits—this would not contradict the indistinguishability of the output from random (indeed, by the very definition of a hardcore bit). However, what helps us here is that we are using specifically the Goldreich-Levin hardcore bit, computed as $r \cdot x_i$ for a random r. Note that r will be leaked to the adversary before the first output bit is even produced, during its computation as $r \cdot x_n$. But crucially, the adversary will not yet know r during the iterated computation of the durable function, and hence will be unable to tailor its measurement to the particular r. We can then show (using the same error-correcting code techniques for reconstructing x_i as in [13]) that $r \cdot x_i$ is unpredictable given the leakage obtained by the adversary. More details of the proof are deferred to the full version of the paper.

Our second theorem addresses the stronger notion of PO indistinguishability. We have already seen that PO indistinguishable generators can be built out of maximal one-way permutations with natural hardcore bits. However, this assumption may be too strong. What this theorem shows is that as long as there is some way to a build the simplest possible PO indistinguishable generator—the one with one-bit expansion—there is a way to convert it to a PO indistinguishable generator with arbitrary expansion.

Theorem 2. *A PO indistinguishable generator that expands its input by a single bit implies a PO indistinguishable generator with any polynomial expansion.*

Proof. The proof consists of a hybrid argument, but such arguments are more complex in our physically observable setting (in particular, rather than a traditional single "pass" through n intermediate steps —where the first is pseudorandom and the last is truly random— they now require two passes: from 1 to n and back). Details can be found in full version of the paper.

6   Some Further Directions

A NEW ROLE FOR OLDER NOTIONS.   In traditional cryptography, in light of the Goldreich-Levin construction [13], it seemed that finding natural hardcore bits of one-way functions became a nearly pointless endeavor (from which only minimal efficiency could be realized). However, Claim 4.4 changes the state of affairs dramatically. This shows how physically observable cryptography may provide new impetus for research on older subjects.

(Another notion from the past that seemed insignificant was the method of outputting bits backwards in the Blum-Micali generator. It was made irrelevant by the equivalence of unpredictability and indistinguishability. In our new world, however, outputting bits backwards is crucially important for Claim 4.4 and Theorem 1.)

INHERITED VS. GENERATED RANDOMNESS.   Our definitions in the physically observable model do not address the origin of the secret input x for a one-way function $\mathcal{P}$: according to the definitions, nothing about x is observable by F before $\mathcal{P}$ starts running. One may take another view of a one-way function, however: one that includes the generation of a random input x as the first step. While in traditional cryptography this distinction seems unimportant, it is quite crucial in physically observable cryptography: the very generation of a random x may leak information about x. It is conceivable that some applications require a definition that includes the generation of a random x as part of the functionality of $\mathcal{P}$. However, we expect that in many instances it is possible to "hardwire" the secret randomness before the adversary has a chance to observe the machine, and then rely on pseudorandom generation.

DETERMINISTIC LEAKAGE AND REPEATED COMPUTATIONS.   Our definitions allow for repeated computation to leak new information each time. However, the case can be made (e.g., due to proper hardware design) that some devices computing a given function f may leak the same information whenever f is evaluated at the same input x. This is actually implied by making the leakage function deterministic and independent of the adversary measurement. *Fixed-leakage physically observable cryptography* promises to be a very useful restriction of our general model (e.g., because, for memory efficiency, crucial cryptographic quantities are often reconstructed from small seeds, such as in the classical pseudorandom function of [16]).

SIGNATURE SCHEMES. In a forthcoming paper we shall demonstrate that digital signatures provide another example of a crucial cryptographic object constructible in our general model. Interestingly, we shall obtain our result by relying on some old constructions (e.g., [21] and [22]), highlighting once more how old research may play a role in our new context.

Acknowledgment. The work of the second author was partly funded by the National Science Foundation under Grant No. CCR-0311485.

References

1. *Proceedings of the Twenty First Annual ACM Symposium on Theory of Computing*, Seattle, Washington, 15–17 May 1989.
2. D. Agrawal, B. Archambeault, J. R. Rao, and P. Rohatgi. The EM side-channel(s). In *Cryptographic Hardware and Embedded Systems Conference (CHES '02)*, 2002.
3. W. Alexi, B. Chor, O. Goldreich, and C. Schnorr. RSA and Rabin functions: Certain parts are as hard as the whole. *SIAM J. Computing*, 17(2):194–209, 1988.
4. Ross Anderson and Markus Kuhn. Tamper resistance — a cautionary note. In *The Second USENIX Workshop on Electronic Commerce*, November 1996.
5. Ross Anderson and Markus Kuhn. Low cost attacks on tamper resistant devices. In *Fifth International Security Protocol Workshop*, April 1997.
6. Eli Biham and Adi Shamir. Differential fault analysis of secret key cryptosystems. In Burton S. Kaliski, Jr., editor, *Advances in Cryptology—CRYPTO '97*, volume 1294 of *Lecture Notes in Computer Science*, pages 513–525. Springer-Verlag, 1997.
7. M. Blum and S. Micali. How to generate cryptographically strong sequences of pseudo-random bits. *SIAM Journal on Computing*, 13(4):850–863, November 1984.
8. D. Boneh, R. DeMillo, and R. Lipton. On the importance of checking cryptographic protocols for faults. In Walter Fumy, editor, *Advances in Cryptology—EUROCRYPT 97*, volume 1233 of *Lecture Notes in Computer Science*, pages 37–51. Springer-Verlag, 11–15 May 1997.
9. S. Chari, C. Jutla, J. R. Rao, and P. Rohatgi. Towards sound approaches to counteract power analysis attacks. In Wiener [29], pages 398–412.
10. Whitfield Diffie and Martin E. Hellman. New directions in cryptography. *IEEE Transactions on Information Theory*, IT-22(6):644–654, 1976.
11. Shimon Even, Oded Goldreich, and Silvio Micali. On-line/off-line digital signatures. *Journal of Cryptology*, 9(1):35–67, Winter 1996.
12. Rosario Gennaro, Anna Lysyanskaya, Tal Malkin, Silvio Micali, and Tal Rabin. Tamper Proof Security: Theoretical Foundations for Security Against Hardware Tampering. Proceedings of the Theory of Cryptography Conference, 2004.
13. O. Goldreich and L. Levin. A hard-core predicate for all one-way functions. In ACM [1], pages 25–32.
14. Oded Goldreich. *Foundations of Cryptography: Basic Tools*. Cambridge University Press, 2001.
15. Oded Goldreich and Silvio Micali. Unpublished.
16. O. Goldreich, S. Goldwasser, and S. Micali. How to Construct Random Functions. *Journal of the ACM*, 33(4):792–807, October 1986.
17. J. Håstad, R. Impagliazzo, L.A. Levin, and M. Luby. Construction of pseudo-random generator from any one-way function. *SIAM Journal on Computing*, 28(4):1364–1396, 1999.

18. Yuval Ishai, Amit Sahai, and David Wagner. Private circuits: Securing hardware against probing attacks. In Dan Boneh, editor, *Advances in Cryptology—CRYPTO 2003*, Lecture Notes in Computer Science. Springer-Verlag, 2002.

19. Joshua Jaffe, Paul Kocher, and Benjamin Jun. United states patent 6,510,518: Balanced cryptographic computational method and apparatus for leak minimizational in smartcards and other cryptosystems, 21 January 2003.

20. Paul Kocher, Joshua Jaffe, and Benjamin Jun. Differential power analysis. In Wiener [29], pages 388–397.

21. Leslie Lamport. Constructing digital signatures from a one way function. Technical Report CSL-98, SRI International, October 1979.

22. Ralph C. Merkle. A certified digital signature. In G. Brassard, editor, *Advances in Cryptology—CRYPTO '89*, volume 435 of *Lecture Notes in Computer Science*, pages 218–238. Springer-Verlag, 1990, 20–24 August 1989.

23. S. W Moore, R. J. Anderson, P. Cunningham, R. Mullins, and G. Taylor. Improving smartcard security using self-timed circuits. In *Asynch 2002*. IEEE Computer Society Press, 2002.

24. Moni Naor and Moti Yung. Universal one-way hash functions and their cryptographic applications. In ACM [1], pages 33–43.

25. FIPS publication 46: Data encryption standard, 1977. Available from http://www.itl.nist.gov/fipspubs/.

26. Jean-Jacques Quisquater and David Samyde. Electromagnetic analysis (EMA): Measures and counter-measures for smart cards. In *Smart Card Programming and Security (E-smart 2001) Cannes, France*, volume 2140 of *Lecture Notes in Computer Science*, pages 200–210, September 2001.

27. John Rompel. One-way functions are necessary and sufficient for secure signatures. In *Proceedings of the Twenty Second Annual ACM Symposium on Theory of Computing*, pages 387–394, Baltimore, Maryland, 14–16 May 1990.

28. Sergei Skorobogatov and Ross Anderson. Optical fault induction attacks. In *Cryptographic Hardware and Embedded Systems Conference (CHES '02)*, 2002.

29. Michael Wiener, editor. *Advances in Cryptology—CRYPTO '99*, volume 1666 of *Lecture Notes in Computer Science*. Springer-Verlag, 15–19 August 1999.

30. A. C. Yao. Theory and applications of trapdoor functions. In *23rd Annual Symposium on Foundations of Computer Science*, pages 80–91, Chicago, Illinois, 3–5 November 1982. IEEE.

A   Minimal GMR Notation

- *Random assignments.* If S is a probability space, then "$x \leftarrow S$" denotes the algorithm which assigns to x an element randomly selected according to S. If F is a finite set, then the notation "$x \leftarrow F$" denotes the algorithm which assigns to x an element selected according to the probability space whose sample space is F and uniform probability distribution on the sample points.
- *Probabilistic experiments.* If $p(\cdot, \cdot, \cdots)$ is a predicate, the notation $\Pr[x \leftarrow S; y \leftarrow T; \ldots : p(x, y, \cdots)]$ denotes the probability that $p(x, y, \cdots)$ will be true after the ordered execution of the algorithms $x \leftarrow S$, $y \leftarrow T, \ldots$.

Efficient and Universally Composable Committed Oblivious Transfer and Applications

Juan A. Garay[1], Philip MacKenzie[1], and Ke Yang[2]

[1] Bell Labs – Lucent Technologies, Murray Hill, NJ, USA
{garay,philmac}@research.bell-labs.com
[2] Carnegie Mellon University, Pittsburgh, PA, USA
yangke@cs.cmu.edu

Abstract. Committed Oblivious Transfer (COT) is a useful cryptographic primitive that combines the functionalities of bit commitment and oblivious transfer. In this paper, we introduce an extended version of COT (ECOT) which additionally allows proofs of relations among committed bits, and we construct an efficient protocol that securely realizes an ECOT functionality in the universal-composability (UC) framework. Our construction is more efficient than previous (non-UC) constructions of COT, involving only a constant number of exponentiations and communication rounds. Using the ECOT functionality as a building block, we construct efficient UC protocols for general two-party and multi-party functionalities, each gate requiring a constant number of ECOT's.

1 Introduction

Committed Oblivious Transfer (COT) was introduced by Crépeau [17] (under the name "Verifiable Oblivious Transfer") as a natural combination of $\binom{2}{1}$-Oblivious Transfer [21] and Bit Commitment. At the start of the computation Alice is committed to bits a_0 and a_1 and Bob is committed to bit b; at the end Bob is committed to a_b and knows nothing about $a_{\bar{b}}$, while Alice learns nothing about b. One can see that this allows each party engaged in an oblivious transfer to be certain that the other party is performing the oblivious transfer operation on their declared inputs.[1] This has been shown to be useful in [18], who construct a protocol for general secure multi-party computation in the model of [28] using COT.

In this paper we show how to improve on previous constructions of COT in the areas of efficiency and universal composability. In terms of efficiency, the protocol we construct for COT uses only a constant number of exponentiations and communication rounds per transfer.[2] In contrast, the most efficient previously

---

[1] This contrasts with standard oblivious transfer, where some other method (perhaps another cryptographic building block, or verification at some higher layer protocol) is required to guarantee that parties are performing their part of the transfer on their declared inputs.

[2] Security is proved under some standard number theoretic assumptions, discussed later.

M. Naor (Ed.): TCC 2004, LNCS 2951, pp. 297–316, 2004.

known construction of COT [18] uses $O(k)$ invocations of OT (thus implying at least the same number of public-key operations using known constructions) and bit commitments, and $O(k)$ rounds, for k a security parameter. Furthermore, we show that our protocol securely realizes an ideal COT functionality in the recently-proposed *universal composability* (UC) framework by Canetti [9], in the *common reference string* (CRS) model. Recall that to define security in this framework, one first specifies an "ideal functionality" describing the desired behavior of the protocol using a trusted party, and then one proves that a particular protocol operating in the real world "securely realizes" this ideal functionality, by showing that no "environment" would be able to distinguish (1) an adversary operating in the real world with parties running this protocol from (2) an "ideal adversary" operating in an ideal process consisting of dummy parties that simply call the ideal functionality. A main virtue of this framework is that the security of protocols thus defined is preserved under a general composition operation called "universal composition," which essentially means that protocols remain secure even when composed with other protocols that may be running concurrently in the same system. We give a more detailed review of the UC framework later in the paper. We note that a similar framework was independently proposed by Pfitzmann and Waidner [37,38]. Intuitively, these two frameworks are similar, although there are a number of technical differences. We choose to use the UC framework in this paper.[3]

Our protocol actually realizes an enhanced COT functionality, which we call *ECOT*, where in addition to oblivious transfer, one can prove certain relations among committed bits (in particular, among three bits). To demonstrate the usefulness of this functionality, we show that using ECOT as a building block, any well-formed two-party and multi-party functionality can be securely realized *efficiently* in the universal composability framework. Plugging in our protocol for realizing the ECOT into this construction, we have an efficient protocol for any well-formed two-party and multi-party functionality in the CRS model.

Canetti *et al.* [11] were the first to show that such functionalities are indeed realizable in this model, even under general cryptographic assumptions and regardless of the number of corrupted parties. More specifically, [11] follows the general "two-phase" approach of [27] of first designing a solution for the case of honest-but-curious parties, and then turning it into a solution for the actively malicious adversary, using a "compiler." The compiler adds a zero-knowledge proof to every message, proving that it is consistent with the history and the (committed) private input and the randomness. Notice that since the "consistency" proofs are for relations involving the execution of Turing machines, they are quite complex and it is unlikely that they admit efficient protocols; rather, proofs for general NP statements are used (which involve a reduction to an

---

[3] The ideal-process/real-world formulation of security and the simulator-based paradigm were initiated by Goldreich *et al.* [27]. From then on, there have been many definitions in this (now standard) paradigm, with emphasis on different aspects. For a number of examples, see Goldwasser and Levin [30], Micali and Rogaway [32], Beaver [2,3], and Canetti [8], for the formulations that preceed the UC framework.

NP-complete problem like Hamiltonian Cycle), making the compiler a major source of inefficiency. Canetti *et al.* make the protocol in [27] secure in the UC framework by replacing the basic primitives (namely, oblivious transfer, bit commitment, and zero-knowledge) with their universally composable counterparts. The resultant protocol becomes universally composable, but remains rather inefficient. In this paper we follow a different approach. By incorporating stronger security into the basic building block (i.e., ECOT), we are able to build protocols secure against adaptive and malicious adversaries *directly*, eliminating the need for a (normally inefficient) compiler. In this way, we are able to construct protocols that are efficient and at the same time enjoy a high level of security.

Our results. We now present a more detailed account of our results. We start by defining an ECOT functionality ($\mathcal{F}_{\mathrm{ECOT}}$), which, as mentioned above, additionally allows the sender to prove relations on three committed bits to the receiver. Then we construct a protocol to realize the ECOT functionality. The starting point for our construction is the standard Pedersen commitment scheme [35]. Then we build an OT protocol over these commitments that is loosely based on the (non-concurrent version of the) OT protocol of Garay and MacKenzie [23] (which in turn is based on the OT protocol of Bellare and Micali [4]). Zero-knowledge (ZK) proofs are required in this OT protocol, and thus we work in a hybrid model with ideal ZK functionalities. Naturally, the constructions for proving relations on three committed bits also use these ideal ZK functionalities. Finally, to construct efficient protocols that securely realize these ZK functionalities, we construct a special type of honest-verifier ZK protocol for each desired relations, and then we use a result by Garay *et al.* [24] that shows how to convert this special type of honest-verifier ZK protocol into a universally-composable ZK protocol. These results are presented in Section 3.

The ECOT functionality can be naturally extended into one that performs $\binom{4}{1}$-transfers (instead of $\binom{2}{1}$)) and proves relations on four committed bits (as opposed to three). We call this extended functionality $\mathcal{F}^4_{\mathrm{ECOT}}$, and show how to construct it using the original $\mathcal{F}_{\mathrm{ECOT}}$ functionality as a building block. Equipped with $\mathcal{F}^4_{\mathrm{ECOT}}$, we then show how to securely realize a two-party functionality that we call *Joint Gate Evaluation* ($\mathcal{F}_{\mathrm{JGE}}$), which, as its name indicates, allows two parties to securely compute any Boolean function over two bits shared between them. Essentially, the protocol realizing this functionality uses a construction similar to that of [27] for the computation of the multiplication gate. However, distinctive features of the protocol are that it deals directly with adaptively malicious parties, and its efficiency: only a constant number of exponentiations and communication rounds per gate evaluation. Joint Gate Evaluation is presented in Section 4.

Finally, we use $\mathcal{F}_{\mathrm{JGE}}$ to securely realize — efficiently — any adaptively well-formed two-party and multi-party functionality, which is expressed by an arithmetic circuit over GF(2), in a universally-composable way. Again, since the realization is directly for the actively malicious adversary, and by means of an efficient building block, the overall computational complexity is a small constant times the number of gates in the representation of the functionality, and the number of rounds is a constant times the depth of the circuit. The treatment of two-party functionalities is presented in Section 5, while the case of multi-party functionalities, with the one-to-many extensions and realizations of the required building blocks, is discussed in Section 6. Putting everything together, we construct efficient and universally composable two-party and multi-party computation protocols that are secure against adaptive adversaries in the *erasing* model, where we allow parties to erase certain information reliably.

As a technical note, we use the gate-by-gate approach from [27], and make sure that each gate is computed efficiently. We do not use the "encrypted circuit" approach due to Yao [40], which yields constant-round protocols but is rather inefficient in terms of communication complexity, since one needs to prove in zero-knowledge that the encrypted circuit is correct and these proofs are unlikely to admit efficient protocols.

Related work. We already mentioned prior work on COT [17,18]. Although the protocols presented there are generic and hence may be implemented with or without computational assumptions (e.g., using primitives based on quantum channels), they are less efficient by at least a factor of k, where k is the security parameter, and furthermore, they are not universally composable. (As a side note, a "stand-alone" version of our ECOT protocol would be substantially simpler, in particular with respect to the implementation of the necessary ZK proofs.)

We can also compare the ECOT functionality to the functionalities defined in [11], who use a "two-phase" approach to construct universally composable two-party/multiple-party computation protocols. In the first phase, where they construct a protocol secure against semi-honest adversaries, an important tool is the OT functionality. In the second phase, where they exhibit a "compiler" that turns protocols in the first phase into ones secure against malicious adversaries, an important tool is the "commit-and-prove" functionality, which proves general NP statements. In some sense, the ECOT functionality may be viewed as a "combination" of the OT functionality and the commit-and-prove functionality. However, we stress that since ECOT only needs to prove very simple relations (among three bits), it can be realized more efficiently.[4]

Recently, Damgård and Nielsen [20] presented efficient universally composable multi-party computation protocols using a different approach. Their construction is based on an efficient MPC protocol by Cramer *et al.* [14], which in turn is based on threshold homomorphic cryptosystems. Compared to our result, the Damgård-Nielsen construction works in a slightly stronger model, namely the *public key infrastructure* (PKI) model, where a trusted party not only generates a common reference string (which contains the public keys of all the paries), but

---

[4] We note that a commitment functionality with the capability to perform proofs on committed bits was also proposed by Damgård and Nielsen [19], along with efficient protocols realizing it under some specific number-theoretic assumptions. However, it was not shown that their functionality could be used in constructing protocols for general secure multi-party computation, and more specifically, oblivious transfer.

also a private string for each party (as the party's secret key). On the other hand, their protocol is secure against adaptive adversaries in the so-called *non-erasing* model, where the parties are not allowed to erase any information, while our construction is secure in the erasing model only.

Due to space limitation, proofs are omitted from this extended abstract, but may be found in the full version of this paper [25].

2   Preliminaries and Definitions

All our results are in the *common reference string* (CRS) model, which assumes that there is a string uniformly generated from some distribution and is available to all parties at the start of a protocol. This is a generalization of the *public random string* model, where a uniform distribution over fixed-length bit strings is assumed.

For a distribution Δ, we say $a \in \Delta$ to denote any element that has non-zero probability in Δ, i.e., any element in the support of Δ. We say $a \xleftarrow{R} \Delta$ to denote a is randomly chosen according to distribution Δ. For a set S, we say $a \xleftarrow{R} S$ to denote that a is uniformly drawn from S.

Ω-protocols. We will use a special type of zero-knowledge protocols, namely, *Ω-protocols* [24], which are variants of the so-called Σ-protocols [15,13]. Very roughly speaking, Σ-protocols are three-round, public-coin, honest-verifier zero-knowledge protocols, and Ω-protocols are proof-of-knowledge Σ-protocols with a straight-line extractor. See [24,25] for a detailed description of Ω-protocols.

The universal composability framework. The universal composability framework was suggested by Canetti for defining the security and composition of protocols [9]. In this framework one first defines an "ideal functionality" of a protocol, and then proves that a particular implementation of this protocol operating in a given computational environment securely realizes this ideal functionality. The basic entities involved are n players $P_1, \ldots, P_n$, an adversary $\mathcal{A}$, and an environment $\mathcal{Z}$. The real execution of a protocol π, run by the players in the presence of $\mathcal{A}$ and an environment machine $\mathcal{Z}$, with input z, is modeled as a sequence of *activations* of the entities. The environment $\mathcal{Z}$ is activated first, generating in particular the inputs to the other players. Then the protocol proceeds by having $\mathcal{A}$ exchanging messages with the players and the environment. Finally, the environment outputs one bit, which is the output of the protocol.

The security of the protocols is defined by comparing the real execution of the protocol to an ideal process in which an additional entity, the ideal functionality $\mathcal{F}$, is introduced; essentially, $\mathcal{F}$ is an incorruptible trusted party that is programmed to produce the desired functionality of the given task. Let $\mathcal{S}$ denote the adversary in this idealized execution. The players are replaced by dummy players, who do not communicate with each other; whenever a dummy player is activated, its input is forwarded to $\mathcal{F}$ by $\mathcal{S}$, who can see the "public header" of the input.[5] As in the real-life execution, the output of the protocol execution is the one-bit output of $\mathcal{Z}$. Now a protocol π *securely realizes* an ideal functionality $\mathcal{F}$ if for any real-life adversary $\mathcal{A}$ there exists an ideal-execution adversary $\mathcal{S}$ such that no environment $\mathcal{Z}$, on any input, can tell with non-negligible probability whether it is interacting with $\mathcal{A}$ and players running π in the real-life execution, or with $\mathcal{S}$ and $\mathcal{F}$ in the ideal execution. More precisely, if the two binary distribution ensembles, $\text{REAL}_{\pi,\mathcal{A},\mathcal{Z}}$ and $\text{IDEAL}_{\mathcal{F},\mathcal{S},\mathcal{Z}}$, describing $\mathcal{Z}$'s output after interacting with adversary $\mathcal{A}$ and players running protocol π (resp., adversary $\mathcal{S}$ and ideal functionality $\mathcal{F}$), are computationally indistinguishable (denoted $\text{REAL}_{\pi,\mathcal{A},\mathcal{Z}} \stackrel{c}{\approx} \text{IDEAL}_{\mathcal{F},\mathcal{S},\mathcal{Z}}$).

Protocols typically invoke other sub-protocols. In this framework the *hybrid model* is like a real-life execution, except that some invocations of the sub-protocols are replaced by the invocation of an instance of an ideal functionality $\mathcal{F}$; this is called the "$\mathcal{F}$-hybrid model." We are designing and analyzing protocols in the CRS model, and so they will be operating in the $\mathcal{F}_{\text{CRS}}^{\mathcal{D}}$-hybrid model, where $\mathcal{F}_{\text{CRS}}^{\mathcal{D}}$ is the functionality that chooses a string from distribution $\mathcal{D}_k$ and hands it to all parties. Further, we will consider the "multi-session extension of $\mathcal{F}$" of Canetti and Rabin [12], denoted $\hat{\mathcal{F}}$, which runs multiple copies of $\mathcal{F}$ by identifying each copy by a special *sub-session identifier*.

The definition of $\hat{\mathcal{F}}_{\text{ZK}}^{R}$, the multi-session extension of $\mathcal{F}_{\text{ZK}}^{R}$, is shown below. Note the two types of indices: the *sid*, which differentiates messages to $\hat{\mathcal{F}}_{\text{ZK}}^{R}$ from messages sent to other functionalities, and *ssid*, the sub-session identifier, which is unique per input message (or proof).

Functionality $\hat{\mathcal{F}}_{\text{ZK}}^{R}$

$\hat{\mathcal{F}}_{\text{ZK}}^{R}$ proceeds as follows, running with security parameter k, parties $P_1, \ldots, P_n$, and an adversary $\mathcal{S}$:

- Upon receiving (zk-prover, $sid, ssid, P_i, P_j, x, w$) from P_i: If $R(x, w)$ then send (ZK-PROOF, $sid, ssid, P_i, P_j, x$) to P_j and $\mathcal{S}$ and halt. Otherwise, ignore.

Refer to [9,11] for further description of the UC framework.

3   Universally Composable Committed Oblivious Transfer

In this section we present the $\mathcal{F}_{\text{ECOT}}$ functionality, an extension of COT where in addition to the oblivious transfer, the sender can prove to the receiver (Boolean) relations among the committed bits. We will later use this functionality to implement an efficient *Joint Gate Evaluation* functionality, which in turn will enable efficient and universally composable multi-party computation. The functionality $\mathcal{F}_{\text{ECOT}}$ is shown below. Informally, a party P_i commits to a bit b by sending an ecot-commit message to the ideal functionality $\mathcal{F}_{\text{ECOT}}$, and P_i can later open this bit by sending an ecot-open message with appropriate commitment identifier

---

[5] This feature was added to the UC framework in [11].

(cid) value. For P_i to obliviously transfer a bit to P_j, P_i needs to commit two bits b_0 and b_1 and P_j needs to commit to one bit b_t; after sending an ecot-transfer to $\mathcal{F}_{\text{ECOT}}$, the bit b_{b_t} is transferred to P_j and automatically committed by $\mathcal{F}_{\text{ECOT}}$ on behalf of P_j. Meanwhile, P_i does not learn anything, except that a transfer took place. Furthermore, the functionality also allows a party P_i to prove to P_j that three bits b_0, b_1, and b_2 it committed to satisfy a particular binary relation by sending an ecot-prove message to $\mathcal{F}_{\text{ECOT}}$.

As a convention, we use $\text{op}_m^{(2)}$ to denote a function on two bits, where $m \in \{0,1\}^4$ is the string of bits of the Boolean function's truth table (output column). We also often identify m with the integer whose binary representation is m. (For example, $m = 1$ represents the AND function, whose truth table is 0001.)

As a technical note, we note that the Open phase is not strictly necessary since it can be simulated by the Prove phase. Take $\text{op}_{0000}^{(2)}$ and $\text{op}_{1111}^{(2)}$, which correspond to the all-zero and all-one functions. Then, by proving that $\text{op}_{0000}^{(2)}(b_0, b_1) = b_2$ for arbitrary bits b_0 and b_1, one essentially opens bit b_2 to 0; similarly, by proving that $\text{op}_{1111}^{(2)}(b_0, b_1) = b_2$, one opens b_2 to 1. We choose to include the Open phase in the functionality for clarity and efficiency (the Open phase can be realized more efficiently than the simulated Prove phase).

Functionality $\mathcal{F}_{\text{ECOT}}$

$\mathcal{F}_{\text{ECOT}}$ proceeds as follows, running with parties $P_1, ..., P_n$ and an adversary $\mathcal{S}$.

- **Commit phase:** When receiving from P_i a message $\langle \text{ecot-commit}, sid, cid, P_j, b \rangle$, record $\langle cid, P_i, P_j, b \rangle$, send message $\langle \text{ECOT-RECEIPT}, sid, cid, P_i, P_j \rangle$ to P_i, P_j and $\mathcal{S}$, and ignore all future messages of the form $\langle \text{ecot-commit}, sid, cid, P_j, * \rangle$ from P_i and $\langle \text{ecot-transfer}, sid, cid, *, *, *, P_i \rangle$ from P_j.
- **Prove phase:** When receiving from P_i a message $\langle \text{ecot-prove}, sid, ssid, cid_0, cid_1, cid_2, P_j, m \rangle$, if the following three tuples, $\langle cid_0, P_i, P_j, b_0 \rangle$, $\langle cid_1, P_i, P_j, b_1 \rangle$, $\langle cid_2, P_i, P_j, b_2 \rangle$, are all recorded, and $\text{op}_m^{(2)}(b_0, b_1) = b_2$, then send message $\langle \text{ECOT-PROOF}, sid, ssid, cid_0, cid_1, cid_2, P_i, m \rangle$ to P_j and $\mathcal{S}$; otherwise do nothing.
- **Transfer phase:** When receiving from P_i a message $\langle \text{ecot-transfer}, sid, cid, cid_0, cid_1, tcid, P_j \rangle$, if the following three tuples $\langle cid_0, P_i, P_j, b_0 \rangle$, $\langle cid_1, P_i, P_j, b_1 \rangle$, and $\langle tcid, P_j, P_i, b_t \rangle$, are all recorded, send message $\langle \text{ECOT-DATA}, sid, cid, P_i, P_j, cid_0, cid_1, tcid, b_{b_t} \rangle$ to P_j, record tuple $\langle cid, P_j, P_i, b_{b_t} \rangle$, and send message $\langle \text{ECOT-RECEIPT}, sid, cid, P_i, P_j, cid_0, cid_1, tcid \rangle$ to P_i and $\mathcal{S}$, and ignore all future messages of the form $\langle \text{ecot-commit}, sid, cid, P_i, * \rangle$ from P_i and $\langle \text{ecot-transfer}, sid, cid, *, *, *, P_j \rangle$ from P_j. Otherwise, do nothing.
- **Open phase:** When receiving from P_i a message $\langle \text{ecot-open}, sid, cid, P_i, P_j \rangle$, if the tuple $\langle cid, P_i, P_j, b \rangle$ is recorded, send message $\langle \text{ECOT-DATA}, sid, cid, P_i, P_j, b \rangle$ to both $\mathcal{S}$ and P_j; otherwise, do nothing.

Before presenting a protocol that securely realizes $\mathcal{F}_{\text{ECOT}}$, we first discuss some preliminary constructions that will be used as building blocks.

3.1   Building Blocks

In [24], Garay *et al.* introduced a technique to transform any Ω-protocol into a universally composable protocol by using a digital signature scheme that is existentially unforgeable against adaptive chosen-message attacks. Their transformation is efficient, if the digital signature scheme admits an efficient proof of knowledge protocol. In particular, they proved the following result.

Theorem 1 ([24]). *Under the strong RSA assumption or the DSA assumption, for every relation R that admits an Ω-protocol Π, there exists a three-round protocol $\mathsf{UC}[\Pi]$ that securely realizes the $\hat{\mathcal{F}}_{\text{ZK}}^{R}$ ideal functionality in the $\mathcal{F}_{\text{CRS}}$-hybrid model against adaptive adversaries, assuming erasing. Furthermore, the (additive) overhead of $\mathsf{UC}[\Pi]$ to Π is constant number of exponentiations plus the generation of a signature.*

See [25] for discussion on the Strong RSA assumption.

Drawing from standard techniques in the literature (e.g., [6,7,22,31,24]), we are able to construct efficient Ω-protocols for the following relations; by then "plugging" them into Theorem 1, we obtain efficient universally composable zero-knowledge protocols for these relations. Due to space limitations, the detailed construction of these Ω-protocols appears in the full version [25].

1. **"OR" of two discrete logs:**

$$R_{\text{OR-DL}}((y_0, g_0, y_1, g_1), (x_0, x_1)) = R_{\text{DL}}((y_0, g_0), x_0) \vee R_{\text{DL}}((y_1, g_1), x_1)$$

2. **"OR"/"AND" relation of six discrete logs:**

$$R_{\text{OR-N-DL}}((y_0, y_1, y_2, y_3, y_4, y_5, g), (x_0, x_1, x_2, x_3, x_4, x_5)) =$$
$$((R_{\text{DL}}((y_0, g), x_0) \vee R_{\text{DL}}((y_1, g), x_1)) \wedge R_{\text{DL}}((y_2, g), x_2)) \vee$$
$$(R_{\text{DL}}((y_3, g), x_3) \wedge R_{\text{DL}}((y_4, g), x_4) \wedge R_{\text{DL}}((y_5, g), x_5))$$

3. **Partial equality of representations:**

$$R_{\text{PEREP}}((x_0, g_0, g_1, x_1, g_2, g_3), (\alpha_0, \alpha_1, \alpha_2))$$

4. **"OR" of partial equality of representations:**

$$R_{\text{OR-PEREP}}((x_0, g_0, g_1, x_1, g_2, g_3, y_0, h_0, h_1, y_1, h_2, h_3), (\alpha_0, \alpha_1, \alpha_2, \beta_0, \beta_1, \beta_2)) =$$
$$R_{\text{PEREP}}((x_0, g_0, g_1, x_1, g_2, g_3), (\alpha_0, \alpha_1, \alpha_2)) \vee$$
$$R_{\text{PEREP}}((y_0, h_0, h_1, y_1, h_2, h_3), (\beta_0, \beta_1, \beta_2))$$

3.2   The UCECOT Protocol

We now present UCECOT, a protocol that securely realizes the $\mathcal{F}_{\text{ECOT}}$ ideal functionality in the $(\mathcal{F}_{\text{CRS}}, \hat{\mathcal{F}}_{\text{ZK}}^{R_{\text{OR-DL}}}, \hat{\mathcal{F}}_{\text{ZK}}^{R_{\text{OR-N-DL}}}, \hat{\mathcal{F}}_{\text{ZK}}^{R_{\text{PEREP}}}, \hat{\mathcal{F}}_{\text{ZK}}^{R_{\text{OR-PEREP}}})$-hybrid model, where the CRS consists of (p, q, g, h) such that q and p are primes satisfying $q|(p-1)$ and $g, h \in \mathbb{Z}_p^*$ are random elements satisfying $\text{order}(g) = \text{order}(h) = q$. p and q will also serve as the public parameters in the relations $R_{\text{DL}}, R_{\text{PEREP}}$, and their compositions.

We first describe the protocol.

Commit phase: On receiving private input $\langle \text{ecot-commit}, sid, cid, P_j, b \rangle$, assuming that cid is not used before, party P_i picks a random $r \xleftarrow{R} \mathbb{Z}_q$, computes $B \leftarrow g^r \cdot h^b \mod p$, sends message $(\text{ucecot-commit}, sid, cid, B)$ to party P_j, message $(\text{zk-prover}, sid, cid, P_i, P_j, (B, g, B/h, g), (r, r))$ to $\hat{\mathcal{F}}_{\text{ZK}}^{R_{\text{OR-DL}}}$, and outputs $\langle \text{ECOT-RECEIPT}, sid, cid, P_i, P_j \rangle$. After receiving the messages from P_i and $\hat{\mathcal{F}}_{\text{ZK}}^{R_{\text{OR-DL}}}$ respectively, P_j outputs $\langle \text{ECOT-RECEIPT}, sid, cid, P_i, P_j \rangle$. Essentially P_i sends a Pedersen commitment [35] of bit b to P_j and uses the $\hat{\mathcal{F}}_{\text{ZK}}^{R_{\text{OR-DL}}}$ ideal functionality to prove that he either knows the discrete log of B (in which case P_i is committing to bit 0) or the discrete log of B/h base g (in which case P_i is committing to bit 1).

Prove phase: Suppose P_i has committed bits b_0, b_1, and b_2 to P_j using cids cid_0, cid_1, and cid_2, respectively. Further assume that their corresponding Pedersen commitments are $B_0 = g^{r_0} \cdot h^{b_0}$, $B_1 = g^{r_1} \cdot h^{b_1}$, and $B_2 = g^{r_2} \cdot h^{b_2}$. Now, upon receiving private input $\langle \text{ecot-prove}, sid, ssid, cid_0, cid_1, cid_2, P_j, m \rangle$, P_i is to prove to P_j that $\text{op}_m^{(2)}(b_0, b_1) = b_2$, using sub-session id $ssid$. We first consider the situation where $m = 1110$, in which case $\text{op}_m^{(2)}$ is the NAND operation. In this situation, P_i sends message $(\text{ucecot-prove}, sid, ssid, cid_0, cid_1, cid_2, m)$ to P_j and sends message $(\text{zk-prover}, sid, ssid, P_i, P_j, (B_0, B_1, B_2/h, B_0/h, B_1/h, B_2, g), (r_0, r_1, r_2, r_0, r_1, r_2))$ to $\hat{\mathcal{F}}_{\text{ZK}}^{R_{\text{OR-N-DL}}}$. After receiving the corresponding message from $\hat{\mathcal{F}}_{\text{ZK}}^{R_{\text{OR-N-DL}}}$, P_j outputs $\langle \text{ECOT-PROOF}, sid, ssid, cid_0, cid_1, cid_2, P_i, m \rangle$. Intuitively, P_i is proving that $(((b_0 = 0) \vee (b_1 = 0)) \wedge (b_2 = 1)) \vee ((b_0 = 1) \wedge (b_1 = 1) \wedge (b_2 = 0))$.

In the case of any other binary operations $\text{op}_m^{(2)}$, it can be written as a composition of NANDs and then proved step by step. P_i will need to commit to all the intermediate bits and prove each NAND operation is correct. For example, consider the case where $m = 0001$ is the AND operation. Notice that $x \wedge y = \overline{\overline{x \wedge y} \wedge \overline{x \wedge y}}$ Therefore, to prove that $b_2 = b_0 \wedge b_1$, P_i needs to commit to a new bit $b_3 = \overline{b_0 \wedge b_1}$ using the protocol in the Commit phase, and then prove that both $b_3 = \overline{b_0 \wedge b_1}$ and that $b_2 = \overline{b_3 \wedge b_3}$.

Transfer phase: Suppose P_i has committed bits b_0 and b_1, and P_j has committed bit b_t, using identifiers cid_0, cid_1, and $tcid$, respectively. Further assume that the corresponding Pedersen commitments are $B_0 = g^{r_0} \cdot h^{b_0}$, $B_1 = g^{r_1} \cdot h^{b_1}$, and $B_t = g^{r_t} \cdot h^{b_t}$. Now, upone receiving private input ecot-transfer, $sid, cid, cid_0, cid_1, tcid, P_j\rangle$, assuming that cid is not used before, P_i is to obliviously transfers bit b_{b_t} to P_j, using session id sid and the commitment id cid for the new bit b_{b_t}. Intuitively, P_i sends two Pedersen commitments, C_0 and C_1, where C_0 is a commitment to b_0 using base B_t, and C_1 is a commitment to b_1 using base B_t/h. It also sends A_0 and A_1 generated using the same randomness as C_0 and C_1. If $b_t = 0$, then P_j knows the discrete log of B_t and can check if C_0 is a commitment to zero or not, and if $b_t = 1$, then P_j knows the discrete log of B_t/h and can check if C_1 is a commitment to zero or not.

Now we proceed to the details. P_i randomly picks $a_0, a_1 \overset{R}{\leftarrow} \mathbb{Z}_q$ and computes $A_0 \leftarrow g^{a_0}$, $A_1 \leftarrow g^{a_1}$, $C_0 \leftarrow B_t^{a_0} \cdot h^{b_0}$, and $C_1 \leftarrow (B_t/h)^{a_1} \cdot h^{b_1}$. P_i then sends message (ucecot-transfer, $sid, cid, cid_0, cid_1, tcid, A_0, A_1, C_0, C_1$) to P_j and sends the following four messages to the ideal functionality $\hat{\mathcal{F}}_{\text{ZK}}^{R_{\text{PEREP}}}$.[6]

$$\text{(zk-prover}, sid, cid \circ 00, P_i, P_j, (C_0, h, B_t, B_0, h, g), (b_0, a_0, r_0))$$
$$\text{(zk-prover}, sid, cid \circ 01, P_i, P_j, (C_1, h, B_t/h, B_1, h, g), (b_1, a_1, r_1))$$
$$\text{(zk-prover}, sid, cid \circ 10, P_i, P_j, (A_0, g, 1, C_0, B_t, h), (a_0, 0, b_0))$$
$$\text{(zk-prover}, sid, cid \circ 11, P_i, P_j, (A_1, g, 1, C_1, B_t/h, h), (a_1, 0, b_1))$$

After this, P_i erases a_0 and a_1.

After receiving the message from P_i and four messages from the ideal functionality $\hat{\mathcal{F}}_{\text{ZK}}^{R_{\text{PEREP}}}$, P_j does the following (otherwise P_j aborts).
If $b_t = 0$, then check if $A_0^{r_t} = C_0 \bmod p$, and set $b \leftarrow 0$ if yes and $b \leftarrow 1$ otherwise; if $b_t = 1$, then check if $A_1^{r_t} = C_1 \bmod p$, and sets $b \leftarrow 0$ if yes and $b \leftarrow 1$ otherwise. Now b is the bit P_j receives.

Next, P_j picks a random $r \overset{R}{\leftarrow} \mathbb{Z}_q^*$ and sets $B \leftarrow g^r \cdot h^b \bmod p$, sends message (ecot-commit, sid, cid, B) to party P_i, sends message (zk-prover, $sid, cid, P_j, P_i, (C_0, h, A_0, B, h, g, C_1, h, A_1, B, h, g), (b, r_t, r, b, r_t, r))$ to ideal functionality $\hat{\mathcal{F}}_{\text{ZK}}^{R_{\text{OR-PEREP}}}$, and outputs $\langle$ECOT-DATA, $sid, cid, P_i, P_j, cid_0, cid_1, tcid, b\rangle$. Finally, after receiving messages from P_j and $\hat{\mathcal{F}}_{\text{ZK}}^{R_{\text{OR-PEREP}}}$, P_i outputs $\langle$ECOT-RECEIPT, $sid, cid, P_i, P_j, cid_0, cid_1, tcid\rangle$.

Open phase: Suppose P_i has committed a bit b to P_j using session id sid, and commitment id cid. Further assume that the commitment is $B = g^r \cdot h^b \bmod p$. Now upon receiving private input $\langle$ecot-open, $sid, cid, P_i, P_j\rangle$, P_i opens the bit b by sending message (ucecot-open, sid, cid, b, r) to P_j, who then verifies that $B = g^r \cdot h^b \bmod p$, and outputs (ECOT-DATA, sid, cid, P_i, P_j, b) if the verification is valid.

This is exactly the opening of a Pedersen commitment.

In the full version, we show:

---

[6] We assume that all the id's are binary strings, and we use "$a \circ b$" to indicate the concatenation of string a with string b.

Theorem 2. *Under the DDH assumption, protocol* UCECOT *securely realizes the* $\mathcal{F}_{\mathrm{ECOT}}$ *ideal functionality in the* $(\mathcal{F}_{\mathrm{CRS}}, \hat{\mathcal{F}}_{\mathrm{ZK}}^{R_{\mathrm{OR-DL}}}, \hat{\mathcal{F}}_{\mathrm{ZK}}^{R_{\mathrm{OR-N-DL}}}, \hat{\mathcal{F}}_{\mathrm{ZK}}^{R_{\mathrm{PEREP}}}$, $\hat{\mathcal{F}}_{\mathrm{ZK}}^{R_{\mathrm{OR-PEREP}}})$-*hybrid model against adaptive, malicious adversaries, assuming erasing.*

4   Joint Gate Evaluation

In this section we show how to securely realize a two-party functionality that we call *Joint Gate Evaluation* ($\mathcal{F}_{\mathrm{JGE}}$) in the $\mathcal{F}_{\mathrm{ECOT}}$-hybrid model in the presence of a malicious, adaptive adversary. Informally, $\mathcal{F}_{\mathrm{JGE}}$ allows two parties to jointly evaluate any binary operation on two bits, and this will allow us to construct general two-party computation protocols on top of $\mathcal{F}_{\mathrm{JGE}}$. We first present the functionality, shown below.

Functionality $\mathcal{F}_{\mathrm{JGE}}$

$\mathcal{F}_{\mathrm{JGE}}$ proceeds as follows, running with parties $P_1, ..., P_n$, and adversary $\mathcal{S}$.

- **Commit phase:** When receiving from P_i a message $\langle \mathsf{commit}, sid, cid, P_j, b \rangle$, record $\langle cid, \{P_i, P_j\}, b \rangle$, send message $\langle \mathsf{RECEIPT}, sid, cid, P_i, P_j \rangle$ to P_i, P_j and $\mathcal{S}$, and ignore all further messages of the form $\langle \mathsf{commit}, sid, cid, x, * \rangle$ and $\langle \mathsf{eval}, sid, cid, *, *, x, * \rangle$ from P_j or P_j, where $x \in \{P_i, P_j\}$.
- **Evaluate phase:** When receiving from P_i a message $\langle \mathsf{eval}, sid, cid, cid_0, cid_1, P_j, m \rangle$, if both $\langle cid_0, \{P_i, P_j\}, b_0 \rangle$ and $\langle cid_1, \{P_i, P_j\}, b_1 \rangle$ are recorded, then compute $b = \mathrm{op}_m^{(2)}(b_0, b_1)$, record $\langle cid, \{P_i, P_j\}, b \rangle$, send message $\langle \mathsf{EVAL\text{-}RECEIPT}, sid, cid, cid_0, cid_1, P_i, P_j, m \rangle$ to P_i, P_j and $\mathcal{S}$, and ignore all further messages of the form $\langle \mathsf{commit}, sid, cid, x, * \rangle$ and $\langle \mathsf{eval}, sid, cid, *, *, x, * \rangle$ from P_i or P_j, where $x \in \{P_i, P_j\}$. Otherwise, do nothing.
- **Open phase:** When receiving from P_i a message $\langle \mathsf{open}, sid, cid, P_j \rangle$, if the tuple $\langle cid, \{P_i, P_j\}, b \rangle$ is recorded, then send message $\langle \mathsf{DATA}, sid, cid, P_i, P_j, b \rangle$ to P_j; otherwise, do nothing.

At a high level, the approach we will use to realize functionality $\mathcal{F}_{\mathrm{JGE}}$ is similar to that in [26,11]. In particular, each bit stored in $\mathcal{F}_{\mathrm{JGE}}$ will be XOR-shared by P_i and P_j, and each gate evaluation will be done by a $\binom{4}{1}$-oblivious transfer. However, our resulting construction is directly secure against a malicious, adaptive adversary, and therefore we do not need the "compiler" used in [26, 11]. This "direct" (as opposed to the "two-phase") approach makes our protocol much more efficient.

In particular, we will realize the $\mathcal{F}_{\mathrm{JGE}}$ functionality using a further generalization of the $\mathcal{F}_{\mathrm{ECOT}}$ functionality, which we call $\mathcal{F}_{\mathrm{ECOT}}^4$. The Commit and Open phases of $\mathcal{F}_{\mathrm{ECOT}}^4$ are identical to those of $\mathcal{F}_{\mathrm{ECOT}}$, but the Transfer phase performs a $\binom{4}{1}$-transfer (instead of $\binom{2}{1}$), while the Prove phase proves relations consisting of Boolean functions of *three bits* (as opposed to two).

The detailed descriptions of $\mathcal{F}^4_{\text{ECOT}}$ and a protocol that securely realizes it in the $\mathcal{F}_{\text{ECOT}}$-hybrid model appear in [25].

We now give a high-level idea of how the protocol will realize the $\mathcal{F}_{\text{JGE}}$ functionality in the $\mathcal{F}^4_{\text{ECOT}}$-hybrid model. In the protocol, each bit b of identifier cid stored in $\mathcal{F}_{\text{JGE}}$ is shared between P_i and P_j additively. More precisely, P_i has a bit b_1 and P_j has a bit b_2 such that $b = b_1 \oplus b_2$. Furthermore, each of b_1 and b_2 is a random bit by itself. Both P_i and P_j will commit to their bits to each other using identifier cid. To open this bit to P_i, P_j opens its share, b_2, to P_i, who then computes $b = b_1 \oplus b_2$.

In order to evaluate $c = \mathsf{op}_m^{(2)}(a,b)$, suppose P_i holds a_1 and b_1 as shares of a and b, and P_j holds a_2 and b_2, respectively. Then, P_i generates a random bit $c_1 \xleftarrow{R} \{0,1\}$ and computes four bits $o_{00}, o_{01}, o_{10}, o_{11}$, which are the "candidate bits" for c_2, P_j's share of bit c. Which bit is c_2 depends on P_j's shares a_2 and b_2. The actual bits are computed as in the table below.

(a_2, b_2)	P_j's output c_2
$(0,0)$	$o_{00} = c_1 \oplus \mathsf{op}_m^{(2)}(a_1, b_1)$
$(0,1)$	$o_{01} = c_1 \oplus \mathsf{op}_m^{(2)}(a_1, (b_1 \oplus 1))$
$(1,0)$	$o_{10} = c_1 \oplus \mathsf{op}_m^{(2)}((a_1 \oplus 1), b_1)$
$(1,1)$	$o_{11} = c_1 \oplus \mathsf{op}_m^{(2)}((a_1 \oplus 1), (b_1 \oplus 1))$

P_i then commits to the bits $c_1, o_{00}, o_{01}, o_{10}, o_{11}$ and proves to P_j the relations in the table using the Prove phase of $\mathcal{F}^4_{\text{ECOT}}$. (We use m_0, m_1, m_2, m_3 to denote the encodings of these relations.) Next, P_i and P_j engage in a $\binom{4}{1}$-oblivious transfer so that P_j receives bit $o_{a_2 b_2}$, which is P_j's share of bit c.

The full description of UCJGE, the protocol that securely realizes $\mathcal{F}_{\text{JGE}}$ in the $\mathcal{F}^4_{\text{ECOT}}$-hybrid model, as well as the proof of the following theorem, appear in [25].

Theorem 3. *Protocol* UCJGE *securely realizes the* $\mathcal{F}_{\text{JGE}}$ *functionality in the* $\mathcal{F}^4_{\text{ECOT}}$-*hybrid model against malicious, adaptive adversaries.*

5   Efficient and Universally Composable Two-Party Computation

In this section we show how to securely realize any adaptively well-formed two-party functionality in the presence of malicious adaptive adversaries in the $\mathcal{F}_{\text{JGE}}$-hybrid model. Our construction is similar to the constructions in [27,26,11] for semi-honest adversaries. However, since our $\mathcal{F}_{\text{JGE}}$ functionality is secure in the presence of malicious adversaries, we are able to obtain a two-party protocol secure against malicious adversaries directly.

We first review some of the assumptions about two-party functionalities we use in our paper, which are also used in [11]. We let $\mathcal{F}$ be an ideal two-party functionality, and we let P_1 and P_2 be the participating parties. We assume that $\mathcal{F}$ may be represented via a family $\mathcal{C_F}$ of Boolean circuits, the kth circuit representing an activation of $\mathcal{F}$ with security parameter k. Without loss of generality, we assume the circuits are composed entirely of NAND gates.[7]

For simplicity, we assume that in each activation, (1) at most one party has an input to $\mathcal{F}$ with at most k bits, (2) each party may receive at most k bits as output from $\mathcal{F}$, (3) $\mathcal{F}$ is a deterministic function, and (4) the local state of $\mathcal{F}$ after each activation can be described by at most k bits. The initial state of $\mathcal{F}$ is described by k zero bits. We assume that messages sent from $\mathcal{A}$ to $\mathcal{F}$ are ignored, and there are no messages from $\mathcal{F}$ to $\mathcal{A}$.

We note that the "deterministic function" assumption about $\mathcal{F}$ is without loss of generality, since we can always realize a probabilistic functionality $\mathcal{F}$ using a deterministic one $\mathcal{F}'$ as follows. Assuming that $\mathcal{F}$ needs k random bits, then $\mathcal{F}'$ receives a k-bit string as auxiliary input from each participating party upon the first activation, and then runs $\mathcal{F}$ using the XOR of these strings as the random bit string. It is easy to see that the simple protocol where each party sends a random k-bit string as the auxiliary input to $\mathcal{F}'$ securely realizes the ideal functionality $\mathcal{F}$ in the $\mathcal{F}'$-hybrid model.[8]

The following protocol $\Pi_{\mathcal{F}}$ realizes an activation of $\mathcal{F}$ when P_1 sends a message to $\mathcal{F}$. (The case for P_2 is analogous.) We assume that both P_1 and P_2 hold an sid as auxiliary input. When P_1 is activated with input (sid, v), it initiate a protocol with P_2 to perform a joint gate-by-gate evaluation of the appropriate circuit in $\mathcal{C_F}$.

Formally, they carry out the following protocol.

Initialization: When P_1 receives (sid, v), it checks if this is the first activation of $\mathcal{F}$, and if so it sets up the internal state. Then it commits to its private input.

> **Setting up the internal state:** For $i = 1, 2, ..., k$, P_1 sends messages $\langle \mathsf{commit}, sid, cid_i, P_2, 0 \rangle$ and then $\langle \mathsf{open}, sid, cid_i, P_2 \rangle$ to $\mathcal{F}_{\mathrm{JGE}}$. P_1 waits to receive the appropriate receipts. P_2 aborts if any of the bits are not zero. Effectively, P_1 commits to the initial internal state of $\mathcal{F}$ (which is all zeros), and by opening them immediately, it proves to P_2 that these bits are indeed all-zero.[9]

> **Committing to the private input:** For $i = 1, 2, ..., k$, P_1 sends messages $\langle \mathsf{commit}, sid, cid_i, P_1, v_i \rangle$ to $\mathcal{F}_{\mathrm{JGE}}$ and waits to receive the appropriate

---

[7] This is entirely for simplicity. Note that the $\mathcal{F}_{\mathrm{JGE}}$ functionality can be used to evaluate any gate of fan-in two.

[8] Note that if adaptive corruptions are allowed, then this is actually only true for adaptively well-formed functionalities. See [11] for a discussion on this point, and the modifications necessary for an ideal adversary in the case of probabilistic functions.

[9] Note that the cid's used here and elsewhere in the protocol must all be unique bit strings that indicate the bit's use in the circuit. For instance, the cid_i here could be the bit encoding of $\langle \mathsf{state}, i \rangle$.

receipts. Here we assume that $v = v_1 v_2 \cdots v_k$.[10] P_2 simply records the receipts received from $\mathcal{F}_{\mathrm{JGE}}$.

Gate-by-gate evaluation: For each NAND gate in the circuit, P_1 determines the commitment identifiers associated with the inputs to that NAND gate, say cid_0 and cid_1, creates a new unique commitment identifier cid, sends message $\langle \mathsf{eval}, sid, cid, cid_0, cid_1, P_2, 1110 \rangle$ to $\mathcal{F}_{\mathrm{JGE}}$, and waits for the appropriate receipt. Here $m = 1110$ is the encoding of the NAND operation. P_2 simply records the receipts received from $\mathcal{F}_{\mathrm{JGE}}$.

Output: P_2 verifies from all its receipts that P_1 had $\mathcal{F}_{\mathrm{JGE}}$ perform the correct computation on the appropriate bits. Then for each output bit of $\mathcal{F}$, it is either an internal state bit, or a bit addressed to either P_1 or P_2 (we have assumed that $\mathcal{F}$ does not communicate with $\mathcal{A}$). In the former case, P_1 and P_2 do not need to do anything. They simply store the identifier of this bit, so that they can use it in the next activation. In the latter case, assuming that this bit, with identifier cid, is addressed to P_2, P_1 sends a message $\langle \mathsf{open}, sid, cid, P_2 \rangle$ to $\mathcal{F}_{\mathrm{JGE}}$ and P_2 extracts the bit b from the message $\langle \mathsf{DATA}, sid, cid, \{P_1, P_2\}, b \rangle$ received from $\mathcal{F}_{\mathrm{JGE}}$. The protocol for the case for a bit addressed to P_1 is the same, but with P_1 and P_2 switched.

Messages that are out of order are dealt with using tagging, as in [11].

Theorem 4. *Let $\mathcal{F}$ be a two-party adaptively well-formed functionality. Then $\Pi_{\mathcal{F}}$ securely realizes $\mathcal{F}$ in the $\mathcal{F}_{\mathrm{JGE}}$-hybrid model, in the presence of malicious adaptive adversaries.*

Proof appears in [25].

6   Efficient and Universally Composable Multi-party Computation

In this section we show how to extend the results from previous sections to securely realize any well-formed multi-party functionality in the presence of malicious adaptive adversaries corrupting an arbitrary number of parties. Our construction is similar to that in [11] for semi-honest adversaries. But, again as in the two-party case, we are able to construct building blocks that can withstand malicious adversaries, and therefore our construction is secure against malicious, adaptive adversaries directly.

In order to securely realize $\mathcal{F}$, we basically follow the same approach as in the two-party case. However, we first need to extend some of our constructions from previous sections to suit the multiple-party case.

---

[10] To indicate the use of each of these bits in the circuit, one could, for instance, set cid_i to be the bit encoding of $\langle \mathsf{input}, P_1, a, i \rangle$, where a is the activation number.

6.1 Broadcast and the One-to-Many ZK Functionalities

We assume an *authenticated broadcast* channel available to all participating parties. The channel is modeled by the broadcast functionality $\mathcal{F}_{BC}$ below. The functionality guarantees the authenticity of a message, i.e., that no party P_i can fake a message from P_j. This is also the assumption used in [11], and we refer the readers to [11,29] for more in-depth discussions.

Functionality $\mathcal{F}_{BC}$

$\mathcal{F}_{BC}$ proceeds as follow, running with parties $P_1, ..., P_n$ and an adversary $\mathcal{S}$.

  – Upon receiving a message (broadcast, $sid, \mathcal{P}, x$) from P_i, where $\mathcal{P}$ is a set of parties, send (BCAST-MSG, $sid, P_i, \mathcal{P}, x$) to all parties in $\mathcal{P}$ and $\mathcal{S}$, and halt.

We also need an extension of the ZK functionality, namely the one-to-many ZK functionality, denoted by $\mathcal{F}_{mZK}$. Intuitively, this functionality allows a single prover to prove a theorem to multiple verifiers simultaneously. We give the formal definition in [25].

We observe that the UCZK construction by Garay *et al.* [24] can be naturally extended to a one-to-many UCZK protocol with the additional broadcast functionality. Roughly speaking, P_i (the prover) runs an independent copy of the two-party UCZK protocol with every party $P_j \in \mathcal{P}$ using a unique sid, and all messages are broadcast. Each P_j accepts if and only if all the conversations are accepting. It is straightforward to construct an ideal adversary $\mathcal{S}$. If the prover is uncorrupted, $\mathcal{S}$ simply runs a multi-party UCZK simulator for every copy of the UCZK protocol. If the prover is corrupted and there is at least one uncorrupted verifier, $\mathcal{S}$ can extract the witness. If all parties are corrupted, the simulation is straightforward. The conversion remains efficient. Therefore we have the following theorem.

Theorem 5. *Under the strong RSA assumption or the DSA assumption, for every relation R that admits an Ω-protocol Π, there exists a three-round protocol* UC$[\Pi]$ *that securely realizes the $\mathcal{F}_{mZK}^R$ ideal functionality in the $(\mathcal{F}_{CRS}, \mathcal{F}_{BC})$-hybrid model against adaptive adversaries, assuming erasing. Furthermore, the computation complexity of* UC$[\Pi]$ *is that of Π plus constant number of exponentiations and the generation of a signature, times the number of receiving parties.*

6.2 Multi-party ECOT

We also extend the $\mathcal{F}_{ECOT}$ functionality to the multi-party case, where the proof phase is replaced by a one-to-many proof and the receipts are sent to all participating parties. A formal definition of $\mathcal{F}_{mECOT}$ appears in [25].

It is straightforward to extend the UCECOT protocol to the multiple-party case. One simply replaces the $\mathcal{F}_{ZK}$ functionalities by the $\mathcal{F}_{mZK}$ functionalities and replaces the point-to-point messages by broadcast messages. We denote the extended protocol by UCmECOT, and we have the following theorem.

Theorem 6. *Under the DDH assumption, protocol* UCmECOT *securely realizes the* $\mathcal{F}_{\mathrm{mECOT}}$ *ideal functionality in the* $(\mathcal{F}_{\mathrm{CRS}}, \mathcal{F}_{\mathrm{BC}}, \hat{\mathcal{F}}_{\mathrm{mZK}}^{R_{\mathrm{OR\text{-}DL}}}, \hat{\mathcal{F}}_{\mathrm{mZK}}^{R_{\mathrm{OR\text{-}N\text{-}DL}}}, \hat{\mathcal{F}}_{\mathrm{mZK}}^{R_{\mathrm{PEREP}}},$ $\hat{\mathcal{F}}_{\mathrm{mZK}}^{R_{\mathrm{OR\text{-}PEREP}}})$-*hybrid model against adaptive adversaries, assuming erasing.*

6.3   Multi-party Joint Gate Evaluation

We extend the joint gate evaluation functionality to the multi-party case. Functionality $\mathcal{F}_{\mathrm{mJGE}}$ is shown below. The only changes with respect to the two-party case are that the receipts are sent to all participating parties, and that all parties have to agree for the opening to take place.

Functionality $\mathcal{F}_{\mathrm{mJGE}}$

$\mathcal{F}_{\mathrm{JGE}}$ proceeds as follows, running with parties $P_1, ..., P_n$, and adversary $\mathcal{S}$.

- **Commit phase:**   When receiving from P_i a message $\langle \mathrm{commit}, sid, cid, \mathcal{P}, b \rangle$, if $P_i \in \mathcal{P}$, then record $\langle cid, \mathcal{P}, b \rangle$, send message $\langle \mathrm{RECEIPT}, sid, cid \rangle$ to all parties in $\mathcal{P}$ and $\mathcal{S}$, and ignore all further messages of the form $\langle \mathrm{commit}, sid, cid, *, * \rangle$ and $\langle \mathrm{eval}, sid, cid, *, *, *, * \rangle$.
- **Evaluate phase:**   When receiving from P_i a message $\langle \mathrm{eval}, sid,$ $cid, cid_0, cid_1, \mathcal{P}, m \rangle$, if $P_i \in \mathcal{P}$ and both $\langle cid_0, \mathcal{P}, b_0 \rangle$ and $\langle cid_1, \mathcal{P}, b_1 \rangle$ are recorded, then compute $b = \mathrm{op}_m^{(2)}(b_0, b_1)$, record $\langle cid, \mathcal{P}, b \rangle$, send message $\langle \mathrm{EVAL\text{-}RECEIPT}, sid, cid, cid_0, cid_1, P_i, \mathcal{P}, m \rangle$ to all parties in $\mathcal{P}$ and $\mathcal{S}$, and ignore all further messages of the form $\langle \mathrm{commit}, sid, cid, *, * \rangle$ and $\langle \mathrm{eval}, sid, cid, *, *, *, * \rangle$; otherwise, do nothing.
- **Open phase:**   When receiving from P_i a message $\langle \mathrm{open}, sid, cid, P_j \rangle$, if $P_i \in \mathcal{P}$, $P_j \in \mathcal{P}$, and the tuple $\langle cid, \mathcal{P}, b \rangle$ is recorded, then record tuple $\langle \mathrm{openreq}, sid, cid, P_j \rangle$. When a tuple $\langle \mathrm{openreq}, sid, cid, P_i, P_j \rangle$ is recorded for every $P_j \in \mathcal{P}$, then send message $\langle \mathrm{DATA}, sid, cid, b \rangle$ to P_i.

In fact, we only need a "weakened" version of the $\mathcal{F}_{\mathrm{mJGE}}$ functionality for general multi-party computation. The weakened version, denoted by $\mathcal{F}_{\mathrm{wmJGE}}$, has the additional constraint that only XOR and AND operations are allowed in the evaluation phase. It is obvious that since $\{\mathrm{XOR}, \mathrm{AND}\}$ is a complete set of Boolean operations, $\mathcal{F}_{\mathrm{wmJGE}}$ is powerful enough to realize any multi-party functionality.

As in the two-party case, we also need an extension of the $\mathcal{F}_{\mathrm{mECOT}}$ functionality, denoted by $\mathcal{F}_{\mathrm{mECOT}}^4$, that performs $\binom{4}{1}$-oblivious transfer and proves relations among four bits. We only state the following theorem and omit the details.

Theorem 7. *There exists an efficient protocol that securely realizes the* $\mathcal{F}_{\mathrm{mECOT}}^4$ *functionality in the* $\mathcal{F}_{\mathrm{mECOT}}$-*hybrid model against malicious, adaptive adversaries.*

Next, we briefly sketch a protocol UCmJGE that securely realizes $\mathcal{F}_{\mathrm{wmJGE}}$ in the $\mathcal{F}_{\mathrm{mECOT}}^4$-hybrid model. This protocol is essentially a multi-party extension to the UCJGE protocol. In UCmJGE, a bit b is now shared among all participating parties: party P_i has bit b_i such that $\sum_{i=1}^n b_i = b \mod 2$. In the following description, we omit some details in the protocol such as the format of the messages and the identifiers of the bits. These details should be clear from the context.

Commit phase: For party P_i to commit to a bit b, it generates random bits $b_1, b_2, ..., b_{n-1} \xleftarrow{R} \{0,1\}$ and $b_n \leftarrow b \oplus b_1 \oplus \cdots \oplus b_{n-1}$. Then P_i commits to b_i through $\mathcal{F}^4_{\mathrm{mECOT}}$, sends bits b_j to party P_j for all $j \neq i$. Then each P_j commits to b_j through the $\mathcal{F}^4_{\mathrm{mECOT}}$ and opens it to P_i immediately.

Evaluate phase: Assume the two bits to be computed are a and b, and P_i holds bits a_i, b_i as their shares. Naturally we have $a = \sum a_i \mod 2$ and $b = \sum b_i \mod 2$. We assume the result bit is c and each party should hold a share c_i at the end of this phase. We consider two cases according to the operation performed.

XOR: To compute the XOR of bit a and b, each party simply computes $c_i = a_i \oplus b_i$. No messages are needed.

AND: To compute the AND of bit a and b, we follow the approach in [26, 11]. Observe that AND is the multiplication modulo 2, and we have the following equality.

$$\left(\sum_{i=1}^n a_i \right) \cdot \left(\sum_{i=1}^n b_i \right) = n \cdot \sum_{i=1}^n a_i \cdot b_i + \sum_{1 \leq i < j \leq n} (a_i + a_j) \cdot (b_i + b_j) \mod 2$$

(see [26] for the justification of this equality). Therefore, each party P_i can compute $n \cdot a_i \cdot b_i$ by itself, and each pair P_i and P_j can jointly compute $(a_i + a_j) \cdot (b_i + b_j)$ as in the two-party case, by invoking multiple transfer phases of the $\mathcal{F}^4_{\mathrm{mECOT}}$ functionality.

Open phase: To open a bit b, shared as $b = \sum_{i=1}^n b_i$, to party P_i, every P_j opens its share b_j through $\mathcal{F}^4_{\mathrm{mECOT}}$. Then P_i sums up all the shares to obtain b.

Abort: In case any party aborts and/or deviates from the protocol, all parties abort the protocol.

Theorem 8. *Protocol* UCmJGE *securely realizes functionality* $\mathcal{F}_{\mathrm{mJGE}}$ *in the* $\mathcal{F}^4_{\mathrm{mECOT}}$-*hybrid model against malicious, adaptive adversaries.*

The proof is very similar to that of Theorem 3. Next, for any multi-party functionality $\mathcal{F}$, we construct a protocol $\Pi_{\mathcal{F}}$ that securely realizes $\mathcal{F}$ in the $\mathcal{F}_{\mathrm{mJGE}}$-hybrid model. The construction is almost identical to the two-party case, except that since we assume the circuit computing $\mathcal{F}$ consists of AND and XOR gates, instead of NAND gates, the gate-by-gate evaluation will invoke the $\mathcal{F}_{\mathrm{mJGE}}$ functionality with different encodings of functions. Again, we defer the detailed construction and proof to the full version of this paper.

Theorem 9. *Let* $\mathcal{F}$ *be a multi-party adaptively well-formed functionality. Then* $\Pi_{\mathcal{F}}$ *securely realizes* $\mathcal{F}$ *in the* $\mathcal{F}_{\mathrm{mJGE}}$-*hybrid model, in the presence of malicious adaptive adversaries.*

Acknowledgements. The authors thank the anonymous reviewers for TCC'04 for the many valuable comments.

References

1. N. Barić and B. Pfitzmann. Collision-free accumulators and fail-stop signature schemes without trees. In *Advances in Cryptology–Eurocrypt '97*, pp.480–494, 1997.
2. D. Beaver. Foundations of Secure Interactive Computing. In *Advances in Cryptology – CRYPTO '91*, pp. 377–391, 1991.
3. D. Beaver. Secure Multiparty Protocols and Zero-Knowledge Proof Systems Tolerating a Faulty Minority. In *Journal of Cryptology* 4(2), pp. 75–122, 1991.
4. M. Bellare and S. Micali. Non-interactive oblivious transfer and applications. *Advances in Cryptology—CRYPTO '89*, pp. 547–557, volume 435 of *Lecture Notes in Computer Science*, Springer-Verlag, 1990.
5. D. Boneh. The decision Diffie-Hellman problem. In *Proceedings of the Third Algorithmic Number Theory Symposium* (LNCS 1423), pp. 48–63, 1998.
6. F. Boudot. Efficient Proofs that a Committed Number Lies in an Interval. In *EUROCRYPT 2000*, pp. 431–444, 2000.
7. J. Camenisch and M. Michels. Separability and efficiency for generic group signature schemes. In *Advances in Cryptology—CRYPTO '99*, volume 1666 of *Lecture Notes in Computer Science*, pages 414–430, Springer-Verlag, 1999.
8. R. Canetti. Security and Composition of Multiparty Cryptographic Protocols. In *Journal of Cryptology* 13(1), pp. 143–202, 2000.
9. R. Canetti. Universally composable security: A new paradigm for cryptographic protocols. In *42nd FOCS*, pp. 136–145, 2001.
10. R. Canetti and M. Fischlin. Universally composable commitments. In *CRYPTO 2001* (LNCS 2139), pp. 19–40, 2001.
11. R. Canetti, Y. Lindell, R. Ostrovsky and A. Sahai. Universally composable two-party computation. In *STOC '02*, pp. 494–503, 2002. Full version in *Cryptology ePrint Archive*, Report 2002/140.
12. R. Canetti and T. Rabin. Universal Composition with Joint State In *Cryptology ePrint Archive*, Report 2002/047, http://eprint.iacr.org/, 2002.
13. R. Cramer. Modular Design of Secure yet Practical Cryptographic Protocols. Ph.D. Thesis. CWI and University of Amsterdam, 1997.
14. R. Cramer, I. Damgård, and J. Nielsen. Multiparty Computation from Threshold Homomorphic Encryption In *Advances in Cryptology–EuroCrypt '01*, volume 2045 of *Lecture Notes in Computer Science*, pp. 280–300, Springer-Verlag, 2001.
15. R. Cramer, I. Damgård, and B. Schoenmakers. Proofs of partial knowledge and simplified design of witness hiding protocols. In *Advances in Cryptology–CRYPTO '94* (LNCS 839), pages 174–187, 1994.
16. R. Cramer and V. Shoup. Signature scheme based on the strong RSA assumption. In *ACM Transactions on Information and System Security (ACM TISSEC)* 3(3):161-185, 2000.
17. C. Crépeau. Verifiable disclosure of secrets and applications. In *Eurocrypt '89*, LNCS 434, pp 181 – 191, 1990.
18. C. Crépeau, J. van de Graaf, and A. Tapp. Committed oblivious transfer and private multi-party computation. In *Advances in Cryptology—CRYPTO '95*, volume 963 of *Lecture Notes in Computer Science*, pages 110–123. Springer-Verlag, 27–31 Aug. 1995.

19. I. Damgård and J. Nielsen. Perfect hiding and perfect binding universally composable commitment schemes with constant expansion factor. In *CRYPTO 2002* (LNCS 2442), pp. 581–596, 2002. A later version in *Cryptology ePrint Archive*, Report 2001/091. http://eprint.iacr.org/, 2001.

20. I. Damgård, and J. Nielsen. Universally Composable Efficient Multiparty Computation from Threshold Homomorphic Encryption. In *Advances in Cryptology–CRYPTO '03*, 2003.

21. S. Even, O. Goldreich, and A. lempel, A Randomized Protocol for Signing Contracts. In *Communications of the ACM*, 28:637-647 (1985).

22. E. Fujisaki and T. Okamoto. Statistical zero knowledge protocols to prove modular polynomial relations. In *Advances in Cryptology–CRYPTO '97*, pp. 16-30, 1997.

23. J. Garay and P. MacKenzie. Concurrent Oblivious Transfer. In *FOCS 2000*, pp. 314-324, Redondo Beach, CA, November 2000.

24. J. Garay, P. MacKenzie and K. Yang. Strengthening Zero-Knowledge Protocols using Signatures. In *Advances in Cryptology–Eurocrypt 2003*, Warsaw, Poland, LNCS 2656, pp.177-194, 2003. Full version available from *Cryptology ePrint Archive*, Report 2003/037, http://eprint.iacr.org/2003/037, 2003.

25. J. Garay, P. MacKenzie and K. Yang. Efficient and Universally Composable Committed Oblivious Transfer and Applications (full paper). To appear in *Cryptology ePrint Archive*.

26. O. Goldreich. Secure Multi-Party Computation (Working Draft, Version 1.2), March 2000. Available from http://www.wisdom.weizmann.ac.il/~oded/pp.html.

27. O. Goldreich, S. Micali and A. Wigderson. How to play any mental game or a completeness theorem for protocols with honest majority. In *19th ACM Symposium on the Theory of Computing*, pp. 218–229, 1987.

28. S. Goldwasser and L. Levin. Fair computation of general functions in presence of immoral majority, In *Advances in Cryptology-CRYPTO '90*, pp. 77-93, Springer-Verlag, 1991.

29. S. Goldwasser and Y. Lindell. Secure Computation Without Agreement. In 16th *DISC*, Springer-Verlag (LNCS 2508), pages 17-32, 2002.

30. S. Goldwasser and L. Levin. Fair computation of general functions in presence of immoral majority, In *Advances in Cryptology–CRYPTO '90*, pp. 77-93, Springer-Verlag, 1991.

31. P. MacKenzie and M. Reiter. Two-Party Generation of DSA Signatures. In *Advances in Cryptology–CRYPTO '01*, pp 137–154, 2001.

32. S. Micali and P. Rogaway. Secure Computation (Abstract). In *Advances in Cryptology – CRYPTO '91*, pp. 392–404, 2001.

33. T. Osamoto and S. Uchiyama. A new public-key cryptosystem as secure as factoring. In *Advances in Cryptology–Eurocrypt '98*, pp.380–318, 1998.

34. P. Paillier. Public-key cryptosystems based on composite degree residue classes. In *Advances in Cryptology–Eurocrypt '99*, pp.223–238, 1999.

35. T. P. Pedersen. Non-Interactive and Information-Theoretic Secure Verifiable Secret Sharing. In *CRYPTO 1991*, pp. 129–140, 1991.

36. B. Pfitzmann, M. Schunter, and M. Waidner. Provably Secure Certified Mail. In *IBM Research Report RZ 3207 (#93253) 02/14/00*, IBM Research Division, Zürich, August 2000.

37. B. Pfitzmann and M. Waidner. Composition and integrity preservation of secure reactive systems. In *ACM Conference on Computer and Communications Security (CCS 2000)*, pp. 245–254, 2000.

38. B. Pfitzmann and M. Waidner. A Model for Asynchronous Reactive Systems and its Application to Secure Message Transmission. In *IEEE Symposium on Security and Privacy*, pp. 184–200, 2001.
39. P. Rogaway. The round complexity of secure protocols. Ph.D. Thesis, MIT, June 1991.
40. A. Yao. Protocols for Secure Computation. In *FOCS 1982*, pages 160–164, 1982.

A Universally Composable Mix-Net

Douglas Wikström[1,2]

[1] Royal Institute of Technology (KTH)
KTH, Nada, S-100 44 Stockholm, Sweden
[2] Swedish Institute of Computer Science (SICS)
Box 1263, S-164 29 Kista, Sweden
douglas@sics.se

Abstract. A mix-net is a cryptographic protocol executed by a set of mix-servers that provides anonymity for a group of senders. The main application is electronic voting.

Numerous mix-net constructions and stand-alone definitions of security are proposed in the literature, but only partial proofs of security are given for most constructions and no construction has been proved secure with regards to any kind of composition.

We define an ideal mix-net in the universally composable security framework of Canetti [6]. Then we describe a mix-net based on Feldman [13] and using similar ideas as Desmedt and Kurosawa [10], and prove that it securely realizes the ideal mix-net with respect to static adversaries that corrupt a minority of the mix-servers and arbitrarily many senders.

The mix-net executes in a hybrid model with access to ideal distributed key generation, but apart from that our only assumption is the existence of a group in which the Decision Diffie-Hellman Problem is hard.

If there are relatively few mix-servers or a strong majority of honest mix-servers our construction is practical.

1 Introduction

The notion of a mix-net was invented by Chaum [7]. Properly constructed a mix-net takes a list of cryptotexts and outputs the cleartexts permuted using a secret random permutation. Usually a mix-net is realized by a set of mix-servers organized in a chain that collectively execute a protocol. Each mix-server receives a list of encrypted messages from the previous mix-server, transforms them, using partial decryption or random re-encryption, reorders them, and outputs the result. The secret permutation is shared by the mix-servers.

1.1 Previous Work

Chaum's original "anonymous channel" [7,36] enables a sender to send mail anonymously. When constructing election schemes [7,14,37,43,35] a mix-net can be used to ensure that the vote of a given voter can not be revealed. Abe gives an efficient construction of a general mix-net [1], and argues about its properties. Jakobsson has written (partly with Juels) more general papers on the topic of

M. Naor (Ed.): TCC 2004, LNCS 2951, pp. 317–335, 2004.
© Springer-Verlag Berlin Heidelberg 2004

mixing [24,25,26] focusing on efficiency. Furukawa and Sako [15], and Neff [33] respectively have recently found efficient proofs of a correct shuffle, but these proposals have incomplete or flawed analysis. Groth [23] builds on Neff's ideas to form an abstract protocol for any homomorphic cryptosystem.

Desmedt and Kurosawa [10] describe an attack on a protocol by Jakobsson [24]. Similarly Mitomo and Kurosawa [32] exhibit a weakness in another protocol by Jakobsson [25]. Pfitzmann has given some general attacks on mix-nets [40,39], and Michels and Horster give additional attacks in [31]. Wikström [46] gives several attacks for a protocol by Golle et al. [22]. He also gives attacks for the protocols by Jakobsson [25] and Jakobsson and Juels [27]. Abe [2] has independently found related attacks.

Canetti [6] and independently Pfitzmann and Waidner [41], proposed security frameworks for reactive processes. We use the former framework. Both frameworks has composition theorems, and are based on older definitional work. The initial ideal-model based definitional approach for secure function evaluation is informally proposed by Goldreich, Micali, and Wigderson in [18]. The first formalizations appear in Goldwasser and Levin [19], Micali and Rogaway [30], and Beaver [3]. Canetti [5] presents the first definition of security that is preserved under composition. See [5,6] for an excellent background on these definitions.

1.2 Contribution

The large number of attacks and flawed analysis for mix-net constructions, e.g. [10,32,40,39,31,46,2] and [33,15] respectively, suggest that constructing a secure mix-net is hard. Previous work on mix-nets gives ad-hoc definitions of security, and most provide proofs in heuristic models. We take a broader view and present the first mix-net *provably secure* in the UC-security framework. To achieve this we introduce a natural definition of a UC-secure mix-net, and avoid all two-party proofs of knowledge. Instead we introduce multi-verifier proofs of knowledge that exploit the potential of an honest majority of mix-servers.

1.3 Outline of the Paper

The paper is organized as follows. First we define ideal functionalities corresponding to the notions of a mix-net, a bulletin board, distributed key generation, and multi-verifier zero-knowledge. Then we describe a generic mix-net running in a hybrid model with access to these ideal functionalities (except the ideal mix-net) that securely realizes the ideal mix-net. This is followed by protocols that securely realize a proof of knowledge of a cleartext of an El Gamal cryptotext, and a proof of knowledge of the correctness of a decrypt-shuffle respectively. Finally we use the composition theorem of Canetti [6] to compose our protocols with each other and with the universally composable authenticated broadcast presented by Goldwasser and Lindell [20]. This gives a universally composable mix-net in a hybrid model with ideal distributed key generation. In this conference version we only give shortened proofs of Lemma 2 and Lemma 4. The full version of this paper [47] provides proofs of all claims.

1.4   Notation

Throughout $S_1, \ldots, S_N$ will denote senders and $M_1, \ldots, M_k$ mix-servers. All participants are modeled as interactive Turing machines. We abuse notation and use P_i and M_j to denote both the machines themselves and their identity. We denote the set of permutations of N elements by Σ_N. We use the term "randomly" instead of "uniformly and independently at random". We assume that G_q is a group of prime order q with generator g for which the Decision Diffie-Hellman Assumption holds. Informally the assumption says that it is hard to distinguish the distributions $(g^\alpha, g^\beta, g^{\alpha\beta})$ and $(g^\alpha, g^\beta, g^\gamma)$ when $\alpha, \beta, \gamma \in \mathbb{Z}_q$ are randomly chosen.

We review the El Gamal [12] cryptosystem employed in G_q. The private key x is generated by choosing $x \in \mathbb{Z}_q$ randomly. The corresponding public key is $y = g^x$. Encryption of a message $m \in G_q$ using the public key y is given by $E_y(m, r) = (g^r, y^r m)$, where r is chosen randomly from $\mathbb{Z}_q$, and decryption of a cryptotext on the form $(u, v) = (g^r, y^r m)$ using the private key x is given by $D_x(u, v) = u^{-x} v = m$. Tsionis and Yung [45] shows that the El Gamal cryptosystem is semantically secure [21,29] under the DDH-assumption.

1.5   The UC-Security Framework

In this conference version we only give a short informal review of the UC-framework. For details we refer the reader to Canetti [6] or the full version of this paper [47].

The core of the framework consists of the real model, the ideal model, and many different hybrid models. In all models the corresponding adversary may corrupt a certain fraction of the parties.

The real model is a model of real world computing, i.e. a list of interactive Turing machines execute a protocol over an asynchronous authenticated open network. The real adversary can see all communication and decide when messages are delivered. The ideal model contains an ideal functionality, i.e. a trusted party, that defines a service we wish to implement. Thus a protocol in the ideal model is trivial and consists of machines that forwards any input to the ideal functionality, and gives any output from the ideal functionality as output. The ideal adversary decides when messages are delivered from the ideal functionality but it can not see any contents. An ideal functionality is considered secure by definition. To be able to seamlessly move from a real model to an ideal model there are many hybrid models. A protocol running in a hybrid model is a list of interactive Turing machines that has access to some set of ideal functionalities.

The definition of security is based on the simulation paradigm. A protocol is said to securely realize an ideal functionality if for any real adversary in the real model, there is an ideal adversary in the ideal model that has the same advantage. In contrast to classical definitions the distinguisher is present during the execution and may influence the adversary based on part of the transcript.

The definition of security allows secure composition of protocols, i.e. given a protocol secure in a hybrid model, and protocols that securely realize all ideal functionalities in use, it is trivial to construct a secure protocol in the real model.

The notion of a communication model, $\mathcal{C}_\mathcal{I}$, used below is not explicit in Canetti [6]. It works as a router between participants and between participants and ideal functionalities. Given input $(A, B, C, \dots)$ it interprets A as the receiver of $(B, C, \dots)$. The adversary can not read the correspondence with ideal functionalities, but it has full control over when a message is delivered.

Throughout we consider the adversary model below, and we explicitly say when a result holds only with regards to blocking adversaries.

Definition 1. *We define* $\mathcal{M}_{B(k)}$ *to be the set of* static adversaries *that corrupt less than* $B(k)$ *participants of the mix-server type* M_j, *and arbitrarily many participants of the sender type* P_i.

2   Ideal Functionalities

No definition of an ideal mix-net in the UC-security framework has been given in the literature. Below we give a natural definition corresponding to a mix-net that outputs the cleartexts. The term mix-net is sometimes used also for constructions that do not decrypt the inputs, but we do not consider this here. We assume that each sender only sends one message.

Throughout we implicitly assume that a message handed to an ideal functionality that is not on the forms prescribed in its definition is returned to the sender immediately. In particular this includes verifying membership in G_q when appropriate. We use the same convention for definitions of protocols.

Functionality 1 (Mix-Net). The ideal functionality for a *mix-net*, $\mathcal{F}_{\mathrm{MN}}$, running with mix-servers $M_1, \dots, M_k$, senders $P_1, \dots, P_N$, and ideal adversary $\mathcal{S}$ proceeds as follows

1. Initialize a list $L = \emptyset$, and set $J_P = \emptyset$ and $J_M = \emptyset$.
2. Suppose $(P_i, \mathtt{Send}, m_i)$, $m_i \in G_q$, is received from $\mathcal{C}_\mathcal{I}$. If $i \notin J_P$, set $J_P \leftarrow J_P \cup \{i\}$, and append m_i to the list L. Then hand $(\mathcal{S}, P_i, \mathtt{Send})$ to $\mathcal{C}_\mathcal{I}$.
3. Suppose $(M_j, \mathtt{Run})$ is received from $\mathcal{C}_\mathcal{I}$. Set $J_M \leftarrow J_M \cup \{j\}$. If $|J_M| \geq k/2$, then sort the list L lexicographically to form a list L', and hand $((\mathcal{S}, M_j, \mathtt{Output}, L'), \{(M_l, \mathtt{Output}, L')\}_{l=1}^k)$ to $\mathcal{C}_\mathcal{I}$. Otherwise, hand $\mathcal{C}_\mathcal{I}$ the list $(\mathcal{S}, M_j, \mathtt{Run})$.

Most constructions given in the literature assume the existence of an authenticated bulletin board, but this assumption is rarely formalized.

Functionality 2 (Bulletin Board). The ideal *bulletin board* functionality, $\mathcal{F}_{\mathrm{BB}}$, running with participants $P_1, \dots, P_k$ and ideal adversary $\mathcal{S}$.

1. $\mathcal{F}_{\mathrm{BB}}$ holds a database indexed on integers. Initialize a counter $c = 0$.
2. Upon receiving $(P_i, \mathtt{Write}, m_i)$, $m_i \in \{0, 1\}^*$, from $\mathcal{C}_\mathcal{I}$, store (P_i, m_i) under the index c in the database, hand $(\mathcal{S}, \mathtt{Write}, c, P_i, m_i)$ to $\mathcal{C}_\mathcal{I}$, and set $c \leftarrow c+1$.
3. Upon receiving $(P_j, \mathtt{Read}, c)$ from $\mathcal{C}_\mathcal{I}$ check if a tuple (P_i, m_i) is stored in the database under c. If so hand $((\mathcal{S}, P_j, \mathtt{Read}, c, P_i, m), (P_j, \mathtt{Read}, c, P_i, m_i))$ to $\mathcal{C}_\mathcal{I}$. If not, hand $((\mathcal{S}, P_j, \mathtt{NoRead}, c), (P_j, \mathtt{NoRead}, c))$ to $\mathcal{C}_\mathcal{I}$.

Goldwasser and Lindell [20] show that an authenticated broadcast can be securely realized with respect to *blocking* $\mathcal{M}_{k/2}$-adversaries. On the other hand Lindell, Lysyanskaya and Rabin [28] show that composable authenticated broadcast can not be realized for *non-blocking* $\mathcal{M}_B$-adversaries if $B > k/3$. The following lemma follows from [20].

Lemma 1. *There exists a protocol π_{BB} that securely realizes $\mathcal{F}_{BB}$ with respect to blocking $\mathcal{M}_{k/2}$-adversaries.*

The mix-servers must somehow set up distributed El Gamal keys, but we do not consider this problem here. We only note that the problem was first addressed by Pedersen [38], and that Gennaro et al. [17] discovered a flaw in his approach, and a solution to the problem. Unfortunately their protocol is given in a different model, and can not be applied here directly. Below, the joint secret key $x = \sum_{j=1}^{k} x_j$ and the corresponding public key $y = \prod_{j=1}^{k} y_j = g^x$ are implicit. Any individual participant can compute y, but not x.

Functionality 3 (Distributed El Gamal Key Generation). The ideal *Distributed El Gamal Key Generation over G_q*, $\mathcal{F}_{KG}$, running with mix-servers $M_1, \dots, M_k$, senders $P_1, \dots, P_N$, and ideal adversary $\mathcal{S}$ proceeds as follows.

1. Initialize sets $J_j = \emptyset$ for $j = 0, \dots, k$.
2. Until $|J_0| = k$ wait for $(M_j, \mathtt{MyKey}, x_j, y_j)$ from $\mathcal{C}_{\mathcal{I}}$ such that $x_j \in \mathbb{Z}_q$, $y_j = g^{x_j}$, and $j \notin J_0$. Set $J_0 \leftarrow J_0 \cup \{j\}$.
3. Hand $((\mathcal{S}, \mathtt{PublicKeys}, y_1, \dots, y_k), \{(P_j, \mathtt{PublicKeys}, y_1, \dots, y_k)\}_{j=1}^{N},$ $\{(M_j, \mathtt{Keys}, x_j, y_1, \dots, y_k)\}_{j=1}^{k})$ to $\mathcal{C}_{\mathcal{I}}$.
4. If $(M_j, \mathtt{Recover}, M_l)$ is received from $\mathcal{C}_{\mathcal{I}}$, set $J_l \leftarrow J_l \cup \{j\}$. If $|J_l| \geq k/2$, then hand $((\mathcal{S}, \mathtt{Recovered}, M_l, x_l), \{(M_j, \mathtt{Recovered}, M_l, x_l)\}_{j=1}^{k})$ to $\mathcal{C}_{\mathcal{I}}$, and otherwise hand $(\mathcal{S}, M_j, \mathtt{Recover}, M_l)$ to $\mathcal{C}_{\mathcal{I}}$.

We need two different zero-knowledge proofs of knowledge. Following Canetti et al. [8] we define a single ideal zero-knowledge functionality taking a relation R as a parameter, and then give two polynomial-time recognizable relations R_C, and R_{DS} for the functionalities we need.

Functionality 4 (Zero-Knowledge Proof of Knowledge). Let $\mathcal{L}$ be a language given by a binary relation R. The ideal *zero-knowledge proof of knowledge* functionality of a witness w to an element $x \in \mathcal{L}$, running with provers $P_1, \dots, P_N$, and verifiers $M_1, \dots, M_k$, proceeds as follows.

1. Upon receipt of $(P_i, \mathtt{Prover}, x, w)$ from $\mathcal{C}_{\mathcal{I}}$, store w under the tag (P_i, x), and hand $(\mathcal{S}, P_i, \mathtt{Prover}, x, R(x, w))$ to $\mathcal{C}_{\mathcal{I}}$. Ignore further messages from P_i.
2. Upon receipt of $(M_j, \mathtt{Question}, P_i, x)$ from $\mathcal{C}_{\mathcal{I}}$, let w be the string stored under the tag (P_i, x) (the empty string if nothing is stored), and hand $((\mathcal{S}, M_j, \mathtt{Verifier}, P_i, x, R(x, w)), (M_j, \mathtt{Verifier}, P_i, R(x, w)))$ to $\mathcal{C}_{\mathcal{I}}$.

The first relation corresponds to knowledge of the cleartext m, when (u, v) is interpreted as $(g^r, y^r m)$. This may be viewed as the ideal counterpart of the proof of knowledge in the heuristically non-malleable version of El Gamal described both by Tsionis and Yung [45] and Schnorr and Jakobsson [44].

Definition 2 (Knowledge of Cleartext). *Define a relation* $R_C \subset G_q^4 \times \mathbb{Z}_q$, *by* $((g, y, u, v), r) \in R_C$ *precisely when* $\log_g u = r$.

Although neither y nor v plays any role in the definition we keep them to emphasize the similarity with older work.

The second relation corresponds to a correct partial decryption, permutation and re-encryption of a list of El Gamal cryptotexts. This may be viewed as the ideal counterpart to the honest verifier zero-knowledge proof of knowledge presented by Furukawa et al. [16], or that of Neff [34].

Definition 3 (Knowledge of Correct Decrypt-Shuffle). *Define for each* N *a relation* $R_{DS} \subset (G_q^3 \times G_q^{2N} \times G_q^{2N}) \times (\mathbb{Z}_q \times \Sigma_N \times \mathbb{Z}_q^N)$, *by*

$$((g, h, y, \{(u_i, v_i)\}_{i=1}^N, \{(u_i', v_i')\}_{i=1}^N), (x, \pi, \{r_i\}_{i=1}^N)) \in R_{DS}$$

precisely when $(u_i', v_i') = (g^{r_i} u_{\pi^{-1}(i)}, h^{r_i} v_{\pi^{-1}(i)} u_{\pi^{-1}(i)}^{-x})$ *for* $i = 1, \ldots, N$, *and* $\log_g y = x$.

In an application the prover M_j holds π, r_i, and x such that $y = g^x$, and h corresponds to the remaining part of a shared key.

3   A Generic Mix-Net in a Hybrid Model

We describe a generic mix-net protocol in the $(\mathcal{F}_{BB}, \mathcal{F}_{KG}, \mathcal{F}_{ZK}^{R_C}, \mathcal{F}_{ZK}^{R_{DS}})$-hybrid model, i.e. the participants use an ideal bulletin board, ideal distributed El Gamal key generation, and ideal zero-knowledge proof systems for the relations R_C and R_{DS}. The structure of our mix-net corresponds closely to the mix-net implemented by Furukawa et al. [16]. Other researchers, e.g. Neff [34], have had similar ideas. Our mix-net is secure as long as a majority of the mix-servers M_j are honest. There is no bound on the number of corrupted senders P_i.

In the other common structure of a mix-net each mix-server performs a random re-encryption and permutation, and then the mix-servers jointly decrypt the output of the last mix-server. We believe that our results may be generalized to hold for such a protocol.

We abuse notation. When a message is received via a copy of the ideal communication model $\mathcal{C}_I$, we say that it is received directly from an ideal functionality.

Informally the mix-net works as follows. Each sender encrypts its message using the El Gamal cryptosystem and proves that it knows the randomness used to do this. Then the mix-servers take turns to partially decrypt, permute, and re-encrypt the elements in the list. The output of the last mix-server is a list of permuted cleartexts.

Protocol 1 (Generic Mix-Net). The generic mix-net protocol $\pi = (P_1, \ldots, P_N, M_1, \ldots, M_k)$ consists of senders P_i, and mix-servers M_j.

SENDER P_i. Each sender P_i proceeds as follows.

1. Wait for (PublicKeys, $y_1, \ldots, y_k$) from $\mathcal{F}_{KG}$, and compute $y = \prod_{\iota=1}^k y_\iota$.

2. Wait for an input $(\mathtt{Send}, m_i)$, $m_i \in G_q$. Then choose $r_i \in \mathbb{Z}_q$ randomly and compute $(u_i, v_i) = E_y(m_i, r_i)$.

3. Hand $(\mathtt{Prover}, (g, y, u_i, v_i), r_i)$ to $\mathcal{F}_{\mathrm{ZK}}^{R_C}$.

4. Hand $(\mathtt{Write}, (u_i, v_i))$ to $\mathcal{F}_{\mathrm{BB}}$.

MIX-SERVER M_j. Each mix-server M_j proceeds as follows.

1. Choose $x_j \in \mathbb{Z}_q$ randomly and hand $(\mathtt{MyKey}, x_j, g^{x_j})$ to $\mathcal{F}_{\mathrm{KG}}$.

2. Wait for $(\mathtt{Keys}, x_j, y_1, \ldots, y_k)$ from $\mathcal{F}_{\mathrm{KG}}$, compute $h_l = \prod_{j=l}^{k} y_j$ for $l = 1, \ldots, k$, and set $y = h_1$.

3. Wait for an input $(\mathtt{Run})$, and then hand $(\mathtt{Write}, \mathtt{Run})$ to $\mathcal{F}_{\mathrm{BB}}$.

4. Wait until at least $k/2$ different mix-servers has written $\mathtt{Run}$ on $\mathcal{F}_{\mathrm{BB}}$, and let the last entry of this type be $(c_{\mathrm{Run}}, M_i, \mathtt{Run})$.

5. Form the list $L_* = \{(u_\gamma, v_\gamma)\}_{\gamma \in I_*}$, for some index set I_*, from the set of entries on $\mathcal{F}_{\mathrm{BB}}$ on the form $(c, P_\gamma, (u_\gamma, v_\gamma))$, where $0 \le c < c_{\mathrm{run}}$, $\gamma \in \{1, \ldots, N\}$, and $u_\gamma, v_\gamma \in G_q$.

6. For each $\gamma \in I_*$ do the following,

   a) Hand $(\mathtt{Question}, P_\gamma, (g, y, u_\gamma, v_\gamma))$ to $\mathcal{F}_{\mathrm{ZK}}^{R_C}$.

   b) Wait for $(\mathtt{Verifier}, P_\gamma, b_\gamma)$ from $\mathcal{F}_{\mathrm{ZK}}^{R_C}$.

   Then form $L_0 = \{(u_{0,i}, v_{0,i})\}_{i=1}^{N'}$ consisting of pairs (u_γ, v_γ) such that $b_\gamma = 1$.

7. For $l = 1, \ldots, k$ do:

   a) If $l \ne j$, then do:

      i. Wait until an entry $(c, M_l, (\mathtt{List}, L_l))$ appears on $\mathcal{F}_{\mathrm{BB}}$, where L_l is on the form $\{(u_{l,i}, v_{l,i})\}_{i=1}^{N'}$ for $u_{l,i}, v_{l,i} \in G_q$.

      ii. Hand $(\mathtt{Question}, M_l, (g, h_{l+1}, y_l, L_{l-1}, L_l))$ to $\mathcal{F}_{\mathrm{ZK}}^{R_{DS}}$, and wait for $(\mathtt{Verifier}, M_l, b_l)$ from $\mathcal{F}_{\mathrm{ZK}}^{R_{DS}}$.

      iii. If $b_l = 0$, then hand $(\mathtt{Recover}, M_l)$ to $\mathcal{F}_{\mathrm{KG}}$, and wait for $(\mathtt{Recovered}, M_l, x_l)$ from $\mathcal{F}_{\mathrm{KG}}$. Then define $L_l = \{(u_{l,i}, v_{l,i})\}_{i=1}^{N'} = \{D_{x_j}(u_{l-1,i}, v_{l-1,i})\}_{i=1}^{N'} = \{(u_{l-1,i}, v_{l-1,i} u_{l-1,i}^{-x_l})\}_{i=1}^{N'}$.

   b) If $l = j$, then choose $r_{j,i} \in \mathbb{Z}_q$ and $\pi_j \in \Sigma_{N'}$ randomly, and compute

$$
L_j = \{(u_{j,i}, v_{j,i})\}_{i=1}^{N'} = \left\{ \left(g^{r_{j,i}} u_{j-1, \pi_j^{-1}(i)}, h_{j+1}^{r_{j,i}} \frac{v_{j-1, \pi_j^{-1}(i)}}{u_{j-1, \pi_j^{-1}(i)}^{x_j}} \right) \right\}_{i=1}^{N'}.
$$

Finally hand $(\mathtt{Prover}, (g, h_{j+1}, y_j, L_{j-1}, L_j), (x_j, \pi_j, \{r_{j,i}\}_{i=1}^{N'}))$ to $\mathcal{F}_{\mathrm{ZK}}^{R_{DS}}$, and hand $(\mathtt{Write}, (\mathtt{List}, L_j))$ to $\mathcal{F}_{\mathrm{BB}}$.

8. Sort $\{v_{k,i}\}_{i=1}^{N'}$ lexicographically to form a list L' and output $(\mathtt{Output}, L')$.

Lemma 2. *Protocol 1 securely realizes the ideal functionality $\mathcal{F}_{\mathrm{MN}}$ in the $(\mathcal{F}_{\mathrm{BB}}, \mathcal{F}_{\mathrm{KG}}, \mathcal{F}_{\mathrm{ZK}}^{R_C}, \mathcal{F}_{\mathrm{ZK}}^{R_{DS}})$-hybrid model with respect to $\mathcal{M}_{k/2}$-adversaries under the DDH-assumption in G_q.*

Each mix-server computes $3N$ exponentiations in G_q.

Lemma 2 reduces the problem of constructing a UC-secure mix-net to the problem of constructing UC-secure realizations of the ideal functionalities $\mathcal{F}_{\text{BB}}$, $\mathcal{F}_{\text{KG}}$, $\mathcal{F}_{\text{ZK}}^{R_C}$ and $\mathcal{F}_{\text{ZK}}^{R_{\text{DS}}}$. The lemma can also viewed as an argument of the security of mix-nets where the ideal functionalities $\mathcal{F}_{\text{ZK}}^{R_C}$ and $\mathcal{F}_{\text{ZK}}^{R_{\text{DS}}}$ are heuristically, but efficiently, realized, e.g. by zero-knowledge proofs of knowledge in the common random string model or the random oracle model (cf. [33,15,16,23]).

Pfitzmann [39,40] shows that the cryptotexts handed to a mix-net must be non-malleable [11] and a common way to ensure this is to use the cryptosystem suggested by Tsionis and Yung [45] and Schnorr and Jakobsson [44], or the Cramer-Shoup cryptosystem [9]. Both constructions are efficient and may be viewed as El Gamal augmented with a proof of knowledge, but only the latter is provably secure and both lack the extraction requirements of the UC-framework.

4   Secure Realizations of $\mathcal{F}_{\text{ZK}}^{R_C}$ and $\mathcal{F}_{\text{ZK}}^{R_{\text{DS}}}$

We securely realize the ideal functionalities $\mathcal{F}_{\text{ZK}}^{R_C}$ and $\mathcal{F}_{\text{ZK}}^{R_{\text{DS}}}$ in the $\mathcal{F}_{\text{BB}}$-hybrid model in a reasonably practical way as long as the number of mix-servers is relatively small. A key observation is that since we are considering $\mathcal{M}_{B(k)}$-adversaries, the prover may well disclose its secret witness to all subsets consisting of at least $B(k)$ verifiers as long as it does not disclose it to compute subset consisting of less than $B(k)$ verifiers.

4.1   A Realization of $\mathcal{F}_{\text{ZK}}^{R_C}$ in the $\mathcal{F}_{\text{BB}}$-Hybrid Model

We observe that we may view the verifiable secret sharing scheme (VSS) of Feldman [13] as a multi-verifier proof of knowledge of a logarithm, since his scheme only leaks information on the secret that is already known in our setting! Note that this protocol does *not* securely realize any natural ideal VSS functionality. The simulatability properties of the UC-framework are not satisfied.

Intuitively, the protocol works as follows. A prover shares his witness to the relation R_C, and uses a semantically secure cryptosystem over the authenticated bulletin board $\mathcal{F}_{\text{BB}}$ to distribute the shares. The verifiers check their shares, and write the result of their verification on the bulletin board. Each verifier then checks that all verifiers accepted their shares.

Protocol 2 (Zero-Knowledge Proof of Knowledge of Cleartext). Let $t = \lceil k/2 - 1 \rceil$. The zero-knowledge proof of knowledge of a cleartext protocol $\pi = (P_1, \dots, P_N, M_1, \dots, M_k)$ consists of provers P_i, and verifiers M_j.

PROVER P_i.

1. Wait until $(\cdot, M_j, \textsf{Keys}, y_{j,1}, \dots, y_{j,N})$ appears on $\mathcal{F}_{\text{BB}}$ for $j = 1, \dots, k$.
2. Wait for input $(\textsf{Prover}, (g, y, u_i, v_i), r_i)$, where $g, y, u_i, v_i \in G_q$ and $r_i \in \mathbb{Z}_q$.
3. Choose $a_{i,l} \in \mathbb{Z}_q$ randomly, define $p_i(x) = r + \sum_{l=1}^{t} a_{i,l} x^l$, and compute

$$\alpha_{i,l} = g^{a_{i,l}} \text{ for } l = 1, \dots, t, \quad s_{i,j} = p_i(j) \text{ for } j = 1, \dots, k \ , \quad \text{and}$$
$$C_{i,j} = E_{y_{j,i}}(s_{i,j}), \quad \text{for } j = 1, \dots, k \ .$$

4. Hand $(\texttt{Write}, \texttt{Proof}, (g, y, u_i, v_i), (\alpha_{i,1}, \dots, \alpha_{i,t}, C_{i,1}, \dots, C_{i,k}))$ to $\mathcal{F}_{\text{BB}}$.

VERIFIER M_j.

1. Generate El Gamal keys $(x_{j,i}, y_{j,i})$ for $i = 1, \dots, N$, and hand $(\texttt{Write}, \texttt{Keys}, y_{j,1}, \dots, y_{j,N})$ to $\mathcal{F}_{\text{BB}}$.
2. On input $(\texttt{Question}, P_i, (g, y, u_i, v_i))$ do:
   a) If $(\cdot, P_i, \texttt{Proof}, (g, y, u_i, v_i), (\alpha_{i,1}, \dots, \alpha_{i,t}, C_{i,1}, \dots, C_{i,k}))$ can not be found on $\mathcal{F}_{\text{BB}}$, then output $(\texttt{Verifier}, P_i, 0)$. Otherwise continue.
   b) Compute $s_{i,j} = D_{x_{j,i}}(C_{i,j})$, and verify that $g^{s_{i,j}} = u_i \prod_{l=1}^{t} \alpha_{i,l}^{j^l}$. If so set $b_{j,i} = 1$, otherwise $b_{j,i} = x_{j,i}$. Hand $(\texttt{Write}, \texttt{Judgement}, P_i, b_{j,i})$ to $\mathcal{F}_{\text{BB}}$.
   c) Wait until $(\cdot, M_l, \texttt{Judgement}, P_i, b_{l,i})$ appears on $\mathcal{F}_{\text{BB}}$ for $l = 1, \dots, k$.
   d) Do the following for $l = 1, \dots, k$:
      i. If $b_{l,i} = 1$, then set $b'_{l,i} = 1$.
      ii. If $b_{l,i} \neq 1$ then check if $y_{l,i} = g^{b_{l,i}}$. If not set $b'_{l,i} = 1$. If so compute $s_{i,l} = D_{b_{l,i}}(C_{i,l})$, and verify that $g^{s_{i,l}} = u_i \prod_{l=1}^{t} \alpha_{i,l}^{l^l}$. If so set $b'_{l,i} = 1$ and otherwise set $b'_{l,i} = 0$.
   e) If $\sum_{l=1}^{k} b'_{l,i} = k$ set $b = 1$ and otherwise 0. Then output $(\texttt{Verifier}, P_i, b)$.

Lemma 3. *Protocol 2 securely realizes the ideal functionality $\mathcal{F}_{\text{ZK}}^{R_C}$ in the $\mathcal{F}_{\text{BB}}$-hybrid model with respect to $\mathcal{M}_{k/2}$-adversaries under the DDH-assumption in G_q.*

Each prover computes $2k + t$ full exponentiations in G_q. Each verifier computes 2 full exponentiations in G_q for each prover.

The above protocol differs from the original protocol of Feldman [13] in that it does not require any interaction from the prover. To achieve this each verifier must generate an El Gamal key for each prover.

In order to use a single key for each mix-server we would need a cryptosystem secure against adaptive Chosen Ciphertext Attacks (CCA-attacks) in the sense of Rackoff and Simon [42]. Cramer and Shoup [9] show that their cryptosystem is CCA-secure under the DDH-assumption, so there exists such a cryptosystem. There are two drawbacks of this approach. Firstly, the complexity of the prover increases. Secondly, a verifier is no longer able to verify the correctness of a false complaint, since the complaining verifier is unable to reveal its private key (revealing the key reveals the witnesses of honest provers). It can be shown that this variant is only secure for $\mathcal{M}_{n/3}$-adversaries.

If there are very few corrupted provers a combination of the two methods is possible. For the provers a CCA-secure cryptosystem is used, but instead of revealing the key to complain, a verifier proves the correctness of its claim in zero-knowledge to the other verifiers, but using a protocol similar to the above.

A CCA-secure cryptosystem that has the property that a decryptor can show directly to a third party the contents of a cryptotext without revealing its key would also solve the problem. Such a cryptosystem can be constructed under strong assumptions (cf. [4]).

4.2   A Realization of $\mathcal{F}_{ZK}^{R_{DS}}$ in the $\mathcal{F}_{BB}$-Hybrid Model

Neff [33] and independently Furukawa and Sako [15] presents elegant ideas for proving the correctness of a shuffle, and Groth [23] recently refined the ideas of Neff [33], and gave a more rigorous analysis. Presently we are unable to transform any of these protocols into a UC-secure zero-knowledge proof without loosing the efficiency of the original protocol. The approach of Desmedt and Kurosawa [10] is better suited to the extraction requirements of the UC-framework, but their protocol allows malicious verifiers to make honest verifiers reject the "proof" of an honest prover. This means that their "proof" is not a realization of a proof of knowledge according to Functionality 4. They use global properties to avoid this difficulty, but in our modularized approach this is difficult. Furthermore, we need a proof of correctness of a decrypt shuffle instead of a re-encryption shuffle.

We construct a secure realization of $\mathcal{F}_{ZK}^{R_{DS}}$, using similar ideas as Desmedt and Kurosawa, that is practical if the number of verifiers is small, or if a strong majority of the mix-servers are honest. The following definition uses several different partitions of the verifiers such that there is one partition such that each block contains at least one honest verifier, and such that all partitions have the property that there is one block that contains no corrupt verifiers.

Definition 4 ((k,t)-set system). Let $S = \{M_1, \dots, M_k\}$ be a set. A (k,t)-set system is a family $F = \{T_1, \dots, T_d\}$ of $(t+1)$-partitions $T_i = \{W_{i,1}, \dots, W_{i,t+1}\}$ of S, such that $\forall A \subset S$, $|A| = t$, $\exists T \in F$ such that $\forall W \in T$ we have $W \not\subset A$.

If there exists a (t,k)-set system, there exists such a set system with a minimal value of d. It is not hard to see that d grows exponentially with k when t/k is constant. However, if $k = (t+1)(t+1)$ any partition T_1 such that $|W_{1,j}| = t+1$ suffices, and for some practical values of k and t the value of d is not terribly large, i.e. (k,t)-set system can be found by brute force search. For example if $k = 10$, $t = 4$ then $F = \{T_0, \dots, T_4\}$, where $T_i = \{\{j + i \mod 5, j + 5\}\}_{j=0}^{9}$, suffices and $d = 5$. More details on set systems can be found in [10].

Our protocol is based on a (k,t)-set system and works as follows. The prover constructs a chain $L = \overline{L}_0, \overline{L}_1, \dots, \overline{L}_{t+1} = L'$ of lists and a list $(\alpha_1, \dots, \alpha_{t+1})$ for each partition in the set system. The α_l:s are randomly chosen under the restriction $\prod_{l=1}^{t+1} \alpha_l = y$. The lists are randomly chosen under the restriction $((g, h \prod_{\iota=l+1}^{t+1} \alpha_\iota, \alpha_l, \overline{L}_{l-1}, \overline{L}_l), w_l) \in R_{DS}$ for $l = 1, \dots, t+1$. The witnesses w_l of the relations in a chain are encrypted with a semantically secure cryptosystem using the keys of the verifiers, and written on the bulletin board. The length of each chain is $t+1$, which ensures that t corrupted verifiers gets no information. The number of chains and how the links are revealed are determined by the (k,t)-set system in such a way that there is at least one chain in which all links are revealed to the set of honest verifiers. This ensures the immediate extraction required by the UC-framework.

Protocol 3 (Zero-Knowledge Proof of Correct Decrypt-Shuffle). The proof protocol $\pi = (P_1, \dots, P_k, M_1, \dots, M_k)$ consists of provers P_j, and verifiers

M_j. Let $t = B - 1$ and $F = \{T_1, \ldots, T_d\}$, where $T_i = \{W_{i,1}, \ldots, W_{i,t+1}\}$, be a (k, t)-set system known by all participants.

PROVER P_i.

1. Wait until $(\cdot, M_j, \textsf{Keys}, y_{j,1}, \ldots, y_{j,k})$ appears on $\mathcal{F}_{\text{BB}}$ for $j = 1, \ldots, k$.
2. Wait for input $(\textsf{Prover}, (g, h, y, L, L'), (x, \pi, L_R))$.
3. Do the following for $\gamma = 1, \ldots, d$:
   a) Set $\overline{L}_{\gamma,0} = L$, and $\overline{L}_{\gamma,t+1} = L'$.
   b) Choose $a_{\gamma,1}, \ldots, a_{\gamma,t+1} \in \mathbb{Z}_q$ randomly under the restriction that $x = \sum_{l=1}^{t+1} a_{\gamma,l}$, and define $\alpha_{\gamma,l} = g^{a_{\gamma,l}}$, and $\beta_{\gamma,\iota} = \prod_{l=\iota}^{t+1} \alpha_{\gamma,l}$.
   c) For $l = 1, \ldots, t$ choose a list $\overline{L}_{\gamma,l}$ randomly under the restriction that $((g, h\beta_{\gamma,l+1}, \alpha_{\gamma,l}, \overline{L}_{\gamma,l-1}, \overline{L}_{\gamma,l}), w_{\gamma,l}) \in R_{\text{DS}}$ for some witness $w_{\gamma,l}$.
   d) Let $w_{\gamma,t+1}$ be defined by $((g, h, \alpha_{\gamma,t+1}, \overline{L}_{\gamma,t}, \overline{L}_{\gamma,t+1}), w_{\gamma,t+1}) \in R_{\text{DS}}$.
   e) Compute $C_{\gamma,j} = E_{y_{j,i}}(w_{\gamma,l})$ where the relation between j and l is given by $j \in W_{\gamma,l}$, for $j = 1, \ldots, k$ and $l = 1, \ldots, t+1$.
4. Hand $(\textsf{Write}, \textsf{Proof}, \{\alpha_{\gamma,t+1}, \{\alpha_{\gamma,l}, \overline{L}_{\gamma,l}\}_{l=1}^{t}, \{C_{\gamma,j}\}_{j=1}^{k}\}_{\gamma=1}^{d})$ to $\mathcal{F}_{\text{BB}}$.

VERIFIER M_j.

1. Generate El Gamal keys $(x_{j,i}, y_{j,i})$ for $i = 1, \ldots, k$, and hand $(\textsf{Write}, \textsf{Keys}, y_{j,1}, \ldots, y_{j,k})$ to $\mathcal{F}_{\text{BB}}$.
2. On input $(\textsf{Question}, P_i, (g, h, y, L, L'))$ do:
   a) If $(\cdot, P_i, \textsf{Proof}, \{\alpha_{\gamma,t+1}, \{\alpha_{\gamma,l}, \overline{L}_{\gamma,l}\}_{l=1}^{t}, \{C_{\gamma,j'}\}_{j'=1}^{k}\}_{\gamma=1}^{d})$ can not be found on $\mathcal{F}_{\text{BB}}$ output $(\textsf{Verifier}, P_i, 0)$. Otherwise continue.
   b) Do the following for $\gamma = 1, \ldots, d$:
      i. Set $\overline{L}_{\gamma,0} = L$, and $\overline{L}_{\gamma,t+1} = L'$.
      ii. Compute $w_{\gamma,l} = D_{x_{j,i}}(C_{\gamma,j})$, where l is defined by $j \in W_{\gamma,l}$.
      iii. Verify that $y = \prod_{\iota=1}^{t+1} \alpha_{\gamma,\iota}$, and $((g, h\beta_{\gamma,l+1}, \alpha_{\gamma,l}, \overline{L}_{\gamma,l-1}, \overline{L}_{\gamma,l}), w_{\gamma,l}) \in R_{\text{DS}}$. If so, set $b_{j,\gamma} = 1$ and otherwise $b_{j,\gamma} = x_{j,i}$.
   c) Hand $(\textsf{Write}, \textsf{Judgement}, P_i, \{b_{j,\gamma}\}_{\gamma=1}^{d})$ to $\mathcal{F}_{\text{BB}}$
   d) Wait until $(\cdot, M_{j'}, \textsf{Judgement}, P_i, \{b_{j',\gamma}\}_{\gamma=1}^{d})$ appears on $\mathcal{F}_{\text{BB}}$ for $j' \neq j$.
   e) Do the following for $\gamma = 1, \ldots, d$ and $j' = 1, \ldots, k$:
      i. If $b_{j',\gamma} = 1$, set $b'_{j',\gamma} = 1$.
      ii. If $b_{j',\gamma} \neq 1$, check if $b_{j',\gamma}$ is the private key corresponding to $y_{j',i}$. If not set $b'_{j',\gamma} = 1$. If so, compute $w_{\gamma,l} = D_{b_{j',\gamma}}(C_{\gamma,j})$, where l is defined by $j' \in W_{\gamma,l}$, and check if $((g, h\beta_{\gamma,l+1}, \alpha_{\gamma,l}, \overline{L}_{\gamma,l-1}, \overline{L}_{\gamma,l}), w_{\gamma,l}) \in R_{\text{DS}}$ and $y = \prod_{\iota=1}^{t+1} \alpha_{\gamma,\iota}$. If so set $b'_{j',\gamma} = 1$, and otherwise set $b'_{j',\gamma} = 0$.
   f) If $\sum_{j'=1}^{k} \sum_{\gamma=1}^{d} b'_{j',\gamma} = kd$ then set $b = 1$ and otherwise $b = 0$. Then output $(\textsf{Verifier}, P_i, b)$.

Lemma 4. *Let $B \leq k/2$. Protocol 3 securely realizes the ideal functionality $\mathcal{F}_{\text{ZK}}^{R_{\text{DS}}}$ in the $\mathcal{F}_{\text{BB}}$-hybrid model with respect to $\mathcal{M}_B$-adversaries under the DDH-assumption in G_q.*

Each prover computes $O(5dtN)$ exponentiations in G_q, and each verifier computes $O(4dN)$ exponentiations in G_q for each prover.

In both Protocol 2 and 3 the El Gamal cryptosystem could be replaced by any semantically secure cryptosystem, under potentially stronger assumptions. Alternatively the ideal functionality for secure single message transmission could be used since each key is only used once, but that would require that the ideal functionality is altered to allow a receiver to "publish its private key".

The value of d, and the complexity of the protocol grows exponentially with the number of mix-servers if t/k is constant, but when the number of mix-servers is small, e.g. $k = 14$ and $t = 6$, or if there is a strong majority of honest mix-servers, e.g. $t = \sqrt{k}$, our scheme is practical.

5   Combining the Results

At this point combining the results to show that we have securely realized a universally composable mix-net is easy.

Theorem 1. *Let π be the composition of Protocol 1, with Protocol 2 and Protocol 3. Then π securely realizes $\mathcal{F}_{\mathrm{MN}}$ in the $(\mathcal{F}_{\mathrm{BB}}, \mathcal{F}_{\mathrm{KG}})$-hybrid model with respect to $\mathcal{M}_{k/2}$-adversaries under the DDH-assumption in G_q.*

Corollary 1. *The composition of π and π_{BB} securely realizes $\mathcal{F}_{\mathrm{MN}}$ in the $\mathcal{F}_{\mathrm{KG}}$-hybrid model with respect to blocking $\mathcal{M}_{k/2}$-adversaries under the DDH-assumption in G_q.*

Our mix-net is not "universally verifiable", i.e. an individual outsider can not verify the correctness of an execution. On the other hand nothing prevents the mix-servers to prove the correctness of a decrypt-shuffle to any set of outside verifiers such that the majority are honest. Furthermore, in some scenarios the assumption on the maximum number of corrupted mix-servers is well founded.

We require an ideal distributed key generation functionality. The natural next step is to try to find a protocol that securely realizes this functionality under various reasonable assumptions. Another interesting line of research is to find more efficient secure realizations of $\mathcal{F}_{\mathrm{ZK}}^{R_C}$ and $\mathcal{F}_{\mathrm{ZK}}^{R_{\mathrm{DS}}}$ in various models. Scenarios where the number of mix-servers is large should also be considered.

Acknowledgments. I am grateful to Johan Håstad for his advice and support. I had discussions with Gunnar Sjödin. My discussions with Rafael Pass encouraged me to do this work. Andy Neff and Jun Furukawa kindly answered all my questions about their respective constructions. I also thank the anonymous referees for their advise.

References

1. M. Abe, *Universally Verifiable mix-net with Verification Work Independent of the Number of Mix-centers*, Eurocrypt '98, pp. 437–447, LNCS 1403, 1998.

2. M. Abe, *Flaws in Some Robust Optimistic Mix-Nets*, In Proceedings of Information Security and Privacy, 8th Australasian Conference, LNCS 2727, pp. 39–50, 2003.
3. D. Beaver, *Foundations of secure interactive computation*, Crypto '91, LNCS 576, pp. 377–391, 1991.
4. R. Canetti, *Towards realizing random oracles: Hash functions that hide all partial information*, Crypto '97, LNCS 1294, pp. 455–469, 1997.
5. R. Canetti, *Security and composition of multi-party cryptographic protocols*, Journal of Cryptology, Vol. 13, No. 1, winter 2000.
6. R. Canetti, *Universally Composable Security: A New Paradigm for Cryptographic Protocols*, http://eprint.iacr.org/2000/067 and ECCC TR 01–24. Extended abstract appears in 42nd FOCS, IEEE Computer Society, 2001.
7. D. Chaum, *Untraceable Electronic Mail, Return Addresses and Digital Pseudonyms*, Communications of the ACM - CACM '81, Vol. 24, No. 2, pp. 8-4-88, 1981.
8. R. Canetti, Y. Lindell, R. Ostrovsky, A. Sahai, *Universally Composable Two-Party and Multi-Party Secure Computation*, 34th STOC, pp. 494–503, 2002.
9. R. Cramer, V. Shoup, *A Practical Public Key Cryptosystem Provably Secure against Adaptive Chosen Ciphertext Attack*, Crypto '98, pp. 13–25, LNCS 1462, 1998.
10. Y. Desmedt, K. Kurosawa, *How to break a practical MIX and design a new one*, Eurocrypt 2000, pp. 557-572, LNCS 1807, 2000.
11. D. Dolev, C. Dwork, M. Naor, *Non-Malleable Cryptography*, 23rd STOC, pp. 542–552, 1991.
12. T. El Gamal, *A Public Key Cryptosystem and a Signature Scheme Based on Discrete Logarithms*, IEEE Transactions on Information Theory, Vol. 31, No. 4, pp. 469–472, 1985.
13. P. Feldman, *A practical scheme for non-interactive verifiable secret sharing*, In Proceedings of the 28th FOCS, pages 427–438, 1987.
14. A. Fujioka, T. Okamoto and K. Ohta, *A practical secret voting scheme for large scale elections*, Auscrypt '92, LNCS 718, pp. 244–251, 1992.
15. J. Furukawa, K. Sako, *An efficient scheme for proving a shuffle*, Crypto 2001, LNCS 2139, pp. 368–387, 2001.
16. J. Furukawa, H. Miyauchi, K. Mori, S. Obana, K. Sako, *An implementation of a universally verifiable electronic voting scheme based on shuffling*, Financial Cryptography '02, 2002.
17. R. Gennaro, S. Jarecki, H. Krawczyk, T. Rabin, *Secure Distributed Key Generation for Discrete-Log Based Cryptosystems*, Eurocrypt '99, LNCS 1592, pp. 295–310, 1999.
18. O. Goldreich, S. Micali, and A. Wigderson, *How to Play Any Mental Game*, 19th STOC, pp. 218–229, 1987.
19. S. Goldwasser, L. Levin, *Fair computation of general functions in presence of immoral majority*, Crypto '90, LNCS 537, pp. 77–93, 1990.
20. S. Goldwasser, Y. Lindell, *Secure Multi-Party Computation Without Agreement*, In Proceedings of the 16th DISC, LNCS 2508, pp. 17–32, 2002.
21. S. Goldwasser, S. Micali, *Probabilistic Encryption*, Journal of Computer and System Sciences (JCSS), Vol. 28, No. 2, pp. 270–299, 1984.
22. P. Golle, S. Zhong, D. Boneh, M. Jakobsson, A. Juels, *Optimistic Mixing for Exit-Polls*, Asiacrypt 2002, LNCS, 2002.
23. N. Groth, *A Verifiable Secret Shuffle of Homomorphic Encryptions*, PKC 2003, pp. 145–160, LNCS 2567, 2003.
24. M. Jakobsson, *A Practical Mix*, Eurocrypt '98, LNCS 1403, pp. 448–461, 1998.

25. M. Jakobsson, *Flash Mixing*, In Proceedings of the 18th ACM Symposium on Principles of Distributed Computing - PODC '98, pp. 83–89, 1998.

26. M. Jakobsson, A. Juels, *Millimix: Mixing in small batches*, DIMACS Techical report 99-33, June 1999.

27. M. Jakobsson, A. Juels, *An optimally robust hybrid mix network*, In Proceedings of the 20th ACM Symposium on Principles of Distributed Computing - PODC '01, pp. 284–292, 2001.

28. Y. Lindell, A. Lysyanskaya, T. Rabin, *On the Composition of Authenticated Byzantine Agreement*, 34th STOC, pp. 514–523, 2002.

29. S. Micali, C. Rackoff, B. Sloan, *The notion of security for probabilistic cryptosystems*, SIAM Journal of Computing, Vol. 17, No. 2, pp. 412–426, 1988.

30. S. Micali, P. Rogaway, *Secure Computation*, Crypto '91, LNCS 576, pp. 392–404, 1991.

31. M. Michels, P. Horster, *Some remarks on a reciept-free and universally verifiable Mix-type voting scheme*, Asiacrypt '96, pp. 125–132, LNCS 1163, 1996.

32. M. Mitomo, K. Kurosawa, *Attack for Flash MIX*, Asiacrypt 2000, pp. 192–204, LNCS 1976, 2000.

33. A. Neff, *A verifiable secret shuffle and its application to E-Voting*, In Proceedings of the 8th ACM Conference on Computer and Communications Security - CCS 2001, pp. 116–125, 2001.

34. A. Neff, *Personal communication*, 2003.

35. V. Niemi, A. Renvall, *How to prevent buying of votes in computer elections*, Asiacrypt'94, LNCS 917, pp. 164–170, 1994.

36. W. Ogata, K. Kurosawa, K. Sako, K. Takatani, *Fault Tolerant Anonymous Channel*, Information and Communications Security - ICICS '97, pp. 440–444, LNCS 1334, 1997.

37. C. Park, K. Itoh, K. Kurosawa, *Efficient Anonymous Channel and All/Nothing Election Scheme*, Eurocrypt '93, LNCS 765, pp. 248–259, 1994.

38. T. Pedersen, *A threshold cryptosystem without a trusted party*, Eurocrypt '91, LNCS 547, pp. 522–526, 1991.

39. B. Pfitzmann, *Breaking an Efficient Anonymous Channel*, Eurocrypt '94, LNCS 950, pp. 332–340, 1995.

40. B. Pfitzmann, A. Pfitzmann, *How to break the direct RSA-implementation of mixes*, Eurocrypt '89, LNCS 434, pp. 373–381, 1990.

41. B. Pfitzmann, M. Waidner, *Composition and Integrity Preservation of Secure Reactive Systems*, 7th Conference on Computer and Communications Security of the ACM, pp. 245–254, 2000.

42. C. Rackoff, D. Simon, *Noninteractive zero-knowledge proofs of knowledge and chosen ciphertext attacks*, 22nd STOC, pp. 433–444, 1991.

43. K. Sako, J. Killian, *Reciept-free Mix-Type Voting Scheme*, Eurocrypt '95, LNCS 921, pp. 393–403, 1995.

44. C. Schnorr, M. Jakobsson, *Security of Signed El Gamal Encryption*, Asiacrypt 2000, LNCS 1976, pp. 73–89, 2000.

45. Y. Tsiounis, M. Yung, *On the Security of El Gamal based Encryption*, International workshop on Public Key Cryptography, LNCS 1431, pp. 117–134, 1998.

46. D. Wikström, *Five Practical Attacks for "Optimistic Mixing for Exit-Polls"*, to appear in proceedings of Selected Areas of Cryptography (SAC), LNCS, 2003.

47. D. Wikström, *A Universally Composable Mix-Net*, manuscript will be available at http://eprint.iacr.org/.

A   Proofs

Because of space restrictions we are unable to present proofs of all claims in this conference version. We present shortened proofs of Lemma 2 and Lemma 4. Proofs of all claims are given in the full version of this paper [47].

Proof (Lemma 2). We describe an ideal adversary $\mathcal{S}(\cdot)$ that runs any hybrid adversary $\mathcal{A}' = \mathcal{A}^{(\mathcal{S}_{BB}, \mathcal{S}_{KG}, \mathcal{S}_{ZK}^{R_C}, \mathcal{S}_{ZK}^{R_{DS}})}$ as a black-box. Then we show that if $\mathcal{S}$ does not imply that the protocol is secure, then we can break the DDH-assumption.

THE IDEAL ADVERSARY $\mathcal{S}$. Let I_P and I_M be the set of indices of participants corrupted by $\mathcal{A}$ of the sender type and the mix-server type respectively. The ideal adversary $\mathcal{S}$ corrupts the dummy participants $\tilde{P}_i$ for which $i \in I_P$, and the dummy participants $\tilde{M}_i$ for which $i \in I_M$. The ideal adversary is best described by starting with a copy of the original hybrid ITM-graph

$$(V, E) = \mathcal{Z}'(\mathcal{H}(\mathcal{A}', \pi^{(\tilde{\pi}_1^{\mathcal{F}_{BB}}, \tilde{\pi}_2^{\mathcal{F}_{KG}}, \tilde{\pi}_3^{\mathcal{F}_{ZK}^{R_C}}, \tilde{\pi}_4^{\mathcal{F}_{ZK}^{R_{DS}}})}))), \text{ where } \mathcal{Z} \text{ is replaced by a machine}$$
$\mathcal{Z}'$.

The adversary $\mathcal{S}$ simulates all machines in V except those in $\mathcal{A}'$, and the corrupted machines P_i for $i \in I_P$ and M_i for $i \in I_M$ under $\mathcal{A}'$:s control. We now describe how each machine is simulated.

$\mathcal{S}$ simulates the machines P_i, $i \notin I_P$, and the ideal functionalities $\mathcal{F}_{BB}$, $\mathcal{F}_{ZK}^{R_C}$ and $\mathcal{F}_{KG}$ honestly. All M_j for $j \notin I_M$ are also simulated honestly, except for M_l, where l is chosen as the maximal index not in I_M, i.e. the last honest mix-server. The machine M_l plays a special role.

Simulation of Links $(\mathcal{Z}, \mathcal{A})$, $(\mathcal{Z}, P_i)$ for $i \in I_P$, and $(\mathcal{Z}, M_j)$ for $j \in I_M$. $\mathcal{S}$ simulates $\mathcal{Z}'$, $\tilde{P}_i$, for $i \in I_P$, and $\tilde{M}_j$ for $j \in I_M$, such that it appears as if $\mathcal{Z}$ and $\mathcal{A}$, $\mathcal{Z}$ and P_i for $i \in I_P$, and $\mathcal{Z}$ and M_j for $j \in I_M$ are linked directly. For details on this see [47].

Extraction from Corrupt Mix-Servers and Simulation of Honest Mix-Servers. When a corrupt mix-server M_j, for $j \in I_M$, writes Run on $\mathcal{F}_{BB}$, $\mathcal{S}$ must make sure that $\tilde{M}_j$ sends (Run) to $\mathcal{F}_{MN}$. Otherwise it may not be possible to deliver an output to honest mix-servers. If an honest dummy mix-server $\tilde{M}_j$, for $j \notin I_M$, receives (Run) from $\mathcal{Z}$, $\mathcal{S}$ must make sure that M_j receives (Run) from $\mathcal{Z}'$. If an honest mix-server M_j, for $j \notin I_M$, outputs (Output, L'), $\mathcal{S}$ must make sure that $\tilde{M}_j$ does the same. This is done as follows.

1. Let $j \in I_M$. If $(\cdot, M_j, \text{Run})$ appears on $\mathcal{F}_{BB}$ $\tilde{M}_j$ hands (Run) to $\mathcal{F}_{MN}$. When $\mathcal{S}$ receives $(\mathcal{S}, \tilde{M}_j, \text{Run})$ or $((\mathcal{S}, \tilde{M}_j, \text{Output}, L'), \{(\tilde{M}_l, \tau_l)\}_{l=1}^k)$ from $\mathcal{C}_{\mathcal{I}}$ the simulation of $\mathcal{F}_{BB}$ is continued.
2. Let $j \notin I_M$. If $\mathcal{S}$ receives $(\mathcal{S}, \tilde{M}_j, \text{Run})$ or $((\mathcal{S}, M_j, \text{Output}, L'), \{(M_l, \tau_l)\}_{l=1}^k)$ from $\mathcal{F}_{MN}$, $\mathcal{Z}'$ hands (Run) to M_j.
3. Let $j \notin I_M$. If $\mathcal{Z}'$ receives (Output, L') from M_j, $\mathcal{S}$ instructs $\mathcal{C}_{\mathcal{I}}$ to deliver (Output, L') to $\tilde{M}_j$.

Extraction from Corrupt Senders and Simulation of Honest Senders. If a corrupt sender P_i, for $i \in I_P$, in the hybrid protocol produces a cryptotext and informs

$\mathcal{F}_{\text{ZK}}^{R_C}$ such that its input is deemed valid, then $\mathcal{S}$ must make sure that this message is extracted and given as input to $\mathcal{F}_{\text{MN}}$ by $\tilde{P}_i$.

When an honest dummy sender $\tilde{P}_i$, for $i \notin I_P$, receives a message m_i from $\mathcal{Z}$, $\mathcal{S}$ must ensure that P_i receives some message m_i' from $\mathcal{Z}'$. But $\mathcal{S}$ can not see m_i, and must therefore hand some other message $m_i' \neq m_i$ to P_i, and then later fix this flaw in the simulation before $\mathcal{A}'$ or $\mathcal{Z}$ notice it. This is done as follows.

1. Let $i \in I_P$. Until $\mathcal{S}$ receives $((\mathcal{S}, M_j, \texttt{Output}, L'), \{(M_l, \tau_l)\}_{l=1}^k)$ from $\mathcal{C}_\mathcal{I}$.
   a) If $\mathcal{F}_{\text{ZK}}^{R_C}$ receives $(P_i, \texttt{Prover}, (g, y, u_i, v_i), r_i)$ such that $((g, y, u_i, v_i), r_i) \in R_{\text{DS}}$, then consult the storage of $\mathcal{F}_{\text{BB}}$ and look for a pair $(c, P_i, (u_i, v_i))$.
   b) If $\mathcal{F}_{\text{BB}}$ receives $(P_i, \texttt{Write}, (u_i, v_i))$ then look if $\mathcal{F}_{\text{ZK}}^{R_C}$ stored r_i under $(P_i, (g, y, u_i, v_i))$ such that $((g, y, u_i, v_i), r_i) \in R_{\text{DS}}$.
   If such a pair $[(c, P_i, (u_i, v_i)), (P_i, (g, y, u_i, v_i), r_i)]$ is found then $\tilde{P}_i$ sends $m_i = v_i y^{-r_i}$ to $\mathcal{F}_{\text{MN}}$ and ignores further such pairs. When $\mathcal{F}_{\text{MN}}$ writes $(\tilde{P}_i, \texttt{Send})$ to $\mathcal{S}$, the simulation, of $\mathcal{F}_{\text{ZK}}^{R_C}$ or $\mathcal{F}_{\text{BB}}$ respectively, is continued.
2. Let $i \notin I_P$. When $\mathcal{S}$ receives $(\tilde{P}_i, \texttt{Send})$ from $\mathcal{F}_{\text{MN}}$, then $\mathcal{Z}'$ sends a randomly chosen message $m_i' \in G_q$ to P_i.

How M_l and $\mathcal{F}_{\text{ZK}}^{R_{\text{DS}}}$ fix the flaw in the simulation. $\mathcal{S}$ must make sure that the faulty messages $m_i' \neq m_i$ introduced during simulation of honest senders, because it does not know the real messages m_i of the honest dummy participants $\tilde{P}_i$ for $i \in i_P$, are not noticed. This is done by modifying M_l and $\mathcal{F}_{\text{ZK}}^{R_{\text{DS}}}$ as follows.

1. If $\mathcal{F}_{\text{ZK}}^{R_{\text{DS}}}$ receives a tuple $(M_j, \texttt{Question}, M_l, (g, h_{l+1}, y_l, L_{l-1}, L_l))$ it verifies that a tuple on the form $(M_l, \texttt{Prover}, (g, h_{l+1}, y_l, L_{l-1}, L_l), \cdot)$ has been received. If so it sets $b = 1$ and otherwise $b = 0$. Finally it hands to $\mathcal{C}_\mathcal{I}$ $((\mathcal{S}, M_j, \texttt{Verifier}, M_l, (g, h_{l+1}, y_l, L_{l-1}, L_l), b), (M_j, \texttt{Verifier}, M_l, b))$.
2. M_l does the following instead of Step 7b in the protocol. Let $L' = \{m_i\}_{i=1}^{N'}$, and note that by construction $\mathcal{S}$ has received $((\mathcal{S}, M_j, \texttt{Output}, L'), \dots)$, i.e. it knows L'. M_l chooses $r_{l,i} \in \mathbb{Z}_q$, and $\pi_l \in \Sigma_N$ randomly, and computes the list $L_l = \{(u_{l,i}, v_{l,i})\}_{i=1}^{N'} = \{(g^{r_{l,i}}, h_{l+1}^{r_{l,i}} m_{\pi_l^{-1}(i)})\}_{i=1}^{N'}$. Finally it hands $(\texttt{Prover}, (g, h_{l+1}, y_l, L_{l-1}, L_l), \cdot)$ to $\mathcal{F}_{\text{ZK}}^{R_{\text{DS}}}$, and $(\texttt{Write}, (\texttt{List}, L_l))$ to $\mathcal{F}_{\text{BB}}$.

The first step ensures that $\mathcal{F}_{\text{ZK}}^{R_{\text{DS}}}$ plays along with M_l and pretends to other M_j that M_l did prove his knowledge properly. The second step ensures that M_l fixes the flaw in the simulation introduced by $\mathcal{S}$ at the point when it did not know the messages sent by honest dummy participants $\tilde{P}_i$, for $i \notin I_P$.

This concludes the definition of the ideal adversary $\mathcal{S}$.

REACHING A CONTRADICTION. Next we show, using a hybrid argument, that if the ideal adversary $\mathcal{S}$ defined above does not imply the security of Protocol 1, then we can break the DDH-assumption.

Suppose that $\mathcal{S}$ does not imply the security of the protocol. Then there exists a hybrid adversary $\mathcal{A}' = \mathcal{A}^{(\mathcal{S}_{\text{BB}}, \mathcal{S}_{\text{KG}}, \mathcal{S}_{\text{ZK}}^{R_C}, \mathcal{S}_{\text{ZK}}^{R_{\text{DS}}})}$, an environment $\mathcal{Z}$ with auxiliary input $z = \{z_n\}$, a constant $c > 0$ and an infinite index set $\mathcal{N} \subset \mathbb{N}$ such that for

$n \in \mathcal{N}: |\Pr[\mathcal{Z}_z(\mathcal{I}(\mathcal{S}, \tilde{\pi}^{\mathcal{F}_{\mathrm{MN}}})) = 1] - \Pr[\mathcal{Z}_z(\mathcal{H}(\mathcal{A}', \pi^{(\tilde{\pi}_1^{\mathcal{F}_{\mathrm{BB}}}, \tilde{\pi}_2^{\mathcal{F}_{\mathrm{KG}}}, \tilde{\pi}_3^{\mathcal{F}_{\mathrm{ZK}}^{R_C}}, \tilde{\pi}_4^{\mathcal{F}_{\mathrm{ZK}}^{R_{\mathrm{DS}}}})})) =$
$1]| \geq \frac{1}{n^c}$, where $\mathcal{S}$ runs $\mathcal{A}'$ as a black-box as described above, i.e. $\mathcal{S} = \mathcal{S}(\mathcal{A}')$.

Defining the Hybrids. Without loss we assume that $\{1, \ldots, N\} \setminus I_P = \{1, \ldots, \eta\}$, and define an array of hybrid machines $T_0, \ldots, T_\eta$. Set $T_0 = \mathcal{Z}_z(\mathcal{I}(\mathcal{S}(\mathcal{A}'), \tilde{\pi}^{\mathcal{F}_{\mathrm{MN}}}))$, and then define T_s by the following modification to T_0.

1. When $\mathcal{S}$ receives $(\tilde{P}_i, \mathsf{Send})$ from $\mathcal{F}_{\mathrm{MN}}$, for $i \notin I_P$, it checks if $i \in \{1, \ldots, s\}$. If so it consults the storage of $\mathcal{F}_{\mathrm{MN}}$ to find the message m_i sent by $\tilde{P}_i$. Then $\mathcal{Z}'$ sends m_i to P_i. Otherwise $\mathcal{Z}'$ sends a random message $m_i' \in \mathbb{Z}_q$ to P_i.

By inspection of the constructions we see that the output of T_η is identically distributed to the output of $\mathcal{Z}_z(\mathcal{H}(\mathcal{A}', \pi^{(\tilde{\pi}_1^{\mathcal{F}_{\mathrm{BB}}}, \tilde{\pi}_2^{\mathcal{F}_{\mathrm{KG}}}, \tilde{\pi}_3^{\mathcal{F}_{\mathrm{ZK}}^{R_C}}, \tilde{\pi}_4^{\mathcal{F}_{\mathrm{ZK}}^{R_{\mathrm{DS}}}})}))$ since the only essential difference is that M_l does not hand knowledge of his transformation to $\mathcal{F}_{\mathrm{ZK}}^{R_{\mathrm{DS}}}$, but $\mathcal{F}_{\mathrm{ZK}}^{R_{\mathrm{DS}}}$ ignores M_l's inability so this is not discovered by $\mathcal{A}$ or $\mathcal{Z}$.

If we set $p_s = \Pr[T_s = 1]$, we have $\frac{1}{n^c} \leq |p_0 - p_\eta| \leq \sum_{i=1}^{\eta} |p_{s-1} - p_s|$, which implies that there exists some fixed $0 < s \leq \eta$ such that $|p_{s-1} - p_s| \geq \frac{1}{\eta n^c} \geq \frac{1}{N n^c}$.

Defining a Distinguisher. We are now finally ready to define a distinguisher D.

D is confronted with the following test. An oracle first chooses $\alpha, \beta, \gamma \in \mathbb{Z}_q$ and a bit $b \in \{0, 1\}$ randomly and defines $(y_l', u, v) = (g^\alpha, g^\beta, g^{b\alpha\beta + (1-b)\gamma})$. Then D is given (y_l', u, v) and the task is to guess b. D does the following. It replaces y_l in M_l:s key generation by y_l'. This does not change the distribution of this key and thus does not change any of the hybrids. Since M_l appears to behave honestly (with the help of $\mathcal{F}_{\mathrm{ZK}}^{R_{\mathrm{DS}}}$), the fact that M_l does not know $\alpha = \log_g y_l'$ is never revealed, and since less than $k/2$ mix-servers are corrupted α need never be recovered. D then simulates T_s until P_s receives the message (Send, m_s), at which point it forms $(u', v') = (u, u^{\sum_{j \neq l} x_j} v m_s)$. Then P_s is modified to hand $(\mathsf{Write}, (u', v'))$ to $\mathcal{F}_{\mathrm{BB}}$, and $(\mathsf{Prover}, (g, y, u', v'), 1)$ to $\mathcal{F}_{\mathrm{ZK}}^{R_C}$. Furthermore, $\mathcal{F}_{\mathrm{ZK}}^{R_C}$ is modified to a handle this message as if $((g, y, u', v'), 1) \in R_C$, i.e. it will essentially lie on P_i's behalf. D then continues the simulation of T_s until it outputs a bit b', which is then output by D.

If (y_l', u, v) is a Diffie-Hellman triple, then (u', v') is a valid encryption of m_s and the output of D is identically distributed to the output of T_s. If on the other hand (y_l', u, v) is a random triple, then (u', v') corresponds to an encryption of a random message m_s', i.e. the output of D is identically distributed to T_{s-1}. We conclude that $|\Pr[D(g^\alpha, g^\beta, g^\gamma) = 1] - \Pr[D(g^\alpha, g^\beta, g^{\alpha\beta}) = 1]| = |p_{s-1} - p_s| \geq \frac{1}{N n^c}$, which contradicts the DDH-Assumption, and the theorem is true.

Proof (Lemma 4). We describe an ideal adversary $\mathcal{S}(\cdot)$ that runs any hybrid adversary $\mathcal{A}' = \mathcal{A}^{(\mathcal{S}_{\mathrm{BB}}, \mathcal{S}_{\mathrm{KG}})}$ as a black-box. Then we show that if $\mathcal{S}$ does not imply that the protocol is secure, then we can break the DDH-assumption.

THE IDEAL ADVERSARY $\mathcal{S}$. Let I_P and I_M be the set of indices of participants corrupted by $\mathcal{A}$ of the sender type and the mix-server type respectively. The ideal adversary $\mathcal{S}$ corrupts the dummy participants $\tilde{P}_i$ for which $i \in I_P$, and the dummy participants $\tilde{M}_j$ for which $j \in I_M$. The ideal adversary is best described by starting with a copy of the original hybrid ITM-graph $(V, E) =$

$\mathcal{Z}'(\mathcal{H}(\mathcal{A}', \pi^{\tilde{\pi}^{\mathcal{F}_{BB}}}))$, where we have replaced $\mathcal{Z}$ by a machine $\mathcal{Z}'$. The adversary $\mathcal{S}$ simulates all machines in V except for those in $\mathcal{A}'$, and the corrupted machines P_i for $i \in I_P$ and M_i for $i \in I_M$ under $\mathcal{A}'$:s control. $\mathcal{S}$ simulates $\mathcal{F}_{BB}$ honestly.

Simulation of Links $(\mathcal{Z}, \mathcal{A})$, $(\mathcal{Z}, P_i)$ *for* $i \in I_P$, *and* $(\mathcal{Z}, M_j)$ *for* $j \in I_M$. $\mathcal{S}$ simulates $\mathcal{Z}'$, $\tilde{P}_i$, for $i \in I_P$, and $\tilde{M}_j$ for $j \in I_M$, such that it appears as if $\mathcal{Z}$ and $\mathcal{A}$, $\mathcal{Z}$ and P_i for $i \in I_P$, and $\mathcal{Z}$ and M_j for $j \in I_M$ are linked directly. For details on this see [47].

Simulation of Honest Verifiers. When an honest verifier $\tilde{M}_j$, for $j \notin I_M$, receives $(\texttt{Question}, P_i, (g, h, y, L, L'))$ from $\mathcal{F}_{ZK}^{R_{DS}}$, $\mathcal{S}$ must ensure that the simulated honest verifier M_j receives $(\texttt{Question}, P_i, (g, h, y, L, L'))$ from $\mathcal{Z}'$. When the simulated honest verifier M_j hands $(\texttt{Verifier}, P_i, b)$ to $\mathcal{Z}'$, $\mathcal{S}$ must ensure that $(\texttt{Verifier}, P_i, b)$ is delivered to $\tilde{M}_j$. This is done as follows.

1. Let $j \notin I_M$. If $\mathcal{S}$ receives $((\mathcal{S}, \tilde{M}_j, \texttt{Verifier}, \tilde{P}_i, (g, h, y, L, L'), b), (\tilde{M}_j, \tau_j))$ from $\mathcal{C}_\mathcal{I}$, $\mathcal{Z}'$ hands $(\texttt{Question}, P_i, (g, h, y, L, L'))$ to M_j.
2. Let $j \notin I_M$. If $\mathcal{Z}'$ receives $(\texttt{Verifier}, P_i, b)$ from M_j, $\mathcal{S}$ hands $(1, \tau_j)$ to $\mathcal{C}_\mathcal{I}$, i.e. $\mathcal{S}$ instructs $\mathcal{C}_\mathcal{I}$ to deliver $(\texttt{Verifier}, \tilde{P}_i, b)$ to $\tilde{M}_j$.

Simulation of Honest Provers. If an honest dummy prover $\tilde{P}_i$, for $i \notin I_P$, receives a message $(\texttt{Prover}, (g, h, y, L, L'), w)$ from $\mathcal{Z}$, $\mathcal{S}$ must ensure that P_i constructs a simulated proof deemed valid by the verifiers M_j despite that $\mathcal{S}$ does not know w. To be able to do this $\mathcal{S}$ must ensure that the honest mix-servers M_j, for $j \notin I_M$, do not complain. This is done as follows.

1. Let $j \notin I_M$. M_j follows its program except that if $i \notin I_P$ it always sets $b_{j,\gamma} = 1$ in Step 2(b)iii (i.e. it never decrypts anything encrypted with $y_{j,i}$).
2. Suppose that $\mathcal{S}$ receives $(\mathcal{S}, \tilde{P}_i, \texttt{Prover}, (g, h, y, L, L'), 1)$ from $\mathcal{C}_\mathcal{I}$ for $i \notin I_P$. By construction there exists for each γ some partition $W_{\gamma, \zeta_\gamma} \cap I_M = \emptyset$. $\mathcal{S}$ hands $(\texttt{Prover}, (g, h, y, L, L'), \cdot)$ to P_i, where Step 3 in the program of P_i is replaced by the following. For $\gamma = 1, \ldots, d$:
   a) Set $\overline{L}_{\gamma, 0} = L$, and $\overline{L}_{\gamma, t+1} = L'$.
   b) Choose $a_{\gamma, l} \in \mathbb{Z}_q$, for $l \neq \zeta_\gamma$, randomly and define $\alpha_{\gamma, l} = g^{a_{\gamma, l}}$ for $l \neq \zeta_\gamma$, $\alpha_{\gamma, \zeta_\gamma} = y(\prod_{l \neq \zeta_\gamma} \alpha_{\gamma, l})^{-1}$, and $\beta_{\gamma, \iota} = \prod_{l=\iota}^{t+1} \alpha_{\gamma, l}$.
   c) For $l = 1, \ldots, \zeta_\gamma - 1$ choose a list $\overline{L}_{\gamma, l}$ randomly under the restriction that $((g, h\beta_{\gamma, l+1}, \alpha_{\gamma, l}, \overline{L}_{\gamma, l-1}, \overline{L}_{\gamma, l}), w_{\gamma, l}) \in R_{DS}$ for some witness $w_{\gamma, l}$. For $l = t, \ldots, \zeta_\gamma$ choose a list $\overline{L}_{\gamma, l}$ randomly under the restriction that $((g, h\beta_{\gamma, l+2}, \alpha_{\gamma, l+1}, \overline{L}_{\gamma, l}, \overline{L}_{\gamma, l+1}), w_{\gamma, l+1}) \in R_{DS}$ for some witness $w_{\gamma, l+1}$.
   d) Define $w_{\gamma, \zeta_\gamma} = (1, 1, \ldots, 1)$.
   e) Compute $C_{\gamma, j} = E_{y_{j,i}}(w_{\gamma, l})$ where the relation between j and l is given by $j \in W_{\gamma, l}$, for $j = 1, \ldots, k$ and $l = 1, \ldots, t+1$.

Note that all components of the (corrupt) proof of P_i above except $C_{\gamma, j}$ for $j \in W_{\gamma, \zeta_\gamma}$ and $\gamma = 1, \ldots, d$ are identically distributed to the proof of a prover following its program.

Extraction from Corrupt Provers. If a corrupt prover P_i, for $i \in I_P$, constructs a valid proof of knowledge, $\mathcal{S}$ must extract the knowledge and forward it to $\mathcal{F}_{ZK}^{R_{DS}}$.

$\mathcal{S}$ does this as follows. By construction there exists an $0 < \alpha \le d$ and a list $M_{\omega_1}, \ldots, M_{\omega_{t+1}}$, such that $M_{\omega_l} \in W_{\alpha,l}$, and $M_{\omega_l} \notin I_P$ for $l = 1, \ldots, t+1$.

1. Suppose that $(\cdot, P_i, \texttt{Proof}, \{\alpha_{\gamma,t+1}, \{\alpha_{\gamma,l}, \overline{L}_{\gamma,l}\}_{l=1}^t, \{C_{\gamma,j}\}_{j=1}^k\}_{\gamma=1}^d)$ for $i \in I_P$, appears on $\mathcal{F}_{\mathrm{BB}}$. $\mathcal{S}$ interrupts the simulation of $\mathcal{F}_{\mathrm{BB}}$ when $\mathcal{F}_{\mathrm{BB}}$ receives a message on the form $(\texttt{Write}, \texttt{Verifier}, P_i, \{b_{j,\gamma}\}_{\gamma=1}^d)$ from M_j and such messages has been received from all other mix-servers.
   $\mathcal{S}$ then checks if the proof is deemed valid by the provers by performing the tests of Step 2(e)ii. If so $\mathcal{S}$ does the following.
   a) It computes $w_{\alpha,l} = D_{x_{\omega_l,i}}(C_{\alpha,\omega_l})$ for $l = 1, \ldots, t+1$.
   b) From $w_{\alpha,1}, \ldots, w_{\alpha,t+1}$ it is trivial to compute a witness w such that $((g, h, y, L, L'), w) \in R_{\mathrm{DS}}$.
   c) Finally $\mathcal{S}$ hands $(\texttt{Prover}, (g, h, y, L, L'), w)$ to $\tilde{P}_i$ (who forwards it to $\mathcal{F}_{\mathrm{ZK}}^{R_{\mathrm{DS}}}$). When $\mathcal{S}$ receives $(\mathcal{S}, \tilde{P}_i, \texttt{Prover}, (g, h, y, L, L'), 1)$ from $\mathcal{F}_{\mathrm{ZK}}^{R_{\mathrm{DS}}}$ it continues the simulation of $\mathcal{F}_{\mathrm{BB}}$.

REACHING A CONTRADICTION. Next we show, using a hybrid argument, that if the ideal adversary $\mathcal{S}$ defined above does not imply that Protocol 3 is secure, then we can break the DDH-assumption.

Suppose that $\mathcal{S}$ does not imply the security of the protocol. Then there exists a hybrid adversary $\mathcal{A}' = \mathcal{A}^{\mathcal{S}_{\mathrm{BB}}}$, an environment $\mathcal{Z}$ with auxiliary input $z = \{z_n\}$, a constant $c > 0$ and an infinite index set $\mathcal{N} \subset \mathbb{N}$ such that for $n \in \mathcal{N}$: $|\Pr[\mathcal{Z}_z(\mathcal{I}(\mathcal{S}, \tilde{\pi}^{\mathcal{F}_{\mathrm{ZK}}^{R_{\mathrm{DS}}}})) = 1] - \Pr[\mathcal{Z}_z(\mathcal{H}(\mathcal{A}', \pi^{\tilde{\pi}^{\mathcal{F}_{\mathrm{BB}}}})) = 1]| \ge \frac{1}{n^c}$, where $\mathcal{S}$ runs $\mathcal{A}'$ as a black-box as described above, i.e. $\mathcal{S} = \mathcal{S}(\mathcal{A}')$.

Defining the Hybrids. Without loss we assume that $\{1, \ldots, N\} \setminus I_P = \{1, \ldots, \eta\}$. We define $T_0 = \mathcal{Z}_z(\mathcal{I}(\mathcal{S}(\mathcal{A}'), \tilde{\pi}^{\mathcal{F}_{\mathrm{ZK}}^{R_{\mathrm{DS}}}}))$, and then define T_s by the following modifications to T_0.

1. When $\mathcal{S}$ receives $(\texttt{Prover}, \tilde{P}_i, (g, h, y, L, L'), 1)$ for $i \notin I_M$, it checks if $i \in \{1, \ldots, s\}$. If so, $\mathcal{S}$ consults the internal storage of $\mathcal{F}_{\mathrm{ZK}}^{R_{\mathrm{DS}}}$ and finds the w stored under the tag $(\tilde{P}_i, (g, h, y, L, L'))$. Then it runs a P_i following the protocol on input $(\texttt{Prover}, (g, h, y, L, L'), w)$. If $i \notin \{1, \ldots, s\}$, then the simulation of P_i proceeds as outlined above.

By inspection of the constructions we see that T_η is identically distributed to $\mathcal{Z}_z(\mathcal{H}(\mathcal{A}', \pi^{\tilde{\pi}^{\mathcal{F}_{\mathrm{BB}}}}))$, since the only essential difference is that honest verifiers do not verify the proofs of honest provers, but this is never noticed by $\mathcal{A}'$ or $\mathcal{Z}$.

If we set $p_s = \Pr[T_s = 1]$, we have $\frac{1}{n^c} \le |p_0 - p_\eta| \le \sum_{s=1}^\eta |p_{s-1} - p_s|$, which implies that there exists some fixed $0 < s \le \eta$ such that $|p_{s-1} - p_s| \ge \frac{1}{\eta n^c} \ge \frac{1}{N n^c}$.

Completing the Proof. We only argue informally for the remainder of the proof. For a formal proof we refer the reader to [47]. Informally we have shown that there is an adversary and an environment that can distinguish executions where the s:th prover follows its program and encrypts real shares of its proof, and executions where the s:th prover encrypts $(1, 1, \ldots, 1)$, for the honest verifiers. From this observation we construct a distinguisher. A hybrid argument shows that this distinguisher violates the DDH-assumption.

A General Composition Theorem
for Secure Reactive Systems

Michael Backes, Birgit Pfitzmann, and Michael Waidner

IBM Zurich Research Lab
{mbc,bpf,wmi}@zurich.ibm.com

Abstract. We consider compositional properties of reactive systems that are secure in a cryptographic sense. We follow the well-known simulatability approach of modern cryptography, i.e., the specification is an ideal system and a real system should in some sense simulate this ideal one. We show that if a system consists of a polynomial number of arbitrary ideal subsystems such that each of them has a secure implementation in the sense of blackbox simulatability, then one can securely replace all ideal subsystems with their respective secure counterparts without destroying the blackbox simulatability relation. We further prove our theorem for universal simulatability by showing that blackbox simulatability implies universal simulatability under reasonable assumptions. We show all our results with concrete security.

1 Introduction

In recent times, the analysis of cryptographic protocols has been getting more and more attention, and thus the demand for general frameworks for representing cryptographic protocols and their security requirements has been rising. To enable a cryptographically correct analysis of cryptographic protocols, such frameworks have to capture probabilistic behaviors, complexity-theoretically bounded adversaries as well as a reactive environment of the protocol, i.e., continuous interaction with users and an adversary, e.g., in many protocol runs. Clearly, such frameworks further have to be rigorously defined to avoid ambiguities and to enable convincing proofs. Moreover, it is highly desirable that such frameworks provide a link to formal methods, i.e., to tool-supported verification of cryptographic protocols. Tool support can minimize flaws, which occur quite often if the distributed-systems aspects of cryptographic protocols are analyzed by hand. One ingredient for this is that the model should contain an abstract machine model besides Turing machines. The model of Pfitzmann and Waidner [31] is suitable for all these requirements and we use it as a rigorous foundation of this work.

The model of [31] introduced a notion of security-preserving refinement, called *reactive simulatability*. This notion captures the idea of refinement that preserves not only integrity properties but also confidentiality properties. Intuitively it can be stated as follows, when applied to the relation between a real and an ideal system:[1] Everything that can happen to users of the real system in the presence of an arbitrary adversary A' can also happen to the same users with the ideal system, where attack capabilities are

---

[1] Other terms are implementation and specification, or in special cases cryptographic and abstract system.

M. Naor (Ed.): TCC 2004, LNCS 2951, pp. 336–354, 2004.

usually much more restricted, in the presence of another adversary A. In particular, it comprises confidentiality because the notion of what happens to users, called their *view*, not only includes their in- and outputs to the system, but also their communication with the adversary. This includes whether the adversary can guess secrets of the users or partial information about them. As it is often desirable to impose further restrictions on how the adversary A against the ideal service is constructed, simulatability comes in different flavors. The two most prominent ones (besides general simulatability as described above, which does not impose any restriction on A) are *universal simulatability*, which states that A has to be independent of the actual users of the protocol, and the (seemingly) more restrictive notion of *black-box simulatability*, which states that A consists of the original adversary A' and a simulator that may only depend on the protocol itself.

One of the key results in the considered model is a composition theorem [31]. It states that if a larger system is designed based on a specification of a subsystem, and the implementation of the subsystem is later plugged in, the entire implementation of the larger system is as secure as its design in the same sense of reactive simulatability. This theorem (as well as its predecessor [30] for a synchronous reactive model) holds for all variants of simulatability (general, universal, and blackbox), but it is restricted to replacing one system. Obviously, a constant number of systems can then be replaced by applying the theorem multiple times.

In this work, we present a more comprehensive composition theorem for black-box simulatability by showing that a *polynomial number* (in a security parameter) of *arbitrary* systems can be composed without destroying the simulatability relation. The proof relies on what is often called a "standard hybrid argument" as first used in [15]. We further show that universal simulatability implies black-box simulatability under reasonable assumptions. This is of independent interest, but it in particular allows us to prove our theorem also for universal simulatability. We show all our results with concrete security.

Related Literature. Simulatability was first sketched for secure multi-party function evaluation, i.e., for the computation of one output tuple from one tuple of secret inputs from each participant in [33] and defined (with different degrees of generality and rigorosity) in [14,6,27,9]. While composition theorems for special cases were proven in [6, 27], the first general composition theorem for non-reactive simulatability was proven in [9].

An important step towards compositionality results of reactive systems was taken in [19,20], where the cryptographic security of specific systems was directly defined and verified using a formal language, the π-calculus, and security was expressed using observational equivalence. This notion is even stronger than reactive simulatability because the entire environment (corresponding to users and adversary together for reactive simulatability) must not be able to distinguish the implementation and the specification. Correspondingly, the concrete specifications used were not abstract; they essentially comprise the actual protocols including all cryptographic details. Composition was defined in the calculus by defining processes with "holes" for other processes, which then allows for composing a constant number of systems.

A reactive simulatability definition was first proposed (after some earlier sketches, in particular in [13,29,9]) in [16]. It is synchronous, covers a restricted class of protocols (straightline programs with restricted operators, in view of the constructive result of this paper), and simulatability is defined for the information-theoretic case only, where it can be done with a quantification over input sequences instead of active honest users.

The first composition theorem for reactive simulatability was given in [30] for a general synchronous reactive model, followed by essentially the same composition theorem [31] in the corresponding asynchronous model. Later than [31] but independently, another model of asynchronous reactive systems together with a composition theorem for reactive simulatability was developed in [10]. The theorem is specific for universal simulatability, but for this case it is more general than the ones in [30,31] since it additionally allows for securely composing a polynomial number of copies of an ideal service, which naturally correspond to different protocol instances in the real implementation. We stress that our composition theorem in this paper not only captures secure composition of a polynomial number of copies of one single ideal system but also of a polynomial number of truly arbitrary systems. However, our work was inspired by [10].

Besides considering composition as secure refinement, property-based composition has received interest in the literature: It considers the question whether systems that individually provide certain security properties still have these properties when they are run in parallel with other systems. For safety and liveness, general theories of this kind of compositionality exist [28,32,1], which are sufficient to reason about most functional system properties. However, many security properties are not safety and liveness properties, in particular confidentiality. Compositional information flow properties were first investigated in [23]. After that, much work has been devoted to identifying properties which are preserved under composition like, e.g., restrictiveness [23,24], forward correctability [18], or separability [25]. For certain security properties that are in general not preserved under composition, it is known how to restrict composition in order to preserve these properties [25,26]. More recent work concentrated on a uniform basis to reason about property-based composition [22,11].

Somewhere between both notions of composition, so-called preservation theorems exist, which state that specific properties are preserved under (reactive) simulatability. Such theorems exist for integrity [2], transitive and non-transitive non-interference [3, 4], i.e., absence of information flow, and a class of liveness properties [5].

Outline. In Section 2 we review the model of reactive systems in asynchronous networks. Section 3 contains our composition theorem and its proof for black-box simulatability. In Section 4, we show that universal simulatability implies black-box simulatability and reasonable assumptions. In particular, this can be used to carry over our composition theorem for universal simulatability.

2   Asynchronous Reactive Systems

In this section, we review our model for secure reactive systems in an asynchronous network from [31]. Several definitions are only sketched whereas those that are important for understanding our results are given in full detail. All other details can be looked up in the original paper.

2.1   General System Model

Systems mainly consist of several interactive machines. Machines communicate via *ports* (local endpoints for different potential channels) and messages are strings over

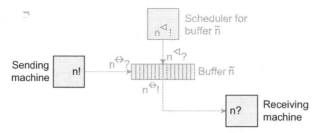

Fig. 1. Ports and buffers. Specifications only need to spell out the black part

an alphabet Σ. Inspired by the CSP-Notation [17], we write output and input ports as q! and q? respectively. As in similar models, channels are defined implicitly by naming convention (and not by a separate graph), that is port q! sends messages to q?. For asynchronous timing, a message is not immediately delivered to its recipient, but first stored in a special machine $\tilde{q}$ called a buffer. If a machine wants to schedule the i-th message of buffer $\tilde{q}$, it must have the unique clock-out port $q^{\triangleleft}!$, and it sends i at $q^{\triangleleft}!$, see Figure 1. The buffer then outputs and deletes its i-th message. For a port p, we write p^c to denote the port which it connects to according to Figure 1, i.e., $q!^c = q^{\leftrightarrow}?, q^{\leftrightarrow}!^c = q?,$ $q^{\triangleleft}!^c = q^{\triangleleft}?$ and vice versa. The in- and output ports in a port set or port sequence P are denoted $in(P)$ and $out(P)$.

Our primary machine model is probabilistic state-transition machines, similar to probabilistic I/O automata as in Lynch [21] (and also essentially in [6,27]). If a machine is switched, it receives an input tuple at its input ports and performs its transition function. This yields a new state and an output tuple in the deterministic case, or a finite distribution over such pairs in the probabilistic case. Moreover, each machine has a function bounding the length of the considered inputs; this allows flexible time bounds independent of the environment.

Definition 1. *(Machines) A machine is a tuple*

$$M = (name_M, Ports_M, States_M, \delta_M, l_M, Ini_M, Fin_M)$$

of a name $name_M \in \Sigma^+$, a finite sequence $Ports_M$ of ports, a set $States_M \subseteq \Sigma^*$ of states, a probabilistic state-transition function δ_M, a length function $l_M : States_M \to (\mathbb{N} \cup \{\infty\})^{|in(Ports_M)|}$, and sets $Ini_M, Fin_M \subseteq States_M$ of initial and final states. Its input set is $\mathcal{I}_M := (\Sigma^*)^{|in(Ports_M)|}$; the i-th element of an input tuple denotes the input at the i-th in-port. Its output set is $\mathcal{O}_M := (\Sigma^*)^{|out(Ports_M)|}$. The empty word, ϵ, denotes no in- or output at a port. δ_M probabilistically maps each pair $(s, I) \in States_M \times \mathcal{I}_M$ to a pair $(s', O) \in States_M \times \mathcal{O}_M$.

Two restrictions apply to δ_M: Every output distribution has to be finite and if $I = (\epsilon, \ldots, \epsilon)$, then $\delta_M(s, I) = (s, (\epsilon, \ldots, \epsilon))$. Inputs are ignored beyond the length bounds, i.e., $\delta_M(s, I) = \delta_M(s, I\lceil_{l_M(s)})$ for all $I \in \mathcal{I}_M$, where $r\lceil_l$ for $l \in \mathbb{N}, r \in \Sigma^*$ denotes the l-symbol prefix, and the notation is lifted to tuples. We further demand $l_M(s) = (0, \ldots, 0)$ for every $s \in Fin_M$. ◇

In the text, we often write "M" for $name_M$. The set (in contrast to the sequence) of ports of a machine M is denoted by $ports(M)$, and similar for sets of machines.

A *collection* $\hat{C}$ of machines is a set of machines with pairwise different machine names and disjoint sets of ports. The *completion* $[\hat{C}]$ of a collection $\hat{C}$ is the union of all machines of $\hat{C}$ and the buffers needed for every channel. A port of a collection is called *free* if its connecting port is not in the collection. These ports will be connected to the users and the adversary. The free ports of a completion $[\hat{C}]$ are denoted as $\mathrm{free}([\hat{C}])$. A collection $\hat{C}$ is called *closed* if its completion $[\hat{C}]$ has no free ports except a special master clock-in port $\mathsf{clk}^{\lhd}?$.

A closed collection represents a "runnable" system and a probability space of *runs* (sometimes called *traces* or *executions*) is defined for it. Machines switch sequentially, i.e., we have exactly one active machine M at any time. If this machine has clock out-ports, it can select the next message to be delivered by scheduling a buffer via one of these clock out-ports. If the buffer contains a message at the selected position, it delivers this message, and the receiving machine is the next active machine. If M tries to schedule multiple messages, only one is taken, and if it schedules none or the message does not exist, the master scheduler X becomes active. Formally, runs are defined as follows.

Definition 2. *(Runs and Views) Let $\hat{C}$ be a closed collection with master scheduler X. Runs and their probability spaces are defined inductively by the following algorithm for each tuple $ini \in \times_{\mathsf{M} \in \hat{C}} Ini_{\mathsf{M}}$ of initial states. The algorithm maintains variables for the state of each machine and treats each port as a variable over Σ^*, initialized with ϵ except for $\mathsf{clk}^{\lhd}? := 1$. It further maintains a variable $\mathsf{M_{CS}}$ ("current scheduler") over machine names, initially $\mathsf{M_{CS}} := \mathsf{X}$, for the currently active non-buffer machine, and a variable r for the resulting run, an initially empty list. The algorithm has five phases. Probabilistic choices only occur in Phase 1.*

1. Switch current scheduler: *Switch the current machine $\mathsf{M_{CS}}$, i.e., set $(s', O) \leftarrow \delta_{\mathsf{M_{CS}}}(s, I)$ for its current state s and in-port values I. Then assign ϵ to all in-ports of $\mathsf{M_{CS}}$.*
2. Termination: *If X is in a final state, the run stops. (As X made no outputs in this case, this only prevents repeated master clock inputs.)*
3. Store outputs: *For each simple out-port o! of $\mathsf{M_{CS}}$ with o! $\neq \epsilon$, in their given order, switch buffer $\tilde{\mathsf{o}}$ with input $\mathsf{o}^{\leftrightarrow}? := $ o!. Then assign ϵ to these ports o! and $\mathsf{o}^{\leftrightarrow}?$.*
4. Clean up scheduling: *If at least one clock out-port of $\mathsf{M_{CS}}$ has a value $\neq \epsilon$, let $\mathsf{n}^{\lhd}!$ denote the first such port and assign ϵ to the others. Otherwise let $\mathsf{clk}^{\lhd}? := 1$ and $\mathsf{M_{CS}} := \mathsf{X}$ and go to Phase 1.*
5. Deliver scheduled message: *Switch buffer $\tilde{\mathsf{n}}$ with input $\mathsf{n}^{\lhd}? := \mathsf{n}^{\lhd}!$, set $\mathsf{n}? := \mathsf{n}^{\leftrightarrow}!$ and then assign ϵ to all ports of $\tilde{\mathsf{n}}$ and to $\mathsf{n}^{\lhd}!$. If $\mathsf{n}? = \epsilon$ let $\mathsf{clk}^{\lhd}? := 1$ and $\mathsf{M_{CS}} := \mathsf{X}$. Else let $\mathsf{M_{CS}} := \mathsf{M}'$ for the unique machine M' with $\mathsf{n}? \in \mathrm{ports}(\mathsf{M}')$. Go to Phase 1.*

Whenever a machine (this may be a buffer) M switches from (s, I) to (s', O), we add a step $(name_{\mathsf{M}}, s, I, s', O)$ to the run r with the following two restrictions. First, we cut each input according to the respective length function, i.e., we replace I by $I' := I\lceil_{l_{\mathsf{M}}(s)}$. Secondly, we do not add the step to the run if $I' = (\epsilon, \ldots, \epsilon)$, i.e., if nothing happens in reality. This gives a random variable $run_{\hat{C},ini}$ for each tuple $ini \in \times_{\mathsf{M} \in \hat{C}}$ of initial states, and similarly for l-step prefixes $run_{\hat{C},ini,l}$.

The view *of a subset $\hat{M} \subseteq \hat{C}$ of machines in a run r is the subsequence of r consisting of those steps where a machine of $\hat{M}$ switches. This gives a random variable $view_{\hat{C},ini}(\hat{M})$ for each tuple ini of initial states, and similarly for l-step prefixes*

$view_{\hat{C},ini,l}(\hat{M})$ of the view. For a singleton $\hat{M} = \{H\}$ we write $view_{\hat{C},ini}(H)$ for $view_{\hat{C},ini}(\{H\})$. $\qquad\diamond$

2.2 Security-Specific System Model

We now define specific collections for security purposes. We start with the definition of *structures*. Intuitively, these are the machines that execute a security protocol. They have a distinguished set of *service ports*. This is a subset of the free ports where, intuitively, a certain service is guaranteed, while remaining free ports are meant only for the adversary. Typical examples of inputs at service ports are "send message m to participant id" for a message transmission system or "pay amount x to participant id" for a payment system, while typical non-service ports are those of insecure network connections in a real system. For cryptographic purposes, the initial state of all machines in a structure is a security parameter k in unary representation.

Definition 3. *(Structures and Service Ports) A* structure *is a pair* $struc = (\hat{M}, S)$ *where* $\hat{M}$ *is a collection of simple machines (i.e., with only normal in- and out-ports and clock out-ports) with* $\{1\}^* \subseteq Ini_M$ *for all* $M \in \hat{M}$, *and* $S \subseteq \text{free}([\hat{M}])$. *The set* S *is called* service ports. $\qquad\diamond$

Forbidden ports for users of a structure are those that clash with port names of given machines and those that would link the user to a non-service port.

Definition 4. *(Forbidden Ports) For a structure* $(\hat{M}, S)$ *let* $\bar{S}_{\hat{M}} := \text{free}([\hat{M}]) \setminus S$. *We call* $\text{forb}(\hat{M}, S) := \text{ports}(\hat{M}) \cup \bar{S}_{\hat{M}}^c$ *the* forbidden ports. $\qquad\diamond$

A *system* is a set of structures. The idea behind systems is that there may be different actual structures depending on the set of actually malicious participants.

Definition 5. *(Systems) A* system *Sys is a set of structures.* $\qquad\diamond$

A structure can be complemented to a *configuration* by adding a *user* machine and an *adversary* machine. The user is restricted to connecting to the service ports. The adversary closes the collection, i.e., it connects to the remaining service ports, the other free ports $\bar{S}_{\hat{M}}$ of the collection, and the free ports of the user. Thus, user and adversary can interact, e.g., for modeling active attacks.

Definition 6. *(Configurations) A* configuration *of a structure* $(\hat{M}, S)$ *is a tuple* $conf = (\hat{M}, S, H, A)$ *where*

- H *is a machine called* user *with* $\text{ports}(H) \cap \text{forb}(\hat{M}, S) = \emptyset$ *and* $\{1\}^* \subseteq Ini_H$,
- A *is a machine called* adversary *with* $\{1\}^* \subseteq Ini_A$,
- *and the completion* $\hat{C} := [\hat{M} \cup \{H, A\}]$ *is a closed collection.*

The set of configurations of $(\hat{M}, S)$ *is written* $\text{Conf}(\hat{M}, S)$. *The notation* $\text{Conf}()$ *is lifted to sets of structures, i.e., systems. We write* $conf.\hat{M}$ *for* $conf[1]$ *(component selection function) and similarly* $conf.S$, $conf.H$, *and* $conf.A$, *and* $conf.struc$ *for* $conf[1, 2]$. $\diamond$

2.3   Parametrized Systems

In many typical systems, the structures only depend on the trust model, but not on the security parameter k. In a *parametrized* system this is different. Hence such a system is partitioned into different subsystems for different values of k. "Normal" systems can naturally be identified with parametrized systems where all subsystems are equal.

Definition 7. *(Parametrized Systems) A* parametrized system *is a system Sys together with a partitioning* $(Sys_k)_{k \in \mathbb{N}}$, *i.e., the elements* Sys_k *are pairwise disjoint systems with* $Sys = \bigcup_{k \in \mathbb{N}} Sys_k$. *In slight abuse of notation we also call the sequence of partitions Sys, and if the system is called Sys, the notation* Sys_k *always refers to the k-th element in the partition sequence.*

A bounding function *for a parametrized system is a function* P *such that for all* $k \in \mathbb{N}$ *and* $(\hat{M}, S) \in Sys_k$ *we have* $|\hat{M}| \leq P(k)$ *and the runtime of every* $\mathsf{M} \in \hat{M}$ *on initial input* 1^k *is bounded by* $P(k)$ *in the sense of circuit complexity (more precisely, circuit size). A parametrized system is* polynomial-time *if it has a polynomial bounding function.*   ◇

Circuit complexity, i.e., non-uniform complexity, is natural for this definition because one can consider every machine M, used only for security parameter k, as a separate circuit. As we want to bound the overall runtime of a machine with respect to its initial input length, just as in the uniform case, this can be defined by one normal non-cyclic circuit for each machine. Meaningful uniform complexity for such a definition requires a universal machine that simulates all these structures, and a generation algorithm for structures. However, our results are reductions with concrete security (as first introduced as a general concept with special notation in [8]), and usable for a wide range of complexity measures. In those reductions we actually work with Turing complexity because it is defined in full detail for our interacting machines.

A parametrized system considers the potentially used subsystems as potentially available from the start. This is also implicitly the case in [10] because although a subsystem is said to be generated there, it springs up magically in distributed locations by this operation. This means that all the connections must be assumed to be predefined. A truly dynamic system would need to distribute port or machine names of new machines, like the π-calculus does. We do not see any specific reason while our theorem should not hold for this case but it would require a rigorous definition first.

We now define user and adversary of a parametrized system.

Definition 8. *(User and Adversary of a Parametrized System) A* user *and an* adversary *of a parametrized system Sys are families* $(\mathsf{H}_{struc})_{struc \in Sys}$, $(\mathsf{A}_{struc})_{struc \in Sys}$ *such that* $(\hat{M}, S, \mathsf{H}_{(\hat{M},S)}, \mathsf{A}_{(\hat{M},S)}) \in \mathsf{Conf}(Sys)$ *for all* $(\hat{M}, S) \in Sys$.   ◇

To reason about the complexity of users and adversaries, or more generally families of machines, we define the parametrized complexity.

Definition 9. *(Parametrized Complexity) Let* $X = \bigcup_{k \in \mathbb{N}} X_k$ *be a partitioned index set (with the same conventions as for systems) and let* $A = (A_x)_{x \in X}$ *be a family of machines with* $\{1\}^* \subseteq Ini_{A_x}$ *for every* $x \in X$. *We say that A is of* complexity $t \colon \mathbb{N} \to \mathbb{N}$ *if for all* $x \in X_k$, *the runtime of* A_x *on initial input* 1^k *is bounded by* $t(k)$ *in the sense of circuit complexity. We sometimes write* t_A *for "the" complexity of A.*   ◇

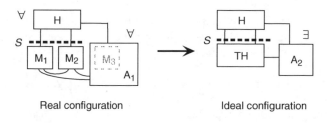

Real configuration   Ideal configuration

Fig. 2. Example of simulatability. The view of H is compared.

2.4 Defining Security with Simulatability

Reactive simulatability essentially means that whatever might happen to an honest user in a real system Sys_1 can also happen in an ideal system Sys_2. More precisely, for every configuration $conf_1$ of Sys_1, there exists a configuration $conf_2$ of Sys_2 with the same user yielding *indistinguishable views* for this user. A typical situation is illustrated in Figure 2.

However, we do not want to compare a structure of Sys_1 with arbitrary structures of Sys_2, but only with certain suitable ones. What suitable means in a concrete situation can be defined by a mapping f from Sys_1 to Sys_2. The mapping f is called *valid* if it maps structures with the same service ports, so that the same user can connect.

Definition 10. *(Valid Mappings) A* valid mapping *between two systems Sys_1 and Sys_2 is a function $f\colon Sys_1 \to Sys_2$ with $(\hat{M}_2, S_2) = f((\hat{M}_1, S_1)) \Rightarrow S_1 = S_2$. We call $f((\hat{M}_1, S_1))$ the* corresponding structure *of $(\hat{M}_1, S_1)$. If the systems are parametrized, we also require $f(Sys_{1,k}) \subseteq Sys_{2,k}$ for all $k \in \mathbb{N}$.* ◇

A technical problem for reactive simulatability is that a correct user of a structure from Sys_1 might have forbidden ports in the corresponding structure. Configurations where this does not happen are called *suitable*; we restrict the simulatability definition to those. We omit a rigorous definition for brevity. For a valid mapping $f\colon Sys_1 \to Sys_2$, let $\mathrm{Conf}^f(Sys_1)$ be the set of suitable configurations.

We present the definition of *indistinguishability* for two families of random variables with a common partitioned index set and with versions for concrete security, following [34,7,12].

Definition 11. *(Indistinguishability) Let two families $(\mathrm{var}_x)_{x \in X}$ and $(\mathrm{var}'_x)_{x \in X}$ of discrete probability distributions (random variables)*

- *They are called* perfectly indistinguishable *iff $\mathrm{var}_x = \mathrm{var}'_x$ for all $x \in X$.*
- *They are called* statistically δ-indistinguishable *for a function $\delta\colon \mathbb{N} \to \mathbb{R}_{\geq 0}$ iff the statistical distance $\Delta_{\mathrm{stat}}(\mathrm{var}_x, \mathrm{var}'_x) := \frac{1}{2}\sum_{d \in D_x} |\mathrm{Pr}(\mathrm{var}_x = d) - \mathrm{Pr}(\mathrm{var}'_x = d)|$ is at most $\delta(k)$ for all k and all $x \in X_k$.*
- *An algorithm* Dis *is called a (t, δ)-distinguisher for var_x and var'_x for $t \in \mathbb{N}$, $\delta \in \mathbb{R}_{\geq 0}$, and $x \in X_k$ iff its complexity is at most t and*

$$\delta_x^{\mathrm{Dis}} := |\mathrm{Pr}(\mathrm{Dis}(1^k, \mathrm{var}_x) = 1) - \mathrm{Pr}(\mathrm{Dis}(1^k, \mathrm{var}'_x) = 1)| \geq \delta.$$

– *The distributions are called* polynomially indistinguishable *iff for all polynomials t and all distinguishers* $(\mathsf{Dis}_x)_{x \in X}$ *with complexity t in their first parameter, there exists a negligible function δ such that $\delta_x^{\mathsf{Dis}} \leq \delta(k)$ for all k and all $x \in X_k$.*   ◇

We write "$\approx_y$" for indistinguishability with $y = \mathsf{perf}$, δ, or poly, respectively. We write "$\approx$" if we want to treat all cases together, and we often write "$=$" for "$\approx_{\mathsf{perf}}$".

We later need that indistinguishability of families of random variables implies indistinguishability of functions of them, e.g., of "parts" of the random variables.

Lemma 1. *(Indistinguishability of Derived Distributions) Let* var, var′ *be families of probability distributions with partitioned index set X and a common family of domains D, and let $\phi = (\phi_x)_{x \in X}$ be a family of functions ϕ_x on D_x (to strings, but encoding domains as strings is not made explicit). Then the following holds:*

– var $\approx_y$ var′ $\Rightarrow$ $\phi(\mathsf{var}) \approx_y \phi(\mathsf{var}')$ *if y is* perf, *or a function δ.*
– *Every (t, δ)-distinguisher Dis_ϕ for $\phi(\mathsf{var}_x)$ and $\phi(\mathsf{var}'_x)$ gives rise to a (t', δ)-distinguisher Dis for var_x and var'_x with $t' = t + t_\phi(b(k))$, where $t_\phi \colon \mathbb{N} \to \mathbb{N}$ denotes the complexity of ϕ, and $b \colon \mathbb{N} \to \mathbb{N}$ bounds the length of the random variables, i.e., $|v| \leq b(k)$ for all $v \in D_x$ and $x \in X_k$.*
– var $\approx_{\mathsf{poly}}$ var′ $\Rightarrow$ $\phi(\mathsf{var}) \approx_{\mathsf{poly}} \phi(\mathsf{var}')$ *if the random variables are of polynomial length, and ϕ is of polynomial complexity.*   □

This is clear for the perfect case, and can be easily shown by computations on statistical distances for the statistical case. For concrete complexity and the computational case, the distinguisher family Dis for the original distributions is defined by $\mathsf{Dis}_x(1^k, v) := \mathsf{Dis}_{\phi,x}(1^k, \phi(v))$ for all k and $x \in X_k$, and for v of length at most $b(k)$.

We are now ready to define reactive simulatability for parametrized systems. We require that there exists an extension f_C of the valid structure mapping f to a configuration mapping that leaves the user unchanged, i.e., we skolemize the existence of corresponding adversaries in Figure 2. We then consider the families of user views $view_{conf_1}(\mathsf{H})$ and $view_{f_C(conf_1)}(\mathsf{H})$ where all machines have initial input 1^k for the security parameter k to which this configuration belongs. Each of these two families contains one well-defined probability distribution for each configuration $conf_1$. Overall these are two families of distributions with the partitioned index set $\mathsf{Conf}^f(Sys_1) = \bigcup_{k \in \mathbb{N}} \mathsf{Conf}^f(Sys_{1,k})$. Similarly, we obtain two families $view_{conf_1, l}(\mathsf{H})$ and $view_{f_C(conf_1), l}(\mathsf{H})$ for l-step prefixes of user views.

Definition 12. *(Reactive Simulatability) Let parametrized systems Sys_1 and Sys_2 with a valid mapping f be given. For reactive simulatability, we require that there exists a function $f_C \colon \mathsf{Conf}^f(Sys_1) \to \mathsf{Conf}(Sys_2)$ with $f_C(conf_1).struc = f(conf_1.struc)$ and $f_C(conf_1).\mathsf{H} = conf_1.\mathsf{H}$ for all $conf_1 \in \mathsf{Conf}^f(Sys_1)$, and with the following properties. We say that f_C is a τ-mapping for a structure $struc_1$ and a function $\tau \colon \mathbb{N} \to \mathbb{N}$ if the complexity $t_{f_C(conf_1).\mathsf{A}}$ is bounded by $\tau(t_{conf_1.\mathsf{A}})$ for all $conf_1 \in \mathsf{Conf}(struc_1)$. The entire f_C is a τ-mapping for a function $\tau \colon \mathbb{N}^2 \to \mathbb{N}$ if for all $conf_1 \in \mathsf{Conf}^f(Sys_1)$ we have $t_{f_C(conf_1).\mathsf{A}} \leq \tau(k, t_{conf_1})$.*

We say that $Sys_1 \geq_{\mathsf{sec}}^{f,y} Sys_2$, spoken "$y$'-at least as secure as", under the following conditions for different cases of y and y', where we abbreviate $\mathsf{H} := conf_1.\mathsf{H}$:

a) $y = \mathsf{perf}$ and $y' =$ "perfectly" iff $view_{conf_1}(\mathsf{H})$ and $view_{f_C(conf_1)}(\mathsf{H})$ are perfectly indistinguishable for every $conf_1 \in \mathsf{Conf}^f(Sys_1)$.

b) $y = \delta$ and $y' =$ "δ-statistically" for a function $\delta \colon \mathbb{N}^2 \to \mathbb{R}_{\geq 0}$ iff for every $conf_1 \in \mathsf{Conf}^f(Sys_{1,k})$ and every $l \in \mathbb{N}$ we have $view_{conf_1,l}(\mathsf{H}) \approx_{\delta(k,l)} view_{f_C(conf_1),l}(\mathsf{H})$.

c) Concrete security: An algorithm Dis is called a (t, δ)-distinguisher for $conf_1 \in \mathsf{Conf}^f(Sys_{1,k})$ and $f_C(conf_1)$ where $t \in \mathbb{N}$ and $\delta \in \mathbb{R}_{\geq 0}$ iff its complexity is at most t and $\delta^{\mathsf{Dis}}_{conf_1} \geq \delta$ where

$$\delta^{\mathsf{Dis}}_{conf_1} := |\Pr(\mathsf{Dis}(1^k, view_{conf_1}(\mathsf{H})) = 1) - \Pr(\mathsf{Dis}(1^k, view_{f_C(conf_1)}(\mathsf{H})) = 1)|.$$

e) $y = \mathsf{poly}$ and $y' =$ "polynomially" iff for all users H and adversary A of polynomial complexity, the views $(view_{(\hat{M},S,\mathsf{H}_{(\hat{M},S)},\mathsf{A}_{(\hat{M},S)})}(\mathsf{H}_{(\hat{M},S)}))_{(\hat{M},S) \in Sys_1}$ and $(view_{f_C((\hat{M},S,\mathsf{H}_{(\hat{M},S)},\mathsf{A}_{(\hat{M},S)}))}(\mathsf{H}_{(\hat{M},S)}))_{(\hat{M},S) \in Sys_1}$ are polynomially indistinguishable and f_C is a P-mapping for a polynomial P.

Universal simulatability means that $f_C(conf_1).\mathsf{A}$ (i.e., A_2 in Figure 2) for $conf_1 = (\hat{M}_1, S, \mathsf{H}, \mathsf{A}_1)$ only depends on $\hat{M}_1$, S, and A_1. We write $\geq^{\mathsf{uni},f,y}_{\mathsf{sec}}$ instead of $\geq^{f,y}_{\mathsf{sec}}$ if we want to emphasize this case. $\diamond$

Where the difference between the types of security is irrelevant, we only write $\geq^f_{\mathsf{sec}}$, and we omit the indices f and sec if they are clear from the context.

An essential ingredient in the composition theorem and other uses of the model is a notion of combining several machines into one, and a lemma that this makes no essential difference in views. The combination is defined in a canonical way by considering a combined state space and letting each transition function operate on its respective part. We omit details for brevity. The combination of a set $\hat{M}$ of machines is written $\mathsf{comb}(\hat{M})$ and we sometimes write $\mathsf{comb}(\mathsf{M}_1, \ldots, \mathsf{M}_j)$ for $\mathsf{comb}(\{\mathsf{M}_1, \ldots, \mathsf{M}_j\})$.

Lemma 2. (Machine Combination) Let $\hat{C}$ be a collection without buffers, and $\hat{D} \subseteq \hat{C}$. The view of every set of original machines in $(\hat{C} \setminus \hat{D}) \cup \{\mathsf{comb}(\hat{D})\}$ is the same as in $\hat{C}$. This includes the view of the submachines in $\mathsf{comb}(\hat{D})$, which is well-defined given $\hat{C}$ and $\hat{D}$. The Turing complexity of $\mathsf{comb}(\hat{D})$ is the sum of the complexities of the machines in $\mathsf{comb}(\hat{D})$. $\square$

We can now add the notion of blackbox simulatability to Definition 12. Here A_2 is given as the combination of a fixed "simulator" Sim and a machine A'_1 that is identical to A_1 up to port renaming.

Definition 13. (Blackbox Simulatability) With the notation of Definition 12, blackbox simulatability means that we have functions f_{Sim} from Sys_1 to machines (the simulators for the structures) and f_σ from Sys_1 to port renaming functions such that for all $conf_1 = (\hat{M}_1, S, \mathsf{H}, \mathsf{A}_1) \in \mathsf{Conf}^f(Sys_1)$ we have $f_C(conf_1) = (\hat{M}_2, S, \mathsf{H}, \mathsf{A}_2)$ with $(\hat{M}_2, S) = f((\hat{M}_1, S))$ and $\mathsf{A}_2 = \mathsf{comb}(\mathsf{Sim}, \mathsf{A}'_1)$ with $\mathsf{Sim} := f_{\mathsf{Sim}}((\hat{M}_1, S_1))$ and $\mathsf{A}'_1 := f_\sigma((\hat{M}_1, S_1))(\mathsf{A}_1)$. For computational security, we require that Sim is polynomial-time, i.e., that the parametrized complexity of $(f_{\mathsf{Sim}}((\hat{M}_1, S)))_{(\hat{M}_1,S) \in Sys_1}$ is polynomially bounded. We write $\geq^{\mathsf{bb}}_{\mathsf{sec}}$ instead of $\geq_{\mathsf{sec}}$ if we want to emphasize this case (with the respective superscripts). $\diamond$

2.5   Composition

When composing several systems, one typically does not want to compose every structure of one system with every structure of the others, but only with certain matching ones. For instance, if the individual machines of Sys_2 are implemented on the same physical devices as those of Sys_1, as usual in a layered distributed system, we only compose structures corresponding to the same set of corrupted physical devices. However, this is not the only conceivable situation. Hence we do not define a composition operator that produces one specific composition, but a set of possible compositions.

Definition 14. *(Composability and Composition of Structures) We call structures* $(\hat{M}_1, S_1), \dots, (\hat{M}_n, S_n)$ *composable if* $\text{ports}(\hat{M}_i) \cap \text{forb}(\hat{M}_j, S_j) = \emptyset$ *and* $S_i \cap \text{free}([\hat{M}_j]) = S_j \cap \text{free}([\hat{M}_i])$ *for all* $i \neq j$.[2] *We then define their composition as* $(\hat{M}_1, S_1)\| \dots \|(\hat{M}_n, S_n) := (\hat{M}, S)$ *with* $\hat{M} := \hat{M}_1 \cup \dots \cup \hat{M}_n$ *and* $S := (S_1 \cup \dots \cup S_n) \cap \text{free}([\hat{M}])$. $\Diamond$

We now define the composition of variably many systems, i.e., there is a potentially infinite supply of systems from which a finite number $P(k)$ is chosen for composition for each security parameter k.

Definition 15. *(Parametrized Composition of Systems) Let a sequence* $Sysseq = (Sys^{(i)})_{i\in\mathbb{N}}$ *be given where each* $Sys^{(i)}$ *is a parametrized system, and let* $P\colon \mathbb{N} \to \mathbb{N}$ *be a function. Then a* P-*sized composition of* $Sysseq$ *is a parametrized system* Sys^* *where for all* $k \in \mathbb{N}$, *every structure* $(\hat{M}^*, S^*) \in Sys^*_k$ *has a unique representation* $(\hat{M}^*, S^*) = (\hat{M}_1, S_1)\| \dots \|(\hat{M}_{P(k)}, S_{P(k)})$ *with composable structures* $(\hat{M}_i, S_i) \in Sys^{(i)}_k$ *for* $i = 1, \dots, P(k)$. *We call* $(\hat{M}_i, S_i)$ *the restriction of* $(\hat{M}^*, S^*)$ *to* $Sys^{(i)}$ *and write* $(\hat{M}_i, S_i) = (\hat{M}^*, S^*)\lceil_{Sys^{(i)}}$. $\Diamond$

If the systems $Sys^{(i)}$ have a joint bounding function Q, then $P \cdot Q$ is a bounding function for Sys^*. In particular, if P and Q are polynomials, then Sys^* is polynomial-time.

3   General Composition Theorem for Blackbox Simulatability

In this section, we show that reactive blackbox simulatability is consistent with the composition of a parametrized number of systems, in particular polynomially many in the computational case. The basic idea is the following: Assume that we have proven that a potentially infinite supply of systems $Sys^{(i)}$ are as secure as systems $Sys'^{(i)}$ in the sense of black-box simulatability. Now we want to use $Sys^{(i)}$ as a secure replacement for $Sys'^{(i)}$, i.e., as an implementation of the ideal system $Sys'^{(i)}$. The following theorem shows that such modular proofs are possible. The situation is shown in the upper part of Figure 3.

Additional conditions in the theorem are that all corresponding structures are composable and that, for the polynomial case, the security of the system is in certain sense uniform.

---

[2] The first condition makes one structure a valid user of another. The second one excludes cases where $p \in \text{free}([\hat{M}_i]) \cap \text{free}([\hat{M}_j])$ (e.g., a clock port for a connection between these structures) and $p \in S_i$ but $p \notin S_j$.

Theorem 1. *(Secure Parametrized Composition, Blackbox Case) Let $Sysseq = (Sys^{(i)})_{i \in \mathbb{N}}$ and $Sysseq' = (Sys'^{(i)})_{i \in \mathbb{N}}$ be sequences of parametrized systems. Let $f = (f^{(i)})_{i \in \mathbb{N}}$ be a sequence of valid mappings $f^{(i)}: Sys^{(i)} \to Sys'^{(i)}$, and let $Sys^{(i)} \geq_{\mathsf{sec}}^{\mathsf{bb}, f^{(i)}, y_i} Sys'^{(i)}$ for all $i \in \mathbb{N}$.*

Let $P: \mathbb{N} \to \mathbb{N}$, and let $Sys^{\#}$ and Sys^* denote the P-sized compositions of $Sysseq$ and $Sysseq'$, respectively. Assume that the following structural conditions hold for all $k \in \mathbb{N}$ and every structure $(\hat{M}^{\#}, S) \in Sys_k^{\#}$: Let its restrictions be $(\hat{M}_i, S_i) := (\hat{M}^{\#}, S)\lceil_{Sys^{(i)}}$ and the corresponding structures $(\hat{M}_i', S_i) := f^{(i)}((\hat{M}_i, S_i))$ for all $i \leq P(k)$. Then the composition

$$f^{\#}((\hat{M}^{\#}, S)) := (\hat{M}_1', S_1) \parallel \cdots \parallel (\hat{M}_{P(k)}', S_{P(k)})$$

exists and lies in Sys_k^*. Furthermore, $(\hat{M}_i, S_i)$ and $(\hat{M}_j', S_j)$ must be composable for $j \neq i$, and $\mathsf{ports}(\hat{M}_i') \cap S_j^c = \mathsf{ports}(\hat{M}_i) \cap S_j^c$ for all $j \neq i$. Then we have

$$Sys^{\#} \geq_{\mathsf{sec}}^{\mathsf{bb}, f^{\#}, y} Sys^*$$

a) *with $y = \mathsf{perf}$ if $y_i = \mathsf{perf}$ for all $i \in \mathbb{N}$.*
b) *with $y = P(k) \cdot \delta(k, b(k))$ if all y_i are bounded by a function $\delta: \mathbb{N}^2 \to \mathbb{R}_{\geq 0}$, and where $b(k)$ is the sum of the complexity of the systems, the user, and the simulators.*
c) *With concrete complexity: For every $\mathit{conf}^{\#} \in \mathsf{Conf}^{f^{\#}}(Sys_k^{\#})$, a (t, δ)-distinguisher for $\mathit{conf}^{\#}$ and $f_{\mathsf{C}}(\mathit{conf}^{\#})$ gives rise to a (t', δ')-distinguisher for $\mathit{conf}^{(i)}$ and $f_{\mathsf{C}}(\mathit{conf}^{(i)})$ for a $\mathit{conf}^{(i)} \in \mathsf{Conf}(Sys_k^{(i)})$ with $\delta' = \frac{\delta}{P(k)}$ and $t' = t + b'(k)$, where $b'(k)$ is a polynomial independent of $t_{\mathit{conf}^{\#}}.\mathsf{A}$. (Details are given in the proof.)*
d) *with $y = \mathsf{poly}$ if $y_i = \mathsf{poly}$ for all $i \in \mathbb{N}$ and under the following conditions: The function P is polynomially bounded, and the systems $Sys^{(i)}$ have a joint bounding polynomial Q. The complexities of the simulator families induced by the mappings $f_{\mathsf{Sim}}^{(i)}$ are bounded by a joint polynomial Q_{Sim}. The distinguishing probabilities of the system pairs $(Sys^{(i)}, Sys'^{(i)})$ are uniformly bounded, i.e., for all polynomials t there exists a negligible function δ such that for all distinguishers Dis, all $i, k \in \mathbb{N}$, and all $\mathit{conf} = (\hat{M}_i, S_i, \mathsf{H}, \mathsf{A}) \in \mathsf{Conf}^{f^{(i)}}(Sys_k^{(i)})$ we have $(t_{\mathsf{Dis}} \leq t(k) \wedge t_{\mathsf{H}} \leq t(k) \wedge t_{\mathsf{A}} \leq t(k)) \Rightarrow \delta_{\mathit{conf}}^{\mathsf{Dis}} \leq \delta(k)$ (recall Definition 12d).* $\qquad \square$

The first statement to be proved is extracted into the following lemma.

Lemma 3. *Under the conditions of Theorem 1, the mapping $f^{\#}$ is a valid mapping between $Sys^{\#}$ and Sys^*.* $\qquad \square$

The proof is straightforward as in [30], but heavy on notation. Hence we omit it in this short version. Recall that blackbox simulatability was defined by a function that selects one fixed simulator for each structure (Definition 13).

Definition 16. *(Simulator and Corresponding Configurations) Under the conditions of Theorem 1 and for all $i \in \mathbb{N}$, let $f_{\mathsf{Sim}}^{(i)}$ and $f_{\mathsf{A}}^{(i)}$ be the simulator and renaming functions from which $f_{\mathsf{C}}^{(i)}$ is composed by blackbox simulatability. We compose them*

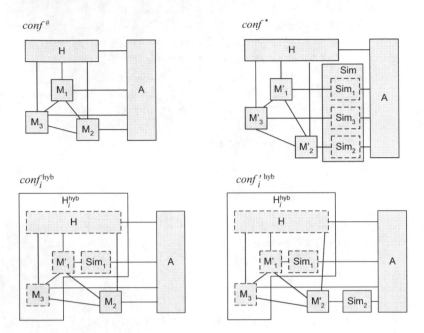

Fig. 3. Configurations in the composition theorem for blackbox simulatability.

into functions $f_{\text{Sim}}^{\#}$ *and* $f_{\text{A}}^{\#}$ *on* $Sys^{\#}$ *as follows: Given* $k \in \mathbb{N}$ *and* $(\hat{M}^{\#}, S) \in Sys_k^{\#}$, *let* $\text{Sim}_i := f_{\text{Sim}}^{(i)}((\hat{M}_i, S_i))$ *for all* $i \leq P(k)$, *and let*

$$f_{\text{Sim}}^{\#}((\hat{M}^{\#}, S)) := \text{comb}(\text{Sim}_1, \ldots, \text{Sim}_{P(k)});$$

further let $f_{\text{A}}^{\#} := f_{\text{A}}^{(P(k))} \circ \cdots \circ f_{\text{A}}^{(1)}$. *Let* $f_{\text{C}}^{\#}$ *be constructed from* $f^{\#}$, $f_{\text{Sim}}^{\#}$, *and* $f_{\text{A}}^{\#}$ *by the equations in Definition 13 (blackbox simulatability).* $\diamondsuit$

The complexity t_{Sim} of the simulator is $t_{\text{Sim}}(k) = \sum_{i=1}^{P(k)} t_{\text{Sim}_i}(k)$ by Lemma 2. In the polynomial case, there exists a polynomial Q_{Sim} such that $t_{\text{Sim}_i} \leq Q_{\text{Sim}}$ for all i, hence $t_{\text{Sim}}(k)$ is polynomially bounded by $P(k) \cdot Q_{\text{Sim}}(k)$.

We also omit the technical proof that indeed $f_{\text{C}}^{\#} : \text{Conf}^{f^{\#}}(Sys^{\#}) \to \text{Conf}(Sys^{*})$ in Definition 16. It is nevertheless interesting that these proof parts that verify the compatibility of channels and the difference of service ports and adversary ports in compositions make up the major part of a rigorous proof, while the cryptographic aspects are shorter and more standard.

Now we can concentrate on proving that the simulator simulates correctly. The proof consists of a hybrid argument as first used in [15], i.e., we construct intermediate configurations that differ only in the machines of one system.

Proof (Theorem 1). Let a configuration $conf^{\#} = (\hat{M}^{\#}, S, \text{H}, \text{A}) \in \text{Conf}^{f^{\#}}(Sys_k^{\#})$ be given and $conf^{*} := f_{\text{C}}^{\#}(conf^{\#})$ the corresponding configuration according to Definition 16. Let the sub-structures $(\hat{M}_i, S_i)$ and $(\hat{M}_i', S_i')$, the simulators Sim_i, and functions f_z^x with various indices be defined as in the formulation of the theorem and Definition 16.

Furthermore, let $(\hat{M}^*, S) := f^*((\hat{M}^\#, S))$ and $\mathsf{Sim} := f_{\mathsf{Sim}}^\#((\hat{M}^\#, S))$. Then we have $conf^* = (\hat{M}^*, S, \mathsf{H}, \mathsf{comb}(\mathsf{Sim}, f_\mathsf{A}^\#(\mathsf{A})))$; recall that $f_\mathsf{A}^\#$ is just a port renaming; hence Figure 3 simplifies it to A.

The outline of the hybrid argument is as follows.

1. We define *hybrid configurations* $conf_i^{\mathsf{hyb}}$ of $Sys^{(i)}$ and $conf_i'^{\mathsf{hyb}}$ of $Sys'^{(i)}$ for $i = 1, \dots, P(k)$. In $conf_i^{\mathsf{hyb}}$ the first $i-1$ real structures have already been replaced with their ideal counterparts, while in $conf_i'^{\mathsf{hyb}}$ also the i-th structure has been replaced. To make these configurations correct configurations of the respective systems, all other machines are grouped into an overall hybrid user $\mathsf{H}_i^{\mathsf{hyb}}$ as shown at the bottom of Figure 3 for $i = 2$ and $P(k) = 3$.

2. We show that these are correct and corresponding configurations with respect to the given blackbox simulatability between $Sys^{(i)}$ and $Sys'^{(i)}$.

3. We show that the views of H in $conf_i'^{\mathsf{hyb}}$ and $conf_{i+1}^{\mathsf{hyb}}$ are equal for $i = 1, \dots, P(k) - 1$. Moreover, we show that the views of H are equal in $conf^\#$ and $conf_1^{\mathsf{hyb}}$, and in $conf_{P(k)}'^{\mathsf{hyb}}$ and $conf^*$. This gives a kind of indistinguishability chain (for one configuration)

$$view_{conf^\#}(\mathsf{H}) \approx view_{conf_1^{\mathsf{hyb}}}(\mathsf{H}) \approx \cdots \approx view_{conf_{P(k)}'^{\mathsf{hyb}}}(\mathsf{H}) \approx view_{conf^*}(\mathsf{H}).$$

4. We show that this implies indistinguishability between first and last elements.

We now explain these steps in more detail.

Step 1: For $i = 1, \dots, P(k)$, let the machine collection for the i-th hybrid user be $\hat{H}_i := \{\mathsf{H}\} \cup \bigcup_{1 \le j < i} \hat{M}_j' \cup \{\mathsf{Sim}_j \mid 1 \le j < i\} \cup \bigcup_{i < j \le P(k)} \hat{M}_j$, and let $\mathsf{H}_i^{\mathsf{hyb}} := \mathsf{comb}(\hat{H}_i)$. Furthermore let $\mathsf{A}_i := f_\mathsf{A}^{(i-1)} \circ \cdots \circ f_\mathsf{A}^{(1)}(\mathsf{A})$ and $\mathsf{A}_i' := f_\mathsf{A}^{(i)}(\mathsf{A}_i)$. Then we define the *hybrid configurations* as

$$conf_i^{\mathsf{hyb}} := (\hat{M}_i, S_i, \mathsf{H}_i^{\mathsf{hyb}}, \mathsf{A}_i);$$
$$conf_i'^{\mathsf{hyb}} := (\hat{M}_i', S_i, \mathsf{H}_i^{\mathsf{hyb}}, \mathsf{comb}(\mathsf{Sim}_i, \mathsf{A}_i')).$$

For the computational case, we have to show that the family of $\mathsf{H}_i^{\mathsf{hyb}}$ is polynomial-time. This holds since $t_{\mathsf{H}_i^{\mathsf{hyb}}} \le t_\mathsf{H} + t_{\mathsf{Sim}} + t_{\hat{M}^\#} + t_{\hat{M}^*}$ by Lemma 2, where each addend is polynomially bounded by assumption.

Step 2: We have to show that $conf_i^{\mathsf{hyb}} \in \mathsf{Conf}^{f_i}(Sys_i)$ and $conf_i'^{\mathsf{hyb}} \in \mathsf{Conf}(Sys_i')$, i.e., essentially that the hybrid users do not use non-service ports. In this short version, we omit this proof. Then the definition of $conf_i^{\mathsf{hyb}}$ and $conf_i'^{\mathsf{hyb}}$ immediately implies

$$conf_i'^{\mathsf{hyb}} = f_\mathsf{C}^{(i)}(conf_i^{\mathsf{hyb}}), \tag{1}$$

i.e., these are indistinguishable configurations under the given blackbox simulatability between $Sys^{(i)}$ and $Sys'^{(i)}$.

Step 3: The configurations $conf_i^{\prime\text{hyb}}$ and $conf_{i+1}^{\text{hyb}}$ consist of the same collection of machines $\hat{C}_i := \hat{H}_i \cup \{\hat{M}'_i, \text{Sim}_i, \mathsf{A}'_i\}$. Combining them in different ways does not alter the view of H by Lemma 2. Thus we have

$$view_{conf_i^{\prime\text{hyb}}}(\mathsf{H}) = view_{conf_{i+1}^{\text{hyb}}}(\mathsf{H}) \tag{2}$$

for all $i \in \{1, \dots, P(k)\}$, and similarly

$$view_{conf^\#}(\mathsf{H}) = view_{conf_1^{\text{hyb}}}(\mathsf{H}) \wedge view_{conf_{P(k)}^{\text{hyb}}}(\mathsf{H}) = view_{conf^*}(\mathsf{H}). \tag{3}$$

Step 4: We now distinguish the type of the given simulatability relations $Sys^{(i)} \geq_{\text{sec}}^{\text{bb}, f^{(i)}, y_i} Sys^{\prime(i)}$.

For perfect simulatability, Equation (1) gives us $view_{conf_i^{\text{hyb}}}(\mathsf{H}) = view_{conf_i^{\prime\text{hyb}}}(\mathsf{H})$ for all i. With Equations (2) and (3) this yields $view_{conf^\#}(\mathsf{H}) = view_{conf^*}(\mathsf{H})$. This result for an arbitrary fixed configuration $conf^\#$ implies equality of all families of such views.

For statistical simulatability, let $Sys^{(i)}$ be δ_i-statistically at least as secure as $Sys^{\prime(i)}$. Let $l \in \mathbb{N}$. For prefixes of length l and v ranging over the potential views of this length, we abbreviate $q_v^\# := \Pr(view_{conf^\#, l}(\mathsf{H}) = v)$, and $q_v^* := \Pr(view_{conf^*, l}(\mathsf{H}) = v)$, and $q_{i,v} := \Pr(view_{conf_i^{\text{hyb}}, l}(\mathsf{H}) = v)$ and $q'_{i,v} := \Pr(view_{conf_i^{\prime\text{hyb}}, l}(\mathsf{H}) = v)$ for all i. For all potential views v, we have $q'_{i,v} = q_{i+1,v}$ and $q_v^\# = q_{1,v}$ and $q'_{P(k),v} = q_v^*$ by Equations (2) and (3). The desired statistical distance is

$$\delta_{\text{stat}}(conf^\#) := \frac{1}{2} \sum_v |q_v^\# - q_v^*|$$

$$= \frac{1}{2} \sum_v |q_{1,v} - q_{2,v} + q_{2,v} - q_{3,v} + \cdots + q_{P(k),v} - q'_{P(k),v}|$$

$$\leq \frac{1}{2} \sum_v (|q_{1,v} - q_{2,v}| + |q_{2,v} - q_{3,v}| + \cdots + |q_{P(k),v} - q'_{P(k),v}|)$$

$$= \sum_{i=1}^{P(k)} \frac{1}{2} \sum_v |q_{i,v} - q'_{i,v}|$$

$$= \sum_{i=1}^{P(k)} \Delta_{\text{stat}}(view_{conf_i^{\text{hyb}}, l}(\mathsf{H}), view_{conf_i^{\prime\text{hyb}}, l}(\mathsf{H})).$$

With Lemma 1 this gives

$$\delta_{\text{stat}}(conf^\#) \leq \sum_{i=1}^{P(k)} \Delta_{\text{stat}}(view_{conf_i^{\text{hyb}}, l_i}(\mathsf{H}_i^{\text{hyb}}), view_{conf_i^{\prime\text{hyb}}, l_i}(\mathsf{H}_i^{\text{hyb}})) \leq \sum_{i=1}^{P(k)} \delta(k, l_i),$$

where the l_i are sufficiently large numbers to ensure that the l-step prefix of the view of H in $conf_i^{\text{hyb}}$ is a subsequence of the l_i-step prefix of the view of $\mathsf{H}_i^{\text{hyb}}$. A general bound is the complexity of H_i^{hyb}, which is bounded by $b := t_{\text{H}} + t_{\hat{M}\#} + t_{\hat{M}*} + t_{\text{Sim}}$. This implies $\delta_{\text{stat}}(conf^\#) \leq P(k) \cdot \delta(k, b(k))$ as desired.

For concrete complexity and for a (t, Δ^{Dis})-distinguisher Dis, we have by definition

$$\Delta^{\text{Dis}} \leq |\text{Pr}(\text{Dis}(1^k, view_{conf\#}(\text{H})) = 1) - \text{Pr}(\text{Dis}(1^k, view_{conf*}(\text{H})) = 1)|.$$

We abbreviate $q^\# := \text{Pr}(\text{Dis}(1^k, view_{conf\#}(\text{H})) = 1)$ and $q^* := \text{Pr}(\text{Dis}(1^k, view_{conf*}(\text{H})) = 1)$, and $q_i := \text{Pr}(\text{Dis}(1^k, view_{conf_i^{\text{hyb}}}(\text{H})) = 1)$ and $q_i' := \text{Pr}(\text{Dis}(1^k, view_{conf_i'^{\text{hyb}}}(\text{H})) = 1)$ for all i, and $\Delta_i := |q_i - q_i'|$. Now Equations (2) and (3) yield

$$\Delta^{\text{Dis}} = |q^\# - q^*| = |q_1 - q_2 + q_2 - q_3 + q_3 + \cdots + q_{P(k)} - q_{P(k)}'|$$
$$\leq |q_1 - q_2| + |q_2 - q_3| + \cdots + |q_{P(k)} - q_{P(k)}'| = \Delta_1 + \Delta_2 + \cdots + \Delta_{P(k)}.$$

This implies that there exists some i with $\Delta_i \geq \frac{\Delta^{\text{Dis}}}{P(k)}$.

We can now consider Dis as a (t, Δ_i)-distinguisher $\text{Dis}_\phi^{(i)}$ of a function ϕ of views of the actual user H_i^{hyb} of the i-th hybrid systems. Here ϕ is defined by $\phi(v) := v\lceil_{\text{H}}$, i.e., the restriction to the view of H. The complexity t_ϕ of ϕ is linear. Hence Lemma 1 implies that there exists a (t_i, Δ_i)-distinguisher $\text{Dis}^{(i)}$ for $view_{conf_i^{\text{hyb}}}(H_i^{\text{hyb}})$ and $view_{conf_i'^{\text{hyb}}}(H_i^{\text{hyb}})$ with $t_i = t + b'(k)$, where $b'(k)$ bounds the length of the views of H_i^{hyb}. The complexity $t_{H_i^{\text{hyb}}}$ of H_i^{hyb} is bounded by $b = t_{\text{H}} + t_{\hat{M}\#} + t_{\hat{M}*} + t_{\text{Sim}}$, and above we showed $t_{\text{Sim}} \leq P \cdot Q_{\text{Sim}}$. The length of runs and thus views in our current representation is bounded by the square of this complexity (but this might be improvable by tighter encoding). This yields the desired polynomial bound $b'(k)$ independent of the adversary complexity.

For polynomial simulatability, let H, A be a user and an adversary for $Sys^\#$ of complexity t_{H} and t_{A}, and let t be a polynomial and Dis a distinguisher family of complexity t. Then the functions $t_{H_i^{\text{hyb}}}$, t_i, and $t_{\text{A}_i} = t_{\text{A}}$ are polynomials. By assumption, there exists a negligible function δ that uniformly bounds the advantage of distinguishers for the given system pairs for the complexity function $\max(t_i, t_{H_i^{\text{hyb}}}, t_{\text{A}_i})$. Now let a configuration $conf^\# = (\hat{M}^\#, S, H_{(\hat{M}\#, S)}, A_{(\hat{M}\#, S)})$ be given. The concrete security considerations and Equation (1) imply $\Delta_i = \delta_{conf_i^{\text{hyb}}}^{\text{Dis}^{(i)}} \leq \delta(k)$, and therefore $\delta_{conf\#}^{\text{Dis}} \leq P(k) \cdot \delta(k)$ is negligible. This proves the desired polynomial indistinguishability of the families of user views over $Sys^\#$ and Sys^*. $\blacksquare$

4   From Black-Box to Universal Simulatability

We now show a relation between universal simulatability and black-box simulatability. It allows us to apply our general composition theorem to universal simulatability under reasonable assumptions, but it also is of independent interest. More precisely, we show that universal simulatability for two parametrized systems Sys_1 and Sys_2 is equivalent to black-box simulatability if Sys_1 fulfills the following structural requirements: Whenever a clock-out port of a structure $(\hat{M}_1, S_1) \in Sys_1$ is contained in $\bar{S}_1^c$, then so is either the corresponding input or output port. This means that the adversary is not allowed to schedule messages of a connection where it is neither the sender nor the recipient. This condition is naturally fulfilled for insecure channels, since the adversary is inserted between the connections of two machines of the system.

Theorem 2. *(Relating Black-box and Universal Simulatability) Let Sys_1, Sys_2 be two parametrized systems with a valid mapping f, where for every structure $(\hat{M}_1, S_1) \in Sys_1$, we have $\mathsf{p}^{\lhd}! \in \bar{S}_1^c \Rightarrow (\mathsf{p}? \in \bar{S}_1^c \vee \mathsf{p}! \in \bar{S}_1^c)$. Then $Sys_1 \geq_{sec}^{bb,f,y} Sys_2$ iff $Sys_1 \geq_{sec}^{uni,f,y} Sys_2$ for $y = \mathsf{perf}$ or a function δ and also for $y = \mathsf{poly}$ if Sys_1 is polynomial-time.*

For concrete security, if $\geq_{sec}^{uni,f}$ is given with a τ-mapping f_C, then we obtain $\geq_{sec}^{bb,f}$ with simulator complexity $\tau(t_{Sys_1})$, and a (t, δ)-distinguisher for the views in the black-box case gives rise to a (t', δ)-distinguisher for the views in the universal case where t' is the sum of t and the view length of H and A. □

Proof. The left-to-right direction is clear by definition. The difficult direction is to show that universal simulatability implies black-box simulatability. Due to lack of space, we can only present a short sketch. This direction essentially consists of four steps:

1. Let a configuration $conf_1 = (\hat{M}_1, S, \mathsf{H}, \mathsf{A}_1)$ of the sub-system $Sys_{1,k}$ be given. We first derive another configuration $conf_1^{uni} = (\hat{M}_1, S, \mathsf{H}^{uni}, \mathsf{A}'_1)$ of Sys_1 as follows: We insert a machine $\mathsf{TS}_{P,b,k}$, called *transparent scheduler*, into the connections between A_1 and the simple ports in $\bar{S}_1$. It forwards messages between machines of the structure and the adversary. Its parameters P and b correspond to the ports that the transparent scheduler connects to and a bound on its runtime, which is the joint runtime of the machines in $\hat{M}_1$. This machine only depends on $\hat{M}_1$, S, and k. The new user is the combination $\mathsf{H}^{uni} := \mathsf{comb}(\mathsf{H}, \mathsf{A}_1)$, and the new adversary is $\mathsf{A}'_1 := \mathsf{TS}_{P,b,k}$. We show that the views of both H and A_1 are identical in the two configurations.

2. We now show that $conf_1^{uni} \in \mathsf{Conf}^f(Sys_1)$ and apply the precondition $Sys_1 \geq_{sec}^{uni,f} Sys_2$. This yields an indistinguishable configuration $conf_2^{uni}$ of Sys_2 with a new adversary A_2. By the definition of universal simulatability, A_2 only depends on $\hat{M}_1$, S and on $\mathsf{A}'_1 = \mathsf{TS}_{P,b,k}$. Since $\mathsf{TS}_{P,b,k}$ only depends on $\hat{M}_1$ and S, the adversary A_2 also only depends on $\hat{M}_1$ and S.

3. We obtain a configuration $conf_2$ with the original user and a simulator from $conf_2^{uni}$ by reversing the combination of H and A_1 into H^{uni}, and by defining the simulator as $\mathsf{Sim} := \mathsf{A}_2$. We show that this does not affect the view of H.

4. Combining several equalities between views of H in different configurations and one indistinguishability gives the same class of indistinguishability.

Summarized statements follow from this treatment per configuration, i.e., with concrete security (although details are omitted here), as usual. ∎

Acknowledgments. We thank *Anupam Datta, Dennis Hofheinz, Ralf Küsters, John Mitchell, Jörn Müller-Quade, Dusko Pavlovic* and *Rainer Steinwandt* for interesting discussions.

References

1. M. Abadi and L. Lamport. Conjoining specifications. *ACM Transactions on Programming Languages and Systems*, 17(3):507–534, 1995.
2. M. Backes and C. Jacobi. Cryptographically sound and machine-assisted verification of security protocols. In *Proc. 20th Annual Symposium on Theoretical Aspects of Computer Science (STACS)*, volume 2607 of *LNCS*, pages 675–686. Springer, 2003.
3. M. Backes and B. Pfitzmann. Computational probabilistic non-interference. In *Proc. 7th European Symposium on Research in Computer Security (ESORICS)*, volume 2502 of *LNCS*, pages 1–23. Springer, 2002.
4. M. Backes and B. Pfitzmann. Intransitive non-interference for cryptographic purposes. In *Proc. 24th IEEE Symposium on Security & Privacy*, pages 140–152, 2003.
5. M. Backes, B. Pfitzmann, M. Steiner, and M. Waidner. Polynomial fairness and liveness. In *Proc. 15th IEEE Computer Security Foundations Workshop (CSFW)*, pages 160–174, 2002.
6. D. Beaver. Secure multiparty protocols and zero knowledge proof systems tolerating a faulty minority. *Journal of Cryptology*, 4(2):75–122, 1991.
7. M. Bellare, J. Killian, and P. Rogaway. The security of cipherblock chaining. In *Advances in Cryptology: CRYPTO '94*, volume 839 of *LNCS*, pages 341–358. Springer, 1994.
8. M. Bellare and P. Rogaway. Optimal asymmetric encryption. In *Advances in Cryptology: EUROCRYPT '94*, volume 950 of *LNCS*, pages 92–111. Springer, 1994.
9. R. Canetti. Security and composition of multiparty cryptographic protocols. *Journal of Cryptology*, 3(1):143–202, 2000.
10. R. Canetti. Universally composable security: A new paradigm for cryptographic protocols. In *Proc. 42nd IEEE Symposium on Foundations of Computer Science (FOCS)*, pages 136–145, 2001. Extended version in Cryptology ePrint Archive, Report 2000/67, http://eprint.iacr.org/.
11. A. Datta, A. Derek, J. C. Mitchell, and D. Pavlovic. Secure protocol composition (extended abstract). In *Proc. 1st ACM Workshop on Formal Methods in Security Engineering (FMSE)*, pages 11–23, 2003.
12. O. Goldreich. *Foundations of Cryptography: Basic Tools*. Cambridge University Press, 2001.
13. O. Goldreich, S. Micali, and A. Wigderson. How to play any mental game – or – a completeness theorem for protocols with honest majority. In *Proc. 19th Annual ACM Symposium on Theory of Computing (STOC)*, pages 218–229, 1987.
14. S. Goldwasser and L. Levin. Fair computation of general functions in presence of immoral majority. In *Advances in Cryptology: CRYPTO '90*, volume 537 of *LNCS*, pages 77–93. Springer, 1990.
15. S. Goldwasser and S. Micali. Probabilistic encryption. *Journal of Computer and System Sciences*, 28:270–299, 1984.
16. M. Hirt and U. Maurer. Player simulation and general adversary structures in perfect multiparty computation. *Journal of Cryptology*, 13(1):31–60, 2000.
17. C. A. R. Hoare. *Communicating Sequential Processes*. International Series in Computer Science, Prentice Hall, Hemel Hempstead, 1985.
18. D. M. Johnson and F. Javier Thayer. Security and the composition of machines. In *Proc. 1st IEEE Computer Security Foundations Workshop (CSFW)*, pages 72–89, 1988.
19. P. Lincoln, J. Mitchell, M. Mitchell, and A. Scedrov. A probabilistic poly-time framework for protocol analysis. In *Proc. 5th ACM Conference on Computer and Communications Security*, pages 112–121, 1998.
20. P. Lincoln, J. Mitchell, M. Mitchell, and A. Scedrov. Probabilistic polynomial-time equivalence and security analysis. In *Proc. 8th Symposium on Formal Methods Europe (FME 1999)*, volume 1708 of *LNCS*, pages 776–793. Springer, 1999.

21. N. Lynch. *Distributed Algorithms*. Morgan Kaufmann Publishers, San Francisco, 1996.
22. H. Mantel. On the composition of secure systems. In *Proc. 23rd IEEE Symposium on Security & Privacy*, pages 88–101, 2002.
23. D. McCullough. Specifications for multi-level security and a hook-up property. In *Proc. 8th IEEE Symposium on Security & Privacy*, pages 161–166, 1987.
24. D. McCullough. A hookup theorem for multilevel security. *IEEE Transactions on Software Engineering*, 16(6):563–568, 1990.
25. J. McLean. A general theory of composition for trace sets closed under selective interleaving functions. In *Proc. 15th IEEE Symposium on Security & Privacy*, pages 79–93, 1994.
26. J. McLean. A general theory of composition for a class of "possibilistic" security properties. *IEEE Transactions on Software Engineering*, 22(1):53–67, 1996.
27. S. Micali and P. Rogaway. Secure computation. In *Advances in Cryptology: CRYPTO '91*, volume 576 of *LNCS*, pages 392–404. Springer, 1991.
28. J. Misra and K. M. Chandy. Proofs of network of processes. *IEEE Transactions on Software Engineering*, 7(4):417–426, 1981.
29. B. Pfitzmann and M. Waidner. A general framework for formal notions of "secure" systems. Research Report 11/94, University of Hildesheim, Apr. 1994.
   http://www.semper.org/sirene/lit/abstr94.html\#PfWa_94.
30. B. Pfitzmann and M. Waidner. Composition and integrity preservation of secure reactive systems. In *Proc. 7th ACM Conference on Computer and Communications Security*, pages 245–254, 2000. Extended version (with Matthias Schunter) IBM Research Report RZ 3206, May 2000, http://www.semper.org/sirene/publ/PfSW1_00ReactSimulIBM.ps.gz.
31. B. Pfitzmann and M. Waidner. A model for asynchronous reactive systems and its application to secure message transmission. In *Proc. 22nd IEEE Symposium on Security & Privacy*, pages 184–200, 2001. Extended version in Cryptology ePrint Archive, Report 2000/066, http://eprint.iacr.org/.
32. J. Widom, D. Gries, and F. B. Schneider. Trace-based network proof systems: Expressiveness and completeness. *ACM Transactions on Programming Languages and Systems*, 14(3):396–416, 1992.
33. A. C. Yao. Protocols for secure computations. In *Proc. 23rd IEEE Symposium on Foundations of Computer Science (FOCS)*, pages 160–164, 1982.
34. A. C. Yao. Theory and applications of trapdoor functions. In *Proc. 23rd IEEE Symposium on Foundations of Computer Science (FOCS)*, pages 80–91, 1982.

Unfair Noisy Channels and Oblivious Transfer

Ivan Damgård[1], Serge Fehr[2]*, Kirill Morozov[1], and Louis Salvail[1]**

[1] BRICS***, FICS [†], Aarhus University, Denmark
{ivan,kirill,salvail}@brics.dk
[2] ACAC[‡], Department of Computing, Macquarie University, Australia
sfehr@ics.mq.edu.au

Abstract. In a paper from EuroCrypt'99, Damgård, Kilian and Salvail show various positive and negative results on constructing Bit Commitment (BC) and Oblivious Transfer (OT) from Unfair Noisy Channels (UNC), i.e., binary symmetric channels where the error rate is only known to be in a certain interval $[\gamma..\delta]$ and can be chosen adversarially. They also introduce a related primitive called *PassiveUNC*. We prove in this paper that any OT protocol that can be constructed based on a *PassiveUNC* and is secure against a passive adversary can be transformed using a generic "compiler" into an OT protocol based on a *UNC* which is secure against an active adversary. Apart from making positive results easier to prove in general, this also allows correcting a problem in the EuroCrypt'99 paper: There, a positive result was claimed on constructing from UNC an OT that is secure against active cheating. We point out that the proof sketch given for this was incomplete, and we show that a correct proof of a much stronger result follows from our general compilation result and a new technique for transforming between weaker versions of OT with different parameters.

1 Introduction

Bit Commitment (BC) and Oblivious Transfer (OT) are the most fundamental primitives in cryptographic protocol design [8,1,3,9,10]. But in a scenario with only two players, neither primitive can be implemented with unconditional security based only on standard, error free communication. Even quantum communication does not help [14,13]. However, Crépeau and Kilian have shown that both primitives can be implemented based on a binary symmetric channel (BSC) [5]. A BSC is a channel for transmitting single bits, and for every bit transmitted, the channel decides with some fixed probability to flip the bit before it is

---

* Most of this work was done while at BRICS, Aarhus University, Denmark.
** Research funded by European project PROSECCO.
*** Basic Research in Computer Science (www.brics.dk), funded by the Danish National Research Foundation.
[†] FICS, Foundations in Cryptography and Security, funded by the Danish Natural Sciences Research Council.
[‡] Centre for Advanced Computing - Algorithms and Cryptography.

M. Naor (Ed.): TCC 2004, LNCS 2951, pp. 355–373, 2004.

given to the receiver. Unfortunately, results based on BSCs do not give realistic security guarantees. The reason for this is that one must expect that a cheating player will try to influence the channel and have this work to his/her advantage, for instance by lowering the noise rate in order to learn more than expected about what the other party sent or received. Note that one can always hide the fact that the channel was made less noisy by pretending to have sent(received) a more noisy signal than the one actually sent(received). Moreover, even in the absence of such attacks, it is hardly realistic to assume that the noise rate is known exactly.

In [7], Damgård, Kilian and Salvail introduce the Unfair Noisy Channel (UNC) as a model of a noisy channel that is more realistic in cryptographic applications than a BSC. A (γ, δ)-UNC is basically a BSC, where, however, the noise rate is only known to be in a certain interval $[\gamma..\delta]$, and where if the sender or receiver has been corrupted by an adversary, the adversary can set the noise rate to any desired value in the interval. So a UNC models active cheating directed against the way a physical channel works in order to manipulate the error rate. If the channel is a radio link, for instance, the adversary could invest in more sophisticated receiving equipment without telling the other party and thereby lowering the noise rate from his point of view. However, it may still be realistic to assume that he cannot remove *all* noise from the channel, so such a case can be captured in the UNC model.

Another primitive was also introduced, namely a (γ, δ)-PassiveUNC. This is a BSC with error rate δ, but where the adversary gets for every transmission some side information z with the property that given z, the bit received/sent by the other (honest) player can be guessed with error probability γ. In other words, knowledge of z brings the error rate down to γ from the adversary's point of view. This models a passive, i.e., "honest but curious" adversary, who measures somewhere "in the middle" of the channel, and then later uses the information obtained to compute data he should not have access to.

In [7], it was proved that Bit Commitment (BC) can be implemented with unconditional security based on a (γ, δ)-UNC if and only if the interval $[\gamma..\delta]$ is not too wide, more precisely, if and only if $\delta < 2\gamma(1 - \gamma)$. It was also shown that one cannot base Oblivious Transfer (OT) on a (γ, δ)-UNC (nor on a PassiveUNC) if $\delta \geq 2\gamma(1 - \gamma)$. On the positive side, it was shown that if γ and δ satisfy a rather complex condition (stronger than $\delta < 2\gamma(1 - \gamma)$), then OT (with *passive* security) can be based on a (γ, δ)-PassiveUNC.

Finally, it was claimed that this same result also holds when using a (γ, δ)-UNC, and with security against *active* cheating. This was based on a standard idea where the players use bit commitments to commit to all private data, including what is sent and received on the channel, and then use generic zero-knowledge techniques to demonstrate that they follow the protocol. This technique indeed works assuming that we can force a cheating player to commit to the bits he actually sends or receives over the channel (except with arbitrarily small probability). This assumption is true for a BSC: for instance the sender S can be instructed to commit to bits $b_i, i = 1..n$, and send them over the BSC with noise rate, say, δ. Having received bits $\hat{b}_i, i = 1..n$, the receiver R then asks to have all committed bits opened except one, say b_j. If S was honest, we expect that a fraction of about δ of the opened bits will be different from the received bits $\hat{b}_i, i = 1..n$. So R is instructed to reject if the fraction of disagreement is significantly larger than δ. If R does not reject, this means intuitively that he believes that the committed bit b_j really is the bit that was sent over the channel and resulted in R receiving $\hat{b}_j$. This is justified since it follows from standard probability theory that the probability of having b_j different from the j'th bit actually sent and still have the receiver accept, can be made arbitrarily small by increasing n.

Unfortunately, no such technique can work for a UNC. We show below that for any protocol that aims to implement a "committed UNC", the probability of error is at least a constant, namely $(\delta - \gamma)/(1 - 2\gamma)$. This problem was not taken care of in [7].

In this paper, we show a different (and correct) way to apply the idea of using commitments and zero-knowledge proofs to enforce correct behavior. This turns out to lead to a result that is much more general than what was claimed in [7] and which can be informally stated as follows: Any two-party protocol that, based on a (γ, δ)-PassiveUNC, implements an OT secure against passive cheating, can be transformed using a generic "compiler" into a protocol that uses a (γ, δ)-UNC for communication and builds an OT secure against active cheating.

The opposite direction of this result is also true, and trivial to prove. So this implies that, to prove positive or negative results, on building OT from UNC or PassiveUNC, we can now concentrate only on the case of PassiveUNC and passive cheating - which is clearly much simpler. It also immediately implies a complete proof of the claim made in [7].

In the final part of the paper we exploit this, and a new technique for transforming between the weaker versions of OT, in order to prove a stronger positive OT result than the one claimed in [7]. In other words, there is now a much larger range of (γ, δ)-values for which we can implement OT based on a (γ, δ)-UNC. For instance we can now show that robust OT follows from a (γ, δ)-UNC with *any* value of δ between 0 and $1/2$, provided γ is close enough to δ.

Due to space limitations, some proofs could not be included in this proceedings version of the paper. They can be found in the full paper [6].

2   Models of Communication and Adversaries

Our protocols throughout the paper take place in a model with two players A, B connected by an error free channel and also by a noisy channel with some particular characteristic, such as a UNC or a PassiveUNC. We assume a bounded delay in message delivery for all channels such that failure to send a message can be detected.

In order to specify formally the channels and reductions we study, we will use the universally composable framework of Canetti [2]. In this framework, players in a protocol can be given access to one or more *ideal functionalities*. Such a functionality can be thought of as a trusted party T with whom every player can communicate privately. There is a number of commands specified that T will execute. Every player can send a command to T, and T will faithfully carry out the command according to its specification, and may send results back to (some of) the players. Many cryptographic constructions – including ours – actually aim at building a protocol for the players only (without a trusted party) that does "the same thing" as some ideal functionality T, even if an adversary can corrupt some of the players and make them behave as he likes. The framework provides a precise definition of what it means that a protocol π in this way securely implements T. If this definition is satisfied, then any protocol that is secure when using T is also secure if T is replaced by π. In its full generality, the definition is robust against adaptive adversaries and concurrent composition of protocols.

All our protocols are in the 2-player case with information theoretic security. Here, the standard approach in previous research to security proofs has been to assume that either A or B is cheating, then prove some relevant security properties, and finally to prove that if both parties are honest, then the protocol "works correctly". We express this in the UC framework by assuming an infinitely powerful non-adaptive adversary who from the start has corrupted no one, or either A or B. While we believe that our results extend to adaptive adversaries, we do not prove or claim this in this paper. Furthermore, if the noisy channel is a UNC, then the adversary is assumed to be active, i.e., can decide the corrupted player's behavior. If the channel is a PassiveUNC, the adversary is passive.

Another consequence of being in the two-player case, is that we do not think of our protocols as subroutines in a multiplayer protocol, nor are we worried about external observers, only about what a corrupted A or B might do or learn. We therefore assume that unless the adversary corrupts a player, he gets no information about the communication between A and B. At the cost of more complex proofs, our results extend to the case where the adversary always eavesdrops the error free channel.

To prove that a protocol π satisfies the UC definition, one has to construct, for every adversary Adv attacking the protocol in question, an ideal model adversary, or *simulator S*, which gets to attack an ideal scenario where only the players and T are present. The goal of S is to achieve "the same" as Adv could have achieved by an attack on the real protocol. In the framework, this is formalized by assuming an *environment machine Z* which can communicate in a real life attack with Adv and the honest players, and in the ideal model with S and the honest players. The protocol is said to be secure if for every adversary Adv there exists a simulator S, such that Z cannot tell if it is in the real-life or the ideal model. For details, see [2].

In proofs of this type of security, S usually works by running internally a copy of the adversary Adv, and passing interaction back and forth between Z and Adv with no change. If S can simulate with an indistinguishable distribution both the view of Adv attacking π and simultaneously make the input/output behavior of the honest players be as in the real attack, then Z will not be able to tell any difference.

The noisy channels we study in this paper can very conveniently be modeled as ideal functionalities, and reductions that build one type of channel from another can be proved secure in this framework. Since the results we prove are information theoretic in nature, we modify the UC model as given in [2] by allowing our adversaries and simulators infinite computing power - but we stress that honest players can execute our protocols efficiently.

3   Some Functionalities

We can now specify our basic types of channels precisely but for completeness we start by describing the functionality for standard (1-out-of-2) OT as well as for a weak version as introduced in [7] with parameters $0 \le p, q \le 1$ and $0 \le \epsilon \le 1/2$:

Functionality OT

Send (b_0, b_1): The issuer of the Send command is called the sender, the other party is the receiver. On receipt of this command, the functionality records (b_0, b_1) and outputs "which bit?" to the receiver. It ignores all further commands until the receiver sends a "Choice" command.

Choice c: Receiving this command from the receiver, the functionality sends b_c to the receiver if $c \in \{0, 1\}$ and otherwise ignores the command.

For later convenience, we call the receiver's choice c the *selection bit* and the bit b_{1-c} (which is not revealed to the receiver) the *secret bit*.

Functionality (p, q, ϵ)-**WOT**

Send (b_0, b_1): The functionality's action on this command is the same as in OT.
Choice c: If $c \notin \{0, 1\}$ then the functionality ignores the command. Otherwise, it chooses $\tilde{b}_c \in \{0, 1\}$ such that $Pr(\tilde{b}_c \ne b_c) = \epsilon$ and sends it to the receiver. Additionally, if the sender is corrupted, then with probability p it sends c to the sender, and if the receiver is corrupted, then with probability q it sends b_{1-c} to the receiver.

A (γ, δ)-UNC is specified by the following functionality.

Functionality (γ, δ)-**UNC**

Send b: The issuer of the Send command is called the sender, the other party is the receiver. On receipt of this command, the functionality records b and outputs a string "which error probability?" to the adversary. It ignores all further commands until the adversary sends an "Error probability" command.
Error probability ϵ: Receiving this command from the adversary, the functionality checks if $\gamma \le \epsilon \le \delta$. If not, the command is ignored. Otherwise, it chooses a random bit b', such that $Pr(b' = 1) = \epsilon$, and sends $\hat{b} = b \oplus b'$ to the receiver.

What we want to model here is intuitively that a corrupted player may influence the error rate or even block the channel. But if both players are honest, transmissions will always go through, however, the error rate will fluctuate in some arbitrary way in the given interval. We therefore assume throughout about the adversary that if both players are honest, then the adversary will always give a legal error probability back when receiving a request from the UNC.

As mentioned, the adversary is allowed to set the error probability to any value in $[\gamma..\delta]$ for every transmission. However, if the adversary corrupts a player, any attack he can do following, say, algorithm Alg can be simulated perfectly by an adversary that sets the error rate to γ always, but adds artificial noise to any bit sent(received) in case Alg wanted a larger error rate. We may therefore always assume that an active adversary who corrupts A or B always sets the error rate of the UNC to γ.

We introduce some notation that will be convenient: if we cascade a BSC with error rate x and a BSC with error rate y, the result is again a BSC, we define $x \boxplus y$ to be the resulting error rate, $x(1 - y) + (1 - x)y$. Note that the operator $\boxplus$ is commutative, associative and satisfies that if $|x - x'| < \nu$, then $|x \boxplus y - x' \boxplus y| < \nu$ for all y.

Functionality (γ, δ)-PassiveUNC

Send b: The issuer of the Send command is called the sender, the other party is the receiver. On receipt of this command, the functionality chooses random bits b', b'', such that $Pr(b' = 1) = \gamma$ and $Pr(b'' = 1) = \nu$, where $\nu \boxplus \gamma = \delta$. This ensures that $Pr(b' \oplus b'' = 1) = \delta$. The functionality sends $\hat{b} = b \oplus b' \oplus b''$ to the receiver. If the adversary has corrupted a player, it sends to the adversary a bit z, where $z = b \oplus b''$ if the sender is corrupted, and $z = b \oplus b'$ if the receiver is corrupted. Intuitively, given z, the noise rate goes down to γ.

We need to consider the use of commitments and zero-knowledge proofs in our protocols. This can also be modeled by an ideal functionality, where one commits simply by giving the bit to the trusted party, who will then later open it on request from the committer. Furthermore, the trusted party will confirm that committed bits satisfy a given formula, if this is indeed true.

Functionality Commit-and-prove (CaP)

Commit cID, b: Receiving this command, where cID is a bitstring and b is a bit, do as follows: if no message containing cID has been received yet, record the value of cID, b and send as output $Commit, cID$ to all players.

Open cID: if cID, b has been received earlier from the player issuing this command, send b to all players.

Prove L, Φ: Receiving this command, where L is a list of bit strings and Φ is a Boolean formula, check if L contains only strings that has been used as identifiers for bits committed to by the issuer of the Prove command. If so, find the corresponding bits and check if they satisfy Φ. If so, sends (OK, L, Φ) to all players. Else, send $(Fail, L, \Phi)$.

As bit commitment scheme in our protocols, we will use the UNC-based construction from [7], which works assuming $\delta < 2\gamma(1-\gamma)$ which we will assume throughout. This scheme is statistically close to perfect, regardless of A and B's computing power. Furthermore, given any commitment scheme, one can always construct a new one, where one can prove in zero-knowledge that committed bits satisfy a given Boolean formula (see [11]). It follows that in any protocol where we assume access to a UNC, we may assume also a CaP without loss of generality.

A final functionality that will come in handy is the ability to choose random bits and numbers with a prescribed distribution:

Functionality RandomChoice

Flip sID, ν: Here sID is a session ID and ν must be a probability. Once the functionality has received this command from every player containing identical values of sID, ν, it chooses a bit b at random such that $Pr(b = 1) = \nu$ and sends b to all players.

Uniform, sID, j: Here sID is a session ID and j must be a natural number. Once the functionality has received this command from every player containing identical values of sID, j, it chooses i uniformly from $[0..j - 1]$ and sends i to all players.

Using standard techniques, one can implement this functionality based on the CaP, with a statistically good simulation. It should be noted that in our two-player scenario, functionalities such as RandomChoice can only be realized if the adversary is allowed to abort after seeing the output. But this is consistent with the UC framework, where adversary and simulator are indeed allowed to abort any time.

4   Committed (Passive)UNC

We first define informally the notion of a *committed UNC*. This is a protocol for players A, B, using a (γ, δ)-UNC and an error free channel. We will assume that $\delta < 2\gamma(1 - \gamma)$, so that bit commitment can be done, based on the UNC. Note that if the UNC can only send bits from A to B, we can still simulate a UNC in the opposite direction using the error free channel, so that we can assume that both A and B can commit to bits without loss of generality.

Intuitively, the purpose of a committed UNC is to act just like an ordinary UNC, but such that players are committed to the bits they send/receive on the UNC, at least except with some bounded probability.

We now define this concept more formally: a committed UNC protocol may halt because A or B reject. Otherwise it outputs two commitments, one from A containing a bit b_A, and one from B containing a bit b_B. Finally, the output designates one of the transmissions that were made over the UNC from A to B. Let s_A resp. r_B be the bit sent, respectively received in this transmission.

We require that if A, B both follow the protocol, then both players accept except with probability negligible in the security parameter k. Also, whenever A is honest, we have that b_A is uniformly random and $b_A = s_A$. Whenever B is honest, we have $r_B = b_B$. When A is corrupted and B is honest, we let p_A be the probability of the event that B accepts and $b_A \neq s_A$. Similarly, when B is corrupted and A is honest, we let p_B be the probability that A accepts and $r_B \neq b_B$. In general, the error probabilities p_A, p_B will be functions of γ, δ and the security parameter k.

The argument sketched in [7] on constructing OT from UNC took as point of departure a protocol that builds OT from a (γ, δ)-PassiveUNC for certain values of γ, δ and is secure assuming that players cheat only passively, i.e., are honest, but curious. It was then noted that one can replace the PassiveUNC with a UNC, still assuming that only passive cheating occurs. The final idea was then to replace the UNC with a committed UNC (although this notion was not formally defined there) and have players prove in ZK that they were following the protocol. If the error probabilities of the committed UNC could be made arbitrarily small with increasing k, then this would result in an OT secure against active cheating for essentially the same values of γ, δ that could be handled in the passive case. But unfortunately, this is impossible:

Theorem 1. *Any committed UNC as defined above, based on a (γ, δ)-UNC must have $p_A, p_B \geq \frac{\delta - \gamma}{1 - 2\gamma}$.*

Proof. Suppose, for instance, that A is cheating. Then A sets always the minimal noise level for the UNC, but adds artificial noise to each transmission with noise rate $\frac{\delta - \gamma}{1 - 2\gamma}$ such that the total error probability for each transmission is $\frac{\delta - \gamma}{1 - 2\gamma} \boxplus \gamma = \delta$. On the resulting transmissions, he runs a copy A_0 of the *honest* algorithm for A. Clearly, B (who is honest) cannot distinguish this from an all honest situation where the noise rate happens to be δ all the time, and so he must accept with overwhelming probability. However, it now holds for every transmission that the bit committed to and also sent by A_0, differs from the one A actually sent with probability $\frac{\delta - \gamma}{1 - 2\gamma}$. The theorem follows.   □

Theorem 1 essentially says that we cannot force a player to commit to the bit he *physically* sends on a UNC. To get around this problem, we take a different point of view: we will create a new virtual channel from the UNC, where a bit committed to by the sender is *by definition* the bit sent on the new channel. Any difference between the committed bit and what is sent on the original UNC is regarded as noise. With appropriate checking that a cheating player does not introduce too much noise this way, it turns out that we obtain something that behaves as essentially like a PassiveUNC, *even in presence of active cheating*. We model this by an ideal functionality called $(\gamma, \delta, q())$-Committed PassiveUNC (CPUNC). It combines a functionality similar to the PassiveUNC with the Commit-and-Prove functionality. In particular, it allows to commit to bits with or without sending them on the channel. But if they are sent, sender and receiver will be committed to what they send/receive. With security parameter k, the error rate will be in the range $\delta \pm 1/q(k)$, but will drop to γ

given the view of a cheating player. Note that a CPUNC is not a committed UNC, and so Theorem 1 does not forbid the existence of a secure implementation.

Functionality $(\gamma, \delta, q())$-CPUNC

Stop. On receiving this command from the adversary, the CPUNC stops working and ignores all further commands.

Send cID, b: CPUNC comes with parameters $0 \leq \gamma \leq \delta \leq 1/2$, a security parameter value k and a polynomial $q()$. The issuer of the Send command is called the sender, the other party is the receiver. The string cID must not have been used before to identify a sent, received or committed bit, else the command is ignored. On receipt of this command from A or B, the functionality records cID, b and outputs a string "which error probability?" to the adversary, it ignores all further commands until the adversary sends an "Error probability" command.

Error probability κ': Receiving this command from the adversary, the functionality checks if $|\delta - \kappa'| \leq 1/q(k)$. If not, the command is ignored. Otherwise, the functionality chooses random bits b', b'', such that $Pr(b' = 1) = \gamma$ and $Pr(b'' = 1) = \nu$, where $\nu \boxplus \gamma = \kappa'$. This ensures that $Pr(b' \oplus b'' = 1) = \kappa'$. The functionality sets $\hat{b} = b \oplus b' \oplus b''$. If the adversary has corrupted a player, it sends to the adversary a bit z, where $z = b \oplus b''$ if the sender is corrupted, and $z = b \oplus b'$ if the receiver is corrupted. It records cID, b as if the sender had committed to b. It then sends cID to all players, and ignores all further commands until the receiver sends a "ReciptID" command.

ReceiptID $c\hat{I}D$: This command is ignored if $c\hat{I}D$ has been used to identify any committed, sent or received bit earlier. If this is not the case, the CPUNC records $c\hat{I}D, \hat{b}$ as if the receiver had committed to $\hat{b}$, it sends $c\hat{I}D$ to all players and $\hat{b}$ to the receiver.

Commit cID, b: Receiving this command, where cID is a bitstring and b is a bit, do as follows: if cID has not been used to identify a sent, received or committed bit before, record the value of cID, b and send as output $Commit, cID$ to all players.

Open cID: if cID, b has been recorded as a commitment from the player issuing this command, send b to all players.

Prove L, Φ: Receiving this command, where L is a list of bit strings and Φ is a Boolean formula, check if L contains only strings that has been used as identifiers for bits committed to by the issuer of the Prove command. If so, find the corresponding bits and check if they satisfy Φ. If so, sends (OK, L, Φ) to all players. Else, send $(Fail, L, \Phi)$.

We now describe a protocol that securely realizes the functionality we just described. We assume that the protocol has access to the UNC, CaP and RandomChoice functionalities. The protocol is described by specifying how each of the commands are implemented. The amount of work done in the protocol is specified by a polynomial $p(k)$, where k is the security parameter.

Stop. This command has no direct implementation, the idea is that whenever the adversary behaves such that the honest party detects cheating and aborts, this is equivalent to sending a Stop command in the ideal scenario.

Send (Transmission Step). We describe how A will send a bit b to B.

1. A commits to b
2. A chooses at random bits $\bar{B} = b_1, ..., b_{kp(k)^3}$, commits to each bit and sends each bit to B over the UNC. B commits to every bit $\hat{B} = \hat{b}_1, ..., \hat{b}_{kp(k)^3}$ he receives.
3. Call RandomChoice $kp(k)^2$ times to generate integers j_i chosen uniformly in the range $[1..kp(k)^3]$, for $i = 1, ..., kp(k)^2$.
4. All bits $b_{j_i}, \hat{b}_{j_i}$ are opened. Let κ be the fraction of the $kp(k)^2$ opened positions where $b_{j_i} \neq \hat{b}_{j_i}$. A and B check that $\kappa \leq \delta + 1/p(k)$. They abort all interaction if this is not satisfied.
5. Call RandomChoice to generate an integer j uniformly chosen among the indices of positions that were not opened in the previous step. A sends $b' = b \oplus b_j$ using error free transmission and proves (using CaP) that this value is correct.
6. Let μ be defined by $\kappa \boxplus \mu = \delta + 1/p(k)$. By a call to RandomChoice, generate a bit c such that $Pr(c = 1) = \mu$.
7. B defines the bit he receives as $\hat{b} = \hat{b}_j \oplus b' \oplus c$. He commits to $\hat{b}$ and proves (using CaP) that the committed value is correct.

If B wants to send a bit to A, we implement this in the same way as above, by interchanging the roles of A and B and of b_j and $\hat{b}_j$.

Commit, Open, Prove. Each of these commands correspond directly to commands that are already available in the Commit-and-Prove functionality we assume we have access to. Therefore these commands are implemented by directly calling the corresponding command with the same input in the Commit-and-Prove. Note that inputs to the Prove or Open command may include bits that were sent or received during a Send command, since these are also committed to.

Before proving anything about this construction, we describe first the intuition behind it: for bit strings X, Y of equal length, let $err(X, Y)$ be the fraction of positions where X disagrees with Y. Now, if both parties are honest, the expected value of $err(\bar{B}, \hat{B})$ is at most δ, so allowing the estimate κ to be up to $\delta + 1/p(k)$ implies that we reject with negligible probability, as we shall see. Then assume that one player, say A, is corrupted, and let $\tilde{B} = \tilde{b}_1, ..., \tilde{b}_{kp(k)^3}$ be the bits actually sent by A on the UNC when a bit is transmitted. Let $\epsilon = err(\bar{B}, \tilde{B})$. Since the UNC introduces errors with probability γ independently of anything else, we expect that $\epsilon \boxplus \gamma \approx err(\bar{B}, \hat{B}) \approx \kappa$, and hence that $\epsilon \boxplus \gamma \boxplus \mu \approx \kappa \boxplus \mu \approx \delta$. Here, $\approx$ means equality up to a $1/poly()$ term.

We can now see that after doing the transmission step, A is actually in a position approximately equivalent to having sent b on a (γ, δ)-PassiveUNC: we have that the bit b sent is related to the bit $\hat{b}$ received as $b = \hat{b} \oplus (b_j \oplus \tilde{b}_j) \oplus c \oplus n_j$, where n_j is a noise bit chosen by the UNC, such that $Pr(n_j = 1) = \gamma$. By the choice of c, and random choice of j, we have

$$Pr(b \neq \hat{b}) = Pr((b_j \oplus \tilde{b}_j) \oplus c \oplus n_j = 1) \approx \epsilon \boxplus \mu \boxplus \gamma \approx \kappa \boxplus \mu \approx \delta.$$

But since the adversary knows $(b_j \oplus \tilde{b}_j) \oplus c$, the error rate from his point of view is only what is introduced by the UNC, namely γ.

In the full paper [6] we show the theorem below. First, some terminology to state the result: we say that a simulator (in the UC framework) is non-blocking, if it stops the CPUNC (by sending a stop command or refusing to give correct input when asked for it) with only negligible probability.

Theorem 2. *The Committed Passive UNC protocol securely realizes the $(\gamma, \delta, q())$-CPUNC functionality when given access to ideal (γ, δ)-UNC, CaP and RandomChoice functionalities, and for any polynomial $q()$, provided we choose the polynomial $p()$ measuring the work done in the protocol as $p(k) = 4q(k)$. Moreover, for the case where both players are honest, the simulator is non-blocking.*

Remark 1. The last claim in the theorem is a way to state in the UC framework the traditional completeness property for a 2-party protocol: if both players are honest, the protocol completes successfully with overwhelming probability.

5   From Passive to Active Security

In this section, we sketch a proof of the following result:

Theorem 3. *Let π be any protocol that securely realizes OT based on a (γ, δ)-PassiveUNC assuming a passive adversary. Then there exists a protocol with complexity polynomial in that of π that also securely realizes OT based on a (γ, δ)-UNC, assuming an active adversary.*

So we assume we have a protocol π that implements Oblivious Transfer given access to a (γ, δ)-PassiveUNC functionality, and that this protocol is secure against a passive adversary.

We then note that the previous section showed how to implement the CPUNC functionality based on the UNC. Therefore from π, we may construct a protocol $\bar{\pi}$ as follows: active cheating is prevented by first making players commit to all inputs, and furthermore, the random coins of a player are decided using a standard trick: the player in question commits to a random string a, the other player sends a random string b in the clear and the random coins to be used are $a \oplus b$. Second, all transmissions over the PassiveUNC now take place using the CPUNC, and each time something is sent, you use the CPUNC to prove that what was sent was computed according to π with the given (committed) inputs, random coins and messages received earlier.

Note that a player trying to send an incorrect message will be caught with certainty. Therefore, the views obtained by the players are always (a possibly truncated version of) what would be obtained in presence of a passive adversary.

Our first goal will be to show that $\bar{\pi}$ implements a weak form of OT (which then implies standard OT), namely a (p, q, ϵ)-WOT as defined in Section 3.

Lemma 1. $\bar{\pi}$ *as described above realizes (with statistically good simulation) a* (p, q, ϵ)-*WOT with* $p = q = \epsilon = 3/k$, *when* $\bar{\pi}$ *is executed with security parameter value* k.

Proof. (Sketch) The above discussion implies that we only have to show the lemma for a passive adversary: the only difference between a passive and an active attack on $\bar{\pi}$ is that the adversary may stop early in the active case, and this can never be prevented in an active attack. Assuming a passive adversary, the only difference between $\bar{\pi}$ and π is that $\bar{\pi}$ does not use a (γ, δ)-PassiveUNC but a $(\gamma, \delta, f())$-CPUNC where the adversary can make the error probability fluctuate slightly around δ. This fluctuation is not negligible, namely it is of size $1/f(k)$. However, by Theorem 2, we can choose $f()$ to be any polynomial we like, so assuming π calls the PassiveUNC $t(k)$ times, for some polynomial $t()$, we choose $f(k) = kt(k)$.

Consider the view of a (passively) corrupted sender in π, represented by random variable V. Let $adv_\pi(k, v)$ be the advantage over $1/2$ with which the selection bit can be guessed given that $V = v$ and the protocol was executed with security parameter value k. Let $adv_\pi(k) = \sum_v Pr(V = v) \cdot adv_\pi(k, v)$ be the expected value. Since π was assumed to be secure, $adv_\pi(k)$ is negligible in k (this is equivalent to asserting that the mutual information between the selection bit and V is negligible). Then define a particular possible value v of V to be *good* if $adv_\pi(k, v) \leq \sqrt{adv_\pi(k)}$, and let E be the event that V takes a bad value. Then clearly, E occurs with probability at most $\sqrt{adv_\pi(k)}$. We now define $t(k) + 1$ hybrids that are in between π and $\bar{\pi}$: namely in the i'th hybrid, where $i = 0..t(k)$, we run the normal protocol, but for communication, we use a (γ, δ)-PassiveUNC for the first i calls to the communication channel, and then the (γ, δ)-CPUNC for the rest. Then hybrid 0 is $\bar{\pi}$ while hybrid $t(k)$ is π. When executing hybrid i, we define E_i to be the event that the information contained in the sender's view about the selection bit is larger than $\sqrt{adv_\pi(k)}$. Let ϵ_i be the probability that E_i occurs. Of course $\epsilon_{t(k)} = Pr(E) \leq \sqrt{adv_\pi(k)}$. Also, the only difference between hybrid i and $i + 1$ is that in the $i + 1$'st call to the communication channel, the results returned by the channel have distributions with statistical difference at most $2/f(k)$ between them. It follows that $|\epsilon_i - \epsilon_{i+1}| \leq 2/f(k)$, and hence $\epsilon_0 \leq \epsilon_{t(k)} + 2t(k)/f(k) \leq \sqrt{adv_\pi(k)} + 2/k$. The "OT", that $\bar{\pi}$ implements is therefore no worse than a protocol that with probability, say $3/k$ reveals the selection bit to the sender, and otherwise leaks a negligible amount of information. A similar argument holds for the view of a corrupted receiver; also this type of argument shows that an honest receiver will receive the correct bit, except with probability at most $3/k$. Thus what we have is statistically indistinguishable from a (p, q, ϵ)-WOT, with $p = q = \epsilon = 3/k$. □

We can then complete the argument for the theorem: In [7], a reduction is shown that implements OT based on any (p, q, ϵ)-WOT, as long as $p + q + 2\epsilon < 0.45$. Moreover, it is easy to verify that by choosing k large enough the reduction implements OT efficiently, i.e., it only makes a polynomial number of calls to the underlying WOT. Therefore, by the above lemma, we can replace the WOT by $\bar{\pi}$ and still obtain a secure OT (even though $\bar{\pi}$ is only statistically close to the required WOT). This implies the result we wanted.

6 Extended Positive Results

In this section, we shall assume the result of Theorem 3 and focus on reducing OT to (γ, δ)-PassiveUNC securely against passive adversaries. The strategy of [7] is as follows. First, the (γ, δ)-PassiveUNC is used to construct an imperfect version of OT which may leak information about the parties' private inputs. This imperfect OT is modeled by a WOT. OT is then shown to be reducible to WOT for certain values of (γ, δ).

However, WOT does not precisely capture the imperfect OT obtained in the construction: In WOT the corrupted sender/receiver gets the selection/secret bit (which he is not supposed to see) with a certain probability, while in the imperfect OT obtained the corrupted sender/receiver only gets *some information* about that bit with a certain probability. As a consequence, in order to fit the imperfect OT into the WOT model, it is assumed in [7] that every time the dishonest sender/receiver gets some information about the selection/secret bit, he actually gets full information. Hence, the information leakage is overestimated in [7]. We introduce a new *Generalized Weak Oblivious Transfer (GWOT)* primitive which allows to model imperfect OTs which leak information about the parties' private inputs in a much more general way than WOTs, without overestimating the information leakage. In particular, it precisely captures the imperfect OT resulting from the construction of [7]. Informally, in a GWOT the corrupted sender/receiver gets the selection/secret bit over a BSC with some error probability which is chosen according to some distribution (and announced to the corrupted party). Formally, consider parameters $\{s_i, \alpha_i\}_i$ and $\{r_i, \beta_i\}_i$, where $i = 1, \ldots, N$, and ϵ such that $\{s_i\}_i$ and $\{r_i\}_i$ are probability distributions (over $\{1, \ldots, N\}$) and $0 \leq \alpha_i, \beta_i, \epsilon \leq 1/2$ for $i = 1, \ldots, N$. A GWOT with respect to these parameters is specified by a functionality of the following kind.
Functionality $\left(\{(s_i, \alpha_i)\}_{i=1}^N; \{(r_i, \beta_i)\}_{i=1}^N; \epsilon\right)$**-GWOT**

Send (b_0, b_1): The functionality's action on this command is the same as in OT.
Choice c: If $c \notin \{0, 1\}$ then the functionality ignores the command. Otherwise, it chooses $\tilde{b}_c \in \{0, 1\}$ such that $Pr(\tilde{b}_c \neq b_c) = \epsilon$ and sends it to the receiver. Additionally, if the sender is corrupted, then it chooses $I \in \{1, \ldots, N\}$ and $\tilde{c} \in \{0, 1\}$ such that $Pr(I = i) = s_i$ and $Pr(\tilde{c} \neq c \,|\, I = i) = \alpha_i$, and it sends I and $\tilde{c}$ to the sender. And/or, if the receiver is corrupted, then it chooses $I \in \{1, \ldots, N\}$, and $\tilde{b}_{1-c} \in \{0, 1\}$ such that $Pr(I = i) = r_i$ and $Pr(\tilde{b}_{1-c} \neq b_{1-c} \,|\, I = i) = \beta_i$, and it sends I and $\tilde{b}_{1-c}$ to the receiver.

We will say that a corrupted sender gets c "sent through $\{(s_i, \alpha_i)\}_{i=1}^N$" and similarly a corrupted receiver gets b_{1-c} "sent through $\{(r_i, \beta_i)\}_{i=1}^N$".

Note that there is some ambiguity in the functionality's action in that it is not required that $\tilde{b}_c$ is chosen independently of I and $\tilde{c}$, respectively of I and $\tilde{b}_{1-c}$, as long as the marginal distribution of $\tilde{b}_c$ is correct. Furthermore, a (p, q, ϵ)-WOT coincides obviously with a $\big(\{(p, 0), (1 - p, 1/2)\}; \{(q, 0), (1 - q, 1/2)\}; \epsilon\big)$-GWOT.

It will be convenient to introduce a GWOT of a very particular form, a *Special Generalized Oblivious Transfer (SGWOT)*. Informally, in a SGWOT the corrupted sender/receiver either gets no information on the selection/secret bit or he receives it over a BSC with a certain (fixed) error probability. Formally, for parameters $s, \alpha, r, \beta, \epsilon$ with $0 \leq s, r \leq 1$ and $0 \leq \alpha, \beta \leq 1/2$,

$$((s, \alpha), (r, \beta), \epsilon)\text{-SGWOT} \overset{def}{=} \big(\{(s, 1/2), (1 - s, \alpha)\}; \{(r, 1/2), (1 - r, \beta)\}; \epsilon\big)\text{-GWOT}.$$

Consider the reduction of WOT to (γ, δ)-PassiveUNC given in Appendix A of [7]. As mentioned above, this construction actually results in a GWOT (which is modeled by a WOT by giving away information to the adversary). As a matter of fact, as can easily be seen, it results in a SGWOT. The following Lemma expresses the parameters of the resulting SGWOT as a function of (γ, δ). For convenience, we write $\mu = \frac{\delta - \gamma}{1 - 2\gamma}$, such that $\gamma \boxplus \mu = \delta$. The proof of the Lemma follows by straightforward analysis of reduction WOTfromPassiveUNC of [7].

Lemma 2. *When run with a (γ, δ)-UNC, reduction WOTfromPassiveUNC defined in [7] produces a $\big((s, \alpha), (r, \beta), \epsilon\big)$-SGWOT with the following parameters:*

$$s = \frac{\gamma(1 - \gamma)(\gamma^2 + (1 - \gamma)^2)(\mu^4 + 6\mu^2(1 - \mu)^2 + (1 - \mu)^4)}{\delta(1 - \delta)(\delta^2 + (1 - \delta)^2)} \quad , \; \alpha = \frac{4\gamma^2(1 - \gamma)^2}{\gamma^4 + 6\gamma^2(1 - \gamma^2) + (1 - \gamma^4)}, \quad (1)$$

$$r = \frac{\gamma(1 - \gamma)(\mu^2 + (1 - \mu)^2)}{\delta(1 - \delta)} \quad , \; \beta = \frac{\gamma^2}{\gamma^2 + (1 - \gamma)^2}, \quad (2)$$

$$\epsilon = \frac{\delta^2}{\delta^2 + (1 - \delta)^2}. \quad (3)$$

We have expressed the parameters of $\big((s, \alpha), (r, \beta), \epsilon\big)$-SGWOT with that of the underlying (γ, δ)-PassiveUNC. Now we would like to exploit the machinery of [7] in order to reduce OT to SGWOT. A composition of three basic reductions is used in order to transform a WOT into an OT. The first reduction, S-Red(l) decreases the sender's information about the selection bit by executing WOT l times such that the final selection bit is the parity of all selection bits used during the l executions (this reduction was introduced in [5]). The second reduction, R-Red(l), decreases the receiver's information about the bit that was not selected by encoding it into the parity of l transmissions. The final reduction, E-Red(l), decreases the error rate by executing l identical transmissions through a WOT. Every of these reductions transforms the WOT into a new one (with new parameters), and it is shown in [7] that for certain initial parameters the sequence of WOTs converges to an OT (in some well defined meaningful sense).

In [7], the $\big((s, \alpha), (r, \beta), \epsilon\big)$-SGWOT obtained after invoking WOTfromPassiveUNC was modeled by a $(1 - s, 1 - r, \epsilon)$-WOT. I.e., in order to fit the imperfect OT into the WOT framework, the error probabilities α and β were assumed to be zero by giving the corrupted party some information for free. Clearly, a tighter analysis should avoid this kind of strengthening of the corrupted party for proof-technical conveniences. A straight forward approach would be to try to show that for certain initial parameters, the sequence of GWOTs, resulting by applying the S-, R- and E-Red reductions to the initial SGWOT, converges to an OT. Unfortunately, as the reduction of OT to WOT defined in [7] is executed, the shape of the GWOTs becomes quickly very complex and difficult to analyze. In order to avoid this problem, we give a generic way to replace a (possibly very complex) GWOT by another (ideally simpler) one such that if the new GWOT allows for OT then the initial GWOT also allows for OT; however, in contrast to the strategy of [7] of simply setting the error probabilities to zero, we are trying to be much more tight.

Next definition introduces a partial ordering "$\preceq$" among probability distributions over BSCs, i.e. among sets of the form $\{(s_i, \alpha_i)\}_i$ or $\{(r_i, \beta_i)\}_i$ as considered above, that will be shown (in Lemma 3) to capture the relative difficulty to generate OT using the reduction considered in [7]. Intuitively, we say that $S \preceq S'$ if S can be transformed into S' by removing BSCs in S and replacing each of them by a Bernoulli distribution over 2 BSCs such that the *average* guessing probability for the bit sent through S is the same as when sent through S'.

Definition 1. *Let* $S = \{(p_i, \epsilon_i)\}_{i=1}^N$ *and* S' *be two probability distributions over BSCs. We say that* $S \preceq S'$ *if there exists* $1 \leq \ell \leq N$ *as well as* $0 \leq \delta \leq 1$ *and* $0 \leq \epsilon^- \leq \epsilon \leq \epsilon^+ \leq 1/2$ *such that*

1. *S' is of the form* $S' = S \setminus \{(p_\ell, \epsilon_\ell)\} \cup \{((1-\delta)p_\ell, \epsilon^-), (\delta p_\ell, \epsilon^+)\}$ *and*
2. $\epsilon_\ell = \epsilon = (1 - \delta) \cdot \epsilon^- + \delta \cdot \epsilon^+,$

or if there exists a sequence $S = S_0, S_1, \ldots, S_k = S'$ *of probability distributions over BSCs such that* $S_{\kappa-1} \preceq S_\kappa$ *in the above sense for* $\kappa = 1, \ldots, k.$

Note that in case $\epsilon_j = \epsilon_k$ for some $1 \leq j < k \leq N$, we identify $S = \{(p_i, \epsilon_i)\}_{i=1}^N$ with $S^* = S \setminus \{(p_j, \epsilon_j), (p_k, \epsilon_k)\} \cup \{(p_j + p_k, \epsilon_j)\}$. This is justified in that it is immaterial in our context whether a bit is sent thorough S or through S^*.

The next lemma, a proof of which can be found in the full paper [6], shows that the partial ordering $S \preceq S'$ means that as long as reductions S-Red, R-Red, and E-Red are concerned, S is *easier* to deal with than S'.

Lemma 3. *If OT can be reduced to* $(S'; R'; \epsilon)$*-GWOT by a sequence of reductions S-Red, R-Red, and E-Red, then OT can be reduced to any* $(S; R; \epsilon)$*-GWOT with* $S \preceq S'$ *and* $R \preceq R'$.

One application of Lemma 3 allows to improve the analysis of [7]. As we have seen in Lemma 2, the imperfect OT obtained from a UNC using reduction WOTfromPassiveUNC produces a $((s, \alpha), (r, \beta), \epsilon)$-SGWOT. Using Lemma 3 it is straightforward to verify that we can replace this SGWOT by a (p_s, q_r, ϵ)-WOT with $p_s = (1 - s)(1 - 2\alpha)$ and $q_r = (1 - r)(1 - 2\beta)$. Indeed, for instance the corrupted sender's guessing probability for the selection bit is in the first case $s/2 + (1 - s)(1 - \alpha) = 1 - s/2 - \alpha + s\alpha$ and in the second case $p_s + (1 - p_s)/2 = 1 - s/2 - \alpha + s\alpha$. Applying Lemma 5 of [7] (OT is possible based on (p, q, ϵ)-WOT if $p + q + 2\epsilon \leq 0.45$) to the transformed SGWOT results in the following Lemma.

Lemma 4. *The reduction from OT to WOT of [7] implements OT from any $((s, \alpha), (r, \beta), \epsilon)$-SGWOT with $p_s + q_r + 2\epsilon \leq 0.45$, where $p_s = (1 - s)(1 - 2\alpha)$ and $q_r = (1 - r)(1 - 2\beta)$.*

Combining Lemmas 4 and 2, gives directly the following result:

Lemma 5. *OT may be reduced to (γ, δ)-PassiveUNC if $p_s + q_r + 2\epsilon \leq 0.45$, where $p_s = (1 - s)(1 - 2\alpha)$, $q_r = (1 - r)(1 - 2\beta)$ and s, α, r, β, ϵ are defined by equations (1)–(3).*

Note that [7] only guarantees that OT can be achieved if $p + q + 2\epsilon \leq 0.45$ where $p = 1 - s$ and $q = 1 - r$. Hence, the possibility range given in Lemma 5 strictly contains the one obtained in [7].

Despite this improvement, Lemma 5 still shares the following restriction with [7]. OT cannot be provably achieved for $\delta > 0.35$ even when γ is almost equal to δ (i.e. the resulting UNC has almost no unfairness) since in that case $\epsilon > 0.45$ (see Figure 1). This stands somewhat in contrast to the fact that OT can be achieved based on any (non-trivial) BSC [4,12,15]. Hence, one would expect that OT can be achieved based on any (non-trivial) UNC as long as the unfairness is small enough. The following lemma shows that this is indeed true.

Lemma 6. *There exists a reduction from OT to any (γ, δ)-PassiveUNC that satisfies $1 - (1 - p_s)^l + 1 - (1 - q_r)^l + 2\frac{\epsilon^l}{\epsilon^l + (1 - \epsilon)^l} \leq 0.45$ for some $l \geq 1$, where $p_s = (1 - s)(1 - 2\alpha)$ and $q_r = (1 - r)(1 - 2\beta)$ with $s, \alpha, r, \beta, \epsilon$ defined by (1)–(3).*

Clearly, for any $0 < \delta < 1/2$, for l large enough, and for γ close enough to δ (where the closer δ is to $1/2$, the closer γ has to be to δ), the values p_s and q_r are small enough for the condition expressed in Lemma 6 to be satisfied. Hence, OT is possible based on (γ, δ)-PassiveUNC's for any $0 < \delta < 1/2$ as long as γ is close enough to δ (see Figure 1). This further improves on [7].

Proof. We implement a $((s, \alpha), (r, \beta), \epsilon)$-SGWOT from the (γ, δ)-PassiveUNC according to Lemma 2. Then, by Lemma 3, we convert it into a (p_s, q_r, ϵ)-WOT before applying the reduction E-Red(l) [7] with parameter l. As shown in [7], this results in a $(1 - (1 - p_s)^l, 1 - (1 - q_r)^l, \frac{\epsilon^l}{\epsilon^l + (1 - \epsilon)^l})$-WOT. The claim now follows from the above. $\qquad\square$

It can be shown by straightforward calculations that the new possibility range includes UNC's for which the techniques of [7] results in a "simulatable" WOT (i.e., a trivial WOT), that is, could not be used to implement OT (see Lemma 1 from [7]). In other words, our approach allows to implement and prove secure OT in a range where it is *provably impossible* using the techniques of [7]. The following example illustrates this.

Example 1. Let $\gamma_0 = 0.39$, $\delta_0 = 0.4$ be the parameters of a PassiveUNC. The $(p(\gamma_0, \delta_0), q(\gamma_0, \delta_0), \epsilon(\delta_0))$-WOT obtained from a (γ_0, δ_0)-PassiveUNC the crude way (by giving away all partial information to the adversary as in [7]) achieves $p(\gamma_0, \delta_0) + q(\gamma_0, \delta_0) + 2\epsilon(\delta_0) \approx 0.869$. It can be shown that from this WOT, any sequence of reductions S-, R- and E-Red generates a simulatable WOT, i.e., OT is not reducible to the $(p(\gamma_0, \delta_0), q(\gamma_0, \delta_0), \epsilon(\delta_0))$-WOT using S-, R- and E-Red. At the same time, the $(p_s(\gamma_0, \delta_0), q_r(\gamma_0, \delta_0), \epsilon(\delta_0))$-WOT (obtained according Lemma 3) achieves $p_s(\gamma_0, \delta_0) + q_r(\gamma_0, \delta_0) + 2\epsilon(\delta_0) \approx 0.671$. Moreover, E-Red(2) applied to this WOT generates a (p', q', ϵ')-WOT with $p' + q' + 2\epsilon' \approx 0.438$, which we know from Lemma 5 implies OT.

There exists an even larger range than the one described in Lemma 6 for which a possibility result can be shown. This follows from the fact that the approach of Lemma 6 still gives information for free to the adversary. Indeed, the SGWOT obtained from a (γ, δ)-PassiveUNC is converted into a (p_s, q_r, ϵ)-WOT before reductions S-Red, R-Red and E-Red are applied. We may benefit from trying preserving the SGWOT through the sequence of reductions.

The problem is that the reductions do not preserve the SGWOT per se but produce more complex GWOTs with a quickly growing set of parameters. An approach is to use Lemma 3 in order to immediately convert any resulting GWOT (which is not a SGWOT) back into a SGWOT. Specifically, a $(\{(s_i, \alpha_i)\}_i; \{(r_i, \beta_i)\}_i; \epsilon)$-GWOT can be replaced by a $((s, \alpha), (r, \beta), \epsilon)$-SGWOT, where $\alpha = \min_i\{\alpha_i\}$ and $\beta = \min_i\{\beta_i\}$, and s and r are appropriately chosen such that $\{(s_i, \alpha_i)\}_i \preceq \{(s, 1/2), (1-s, \alpha)\}$ and $\{(r_i, \beta_i)\}_i \preceq \{(r, 1/2), (1-r, \beta)\}$. This indeed results in an increased possibility range:

Lemma 7. *There exists a range of values (γ, δ) which do not satisfy the conditions of Lemma 6 but where OT can still be implemented from such (γ, δ)-UNC's.*

Proof. (sketch) By brute force analysis for any fixed value of δ_0, $0 < \delta_0 < 1/2$, we find the smallest value of γ_0, such that a SGWOT based on (γ_0, δ_0)-PassiveUNC can be reduced to a SGWOT with $p_s + q_r + 2\epsilon \leq 0.45$ using the reductions S-Red, R-Red and E-Red, and replacing any GWOT by a SGWOT as sketched above.

For example, let $\gamma_0 = 0.365$, $\delta_0 = 0.4$. The value $p_s + q_r + 2\epsilon$ of the SGWOT resulting from (γ_0, δ_0)-PassiveUNC is equal to 0.793. It is easy to check that the conditions of Lemma 6 are not satisfied with respect to this SGWOT. Nonetheless, the sequence of reductions "EERSRESERRSESRERSESERRS" (each with parameter $l = 2$) produces as output a SGWOT with $p_s + q_r + 2\epsilon = 0.329$ which implies OT according Lemma 5. □

Using brute-force analysis, it is possible to find experimentally the range for which the reduction considered in Lemma 7 produces OT. The new range is depicted on Figure 1.

On the other hand, even the approach described above is limited in power. The following example suggests that in order to get a possibility result closer to the (γ, δ)-PassiveUNC simulation bound $\delta = 2\gamma(1 - \gamma)$ from [7], one has to find different reduction methods and/or analytical tools.

Example 2. Let $\gamma_0 = 0.33$, $\delta_0 = 0.4$. A SGWOT based on (γ_0, δ_0)-PassiveUNC has the potential $p_s(\gamma_0, \delta_0) + q_r(\gamma_0, \delta_0) + 2\epsilon(\delta_0) \approx 0.949$. It can be shown by brute force analysis that whatever sequence of reductions S-, R- and E-Reduce

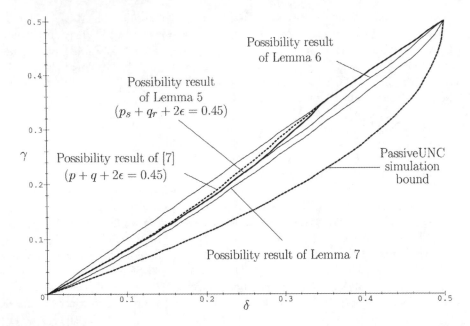

Fig. 1. Positive results on OT from (γ, δ)-PassiveUNC

applied with whatever parameters, it always results at some point a SGWOT with $p_s + q_r + 2\epsilon \geq 1$.

We stress that in contrast to a (p, q, ϵ)-WOT with $p + q + 2\epsilon \geq 1$, a SGWOT with $p_s + q_r + 2\epsilon \geq 1$ is not proven to be simulateable; however, it seems to be a very strong indication that OT cannot be based on such a SGWOT.

7   Conclusion and Open Questions

In this paper, we have shown how to transform any OT protocol secure against passive adversaries given access to a PassiveUNC into one that is secure against active adversaries given access to a standard UNC. This is possible since any non-trivial UNC allows for bit commitment as it was shown in [7]. Our transformation is general enough to be applicable to a wider class of 2-party protocols. Applying it to a passively secure protocol π implementing task T given access to a PassiveUNC produces an actively secure protocol π' that implements T given access to a UNC, however, π' may fail with non-negligible (1/poly) probability. When T is OT, this can be cleaned up using known techniques, in general T can be any task where such "cleaning" is possible.

We have also provided a more refined analysis for the reduction of OT to (γ, δ)-UNC introduced in [7]. As a result, OT is now possible based on a significantly larger range of (γ, δ) than what was known before. Unfortunately, we also show the approach has limits that even a more careful analysis cannot overcome.

Thus, a grey area is left where no positive or negative results are known to apply. Closing this gap is the obvious open problem suggested by this work.

References

1. Brassard, G., Chaum, D., Crépeau, C.: Minimum Disclosure Proofs of Knowledge. J. of Computer and System Sciences, 37(2). Elsevier (1988) 156–189
2. Canetti, R.: Universally Composable Security: A New Paradigm for Cryptographic Protocols. In: 42nd Symposium FOCS, IEEE (2001) 136–145
3. Chaum, D., Damgård, I., van de Graaf, J.: Multi-party Computations Ensuring Privacy of Each Party's Input and Correctness of the Result. In: Advances in Cryptology–CRYPTO '87. LNCS, vol. 293. Springer-Verlag (1987) 462
4. Crépeau, C.: Efficient Cryptographic Protocols Based on Noisy Channels. In: Advances in Cryptology–EUROCRYPT'97. LNCS, vol. 1233. Springer-Verlag (1997) 306–317
5. Crépeau, C., Kilian, J.: Achieving Oblivious Transfer Using Weakened Security Assumptions. In: 29th Symposium FOCS, IEEE (1988) 42–52
6. Damgård, I., Fehr, S., Morozov, K. and Salvail, L.: *Unfair Noisy Channels and Oblivious Transfer*, full version of this paper, BRICS report nr. RS-03-36, (2003) available from www.brics.dk/RS/03/36
7. Damgård, I., Kilian, J., Salvail, L.: On the (Im)possibility of Basing Bit Commitment and Oblivious Transfer on Weakened Security Assumptions. In: Advances in Cryptology–EUROCRYPT '99. LNCS, vol. 1592. Springer-Verlag (1999) 56–73
8. Goldreich, O., Micali, S., Wigderson, A.: Proofs that Yield Nothing but the Validity of the Assertion, and the Methodology of Cryptographic Protocol Design. In: 27th Symposium FOCS. IEEE (1986) 174–187
9. Goldreich, O., Micali, S., Wigderson, A.: How to Play Any Mental Game. In: 19th ACM STOC. ACM Press (1987) 218-229
10. Kilian, J.: Founding Cryptography on Oblivious Transfer. In: 20th ACM STOC. ACM Press (1988) 20–31
11. Kilian, J.: A Note on Efficient Proofs and Arguments. In: 24th ACM STOC. ACM Press (1992) 723–732
12. Korjik, V., Morozov, K.: Generalized Oblivious Transfer Protocols Based on Noisy Channels. In: Proc. Workshop MMM ACNS 2001. LNCS, vol. 2052. Springer-Verlag (2001) 219-229
13. Lo, H.–K., Chau, H. F.: Is Quantum Bit Commitment Really Possible?. Physical Review Letters, vol. 78, no 17, (1997) 3410–3413
14. Mayers, D.: Unconditionally Secure Quantum Bit Commitment is Impossible. Physical Review Letters, vol. 78, no 17, (1997) 3414–3417
15. Stebila, D., Wolf, S.: Efficient Oblivious Transfer From Any Non-Trivial Binary-Symmetric Channel. In: International Symposium on Information Theory (ISIT) (2002) 293

Computational Collapse of Quantum State with Application to Oblivious Transfer

Claude Crépeau[1*], Paul Dumais[1**], Dominic Mayers[2***], and Louis Salvail[3†]

[1] School of Computer Science, McGill University,
{crepeau|dumais}@cs.mcgill.ca
[2] IQI, California Institute of Technology,
dmayers@cs.caltech.edu
[3] BRICS[†], FICS[‡] Dept. of Computer Science, University of Århus,
salvail@brics.dk

Abstract. Quantum 2-party cryptography differs from its classical counterpart in at least one important way: Given blak-box access to a perfect commitment scheme there exists a secure $1-2$ *quantum* oblivious transfer. This reduction proposed by Crépeau and Kilian was proved secure against any receiver by Yao, in the case where perfect commitments are used. However, quantum commitments would normally be based on computational assumptions. A natural question therefore arises: What happens to the security of the above reduction when computationally secure commitments are used instead of perfect ones?

In this paper, we address the security of $1-2$ QOT when computationally binding string commitments are available. In particular, we analyse the security of a primitive called *Quantum Measurement Commitment* when it is constructed from unconditionally concealing but computationally binding commitments. As measuring a quantum state induces an irreversible collapse, we describe a QMC as an instance of "computational collapse of a quantum state". In a QMC a state appears to be collapsed to a polynomial time observer who cannot extract full information about the state without breaking a computational assumption.

We reduce the security of QMC to a *weak* binding criteria for the string commitment. We also show that *secure* QMCs implies QOT using a straightforward variant of the reduction above.

[†] Funded by the Danish National Research Foundation.
[‡] FICS, Foundations in Cryptography and Security, funded by the Danish Natural Sciences Research Council.
[*] Part of this research was done while visiting University of Århus and was funded by Québec's FQRNT and MDER, and Canada's NSERC and MITACS.
[**] Part of this research was funded by NSERC
[***] This work has been supported in part by the National Science Foundation under Grant No. EIA-0086038.
[†] Part of this research was funded by European projects QAIP and PROSECCO.

1   Introduction

Quantum 2-party cryptography differs from its classical counterpart in at least one important way: Given blak-box access to a perfect commitment scheme there exists a secure $1 - 2$ *quantum* oblivious transfer (i.e. 1-2 QOT) scheme[6,3,4]. Classically, it is known that such a reduction is unlikely to exist [10]. By *1-2 QOT* we mean a standard oblivious transfer of two classical messages using quantum communication. In [6], Crépeau and Kilian have shown how 1-2 QOT can be obtained from perfect commitments (i.e. the CK protocol). The security analysis of the CK protocol was provided by Crépeau in [4] with respect to receivers restricted to perform only immediate and complete measurements. The assumption was relaxed in [15] by showing that privacy for the sender is garanteed against any individual measurements applied by the receiver. The security against any receiver was obtained by Yao in [20]. This important paper provides a full proof of security for 1-2 QOT when constructed from perfect commitments under the assumption that the quantum channel is error-free. Yao's result was then generalized by Mayers[13] for the case of noisy quantum channel [3] and where strings are transmitted instead of bits. Mayers then reduced the security of quantum key distribution to the security of such a generalized 1-2 QOT. If 2-party cryptography in the quantum world seems to rely upon weaker assumptions than its classical counterpart, it also shares some of its limits. As it was shown in [12,14,11], no statistically binding and concealing quantum bit commitment can exist. On the other hand, quantum commitments can be based upon physical[17] and computational[8,7] assumptions. A natural question arises: What happens to the security of the CK protocol when computationally secure commitments are used instead of perfect ones? It should be stressed that Yao's proof does not apply in this case since it relies heavily upon the fact that the commitment scheme is modelled by a classical black-box (i.e. one with classical inputs and outputs). The proof is information theoretic provided the sender and the receiver have black-box access to perfect commitments. For Yao's proof to apply, the committing phase should be modelled by the transmission of a *classical bit* to a third party who conceals it to the receiver until the opening phase. Although any unconditionally binding commitment scheme defines such a classical bit, unconditionally concealing commitments do not (i.e. both committed values can be explained by the information provided to the receiver). In this paper, we address the security of 1-2 QOT when computationally binding string commitments are available. In particular, we analyse the security of a primitive called *Quantum Measurement Commitment* (i.e. QMC) when it is constructed from unconditionally concealing but computationally binding commitments. We reduce the security of QMC to a *weak* binding criteria for the string commitment. We also show that *secure* QMCs implies 1-2 QOT using a straightforward variant of the CK protocol. It follows that unlike Yao's proof (and the proof in [15]), our security proof applies when computionally binding commitments are used.

The CK protocol can be seen as a quantum reduction of 1-2 OT to bit commitment. To see how it works, consider the BB84 coding scheme[2,6] for classical bit b into a random state in $\{ |b\rangle_+, |b\rangle_\times \}$. $\theta \in \{+, \times\}$ used to encode b into the quantum state $|b\rangle_\theta$, is called the *transmission basis*. Since only orthogonal quantum states can be distinguished with certainty, the transmitted bit b is not received perfectly by the receiver, Alice, who does not know the transmission basis. The coding scheme also specifies what an honest Alice should be doing with the received state $|b\rangle_\theta$. She picks $\hat{\theta} \in_R \{+, \times\}$ and measures $|b\rangle_\theta$ with measurement $\mathbb{M}_{\hat{\theta}}$ that distinguishes perfectly orthogonal states $|0\rangle_{\hat{\theta}}$ and $|1\rangle_{\hat{\theta}}$. If Bob and Alice follow honestly the BB84 coding scheme then b is received with probability 1 when $\hat{\theta} = \theta$ whereas a random bit is received when $\hat{\theta} \neq \theta$. In other words, If Bob announces the transmission basis a the end of the transmission then the BB84 coding scheme implements a Rabin's oblivious transfer [16] from Bob to Alice provided she is honest. Otherwise, Alice can easily cheat the protocol by postponing the measurement until the basis is announced. In this case she gets the transmitted bit all the time. In order to make the BB84 transmission resistant to active adversaries, the CK protocol uses n BB84 transmissions where for each of them, Alice is asked to commit upon the measurements and outcomes prior the announcement of the transmission bases by Bob.

We call *Quantum Measurement Commitment* (or QMC) the primitive that allows Alice to provide Bob with evidences of measurements she claims having performed on n BB84 qubits before the announcement of $\theta \in \{+, \times\}^n$. Implementing a QMC is simply done by sending a string commitment containing $(\hat{\theta}, \hat{b})$ to Bob where $\hat{\theta} \in \{+, \times\}^n$ is the measurements Alice claims having performed and $\hat{b} \in \{0, 1\}^n$ are the outcomes.

The classical bit encoded in the transmission is defined as the value of some predicate $f(b_1, \ldots, b_n)$. Once the QMC has been performed, Alice should be unable to evaluate $f(b_1, \ldots, b_n)$ even given the knowledge of the transmission bases θ. A *computational collapse* occurred if, given the transmission basis θ, $f(b_1, \ldots, b_n)$ cannot be determined efficiently.

The CK protocol constructs a 1-2 QOT from a QMC with $f(b_1, \ldots, b_n) \equiv \oplus_{i=1}^n b_i$. A QMC is therefore a universal primitive for secure 2-party computation (of classical functions).

Our contribution. In this paper, we address the question of determining how the binding property of the string commitment scheme used for implementing a QMC enforces its security. As already pointed out in [8,7], quantum bit commitment schemes satisfy different binding properties than classical ones. The difference becomes more obvious when string commitments are taken into account. In Sect. 3.1, we generalize the computational binding criteria of [8] to the case where commitments are made to strings of size $\ell \in \Theta(n)$ for n the security parameter, and ℓ some value depending on n. Intuitively, for a class of functions $F \subseteq \{f : \{0,1\}^\ell \to \{0,1\}^m\}$, with $m < \ell$ both depending on n, we say that a string commitment scheme is F–binding if for all $f \in F$, for all commitment prepared by the sender, and for a random $y \in_R \{0,1\}^m$, the commitment cannot be opened efficiently to any $s \in \{0,1\}^\ell$ such that $f(s) = y$ with success probability significantly better than $1/2^m$. The smaller m is compared to ℓ, the weaker is the F–binding criteria. We relate the security of QMC to a weak form of the F–binding property. We assume that a QMC is made using a computationally binding and unconditionally concealing string commitment containing the bases $\hat{\theta} \in \{+, \times\}^n$ and the results $\hat{b} \in \{0, 1\}^n$ obtained by Alice after Bob's transmission of $|b\rangle_\theta$. We then define the security of a QMC by the following game between Alice and Bob. Bob selects a challenge $c \in_R \{0, 1\}$.

If $c = 0$, Alice unveils all measurements and outcomes which Bob verifies (by testing that $\hat{\theta}_i = \theta_i \Rightarrow \hat{b}_i = b_i$). If $c = 1$, Bob announces the transmission basis $\theta \in_R \{+, \times\}^n$ and Alice tries to maximize her bias on b's parity. Let $\tilde{p}_s$ be Alice's probability of success when $c = 0$ and let $\tilde{\epsilon}$ be Alice's expected bias when $c = 1$. First, notice that if $\tilde{p}_s + 2\tilde{\epsilon} = 2$ then the QMC is not accomplishing anything since Alice can always unveil perfectly ($\tilde{p}_s = 1$) and bias the parity of b as she likes ($\tilde{\epsilon} = 1/2$). In this case it is impossible to build a secure OT from that QMC. However, as we will see in Section 3.2, an honest Alice can always achieve $\tilde{p}_s + 2\tilde{\epsilon} = 1$ and thus all adversaries such that $\tilde{p}_s + 2\tilde{\epsilon} \leq 1$ are considered trivial. Our main contribution describes how $\tilde{p}_s$ and $\tilde{\epsilon}$ relate to the $\mathcal{F}_m^n$–binding criteria of the string commitment for $\mathcal{F}_m^n$ a class of functions with *small range* $m \in O(\text{polylog}(n))$. In Sect. 5, we give a black-box reduction of any *good* quantum adversary against QMC into one against the string commitent $\mathcal{F}_m^n$–binding criteria. We show that if $\tilde{p}_s + 4\tilde{\epsilon}^2 \geq 1 + \delta(n)$ for non-negligible $\delta(n)$, then the string commitment is not $\mathcal{F}_m^n$–binding. In Sect. 6, we show that the converse condition $\tilde{\epsilon} \leq \sqrt{1 + \delta(n) - \tilde{p}_s}/2$ (for negligible $\delta(n)$) is sufficient to build a secure 1-2 QOT. We construct a 1-2 QOT along the same lines than the CK protocol by invoking $O(n)$ times a QMC built from a $\mathcal{F}_m^n$-binding string commitment scheme. After making sure that $\tilde{p}_s$ is sufficiently close to 1 for a large fraction of all QMC executions, we show how to obtain a correct and private (according the definition of [4] adapted the obvious way to deal with computational security against the receiver) 1-2 QOT.

Our reduction shows that using computationally binding commitments one can enforce a *computational or apparent collapse of quantum information*. Using such a QMC allows to construct a 1-2 QOT that is unconditionally secure against Bob (i.e. the sender) and computationally secure against Alice (i.e. the receiver) provided the string commitment scheme used to construct the QMC is $\mathcal{F}_m^n$-binding. As for the quantum version of the Goldreich-Levin theorem[1] and the computationally binding commitments of [8] and [7], our result clearly indicates that 2-party quantum cryptography in the computational setting can be based upon different if not weaker assumptions than its classical counterpart.

2   Preliminaries

Notations and Tools. In the following, $\text{poly}(n)$ stands for any polynomial in n. We write $A(n) < \text{poly}(n)$ for "$A(n)$ is smaller than any polynomial provided n is sufficiently large" and $A(n) \leq \text{poly}(n)$ (resp. $A(n) \geq \text{poly}(n)$) means that $A(n)$ is upper bounded by some polynomial (resp. lower bounded by some polynomial). For $w \in \{0, 1\}^n$, $x \preceq w$ means that $x_i = 0$ for all $1 \leq i \leq n$ such that $w_i = 0$

(x belongs to the support of w). We denote by "$\blacklozenge$" the string concatenation operator. For $w \in \{0,1\}^n$, we write $[w] \equiv \oplus_{i=1}^n w_i$. For $w, z \in \{0,1\}^n$, we write $|w|$ for the Hamming weight of w, $\Delta(w, z) = |w \oplus z|$ for the Hamming distance, and $w \odot z \equiv \oplus_{i=1}^n w_i \cdot z_i$ is the boolean inner product. Notation $\|\boldsymbol{u}\|$ denotes the Euclidean norm of $\boldsymbol{u}$ and $\boldsymbol{u}^\dagger$ denotes its complex conjugate transposed. The following well-known identity will be useful,

$$(\forall y \in \{0,1\}^n)[y \neq 0^n \Rightarrow \sum_{x \in \{0,1\}^n} (-1)^{x \odot y} = 0]. \tag{1}$$

Next lemma, for which a proof can be found in [5] , provides a generalization of the parallelogram identity:

Lemma 1. *Let $A \subseteq \{0,1\}^n$ be a set of bitstrings. Let $\{\boldsymbol{v}_{w,z}\}_{w,z}$ be any family of vectors indexed by $w \in \{0,1\}^n$ and $z \in A$ that satisfies,*

$$(\forall s, t \in \{0,1\}^n, s \neq t)[\sum_w \sum_{\substack{z_1 \in A: w \oplus z_1 = s \\ z_2 \in A: w \oplus z_2 = t}} (-1)^{w \odot (z_1 \oplus z_2)} \langle \boldsymbol{v}_{w,z_1}, \boldsymbol{v}_{w,z_2} \rangle = 0] \tag{2}$$

Then,

$$\sum_w \| \sum_{z \in A} (-1)^{w \odot z} \boldsymbol{v}_{w,z} \|^2 = \sum_{w \in \{0,1\}^n} \sum_{z \in A} \| \boldsymbol{v}_{w,z} \|^2. \tag{3}$$

Finally, for $\theta, b \in \{0,1\}^n$, we define $\Delta_\preceq(\theta, b) = \{(\hat{\theta}, \hat{b}) \in \{0,1\}^n \times \{0,1\}^n | (\forall i, 1 \leq i \leq n)[\hat{\theta}_i = \theta_i \Rightarrow \hat{b}_i = b_i]\}$. It is easy to verify that $\#\Delta_\preceq(\theta, b) = 3^n$ and that $(\theta \oplus \tau, b \oplus \beta) \in \Delta_\preceq(\theta, b)$ iff $\beta \preceq \tau$.

Quantum Stuff. The basis $\{ |0\rangle, |1\rangle \}$ denotes the computational or rectilinear or "+" basis for $\mathcal{H}_2$. When the context requires, we write $|b\rangle_+$ to denote the bit b in the rectilinear basis. The diagonal basis, denoted "×", is defined as $\{ |0\rangle_\times, |1\rangle_\times \}$ where $|0\rangle_\times = \frac{1}{\sqrt{2}}(|0\rangle + |1\rangle)$ and $|1\rangle_\times = \frac{1}{\sqrt{2}}(|0\rangle - |1\rangle)$. States $|0\rangle, |1\rangle, |0\rangle_\times$ and $|1\rangle_\times$ are the four BB84 states. For any $x \in \{0,1\}^n$ and $\theta \in \{+, \times\}^n$, the state $|x\rangle_\theta$ is defined as $\otimes_{i=1}^n |x_i\rangle_{\theta_i}$. In the following, we write $\mathbb{P}_{+,0} \equiv \mathbb{P}_0 = |0\rangle\langle 0|$, $\mathbb{P}_{+,1} \equiv \mathbb{P}_1 = |1\rangle\langle 1|$, $\mathbb{P}_{\times,0} = |0\rangle_\times\langle 0|$ and $\mathbb{P}_{\times,1} = |1\rangle_\times\langle 1|$ for the projections along the four BB84 states. We define measurements $\mathbb{M}_+ \equiv \{\mathbb{P}_0, \mathbb{P}_1\}$ and $\mathbb{M}_\times \equiv \{\mathbb{P}_{\times,0}, \mathbb{P}_{\times,1}\}$ allowing to distinguish the BB84 encoded bit in the computational and diagonal basis respectively. For $\theta \in \{+, \times\}^n$, measurement $\mathbb{M}_\theta$ is the composition of measurements $\mathbb{M}_{\theta_i}$ for $1 \leq i \leq n$. In order to simplify the notation, we sometimes associate the rectilinear basis "+" with bit 0 and the diagonal basis with bit 1. We map sequences of rectilinear and diagonal bases into bitstrings the obvious way.

We refer to [8,7] for a more complete description of how quantum protocols are modeled by quantum circuits. We denote by $\mathcal{UG}$ an universal set of quantum gates. The complexity of a quantum circuit C is simply the number $\|C\|_{\mathcal{UG}}$ of elementary gates in C. In the following, we use the two Pauli (unitary) transformations σ_X (bit flip) and σ_Z (conditional phase shift) defined for $b \in \{0,1\}$

as, $\sigma_X : |b\rangle \mapsto |1 - b\rangle$ and $\sigma_Z : |b\rangle \mapsto (-1)^b |b\rangle$. Assuming U is a one qubit operation and $s \in \{0, 1\}^n$, we write $U^{\otimes s} = \otimes_{i=1}^n U_i$ where $U_i = \mathbb{1}_2$ if $s_i = 0$ and $U_i = U$ if $s_i = 1$. $U^{\otimes s}$ is therefore a conditional application of U on each of n registers depending upon the value of s. The maximally entangled state $|\Phi_n^+\rangle = 2^{-n/2} \sum_{x \in \{0,1\}^n} |x\rangle \otimes |x\rangle$ will be useful in our reduction. This state can easily be constructed from scratch by a circuit of $O(n)$ elementary gates.

3   Definitions

3.1   Computationally Binding Quantum String Commitment

In the following we shall always refer to $\mathcal{A}$ as the sender and $\mathcal{B}$ as the receiver of some commitment. Such a scheme can be specified by two families of protocols $\mathcal{C}^{AB} = \{(C_n^A, C_n^B)\}_{n>0}$, and $\mathcal{O}^{AB} = \{(O_n^A, O_n^B)\}_{n>0}$ where each pair defined $\mathcal{A}$'s and $\mathcal{B}$'s circuits for the committing and the opening phase respectively. A ℓ-string commitment allows to commit upon strings of length ℓ for n a security parameter. The committing stage generates the state $|\psi_s\rangle = (C_n^A \odot C_n^B) |s\rangle^A |0\rangle^B$ when $\mathcal{A}$ commits to $s \in \{0, 1\}^\ell$. The opening stage is executed from the shared state $|\psi_s\rangle$ and produces $|\psi_{final}\rangle = (O_n^A \odot O_n^B) |\psi_s\rangle$. In [8], a natural security criteria for computationally binding but otherwise concealing quantum bit commitment schemes was introduced. In the following, we generalize this approach for string commitment schemes.

An adversary $\tilde{\mathcal{A}} = \{(\tilde{C}_n^A, \tilde{O}_n^A)\}_{n>0}$ for the binding condition is such that $|\tilde{\psi}\rangle = (\tilde{C}_n^A \odot C_n^B) |0\rangle^A |0\rangle^B$ is generated during the committing stage. The dishonest opening circuit $\tilde{O}_n^A$ tries to open $s \in \{0, 1\}^l$ given as an extra input in state $|s\rangle^X$. Given the final state $|\tilde{\psi}_{final}\rangle = (\tilde{O}_n^A \odot O_n^B) |s\rangle^X |\tilde{\psi}\rangle^{AB}$ we define $\tilde{p}_s(n)$ as the probability to open $s \in \{0, 1\}^\ell$ with success. More precisely, $\tilde{p}_s(n) = \|\mathbb{Q}_s^B |\tilde{\psi}_{final}\rangle\|^2$ where $\mathbb{Q}_s^B$ is $\mathcal{B}$'s projection operator on the subspace leading to accept the opening of s. The main difference between quantum and classical commitments is the impossibility in the quantum case to determine the committed string s after the committing phase of the protocol. Classically, this can be done by fixing the parties' random tapes so s becomes uniquely determined. In other words, a quantum adversary able to open any string s with probability $p(s)$ is not necessarily able to compute simultaneously the openings of all or even a subset of all strings s. In particular, classical security proof techniques like rewinding have no quantum analogue[9,18]. A committer (to a concealing commitment) can always commit upon any superposition of values for s that will remain such until the opening phase. A honest committer does not necessarily know a single string that can be unveiled with non-negligible probability of success. Suppose a quantum ℓ-string commitment scheme has committing circuit $C_n^A \odot C_n^B$ and let $|\psi(s)\rangle^{AB} = (C_n^A \odot C_n^B) |s\rangle^A |0\rangle^B$. If the committer starts with superposition $\sum_s \sqrt{\tilde{p}_s(n)} |s\rangle$, for any probability distribution $\{(\tilde{p}_s(n), s)\}_{s \in \{0,1\}^\ell}$, then the state obtained after the committing phase would be:

$$\sum_{s\in\{0,1\}^\ell} \sqrt{\tilde{p}_s(n)}\,|\psi(s)\rangle^{AB} = C_n^A \odot C_n^B \left((\sum_{s\{0,1\}^\ell} \sqrt{\tilde{p}_s(n)}\,|s\rangle^A) \otimes |0\rangle^B \right). \quad (4)$$

Equation (4) is a valid commitment to a superposition of strings that will always allow the sender to unveil s with probability $\tilde{p}_s(n)$. The *honest* strategy described in (4) achieves $\sum_s \tilde{p}_s(n) = 1$. In [8], the binding condition is satisfied if no adversary can do significantly better than what is achievable by (4) in the special case $\ell = 1$. More precisely, a bit commitment scheme is computationally binding if for all poly-time adversaries $\tilde{A}$:

$$\tilde{p}_0(n) + \tilde{p}_1(n) < 1 + 1/\text{poly}(n) \quad (5)$$

where $\tilde{p}_b(n)$ is the probability for $\tilde{A}$ to open bit b with success. Extending this definition to the case where $\ell \in \Theta(n)$ must be done with care however. The obvious generalization of (5) to the requirement $\sum_{s\in\{0,1\}^\ell} \tilde{p}_s(n) < 1 + 1/\text{poly}(n)$ is too strong whenever $\ell \in \Theta(n)$. For example, if $\ell = n$ and $\tilde{p}_s(n) = 2^{-n}(1 + \frac{1}{p(n)})$ for all strings $s \in \{0,1\}^n$ then $\tilde{A}$'s behavior is indistinguishable in polynomial time from what is achievable with the *honest* state (4) resulting from distribution $\{(2^{-n}, s)\}_s$. Any such attack that cannot be distinguished from the honest behavior should hardly be considered successful. On the other hand, defining a successful adversary $\tilde{A}$ as one who can open s and s' ($s \neq s'$) such that $\tilde{p}_s(n) + \tilde{p}_{s'}(n) \geq 1 + 1/p(n)$ is in general too weak when one tries to reduce the security of a protocol to the security of the string commitment used by that protocol (as we shall see for QMCs). Breaking a protocol could be reduced to breaking the string commitment scheme in a more subtle way. In general, the possibility to commit upon several strings in superposition can be used by the adversary to make his attack against the binding condition even more peculiar. Instead of trying to open a particular string $s \in \{0,1\}^\ell$, an attacker could be interested in opening any $s \in \{0,1\}^\ell$ such that $f(s) = y$ for some function $f : \{0,1\}^\ell \to \{0,1\}^m$ with $m \leq \ell$. Henceforth, we call such an attack an f-**attack**. We shall see in the following that the *security* of QMC is guaranteed provided the string commitment does not allow the committer to mount such an f-attack for any $f \in F$ where F is a special class of functions. Such an adversary is defined by a family of interactive quantum circuits $\tilde{A}^f = \{(\tilde{C}_n^A, \tilde{O}_n^A)\}_{n>0}$ such that $|\tilde{\psi}\rangle = (\tilde{C}_n^A \odot C_n^B)|0\rangle^A |0\rangle^B$ is the state generated during the committing phase of the protocol and $|\tilde{\psi}(y)\rangle = (\tilde{O}_n^A \odot O_n^B)|y\rangle^X |\tilde{\psi}\rangle^{AB}$ is the state (hopefully) allowing to open $s \in \{0,1\}^\ell$ such that $f(s) = y$. The probability to succeed during the opening stage is,

$$\tilde{p}_y^f(n) = \|\sum_{s\in\{0,1\}^\ell:f(s)=y} \mathbb{Q}_s^B |\tilde{\psi}(y)\rangle\|^2, \quad (6)$$

where $\mathbb{Q}_s^B$ is $\mathcal{B}$'s projector operator leading to accept the opening of $s \in \{0,1\}^\ell$. The following binding criteria takes into account such attacks:

Definition 1. *Let $F \subseteq \{f : \{0,1\}^\ell \to \{0,1\}^m\}$ be a set of functions where $m \leq \ell$. A ℓ-string commitment scheme is* computationally F-binding *if for any $f \in F$ and any adversary $\tilde{\mathcal{A}}^f$ such that $\|\tilde{\mathcal{A}}^f\|_{\mathcal{UG}} \leq poly(n)$, we have*

$$\sum_{y \in \{0,1\}^m} \tilde{p}_y^f(n) < 1 + 1/poly(n) \text{ where } \tilde{p}_y^f(n) \text{ is defined as in (6)}. \tag{7}$$

Notice that all natural attacks can be expressed by an appropriate class of functions F. In general, the smaller m is with respect to ℓ, the weaker is the F–binding criteria. A class of functions of particular interest is built out of $s_1(x,y) = x$, $s_2(x,y) = y$, and $s_3(x,y) = x \oplus y$ for all $x, y \in \{0,1\}$. Let $\mathcal{I}_m^n$ be the set of subsets of $\{1, \ldots, n\}$ having size m. For $I \in \mathcal{I}_m^n$, let $S_I^n = \{s : \{0,1\}^{2n} \to \{0,1\}^m | (\exists j \in \{1,2,3\}^m)(\forall x, y \in \{0,1\}^n)[s(x,y) = \blacklozenge_{h \in I} s_{j_h}(x_h, y_h)]\}$, we define:

$$\mathcal{F}_m^n = \left\{ f : \{0,1\}^{2n} \to \{0,1\}^m | (\exists I \in \mathcal{I}_m^n)[f \in S_I^n] \right\}.$$

In other words, $\mathcal{F}_m^n$ contains the set of functions f such that each of the m output bit of $f(x,y)$ is a bit of either x or y or $x \oplus y$. Notice that no quantum string commitment has been formally shown F-binding for a non-trivial F. We believe however that the commitment of [7] can be turned into a $\mathcal{F}_m^n$-binding string commitment for *small* m but this analysis is beyond the scope of this paper.

3.2   Commitment to Quantum Measurement

Quantum Measurement Commitment (QMC) is a primitive allowing the receiver of random qubits to show the sender that they have been measured without disclosing any further information (i.e. unconditionally) about the measurement and the outcome. As discussed in the Sect. 1, this primitive is the main ingredient in order to provide security in 1-2 QOT against the receiver $\mathcal{A}$. In this paper we restrict our attention to quantum transmission of random BB84 qubits. The measurements performed by the receiver are, for each transmission, independently chosen in $\{\mathbb{M}_+, \mathbb{M}_\times\}$. We model QMCs by the following game between the sender $\mathcal{B}$ and the receiver $\mathcal{A}$:

1. $\mathcal{B}$ sends n random BB84 qubits in state $|b\rangle_\theta$ for $b \in_R \{0,1\}^n$ and $\theta \in_R \{+, \times\}^n$,
2. $\mathcal{A}$ applies measurement $\mathbb{M}_{\hat{\theta}}$ for $\hat{\theta} \in_R \{+, \times\}^n$ producing classical outcome $\hat{b} \in \{0,1\}^n$,
3. $\mathcal{A}$ uses a $2n$-string commitment in order to commit to $(\hat{\theta}, \hat{b})$ toward $\mathcal{B}$,
4. $\mathcal{B}$ picks and announces a random challenge $c \in_R \{0,1\}$,
   - If $c = 0$ then $\mathcal{A}$ opens $(\hat{\theta}, \hat{b})$ and $\mathcal{B}$ verifies that $\hat{b}_i = b_i$ for all i such that $\hat{\theta}_i = \theta_i$, otherwise $\mathcal{B}$ ABORTS,
   - If $c = 1$ then $\mathcal{B}$ announces θ and $\mathcal{A}$ tries to bias $[b]$.

$\mathcal{A}$ wants to maximize both her success probability when unveiling and the bias on $[b]$ whenever θ is announced. This is almost identical to the receiver's situation in the CK protocol[6]. Since we only consider unconditionally concealing string commitments, $\mathcal{B}$ gets information about $\mathcal{A}$'s measurements and results only if they are unveiled. As we shall see next, this flavor of commitments allows $\mathcal{A}$ to postpone her measurement until the unveiling stage. The commitment stage should nevertheless ensure $\mathcal{B}$ that $\mathcal{A}$ cannot use this ability for improving her situation compared to the case where she measures completely before committing. In other words, although this flavor of commitment cannot force $\mathcal{A}$ to measure upon the committing stage, it should do as such through the actions of a computationally bounded $\mathcal{A}$.

We model the adversary $\tilde{\mathcal{A}}$ by a family of interactive quantum circuits $\tilde{\mathcal{A}} = \{(\tilde{C}_n^A, \tilde{O}_n^A, \tilde{E}_n)\}_{n>0}$ where $\tilde{C}_n^A$ and $\tilde{O}_n^A$ are $\tilde{\mathcal{A}}$'s circuits for the committing and the opening phases. Circuit $\tilde{E}_n$ allows to extract the parity of b upon the announcement of basis θ. Circuit $\tilde{C}_n^A$ works upon $\tilde{\mathcal{A}}$'s internal registers H_A together with the register $H_{channel}$ storing the BB84 qubits. We denote by

$$|\psi_{\theta,b}\rangle^{AB} = (\tilde{C}_n^A \odot C_n^B) \, |b\rangle_\theta^{channel}, \tag{8}$$

the resulting state after the committing phase (step 3). This state should allow $\tilde{\mathcal{A}}$ to succeed both challenges with *good* probability. By linearity, we have that for all $\theta, b, x \in \{0,1\}^n$,

$$|\psi_{\theta,b}\rangle = 2^{-\frac{|x|}{2}} \sum_{y:y \preceq x} (-1)^{b\odot x \oplus b \odot y} \, |\psi_{\theta \oplus x, b \oplus y}\rangle, \tag{9}$$

where $\theta \oplus x$ defines a new basis in which $|\psi_{\theta,b}\rangle$ is represented. The probability to open with success $\tilde{p}_{(\theta,b)}^{ok}(n)$, when $|b\rangle_\theta$ was sent, is

$$\tilde{p}_{(\theta,b)}^{ok}(n) = \sum_{(\hat{\theta},\hat{b}) \in \Delta_{\preceq}(\theta,b)} \|\mathbb{Q}_{(\hat{\theta},\hat{b})}^B (\tilde{O}_n^A \odot O_n^B) \, |\psi_{\theta,b}\rangle\|^2 = \|\mathbb{Q}_{(\theta,b)}^* \, |\psi_{\theta,b}\rangle\|^2, \tag{10}$$

for $\mathbb{Q}_{(\hat{\theta},\hat{b})}^B$ the projection operator applied upon $\mathcal{B}$'s registers and leading to a valid opening of $(\hat{\theta}, \hat{b}) \in \{0,1\}^{2n}$. The opening of $(\hat{\theta}, \hat{b})$ is accepted by $\mathcal{B}$ iff $(\hat{\theta}, \hat{b}) \in \Delta_{\preceq}(\theta, b)$. For simplicity, circuits $\tilde{O}_n^A \odot O_n^B$ can be included in the description of $\mathbb{Q}_{(\hat{\theta},\hat{b})}^B$ so the opening process can be seen as a single projection $\mathbb{Q}_{(\theta,b)}^* = \sum_{(\hat{\theta},\hat{b}) \in \Delta_{\preceq}(\theta,b)} \mathbb{Q}_{(\hat{\theta},\hat{b})}^B$. Therefore, the expected probability of success $\tilde{p}^{ok}(n)$ is,

$$\tilde{p}^{ok}(n) = \frac{1}{4^n} \sum_{b \in \{0,1\}^n} \sum_{\theta \in \{+,\times\}^n} \tilde{p}_{(\theta,b)}^{ok}(n). \tag{11}$$

When $c = 1$, $\tilde{\mathcal{A}}$ should be able, given the announcement of θ, to extract information about the parity $[b]$. The extractor $\tilde{E}_n$ has access to an extra register H_Θ storing the basis $\theta \in \{+, \times\}^n$. The extractor stores the guess for $[b]$ in register $H_\oplus$. The bias $\tilde{\varepsilon}_{\theta,b}(n)$ provided by the extractor when the qubits were initially in state $|b\rangle_\theta$ is

$$\frac{1}{2} + \tilde{\varepsilon}_{\theta,b}(n) = \|\mathbb{P}^\oplus_{[b]}(\tilde{E}_n \otimes \mathbf{1}_B)\,|\theta\rangle^\Theta\,|0\rangle^\oplus\,|\psi_{\theta,b}\rangle^{AB}\|^2, \tag{12}$$

where $\mathbb{P}^\oplus_{[b]}$ is applied upon the output register $H_\oplus$. The expected value $\tilde{\varepsilon}(n)$ for the bias provided by $\tilde{E}_n$ is simply,

$$\tilde{\varepsilon}(n) = \frac{1}{4^n} \sum_{b\in\{0,1\}^n} \sum_{\theta\in\{+,\times\}^n} \tilde{\varepsilon}_{\theta,b}(n). \tag{13}$$

We characterize $\tilde{\mathcal{A}}$'s behavior against QMC by both $\tilde{p}^{ok}(n)$ and $\tilde{\varepsilon}(n)$. Independently of the string commitment scheme used, there always exists $\tilde{\mathcal{A}}^*$ preparing a superposition of attacks that 1) succeeds with probability 1 during the opening and 2) provides $[b]$ with certainty. Such an attack can be implemented as follows:

$$|\psi^*_{\theta,b}\rangle = \alpha(C^A_n \odot C^B_n)\,|b\rangle^{channel}_\theta + \beta(C^A_n \odot C^B_n)\,|0^n\rangle^{channel}_{+^n} \tag{14}$$

where $|\alpha|^2 + |\beta|^2 = 1$ and C^A_n and C^B_n are the honest circuits for committing. The state $|\psi^*_{\theta,b}\rangle$ is a superposition of the honest behavior with probability $|\alpha|^2$ and the trivial attack consisting in not measuring the qubits received with probability $|\beta|^2$. The expected probability of success $p^*(n)$ is

$$p^*(n) = |\alpha|^2 + |\beta|^2(\frac{3}{4})^n \approx |\alpha|^2 \tag{15}$$

since with probability $|\alpha|^2$ an honest QMC was executed and with probability $|\beta|^2$ a QMC to the fixed state $|0^n\rangle_\theta$ was made. In the later case, the probability to pass $\mathcal{B}$'s test is $(3/4)^n$. The expected bias satisfies

$$\varepsilon^*(n) = \frac{|\alpha|^2}{2}(\frac{1}{2})^n + \frac{|\beta|^2}{2} \approx \frac{|\beta|^2}{2} \tag{16}$$

since with probability $|\alpha|^2$ a QMC to $|b\rangle_\theta$ is recovered (in which case a nonzero bias on $[b]$ occurs only when $\hat{\theta} = \theta$) and with probability $|\beta|^2$ a QMC to a dummy value is made thus allowing to extract $[b]$ perfectly. Such an attack does not enable the committer to break the binding property of the string commitment but nevertheless achieves: $p^*(n) + 2\varepsilon^*(n) > 1$. We define two flavors of adversaries against QMC. The first flavor captures any adversary that achieves anything better than the trivial adversary $\tilde{\mathcal{A}}^*$ defined in (14). The second flavor captures stronger adversaries for which our reduction will be shown to produce attacks against the $\mathcal{F}^n_m$–binding property of the string commitment.

Definition 2. *An adversary* $\tilde{\mathcal{A}} = \{(\tilde{C}^A_n, \tilde{O}^A_n, \tilde{E}_n)\}_{n>0}$ *against QMC is* $\delta(n)$–*non-trivial if* $\tilde{p}^{ok}(n) + 2\tilde{\varepsilon}(n) \geq 1 + \delta(n)$, *and* $\delta(n)$–*good if* $\tilde{p}^{ok}(n) + 4\tilde{\varepsilon}(n)^2 \geq 1 + \delta(n)$ *for* $\tilde{p}^{ok}(n)$ *and* $\tilde{\varepsilon}(n)$ *defined as in (11) and (13) respectively.*

Notice that if $\tilde{\mathcal{A}}$ is not $\delta(n)$-good (or $\delta(n)$-non-trivial) then an upper bound on the expected bias $\tilde{\varepsilon}(n)$ can be obtained from a lower bound on $\tilde{p}^{ok}(n)$. This is how we use QMCs for implementing oblivious transfer in Sect. 6.

4   The Reduction

Using a *good* adversary $\tilde{\mathcal{A}}$ against QMC, we would like to build an adversary against the $\mathcal{F}_m^n$-binding property of the underlying string commitment. In this section, we provide the first step of the reduction given that $\tilde{\mathcal{A}}$'s parity extractor is perfect (i.e. it always returns the parity of the committed string). We construct a circuit built from $\tilde{\mathcal{A}}$ allowing to prepare a commitment into which any $|\psi_{\theta,b}\rangle$ can be inserted efficiently at the opening stage. In Sect. 5, we show how to use this circuit for attacking the binding property of the string commitment.

4.1   The Switching Circuit

Let $\tilde{\mathcal{A}} = \{(\tilde{C}_n^A, \tilde{O}_n^A, \tilde{E}_n)\}_{n>0}$ be an adversary in QMC. We call H_{Keep} the register kept by $\tilde{\mathcal{A}}$ after the committing phase. We denote by H_B the register containing what is sent by $\mathcal{A}$ and kept by $\mathcal{B}$ after the committing phase. $H_Q \simeq \mathcal{H}_{2^n}$ denotes the register containing the BB84 qubits before the commitment, $H_\Theta \simeq \mathcal{H}_{2^n}$ denotes the register for the basis given as input to the extractor, and $H_\oplus \simeq \mathcal{H}_2$ denotes the register in which the guess on $[b]$ is stored by the extractor.

Instead of running $\tilde{C}_n \equiv (\tilde{C}_n^A \odot C_n^B)$ upon some BB84 qubits, we run it with the maximally entangled state $|\Phi_n^+\rangle$ where the first half is stored in H_Θ and the second half stored in H_Q. Therefore, the basis given as input to the extractor is not a classical state but is rather entangled with register H_Q containing the qubits $\tilde{A}$ is committed upon. After the execution of $\tilde{C}_n |\Phi_n^+\rangle^{\Theta,Q}$, transformations $B^{\otimes b}$ and $T^{\otimes \theta}$ are applied to register H_Θ in order to prepare the input for the extractor where, $B = \sigma_X \sigma_Z$ and $T = \mathtt{H}\sigma_Z$. $\tilde{E}_n$ is then run before σ_Z is applied upon the extractor's output register $H_\oplus$. The transformation is completed by running the extractor in reverse. The resulting circuit, shown in Fig. 1, is called the *switching circuit*. Next, we see that whenever the parity extractor is perfect, the instance of the switching circuit using transformations $B^{\otimes b}$ and $T^{\otimes \theta}$ generates $|\psi_{\theta,b}\rangle$. To see this, we follow its evolution from the initial state $|\Phi_n^+\rangle$. We

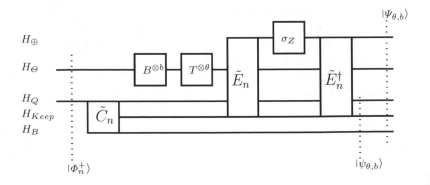

Fig. 1. The Switching Circuit

first look at the state generated before the extractor is applied,

$$|\Phi_n^+\rangle \equiv \sum_s \frac{1}{\sqrt{2}^n} |s\rangle |s\rangle \xrightarrow{\tilde{C}_n} \sum_s \frac{1}{\sqrt{2}^n} |s\rangle |\psi_{+^n,s}\rangle \xrightarrow{B^{\otimes b}} \sum_s \frac{(-1)^{b\odot s}}{\sqrt{2}^n} |b \oplus s\rangle |\psi_{+^n,s}\rangle$$

$$\xrightarrow{T^{\otimes \theta}} \sum_{s,t\,:\,t\preceq\theta} \frac{(-1)^{b\odot s \,\oplus\, b\odot t \,\oplus\, s\odot t}}{\sqrt{2}^{n+|\theta|}} |b \oplus s \oplus t\rangle |\psi_{+^n,s}\rangle \tag{17}$$

$$= \sum_{\substack{t\preceq\theta \\ s,t,v\,:\, v\preceq b\oplus s\oplus t}} \frac{(-1)^{b\odot t \,\oplus\, s\odot v \,\oplus\, s\odot s}}{\sqrt{2}^{n+|\theta|+|b\oplus s\oplus t|}} |b \oplus s \oplus t\rangle |\psi_{b\oplus s\oplus t, s\oplus v}\rangle. \tag{18}$$

The states up to (17) are obtained by definition of $|\Phi_n^+\rangle$, $\tilde{C}_n$, $B^{\otimes b}$, and $T^{\otimes \theta}$. Equation (18) follows after changing the basis from $+^n$ to $b \oplus s \oplus t$ using (9). From (18), we follow the evolution through $\tilde{E}_n^\dagger \sigma_Z \tilde{E}_n$,

$$T^{\otimes\theta}B^{\otimes b}\mathcal{C}_n |\Phi_n^+\rangle \xrightarrow{\tilde{E}_n^\dagger \sigma_z \tilde{E}_n} \sum_{\substack{t\preceq\theta \\ s,t,v\,:\, v\preceq b\oplus s\oplus t}} \frac{(-1)^{b\odot t \,\oplus\, s\odot v \,\oplus\, v\odot v}}{\sqrt{2}^{n+|\theta|+|b\oplus s\oplus t|}} |b \oplus s \oplus t\rangle^{\Theta} |\psi_{b\oplus s\oplus t, s\oplus v}\rangle \tag{19}$$

$$= \sum_{\substack{v\oplus x\oplus y\preceq\theta \\ x,y,v\,:\, v\preceq\theta\oplus x}} \frac{(-1)^{b\odot\theta \,\oplus\, b\odot x \,\oplus\, b\odot y \,\oplus\, v\odot y}}{\sqrt{2}^{n+|\theta|+|\theta\oplus x|}} |\theta \oplus x\rangle^{\Theta} |\psi_{\theta\oplus x, b\oplus y}\rangle \tag{20}$$

$$= \sum_{y\preceq x} \frac{(-1)^{b\odot\theta \,\oplus\, b\odot x \,\oplus\, b\odot y}}{\sqrt{2}^{n+|\theta|+|\theta\oplus x|-2|\theta\wedge\bar{x}|}} |\theta \oplus x\rangle^{\Theta} |\psi_{\theta\oplus x, b\oplus y}\rangle$$

$$= \sum_{y\preceq x} \frac{(-1)^{b\odot\theta \,\oplus\, b\odot x \,\oplus\, b\odot y}}{\sqrt{2}^{n+|x|}} |\theta \oplus x\rangle^{\Theta} |\psi_{\theta\oplus x, b\oplus y}\rangle \tag{21}$$

$$= \sum_x \frac{(-1)^{b\odot\theta}}{\sqrt{2}^n} |\theta \oplus x\rangle^{\Theta} \otimes \sum_{y\,:\,y\preceq x} \frac{(-1)^{b\odot x \,\oplus\, b\odot y}}{\sqrt{2}^{|x|}} |\psi_{\theta\oplus x, b\oplus y}\rangle$$

$$= \sum_x \frac{(-1)^{b\odot\theta}}{\sqrt{2}^n} |\theta \oplus x\rangle^{\Theta} |\psi_{\theta,b}\rangle \equiv |\Psi_{\theta,b}\rangle. \tag{22}$$

Notice that in addition to H_Θ, $\tilde{E}_n$ acts upon another extra register $H_\oplus$ ignored in the above derivation. W.l.g one may assume it is included in the Hilbert space where $|\psi_{\theta,b}\rangle$ belongs. Equation (19) follows from the fact that the extractor is perfect. Equation (20) follows after a reorganizing the terms of the sum. Equation (21) follows after using (1). We finally get (22) using (9).

In conclusion, a perfect extractor allows to produce a commitment inside which any $|\psi_{\theta,b}\rangle$ can be put *efficiently* even when θ and b are chosen after the end of the committing phase.

5   Analysis

We analyze the switching circuit when it is run with imperfect parity extractors. We first show how states $\{|\tilde{\Psi}_{\theta,b}\rangle\}_{\theta,b}$, produced in this case, overlap with states

$\{ |\Psi_{\theta,b}\rangle \}_{\theta,b}$ generated when perfect extractors are available. In Sect. 5.2, we represent the behavior of the switching circuit by a table. In Sect. 5.3, we relate this table to attacks against the $\mathcal{F}_m^n$–binding property of the string commitment.

5.1   Generalization to Imperfect Extractors

Assume the adversary $\tilde{A} = \{(\tilde{C}_n^A, \tilde{O}_n^A, \tilde{E}_n)\}_{n>0}$ has access to an imperfect extractor. In this case, $\tilde{E}_n$ is modeled as follows:

$$\tilde{E}_n |\theta\rangle^\Theta |\psi_{\theta,b}\rangle = |\theta\rangle^\Theta \otimes \left(\gamma_{\theta,b} |[b]\rangle^\oplus |\varphi_{\theta,b}\rangle + \hat{\gamma}_{\theta,b} |1 \oplus [b]\rangle^\oplus |\hat{\varphi}_{\theta,b}\rangle \right). \qquad (23)$$

Without loss of generality, we may assume that both $\gamma_{\theta,b}$ and $\hat{\gamma}_{\theta,b}$ are real positive numbers such that $|\gamma_{\theta,b}|^2 \geq \frac{1}{2}$ (i.e. arbitrary phases can be added to $|\varphi_{\theta,b}\rangle$ and $|\hat{\varphi}_{\theta,b}\rangle$). According (13), the expected bias provided by $\tilde{E}_n$ is,

$$\tilde{\varepsilon}(n) \equiv 4^{-n} \sum_\theta \sum_b \tilde{\varepsilon}_{\theta,b}(n) = 4^{-n} \sum_\theta \sum_b \left| |\gamma_{\theta,b}|^2 - \frac{1}{2} \right|. \qquad (24)$$

Compared to the case where the extractor is perfect, only the effect of transformation $\tilde{E}_n^\dagger \sigma_Z \tilde{E}_n$ needs to be recomputed. From (23), we obtain,

$$(\tilde{E}_n^\dagger \sigma_Z \tilde{E}_n) |\theta\rangle |\psi_{\theta,b}\rangle = (-1)^{[b]} |\theta\rangle \otimes (|\psi_{\theta,b}\rangle + e_{\theta,b}), \qquad (25)$$

where the *error vector* $e_{\theta,b}$ satisfies $|\theta\rangle \otimes e_{\theta,b} \equiv -2\hat{\gamma}_{\theta,b}\tilde{E}_n^\dagger(|\theta\rangle |1 \oplus [b]\rangle^\oplus |\hat{\varphi}_{\theta,b}\rangle)$. The final state $|\tilde{\Psi}_{\theta,b}\rangle$, produced by the switching circuit, can be obtained easily from (19) using (25). We get that $|\tilde{\Psi}_{\theta,b}\rangle = \tilde{E}_n^\dagger \sigma_z \tilde{E}_n T^{\otimes\theta} B^{\otimes b} \mathcal{C}_n |\Phi_n^+\rangle$ satisfies:

$$|\tilde{\Psi}_{\theta,b}\rangle = \sum_{y \preceq x} \frac{(-1)^{b\odot\theta \,\oplus\, b\odot x \,\oplus\, b\odot y}}{\sqrt{2}^{n+|x|}} |\theta \oplus x\rangle \otimes (|\psi_{\theta\oplus x, b\oplus y}\rangle + e_{\theta\oplus x, b\oplus y}). \qquad (26)$$

Splitting the inner sum of (26) after distributing the tensor product gives,

$$|\tilde{\Psi}_{\theta,b}\rangle = |\Psi_{\theta,b}\rangle + F_{\theta,b}. \qquad (27)$$

The first part $|\Psi_{\theta,b}\rangle = (2^{-n/2} \sum_x (-1)^{b\odot\theta} |\theta\rangle) \otimes |\psi_{\theta,b}\rangle$ is exactly what one gets when the switching circuit is run with a perfect extractor (see (22)). The second part is the error term for which next lemma gives a characterization.

Lemma 2. *Consider the switching circuit built from adversary* $\tilde{A} = \{(\tilde{C}_n^A, \tilde{O}_n^A, \tilde{E}_n)\}_{n>0}$. *Then,*

$$4^{-n} \sum_\theta \sum_b \| F_{\theta,b} \|^2 \leq 2 - 4\tilde{\varepsilon}(n).$$

Proof. Let θ be fixed. Using the definition of $\boldsymbol{F}_{\theta,b}$, we get

$$2^{-n} \sum_{b \in \{0,1\}^n} \|\boldsymbol{F}_{\theta,b}\|^2 = 2^{-n} \sum_b \| \sum_{y \preceq x} \frac{(-1)^{b \odot \theta \oplus b \odot x \oplus b \odot y}}{\sqrt{2}^{n+|x|}} |\theta \oplus x\rangle \otimes \boldsymbol{e}_{\theta \oplus x, b \oplus y}\|^2$$

$$= 2^{-n} \sum_b \| \sum_x \frac{(-1)^{b \odot \theta \oplus b \odot x}}{\sqrt{2}^{n+|x|}} |\theta \oplus x\rangle \sum_{y:y \preceq x} (-1)^{b \odot y} \boldsymbol{e}_{\theta \oplus x, b \oplus y}\|^2$$

$$= 2^{-2n-|x|} \sum_x \sum_b \| \sum_{y:y \preceq x} (-1)^{b \odot y} \boldsymbol{e}_{\theta \oplus x, b \oplus y}\|^2, \tag{28}$$

where (28) is obtained from the orthogonality of all $\boldsymbol{e}_{\theta \oplus x, b \oplus y}$ when x varies, and from Pythagoras theorem. We now apply Lemma 1 to (28) with $A = \{y \in \{0,1\}^n | y \preceq x\}$, $w \equiv b, z \equiv y$, and $\boldsymbol{v}_{w,z} \equiv \boldsymbol{e}_{\theta \oplus x, b \oplus y}$. We first verify that the condition expressed in (2) is satisfied:

$$\sum_b \sum_{y_1 \in A: b \oplus y_1 = s} \sum_{y_2 \in A: b \oplus y_2 = t} (-1)^{b \odot (y_1 \oplus y_2)} \langle \boldsymbol{e}_{\theta \oplus x, b \oplus y_1}, \boldsymbol{e}_{\theta \oplus x, b \oplus y_2} \rangle =$$

$$\langle \boldsymbol{e}_{\theta \oplus x, s}, \boldsymbol{e}_{\theta \oplus x, t} \rangle \sum_{\substack{b: \\ b \oplus s \preceq x, b \oplus t \preceq x}} (-1)^{b \odot (s \oplus t)} = 0,$$

from an identity equivalent to (1) since b runs aver all substrings in the support of $s \oplus t \preceq x$. We therefore apply the conclusion of Lemma 1 to get that for all $x \in \{0,1\}^n$,

$$\sum_b \| \sum_{y:y \preceq x} (-1)^{b \odot y} \boldsymbol{e}_{\theta \oplus x, b \oplus y}\|^2 = \sum_{y:y \preceq x} \sum_b \|\boldsymbol{e}_{\theta \oplus x, b \oplus y}\|^2 \le 2^{n+|x|}(2 - 4\tilde{\varepsilon}(n)). \tag{29}$$

The result follows after replacing (29) in (28). $\qquad\square$

Using Lemma 2, we show how the the output of the switching circuit with imperfect extractors approaches the one with perfect extractors. Next lemma gives an upper bound on the expected overlap between the states produced using perfect and imperfect extractors.

Lemma 3. *Let $\tilde{\mathcal{A}} = \{(\tilde{C}_n^A, \tilde{O}_n^A, \tilde{E}_n)\}_{n>0}$ be the circuits for the adversary such that the extractor $\tilde{E}_n$ has expected bias $\tilde{\varepsilon}(n)$. Then, the set of states $\{|\tilde{\Psi}_{\theta,b}\rangle\}_{b,\theta}$ produced by the switching circuit satisfies,*

$$S_{\tilde{\mathcal{A}}} = 4^{-n} \sum_{b,\theta} |\langle \tilde{\Psi}_{\theta,b}|\Psi_{\theta,b}\rangle| \ge 2\tilde{\varepsilon}(n).$$

Proof. According (27), we can write $|\tilde{\Psi}_{\theta,b}\rangle = |\Psi_{\theta,b}\rangle + \boldsymbol{F}_{\theta,b} = (1 - \alpha_{\theta,b})|\Psi_{\theta,b}\rangle + \beta_{\theta,b}|\Psi_{\theta,b}^{\perp}\rangle$, where $1 = \||\tilde{\Psi}_{\theta,b}\rangle\|^2 = |(1 - \alpha_{\theta,b})|^2 + |\beta_{\theta,b}|^2$ and $\langle \Psi_{\theta,b}|\Psi_{\theta,b}^{\perp}\rangle = 0$. Isolating $|\alpha_{\theta,b}|$ and using the fact that $|\alpha_{\theta,b}|^2 + |\beta_{\theta,b}|^2 = \|\boldsymbol{F}_{\theta,b}\|^2$ gives $|\alpha_{\theta,b}| = \frac{\|\boldsymbol{F}_{\theta,b}\|^2}{2}$ which, after invoking Lemma 2, leads to $S_{\tilde{\mathcal{A}}} = \sum_{\theta,b} 4^{-n} |\langle \tilde{\Psi}_{\theta,b}|\Psi_{\theta,b}\rangle| \ge \sum_{\theta,b} 4^{-n}(1 - |\alpha_{\theta,b}|) = 1 - \sum_{\theta,b} 4^{-n} \frac{\|\boldsymbol{F}_{\theta,b}\|^2}{2} \ge 2\tilde{\varepsilon}(n)$. $\qquad\square$

Lemma 3 tells us that with *good* extractors, one can generate states having *large* overlap (in the expected sense) with all QMCs to different BB84 qubits which states are chosen at the beginning of the opening stage (i.e. after the end of the committing phase). It remains to show how to use this ability to break the binding property. This second and last step of our reduction is addressed in next section.

5.2   Representing the Switching Circuit by a Table

In this section, we look at how to invoke the switching circuit in order to attack the binding property of the string commitment. Remember first that $|\psi_{\theta,b}\rangle$ has probability $\tilde{p}^{ok}_{(\theta,b)}(n) = \|\mathbb{Q}^*_{(\theta,b)} |\psi_{\theta,b}\rangle\|^2$ to open a valid QMC to $|b\rangle_\theta$ where $\mathbb{Q}^*_{(\theta,b)}$ is defined as in (10). Remember that a valid opening of $|b\rangle_\theta$ consists in the opening of any $2n$–bit string $(\hat{\theta}, \hat{b}) \in \Delta_{\preceq}(\theta, b)$. We take advantage of the structure of $\Delta_{\preceq}(\theta, b)$ in order to exhibit attacks against the binding condition.

Suppose first that adversary $\tilde{\mathcal{A}}$ has access to a perfect parity extractor E_n. From Sect. 4.1, such an adversary can generate $|\psi_{\theta,b}\rangle$ for any choice of $\theta \in \{+, \times\}^n$ and $b \in \{0, 1\}^n$. Each of 4^n sets of valid announcements $\Delta_{\preceq}(\theta, b)$ is of size $\#\Delta_{\preceq}(\theta, b) = 3^n$. We define a table of positive real numbers having 4^n rows and 3^n columns where each row is labeled by a pair (θ, b). The row (θ, b) contains values $T_{\theta,b}(\tau, \beta) = \|\mathbb{Q}^B_{(\theta \oplus \tau, b \oplus \beta)} |\psi_{\theta,b}\rangle\|^2$ for all (τ, β) such that $(\theta \oplus \tau, b \oplus \beta) \in \Delta_{\preceq}(\theta, b)$. This condition is equivalent to (τ, β) such that $\beta \preceq \tau$. The table values for the case $n = 1$ are shown in Fig. 2. The sum of each row is added to the right. The construction is easily generalized for arbitrary n in which case, each

$$
\begin{array}{ccc|c}
\|\mathbb{Q}^B_{(+,0)} |\psi_{+,0}\rangle\|^2 & \|\mathbb{Q}^B_{(\times,0)} |\psi_{+,0}\rangle\|^2 & \|\mathbb{Q}^B_{(\times,1)} |\psi_{+,0}\rangle\|^2 & \tilde{p}^{ok}_{(+,0)}(n) = \|\mathbb{Q}^*_{(+,0)} |\psi_{+,0}\rangle\|^2 \\
\|\mathbb{Q}^B_{(+,1)} |\psi_{+,1}\rangle\|^2 & \|\mathbb{Q}^B_{(\times,1)} |\psi_{+,1}\rangle\|^2 & \|\mathbb{Q}^B_{(\times,0)} |\psi_{+,1}\rangle\|^2 & \tilde{p}^{ok}_{(+,1)}(n) = \|\mathbb{Q}^*_{(+,1)} |\psi_{+,1}\rangle\|^2 \\
\|\mathbb{Q}^B_{(\times,0)} |\psi_{\times,0}\rangle\|^2 & \|\mathbb{Q}^B_{(+,0)} |\psi_{\times,0}\rangle\|^2 & \|\mathbb{Q}^B_{(+,1)} |\psi_{\times,0}\rangle\|^2 & \tilde{p}^{ok}_{(\times,0)}(n) = \|\mathbb{Q}^*_{(\times,0)} |\psi_{\times,0}\rangle\|^2 \\
\|\mathbb{Q}^B_{(\times,1)} |\psi_{\times,1}\rangle\|^2 & \|\mathbb{Q}^B_{(+,1)} |\psi_{\times,1}\rangle\|^2 & \|\mathbb{Q}^B_{(+,0)} |\psi_{\times,1}\rangle\|^2 & \tilde{p}^{ok}_{(\times,1)}(n) = \|\mathbb{Q}^*_{(\times,1)} |\psi_{\times,1}\rangle\|^2
\end{array}
$$

Fig. 2. The table for the case $n = 1$ and perfect extractor.

column contains 4^n orthogonal projectors applied to the 4^n states $\{ |\psi_{\theta,b}\rangle\}_{\theta,b}$. The sum of all values in the table is simply $4^n \tilde{p}^{ok}(n) = \sum_{\theta,b} \tilde{p}^{ok}_{(\theta,b)}(n)$.

The table is defined similarly for imperfect parity extractors. In this case, table $T_{\tilde{\mathcal{A}}} = \{T_{\theta,b}(\tau, \beta)\}_{\theta,b,\tau,\beta \preceq \tau}$ associated with adversary $\tilde{\mathcal{A}}$ contains elements,

$$
T_{\theta,b}(\tau, \beta) = \|\mathbb{Q}^B_{(\theta \oplus \tau, b \oplus \beta)} |\tilde{\Psi}_{\theta,b}\rangle\|^2. \tag{30}
$$

While for perfect extractors the sum over all elements in the table is at least $4^n \tilde{p}^{ok}(n)$, next theorem shows that any table $T_{\tilde{\mathcal{A}}}$ built from a $\delta(n)$–good adversary adds up to $4^n \text{poly}(\delta(n))$. The proof follows easily from Lemma 3 and can be found in [5].

Theorem 1. *If $\tilde{A} = \{(\tilde{C}_n^A, \tilde{O}_n^A, \tilde{E}_n)\}_{n>0}$ is a $\delta(n)$–good adversary against QMC and $T_{\tilde{A}} = \{T_{\theta,b}(\tau, \beta)\}_{\theta,b,\tau,\beta \preceq \tau}$ is its associated table, then*

$$\sum_{\theta,b,\tau} \sum_{\beta \preceq \tau} T_{\theta,b}(\tau, \beta) \geq \frac{4^n \delta(n)^3}{32}. \tag{31}$$

Theorem 1 establishes the existence of one column in $T_{\tilde{A}}$ providing a *weak* attack since any table with 3^n columns all summing up to more than $\frac{4^n \delta(n)^3}{32}$ has one column exceeding $(\frac{4}{3})^n \frac{\delta(n)^2}{32} \gg 1 + 1/\text{poly}(n)$. Let (τ, β) be such a column and consider the class of functions containing only the identity $\mathbf{1}_{2n}$. For $(y, y') \in \{0, 1\}^{2n}$, the state $|\tilde{\Psi}_{y \oplus \tau, y' \oplus \beta}\rangle$ can be generated using the switching circuit. The probability to unveil (y, y') is $T_{y \oplus \tau, y' \oplus \beta}(\tau, \beta) = \|\mathbb{Q}_{(y,y')}^B |\tilde{\Psi}_{y \oplus \tau, y' \oplus \beta}\rangle\|^2$. By construction, we have $\sum_{(y,y')} \tilde{p}_{(y,y')}^f(n) = \sum_{(y,y')} T_{y \oplus \tau, y' \oplus \beta}(\tau, \beta) > 1 + 1/\text{poly}(n)$ which provides an attack against the string commitment's $\mathbf{1}_{2n}$–binding property in accordance with (7). As we pointed out in Sect. 3.1 however, this attack might not even be statistically distinguishable from the trivial adversary. This implies that proving a string commitment computationally $\mathbf{1}_{2n}$-binding would be impossible. In the next section, we find stronger attacks allowing to relax the binding property required for secure QMC.

5.3   Strong Attacks against the String Commitment

We now show that the table $T_{\tilde{A}}$, built out of any $\delta(n)$–good adversary $\tilde{A}$, contains an attack against the $\mathcal{F}_m^n$–binding property of the $2n$–string commitment with $m \in O(\text{polylog}(n))$ whenever $\delta(n) \geq 1/\text{poly}(n)$. We show this using a counting argument. We cover uniformly the table $T_{\tilde{A}}$ with all attacks in $\mathcal{F}_m^n$. Theorem 1 is then invoked in order to conclude that for some $f \in \mathcal{F}_m^n$, condition (7) does not hold.

Attacking the binding condition according to a function $f \in \mathcal{F}_m^n$ is done by grouping columns in $T_{\tilde{A}}$ as described in (6) and discussed in more details in [5]. The number of lines involved in such an attack is clearly 2^m while the number of columns can be shown to be $2^m 3^{n-m}$ (for information see [5] and Lemma 4 below). This means that any attack in $\mathcal{F}_m^n$ covers $t = 3^{n-m} 4^m$ elements in $T_{\tilde{A}}$. The quality of such an attack is characterized by the sum of all elements in the sub-array defined by the attack since this sum corresponds to the value of (7). Let $t_{\tilde{A}} = 3^n 4^n$ be the total number of elements in $T_{\tilde{A}}$ and let $s_{\tilde{A}}$ be its sum. The following lemma, proved in [5], shows that all attacks in $\mathcal{F}_m^n$ cover $T_{\tilde{A}}$ uniformly:

Lemma 4. *All f-attacks with $f \in \mathcal{F}_m^n$ cover $T_{\tilde{A}}$ uniformly, that is, each element in $T_{\tilde{A}}$ belongs to exactly $a = C(m, n)4^m$ attacks each of size $t = 3^{n-m} 4^m$.*

Let s^* be the maximum of (7) for all f-attacks with $f \in \mathcal{F}_m^n$. Clearly, $a \cdot s^* \geq \frac{a \cdot s_{\tilde{A}}}{t_{\tilde{A}}}$ since by Lemma 4, the covering of $T_{\tilde{A}}$ by $f \in \mathcal{F}_m^n$ is uniform and $a \cdot t/t_{\tilde{A}}$

is the number of times $T_{\tilde{A}}$ is generated by attacks in $\mathcal{F}^n_m$. In other words,

$$a \cdot s^* \geq \frac{a \cdot t \cdot s_{\tilde{A}}}{t_{\tilde{A}}} = \frac{a \cdot t \cdot s_{\tilde{A}}}{3^n 4^n} \Rightarrow s^* \geq \frac{t \cdot s_{\tilde{A}}}{3^n 4^n} = \frac{4^m \cdot s_{\tilde{A}}}{3^m 4^n}. \tag{32}$$

Assuming that $\tilde{A}$ is $\delta(n)$–good, Theorem 1 tells us that $s_{\tilde{A}} \geq \frac{4^n \delta(n)^3}{32}$ so (32) implies that,

$$s^* \geq \frac{\delta(n)^3 4^m}{32 \cdot 3^m} \geq 1 + 1/\text{poly}(n), \tag{33}$$

for any $m \geq \lceil \log_{\frac{4}{3}} \left(\frac{32}{\delta(n)^3} \right) \rceil$. Equation (33) guarantees that for at least one $f \in \mathcal{F}^n_m$, condition (7) is not satisfied thereby providing an attack against the $\mathcal{F}^n_m$–binding criteria. Moreover, since $\delta(n) \geq 1/\text{poly}(n)$ it is sufficient that $m \in O(\text{polylog}(n))$. It follows that at least one f-attack in $\mathcal{F}^n_m$ is statistically distinguishable from any trivial one.

6   The Main Result and Its Application

Putting together Theorem 1 and (33) leads to our main result:

Theorem 2 (Main). *Any $\delta(n)$–good adversary $\tilde{A}$ against QMC can break the $\mathcal{F}^n_m$–binding property of the string commitment it is built upon for $m \in O(\log \frac{1}{\delta(n)})$ using a circuit of size $O(\|\tilde{A}\|_{\mathcal{UG}})$.*

Theorem 2 can be applied for the construction of 1-2 QOT in the computational setting. We can use QMCs for building a weak 1-2 QOT such that:

- the sender has no information about the receiver's selection bit and,
- the receiver, according Theorem 2, can only extract a limited amount of information about both bits.

This *weak flavor* of 1-2 QOT is easily obtained by the following primitive, called $\mathcal{W}_n$, accepting $\mathcal{B}$'s input bits (β_0, β_1) and $\mathcal{A}$'s selection bit s (i.e this construction is very similar to the CK protocol[6]):

Protocol $\mathcal{W}_n$

1. $\mathcal{B}$ and $\mathcal{A}$ run the committing phase of a QMC (i.e. built from a $\mathcal{F}^n_m$-binding string commitment scheme) upon $|b\rangle_\theta$ for $b \in_R \{0,1\}^n, \theta \in_R \{+,\times\}^n$ picked by $\mathcal{B}$,
2. $\mathcal{B}$ chooses $c \in_R \{0,1\}$ and announces it to $\mathcal{A}$,
    - if $c = 0$ then $\mathcal{A}$ unveils the QMC, if UNVEIL SUCCEEDS then $\mathcal{A}$ and $\mathcal{B}$ return to 1 otherwise $\mathcal{B}$ ABORTS,
    - if $c = 1$ then $\mathcal{B}$ announces θ, $\mathcal{A}$ announces a partition $I_0, I_1 \subseteq \{1, \ldots, n\}$ such that for all $i \in I_s$ the measurements were made in basis $\hat{\theta}_i = \theta_i$, then $\mathcal{B}$ announces $a_0, a_1 \in \{0,1\}$ s.t. $\beta_0 = a_0 \oplus_{i \in I_0} b_i$ and $\beta_1 = \oplus_{i \in I_1} b_i$:
        - $\mathcal{A}$ does her best to guess $(\hat{b}_0, \hat{b}_1) \approx (\bigoplus_{i \in I_0} b_i, \bigoplus_{i \in I_1} b_i)$.

Clearly, $\mathcal{W}_n$ is a correct 1-2 QOT since an honest receiver $\mathcal{A}$ can always get bit $\beta_s = b_s \oplus a_s$. $\tilde{\mathcal{A}}$'s information about the other bit can be further reduced using the following simple protocol accepting $\mathcal{B}$'s input bits (β_0, β_1) and the selection bit s for the honest receiver:

Protocol R-Reduce$(t, \mathcal{W}_n)$

1. $\mathcal{W}$ is executed t times, with random inputs $(\beta_{0i}, \beta_{1i}), i = 1..t$ for the sender and input s for the receiver such that $\beta_{01} \oplus \ldots \oplus \beta_{0t} = \beta_0$ and $\beta_{11} \oplus \ldots \oplus \beta_{1t} = \beta_1$.
2. The receiver computes the XOR of all bits received, that is $\beta_s = \oplus_{i=1}^{t} \beta_{si}$.

Classically, it is straightforward to see that the receiver's information about one-out-of-two bit decreases exponentially in t. We say that a quantum adversary $\tilde{\mathcal{A}}$ against R-Reduce$(t, \mathcal{W}_n)$ is *promising* if it runs in poly-time and the probability to complete the execution is non-negligible. Using Theorem 2, it is not difficult to show that $\tilde{\mathcal{A}}$'s information about one of the transmitted bits also decreases exponentially in t whenever $\tilde{\mathcal{A}}$ is promising:

Theorem 3. *For any promising receiver $\tilde{\mathcal{A}}$ in* R-Reduce$(t, \mathcal{W}_n)$ *and for all executions, there exists $\tilde{s} \in \{0, 1\}$ such that $\tilde{\mathcal{A}}$'s expected bias on $\beta_{\tilde{s}}$ is negligible in t (even given β_s).*

A sketch of proof can be found in [5]. It relies upon the fact that any promising adversary must run almost all $\mathcal{W}_n$ with $\tilde{p}^{ok}(n) > 1 - \delta$ for any $\delta > 0$. Using Theorem 2, this means that independently for each of those executions $1 \leq i \leq t$, one bit $\beta_{\tilde{s}i}$ out of (β_{0i}, β_{1i}) cannot be guessed with bias better than $\varepsilon_{max}(\delta) << \frac{1}{2}$. In this case, the bias on $\beta_{\tilde{s}}$ can be shown to be negligible in t.

Clearly, the sender $\mathcal{B}$ in R-Reduce$(t, \mathcal{W}_n)$ cannot get any non-negligible amount of information about $\mathcal{A}$'s selection bit when the commitments are statistically concealing. This remark together with Theorem 3 and the correctness of R-Reduce$(t, \mathcal{W}_n)$ lead to:

Corollary 1. *A correct and private 1-2 QOT can be based upon any $\mathcal{F}_m^n$-binding and statistically concealing quantum string commitment scheme. The resulting 1-2 QOT statistically hides the selection bit and computationally hides one out of two transmitted bits.*

In other words, building 1-2 QOT upon Theorem 2 allows for an easy security proof in the computational setting. Our analysis assumes for simplicity that $\mathcal{A}$ and $\mathcal{B}$ have access to a perfect quantum channel. Nevertheless, noise may be tolerated if we construct 1-2 QOT along the lines of BBCS [3] instead of CK [6].

7 Open Questions

An obvious open problem is how to build $\mathcal{F}_m^n$-string commitments from computationally binding bit commitment schemes. In particular, how one can transform the computationally binding bit commitments of [8] and [7] into $\mathcal{F}_m^n$-binding string commitments? This would show that QMCs and therefore 1-2 QOT can be based upon any one-way permutation[8] and/or any one-way function[7]. It is an open question whether or not Theorem 2 holds for $\delta(n)$–non-trivial adversaries against QMC. Such an extension would show that our reduction from an adversary to QMC into one against the binding condition is to some extent optimal. It is also of interest to find attacks against weaker binding properties.

Finally, it would be very interesting to formally prove the security of the CK protocol using Theorem 2. This would result in a proof of security that, in addition to apply in the computational setting, would be based upon a completely different approach than Yao's proof [20]. Moreover, the CK protocol is more practical than our construction since it only requires a constant number of rounds with fewer qubits transmitted (i.e. $\Theta(n)$ vs. $\Theta(tn)$). It would also be useful to prove Corollary 1 in the case where the quantum channel is noisy.

References

1. ADCOCK, M.,and R. CLEVE, "A Quantum Goldreich-Levin Theorem with Cryptographic Applications", In *proceedings of 19th International Symposium on Theoretical Aspects of Computer Science (STACS 2002)*,LNCS, vol. 2285,Springer-Verlag, 2002, pp. 323–334.
2. BENNETT, C. H., and G. BRASSARD, "Quantum cryptography: Public key distribution and coin tossing", In *Proceedings of IEEE International Conference on Computers, Systems, and Signal Processing*, 1984, pp. 175–179.
3. BENNETT, C. H., G. BRASSARD, C. CRÉPEAU and M.-H. SKUBISZEWSKA, "Practical Quantum Oblivious Transfer", In *Advances in Cryptology –CRYPTO'91 : Proceedings*, LNCS, vol. 576, Springer-Verlag, 1992, pp. 362–371.
4. CRÉPEAU, C., "Quantum Oblivious Transfer", *Journal of Modern Optics*, vol. 41, no 12, 1994, pp. 2445–2454.
5. CRÉPEAU, C.,P. DUMAIS, D. MAYERS, and L. SALVAIL, "Computational Collapse of Quantum State with Application to Oblivious Transfer", full version of this paper, BRICS report nr. RS-03-37, available at www.brics.dk/RS/03/37, 2003.
6. CRÉPEAU, C. and J. KILIAN, "Achieving oblivious transfer using weakened security assumptions", *Proceedings of 29th IEEE Symposium on the Foundations of Computer Science*, 1988, pp. 42–52.
7. CRÉPEAU, C., F. LÉGARÉ, and L. SALVAIL, "How to Convert the Flavor of a Quantum Bit Commitment", In *Advances in Cryptology –EUROCRYPT'01 : Proceedings*, LNCS, vol. 2045, Springer-Verlag, 2001, pp. 60–77.
8. DUMAIS, P., D. MAYERS, and L. SALVAIL, "Perfectly Concealing Quantum Bit Commitment From Any Quantum One-Way Permutation", In *Advances in Cryptology –EUROCRYPT'00 : Proceedings*, LNCS, vol. 1807, Springer-Verlag, 2000, pp. 300–315.
9. VAN DE GRAAF, J., *Towards a Formal Definition of Security for Quantum Protocols*, Ph.D. thesis, Computer Science and Operational Research Department, Université de Montréal, 1997.
10. IMPAGLIAZZO, R. and S. RUDICH, "Limits on Provable Consequences of One-Way Permutations", In *Advances in Cryptology –CRYPTO'88 : Proceedings*, LNCS, vol. 403, Springer-Verlag, 1989, pp. 2–7.
11. LO, H.–K.,and H. F. CHAU, "Is quantum Bit Commitment Really Possible?", *Physical Review Letters*, vol. 78, no 17, 1997, pp. 3410–3413.

12. MAYERS, D., "The Trouble With Quantum Bit Commitment", available at http://xxx.lanl.gov/abs/quant-ph/9603015, 1996.
13. MAYERS, D., "Quantum Key Distribution and String Oblivious Transfer in Noisy Channels", In *Advances in Cryptology –CRYPTO'96 : Proceedings*, LNCS, vol. 1109 , Springer-Verlag, 1996, pp. 343–357.
14. MAYERS, D., "Unconditionally Secure Quantum Bit Commitment is Impossible", *Physical Review Letters*, vol. 78, no 17, 1997, pp. 3414–3417.
15. MAYERS, D., and L. SALVAIL, "Quantum Oblivious Transfer is Secure Against All Individual Measurements", In *Proceedings of the Workshop on Physics and Computationm, PhysComp'94*, Dallas, 1994, pp. 69–77.
16. RABIN, M. O., "How to exchange secrets by oblivious transfer", *Technical Memo TR–81*, Aiken Computation Laboratory, Harvard University, 1981.
17. SALVAIL, L., "Quantum Bit Commitment From a Physical Assumption", In *Advances in Cryptology –CRYPTO'98 : Proceedings*, LNCS, vol. 1462 , Springer-Verlag, 1998, pp. 338–354.
18. WATROUS, J, "Limits on the Power of Quantum Statistical Zero-Knowledge", *Proceedings of the 43rd Annual Symposium on Foundations of Computer Science*, 2002, pp. 495–504.
19. YAO, A. C., "Theory and Applications of Trapdoor Functions", *Proceedings of the 23rd IEEE Symposium on Foundations of Computer Science*, 1982, pp. 80–91.
20. YAO, A. C., "Security of Quantum Protocols Against Coherent Measurements", *Proceedings of the 27th ACM Symposium on Theory of Computing*, 1995, pp. 67–75.

Implementing Oblivious Transfer Using Collection of Dense Trapdoor Permutations

Iftach Haitner

Weizmann Institute of Science, Rehovot, Israel.

Abstract. Until recently, the existence of collection of trapdoor permutations (TDP) was believed (and claimed) to imply almost all of the major cryptographic primitives, including public-key encryption (PKE), oblivious transfer (OT), and non-interactive zero-knowledge (NIZK). It was recently realized, however, that the commonly accepted general definition of TDP needs to be strengthened slightly in order to make the security proofs of TDP-based OT go through. We present an implementation of oblivious transfer based on collection of dense trapdoor permutations. The latter is a collection of trapdoor permutations, with the property that the permutation domains are polynomially dense in the set of all strings of a particular length. Previous TDP-based implementations of oblivious transfer assumed an enhancement of the hardness assumption (of the collection).

1 Introduction

1.1 Oblivious Transfer (OT)

Oblivious transfer (OT), originally defined by Rabin [15], is a fundamental primitive in cryptography. OT has several equivalent formulations [15,7,3,5,2,4]. The version we studied, defined by Even, Goldreich and Lempel [7], is that of one-out-of-two OT. Informally, a (one-out-of-two) OT is a two-party protocol, in which one party (the sender) holds two secrets (σ_0 and σ_1) and the other party (the receiver) holds a secret bit i. If both parties follow the protocol, the receiver learns σ_i. In addition, even a cheating receiver (i.e., one that arbitrarily deviates from the protocol) cannot learn more then a single value in $\{\sigma_0, \sigma_1\}$ and even a cheating sender does not learn anything about i during the run of the protocol.

OT implies key agreement (KA) [15,1], signing contracts [7], and in general any secure multi-party evaluation [17,14,10].

1.2 Collection of Trapdoor Permutations (TDP)

A "collection of trapdoor permutations" (TDP) is among the strongest cryptographic primitives. TDP is a special case of collection of one-way permutations

M. Naor (Ed.): TCC 2004, LNCS 2951, pp. 394–409, 2004.

(OWP). Informally, a collection of permutations is one-way if a permutation chosen from this collection is easy to compute on any input, but hard to invert on the average. Any collection of OWP provides two additional efficient algorithms: The permutation sampler algorithm that samples a random permutation in the collection and the domain sampler algorithm that generates a random element in the domain of a given permutation. We stress that the permutation domains might be arbitrary, as long as there is an efficient domain sampler that generates a random element in them. Such a collection is called TDP, if in addition the permutation sampler algorithm produces a trapdoor information that allows its holder to invert the permutation. (see Subsection 3.4 for details).

1.3   Does TDP Implies OT?

Until recently, the existence of TDP was believed (and claimed) to imply OT. It was recently realized, however, that the commonly accepted general definition of TDP needs to be strengthened slightly in order to make the security proofs of TDP-based OT go through. This is due to the fact that in the standard TDP-based OT protocol, proposed by [7], the (honest-but-curious) `receiver` is expected to sample an element from the permutation domain such that the inverse of this element remains secret from its own point of view. The basic TDP security requirement guarantees secrecy against an external observer (who only observes the sampled element), however, the randomness used by the sampler could potentially be useful for efficient inversion. In fact, an arbitrary sampler could be used to construct a bad one, which first generates a domain element and then applies the permutation to produce the output.

To enable the stronger security feature required by the OT, Goldreich [12] defines a stronger primitive called "enhanced TDP". Specifically, an element produced by the domain sampler of an enhanced TDP should be hard to invert even when given the randomness used to produce it (see Subsection 3.5 for details). It should be noted that this distinction is quite hypothetical, as essentially all of the (very few) known TDP candidates can satisfy the stronger notion under the same assumptions.

1.4   Our Result

We show that OT can be based on any dense-TDP, where the latter is a TDP whose permutation domains are polynomially dense, i.e., contain polynomial fractions of the strings of length k (see Subsection 3.6 for details). We note that density assumption is made in other known constructions, such as the construction of non-interactive zero-knowledge proof of knowledge (NIZKPK) based on dense public-key crypto system [16].

1.5   Our Construction - Main Ideas

Our implementation follows the general ideas of the EGL protocol mentioned above. Recall that the EGL protocol is based on enhanced TDP (rather than a standard TDP) because the (honest-but-curious) `receiver` is expected to sample an element from the permutation domain such that the inverse of this element remains secret from its own point of view. In our construction, the `receiver` does not use the sampler, but rather chooses a random element in $\{0,1\}^n$ and checks whether or not the element is in the permutation domain. The main difficulty in our construction is the fact that it is not guaranteed that one can efficiently do the check above (i.e., check whether a given element is in the permutation domain). In order to overcome this difficulty, we extend a given dense-TDP into a dense-TDP with the extra property that there is an efficient algorithm that *given the permutation trapdoor* checks whether a given element in $\{0,1\}^n$ is inside the permutation domain. (We note that by doing this extension we are penalized, since the extended collection is not guaranteed to be dense-TDP but merely dense-weak-TDP , i.e., the collection's permutations are only guaranteed to be weak-one-way permutations). Then we use the latter TDP to implement a very weak form of OT, where we cannot assure that all the required properties of OT hold, but we can guarantee that they hold with a non-negligible probability. The above construction main idea is that the `sender` helps the `receiver` to check whether a given element is in the permutation domain. The final step of our construction is amplifying the above "weak OT" into a standard one. We note that even though amplifications of information theoretic weak forms of OT are quite common (e.g., [3,6]), amplifications of computational knowledge weak forms of OT, such as our amplification, are rare (in fact we encountered none) and are rather more complicated. Therefore, the amplification part of this paper may have a stand-alone value.

1.6   The Organization of the Rest of the Paper

In Section 2, we give a high level overview of our implementation. Section 3 is where we give the exact definitions of the tools and terms we use in this paper. In Section 4 we give the full implementation of a weak form OT based on dense-TDP and in Section 5 we show how to amplify such a "weak-OT" into a standard one.

2   Overview of Our OT

We present a polynomial time implementation of OT based on the existence of dense-TDP. Our implementation follows the general ideas of the following OT protocol, suggested by [7].

2.1   The EGL OT Protocol

Let (I, D, F) be a TDP, where I is the permutation sampler algorithm, D is the domain sampler algorithm and F and F^{-1} are the evaluation and inverting algorithms respectively (see Subsection 3.4 for details). Recall that the protocol's inputs are: the `sender`'s secrets, σ_0 and σ_1, the `receiver`'s index, i and the security-parameter, n, given in unary.

1. The **sender** uniformly selects a permutation description, α, along with its trapdoor, t, by letting $(\alpha, t) \leftarrow I(1^n)$.
   The **sender** sends α to the **receiver**.
2. The **receiver** uniformly selects two elements, r_0 and r_1, in D_α, as follows: r_{1-i} is selected directly in D_α, using the sampler, D. In order to select r_i, the **receiver** selects a third element, s, in D_α (using the sampler) and then sets r_i to $f_\alpha(s)$.
   Hence, the **receiver** knows the pre-image of r_i (i.e., s), but does not know the pre-image of r_{1-i}. Note that since f_α is a permutation, both r_0 and r_1 have the same distribution and thus, knowing them gives no information about i.
   The **receiver** sends (r_0, r_1) to the **sender**.
3. For both $j = 0, 1$, the **sender** computes $c_j = \sigma_j \oplus b(f_\alpha^{-1}(r_j))$, where b is a hardcore predicate for f_α.
   The **sender** sends (c_0, c_1) to the **receiver**.
4. The **receiver** locally outputs $c_i \oplus b(s)$ (and as $c_i \oplus b(s) = c_i \oplus b(f_\alpha^{-1}(r_i)) = \sigma_i$, it outputs σ_i).
   Note that as the **receiver** does not know the value of $f_\alpha^{-1}(r_{1-i})$, it received no knowledge about σ_{1-i}.

The security of the above protocol relies on the fact that the **receiver** does not know the pre-image of r_{1-i}, even though the **receiver** knows the random coins used by the sampler to select r_{1-i}. Therefore, the above protocol requires that the TDP be an enhanced one.

2.2   Towards the Protocol

We call a given TDP "checkable-domains-TDP", if there is an efficient algorithm that checks whether a given element in $\{0, 1\}^n$ is inside the permutation domain (clearly, a given TDP might not have this property). We start by showing how to implement an OT based on checkable-domains-dense-TDP, and then step-by-step, show how to implement an OT based on a standard dense-TDP.

An OT Based on Checkable-Domains-Dense-TDP. The protocol follows the same lines as the EGL protocol (described in Subsection 2.1), except for Step 2 that has the following form:
2. The **receiver** selects s, r_i and r_{1-i} as follows:

a. s and r_{1-i} are chosen uniformly in $\{0, 1\}^n$.
b. The **receiver** checks whether both s and r_{1-i} are in D_α. If the answer is negative, the **receiver** restarts the protocol (the two parties go back to the first step of the protocol).
c. r_i is set to $f_\alpha(s)$.

It is easy to see that the above construction is indeed an implementation of OT [1]. We stress that since the **receiver** did not use the collection sampler to choose r_{1-i}, the above is still true even if the collection is not enhanced.

Our next step is to implement a dense-TDP based OT with a weaker property than the checkable-domains one. We call a given TDP a "t-checkable-domains-TDP", if there is an efficient algorithm that *given the permutation trapdoor* checks whether a given element in $\{0,1\}^n$ is inside the permutation domain. We do not construct an OT based on t-checkable-domains-dense-TDP directly, but rather construct some weak form of OT. We shall later show how this weak form of OT can be amplified into a standard OT.

2.3   A Weak OT Based on T-Checkable-Domains-Dense-TDP

The first idea is to try and use a similar protocol to Protocol 2.2, where in order to decide whether or not s and r_{1-i} are in D_α, the **receiver** sends both elements to the **sender** in random order, and the **sender** (using the trapdoor) does the check and returns the answer to the **receiver**. If the **sender**'s answer is positive, then the **receiver** sends $f_\alpha(s)$ and r_{1-i} to the **sender** and the protocol proceeds as in Protocol 2.2, otherwise the **receiver** restarts the protocol. It is easy to see, however, that this protocol leaks the value of i to the **sender** (as the **sender** gets both s and $f(s)$).

A better idea is for the **receiver** to send the **sender** $f_\alpha(s)$ [2] and r_{1-i} (instead of s and r_{1-i}) in random order and the **sender** answers whether both elements are in D_α. Only if the **sender**'s answer is positive, the **receiver** reveals the right order of $f_\alpha(s)$ and r_{1-i}, and the protocol proceeds as in Protocol 2.2. At first glance it seems as thought we have a solution; unfortunately this is not the case, as it turns out that not only information about i might leak, but also the **receiver** might miscalculate the value of σ_i. The problem is that even if $f_\alpha(s)$ is in D_α, we are not guaranteed that s is. The reason is that f, when extended to $\{0,1\}^n$, is not necessarily a permutation and therefore s might be outside D_α even if $f_\alpha(s)$ is in D_α. Therefore the **receiver** might miscalculate the value of σ_i. Moreover, as f is not a permutation on $\{0,1\}^n$, $f_\alpha(s)$ and r_{1-i} might have a different distribution and hence, by revealing them to the **sender**, some information about i might leak.

Fortunately, there is a way to overcome the problems above, or more accurately to ensure that the constructed protocol is some weak form of OT. (By a weak form of OT, we mean that even though we cannot assure that all the required properties of OT hold, we can guarantee that they hold with non-negligible probability). The solution is that in addition to checking whether both elements (i.e., $f_\alpha(s)$ and r_{1-i}) are in D_α, the **sender** sends to the **receiver**

---

[1] There is a subtle point regarding the running time of the above protocol, which is not even guaranteed to stop. Due to the density property of the collection, however, this issue can be easily solved.

[2] By $f_\alpha(x)$, where x is not guaranteed to be in D_α, we mean the result of invoking the collection evaluating algorithm, F, with inputs α and x.

some random information [3] about the pre-images (with respect to f_α) of the two elements. The `receiver` checks whether the information it received about the pre-image of $f_\alpha(s)$ is consistent with s. If the answer is negative (or if one of the elements is not in D_α) it restarts the protocol. By keeping the amount of information the `sender` sends about pre-images small [4], we guarantee that only small amount of information about the pre-image of r_{1-i} (and therefore about σ_{1-i}) has leaked to the `receiver`. On the other hand, even though the amount of information is limited, we can guarantee with sufficiently high probability (which depends on the amount of information sent and the density of the collection) that the chosen s is indeed the pre-image of r_i. Hence, the protocol is a weak form of OT where all the required properties hold with sufficiently high probability [5].

We are now ready to construct a "very" weak form of OT (even weaker than the above) based on dense-TDP without any other assumptions.

2.4   A "Very" Weak OT Based on Any Dense-TDP

The main idea is that any dense-TDP can be extended into a t-checkable-domains-dense-TDP. (We note that by doing this extension we are penalized, since the extended collection is not guaranteed to be dense-TDP but merely dense-weak-TDP , i.e., the collection's permutations are only guaranteed to be weak-one-way permutations). The construction of the extended collection is as follows. For each permutation f_α with domain D_α of the original collection, the extended collection has the permutation f'_α with domain D'_α. Where $D_\alpha \subseteq D'_\alpha \stackrel{\text{def}}{=} \{x \in \{0,1\}^n \,|\, f_\alpha(\alpha, (f_\alpha^{-1}(x)) = x\}$ and f'_α is defined to be the natural extension of f_α to D'_α, that is $f'_\alpha(x) \stackrel{\text{def}}{=} F(\alpha, x)$.

By the density property of the collection we have that for any given permutation α, $\frac{|D_\alpha|}{|D'_\alpha|}$ is not negligible, therefore the extended collection's permutations are weak-one-way permutations. Hence, the extended collection is a dense-weak-TDP. Moreover, given an element x in $\{0,1\}^n$ and a permutation trapdoor, one can easily check whether x is in the permutation domain by checking whether $f_\alpha(\alpha, (f_\alpha^{-1}(x)) = x$.

By using Protocol 2.3 with the above dense-weak-TDP as the underlying collection, we construct some weak form of OT. This form of OT is even weaker than the one achieved by Protocol 2.3 as the collection's permutations are only weak one-way and hence, some information about σ_{1-i} might leak to the `receiver` through the run of the protocol. Nevertheless, this weaker form can still be amplified into a standard OT.

---

[3] In our implementation the random information is the output of applying a randomly chosen pairwise independent hash function on the pre-images.

[4] By small amount of information we mean $polylog(n)$ bits of information, where n is the security-parameter of the protocol.

[5] Actually the secrecy of the other secret (i.e., σ_{1-i}) is guaranteed with probability 1.

2.5   The Amplification Step

The amplification of the above "very" weak OT into a standard OT, is done in three consecutive steps. In each step we amplify a different property of the protocol. Hence, after the third step we have a standard OT.

3   Definitions

3.1   The Semi-honest Model

Loosely speaking, a semi-honest party is one that follows the protocol properly with the exception that it keeps a record of all its intermediate computations. In the semi-honest model all parties are assumed to be semi-honest. As far as the implementation of cryptographic protocol is concerned, one can limit oneself to the semi-honest model. The reason is that in [10] it is shown that semi-honest model protocols can be extended to the general (malicious) model, in which nothing is assumed regarding the parties. (For details see [12]).

3.2   Oblivious Transfer (OT)

A (one-out-of-two) OT is a two-party protocol, it has three inputs: the sender's secrets, σ_0 and σ_1, and the receiver's index, i in $\{0, 1\}$. In addition, the protocol receives, as an input, its security-parameter, n, given in unary [6]. The OT has the following properties:

1. Correctness - The receiver almost always learns σ_i. That is, the receiver learns σ_i with probability at least $1 - neg(n)$ ($neg(n)$ stands for negligible function of n), where the probability is over both parties' internal coin tosses.
2. Sender's privacy - The receiver gains no computational knowledge about σ_{1-i}. More formally, let $VIEW_R(\sigma_i, \sigma_{1-i}, i)$ be the random variable defined from the receiver's view of the protocol where σ_i and σ_{1-i} are the sender's input and i is the receiver's input [7]. Then for any polynomial time algorithm M, for any choices of σ_i, i and large enough n,

$$|Pr[M(VIEW_R(\sigma_i, 1, i)) = 1] - Pr[M(VIEW_R(\sigma_i, 0, i)) = 1]| < neg(n)$$

where the probability is over both parties' internal coin tosses.
3. Receiver's privacy- The sender gains no computational knowledge about i.

In this paper we focus in on implementing OT in the semi-honest model (see Subsection 3.1 for details), which by [10] yields an implementation in the general (malicious) model. Furthermore, we limit ourselves to OT whose secrets are one bit long. Implementing this limited version suffices, as by successive use of one bit protocol we construct the non-limited version.

---

[6] We usually omit the security-parameter from the protocol's input parameters list.
[7] The above notation is somewhat misused, as the order of the parameters depends on their values. Nevertheless, the underlying notation is clear, and it is done for the sake of simplicity.

3.3 $(\epsilon_1, \epsilon_2, \epsilon_3) - WOT$

$(\epsilon_1, \epsilon_2, \epsilon_3) - WOT$ is a two-party protocol that serves as an intermediate step in our implementation of OT. $(\epsilon_1, \epsilon_2, \epsilon_3)$–$WOT$ is a relaxed version of OT. Whereas in OT it is required that no knowledge except for the required secret may leak from one party to the other, in $(\epsilon_1, \epsilon_2, \epsilon_3) - WOT$ some amount of knowledge might leak (ϵ_2 is the amount of knowledge that might leak from the sender to the receiver and ϵ_3 is the amount of knowledge that might leak from the receiver to the sender). Furthermore, even the value of the required secret is not guaranteed to pass correctly (it is only guaranteed to pass with probability $1 - \epsilon_1$). Thus the ϵ's measure the weaknesses of the protocol and the smaller they are the better the protocol is. Let us turn to the formal definition.

$(\epsilon_1, \epsilon_2, \epsilon_3) - WOT$ is a two-party protocol, it has three inputs: the sender's secrets, σ_0 and σ_1 in $\{0,1\}$, and the receiver's index, i in $\{0,1\}$. In addition, the protocol receives, as an input, its security-parameter, n, given in unary. $(\epsilon_1, \epsilon_2, \epsilon_3) - WOT$ has the following properties:

1. Correctness - The receiver learns σ_i with probability at least $1 - \epsilon_1$, where the probability is over both parties' internal coin tosses.
2. Sender's privacy - The receiver does not gain more **computational knowledge** about σ_{1-i} than ϵ_2. More formally, let $VIEW_R(\sigma_i, \sigma_{1-i}, i)$ be the random variable defined from the receiver's view of the protocol where σ_i and σ_{1-i} are the sender's input and i is the receiver's input. Then for any polynomial time algorithm M, for any choices of σ_i, i and large enough n,

$$|Pr[M(VIEW_R(\sigma_i, 1, i)) = 1] - Pr[M(VIEW_R(\sigma_i, 0, i)) = 1]| < \epsilon_2$$

   where the probability is over both parties' internal coin tosses.
3. Receiver's privacy - The sender does not gain more **information** about i than ϵ_3. More formally, let $VIEW_S(\sigma_i, \sigma_{1-i}, i)$ be the random variable defined from the sender's view of the protocol where σ_i and σ_{1-i} are the sender's input and i is the receiver's input. Then for any choices of σ_i and σ_{1-i} and large enough n,

$$stat(VIEW_S(\sigma_i, \sigma_{1-i}, 1), VIEW_S(\sigma_i, \sigma_{1-i}, 0)) < \epsilon_3$$

Note that in the above definition, the third parameter (Receiver's privacy) measures information rather than computational knowledge. This strengthening simplifies our construction, as information theoretic reductions are much simpler than computational knowledge reductions.

3.4 Collection of Trapdoor Permutations (TDP)

Collection of trapdoor permutations (uniform complexity version) [11]: Let $\overline{I} \subseteq \{0,1\}^*$ and $\overline{I}_n \stackrel{\text{def}}{=} \overline{I} \cap \{0,1\}^n$. A collection of permutations with indices in $\overline{I}$ is a set $\{f_i : D_i \rightarrow D_i\}_{i \in \overline{I}}$ such that each f_i is one-to-one on the corresponding D_i. Such a collection is called a trapdoor permutation is there exist four probabilistic polynomial-time algorithms I, D, F, F^{-1} such that the following five conditions hold:

1. $Pr[I(1^n) \in \bar{I}_n \times \{0,1\}^*] > 1 - 2^{-n}$.
   That is, I is used to generate a random permutation along with its trapdoor.
2. Selection in domain, for every $n \in \mathbb{N}$ and $i \in \bar{I}_n$
   a) $Pr[D(i) \in D_i] > 1 - 2^{-n}$.
   b) Conditioned on $D(i) \in D_i$, the output is uniformly distributed in D_i.
      Thus $D_i \subseteq \cup_{m \leq poly(|i|)} \{0,1\}^m$. Actually, $D_i \subseteq \{0,1\}^{poly(|i|)}$.
   That is, given a permutation, D is used to generate a random element in the permutation domain.
3. Efficient evaluation, for every $n \in \mathbb{N}, i \in \bar{I}_n$ and $x \in D_i, Pr[F(i,x) = f_i(x)] > 1 - 2^{-n}$.
   That is, given a permutation, F is used to evaluate the permutation on any element in its domain.
4. Hard to invert, let I_n be the random variable describing the distribution of the first element in the output of $I(1^n)$ and $X_n \overset{\text{def}}{=} D(I_n)$, thus, for any polynomial time algorithm M, every polynomial p, and large enough n, $Pr[M(I_n, f_{I_n}(X_n)) = X_n] < \frac{1}{p(n)}$.
5. Inverting with trapdoor, for every $n \in \mathbb{N}$ any pair (i,t) in the range of $I(1^n)$ such that $i \in \bar{I}_n$, and every $x \in D_i, Pr[F^{-1}(t, f_i(x)) = x] > 1 - 2^{-n}$.
   That is, given a permutation along with its trapdoor, F^{-1} is used to find the pre-image of any element in its domain.

3.5   Enhanced Collection of Trapdoor Permutations

The implementation of OT presented by [7], is based on the existence of enhanced collection of trapdoor permutations. The enhancement refers to the hard-to-invert condition; i.e., it is hard to find the pre-image of a random element without knowing the permutation trapdoor. The enhanced condition requires that the hardness still hold *even when the adversary receives, as an additional input, the random coins used to sample the element.* (For more details see [12]).

It is presently unknown whether or not the existence of a TDP implies the existence of an enhanced TDP.

3.6   Collection of Dense Trapdoor Permutations (Dense-TDP)

A collection of dense trapdoor permutations (dense-TDP) is a TDP with one additional requirement. Whereas in an arbitrary TDP, the permutations may have arbitrary domains, here we require that these domains be polynomial fractions of the set of all strings of a particular length. Formally, let D_α be the domain of the permutation named α, then the additional requirement is: There exists a positive polynomial g such that for all $n \in \mathbb{N}$ and all $\alpha \in \bar{I}_n, D_\alpha \subseteq \{0,1\}^n$ and $|D_\alpha| > \frac{2^n}{g(n)}$. We define the density parameter of the collection, ρ, as $\frac{1}{g}$.

An alternative definition might allow D_α to be a subset of $\{0,1\}^{k(n)}$, for some fixed positive polynomial k (rather than a subset of $\{0,1\}^n$). It is easy to see, however, that the two definitions are equivalent.

4   Using Dense-TDP to Construct $\left(\frac{1}{q(n)}, 1 - \frac{\rho(n)^2}{4}, \frac{1}{q(n)}\right) - WOT$

(where ρ is the density parameter of the collection and q is any positive polynomial)

In this section we implement a very weak form of $(\epsilon_1, \epsilon_2, \epsilon_3) - WOT$, as all three parameters are not negligible. Notice that while the second parameter is fixed (equals $1 - \frac{\rho(n)^2}{4}$) and might be rather big, the first and third parameters can be as small as we like (as long as they are polynomial fractions). This freedom in choosing the first and third parameters, is used by the next section in order to construct a stronger protocol.

4.1   Preliminaries

Let (I, D, F) be a dense-TDP with density parameter ρ. For simplicity's sake, we assume that the collection's algorithms are deterministic and errorless, i.e., always return the right answers. Note that in the definition of dense-TDP, the algorithms are probabilistic and might return wrong answers with negligible probability. Extending the following implementation to the general case, however, is rather straightforward. (For details see [13]).

We would like to evaluate $F(\alpha, \cdot)$ and $F^{-1}(\alpha, \cdot)$ on any element in $\{0,1\}^n$ (and not only on elements in D_α). The problem is that nothing is guaranteed about the computation of $F(\alpha, x)$ and $F^{-1}(\alpha, x)$ when x is not in D_α. We can assume, however, that this computation halts in polynomial time and returns some value in $\{0,1\}^n$. Therefore we extend the notations $f_\alpha(x)$ and $f_\alpha^{-1}(x)$ to denote, for all $x \in \{0,1\}^n$, the value of $F(\alpha, x)$ and $F^{-1}(\alpha, x)$ respectively.

4.2   The Protocol's Outline

This protocol is an extension of the EGL protocol (described in Subsection 2.1). The first part of the protocol (Steps 1-3) is similar to the first part (Steps 1-2) of the EGL protocol. In this part, the receiver selects r_{1-i} and s uniformly in $\{0,1\}^n$. Note that either r_{1-i} or s might not be in D_α. This fact reduces the protocol's quality and hence, we are not constructing (in this step) an OT. There is a non-negligible probability, however, that both elements are in D_α, and therefore the protocol can guarantee some weaker requirements.

The middle part of the protocol (Steps 4-5) is where the new key idea lies. The sender helps the receiver to decide whether or not r_0 and r_1 (that the receiver has chosen in the first part of the protocol) "look" as though they have been chosen from the same distribution. In addition, the sender helps the receiver to decide whether or not s is the pre-image (with respect to f_α) of r_i. The above help is given to the receiver without leaking "too much" information about the value of σ_{1-i}. This help is needed, as there is no efficient way to decide whether or not a given element is in D_α. If the receiver concludes that r_0 and r_1 "look" as though they have been chosen from different distributions, or that

s is not the pre-image of r_i, then it restarts the protocol. Hence, the protocol might iterate through its first two parts (Steps 1-5) for quite a while, before it finally reaches its last part (Steps 6-8). It is guaranteed, however, that with very high probability, the protocol halts after a polynomial number of iterations.

The last part of our protocol is similar to the last part (Steps 3-4) of the EGL protocol. The receiver uses the information it received from the sender to calculate σ_i. Note that when s is in D_α (which happens with probability at least ρ), the receiver receives the right value of σ_i.

4.3   The Protocol

The protocol uses a collection of pairwise independent hash functions denoted H_n, where the hash function domain is $\{0,1\}^n$ and their range is $\left\{1, 2, \ldots, \frac{q(n)}{\rho^2(n)}\right\}$ [8]. Recall that the protocol's inputs are: the sender's secrets, σ_0 and σ_1, and the receiver's index, i.

1. The sender uniformly selects a permutation and its trapdoor, α and t, by letting $(\alpha, t) \leftarrow I(1^n)$, and uniformly selects a hash function $h \in H_n$. The sender sends (h, α) to the receiver.
2. The receiver selects s, r_i and r_{1-i} as follows:
   - s is chosen uniformly in $\{0,1\}^n$ and r_i is set to $f_\alpha(s)$.
   - r_{1-i} is chosen uniformly in $\{0,1\}^n$.

   The idea is that when s is in D_α, the receiver knows the value of $f_\alpha^{-1}(r_i)$ (i.e., s), and when r_{1-i} is in D_α, it does not know the value of $f_\alpha^{-1}(r_{1-i})$. Moreover, when both s and r_{1-i} are in D_α, they have the same distribution (as f_α is a permutation on D_α) and thus, knowing them gives no knowledge about i. Note that, if r_{1-i} or s are not in D_α, then the protocol is not guaranteed to work correctly, but with sufficiently high probability, the protocol detects such a situation by itself (Steps 4 - 5).
3. The receiver sends (r_0, r_1) to the sender in random order, i.e., the receiver selects k uniformly in $\{0,1\}$, sets w_0 to r_k and w_1 to r_{1-k}, and sends (w_0, w_1) to the sender.

   By sending r_0 and r_1 in random order, the receiver hides the identity of i. The random order is needed, since r_0 and r_1 might have completely different distributions and thus, sending them in a fixed order might leak information about i. This random ordering step was not taken in the EGL protocol, as in the EGL protocol both r_0 and r_1 were guaranteed to have the same distribution (recall that they were uniformly chosen in D_α). In the current protocol, however, it is not always the case. The reason is that in order to choose r_i we evaluate $f_\alpha(s)$, even though s is not guaranteed to be in D_α. Hence, we can assure nothing about r_i distribution. For example, it might be that for all x not in D_α, $f_\alpha(x)$ equals 0^n.

---

[8] That is, for any n, for any $x, y \in \{0,1\}^n$ and for any $\alpha, \beta \in \left\{1, 2, \ldots, \frac{q(n)}{\rho^2(n)}\right\}$

$$Pr_{h \in_R H_n}[(h(x) = \alpha) \wedge (h(y) = \beta)] = \left(\frac{\rho(n)^2}{q(n)}\right)^2.$$

4. For both $j = 0, 1$, the **sender** checks whether $f_\alpha(f_\alpha^{-1}(w_j))$ is equal to w_j. If the answer is positive it sets v_j to $h(f_\alpha^{-1}(w_j))$, otherwise it **aborts** the current iteration (i.e., the protocol is restarted).

   The **sender** sends (v_0, v_1) to the **receiver**.

5. The **receiver** **aborts** the current iteration, if $v_{i \oplus k}$ is not equal to $h(s)$.

   Motivating comment for Steps 4 and 5: The goal of the last two steps is to ensure, with sufficiently high probability, that the following two requirements hold. The first requirement is that s is the pre-image of r_i and the second requirement is that r_i and r_{1-i} "look" as though they have been chosen from the same distribution. The crucial observation is that when both r_i and r_{1-i} happen to be in D_α (which happens with probability at least $\frac{1}{\rho(n)^2}$), then the above two requirements are guaranteed to hold and the current iteration is not aborted. On the other hand, when one of the above two requirements does not hold, then the current iteration is aborted with probability at least $1 - \frac{1}{q(n)}$. (When s is not the pre-image of r_i then the **receiver** detects it in Step 5 with probability $1 - \frac{1}{q(n)}$, and when s is the pre-image of r_i and the current iteration is not aborted, then both r_i and r_{1-i} are uniformly distributed in the set $D'_\alpha \stackrel{\text{def}}{=} \{x \in \{0,1\}^n \mid f_\alpha(\alpha, (f_\alpha^{-1}(x)) = x\})$.

   We note that even though some information about the pre-image of r_{1-i} (i.e., $v_{(1-i) \oplus k}$) is delivered to the **receiver**, this information is given in a small amount and thus does not enable the **receiver** to compute the pre-image of r_{1-i} by itself.

6. The **receiver** sends k to the **sender**.

   That is, the **receiver** tells the **sender** which of the values, w_0 and w_1, is r_0 and which is r_1. The point is that when we reach this step, r_0 and r_1 have, with substantial probability, the same distribution. Hence, only a small amount of information about i might leak to the **sender**.

7. For both $j = 0, 1$, the **sender** uniformly chooses $y_j \in \{0,1\}^n$ and sets c_j to $b(f_\alpha^{-1}(r_j), y_j) \oplus \sigma_j$, where $b(x, y) \stackrel{\text{def}}{=} < x, y > \mod 2$ (i.e., the inner product of x and y modulus 2).

   The **sender** sends (c_0, c_1, y_0, y_1) to the **receiver**.

   Note that in this protocol, the **sender** XORs σ_0 and σ_1 with the hardcore bits of (r_0, y_0) and (r_1, y_1). The latter hardcore bits are with respect to a specific hardcore predicate (i.e., b) of the trapdoor permutation g_α, defined as $g_\alpha(x, y) \stackrel{\text{def}}{=} (f_\alpha(x), y)$. Recall that in the EGL protocol, the **sender** XORs σ_0 and σ_1 with the hardcore bits of r_0 and r_1, with respect to any given hardcore predicate of $f\alpha$. The reason for this modification is that in our proof of security, we rely on the structure of the above specific hardcore predicate.

8. The **receiver** locally outputs $b(s, y_i) \oplus c_i$.

   Note that when $f_\alpha^{-1}(r_i)$ is equal to s, the **receiver** outputs σ_i. In addition, when r_{1-i} is in D_α, no knowledge about σ_{1-i} leaks to the **receiver**.

Analysis Sketch. In this section we sketch the correctness proof of the above protocol. (A detailed proof can be found at [13]).

We first mention that the protocol is a polynomial one. The reason is that by the density property of the collection, the protocol halts, with very high probability, after $\frac{n}{\rho(n)^2}$ iterations. Thus, without loss of generality, we can assume that the protocol always halts after $\frac{n}{\rho(n)^2}$ iterations and is therefore polynomial.

We say that the protocol had a good-ending, if in its last iteration s was equal to the pre-image of r_i (with respect to f_α). It is not hard to see that the probability for a good-ending of the protocol, is at least $1 - \frac{1}{q(n)}$. The proof of the protocol's first and third properties (i.e., Correctness and Receiver's privacy), is a direct implication of the above result.

The proof of the protocol's second property (Sender's privacy), is proved by contradiction. We assume that the second property does not hold, and construct a polynomial time algorithm that, with non-negligible success, inverts the collection of dense trapdoor permutations. The proof has two major steps. First we construct a polynomial time algorithm, B, that predicts $b(f_\alpha^{-1}(x), y)$ with non-negligible advantage. (Recall that $b(z, w)$ is the inner product of z and w mod 2, and it is a hardcore predicate of the trapdoor permutation g_α, defined as $g_\alpha(z, w) \overset{\text{def}}{=} (f_\alpha(z), w)$. In the second step, we construct a polynomial time algorithm that computes $f_\alpha^{-1}(x)$, by embedding B in the reduction given by [9] in proving *hard-core predicate for any one-way function*.

5   Amplifying $\left(\frac{1}{q(n)}, 1 - \frac{\rho(n)^2}{4}, \frac{1}{q(n)} \right) - WOT$ to OT

(where ρ is the density parameter of the collection and we have the freedom to choose q as any positive polynomial)

In this section we sketch how to amplify a general $\left(\frac{1}{q(n)}, 1 - \frac{1}{t(n)}, \frac{1}{q(n)} \right) - WOT$ to OT, where t is any positive polynomial (not necessarily $\frac{4}{\rho(n)^2}$) and we have the freedom to choose q as any positive polynomial. A detailed construction can be found at [13].

The amplification is done in three independent steps. Each step amplifies some weak form of OT into a stronger form. In Subsection 5.4 we show how to combine these steps to create the desired amplification.

5.1   Using $\left(\frac{1}{nq'(n)t(n)}, 1 - \frac{1}{t(n)}, \frac{1}{nq'(n)t(n)} \right) - WOT$ to Construct $\left(\frac{1}{q'(n)}, neg(n), \frac{1}{q'(n)} \right) - WOT$

(where q' and t are any positive polynomials)

In this step, we show how to reduce (the potentially big) second parameter of $\left(\frac{1}{nq'(n)t(n)}, 1 - \frac{1}{t(n)}, \frac{1}{nq'(n)t(n)} \right) - WOT$ into a negligible function. In the protocol, the sender splits its original pair of secrets into many pairs of secrets, by splitting each of the original secrets into many secrets using a secret sharing scheme. Then, the sender transfers the i'th secret of each new pair to the receiver using $\left(\frac{1}{nq'(n)t(n)}, 1 - \frac{1}{t(n)}, \frac{1}{nq'(n)t(n)} \right) - WOT$. The point is that in order to know the value of σ_j, one should know the j'th secret of each of the new pairs. Thus the amount of knowledge the receiver gains about σ_{1-i} in the following protocol is negligible.

The Protocol. Recall that the protocol's inputs are: the sender's secrets, σ_0 and σ_1, and the receiver's index, i.

1. For both $j = 0, 1$, the sender sets the following values:
   - $\omega_{j,1}, \ldots, \omega_{j,nt(n)-1}$ are uniformly chosen at $\{0, 1\}$.
   - $\omega_{j,nt(n)}$ is set to $\left(\bigoplus_{k=1}^{nt(n)-1} \omega_{j,k}\right) \oplus \sigma_j$.
2. For all $1 \leq k \leq nt(n)$, the sender transfers $\omega_{i,k}$ to the receiver, using $\left(\frac{1}{nq'(n)t(n)}, 1 - \frac{1}{t(n)}, \frac{1}{nq'(n)t(n)}\right) - WOT$.
3. The receiver locally outputs $\bigoplus_{k=1}^{nt(n)} \omega_{i,k}$.

Analysis Sketch. By invoking Yao's XOR lemma, we show that the amount of knowledge the receiver gains about σ_{1-i} through this protocol is negligible and hence, the Sender's privacy is guaranteed. Proving the other properties (Correctness and Receiver's privacy) is rather straightforward. The Correctness property is proved by analyzing the probability that all the invocations of the subprotocol are successful (in a sense that the receiver always computes the right value of $\omega_{i,.}$), and the proof of the Receiver's privacy property is proved by a simple information theoretic argument.

5.2 Using $\left(\frac{1}{nq''(n)}, neg(n), \frac{1}{nq''(n)}\right) - WOT$ to construct $\left(neg(n), neg(n), \frac{1}{q''(n)}\right) - WOT$

(where q'' is any positive polynomial)

In this step, we show how to reduce the first parameter into a negligible function. In the protocol the sender repeatedly transfers σ_i to the receiver, using $\left(\frac{1}{nq''(n)}, neg(n), \frac{1}{nq''(n)}\right) - WOT$. The receiver determines the correct value using majority rule. The point is to decrease the probability that the receiver wrongly determines σ_i.

The Protocol

1. The sender transfers σ_i, n times to the receiver, using $\left(\frac{1}{nq''(n)}, neg(n), \frac{1}{nq''(n)}\right) - WOT$.
2. The receiver decides the value of σ_i by majority rule.

Analysis Sketch. The proof of the Correctness property is immediate by Chernoff bound. The Sender's privacy property is proved by hybrid argument and finally the proof of the Receiver's privacy property is proved by a simple information theoretic argument.

5.3   Using $\left(neg(n), neg(n), \frac{1}{3}\right) - WOT$ to construct $(neg(n), neg(n), neg(n)) - WOT$

In this final step, we reduced the third parameter into a negligible function. The implementation of this step follows the construction presented by Crépeau and Kilian [3].

5.4   Putting It All Together

Given a $\left(\frac{1}{q(n)}, 1 - \frac{1}{t(n)}, \frac{1}{q(n)}\right) - WOT$ protocol, where t is any positive polynomial and we are free to choose q as we like. We start by choosing $q(n)$ to be equal to $3n^2 t(n)$. The second step is to use Step 5.1 to implement $\left(\frac{1}{3n}, neg(n), \frac{1}{3n}\right) - WOT$. In the third step we use Step 5.2 to implement $\left(neg(n), neg(n), \frac{1}{3}\right) - WOT$. In the last step we use Step 5.3 to implement the desired $(neg(n), neg(n), neg(n)) - WOT$.

Recall that by the definition of $(\epsilon_1, \epsilon_2, \epsilon_3) - WOT$, $(neg(n), neg(n), neg(n)) - WOT$ is, in a sense, even a stronger protocol then OT. Since in OT all the requirements are computational knowledge ones and in $(neg(n), neg(n), neg(n)) - WOT$ the Receiver's privacy property is negligible by information-theoretic means [9].

6   Further Issues

A natural question to ask is whether a similar result be obtained even if the permutation requirement is somewhat relaxed. For example can we construct an OT based on dense collection of injective one-way functions? The answer is positive when we consider length-preserving functions. Moreover, exactly the same construction as used in this text can be used. If the functions are not length-preserving, then the size of the function range must be dense both in 2^n and in 2^m (assuming that the function input is n bit long and the output is m bit long), and, again, exactly the same construction as used in this text can be used.

Another natural question to ask is whether an OT can be constructed using "standard" TDP, without any additional requirements? The answer seems to be negative, as it was proved by [8] that OT cannot be Black-Box reduced to collection of injective one-way functions and it seems likely, though not proven yet, that this result can be extended to TDP.

Acknowledgements. I would like to thank my MSc advisor, Oded Goldreich, who introduced me to this subject, and guided me through the writing of this paper.

---

[9] Note that this strengthening also happened in the EGL protocol.

References

1. Manuel Blum, *How to exchange (secret) keys*, ACM Transactions on Computer Systems **1** (1983), no. 2, 175–193.
2. G. Brassard, C. Crepeau, and J.-M. Robert, *Information theoretic reductions among disclosure problems*, 27th Annual Symp. on Foundations of Computer Science (FOCS '86) (Los Angeles, Ca., USA), IEEE, October 1986, pp. 168–173.
3. C. Crépeau and J. Kilian, *Weakening security assumptions and oblivious transfer*, Advances in Cryptology (CRYPTO '88) (Berlin - Heidelberg - New York), Springer, August 1990, pp. 2–7.
4. C. Crépeau and M. Sántha, *On the reversibility of oblivious transfer*, Proceedings of Advances in Cryptology (EUROCRYPT '91) (Berlin, Germany) (Donald W. Davies, ed.), LNCS, vol. 547, Springer, April 1991, pp. 106–113.
5. Claude Crépeau, *Equivalence between two flavours of oblivious transfers*, Advances in Cryptology—CRYPTO '87 (Carl Pomerance, ed.), Lecture Notes in Computer Science, vol. 293, Springer-Verlag, 1988, 16–20 August 1987, pp. 350–354.
6. Ivan Damgård, Joe Kilian, and Louis Salvail, *On the (im)possibility of basing oblivious transfer and bit commitment on weakened security assumptions*, Lecture Notes in Computer Science **1592** (1999), 56–??
7. S. Even, O. Goldreich, and A. Lempel, *A randomized protocol for signing contracts*, Communications of the ACM **28** (1985), no. 6, 637–647.
8. Y. Gertner, S. Kannan, T. Malkin, O. Reingold, and M. Viswanathan, *The relationship between public key encryption and oblivious transfer*, 41st Annual Symp. on Foundations of Computer Science: proceedings: 12–14 November, 2000, Redondo Beach, California (IEEE, ed.), IEEE, 2000, pp. 325–335.
9. O. Goldreich and L. A. Levin, *A hard-core predicate for all one-way functions*, Proceedings of the twenty-first annual ACM Symp. on Theory of Computing, Seattle, Washington, May 15–17, 1989 (New York, NY, USA) (ACM, ed.), ACM Press, 1989, pp. 25–32.
10. O. Goldreich, S. Micali, and A. Wigderson, *How to play any mental game or A completeness theorem for protocols with honest majority*, Proc. 19th Ann. ACM Symp. on Theory of Computing, 1987, pp. 218–229.
11. Oded Goldreich, *Foundations of cryptography: Basic tools*, Cambridge University Press, Cambridge, UK, 2001.
12. _____, *Foundations of cryptography - volume 2*, Working Draft, available at www.wisdom.weizmann.ac.il/oded/foc-vol2.html, 2002.
13. Iftach Haitner, *Implementing oblivious transfer using collection of dense trapdoor permutations*, MSc thesis, available at www.wisdom.weizmann.ac.il/~iftachh/papers/msc.html, 2003.
14. Joe Kilian, *Founding crytpography on oblivious transfer*, Proceedings of the 20th Annual ACM Symp. on the Theory of Computing (Chicago, IL) (Richard Cole, ed.), ACM Press, May 1988, pp. 20–31.
15. M. O. Rabin, *How to exchange secrets by oblivious transfer*, TR-81, Harvard, 1981.
16. A. De Santis and G. Persiano, *Zero-knowledge proofs of knowledge without interaction*, 33rd Annual Symp. on Foundations of Computer Science: October 24–27, 1992, Pittsburgh, Pennsylvania: proceedings [papers] (Silver Spring, MD 20910, USA) (IEEE, ed.), IEEE, 1992, pp. 427–436.
17. Andrew C. Yao, *How to generate and exchange secrets*, Proceedings of the 27th Symp. on Foundations of Computer Science (FOCS), IEEE Computer Society Press, 1986, pp. 162–167.

Composition of Random Systems:
When Two Weak Make One Strong

Ueli Maurer and Krzysztof Pietrzak

ETH Zürich
Department of Computer Science
{maurer,pietrzak}@inf.ethz.ch

Abstract. A new technique for proving the *adaptive* indistinguishability of two systems, each composed of some component systems, is presented, using only the fact that corresponding component systems are *non-adaptively* indistinguishable. The main tool is the definition of a special monotone condition for a random system $\mathbf{F}$, relative to another random system $\mathbf{G}$, whose probability of occurring for a given distinguisher $\mathbf{D}$ is closely related to the distinguishing advantage ε of $\mathbf{D}$ for $\mathbf{F}$ and $\mathbf{G}$, namely it is lower and upper bounded by ε and $\varepsilon(1 + \ln \frac{1}{\varepsilon})$, respectively.

A concrete instantiation of this result shows that the cascade of two random permutations (with the second one inverted) is indistinguishable from a uniform random permutation by adaptive distinguishers which may query the system from both sides, assuming the components' security only against non-adaptive one-sided distinguishers.

As applications we provide some results in various fields as almost k-wise independent probability spaces, decorrelation theory and computational indistinguishability (i.e., pseudo-randomness).

1 Introduction

1.1 Random Systems and the Distinguishing Problem

The statistical distance δ of two random variables A and B has a natural interpretation: The success probability of an optimal distinguisher in telling apart the two random variables A and B is $(1 + \delta)/2$.

It is much more intricate to deal with the indistinguishability of *random systems*[1] which take inputs $X_1, X_2, \ldots$ and generate, for each new input X_i, an output Y_i which depends probabilistically on the inputs and outputs seen so far. As always, we consider a distinguisher $\mathbf{D}$ which may interactively query a random system and, after some number k of queries, outputs a decision bit. For two random systems $\mathbf{F}$ and $\mathbf{G}$ and a distinguisher $\mathbf{D}$ one considers the two random experiments where $\mathbf{D}$ queries $\mathbf{F}$ and where $\mathbf{D}$ queries $\mathbf{G}$, respectively,

---

[1] The term "random" is used here in the same sense as it is used in the term "random variable". It does not imply some kind of uniformity.

M. Naor (Ed.): TCC 2004, LNCS 2951, pp. 410–427, 2004.

for some $k \geq 1$ queries. The advantage of $\mathbf{D}$ in distinguishing $\mathbf{F}$ and $\mathbf{G}$ is defined as difference of the probabilities of $\mathbf{D}$ outputting 1, in both random experiments.

Usually one is interested in the indistinguishability of a random system from some *perfect* random system with respect to *any* distinguisher from some general class of distinguishers (e.g. the class of all adaptive or the class of all non-adaptive distinguishers). In this work we will consider the problem of whether one can compose two or more random systems to obtain a new system whose security is superior to the security of any of its components. This is best illustrated by an example.

1.2   Composition of Random Systems: An Example

Let $\mathbf{E}$ (and likewise $\mathbf{F}$) be a random permutation[2] where the advantage of any *non-adaptive* distinguisher[3] for $\mathbf{E}$ and a uniform random permutation (URP) $\mathbf{P}$ is at most ε_k (where k is the number of queries). We can build a new random permutation $\mathbf{E} \circ \mathbf{F}$ by using $\mathbf{E}$ and $\mathbf{F}$ in a cascade (see Figure 1). Intuitively, this construction should be even "closer" to $\mathbf{P}$ than $\mathbf{E}$ or $\mathbf{F}$ individually. Indeed, Vaudenay [7] proved that the *non-adaptive* indistinguishability of $\mathbf{E} \circ \mathbf{F}$ is $2\varepsilon_k^2$, i.e., the distinguishing advantages are multiplied. The same statement holds if we replace (both occurrences) of non-adaptive with adaptive in the above [8].

If $\mathbf{E}$ and $\mathbf{F}$ are secure against *non-adaptive* distinguishers, can we say something about the *adaptive* security of $\mathbf{E} \circ \mathbf{F}$? The intuition here is that adaptivity cannot help too much as the output of $\mathbf{E}$ in the cascade is obscured by $\mathbf{F}$ and the input to $\mathbf{F}$ is randomized by the leading $\mathbf{E}$. This intuition is indeed correct. We will prove that if the *non-adaptive* security of $\mathbf{E}$ and $\mathbf{F}$ is ε_k, then $\mathbf{E} \circ \mathbf{F}$ has *adaptive* security $2\varepsilon_k(1 + \ln \frac{1}{\varepsilon_k})$. A lower bound of $\Omega(\varepsilon_k)$ for this advantage can easily be shown, in contrast to the above stated $O(\varepsilon_k^2)$ when only non-adaptive security is required. This leaves us (as an open problem) a gap on the order of $\ln \frac{1}{\varepsilon_k}$ between the upper and lower bound.

1.3   From Indistinguishability to Monotone Conditions and Back

The framework of [3] is based on the concept of monotone conditions defined for a random system. Intuitively, after each query to the system, such a condition can either be satisfied or can fail to be satisfied. Monotonicity means that once the condition has failed, it is never satisfied in the future. For example, such a condition could be that at a certain point internally in the system, for example at the input to a component, no collision has occurred. This no-collision condition is obviously monotone.

---

[2] By a random permutation (over some set $\mathcal{X}$) we mean a system which was chosen according to some distribution from all possible permutations over this set. If this distribution is uniform this system is called a *uniform* random permutation (URP).

[3] A non-adaptive distinguisher must choose the queries without seeing the outputs of the invoked system.

Consider two random systems $\mathbf{F}$ and $\mathbf{G}$ with compatible input and output alphabets. In this paper we will consider a monotone condition $\mathcal{A}$ for $\mathbf{F}$, denoted $\mathbf{F}^{\mathcal{A}}$, such that for any fixed input-output behaviour, the probability that $\mathbf{F}$ shows this behaviour *and* the condition occurs is upper bounded by the probability that $\mathbf{G}$ shows this behaviour. This will be denoted as $\mathbf{F}^{\mathcal{A}} \preceq \mathbf{G}$. Lemma 6 shows that if $\mathbf{F}^{\mathcal{A}} \preceq \mathbf{G}$, then for any distinguisher, its advantage in distinguishing $\mathbf{F}$ from $\mathbf{G}$ is upper bounded by the probability that it can make the condition $\mathcal{A}$ fail in $\mathbf{F}$.

One can intuitively think of such a monotone condition as a lamp placed on the system which goes on as soon as the condition fails. More radically, one could think of failure of the condition as a trigger for the system to explode. If the failure of a condition in a system $\mathbf{F}$ is interpreted as such a visible effect, then distinguishing $\mathbf{F}$ from another system $\mathbf{G}$ (without such a trigger) is trivial, provided the trigger event occurs, i.e., the condition fails.

In very many indistinguishability proofs in the literature, such monotone conditions lie at the core of the argument, although this is sometimes obscured in complicated arguments. In [3] it is shown how complex systems with several internal subsystems, each with a monotone condition, can be analysed. However, if one only knows that the two systems are ε-*indistinguishable* from a URF, without knowing a corresponding condition, then the technique of [3] fails. A main goal of this paper is therefore to define a special monotone condition $\mathcal{A}$ (called the maximum condition) for a random system $\mathbf{F}$, relative to a system $\mathbf{G}$, such that $\mathbf{F}^{\mathcal{A}} \preceq \mathbf{G}$ and such that its probability ρ of not occurring (for any distinguisher $\mathbf{D}$) is closely related to the distinguishing advantage ε of $\mathbf{F}$ and $\mathbf{G}$ (for $\mathbf{D}$). More precisely, we provide two lemmas (Lemma 6 mentioned before and Lemma 9) which show that $\varepsilon \leq \rho \leq \varepsilon(1 + \ln \frac{1}{\varepsilon})$. This allows to prove the indistinguishability of two systems consisting of subsystems, knowing only that the subsystems are indistinguishable from a certain ideal system, but using the powerful framework based on monotone conditions.

Continuing the example of Section 1.2, let us discuss intuitively how this maximum condition allows to upper bound the *adaptive* security ε_k of $\mathbf{E} \circ \mathbf{F}$ assuming that the *non-adaptive* security of $\mathbf{E}$ (and likewise of $\mathbf{F}$) is at least γ_k (the k refers to the number of queries the distinguisher is allowed to make). Let $\mathcal{A}$ be the maximum condition for $\mathbf{E}$ relative to a URP $\mathbf{P}$, and let $\mathcal{B}$ be the maximum condition for $\mathbf{F}$ relative to $\mathbf{P}$. One can show (using Lemma 6) that $\varepsilon_k \leq \alpha_k$, where α_k is an upper bound on the maximal success probability of any adaptive distinguisher in making either $\mathcal{A}$ or $\mathcal{B}$ fail when querying $\mathbf{E}^{\mathcal{A}} \circ \mathbf{F}^{\mathcal{B}}$. Then using $\mathbf{E}^{\mathcal{A}} \preceq \mathbf{P}$ and $\mathbf{F}^{\mathcal{B}} \preceq \mathbf{P}$ one can show that this probability is at most the success probability of any *adaptive* distinguisher in making $\mathcal{A}$ fail in $\mathbf{E}^{\mathcal{A}} \circ \mathbf{P}$ plus the probability of making $\mathcal{B}$ fail in $\mathbf{P} \circ \mathbf{F}^{\mathcal{B}}$. But in $\mathbf{E}^{\mathcal{A}} \circ \mathbf{P}$ (and likewise in $\mathbf{P} \circ \mathbf{F}^{\mathcal{B}}$) adaptive strategies cannot be better than non-adaptive ones in making $\mathcal{A}$ fail as the output of $\mathbf{E}^{\mathcal{A}} \circ \mathbf{P}$ is completely independent of the output of the internal system $\mathbf{E}$ on which $\mathcal{A}$ is defined. So $\varepsilon_k \leq 2\beta_k$ where β_k is an upper bound on the probability of any *non-adaptive* distinguisher in making $\mathcal{A}$ fail in $\mathbf{E}$ (and likewise $\mathcal{B}$ in $\mathbf{F}$). As $\mathcal{A}$ and $\mathcal{B}$ are maximum conditions we now obtain (from Lemma 9) $\beta_k \leq \gamma_k(1 + \ln \frac{1}{\gamma_k})$ and thus $\varepsilon_k \leq 2\gamma_k(1 + \ln \frac{1}{\gamma_k})$.

1.4   Outline of the Paper

In Section 2 the definitions of random systems, monotone conditions, the $\preceq$ relation and of distinguishers are given. In Section 3 first the *maximum condition* for two random systems is defined. Then we lower and upper bound (Lemmas 6 and 9) the success probability of a distinguisher in making the maximum condition fail (as described in Section 1.3).

As an application of our framework, in Section 4 we provide two theorems bounding the adaptive security of two systems (parallel execution and XOR of random functions and cascades of permutations) in terms of the non-adaptive security of the component systems. We also give an application for each of the theorems, the first is about k-wise independent sample spaces, the second about the cascade of random involutions. Section 5 discusses some more implications of the results. Section 6 states some open problems.

1.5   Notation

We denote sets by capital calligraphic letters (e.g. $\mathcal{X}$) and the corresponding capital letter X denotes a random variable taking values in $\mathcal{X}$. Concrete values for X are usually denoted by the corresponding small letter x. For a set $\mathcal{X}$ we denote by $\mathcal{X}^k$ the set of ordered k-tuples of elements from $\mathcal{X}$. $X^k = (X_1, X_2, \ldots, X_k)$ denotes a random variable taking values in $\mathcal{X}^k$ and a concrete value is usually denoted by $x^k = (x_1, x_2, \ldots, x_k)$.

Because we will consider different random experiments where the same random variables appear, we extend the standard notation for probabilities and expectations (e.g. $\mathsf{P}_V(v)$, $\mathsf{P}_{V|W}(v, w)$, $\mathsf{E}[V]$) by explicitly writing the considered random experiment $\mathcal{E}$ as a superscript, e.g. $\mathsf{P}_V^{\mathcal{E}}(v)$, $\mathsf{P}_{V|W}^{\mathcal{E}}(v, w)$ and $\mathsf{E}^{\mathcal{E}}[V]$. Equality of distributions means equality for all arguments, e.g.

$$\mathsf{P}_V^{\mathcal{E}_1} = \mathsf{P}_V^{\mathcal{E}_2} \iff \forall v \in \mathcal{V} : \mathsf{P}_V^{\mathcal{E}_1}(v) = \mathsf{P}_V^{\mathcal{E}_2}(v).$$

We sometimes use the notation $\mathsf{P}_{\xi}^{\mathcal{E}}$ instead of $\mathsf{P}^{\mathcal{E}}(\xi)$ to denote the probability of the event ξ.

2   Random Systems, Conditions, and Distinguishers

2.1   Random Systems

Many cryptographic systems correspond to a probabilistic, possibly stateful (but often stateless) system which takes inputs $X_1, X_2, \ldots$ and generates, for each new input X_i, an output Y_i which depends probabilistically on X_i and the internal state.

In communication theory, a memoryless (i.e., stateless) communication channel with input X and output Y is modelled by a conditional probability distribution $P_{Y|X}$. In other words, $P_{Y|X}$ precisely captures the input-output behaviour of the channel, and it is unnecessary to consider the internals of the channel. In the same spirit, a possibly stateful and probabilistic system $\mathbf{F}$ that takes inputs $X_1, X_2, \ldots$ and generates an output Y_i for each new input X_i is modelled as a so-called random system [3], defined as a sequence of conditional probability distributions $P_{Y_i|X_1 \cdots X_i, Y_1 \cdots Y_{i-1}}$.

Definition 1 An $(\mathcal{X}, \mathcal{Y})$-*random system* $\mathbf{F}$ is a (generally infinite) sequence of conditional probability distributions $\mathsf{P}^{\mathbf{F}}_{Y_i|X^i Y^{i-1}}$, for $i \geq 1$. Two systems $\mathbf{F}$ and $\mathbf{G}$ are *equivalent*, denoted $\mathbf{F} \equiv \mathbf{G}$, if they correspond to the same random system, i.e., if $\mathsf{P}^{\mathbf{F}}_{Y_i|X^i Y^{i-1}} = \mathsf{P}^{\mathbf{G}}_{Y_i|X^i Y^{i-1}}$ for all $i \geq 1$.

The sequence $\mathsf{P}^{\mathbf{F}}_{Y_i|X^i Y^{i-1}}$ for $i \geq 1$ also defines the sequence $\mathsf{P}^{\mathbf{F}}_{Y^i|X^i}$ by

$$\mathsf{P}^{\mathbf{F}}_{Y^i|X^i} = \prod_{j=1}^{i} \mathsf{P}^{\mathbf{F}}_{Y_j|X^j Y^{j-1}},$$

and vice versa by

$$\mathsf{P}^{\mathbf{F}}_{Y_i|X^i Y^{i-1}} = \frac{\mathsf{P}^{\mathbf{F}}_{Y^i|X^i}}{\mathsf{P}^{\mathbf{F}}_{Y^{i-1}|X^{i-1}}}.$$

As special classes of random systems we will consider random functions and random permutations, which are stateless random systems.

Definition 2 A *random function* $\mathcal{X} \to \mathcal{Y}$ (*random permutation* on $\mathcal{X}$) is a random variable which takes as values functions $\mathcal{X} \to \mathcal{Y}$ (permutations on $\mathcal{X}$). Throughout the paper the symbols $\mathcal{R}$ and $\mathcal{P}$ are used for the set of all random functions and the set of all random permutations respectively.

A *uniform random function (URF)* $\mathbf{R} : \mathcal{X} \to \mathcal{Y}$ (A *uniform random permutation (URP)* $\mathbf{P}$ on $\mathcal{X}$) is a random function with uniform distribution over all functions from $\mathcal{X}$ to $\mathcal{Y}$ (permutations on $\mathcal{X}$). Throughout the paper, the symbols $\mathbf{R}$ and $\mathbf{P}$ are used exclusively for the systems defined above.

2.2   Monotone Conditions

The concept of *monotone conditions* for random systems was introduced in [3]. A monotone condition $\mathcal{A}$ for a random-system $\mathbf{F}$ is a sequence $a_0, a_1, a_2, \ldots$ of events, where a_0 is the certain event and where a_i ($\overline{a}_i$) denotes the event that the condition is satisfied (failed) after the i'th query to $\mathbf{F}$ has been processed. As described above, monotone means that once the condition has failed, it can never hold again (i.e., $a_i \Rightarrow a_{i-1}$). A natural example of a monotone condition is a no-collision condition. As we are not interested in the behaviour of a random system after the condition has failed, and in fact this behaviour need in general not be defined, the definition below specifies the probability distribution of Y_i, given X^i and Y^{i-1}, only *together* with the event a_i, and conditioned on a_{i-1}. More formally, a random system with a monotone condition is defined like a random system, but the (conditional) probability distributions generally do not sum to 1. We use the term "partial" to denote such distributions which are not actually probability distributions.

Definition 3 An $(\mathcal{X}, \mathcal{Y})$-*random system* $\mathbf{F}$ with a monotone condition $\mathcal{A}$, denoted $\mathbf{F}^{\mathcal{A}}$, is an infinite sequence of partial conditional probability distributions $\mathsf{P}^{\mathbf{F}^{\mathcal{A}}}_{a_i Y_i | X^i Y^{i-1} a_{i-1}}$ for $i \geq 1$.

For any x^i and y^{i-1} we have

$$\mathsf{P}^{\mathbf{F}^{\mathcal{A}}}_{a_i | X^i Y^{i-1} a_{i-1}}(x^i, y^{i-1}) = \sum_{y_i \in \mathcal{Y}} \mathsf{P}^{\mathbf{F}^{\mathcal{A}}}_{a_i Y_i | X^i Y^{i-1} a_{i-1}}(y_i, x^i, y^{i-1}) \leq 1.$$

The sequence $\mathsf{P}^{\mathbf{F}^{\mathcal{A}}}_{a_i Y_i | X^i Y^{i-1} a_{i-1}}$ for $i \geq 1$ also defines the sequence $\mathsf{P}^{\mathbf{F}^{\mathcal{A}}}_{a_i Y^i | X^i}$ by

$$\mathsf{P}^{\mathbf{F}^{\mathcal{A}}}_{a_i Y^i | X^i} = \prod_{j=1}^{i} \mathsf{P}^{\mathbf{F}^{\mathcal{A}}}_{a_j Y_j | X^j Y^{j-1} a_{j-1}},$$

and vice versa.

Definition 4 We introduce a partial order $\preceq$ on input-output compatible random systems with monotone conditions, as follows:

$$\mathbf{F}^{\mathcal{A}} \preceq \mathbf{G}^{\mathcal{B}} \iff \forall i \geq 1 : \; \mathsf{P}^{\mathbf{F}^{\mathcal{A}}}_{a_i Y^i | X^i} \leq \mathsf{P}^{\mathbf{G}^{\mathcal{B}}}_{b_i Y^i | X^i}.$$

In other words, $\mathbf{F}^{\mathcal{A}} \preceq \mathbf{G}^{\mathcal{B}}$ if for all $i \geq 1$ and all $x^i \in \mathcal{X}^i$, $y^i \in \mathcal{Y}^i$, the probability that $\mathbf{F}^{\mathcal{A}}$ outputs y^i on input x^i and the condition $\mathcal{A}$ holds is at most the probability that $\mathbf{G}^{\mathcal{B}}$ will output y^i on input x^i and the condition $\mathcal{B}$ holds. We also define $\mathbf{F}^{\mathcal{A}} \preceq \mathbf{G}$ (here one may think of $\mathbf{G}$ having a condition which never fails):

$$\mathbf{F}^{\mathcal{A}} \preceq \mathbf{G} \iff \forall i \geq 1 : \; \mathsf{P}^{\mathbf{F}^{\mathcal{A}}}_{a_i Y^i | X^i} \leq \mathsf{P}^{\mathbf{G}}_{Y^i | X^i}.$$

2.3   Distinguishers and Their Advantage

Definition 5 A *distinguisher* for an $(\mathcal{X}, \mathcal{Y})$-random systems is a $(\mathcal{Y}, \mathcal{X})$-random system $\mathbf{D}$ which can interactively query $(\mathcal{X}, \mathcal{Y})$-random systems and finally outputs a bit.[4] For an $(\mathcal{X}, \mathcal{Y})$-random system $\mathbf{F}$ we denote by $\mathbf{D} \diamond \mathbf{F}$ the random experiment where $\mathbf{D}$ interactively queries $\mathbf{F}$.

This definition refers to adaptive distinguishers. A non-adaptive distinguisher must fix all inputs $X_1, \ldots, X_k$ before seeing the outputs $Y_1, \ldots, Y_k$.

For the case of random permutations, we will consider mono-directional and bidirectional distinguishers (the latter only in the adaptive version). A bidirectional distinguisher can query the system from both sides.

Definition 6 The *advantage* of $\mathbf{D}$ in distinguishing $\mathbf{F}$ from $\mathbf{G}$, after k queries, denoted $\Delta_k^{\mathbf{D}}(\mathbf{F}, \mathbf{G})$, is the absolute value of the difference of the probability of $\mathbf{D}$ outputting 1 in the two random experiments $\mathbf{D} \diamond \mathbf{F}$ and $\mathbf{D} \diamond \mathbf{G}$.

---

[4] An initial random variable $X_1 \in \mathcal{X}$ must also be defined.

Assuming without loss of generality that, after the query phase, $\mathbf{D}$ makes the optimal decision based on X^k and Y^k, we have[5]

$$\Delta_k^{\mathbf{D}}(\mathbf{F}, \mathbf{G}) = \frac{1}{2} \sum_{\mathcal{X}^k \times \mathcal{Y}^k} \left| \mathsf{P}_{X^k Y^k}^{\mathbf{D} \diamond \mathbf{F}} - \mathsf{P}_{X^k Y^k}^{\mathbf{D} \diamond \mathbf{G}} \right|.$$

We denote the advantages of the best adaptive and the best non-adaptive distinguisher as follows:

$$\Delta_k(\mathbf{F}, \mathbf{G}) \stackrel{\text{def}}{=} \max_{\mathbf{D}} \Delta_k^{\mathbf{D}}(\mathbf{F}, \mathbf{G})$$

and

$$\delta_k(\mathbf{F}, \mathbf{G}) \stackrel{\text{def}}{=} \max_{\text{non-adaptive } \mathbf{D}} \Delta_k^{\mathbf{D}}(\mathbf{F}, \mathbf{G})$$

$$= \max_{x^k \in \mathcal{X}^k} \frac{1}{2} \sum_{y^k \in \mathcal{Y}^k} \left| \mathsf{P}_{Y^k | X^k}^{\mathbf{F}}(y^k, x^k) - \mathsf{P}_{Y^k | X^k}^{\mathbf{G}}(y^k, x^k) \right|.$$

Definition 7 For a random system $\mathbf{F}^{\mathcal{A}}$ with a monotone condition, we let

$$\nu_k^{\mathbf{D}}(\mathbf{F}, \overline{a}_k) \stackrel{\text{def}}{=} 1 - \mathsf{P}_{a_k}^{\mathbf{D} \diamond \mathbf{F}}$$

be the probability that $\mathbf{D}$ makes the condition fail with at most k queries. Furthermore, let

$$\nu_k(\mathbf{F}, \overline{a}_k) \stackrel{\text{def}}{=} \max_{\mathbf{D}} \nu_k^{\mathbf{D}}(\mathbf{F}, \overline{a}_k)$$

be the maximal probability in provoking $\overline{a}_k$ using any adaptive $\mathbf{D}$, and analogously for non-adaptive $\mathbf{D}$:

$$\mu_k(\mathbf{F}, \overline{a}_k) \stackrel{\text{def}}{=} \max_{\text{non-adaptive } \mathbf{D}} \nu_k^{\mathbf{D}}(\mathbf{F}, \overline{a}_k).$$

2.4   Random Systems as Components in Random Experiments

In this section we propose two lemmas which we will need several times in the sequel. Consider the random experiment $\mathcal{E}(\mathbf{F})$ where a random system $\mathbf{F}$, defined by a sequence of distributions $\mathsf{P}_{Y_i | X^i Y^{i-1}}^{\mathbf{F}}$, is interacting with an environment $\mathcal{E}(\cdot)$, given by a sequence of distributions $\mathsf{P}_{X_i | X^{i-1} Y^{i-1}}^{\mathcal{E}(\cdot)}$.[6] Here $\mathcal{E}(\cdot)$ sends a query X_1 to $\mathbf{F}$ which answers with Y_1, then $\mathcal{E}(\cdot)$ sends a query X_2 and so on. So after k queries this random experiment defines a random variable $X^k Y^k$.

---

[5] This definition has a natural interpretation in the random experiment where we first toss a uniform random coin $C \in \{0, 1\}$. Then we let $\mathbf{D}$ (which has no a priori information on C) make k queries to a system $\mathbf{H}$ where $\mathbf{H} \equiv \mathbf{F}$ if $C = 0$ and $\mathbf{H} \equiv \mathbf{G}$ if $C = 1$. Here the expected probability that an optimal guess on C based on the k inputs and outputs of $\mathbf{H}$ will be correct is $1/2 + \Delta_k^{\mathbf{D}}(\mathbf{F}, \mathbf{G})/2$.

[6] This definition of environment $\mathcal{E}(\cdot)$ is exactly the definition of an adaptive distinguisher. We will consider environments where a distinguisher is part of the environment, so as to avoid ambiguities we introduce the term environment here.

Lemma 1 For $\mathcal{E}(.)$ as just defined

$$P_{X^kY^k}^{\mathcal{E}(\mathbf{F})} = P_{X^k|Y^{k-1}}^{\mathcal{E}(\cdot)} P_{Y^k|X^k}^{\mathbf{F}}.$$

Proof: This follows directly from the definition of this random experiment:

$$P_{X^kY^k}^{\mathcal{E}(\mathbf{F})} = \prod_{j=1}^{k} P_{X_j|X^{j-1}Y^{j-1}}^{\mathcal{E}(\cdot)} P_{Y_j|X^jY^{j-1}}^{\mathbf{F}} = P_{X^k|Y^{k-1}}^{\mathcal{E}(\cdot)} P_{Y^k|X^k}^{\mathbf{F}}.$$

$\square$

For example for the random experiment $\mathbf{D}\diamond\mathbf{F}$ (see Definition 5) we have

$$P_{X^iY^i}^{\mathbf{D}\diamond\mathbf{F}} = P_{X^i|Y^{i-1}}^{\mathbf{D}} P_{Y^i|X^i}^{\mathbf{F}}. \tag{1}$$

For $\mathcal{E}(\cdot)$ as just defined we can also consider the random experiment $\mathcal{E}(\mathbf{F}^{\mathcal{A}})$.[7] It is straight-forward to prove the following lemma.

Lemma 2 For $\mathcal{E}(\cdot)$ as above let τ be any event defined on $\mathcal{E}(\cdot)$. Let a_τ be the event that the condition $\mathcal{A}$ holds at the timepoint where τ occurs. If $\mathbf{F}^{\mathcal{A}} \preceq \mathbf{G}$ then

$$P_{\tau \wedge a_\tau}^{\mathcal{E}(\mathbf{F}^{\mathcal{A}})} \leq P_\tau^{\mathcal{E}(\mathbf{G})}$$

3   The Maximum Condition

Definition 8 For two $(\mathcal{X}, \mathcal{Y})$-random systems $\mathbf{F}$ and $\mathbf{G}$, $\mathbf{F}$ with the *maximum condition* (relative to $\mathbf{G}$) is the random system with monotone condition $\mathbf{F}^{\mathcal{A}}$ defined by

$$P_{a_i|X^iY^i}^{\mathbf{F}^{\mathcal{A}}} = \min_{1 \leq j \leq i}^{*} \left\{ \frac{P_{Y_j|X_j}^{\mathbf{G}}}{P_{Y_j|X_j}^{\mathbf{F}}} \right\}$$

and

$$P_{a_iY^i|X^i}^{\mathbf{F}^{\mathcal{A}}} = P_{Y^i|X^i}^{\mathbf{F}} P_{a_i|X^iY^i}^{\mathbf{F}^{\mathcal{A}}}$$

for $i \geq 1$, where $\min^*$ means that the constant 1 is included among the terms to be minimised over, i.e., a $\min^*$ expression is always upper bounded by 1. We denote the maximum condition for $\mathbf{F}$ and $\mathbf{G}$ by $\mathbf{F}\downarrow\mathbf{G}$ and often give it a short name (e.g. $\mathcal{A} := \mathbf{F}\downarrow\mathbf{G}$).

The term "maximum condition" is motivated by the following lemma.

Lemma 3 For $\mathcal{A} := \mathbf{F}\downarrow\mathbf{G}$,

$$\mathbf{F}^{\mathcal{A}} \preceq \mathbf{G}.$$

Moreover, for all $\mathbf{F}^{\mathcal{B}}$,

$$\mathbf{F}^{\mathcal{B}} \preceq \mathbf{G} \implies \mathbf{F}^{\mathcal{B}} \preceq \mathbf{F}^{\mathcal{A}}.$$

---

[7] Note that formally, this is not a random experiment since it is only partially defined, but the notion of a probability of an event in this random experiment is naturally defined, provided the condition that $\mathcal{A}$ holds at the timepoint when the event occurs is taken as part of the event.

Proof: We first observe that the condition is monotone, because of the min-imisation which implies $\mathsf{P}^{\mathbf{F}^{\mathcal{A}}}_{a_i|Y^iX^i} \leq \mathsf{P}^{\mathbf{F}^{\mathcal{A}}}_{a_{i-1}|Y^{i-1}X^{i-1}}$. To prove $\mathbf{F}^{\mathcal{A}} \preceq \mathbf{G}$, observe that $\mathsf{P}^{\mathbf{F}^{\mathcal{A}}}_{a_i|Y^iX^i} \leq \mathsf{P}^{\mathbf{G}}_{Y^i|X^i}/\mathsf{P}^{\mathbf{F}}_{Y^i|X^i}$ implies $\mathsf{P}^{\mathbf{F}^{\mathcal{A}}}_{a_iY^i|X^i} = \mathsf{P}^{\mathbf{F}}_{Y^i|X^i}\mathsf{P}^{\mathbf{F}^{\mathcal{A}}}_{a_i|X^iY^i} \leq \mathsf{P}^{\mathbf{G}}_{Y^i|X^i}$.

To see that $\mathbf{F}^{\mathcal{B}} \preceq \mathbf{G}$ implies $\mathbf{F}^{\mathcal{B}} \preceq \mathbf{F}^{\mathcal{A}}$, note that for the maximum condition $\mathcal{A}$ the distribution $\mathsf{P}^{\mathbf{F}^{\mathcal{A}}}_{a_i|Y^iX^i}$ has everywhere the largest possible value still satis-fying both requirements. So for any $\mathbf{F}^{\mathcal{B}} \preceq \mathbf{G}$ we have $\mathsf{P}^{\mathbf{F}^{\mathcal{B}}}_{b_i|Y^iX^i} \leq \mathsf{P}^{\mathbf{F}^{\mathcal{A}}}_{a_i|Y^iX^i}$ and thus $\mathbf{F}^{\mathcal{B}} \preceq \mathbf{F}^{\mathcal{A}}$. □

For the remainder of this section, let $\mathbf{F}$ and $\mathbf{G}$ be any $(\mathcal{X}, \mathcal{Y})$-random systems. For each $i \geq 0$ we define the function $\lambda_i^{\mathbf{F},\mathbf{G}} : \mathcal{X}^i \times \mathcal{Y}^i \to [0,1]$ as

$$\lambda_i^{\mathbf{F},\mathbf{G}}(x^i, y^i) \stackrel{\text{def}}{=} \max\left\{ \frac{\mathsf{P}^{\mathbf{F}}_{Y^i|X^i}(y^i, x^i) - \mathsf{P}^{\mathbf{G}}_{Y^i|X^i}(y^i, x^i)}{\mathsf{P}^{\mathbf{F}}_{Y^i|X^i}(y^i, x^i)}, 0 \right\}.$$

In a random experiment where the random variables X^i and Y^i are defined we can consider the random variables Z_i and $\widetilde{Z}_i$ defined as

$$Z_i \stackrel{\text{def}}{=} \lambda_i^{\mathbf{F},\mathbf{G}}(X^i, Y^i) \quad \text{and} \quad \widetilde{Z}_i \stackrel{\text{def}}{=} \max_{0 \leq j \leq i} Z_j. \tag{2}$$

The next two lemmas state that the expectation of these random variables in the random experiment $\mathbf{D}\diamond\mathbf{F}$ are the distinguishing advantage of $\mathbf{D}$ for $\mathbf{F}$ and $\mathbf{G}$ and the probability that $\mathbf{D}$ provokes the maximum condition for $\mathbf{F}$ (relative to $\mathbf{G}$) to fail, respectively.

Lemma 4

$$\Delta_k^{\mathbf{D}}(\mathbf{F}, \mathbf{G}) = \mathsf{E}^{\mathbf{D}\diamond\mathbf{F}}[Z_k].$$

Proof:

$$\Delta_k^{\mathbf{D}}(\mathbf{F}, \mathbf{G}) = \frac{1}{2} \sum_{\mathcal{X}^k \times \mathcal{Y}^k} |\mathsf{P}^{\mathbf{D}\diamond\mathbf{F}}_{X^kY^k} - \mathsf{P}^{\mathbf{D}\diamond\mathbf{G}}_{X^kY^k}|$$

$$= \sum_{\mathcal{X}^k \times \mathcal{Y}^k} \max\left\{ \mathsf{P}^{\mathbf{D}\diamond\mathbf{F}}_{X^kY^k} - \mathsf{P}^{\mathbf{D}\diamond\mathbf{G}}_{X^kY^k}, 0 \right\}$$

$$= \sum_{\mathcal{X}^k \times \mathcal{Y}^k} \mathsf{P}^{\mathbf{D}}_{X^k|Y^{k-1}} \max\left\{ \mathsf{P}^{\mathbf{F}}_{Y^k|X^k} - \mathsf{P}^{\mathbf{G}}_{Y^k|X^k}, 0 \right\}$$

$$= \sum_{\mathcal{X}^k \times \mathcal{Y}^k} \mathsf{P}^{\mathbf{D}\diamond\mathbf{F}}_{X^kY^k} \max\left\{ \frac{\mathsf{P}^{\mathbf{F}}_{Y^k|X^k} - \mathsf{P}^{\mathbf{G}}_{Y^k|X^k}}{\mathsf{P}^{\mathbf{F}}_{Y^k|X^k}}, 0 \right\}$$

$$= \mathsf{E}^{\mathbf{D}\diamond\mathbf{F}}[Z_k].$$

□

Lemma 5 For $\mathcal{A} := \mathbf{F}\downarrow\mathbf{G}$,

$$\nu_k^{\mathbf{D}}(\mathbf{F}^{\mathcal{A}}, \overline{a}_k) = \mathsf{E}^{\mathbf{D}\diamond\mathbf{F}}[\widetilde{Z}_k].$$

Proof:

$$\nu_k^{\mathbf{D}}(\mathbf{F}^{\mathcal{A}}, \overline{a}_k) = 1 - \sum_{\mathcal{X}^k \times \mathcal{Y}^k} \mathsf{P}^{\mathbf{D}\Diamond\mathbf{F}^{\mathcal{A}}}_{a_k X^k Y^k}$$

$$= \sum_{\mathcal{X}^k \times \mathcal{Y}^k} \mathsf{P}^{\mathbf{D}\Diamond\mathbf{F}}_{X^k Y^k}(1 - \mathsf{P}^{\mathcal{A}}_{a_k | X^k Y^k})$$

$$= \sum_{\mathcal{X}^k \times \mathcal{Y}^k} \mathsf{P}^{\mathbf{D}\Diamond\mathbf{F}}_{X^k Y^k}\left(1 - \min_{1 \le j \le k}{}^{*}\left\{\frac{\mathsf{P}^{\mathbf{G}}_{Y^j | X^j}}{\mathsf{P}^{\mathbf{F}}_{Y^j | X^j}}\right\}\right)$$

$$= \sum_{\mathcal{X}^k \times \mathcal{Y}^k} \mathsf{P}^{\mathbf{D}\Diamond\mathbf{F}}_{X^k Y^k} \max_{1 \le j \le k}{}^{*}\left\{\frac{\mathsf{P}^{\mathbf{F}}_{Y^j | X^j} - \mathsf{P}^{\mathbf{G}}_{Y^j | X^j}}{\mathsf{P}^{\mathbf{F}}_{Y^j | X^j}}\right\}$$

$$= \mathsf{E}^{\mathbf{D}\Diamond\mathbf{F}}[\widetilde{Z}_k].$$

Here max* means that the constant 0 is included among the terms to be minimised over, i.e., a max* expression is always non-negative.   □

Lemma 6 If $\mathbf{F}^{\mathcal{A}} \preceq \mathbf{G}$, then

$$\Delta_k^{\mathbf{D}}(\mathbf{F}, \mathbf{G}) \le \nu_k^{\mathbf{D}}(\mathbf{F}^{\mathcal{A}}, \overline{a}_k).$$

Proof: Let $\mathcal{B} := \mathbf{F}{\downarrow}\mathbf{G}$. Using the Lemmas 4 and 5 we get

$$\Delta_k^{\mathbf{D}}(\mathbf{F}, \mathbf{G}) = \mathsf{E}^{\mathbf{D}\Diamond\mathbf{F}}[Z_k]$$
$$\le \mathsf{E}^{\mathbf{D}\Diamond\mathbf{F}}[\widetilde{Z}_k]$$
$$= \nu_k^{\mathbf{D}}(\mathbf{F}^{\mathcal{B}}, \overline{b}_k)$$
$$\le \nu_k^{\mathbf{D}}(\mathbf{F}^{\mathcal{A}}, \overline{a}_k).$$

The last step is easily verified using $\mathbf{F}^{\mathcal{A}} \preceq \mathbf{F}^{\mathcal{B}}$, which follows from Lemma 3.   □

Definition 9 A sequence of random variables $V_0, V_1, \ldots$, is a *sub-martingale* if for all $i \ge 0$
$$\mathsf{E}[V_{i+1} | V_0, \ldots, V_i] \ge V_i.$$

The proofs of the Lemmas 7 and 8 below can be found in Appendix A.

Lemma 7 Let $V_0, V_1, \ldots$ be a *sub-martingale* where $0 \le V_i \le 1$ for all i, and let $\widetilde{V}_n \stackrel{\text{def}}{=} \max_{0 \le j \le n} V_j$. Then

$$\mathsf{E}[\widetilde{V}_n] \le \mathsf{E}[V_n] \cdot (1 - \ln(\mathsf{E}[V_n])).$$

Lemma 8 The sequence $Z_0, Z_1, \ldots$ as defined in (2) is a sub-martingale sequence in the random experiment $\mathbf{D}\Diamond\mathbf{F}$, i.e.,

$$\forall i \ge 0: \ \mathsf{E}^{\mathbf{D}\Diamond\mathbf{F}}[Z_{i+1} | Z_0, \ldots, Z_i] \ge Z_i.$$

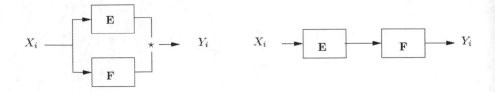

Fig. 1. The random systems $\mathbf{E} \star \mathbf{F}$ (left) and $\mathbf{E} \circ \mathbf{F}$ (right).

Lemma 9 For $\mathcal{A} := \mathbf{F} \downarrow \mathbf{G}$,

$$\nu_k^{\mathrm{D}}(\mathbf{F}^{\mathcal{A}}, \overline{a}_k) \leq \Delta_k^{\mathrm{D}}(\mathbf{F}, \mathbf{G}) \left(1 - \ln\left(\Delta_k^{\mathrm{D}}(\mathbf{F}, \mathbf{G})\right)\right).$$

Proof: Using Lemmas 8 and 7 we get

$$\mathsf{E}^{\mathbf{D} \diamond \mathbf{F}}[\widetilde{Z}_k] \leq \mathsf{E}^{\mathbf{D} \diamond \mathbf{F}}[Z_k] \cdot \left(1 - \ln\left(\mathsf{E}^{\mathbf{D} \diamond \mathbf{F}}[Z_k]\right)\right).$$

Now one can apply the Lemmas 4 and 5. □

4 Stronger Security by Composition

Definition 10 A composition operator $\bowtie$ for a class of random systems $\mathcal{Q}$ is a binary operator $\mathcal{Q} \times \mathcal{Q} \to \mathcal{Q}$ which, given two random systems $\mathbf{E}, \mathbf{F} \in \mathcal{Q}$, defines how to combine $\mathbf{E}$ and $\mathbf{F}$ into a random system $\mathbf{E} \bowtie \mathbf{F} \in \mathcal{Q}$ where, on any invocation of $\mathbf{E} \bowtie \mathbf{F}$, the internal random systems $\mathbf{E}$ and $\mathbf{F}$ are invoked once. In this paper we will consider the two composition operators $\star$ and $\circ$ described below.

- Let $\mathbf{E}, \mathbf{F} \in \mathcal{R}$ be random functions $\mathcal{X} \to \mathcal{Y}$ (see Definition 2) and let $\star$ denote some group operation on $\mathcal{Y}$. We denote by $\mathbf{E} \star \mathbf{F} \in \mathcal{R}$ the random function defined by applying the input to $\mathbf{E}$ and $\mathbf{F}$ and then applying $\star$ to the outputs (see Figure 1, left).
- Let $\mathbf{E}, \mathbf{F} \in \mathcal{P}$ be random permutations over $\mathcal{X}$ (see Definition 2). We denote by $\mathbf{E} \circ \mathbf{F} \in \mathcal{P}$ the random permutation defined by applying the input to $\mathbf{E}$ and $\mathbf{F}$ to the output of $\mathbf{E}$ (see Figure 1, right).

Lemma 10 Consider a class $\mathcal{Q}$ of random systems and a composition operator $\bowtie$ on $\mathcal{Q}$. If there is a random system $\mathbf{I} \in \mathcal{Q}$ such that for all $\mathbf{F} \in \mathcal{Q}$ the following two conditions are satisfied

1. $\mathbf{I} \bowtie \mathbf{I} \equiv \mathbf{I}$.
2. $\nu_k(\mathbf{E}^{\mathcal{A}} \bowtie \mathbf{I}, \overline{a}_k) = \mu_k(\mathbf{E}^{\mathcal{A}} \bowtie \mathbf{I}, \overline{a}_k)$ and $\nu_k(\mathbf{I} \bowtie \mathbf{F}^{\mathcal{B}}, \overline{b}_k) = \mu_k(\mathbf{I} \bowtie \mathbf{F}^{\mathcal{B}}, \overline{b}_k).$[8]

---

[8] This means that whenever one of the two system $\bowtie$ takes as input is the "perfect" system $\mathbf{I}$, then the best adaptive distinguisher has no advantage over the best non-adaptive distinguisher in provoking some event defined on the other system.

Then for any $\mathbf{E}, \mathbf{F} \in \mathcal{Q}$ and any $k \geq 1$ we have

$$\delta_k(\mathbf{E}, \mathbf{I}) \leq \varepsilon \quad \wedge \quad \delta_k(\mathbf{F}, \mathbf{I}) \leq \varepsilon \quad \Longrightarrow \quad \Delta_k(\mathbf{E} \bowtie \mathbf{F}, \mathbf{I}) \leq 2\varepsilon(1 + \ln \tfrac{1}{\varepsilon}).$$

Proof: Let $\mathcal{A}$ ($\mathcal{B}$) be the maximum condition for $\mathbf{E}$ ($\mathbf{F}$), relative to $\mathbf{I}$, i.e.,

$$\mathcal{A} := \mathbf{E} \!\downarrow\! \mathbf{I} \qquad \text{and} \qquad \mathcal{B} := \mathbf{F} \!\downarrow\! \mathbf{I}.$$

Now we have (here $b_{\overline{a}}$, and likewise $a_{\overline{b}}$, denote the event that at any timepoint where the condition $\mathcal{B}$ holds, also the condition $\mathcal{A}$ holds)

$$
\begin{aligned}
\Delta_k(\mathbf{E} \bowtie \mathbf{F}, \mathbf{I}) &= \Delta_k(\mathbf{E} \bowtie \mathbf{F}, \mathbf{I} \bowtie \mathbf{I}) \\
&\leq \nu_k(\mathbf{E}^{\mathcal{A}} \bowtie \mathbf{F}^{\mathcal{B}}, \overline{a}_k \vee \overline{b}_k) \\
&\leq \nu_k(\mathbf{E}^{\mathcal{A}} \bowtie \mathbf{F}^{\mathcal{B}}, \overline{a}_k \wedge b_{\overline{a}}) + \nu_k(\mathbf{E}^{\mathcal{A}} \bowtie \mathbf{F}^{\mathcal{B}}, \overline{b}_k \wedge a_{\overline{b}}) \\
&\leq \nu_k(\mathbf{E}^{\mathcal{A}} \bowtie \mathbf{I}, \overline{a}_k) + \nu_k(\mathbf{I} \bowtie \mathbf{F}^{\mathcal{B}}, \overline{b}_k) \\
&= \mu_k(\mathbf{E}^{\mathcal{A}} \bowtie \mathbf{I}, \overline{a}_k) + \mu_k(\mathbf{I} \bowtie \mathbf{F}^{\mathcal{B}}, \overline{b}_k) \\
&\leq \mu_k(\mathbf{E}^{\mathcal{A}}, \overline{a}_k) + \mu_k(\mathbf{F}^{\mathcal{B}}, \overline{b}_k) \\
&\leq \delta_k(\mathbf{E}, \mathbf{I})(1 - \ln(\delta_k(\mathbf{E}, \mathbf{I}))) + \delta_k(\mathbf{F}, \mathbf{I})(1 - \ln(\delta_k(\mathbf{F}, \mathbf{I}))) \\
&\leq 2\varepsilon(1 + \ln \tfrac{1}{\varepsilon}).
\end{aligned}
$$

The first step above follows from the first condition in the statement of the lemma. As for the second step, let $(\mathbf{E} \bowtie \mathbf{F})^{\mathcal{M}}$ be given by the partial distributions

$$\forall i \;:\; \mathsf{P}^{(\mathbf{E} \bowtie \mathbf{F})^{\mathcal{M}}}_{m_i Y^i | X^i} := \mathsf{P}^{\mathbf{E}^{\mathcal{A}} \bowtie \mathbf{F}^{\mathcal{B}}}_{a_i \wedge b_i Y^i | X^i}.$$

Here $(\mathbf{E} \bowtie \mathbf{F})^{\mathcal{M}} \preceq \mathbf{I} \bowtie \mathbf{I}$ (which follows from $\mathbf{E}^{\mathcal{A}} \preceq \mathbf{I}$ and $\mathbf{F}^{\mathcal{B}} \preceq \mathbf{I}$) and we can apply Lemma 6 as $(\mathbf{E} \bowtie \mathbf{F})^{\mathcal{M}} \leq \nu_k(\mathbf{E}^{\mathcal{A}} \bowtie \mathbf{F}^{\mathcal{B}}, \overline{m}_k) = \nu_k(\mathbf{E}^{\mathcal{A}} \bowtie \mathbf{F}^{\mathcal{B}}, \overline{a}_k \vee \overline{b}_k)$. The third step uses the union bound. Note that $\overline{a}_k \wedge b_{\overline{a}_k}$ is the event that the $\mathcal{A}$-condition fails before the $\mathcal{B}$-condition fails. The fourth step follows from Lemma 2. The fifth step follows by the second condition in the statement of the lemma. The sixth step follows as a non-adaptive distinguisher which queries $\mathbf{E}^{\mathcal{A}}$ (and likewise $\mathbf{F}^{\mathcal{B}}$) can simply "simulate" the system $\mathbf{E}^{\mathcal{A}} \bowtie \mathbf{I}$ ($\mathbf{I} \bowtie \mathbf{F}^{\mathcal{B}}$).[9] The seventh step follows from Lemma 9, and the final step from the assumption of the lemma. $\qquad\square$

Theorem 1 For random functions $\mathbf{E}, \mathbf{F} \in \mathcal{R}$ and $\star$ as in Definition 10,

$$\delta_k(\mathbf{E}, \mathbf{R}) \leq \varepsilon \quad \wedge \quad \delta_k(\mathbf{F}, \mathbf{R}) \leq \varepsilon \quad \Longrightarrow \quad \Delta_k(\mathbf{E} \star \mathbf{F}, \mathbf{R}) \leq 2\varepsilon(1 + \ln \tfrac{1}{\varepsilon}).$$

Proof: The Theorem follows from Lemma 10 by setting $\mathbf{I} \leftarrow \mathbf{R}$, $\mathcal{Q} \leftarrow \mathcal{R}$ and $\bowtie \leftarrow \star$. We only have to verify that the two points required by Lemma 10 are satisfied. As for the first point, $\mathbf{R} \star \mathbf{R} \equiv \mathbf{R}$ clearly holds. For the second point,

---

[9] Here we need that a query to $\mathbf{E}^{\mathcal{A}} \bowtie \mathbf{I}$ results in exactly one invocation of each subsystem. This guarantees we have no feedback which could not be simulated by a non-adaptive distinguisher.

note that the output of $\mathbf{E}^{\mathcal{A}} \star \mathbf{R}$ is independent of the output of the internal system $\mathbf{E}^{\mathcal{A}}$ on which our event is defined. So seeing the output cannot help in making the condition fail and we have $\nu_k(\mathbf{E}^{\mathcal{A}} \star \mathbf{R}, \overline{a}_k) = \mu_k(\mathbf{E}^{\mathcal{A}} \star \mathbf{R}, \overline{a}_k)$. By symmetry, also $\nu_k(\mathbf{R} \star \mathbf{F}^{\mathcal{B}}, \overline{b}_k) = \mu_k(\mathbf{R} \star \mathbf{F}^{\mathcal{B}}, \overline{b}_k)$ holds.   □

As an application for this theorem one can consider an adaptive version of almost k-wise independent distributions (see [5], and [1] for simpler constructions). These are distributions over $\{0,1\}^n$ such that the bits at any k fixed positions are close (say some $\varepsilon > 0$ far away) to uniform.

It is natural to consider an adaptive version of ε-almost k-wise independence where the positions can be chosen adaptively by a distinguisher.

Definition 11 A distribution over $\{0,1\}^n$ is *adaptively ε-almost k-wise independent* if even an adaptive distinguisher, selecting the k positions adaptively, cannot distinguish the k bits from uniformly random with advantage more than ε.

Corollary 1. The distribution over $\{0,1\}^n$ defined by XOR-ing two ε-almost k-wise independent distributions is adaptively $2\varepsilon(1 + \ln \frac{1}{\varepsilon})$-almost k-wise independent.

The following theorem is inspired by Lemma 3 from [4]. We use the notation of [3] to denote bidirectional random permutations. If $\mathbf{F}$ is a random permutation, then $\langle \mathbf{F} \rangle$ is like $\mathbf{F}$, but it can be queried from both sides. The distinguisher can thus also issue a direction bit, in addition to the query, to indicate from which side it is supposed to be applied as input.

Theorem 2 For two random permutations $\mathbf{E}, \mathbf{F} \in \mathcal{P}$ and $\circ$ as in Definition 10,

$$\delta_k(\mathbf{E}, \mathbf{P}) \leq \varepsilon \quad \wedge \quad \delta_k(\mathbf{F}, \mathbf{P}) \leq \varepsilon \quad \Longrightarrow \quad \Delta_k(\mathbf{E} \circ \mathbf{F}, \mathbf{P}) \leq 2\varepsilon \left(1 + \ln \frac{1}{\varepsilon} \right).$$

If we take the inverse $\mathbf{F}^{-1}$ of $\mathbf{F}$ as the second element in the cascade, we additionally obtain security against bidirectional distinguishers:

$$\delta_k(\mathbf{E}, \mathbf{P}) \leq \varepsilon \quad \wedge \quad \delta_k(\mathbf{F}, \mathbf{P}) \leq \varepsilon \quad \Longrightarrow \quad \Delta_k(\langle \mathbf{E} \circ \mathbf{F}^{-1} \rangle, \langle \mathbf{P} \rangle) \leq 2\varepsilon \left(1 + \ln \frac{1}{\varepsilon} \right).$$

Proof: The first statement of the theorem follows from Lemma 10 by setting $\mathcal{Q} \leftarrow \mathcal{P}$, $\mathbf{I} \leftarrow \mathbf{P}$ and $\bowtie \leftarrow \circ$. For the second statement we must set $\mathcal{Q} \leftarrow \mathcal{P}$, $\mathbf{I} \leftarrow \langle \mathbf{P} \rangle$ and $\bowtie$ to be the mapping $\mathbf{E}, \mathbf{F} \rightarrow \langle \mathbf{E} \circ \mathbf{F}^{-1} \rangle$.

We will only prove the (slightly more involved) second statement of the theorem. Note that this statement is somewhat stronger than a direct application of Lemma 10 would imply: the precondition is $\delta_k(\mathbf{E}, \mathbf{P}) \leq \varepsilon \wedge \delta_k(\mathbf{F}, \mathbf{P}) \leq \varepsilon$, and not $\delta_k(\langle \mathbf{E} \rangle, \langle \mathbf{P} \rangle) \leq \varepsilon \wedge \delta_k(\langle \mathbf{F} \rangle, \langle \mathbf{P} \rangle) \leq \varepsilon$ as one would expect (we will come back to that point later).

We must verify that the two points required by Lemma 10 are satisfied. As for the first point, $\langle \mathbf{P} \circ \mathbf{P}^{-1} \rangle \equiv \langle \mathbf{P} \rangle$ clearly holds. For the second point, note that in $\langle \mathbf{E}^{\mathcal{A}} \circ \mathbf{P}^{-1} \rangle$ a query from the $\mathbf{P}^{-1}$ side results in a random value on the input and output of $\mathbf{E}^{\mathcal{A}}$. Thus a query from this side can be replaced by a random query from the $\mathbf{E}^{\mathcal{A}}$ side without changing the probability of an event defined on

$\mathbf{E}^{\mathcal{A}}$, and we have $\nu_k(\langle \mathbf{E}^{\mathcal{A}} \circ \mathbf{P}^{-1} \rangle, \overline{a}_k) = \nu_k(\mathbf{E}^{\mathcal{A}} \circ \mathbf{P}^{-1}, \overline{a}_k)$. Now the output of $\mathbf{E}^{\mathcal{A}} \circ \mathbf{P}^{-1}$ is completely independent of the output of the internal system $\mathbf{E}^{\mathcal{A}}$. So adaptive strategies cannot help in provoking an event defined on $\mathbf{E}^{\mathcal{A}}$, i.e., $\nu_k(\mathbf{E}^{\mathcal{A}} \circ \mathbf{P}^{-1}, \overline{a}_k) = \mu_k(\mathbf{E}^{\mathcal{A}} \circ \mathbf{P}^{-1}, \overline{a}_k)$. We have shown that $\nu_k(\langle \mathbf{E}^{\mathcal{A}} \circ \mathbf{P}^{-1} \rangle, \overline{a}_k) = \mu_k(\mathbf{E}^{\mathcal{A}} \circ \mathbf{P}^{-1}, \overline{a}_k)$, and by symmetry we get $\nu_k(\langle \mathbf{P} \circ (\mathbf{F}^{\mathcal{B}})^{-1} \rangle, \overline{a}_k) = \mu_k(\mathbf{F}^{\mathcal{B}} \circ \mathbf{P}^{-1}, \overline{a}_k)$. This is more than what is actually required by the second condition of Lemma 9. An inspection of the proof of the lemma shows that with this we also get a stronger statement (as mentioned before). □

As an application of this theorem, consider the cascade of two uniform random involutions over $\mathcal{X}$. An involution is a permutation which is its own inverse, and a uniform random involution (URI) on $\mathcal{X}$ is a permutation selected at random from the set of all involutions on $\mathcal{X}$. A URI $\mathbf{I}$ is non-adaptively indistinguishable from a URP $\mathbf{P}$ (the advantage is very small even for a large number of queries, actually $O(\sqrt{|\mathcal{X}|})$ queries are required to achieve a constant advantage), but an adaptive distinguisher can easily distinguish $\mathbf{I}$ from $\mathbf{P}$ simply by using any query X_1, setting $X_2 := Y_1$, and checking whether $Y_2 = X_1$. For a URI, this condition is always satisfied, whereas for a URP, it is satisfied only with exponentially small probability. We get the following corollary from Theorem 2

Corollary 1 Any adaptive bidirectional distinguisher must make in the order of $\sqrt{|\mathcal{X}|}$ queries to achieve a constant distinguishing advantage for a cascade of two uniform random involutions over $\mathcal{X}$ and a uniform random permutation over $\mathcal{X}$.

5   Discussion

We discuss a few implications of the results of this paper.

5.1   Pseudorandomness

As discussed in [3], essentially all proofs of computational indistinguishability of random systems consist basically of an information-theoretic indistinguishability proof. The results of this paper therefore have direct applications to computational settings. For example, in order to design a bidirectionally secure pseudorandom permutation (i.e., a block cipher secure against a combined chosen-message and chosen-ciphertext attack) from any pseudorandom function, it suffices to design an only non-adaptively secure random permutation $\mathbf{F}$ from a random function, then to replace the random function by a pseudorandom function, and to apply the construction twice with one of them inverted. More generally, this paper allows for new constructions of quasi-random systems, as discussed in [3].

5.2   Generalizing Indistinguishability Theory

This paper proposes two generalisations of the framework of [3], where the following technique to bound the indistinguishability $\Delta_k(\mathbf{F}, \mathbf{G})$ of two random systems $\mathbf{F}$ and $\mathbf{G}$ is used:

– Find conditions $\mathcal{A}$ and $\mathcal{B}$ such that $\mathbf{F}^{\mathcal{A}} \equiv \mathbf{G}^{\mathcal{B}}$, which is defined as

$$\mathbf{F}^{\mathcal{A}} \equiv \mathbf{G}^{\mathcal{B}} \quad \Longleftrightarrow \quad \forall i \geq 1: \quad \mathsf{P}^{\mathbf{F}^{\mathcal{A}}}_{a_i Y_i | X^i Y^{i-1} a_{i-1}} = \mathsf{P}^{\mathbf{G}^{\mathcal{B}}}_{b_i Y_i | X^i Y^{i-1} b_{i-1}}.$$

– Prove an upper bound on $\nu_k(\mathbf{F}^{\mathcal{A}}, \overline{a}_k)$, the success probability of any distinguisher in making the condition fail with k queries. Now (by Lemma 7 from [3]) $\Delta_k(\mathbf{F}, \mathbf{G}) \leq \nu_k(\mathbf{F}^{\mathcal{A}}, \overline{a}_k)$ and we are done.

The first generalisation is that by Lemma 6 we may replace the requirement $\mathbf{F}^{\mathcal{A}} \equiv \mathbf{G}^{\mathcal{B}}$ with the weaker requirement $\mathbf{F}^{\mathcal{A}} \preceq \mathbf{G}$ and the second point still holds. As $\mathbf{F}^{\mathcal{A}} \equiv \mathbf{G}^{\mathcal{B}}$ implies $\mathbf{F}^{\mathcal{A}} \preceq \mathbf{G}$ but $\mathbf{F}^{\mathcal{A}} \preceq \mathbf{G}$ does not imply the existence of $\mathcal{B}$ such that $\mathbf{F}^{\mathcal{A}} \equiv \mathbf{G}^{\mathcal{B}}$, this requirement is strictly weaker.

The second generalisation is that, due to Lemma 9, one can go from indistinguishability to monotone conditions: If $\Delta_k(\mathbf{F}, \mathbf{G}) \leq \varepsilon$, then there always exists a monotone condition (i.e. the maximum condition for $\mathbf{F}$ and $\mathbf{G}$) $\mathcal{A}$ such that $\mathbf{F}^{\mathcal{A}} \preceq \mathbf{G}$ and $\nu_k(\mathbf{F}^{\mathcal{A}}, \overline{a}_k) \leq \varepsilon(1 + \ln \frac{1}{\varepsilon})$. So using the above framework (with $\mathbf{F}^{\mathcal{A}} \preceq \mathbf{G}$ instead of $\mathbf{F}^{\mathcal{A}} \equiv \mathbf{G}^{\mathcal{B}}$ in the first step) does not inherently restrict the set of provable statements.

This is in sharp contrast to the original $\mathbf{F}^{\mathcal{A}} \equiv \mathbf{G}^{\mathcal{B}}$ requirement, as there are, for any $\varepsilon > 0$, random systems $\mathbf{F}$ and $\mathbf{G}$ where (for some k, or rather some range for k) $\Delta_k(\mathbf{F}, \mathbf{G}) \leq \varepsilon$, but for any conditions $\mathcal{A}$ and $\mathcal{B}$ which satisfy $\mathbf{F}^{\mathcal{A}} \equiv \mathbf{G}^{\mathcal{B}}$ we have $\nu_k(\mathbf{F}^{\mathcal{A}}, \overline{a}_k) \geq 1 - \varepsilon$. For such systems this framework (with the original $\mathbf{F}^{\mathcal{A}} \equiv \mathbf{G}^{\mathcal{B}}$ requirement in the first step) is not applicable.

As an example for such systems, let the first be a source of uniform random bits and the second be a source where each bit is not completely uniform but has some small bias α. Here $\Delta_k(\mathbf{F}, \mathbf{G}) \approx \sqrt{k}\alpha$ (see [6]) and $\nu_k(\mathbf{F}^{\mathcal{A}}, \overline{a}_k) \approx 1 - (1-\alpha)^{k/2} \approx \alpha k/2$. Thus choosing α small and k large enough we can achieve any $\varepsilon > 0$ as described.

5.3   Decorrelation Theory

Decorrelation theory was introduced by Vaudenay as a tool to prove security of block ciphers against d-iterated attacks, this class of attacks includes linear and differential cryptanalysis. Loosely speaking, in a d-iterated attack a distinguisher, which tries to distinguish the block cipher from a uniform random permutation, is limited to look at blocks of at most d queries at the same time. Decorrelation theory is based on different matrix norms. We refer to [7] for the definition of these norms and note that

For a random permutation $\mathbf{E}$ over $\mathcal{M}$ let $[E]^d$ denote the $\mathcal{M}^d \times \mathcal{M}^d$ matrix where the $(x^d, y^d) \in \mathcal{M}^d \times \mathcal{M}^d$ entry of $[E]^d$ is $\mathsf{P}^{\mathbf{E}}_{Y^d | X^d}(x^d, y^d)$. Now let D be a distance over the matrix space $\mathbb{R}^{\mathcal{M}^d \times \mathcal{M}^d}$. The d-wise decorrelation bias of the permutation E is the distance (C^* denotes the distribution of the uniform random permutation)

$$\mathrm{DecP}^d_D(E) = D([E]^d, [C^*]^d).$$

In the above definition the distance D can be replaced by a matrix norm. The matrix norms considered are denoted $|| \cdot ||_\infty$, $|| \cdot ||_a$ and $|| \cdot ||_s$. These norms have a natural interpretation as they are exactly twice the advantage of the best (non-adaptive, adaptive or bidirectional) distinguisher making at most d queries in distinguishing $\mathbf{E}$ from a URP, i.e. (note that here the first terms are in our notation)

$$\delta_d(\mathbf{E}, \mathbf{P}) \quad = \quad \frac{1}{2}||[E]^d - [C^*]^d||_\infty \quad = \quad \frac{1}{2}\mathrm{DecP}^d_\infty(E) \tag{3}$$

$$\Delta_d(\mathbf{E}, \mathbf{P}) \quad = \quad \frac{1}{2}||[E]^d - [C^*]^d||_a \quad = \quad \frac{1}{2}\mathrm{DecP}^d_a(E) \tag{4}$$

$$\Delta_d(\langle\mathbf{E}\rangle, \langle\mathbf{P}\rangle) \quad = \quad \frac{1}{2}||[E]^d - [C^*]^d||_s \quad = \quad \frac{1}{2}\mathrm{DecP}^d_s(E) \tag{5}$$

The main theorem of [7] states that if a block cipher has small $2d$-wise ($|| \cdot ||_\infty, || \cdot ||_a$ or $|| \cdot ||_s$) decorrelation bias it is secure against any d-iterated attack performed by any (non-adaptive, adaptive or bidirectional) distinguisher.

We can plug in (3), (4) and (5) directly into Theorem 1 and get the first nontrivial relations known among this norms.

Corollary 2

$$\mathrm{DecP}^d_\infty(E) \leq \varepsilon \ \wedge \ \mathrm{DecP}^d_\infty(F) \leq \varepsilon \ \Rightarrow \ \mathrm{DecP}^d_a(E \circ F) \leq 2\varepsilon \left(1 + \ln \tfrac{2}{\varepsilon}\right)$$

$$\mathrm{DecP}^d_\infty(E) \leq \varepsilon \ \wedge \ \mathrm{DecP}^d_\infty(F) \leq \varepsilon \ \Rightarrow \ \mathrm{DecP}^d_s(E \circ F^{-1}) \leq 2\varepsilon \left(1 + \ln \tfrac{2}{\varepsilon}\right).$$

The second statement of the corollary now implies that using a block-cipher with small $2d$-wise decorrelation bias in the ∞ norm against non-adaptive chosen plaintext d-iterated attacks in a cascade (with independent keys, the second time in decrypt mode) results in a block cipher which is secure against adaptive combined chosen plaintext and ciphertext $2d$-iterated attacks.

6   Conclusions and Open Problems

It would be interesting to have a similar framework as the one proposed in this paper for the computational setting. For example, the computational analog of Theorem 2 would state that the cascade of two block-ciphers, each secure against non-adaptively chosen plaintext attacks, is secure against adaptive chosen plaintext/ciphertext adversaries.

As already mentioned in the introduction, there is a gap in the order of $\ln \frac{1}{\varepsilon}$ between the $O(\varepsilon \ln \frac{1}{\varepsilon})$ bound proven in Theorems 1 and 2 and an easy to show $\Omega(\varepsilon)$ lower bound for the respective terms. However, Lemmas 6 and 9 can be shown to be tight up to a (small) multiplicative constant, so we cannot hope to close this gap (i.e. showing an upper bound of $O(\varepsilon)$ by improving on them). But trying to find a concrete example (of random systems) for which a matching $\Omega(\varepsilon \ln \frac{1}{\varepsilon})$ lower bound can be proven seems promising to us.

References

1. N. Alon, O. Goldreich, J. Hastad, R. Peralta, Simple construction of almost k-wise independent random variables, *Random Structures and Algorithms*, vol. 3, no. 3, pp. 289–304, 1992.
2. M. Luby and C. Rackoff, How to construct pseudo-random permutations from pseudo-random functions, *SIAM J. on Computing*, vol. 17, no. 2, pp. 373–386, 1988.
3. U. Maurer, Indistinguishability of random systems, *Advances in Cryptology - EUROCRYPT '02*, Lecture Notes in Computer Science, vol. 2332, pp. 110–132, Springer-Verlag, 2002.
4. U. Maurer and K. Pietrzak, The security of many-round Luby-Rackoff pseudo-random permutations, *Advances in Cryptology - EUROCRYPT '03*, Lecture Notes in Computer Science, vol. 2656, pp. 544–561, Springer-Verlag, 2003.
5. J. Naor and M. Naor, Small-bias probability spaces: Efficient constructions and applications, *SIAM Journal on Computing*, vol. 22, no. 4, pp. 838–356, 1993.
6. R. Renner, The Statistical Distance of Independently Repeated Experiments, Manuscript, available at http://www.crypto.ethz.ch/~renner/publications.html
7. S. Vaudenay, Provable security for block ciphers by decorrelation, *Proceedings of STACS'98*, Lecture Notes in Computer Science, vol. 1373, Springer-Verlag, pp. 249–275, 1998.
8. S. Vaudenay, Adaptive-attack norm for decorrelation and super-pseudorandomness, *Proc. of SAC'99*, Lecture Notes in Computer Science, vol. 1758, pp. 49–61, Springer-Verlag, 2000.

A   Martingales

In what follows, let $\widetilde{V}_n \overset{\text{def}}{=} \max_{0 \leq j \leq n} V_j$. The following lemma is known as the Kolmogorov-Doob inequality.

Lemma 11 *Let* $V_0, V_1, \ldots$ *be a sub-martingale sequence where the* V_i *are non-negative. Then, for every* n,

$$P[\widetilde{V}_n \geq \lambda] \leq \frac{E[V_n]}{\lambda}.$$

Proof of Lemma 7: We restate the lemma for the reader's convenience: If $V_0, V_1, \ldots$ is a *sub-martingale* sequence where $0 \leq V_i \leq 1$ for all i, then

$$E[\widetilde{V}_n] \leq E[V_n] \cdot (1 - \ln(E[V_n])).$$

Let $\psi(r)$ denote the function

$$\psi(r) \overset{\text{def}}{=} \begin{cases} 1 & \text{if } r < E[V_n] \\ E[V_n]/r & \text{if } E[V_n] \leq r \leq 1 \\ 0 & \text{if } r > 1 \end{cases}$$

With Lemma 11 and $0 \leq \widetilde{V}_n \leq 1$ (which follows from $0 \leq V_i \leq 1$) we see that

$$\forall r : P[\widetilde{V}_n \geq r] \leq \psi(r).$$

So we can upper bound $\mathsf{E}[\widetilde{V}_n]$ as

$$\mathsf{E}[\widetilde{V}_n] \leq -\int_{-\infty}^{\infty} \psi'(r)\, r\, dr$$

$$= -\int_{\mathsf{E}[V_n]}^{1} \left(\frac{\mathsf{E}[V_n]}{r}\right)' r\, dr + \mathsf{E}[V_n]$$

$$= \int_{\mathsf{E}[V_n]}^{1} \frac{\mathsf{E}[V_n]}{r^2}\, r\, dr + \mathsf{E}[V_n]$$

$$= -\ln(\mathsf{E}[V_n]) \cdot \mathsf{E}[V_n] + \mathsf{E}[V_n].$$

$\square$

Proof of Lemma 8: We restate the lemma for the reader's convenience: $Z_1, Z_2, \ldots$ as defined in (2) is a sub-martingale sequence in the random experiment $\mathbf{D} \diamond \mathbf{F}$, i.e.,

$$\forall i \geq 0 : \mathsf{E}^{\mathbf{D}\diamond\mathbf{F}}[Z_{i+1}|Z_0, \ldots, Z_i] \geq Z_i.$$

Because the $Z_0, \ldots, Z_i$ are determined by $X^i Y^i$, we can prove the (stronger) statement

$$\forall i \geq 0 : \mathsf{E}^{\mathbf{D}\diamond\mathbf{F}}[Z_{i+1}|X^i Y^i] \geq Z_i$$

instead. Below the sums over $\mathcal{X} \times \mathcal{Y}$ always apply to the random variables X_{i+1} and Y_{i+1}. Lemma 1 is used several times.

$$\mathsf{E}^{\mathbf{D}\diamond\mathbf{F}}[Z_{i+1}|X^i Y^i]$$

$$= \sum_{\mathcal{X} \times \mathcal{Y}} \underbrace{\mathsf{P}^{\mathbf{D}\diamond\mathbf{F}}_{X_{i+1}Y_{i+1}|X^i Y^i}}_{\mathsf{P}^{\mathbf{D}}_{X_{i+1}|X^i Y^i}\mathsf{P}^{\mathbf{F}}_{Y_{i+1}|X^{i+1}Y^i}} \overbrace{\max\left\{\underbrace{\frac{\mathsf{P}^{\mathbf{F}}_{Y_{i+1}|X^{i+1}} - \mathsf{P}^{\mathbf{G}}_{Y_{i+1}|X^{i+1}}}{\mathsf{P}^{\mathbf{F}}_{Y_{i+1}|X^{i+1}}}}_{\mathsf{P}^{\mathbf{F}}_{Y_{i+1}|X^{i+1}Y^i}\mathsf{P}^{\mathbf{F}}_{Y^i|X^i}}, 0\right\}}^{Z_{i+1}}$$

$$= \frac{1}{\mathsf{P}^{\mathbf{F}}_{Y^i|X^i}} \sum_{\mathcal{X} \times \mathcal{Y}} \underbrace{\mathsf{P}^{\mathbf{D}}_{X_{i+1}|X^i Y^i}}_{\mathsf{P}^{\mathbf{D}}_{X_{i+1}|Y^i}/\mathsf{P}^{\mathbf{D}}_{X^i|Y^i}} \max\left\{\mathsf{P}^{\mathbf{F}}_{Y_{i+1}|X^{i+1}} - \mathsf{P}^{\mathbf{G}}_{Y_{i+1}|X^{i+1}}, 0\right\}$$

$$= \frac{1}{\mathsf{P}^{\mathbf{D}}_{X^i|Y^i}\mathsf{P}^{\mathbf{F}}_{Y^i|X^i}} \sum_{\mathcal{X} \times \mathcal{Y}} \max\left\{\mathsf{P}^{\mathbf{D}\diamond\mathbf{F}}_{X^{i+1}Y^{i+1}} - \mathsf{P}^{\mathbf{D}\diamond\mathbf{G}}_{X^{i+1}Y^{i+1}}, 0\right\}$$

$$\geq \frac{1}{\mathsf{P}^{\mathbf{D}}_{X^i|Y^i}\mathsf{P}^{\mathbf{F}}_{Y^i|X^i}} \max\left\{\underbrace{\sum_{\mathcal{X} \times \mathcal{Y}} \mathsf{P}^{\mathbf{D}\diamond\mathbf{F}}_{X^{i+1}Y^{i+1}}}_{\mathsf{P}^{\mathbf{D}\diamond\mathbf{F}}_{X^i Y^i}} - \underbrace{\sum_{\mathcal{X} \times \mathcal{Y}} \mathsf{P}^{\mathbf{D}\diamond\mathbf{G}}_{X^{i+1}Y^{i+1}}}_{\mathsf{P}^{\mathbf{D}\diamond\mathbf{G}}_{X^i Y^i}}, 0\right\}$$

$$= \frac{\mathsf{P}^{\mathbf{D}}_{X^i|Y^i}}{\mathsf{P}^{\mathbf{D}}_{X^i|Y^i}} \max\left\{\frac{\mathsf{P}^{\mathbf{F}}_{Y^i|X^i} - \mathsf{P}^{\mathbf{G}}_{Y^i|X^i}}{\mathsf{P}^{\mathbf{F}}_{Y^i|X^i}}, 0\right\}$$

$$= Z_i.$$

Simpler Session-Key Generation from Short Random Passwords

Minh-Huyen Nguyen [*] and Salil Vadhan[**]

Harvard University, Cambridge, MA
{mnguyen,salil}@eecs.harvard.edu

Abstract. Goldreich and Lindell (CRYPTO '01) recently presented the first protocol for password-authenticated key exchange in the standard model (with no common reference string or set-up assumptions other than the shared password). However, their protocol uses several heavy tools and has a complicated analysis.

We present a simplification of the Goldreich–Lindell (GL) protocol and analysis for the special case when the dictionary is of the form $\mathcal{D} = \{0,1\}^d$, i.e. the password is a short random string (like an ATM PIN number). Our protocol can be converted into one for arbitrary dictionaries using a common reference string of logarithmic length. The security bound achieved by our protocol is somewhat worse than the GL protocol. Roughly speaking, our protocol guarantees that the adversary can "break" the scheme with probability at most $O(\mathrm{poly}(n)/|\mathcal{D}|)^{\Omega(1)}$, whereas the GL protocol guarantees a bound of $O(1/|\mathcal{D}|)$.

We also present an alternative, more natural definition of security than the "augmented definition" of Goldreich and Lindell, and prove that the two definitions are equivalent.

1 Introduction

What is the minimal amount of information that two parties must share in order to perform nontrivial cryptography? This fundamental question is at the heart of many of the major distinctions we draw in cryptography. Classical private-key cryptography assumes that the legitimate parties share a long random key. Public-key cryptography mitigates this by allowing the sharing of information to be done through public keys that need not be hidden from the adversary. However, in both cases, the amount of information shared by the legitimate parties (e.g. as measured by mutual information) needs to be quite large. Indeed, the traditional view is that security comes from the adversary's inability to exhaustively search the keyspace.

Thus it is very natural to ask: *can we do nontrivial cryptography using "low-entropy" keys?* That is, using a keyspace that is feasible to exhaustively search.

[*] Supported by NSF grant CCR-0205423.

[**] Supported by NSF grant CCR-0205423 and a Sloan Research Fellowship. Part of this work done while at the Radcliffe Institute for Advanced Study.

M. Naor (Ed.): TCC 2004, LNCS 2951, pp. 428–445, 2004.
© Springer-Verlag Berlin Heidelberg 2004

In addition to being a natural theoretical question, it has clear relevance to the many "real-life" situations where we need security but only have a low-entropy key (e.g. an ATM PIN number, or human-chosen password on a website).

Public-key cryptography provides an initial positive answer to this question: key-exchange protocols, as in [10], do not require *any* prior shared information. However, this holds only for passive adversaries, and it is well known that without any prior shared information between the legitimate parties, an active adversary can always succeed through a person-in-the-middle attack. Thus, it remains an interesting question to achieve security against active adversaries using a low-entropy shared key. This has led researchers to consider the problem of *password-authenticated key exchange*, which we describe next.

Password-Authenticated Key Exchange. The password-authenticated key exchange problem was first suggested by Bellovin and Merritt [4]. We assume that two parties, Alice and Bob, share a password w chosen uniformly at random from a dictionary $\mathcal{D} \subseteq \{0,1\}^n$. This dictionary can be very small, e.g. $|\mathcal{D}| = \text{poly}(n)$, and in particular it may be feasible for an adversary to exhaustively search it. Our aim is to construct a protocol enabling Alice and Bob to generate a "random" session key $K \in \{0,1\}^n$, which they can subsequently use for standard private-key cryptography. We consider an active adversary that completely controls the communication channel between Alice and Bob. The adversary can intercept, modify, drop, and delay messages, and in particular can attempt to impersonate either party through a person-in-the-middle attack.

Our goal is that, even after the adversary mounts such an attack, Alice and Bob will generate a session key that is indistinguishable from uniform even given the adversary's view. However, our ability to achieve this goal is limited by two unpreventable attacks. First, since the adversary can block all communication, it can prevent one or both of the parties from completing the protocol and obtaining a session key. Second, the adversary can guess a random password $\tilde{w} \leftarrow \mathcal{D}$ and attempt to impersonate one of the parties. With probability $1/|\mathcal{D}|$, the guess equals the real password (i.e., $\tilde{w} = w$), and the adversary will succeed in the impersonation and therefore learn the session key. Thus, we revise our goal to effectively limit the adversary to these two attacks. Various formalizations for this problem have been developed through several works [3,15,22,2,7,12]. We follow the definitional framework of Goldreich and Lindell [12], which is described in more detail in Sec. 2.

In addition to addressing what can be done with a minimal amount of shared information, the study of this problem is useful as another testbed for developing our understanding of *concurrency* in cryptographic protocols. The concurrency implicitly arises from the person-in-the-middle attack, which we can view as two simultaneous executions of the protocol, one between Alice and the adversary and the other between Bob and the adversary.

The first protocols for the password-authenticated key exchange problem were proposed in the security literature, based on informal definitions and heuristic arguments (e.g. [5,24]). The first rigorous proofs of security were given in the random oracle model [2,7]. Only recently were rigorous solutions without random oracles given, in independent works by Goldreich and Lindell [12] and Katz, Ostrovsky, and Yung [16]. One of the main differences between these two protocols is that the KOY protocol (and the subsequent protocols of [17,11]) is in the "public parameters model," requiring a string to be generated and published by a trusted third party, whereas the GL protocol requires no set-up assumption other than the shared password. Thus, even though the KOY protocol has a number of practical and theoretical advantages over the GL protocol (which we will not enumerate here), the GL protocol is more relevant to our initial question about the minimal amount of shared information needed for nontrivial cryptography.

The Goldreich–Lindell Protocol. As mentioned above, the Goldreich–Lindell protocol [12] is remarkable in that the only set-up assumption it requires is that the two parties share a password chosen at random from an arbitrary dictionary. Their protocol can be based on general complexity assumptions (the existence of trapdoor permutations), can be implemented in a constant number of rounds (under stronger assumptions), and achieves a nearly optimal security bound (the adversary has probability only $O(1/|\mathcal{D}|)$ of "breaking" the scheme).

Despite giving such a strong result, the Goldreich–Lindell protocol does not leave us with a complete understanding of the password-authenticated key exchange problem. First, the protocol makes use of several "heavy" tools: secure two-party polynomial evaluation (building on [19], who observed that this yields a protocol for password-authenticated key exchange against passive adversaries), nonmalleable commitments (as suggested in [6]), and the specific concurrent zero-knowledge proof of Richardson and Kilian [21]. It is unclear whether all of these tools are really essential for solving the key exchange problem. Second, the proof of the protocol's security is extremely complicated. Goldreich and Lindell do introduce nice techniques for analyzing concurrent executions (arising from the person-in-the-middle attack) of two-party protocols whose security is only guaranteed in the stand-alone setting (e.g. the polynomial evaluation). But these techniques are applied in an intricate manner that seems inextricably tied to the presence of the nonmalleable commitment and zero-knowledge proof. Finally, finding an efficient instantiation of the Goldreich–Lindell protocol would require finding efficient instantiations of all three of the heavy tools mentioned above, which seems difficult. In particular, the Richardson-Kilian zero-knowledge proof is used to prove an **NP** statement that asserts the consistency of a transcript of the nonmalleable commitment, a standard commitment, and the output of an iterated one-way permutation. For such an **NP** statement, it seems difficult to avoid using a generic zero-knowledge proof system for **NP**, which are almost always inefficient due to the use of Cook's theorem.

Our Protocol. Our main result is a simplification of the Goldreich–Lindell protocol and analysis for the special case when the dictionary is of the form $\mathcal{D} = \{0,1\}^d$, i.e. the password is a short random string (like an ATM PIN number). This special case still retains many of the key features of the problem: the person-in-the-middle attack and the resulting concurrency issues are still present, and the adversary can still exhaustively search the dictionary (since we allow the password length d to be as small as $O(\log n)$, where n is the security parameter). Moreover, our protocol can be converted into one for arbitrary dictionaries in the common reference string model (using the common reference string as the seed of a randomness extractor [20]). For dictionaries $\mathcal{D} \subset \{0,1\}^n$, the common reference string is a uniform string of only logarithmic length (specifically, $O(\log n + \log |\mathcal{D}|)$), and thus retains the spirit of minimizing the amount of shared information between the legitimate parties. In contrast, the previous protocols in the public parameters model [16,17,11] require a public string of length $\text{poly}(n)$ with special number-theoretic structure.

The main way in which we simplify the GL protocol is that we remove the nonmalleable commitments and the Richardson–Kilian zero-knowledge proof. Instead, our protocol combines secure polynomial evaluation with a combinatorial tool (almost pairwise independent hashing), in addition to using "lightweight" cryptographic primitives also used in [12] (one-way permutations, one-time MACs, standard commitments). Our analysis is also similarly simpler. While it has the same overall structure as the analysis in [12] and utilizes their techniques for applying the stand-alone properties of the polynomial evaluation in the concurrent setting, it avoids dealing with the nonmalleable commitments and the zero-knowledge proof (which is the most complex part of the GL analysis).

Removing the nonmalleable commitments and the RK zero-knowledge proof has two additional implications. First, finding an efficient implementation of our protocol only requires finding an efficient protocol for secure polynomial evaluation (in fact, only for linear polynomials).[1] Since this is a highly structured special case of secure two-party computation, it does not seem beyond reach to find an efficient protocol. Indeed, Naor and Pinkas [19] have already given an efficient polynomial evaluation protocol for passive adversaries. Second, our protocol can be implemented in a constant number of rounds assuming only the existence of trapdoor permutations, whereas implementing the Goldreich–Lindell protocol in a constant number of rounds requires additional assumptions, such as the existence of claw-free permutations (for [21]) and some sort of exponential hardness assumption (to use [1]).

We note that the security bound achieved by our protocols is somewhat worse than in previous works. Roughly speaking, our protocol guarantees that the adversary can "break" the scheme with probability at most $O\left(\frac{\text{poly}(n)}{|\mathcal{D}|}\right)^{\Omega(1)}$, whereas previous works guarantee a bound of $O(1/|\mathcal{D}|)$.

An additional result in our paper involves the definition of security in [12]. As pointed out by Rackoff (cf., [2]), it is important that a key exchange protocol provide security even if the party who completes the protocol first starts using the generated key in some application before the second party completes the protocol. In order to address this issue, Goldreich and Lindell [12] augmented

---

[1] Actually, we require a slightly augmented form of polynomial evaluation, in which one of the parties commits to its input beforehand and the protocol ensures consistency with this committed input.

their definition with a "session-key challenge", in which the adversary is given either the generated key or a uniform string with probability $1/2$ upon the first party's completion of the protocol. We present an arguably more natural definition that directly models the use of the generated key in an arbitrary application, and prove its equivalence to the augmented definition of Goldreich and Lindell [12]. (This result is analogous to the result of Shoup [22] for non-password-based key exchange protocols.)

2   Definition of Security

We adopt the notation of Goldreich and Lindell and refer the reader to [12] for more details.

- C denotes the probabilistic polynomial time adversary through which the honest parties A and B communicate. We model this communication by giving C oracle access to a single copy of A and a single copy of B. Here the oracles A and B have memory and represent honest parties executing the session-key generation protocol. We denote by $C^{A(x),B(y)}(\sigma)$ an execution of C with auxiliary input σ when it communicates with A and B, with respective inputs x and y. The output of the channel C from this execution is denoted by output $\left(C^{A(x),B(y)}(\sigma)\right)$.
- The security parameter is denoted by n. The password dictionary is denoted by $\mathcal{D} \subseteq \{0,1\}^n$ and we write $\epsilon = \frac{1}{|\mathcal{D}|}$.

We denote by U_n the uniform distribution over strings of length n, by $\mathrm{neg}(n)$ a negligible function and write $x \xleftarrow{\mathrm{R}} S$ when x is chosen uniformly from the set S.

For a function $\gamma : \mathbb{N} \to [0,1]$, we say that the probability ensembles $\{X_n\}$ and $\{Y_n\}$ are $(1-\gamma)$-*indistinguishable* (denoted by $\{X_n\} \overset{\gamma}{\equiv} \{Y_n\}$) if for every nonuniform PPT distinguisher D and all n,

$$|\Pr[D(X_n) = 1] - \Pr[D(Y_n) = 1]| < \gamma(n) + \mathrm{neg}(n) .$$

We say that $\{X_n\}$ and $\{Y_n\}$ are *computationally indistinguishable*, which we denote by $X_n \overset{c}{\equiv} Y_n$, if they are 1-indistinguishable. We say that $\{X_n\}$ is $(1-\gamma)$ *pseudorandom* if it is $(1-\gamma)$ indistinguishable from U_n.

We will now formalize the problem of session-key generation using human passwords. We first follow the presentation of the problem as in [12] and then contrast it with our definition.

2.1   The Initial Definition

The definition in [12] follows the standard paradigm for secure computation: define an ideal functionality (using a trusted third party) and require that every adversary attacking the real protocol can be simulated by an ideal adversary attacking the ideal functionality. Note that in the real protocol, the active adversary C can prevent one or both of the parties A and B from having an output. Thus, in the ideal model, we will allow C_{ideal} to specify two input bits, dec_C^A and dec_C^B, which determine whether A and B obtain a session key or not.

Ideal model. Let A, B be the honest parties and let C_{ideal} be any PPT ideal adversary with auxiliary input σ.

1. A and B receive $w \xleftarrow{\text{R}} \mathcal{D}$.
2. A and B both send w to the trusted party.
3. C_{ideal} sends $(\text{dec}_C^A, \text{dec}_C^B)$ to the trusted party.
4. The trusted party chooses $K \xleftarrow{\text{R}} \{0,1\}^n$. For each party $i \in \{A, B\}$, the trusted party sends K if $\text{dec}_C^i = 1$ and sends $\perp$ if $\text{dec}_C^i = 0$.

The ideal distribution is defined by:

$$\text{IDEAL}_{C_{\text{ideal}}}(\mathcal{D}, \sigma) = (w, \text{output}(A), \text{output}(B), \text{output}(C_{\text{ideal}}(\sigma))) .$$

Real model. Let A, B be the honest parties and let C be any PPT real adversary with auxiliary input σ.

At some initialization stage, A and B receive $w \xleftarrow{\text{R}} \mathcal{D}$. The real protocol is executed by A and B communicating via C. We will augment C's view of the protocol with A and B's decision bits, denoted by dec_A and dec_B, where $\text{dec}_A = \texttt{reject}$ if $\text{output}(A) = \perp$, and $\text{dec}_A = \texttt{accept}$ otherwise (dec_B is defined similarly). (Indeed, in typical applications, the decisions of A and B will be learned by the real adversary C: if A obtains a session key, then it will use it afterwards; otherwise, A will stop communication or try to re-initiate an execution of the protocol.) C's augmented view is denoted by $\text{output}(C^{A(w),B(w)}(\sigma))$.

The real distribution is defined by:

$$\text{REAL}_C(\mathcal{D}, \sigma) = (w, \text{output}(A), \text{output}(B), \text{output}(C^{A(w),B(w)}(\sigma))) .$$

One might want to say that a protocol for password-based session-key generation is secure if the above ideal and real distributions are computationally indistinguishable. Unfortunately, as pointed in [12], an active adversary can guess the password and successfully impersonate one of the parties with probability $\frac{1}{|\mathcal{D}|}$. This implies that the real and ideal distributions are always distinguishable with probability at least $\frac{1}{|\mathcal{D}|}$. Thus we will only require that the distributions be distinguishable with probability at most $O(\gamma)$ where the goal is to make γ as close to $\frac{1}{|\mathcal{D}|}$ as possible. In the case of a passive adversary, we require that the real and ideal distributions be computationally indistinguishable (for all subsequent definitions, this requirement will be implicit).

Definition 1 (Initial definition). *A protocol for password-based authenticated session-key generation is $(1 - \gamma)$-secure for the dictionary $\mathcal{D} \subseteq \{0,1\}^n$ (where γ is a function of the dictionary size $|\mathcal{D}|$ and n) if:*

1. *For every real passive adversary, there exists an ideal adversary C_{ideal} which always sends (1,1) to the trusted party such that for every auxiliary input $\sigma \in \{0,1\}^{\text{poly}(n)}$,*

$$\{\text{IDEAL}_{C_{\text{ideal}}}(\mathcal{D},\sigma)\}_\sigma \overset{c}{\equiv} \{\text{REAL}_C(\mathcal{D},\sigma)\}_\sigma \ .$$

2. *For every real adversary C, there exists an ideal adversary C_{ideal} such that for every auxiliary input $\sigma \in \{0,1\}^{\text{poly}(n)}$,*

$$\{\text{IDEAL}_{C_{\text{ideal}}}(\mathcal{D},\sigma)\}_\sigma \overset{O(\gamma)}{\equiv} \{\text{REAL}_C(\mathcal{D},\sigma)\}_\sigma \ .$$

By the discussion above, the best we can hope for is $\gamma = \frac{1}{|\mathcal{D}|}$. Note that in [12], their definition and protocol refer to any dictionary $\mathcal{D} \subseteq \{0,1\}^n$ and $\gamma = \frac{1}{|\mathcal{D}|}$. In contrast, our protocol will be $(1-\gamma)$-secure for dictionaries of the form $\mathcal{D} = \{0,1\}^d$ and $\gamma = \left(\frac{\text{poly}(n)}{|\mathcal{D}|}\right)^{\Omega(1)}$.

2.2   Augmented Definitions

The above definition is actually not completely satisfying because of a subtle point raised by Rackoff: the adversary controls the scheduling of the interactions (A,C) and (C,B) so the honest parties do not necessarily end at the same time. A might use its session key K_A before the interaction (C,B) is completed: A's use of K_A leaks information which C might use in its interaction with B to learn K_A, K_B or the password w.

In [12], Goldreich and Lindell augment the above definition with a *session-key challenge* to address this issue. Suppose that A completes the protocol first and outputs a session key K, then the adversary is given a session-key challenge K_β, which is the session key K with probability $1/2$ (i.e. $\beta = 1$) or a truly random string K_0 with probability $1/2$ (i.e. $\beta = 0$). The adversary C will be given the session-key challenge in both the ideal and real models, as soon as the first honest party outputs a session-key K. We call the resulting definition *security with respect to the session-key challenge*.

Goldreich and Lindell give some intuition as to why the session-key challenge solves the above flaw. First, note that the ideal adversary cannot distinguish between the case $\beta = 0$ and the case $\beta = 1$ since in the ideal model, both K_0 and K are truly uniform strings. Consider the real adversary who has been given the session-key challenge: if C has been given K_0, then the session-key challenge does not help C in attacking the protocol, since C could generate K_0 on its own. Suppose that instead C has been given K and can somehow use it to attack the protocol (this corresponds to the situation where A uses the session key K; $C(K)$ can simulate A's use of the key), then it would mean that C can tell if it is in the case $\beta = 0$ or $\beta = 1$, which is not possible if the protocol is secure with respect to the session-key challenge.

Our intuitive notion of security is that *no matter how A uses its session key K* before the execution (C, B) is completed, the ideal and real distributions should be $(1 - O(\gamma))$-indistinguishable. Even with the above intuition, it is not immediate that the session-key challenge fully captures this goal. Thus we propose an alternative augmentation to Definition 1 that corresponds more directly to this goal.

We model the different ways the party A could use its session key K by considering an arbitrary probabilistic polynomial time machine Z which is given the key K (as soon as A outputs a session key K) and interacts with the adversary in both the ideal and real models. This is similar to the "application" queries in Shoup's model for (non-password-based) secure key exchange [22], which was later extended to password protocols in [7]. Z can also be thought of in terms of "environment" as in the definition of universal composability by Canetti [8]: Z models an arbitrary environment (or application) in which the key generated by the session-key generation protocol is used.[2]

Examples of environments follow:

1. $Z(K) = \perp$: A does not use its session key.
2. $Z(K) = K$: A publicly outputs its session key.
3. $Z(K) = K$ with probability $1/2$, U_n with probability $1/2$. This corresponds to the session-key challenge.
4. $Z(K) = \text{Enc}_K(0^n)$: A uses its session-key for secure private-key encryption.
5. C sends a query m_1, $Z(K)$ answers with $\text{Enc}_K(m_1)$, C sends a query m_2, $Z(K)$ answers with $\text{Enc}_K(m_2)$ and so on. A uses its key for encryption and the adversary is mounting a chosen plaintext attack.

We call the definition obtained by adding (in both the ideal and real models) the environment Z *security with respect to the environment*. Informally, a real protocol is secure with respect to the environment if every adversary attacking the real protocol and interacting with an arbitrary environment can be simulated, with probability $1 - O(\gamma)$, by an ideal adversary attacking the ideal functionality and interacting with the same environment in the ideal model. (More precisely, for every real adversary, there should be a *single* ideal adversary that simulates it well for *every* environment.)

Note that security with respect to the environment implies security with respect to the session-key challenge since it suffices to consider the PPT $Z(K)$ which generates $\beta \xleftarrow{\text{R}} \{0, 1\}$ and outputs the key K if $\beta = 1$ or a truly random string K_0 if $\beta = 0$. We show that the two definitions are actually equivalent:

Theorem 2. *A protocol (A, B) is $(1 - \gamma)$-secure with respect to the session-key challenge iff it is $(1 - \gamma)$-secure with respect to the environment.*

This is similar to a result of Shoup [22] showing the equivalence of his definition and the Bellare-Rogaway [3] definition for non-password-based key exchange. The "application" queries in Shoup's definition are analogous to our

---

[2] Note that this is not as general as the definition of Canetti since the environment Z is only given the session key and not the password w.

environment Z, and the "test" queries in [3] are analogous to the session-key challenge. Though both of these definitions have been extended to password-authenticated key exchange [7,2], it is not immediate that Shoup's equivalence result extends directly to our setting. For example, the definitions of [3,2] are not simulation-based and do not directly require that the password remain pseudo-random, whereas here we are relating two simulation-based definitions that do ensure the password's secrecy.

Given Theorem 2, the relationship between security with respect to the environment and security with respect to the session-key challenge is analogous to the relationship between semantic security and indistinguishability for encryption schemes [14,18]. Though both are equivalent, the former captures our intuitive notion of security better, but the latter is typically easier to establish for a given protocol (as it involves only taking into account a specific environment Z).

3   An Overview of the Protocol

Before presenting our protocol, we introduce the polynomial evaluation functionality, which is an important tool for the rest of the paper. In [19], it is observed that a secure protocol for polynomial evaluation immediately yields a protocol for session-key generation which is secure against *passive* adversaries. In [12], Goldreich and Lindell work from the intuition (from [6]) that by augmenting a secure protocol for polynomial evaluation with additional mechanisms, one can obtain a protocol for session-key generation which is secure against *active* adversaries. Our protocol also comes from this intuition but the additional tools we are using are different.

3.1   Secure Polynomial Evaluation

In a secure polynomial evaluation, a party A knows a polynomial Q over some field $\mathbb{F}$ and a party B wishes to learn the value $Q(x)$ for some element $x \in \mathbb{F}$ such that A learns nothing about x and B learns nothing else about the polynomial Q but the value $Q(x)$. More specifically, for our problem, we will assume that $\mathbb{F} = \mathrm{GF}(2^n) \approx \{0,1\}^n$, Q is a linear non-constant polynomial over $\mathbb{F}$, and x is a string in $\{0,1\}^n$.

Definition 3 (Polynomial evaluation). *The polynomial evaluation functionality is defined as:*

Inputs *The input of A is a linear non-constant polynomial Q over $\mathrm{GF}(2^n)$. The input of B is a value $x \in \mathrm{GF}(2^n)$.*
Outputs *B receives $Q(x)$. A receives nothing.*

As observed in [19], a secure protocol for polynomial evaluation yields immediately a protocol for session-key generation which is secure against passive adversaries as follows: A chooses a random linear non-constant polynomial Q, and A and B engage in a secure polynomial evaluation protocol, where A inputs Q and B inputs w, so that B obtains $Q(w)$. Since A has both Q and w, A can also obtain $Q(w)$, and the session key is set to be $K = Q(w)$.

This protocol is secure against passive adversaries because the key K is a random string (since Q is a random polynomial), and it can be shown that an eavesdropper learns nothing about w or $Q(w)$ (due to the security of the polynomial evaluation).

However, the protocol is not secure against active adversaries. For example, an active adversary C can input a fixed polynomial Q_C in its interaction with B, say the identity polynomial id, and a fixed password w_C in its interaction with A. A outputs the session key $Q_A(w)$ and B outputs the session key $Q_C(w) = w$. With probability $1 - 2^{-n}$, the two session keys are different, whereas the definition of security requires them to be equal with probability $1 - O(\gamma)$.

3.2   Motivation for Our Protocol

The main deficiency of the secure polynomial evaluation protocol against active adversaries is that it does not guarantee that A and B output the same random session key. Somehow, the parties have to check that they computed the same random session key before starting to use it. It can be shown that A's session key $K_A = Q_A(w)$ is pseudorandom to the adversary, so A can start using it without leaking information. However, B cannot use its key $K_B = Q_C(w)$ because it might belong to a set of polynomial size (for example, if $Q_C = id$, then $Q_C(w) \in \mathcal{D}$ where the dictionary is by definition a small set). Hence Goldreich and Lindell added a validation phase in which A sends a message to B so that B can check if it computed the same session key, say A sends $f^n(K_A)$ where f is a one-way permutation. Since f^n is a 1-1 map, this uniquely defines K_A (the session key used now consists of hardcore bits of $f^i(K_A)$, for $i = 0, \cdots, n - 1$) : B will compute $f^n(K_B)$ and compare it with the value it received.

But it is still not clear that this candidate protocol is secure. Recall that the security of the polynomial evaluation protocol applies only in the stand-alone setting and guarantees nothing in the concurrent setting. In particular, it might be that C inputs a polynomial Q_C in the polynomial evaluation between C and B such that the polynomials Q_A and Q_C are related in some manner, say for any $w \in \mathcal{D}$, it is easy to compute the correct validation message $f^{2n}(Q_C(w))$ given the value of $f^{2n}(Q_A(w))$; yet B's key does not equal A's key.

To prevent this from happening, Goldreich and Lindell force the polynomial Q input in the polynomial evaluation phase to be consistent with the message sent in the validation phase (which is supposedly $f^{2n}(Q(w))$). The parties have to commit to their inputs at the beginning and then prove in a zero-knowledge manner that the messages sent in the validation phase are consistent with these commitments. Because of the person-in-the-middle attack and the concurrency issues mentioned earlier, Goldreich and Lindell cannot use standard commitment schemes and standard zero-knowledge proofs but rather they use nonmalleable commitments and the specific zero-knowledge proof of Richardson and Kilian.

Our approach is to allow C to input a polynomial Q_C related to Q_A, but to prevent C from being able to compute a correct validation message with respect to B's session-key, even given A's validation message. Suppose that the parties have access to a family of pairwise independent hash functions $\mathcal{H}$. In the validation phase, we require A to send $h(f^{2n}(K_A)) = h(f^{2n}(Q_A(w)))$ for some function $h \stackrel{R}{\leftarrow} \mathcal{H}$. Then, even if $K_A = Q_A(w)$ and $K_B = Q_C(w)$ are related (but distinct), the values $h(f^{2n}(K_A))$ and $h(f^{2n}(K_B))$ will be independent and C cannot do much better than randomly guess the value of $h(f^{2n}(K_B))$.

One difficulty arises at this point: the parties have to agree on a common random hash function $h \stackrel{R}{\leftarrow} \mathcal{H}$. But the honest parties A and B only share the randomness coming from the password w so this password w has to be enough to agree on a random hash function. To make this possible, we assume that the password is the form (w, w') where w and w' are chosen independently of one another: w is chosen at random from an arbitrary dictionary $\mathcal{D} \subseteq \{0,1\}^n$ and w' is uniformly distributed in $\mathcal{D}' = \{0,1\}^{d'}$. (For example, these can be obtained by splitting a single random password from $\{0,1\}^{d''}$ into two parts.) The first part of the password, w, will be used in the polynomial evaluation protocol whereas the second part of the password, w', will be used as the index of a hash function. Indeed, if we assume that $\mathcal{D}' = \{0,1\}^{d'}$, there exists a family of almost pairwise independent hash functions $\mathcal{H} = \{h : \{0,1\}^n \to \{0,1\}^m\}$, where each hash function is indexed by a password $w' \in \mathcal{D}'$ and $m = \Omega(d')$.

We formalize these ideas in the protocol described below.

3.3   Description of the Protocol

Like in [12], we will need a secure protocol for an augmented version of polynomial evaluation.

Definition 4 (Augmented polynomial evaluation). *The augmented polynomial evaluation functionality is defined as:*

Earlier phase. *A sends a commitment $c_A = \mathrm{Commit}(Q_A, r_A)$ to a linear non-constant polynomial Q_A for a randomly chosen r_A. B receives a commitment c_B. We assume that the commitment scheme used is perfectly binding and computationally hiding.*

Inputs. *The input of A is a linear non-constant polynomial Q_A, a commitment c_A to Q_A and a corresponding decommitment r_A. The input of B is a commitment c_B and a value $x \in \mathrm{GF}(2^n)$.*

Outputs.
- *In the case of correct inputs, i.e. $c_A = c_B$ and $c_A = \mathrm{Commit}(Q_A, r_A)$, B receives $Q_A(x)$ and A receives nothing.*
- *In the case of incorrect inputs, i.e. $c_A \neq c_B$ or $c_A \neq \mathrm{Commit}(Q_A, r_A)$, B receives a special failure symbol $\perp$ and A receives nothing.*

The other cryptographic tools we will need are:

Commitment scheme: Let Commit be a perfectly binding, computationally
hiding string commitment.

Seed-committed pseudorandom generator: Similarly to [12], we will use
the seed-committed pseudorandom generator

$$G(s) = (b(s)b(f(s)) \cdots b(f^{n+\ell-1}(s)) f^{n+\ell}(s))$$

where f is a one-way permutation with hardcore bit b.

One-time MAC with pseudorandomness property: Let MAC be a message authentication code for message space $\{0,1\}^{p(n)}$ (for a polynomial $p(n)$
to be specified later) using keys of length $\ell = \ell(n)$ that is secure against one
query attack, i.e. a PPT A which queries the tagging algorithm MAC_K on
at most one message of its choice cannot produce a valid forgery on a different message. Additionally, we will require the following pseudorandomness
property:

- Let K be a uniform key of length ℓ.
- The adversary queries the tagging algorithm MAC_K on the message m
  of its choice.
- The adversary selects $m' \neq m$. We require that the value $\mathrm{MAC}_K(m')$ be
  pseudorandom with respect to the adversary's view.

Two examples of such a MAC are:

- $\mathrm{MAC}_s(m) = f_s(m)$ where $\{f_s\}_{s \in \{0,1\}^\ell}$ is a pseudorandom function family
- $\mathrm{MAC}_{a,b}(m) = am + b$ where $\ell(n) = 2p(n)$ and $a, b \in \mathrm{GF}(2^{\ell/2})$.

Almost pairwise independent hash functions: The family of functions
$\mathcal{H} = \{h_{w'} : \{0,1\}^n \to \{0,1\}^m\}_{w' \in \{0,1\}^{d'}}$ is said to be *pairwise δ-dependent*
or *almost pairwise independent* if:

1. (uniformity) $\forall x \in \{0,1\}^n$, when we choose $w' \xleftarrow{\mathrm{R}} \{0,1\}^{d'}$, $h_{w'}(x)$ is uniform over $\{0,1\}^m$.
2. (pairwise independence) $\forall x_1 \neq x_2 \in \{0,1\}^n, \forall y_1, y_2 \in \{0,1\}^m$, when we
   choose $w' \xleftarrow{\mathrm{R}} \{0,1\}^{d'}$,

$$\Pr_{w' \in \{0,1\}^{d'}} [h_{w'}(x_1) = y_1 \wedge h_{w'}(x_2) = y_2] = \frac{1+\delta}{2^{2m}} .$$

We also require that for a fixed $w' \in \{0,1\}^{d'}$, the function $h_{w'}$ is regular, i.e.
it is 2^{n-m} to 1. In other words, $h_{w'}(U_n) \equiv U_m$. Throughout this paper, we
write $\mu \stackrel{\mathrm{def}}{=} \frac{1+\delta}{2^m}$.

Lemma 5. *For the fixed dictionary $\mathcal{D}' = \{0,1\}^{d'} \subseteq \{0,1\}^n$, there exists a
family of almost pairwise independent hash functions $\mathcal{H} = \{h_{w'} : \{0,1\}^n \to \{0,1\}^m\}_{w' \in \mathcal{D}'}$ for $\mu = O\left(\frac{n}{|\mathcal{D}'|^{1/3}}\right)$.*

The formal description of the protocol follows. A schematic diagram of the
protocol is given in Fig. 1.

Protocol 6. 1. **Inputs:** The parties A and B have a joint password (w, w') where w and w' are chosen independently: w is chosen at random from an arbitrary dictionary $\mathcal{D} \subseteq \{0,1\}^n$ and w' is uniformly distributed in $\mathcal{D}' = \{0,1\}^{d'} \subseteq \{0,1\}^n$.

2. **Commitment:** A chooses a random linear non-constant polynomial Q_A over $GF(2^n)$ and coin tosses r_A and sends $c_A = \text{Commit}(Q_A, r_A)$. B receives some commitment c_B.

3. **Augmented polynomial evaluation:**

   a) A and B engage in a polynomial evaluation protocol: A inputs the polynomial Q_A, the commitment c_A and the coin tosses r_A it used for the commitment; B inputs the commitment c_B it received and the password w seen as an element of $GF(2^n)$.

   b) The output of B is denoted Π_B, which is supposed to be equal to $Q_A(w)$.

   c) A internally computes $\Pi_A = Q_A(w)$.

4. **Validation:**

   a) A sends the string $y_A = h_{w'}(f^{n+\ell}(\Pi_A))$.

   b) Let t_A be the session transcript so far as seen by A. A computes $k_1(\Pi_A) = b(\Pi_A) \cdots b(f^{\ell-1}(\Pi_A))$ and sends the string $z_A = \text{MAC}_{k_1(\Pi_A)}(t_A)$.

5. **Decision:**

   a) A always accepts and outputs $k_2(\Pi_A) = b(f^\ell(\Pi_A)) \cdots b(f^{\ell+n-1}(\Pi_A))$

   b) B accepts (this event is denoted by $\text{dec}_B = \texttt{accept}$) if the strings y_B and z_B it received satisfy the following conditions :
   - $y_B = h_{w'}(f^{n+\ell}(\Pi_B))$
   - $\text{Ver}_{k_1(\Pi_B)}(t_B, z_B) = \texttt{accept}$, where t_B is the session transcript so far as seen by B and $k_1(\Pi_B)$ is defined analogously to $k_1(\Pi_A)$.

   If $\Pi_B = \bot$, then B will immediately reject. If B accepts, it outputs $k_2(\Pi_B) = b(f^\ell(\Pi_B)) \cdots b(f^{\ell+n-1}(\Pi_B))$.

4   Security Theorems

Theorem 7. *Protocol 6 is secure for the dictionary $\mathcal{D} \times \mathcal{D}' = \mathcal{D} \times \{0,1\}^{d'}$ against passive adversaries. More formally, for every passive PPT real adversary C, there exists an ideal adversary C_{ideal} which always sends $(\text{dec}_C^A, \text{dec}_C^B) = (1,1)$ to the trusted party such that for every auxiliary input $\sigma \in \{0,1\}^{\text{poly}(n)}$:*

$$\{\text{IDEAL}_{C_{\text{ideal}}}(\mathcal{D} \times \mathcal{D}', \sigma)\}_\sigma \overset{c}{\equiv} \{\text{REAL}_C(\mathcal{D} \times \mathcal{D}', \sigma)\}_\sigma .$$

Theorem 8. *Protocol 6 is $(1-\gamma)$-secure with respect to the session-key challenge for the dictionary $\mathcal{D} \times \mathcal{D}' = \mathcal{D} \times \{0,1\}^{d'}$, for $\gamma = \max\left\{\frac{1}{|\mathcal{D}|}, \left(\frac{\text{poly}(n)}{|\mathcal{D}'|}\right)^{\Omega(1)}\right\}$. More precisely, $\gamma = \max\left\{\frac{1}{|\mathcal{D}|}, O\left(\left(\frac{n^3}{|\mathcal{D}'|}\right)^{1/6}\right)\right\}$.*

A **has** (w, w') **and picks a random** Q_A $\qquad\qquad$ B **has** (w, w')

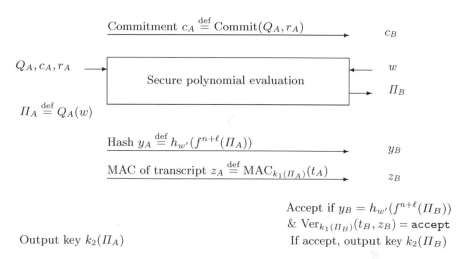

$$\text{Commitment } c_A \overset{\text{def}}{=} \text{Commit}(Q_A, r_A) \longrightarrow c_B$$

$Q_A, c_A, r_A \longrightarrow$ | Secure polynomial evaluation | $\longleftarrow w$

$\longrightarrow \Pi_B$

$\Pi_A \overset{\text{def}}{=} Q_A(w)$

$$\text{Hash } y_A \overset{\text{def}}{=} h_{w'}(f^{n+\ell}(\Pi_A)) \longrightarrow y_B$$

$$\text{MAC of transcript } z_A \overset{\text{def}}{=} \text{MAC}_{k_1(\Pi_A)}(t_A) \longrightarrow z_B$$

Accept if $y_B = h_{w'}(f^{n+\ell}(\Pi_B))$
& $\text{Ver}_{k_1(\Pi_B)}(t_B, z_B) = \text{accept}$

Output key $k_2(\Pi_A)$ $\qquad\qquad$ If accept, output key $k_2(\Pi_B)$

Fig. 1. Overview of our protocol

The shared dictionary of the form $\mathcal{D} \times \{0,1\}^d$ required in Theorem 8 can be realized from several other types of dictionaries $\mathcal{D}''$, achieving security bounds of the form $(\text{poly}(n)/|\mathcal{D}''|)^{\Omega(1)}$ in all cases:

Single Random Password

We can split a single random password from a dictionary $\mathcal{D}'' = \{0,1\}^{d''}$ into two parts, one of length d and one of length d'.

Arbitrary Password with Common Random String

We can convert a password from an arbitrary dictionary $\mathcal{D}'' \subseteq \{0,1\}^n$ into a single random password (as in the previous bullet) in the common random string model. Specifically, we view the common random string $r \in \{0,1\}^\ell$ as the seed for a *randomness extractor* $\text{Ext} : \{0,1\}^n \times \{0,1\}^\ell \to \{0,1\}^{d''}$ [20]. Given password $w \leftarrow \mathcal{D}''$, the honest parties can compute an (almost-uniform) password $\text{Ext}(w, r)$. Using the low min-entropy extractors of [13,23], the length of the common random string need only be $\ell = O(\log n + \log |\mathcal{D}''|)$. (Unlike the protocols of [12] and [16], this requires knowing a lower bound on the size of the dictionary $|\mathcal{D}''|$.)

Two Independent Passwords

If the parties share *two* independent passwords w_1, w_2 coming from arbitrary dictionaries $\mathcal{D}_1'', \mathcal{D}_2'' \subseteq \{0,1\}^n$, then they can apply an extractor for 2 independent weak random sources [9] to convert these into an almost-uniform password. Unfortunately *explicit* constructions for 2-source extractors are only known when $|\mathcal{D}_1''| \cdot |\mathcal{D}_2''| \geq 2^n$, but nonconstructively there exist 2-source extractors that would only require the dictionaries to be of size $\text{poly}(n)$.

5   Overview of the Proof

Like in [12], the main part of the proof of Theorem 8 is the *key-match property*: if $\Pi_A \neq \Pi_B$, then B will reject with probability $1 - O(\gamma)$. Once the key-match property is established, we can easily adapt the proofs in [12] to our specific protocol to build an ideal adversary which simulates the real adversary's view.

The main part of our proof that is new (and simpler than [12]) is the key-match property. As noted in the introduction, the adversary C has total control over the scheduling of the two interactions (A, C) and (C, B). Hence the key-match property will be proved for every possible scheduling case, including those for which these interactions are concurrent. Nevertheless, the key-match property will be established by tools of secure two-party computation, which *a priori* only guarantee security in the stand-alone setting.

Recall that B accepts iff two conditions are satisfied: the string y_B received must equal $h_{w'}(f^{n+\ell}(\Pi_B))$ and the MAC z_B received must be a valid MAC, i.e. $\mathrm{Ver}_{k_1(\Pi_B)}(t_B, z_B) = \mathtt{accept}$. Hence, to establish the key-match property, we can omit the verification of the MAC by B and only consider the probability that C succeeds in sending the value $h_{w'}(f^{n+\ell}(\Pi_B))$ when $\Pi_A \neq \Pi_B$. (Like in [12], the MAC is only used to reduce the simulation of active adversaries to the simulation of passive adversaries plus the key-match property.)

We consider two scheduling cases (see Figures 2 and 3):

Scheduling 1 : C sends the commitment c_B to B *after* A sends the hash value y_A.

The intuition for this case is that we have two sequential executions (A, C) and (C, B). Using the security of the polynomial evaluation (A, C), we show that even if C receives y_A, the hash index w' is $(1 - \epsilon)$ pseudorandom with respect to the adversary's view. Hence, by the uniformity property of the hash functions, C cannot do much better than randomly guess the value of $h_{w'}(f^{n+\ell}(\Pi_B))$.

Scheduling 2 : C sends the commitment c_B to B *before* A sends the hash value y_A.

The almost pairwise independence property means that for fixed values $x_1 \neq x_2 \in \{0,1\}^n$, if the index w' is chosen at random and independently of x_1 and x_2, then given the value $h_{w'}(x_1)$, one cannot do much better than randomly guess the value $h_{w'}(x_2)$. Before y_A is sent, the hash index w' is random (since it has not been used by A). Thus, if we show that the values Π_A and Π_B can be computed before y_A is sent, then w' is independent of $x_1 = f^{n+\ell}(\Pi_A)$ and $x_2 = f^{n+\ell}(\Pi_B)$ and the adversary cannot guess $h_{w'}(x_2)$ even given $y_A = h_{w'}(x_1)$. To show that Π_A and Π_B can be computed before y_A is sent, we use an *ideal* augmented polynomial evaluation (C, B) to extract an opening of the adversary's commitment c_B. (The adversary must input such an opening in the ideal evaluation, else B will reject.)

$A(Q_A, w, w')$ C $B(w, w')$

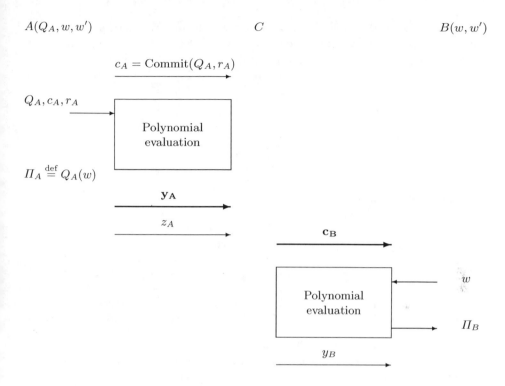

Fig. 2. First scheduling

$A(Q_A, w, w')$ C $B(w, w')$

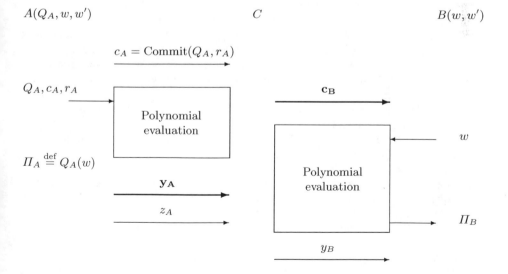

Fig. 3. Second scheduling

Acknowledgments. We thank Oded Goldreich and Yehuda Lindell for their encouragement and an inspiring discussion which led to a substantial simplification of our protocol. We are also grateful to Mihir Bellare for pointing out the extension of our protocol to arbitrary dictionaries in the common random string model.

References

1. Barak, B.: Constant-Round Coin-Tossing With a Man in the Middle or Realizing the Shared Random String Model. IEEE Symposium on Foundations of Computer Science (2002) 345–355
2. Bellare, M., Pointcheval, D., Rogaway, P.: Authenticated Key Exchange Secure against Dictionary Attacks. Advances in Cryptology–Eurocrypt 2000 Proceedings, Lecture Notes in Computer Science **1807** (2000) 139–155
3. Bellare, M., Rogaway, P.: Entity Authentication and Key Distribution. Advances in Cryptology - Crypto 93 Proceedings, Lecture Notes in Computer Science **773** (1994) 232–249
4. Bellovin, S., Merritt, M.: Encrypted Key Exchange: Password-Based Protocols Secure Against Dictionary Attacks. ACM/IEEE Symposium on Research in Security and Privacy (1992) 72–84
5. Bellovin, S., Merritt, M.: Augmented Encrypted Key Exchange: A Password-Based Protocol Secure against Dictionary Attacks and Password File Compromise. ACM Conference on Computer and Communications Security (1993) 244–250
6. Boyarsky, M.: Public-Key Cryptography and Password Protocols: The Multi-User Case. ACM Conference on Computer and Communications Security (1999) 63–72
7. Boyko, V., MacKenzie, P., Patel, S.: Provably Secure Password-Authenticated Key Exchange Using Diffie-Hellman. Advances in Cryptology - Eurocrypt 2000 Proceedings, Lecture Notes in Computer Science **1807** (2000) 156–171
8. Canetti, R.: Universally Composable Security: A New Paradigm for Cryptographic Protocols. IEEE Symposium on Foundations of Computer Science (2001) 136–145
9. Chor, B., Goldreich, O.: Unbiased Bits from Sources of Weak Randomness and Probabilistic Communication Complexity. SIAM Journal on Computing **17:2** (1988) 230–261
10. Diffie, W., Hellman, M.: New Directions in Cryptography. IEEE Transactions on Information Theory **22:6** (1976) 644–654
11. Gennaro, R., Lindell, Y.: A Framework for Password-Based Authenticated Key Exchange. Advances in Cryptology - Eurocrypt 2003 Proceedings, Lecture Notes in Computer Science **2656** (2003) 524–543
12. Goldreich, O., Lindell, Y.: Session-Key Generation Using Human Passwords Only. Advances in Cryptology - Crypto 2001 Proceedings, Lecture Notes in Computer Science **2139** (2001) 408–432
13. Goldreich, O., Wigderson, A.: Tiny Families of Functions with Random Properties: A Quality-Size Trade-off for Hashing. Random Structures and Algorithms **11:4** (1997) 315–343
14. Goldwasser, S., Micali, S.: Probabilistic Encryption. Journal of Computer and System Sciences **28:2** (1984) 270–299
15. Halevi, S., Krawczyk, H.: Public-Key Cryptography and Password Protocols. ACM Conference on Computer and Communications Security (1998) 122–131

16. Katz, J., Ostrovsky, R., Yung, M.: Efficient Password-Authenticated Key Exchange Using Human-Memorable Passwords. Advances in Cryptology - Eurocrypt 2001 Proceedings, Lecture Notes in Computer Science **2045** (2001) 475–494
17. Kobara, K., Imai, H.: Pretty-Simple Password-Authenticated Key-Exchange Under Standard Assumptions. IECIE Trans. **E85-A:10** (2002) 2229–2237
18. Micali, S., Rackoff, C., Sloan, B.: The Notion of Security for Probabilistic Cryptosystems. SIAM Journal on Computing **17** (1988) 412–426
19. Naor, M., Pinkas, B.: Oblivious Transfer and Polynomial Evaluation. ACM Symposium on Theory of Computing. (1999) 245–254
20. Nisan, N., Zuckerman, D.: Randomness is Linear in Space. Journal of Computer and System Sciences **52:1** (1996) 43–52
21. Richardson, R., Kilian, J.: On the Concurrent Composition of Zero-Knowledge Proofs. Advances in Cryptology - Eurocrypt 99 Proceedings, Lecture Notes in Computer Science **1592** (1999) 415–431
22. Shoup, V.: On Formal Models for Secure Key Exchange. Cryptology ePrint Archive (1999) Report 1999/012
23. Srinivasan, A., Zuckerman, D.: Computing with Very Weak Random Sources. IEEE Symposium on Foundations of Computer Science (1994) 264–275
24. Steiner, M., Tsudik, G., Waidner, M.: Refinement and Extension of Encrypted Key Exchange. Operating Systems Review **29:3** (1995) 22–30

Constant-Round Oblivious Transfer
in the Bounded Storage Model

Yan Zong Ding[1], Danny Harnik[2], Alon Rosen[3], and Ronen Shaltiel[2]

[1] College of Computing, Georgia Institute of Technology. 801 Atlantic Drive,
Atlanta, GA 30332-0280.
ding@cc.gatech.edu.
Research supported by NSF Grant CCR-0205423.
[2] Dept. of Computer Science and Applied Math.,
Weizmann Institute of Science. Rehovot 76100, Israel.
{harnik, ronens}@wisdom.weizmann.ac.il.
Research supported in part by a grant from the Israel Science Foundation.
[3] Laboratory for Computer Science, Massachusetts Institute of Technology.
200 Technology Square, Cambridge, MA 02139.[†]
alon@lcs.mit.edu

Abstract. We present a constant round protocol for Oblivious Transfer
in Maurer's *bounded storage model*. In this model, a long random string $\mathcal{R}$
is initially transmitted and each of the parties interacts based on a small
portion of $\mathcal{R}$. Even though the portions stored by the honest parties are
small, security is guaranteed against any malicious party that remembers
almost all of the string $\mathcal{R}$.

Previous constructions for Oblivious Transfer in the bounded storage
model required polynomially many rounds of interaction. Our protocol
has only 5 messages. We also improve other parameters, such as the
number of bits transferred and the probability of immaturely aborting
the protocol due to failure.

Our techniques utilize explicit constructions from the theory of derandomization. In particular, we use constructions of almost t-wise independent permutations, randomness extractors and averaging samplers.

1   Introduction

Oblivious transfer (OT) is one of the fundamental building blocks of modern
cryptography. First introduced by Rabin [Rab81], oblivious transfer can serve
as a basis to a wide range of cryptographic tasks. Most notably, any multi-party
secure computation can be based on the security of OT. This was shown for
various models in several works (cf. [Yao86,GMW87,Kil88]).

Oblivious transfer has been studied in several variants, all of which were
eventually shown to be equivalent. In this paper we consider the one-out-of-two
variant of OT by Even, Goldreich ad Lempel [EGL85], which was shown to be
equivalent to Rabin's variant by Crépeau [Cre87].

[†] Part of this work done while at the Weizmann Institute of Science, Israel.

M. Naor (Ed.): TCC 2004, LNCS 2951, pp. 446–472, 2004.
© Springer-Verlag Berlin Heidelberg 2004

One-out-of-two OT is a protocol between two players, Alice holding two secrets s_0 and s_1, and Bob holding a choice bit c. At the end of the protocol Bob should learn the secret of his choice (i.e., s_c) but learn nothing about the other secret. Alice, on the other hand, should learn nothing about Bob's choice c.

Traditionally, constructions for OT have been based on strong computational assumptions. Either specific assumptions such as factoring or Diffie Hellman (cf. [Rab81,BM89,NP01]) or generic assumption such as the existence of enhanced trapdoor permutations (cf. [EGL85,Gol03,GKM+00]). In contrast, OT cannot be reduced in a black box manner to presumably weaker primitives such as one-way functions [IR89].

This state of affairs motivates the construction of OT in other types of setups. Indeed, protocols for OT were suggested in different models such as under the existence of noisy channels [CK88] or quantum channels [BBCS92]. In this work we follow a direction initiated by Cachin, Crépeau and Marcil [CCM98] and construct OT in the *Bounded Storage model*.

1.1   The Bounded Storage Model

In contrast to the usual approach in modern Cryptography, Maurer's *bounded storage model* [Mau92,Mau93] bounds the *space* (memory size) of dishonest players rather than their running time.

In a typical protocol in the bounded storage model a long random string $\mathcal{R}$ of length N is initially broadcast and the interaction between the polynomial-time participants is conducted based on a short portion of $\mathcal{R}$.[1] What makes such protocols interesting is that, even though the honest players store only a small fraction $k << N$ of the string $\mathcal{R}$, security is guaranteed even against dishonest players with space K where $k << K < N$. Moreover, dishonest players are not restricted to be computationally bounded (This is formalized by allowing dishonest players to choose an arbitrary *memory function* $g^*: \{0,1\}^N \rightarrow \{0,1\}^K$, and store $g^*(\mathcal{R})$. From that moment on, they are not bounded in any way). Naturally, we'd like to maximize K and minimize k. In this paper we have $K = \nu N$ for an arbitrary constant $\nu < 1$ and k will be about $K^{1/2}$.

The bounded storage model has two appealing properties: (1) The security obtained is information theoretic and thus everlasting in the sense that security is guaranteed even if adversaries acquire infinite space after the protocol is executed. (2) Protocols in the bounded storage model need not rely on any assumption except the limitation on the storage capabilities of the adversary.

The latter property should be contrasted with traditional works in Cryptography in which, besides bounding the adversary's computational capabilities, it is also required to rely on unproven hardness assumptions (such as the existence of enhanced trapdoor permutations, or the hardness of factoring large integers).

---

[1] One possible implementation is that $\mathcal{R}$ is broadcast at a very high rate by a trusted party. Another possibility is to have $\mathcal{R}$ transmitted from a satellite. We remark that in our protocol (as in many previous ones) one of the parties can transmit these bits. Furthermore, the assumption that $\mathcal{R}$ is uniformly distributed can be relaxed and it is sufficient that $\mathcal{R}$ has high min-entropy.

We mention that most of the previous work on the bounded storage model concentrated on private key encryption [Mau92,CM97,AR99,ADR02,DR02, DM02,Lu02,Vad03] and key agreement [Mau93,CM97].

1.2   Oblivious Transfer in the Bounded Storage Model

A protocol for OT in the bounded storage model was given in [CCM98]. This protocol requires $k \approx K^{2/3}$ and allows $K = \nu N$ for an arbitrary constant $\nu < 1$. The *error* ϵ in this protocol is rather large $\epsilon = k^{-O(1)}$. (Loosely speaking the error ϵ measures the probability that a dishonest receiver with storage bound K learns both secrets.)

A modified protocol with smaller error ϵ and smaller space k was given in [Din01]. For every constant $c > 0$, it achieves $k = K^{1/2+c}$ and $\epsilon = 2^{-k^{c'}}$ where $c' > 0$ is a constant that depends on c. We mention that the security of [Din01] is proven in a slightly different (and weaker) model, where it is assumed that two random strings $\mathcal{R}_1, \mathcal{R}_2$ of length $6K$ are transmitted one after the other and the bounded receiver chooses what to remember about $\mathcal{R}_2$ as a function of what he remembers about $\mathcal{R}_1$. The work of [Din01] was subsequently extended to deal with one-out-of-k OT for any small constant $k \geq 2$ in [HCR02].[2]

All protocols mentioned above require a lot of interaction. Specifically, for $\epsilon = 2^{-k^{O(1)}}$, they require the exchange of $k^{\Omega(1)}$ messages between the two players.

1.3   Our Results

We give a *constant round* OT protocol in the bounded storage model. Our protocol uses 5 messages following the transmission of the random string $\mathcal{R}$. We achieve parameters k and ϵ similar to that of [Din01] (that is, for every $c > 0$ there exist $c' > 0$ such that our protocol has $k = K^{1/2+c}$ and $\epsilon = 2^{-k^{c'}}$) while working in the stronger model of [CCM98]. Similar to [CCM98] we can achieve $K = \nu N$ for an arbitrary constant $\nu < 1$.

In addition to being constant round our protocol also achieves the following improvements over [CCM98,Din01]:

- The previous protocols are designed to transfer secrets in $\{0, 1\}$. Thus, transferring long secrets requires many messages. Our protocol can handle secrets of length $k^{\Omega(1)}$ in one execution.
- The previous protocols abort unsuccessfully with probability $1/2$ even if both players are honest. Our protocol aborts only with probability $2^{-k^{\Omega(1)}}$.
- For error $\epsilon = 2^{-k^{\Omega(1)}}$, the number of bits communicated in the two previous protocols is at least $K^{1/2}$. In contrast, for error $\epsilon = 2^{-k^c}$ our protocol communicates only $O(k^c)$ bits.

We also give a precise definition for the security of oblivious transfer in the bounded storage model, and point out difficulties arising when trying to consider the more standard notion of a "simulation based" definition.

---

[2] We note that a similar extension can be easily applied to our work.

1.4   Interactive Hashing

An important building block in the OT protocol is a construction of a constant round 2-to-1 *interactive hashing* protocol for unbounded parties. Loosely speaking, in such a protocol Bob holds an input $W \in \{0,1\}^m$, and Alice and Bob want to agree on a pair W_0, W_1 such that $W_d = W$ for some $d \in \{0,1\}$, yet Alice does not know d. It is also required that a dishonest Bob cannot "control" both W_0 and W_1. (See Section 5 for a precise definition.)

As observed in [CCM98], the protocol of Naor, Ostrovsky, Venkatesan and Yung [NOVY98] (originally used in the context of perfectly-hiding commitments) achieves 2-to-1 interactive hashing. One major drawback of the NOVY protocol, however, is that it requires m rounds of interaction. In this paper we give a new 4-message protocol for 2-to-1 interactive hashing that can be used to replace the NOVY protocol in the context of oblivious transfer in the bounded-storage model. Our protocol relies on a construction of almost t-wise independent permutations, such as the construction presented by Gowers in [Gow96].

Organization. Due to space limitation, some of the details and proofs have been omitted from this version. In Section 2 we present an overview of the techniques that were utilized to achieve our results. Some preliminary definitions are given in Section 3. Section 4 provides a definition of OT in the bounded storage model. In Section 5 we define and state our theorem regarding interactive hashing. The OT protocol is presented in Section 6. Sections 7, 8 and 9 give a high level analysis of the protocol. Conclusions and open problems are in Section 10.

2   Overview of the Technique

As motivation for our protocol, we begin by suggesting a simple protocol for OT in the bounded storage model which is bad in the sense that it requires large storage from the honest parties: Alice is required to store *all* of the string $\mathcal{R}$ and Bob is required to store half this string. We partition the N bit long string $\mathcal{R}$ into two equally long parts $\mathcal{R}_0, \mathcal{R}_1$ of length $N/2$. Recall that Alice has two secrets s_0, s_1 and Bob has a "choice bit" c and wants to obtain s_c. Bob will choose which of the two parts $\mathcal{R}_0, \mathcal{R}_1$ to store depending on his "choice bit" c.

Input of Alice: Secrets s_0, s_1.
Input of Bob: Choice bit: $c \in \{0,1\}$.
A random string $\mathcal{R} = (\mathcal{R}_0, \mathcal{R}_1)$ is transmitted.
Alice: Store all of $\mathcal{R}$.
Bob: Store $\mathcal{R}_c$.
Alice: For $i \in \{0,1\}$, send a uniformly chosen seed Y_i, compute $V_i = \mathrm{Ext}(\mathcal{R}_i, Y_i)$
  and $Z_i = V_i \oplus s_i$. Send Y_i, Z_i.
Bob: Compute $V_c = \mathrm{Ext}(\mathcal{R}_c, Y_c)$ and obtain $s_c = V_c \oplus Z_c$.

Fig. 1. A naïve protocol for OT

Intuitively, even if Bob is dishonest and has storage bound νN then there is an $I \in \{0, 1\}$ such that Bob "does not remember" $(1 - \nu)N/2$ bits of information about $\mathcal{R}_I$. This can be formalized by saying that the conditional entropy of $\mathcal{R}_I$ given the memory content of Bob is roughly $(1 - \nu)N/2$. (Actually, in this paper, as in [CCM98,Din01], we work with a variant of entropy called *min-entropy*).

Let $\text{Ext}(X, Y)$ (Ext for *extractor*) denote a function such that whenever X has sufficiently high min-entropy and Y is uniformly distributed then $\text{Ext}(X, Y)$ is close to being uniformly distributed. (The reader is referred to [Nis96,Sha02] for surveys on extractors). To complete the protocol, Alice sends $Z_i = s_i \oplus \text{Ext}(\mathcal{R}_i, Y_i)$ for both $i = 0$ and $i = 1$.

Note that an honest Bob can compute $\text{Ext}(\mathcal{R}_c, Y_c) \oplus Z_c$ and obtain s_c. However, if Bob is dishonest then Z_I is close to uniform from Bob's point of view and reveals no information about s_I.[3] It is easy to prove that even an unbounded dishonest Alice does not learn c.

Using a setup stage before the naïve protocol. The naïve protocol above requires very large storage bounds from the honest parties. In order to instantiate it in a more efficient manner we will first apply a carefully designed *setup stage*. Our goal is that at the end of the setup stage the two players will agree on two small subsets $C_0, C_1 \subseteq [N]$ of size $\ell << N$, such that Alice stores $\mathcal{R}_0 = \mathcal{R}_{C_0}$ and $\mathcal{R}_1 = \mathcal{R}_{C_1}$. (We use $\mathcal{R}_C$ to denote the $|C|$ bit long string obtained by restricting $\mathcal{R}$ to the indices in C.) Bob remembers only one of $\mathcal{R}_0, \mathcal{R}_1$ and cannot remember too much information about the other string. Furthermore, Alice does not know which of the two strings is not known to Bob. Following the setup stage, the two parties can perform OT by using the naïve protocol. We call this second stage the *transfer stage*. As the sets C_0, C_1 are of size $\ell << N$ the storage required by the honest parties at the transfer stage is much smaller than before, and honest players can follow the naïve protocol with space $O(\ell) << N$.

A long random string $\mathcal{R}$ of length N is transmitted.
Alice: Choose random $A \subseteq [N]$ of size n and store $\mathcal{R}_A$.
Bob: Choose random $B \subseteq [N]$ of size n and store $\mathcal{R}_B$.
Alice: Send A to Bob.
Bob: Verify that $C = A \cap B$ is of size at least $\ell = n^2/2N$.
Alice and Bob: Play an interactive hashing protocol where Bob's input is C. Both Alice and Bob obtain $C_0, C_1 \subseteq A$ such that $C \in \{C_0, C_1\}$.
At this point, Alice and Bob use the naïve protocol with $\mathcal{R}_0 = \mathcal{R}_{C_0}$ and $\mathcal{R}_1 = \mathcal{R}_{C_1}$.

Fig. 2. The protocol for the setup stage

---

[3] We mention that the argument above is imprecise. Given the memory content of Bob, the strings Z_0, Z_1 are no longer independent. Thus, to prove security it is not sufficient to prove that Z_I is uniformly distributed given the memory content of Bob. In the technical proof we prove that Z_I is uniformly distributed given the memory content of Bob, Z_{1-I} and Y_0, Y_1.

Implementing the setup stage. An implementation for such a setup stage was suggested in [CCM98]: Alice and Bob each choose a random subset of $[N]$ of size $n = \sqrt{2N\ell}$. We denote them by A and B respectively. When the string $\mathcal{R}$ is transmitted Alice and Bob store $\mathcal{R}_A$ and $\mathcal{R}_B$ respectively. Alice then sends A to Bob. By the birthday paradox, with high probability $C = A \cap B$ is of size roughly ℓ. Note that Bob remembers $\mathcal{R}_C$, and Alice does not know C.

To complete the setup stage, Alice and Bob play an interactive hashing protocol with $W = C$. They obtain sets $C_0, C_1 \subseteq A$ such that $C = C_d$ for some $d \in \{0, 1\}$ and such that Alice does not know d. The security requirement of the interactive hashing can be then used to guarantee that Bob "does not remember a lot of information" about one of the strings $\mathcal{R}_{C_0}, \mathcal{R}_{C_1}$. Thus, the two sets C_0, C_1 satisfy the properties required above and the parties can complete the OT protocol by using the naïve protocol.[4] Note that the setup stage requires the honest parties to store only $k = n = \sqrt{N\ell}$ bits. In this presentation, we did not discuss the security of Bob, however it is easy to show that even an unbounded Alice, which remembers all of $\mathcal{R}$, cannot learn any information about c.

Previous protocols. The protocols of [CCM98,Din01] both use the setup stage described above. They implement interactive hashing using the NOVY-protocol from [NOVY98] which takes $\ell = k^{\Omega(1)}$-rounds. Following the setup stage they perform what can be seen in retrospect as variants of our naïve protocol. (Both papers do not use extractors explicitly, however their strategies can be viewed as some (weak) implementations of extractors.)

Our improvements. Our main improvement comes from replacing the NOVY-protocol for interactive hashing by a new 4-message protocol. This protocol is based on explicit constructions of almost t-wise independent permutations. Some of the additional improvements are given by using competitive explicit constructions of extractors for the naïve protocol above. Another source of improvement comes from allowing Alice to choose the set A using an *averaging sampler* (The reader is referred to [Gol97] for a survey on samplers). Choosing the set A using a competitive averaging sampler reduces the memory requirements of Alice and Bob, as well as the overall communication.[5] We remark that the usefulness of extractors in the bounded storage model was demonstrated in [Lu02], and that of averaging samplers was demonstrated in [Vad03].[6] Our paper can be seen as another example of the usefulness of ideas from the theory of derandomization when designing protocols for the bounded storage model.

---

[4] A subtlety is that Bob has no control whether $C = C_0$ or $C = C_1$. In the actual protocol we allow Bob to ask Alice to "switch" between the roles of C_0, C_1 in order to receive the desired secret.

[5] Note that using a samplers to choose the set B as well, we can further improves the total communication and memory requirements.

[6] It should be noted that the seminal paper of Nisan and Zuckerman [NZ96] which defined extractors, already used them in a very related context to construct pseudorandom generators against bounded space machines.

2.1   The Improved Interactive Hashing Protocol

In an interactive hashing protocol Bob holds an input $W \in \{0,1\}^m$ and at the end of the protocol both parties should agree on W_0, W_1. It is required that there is a $d \in \{0,1\}$ such that $W = W_d$ and that a dishonest Alice cannot learn d. The main requirement is that a dishonest Bob cannot "control" both W_0, W_1. This is captured by the following condition: For every strategy of Bob and every set S of size 2^s (where s is a parameter), If Alice is honest then with high probability Bob cannot force that both W_0 and W_1 are in S.

A naïve solution. A naïve solution to this problem is that Alice sends a random 2-to-1 "hash function" $h : \{0,1\}^m \to \{0,1\}^{m-1}$ and Bob replies with $z = h(W)$. Then the two parties compute the two preimages W_0, W_1 of z under h. Note that for $s > m/2$ this protocol fails even if Alice sends a completely random function $h : \{0,1\}^m \to \{0,1\}^{m-1}$ (By the birthday paradox, for every S of size $2^s > 2^{m/2}$ with high probability over h there are $W_0, W_1 \in S$ such that $h(W_1) = h(W_2)$).

The NOVY-protocol. The NOVY-protocol [NOVY98] for interactive hashing can be thought of as a variant of the naïve solution described above in which Alice does not send "all" of the hash function at once. Alice chooses a random $m \times m$ matrix A with entries in $\{0,1\}$ subject to the restriction that A is invertible. Every such A can be seen as defining a function $h_A(x) = A \cdot x$. It is easy to see that the function h_A is a pairwise independent permutation. In particular, the function $h'_A(x) = (A \cdot x)_{1,\ldots,m-1}$ is 2-to-1. The protocol consists of $m - 1$ rounds. In round i, Alice sends A_i (the i'th row of A), and Bob replies with the $z_i = \langle A_i, W \rangle = h_A(W)_i$. Intuitively, revealing h_A slowly in return to bits z_i restricts Bob in the sense that he has to "choose at least part of his input" before seeing all of h_A.

The new protocol. Viewing the NOVY-protocol this way suggests the following improvement: We replace the family $\{h_A\}_A$ by a family of permutations with stronger independence properties. Namely, we will let π be randomly chosen from a family of m-wise independent permutations. In the new protocol, Alice sends π to Bob and in exchange Bob sends at once $z_1, \cdots, z_v$ where $z_i = \pi(W)_i$ for v close to m. We can show that the independence properties of π "protect Alice" and allow the parties to engage in a new interactive hashing protocol for sending the remaining few $m - v$ bits. By choosing the parameters appropriately, the two parties can use the naïve solution (with a pairwise independent hash function $g : \{0,1\}^{m-v} \to \{0,1\}^{m-v-1}$) after the first round. As a result of that we obtain a 2-round (4-messages) protocol (see Section 5.4).

Unfortunately, we are not aware of any explicit construction of a small sample space of t-wise independent permutations for $t > 3$. Nevertheless, in [Gow96] (see also [NR99] and the references therein) it was shown how to construct a sample space of permutations in which every t elements are close to being independent, and we can carry out the argument with this weaker property.

3   Preliminaries

We use $[N]$ to denote the set $\{1, \ldots, N\}$. We use $X \xleftarrow{r} S$ to denote uniformly choosing X from S. For a set $A \subseteq [N]$ and a string $\mathcal{R} \in \{0,1\}^N$ we let $\mathcal{R}_A$ denote the substring of $\mathcal{R}$ consisting of the bits indexed by A. For a set S and $\ell \leq |S|$, we use $\binom{S}{\ell}$ to denote the set of all subsets $T \subseteq S$ with $|T| = \ell$.

Encoding subsets. We use a method of encoding sets in $\binom{[n]}{\ell}$ into binary strings. The following method was used in [CCM98]:

Theorem 3.1 ([Cov73]) *For every integers $\ell \leq n$ there is a one to one mapping $F : \binom{[n]}{\ell} \to [\binom{n}{\ell}]$ such that both F and F^{-1} can be computed in time polynomial in n and space $O(\log \binom{n}{\ell})$.*

Using Theorem 3.1 we can encode $\binom{[n]}{\ell}$ by binary strings of length $\lceil \log \binom{n}{\ell} \rceil$. However, it could be the case that images of subsets constitute only slightly more than half of the strings above. This is exactly what causes the protocols of [CCM98,Din01] to unsuccessfully abort with probability $1/2$ (and is solved by repeating the protocol until the execution succeeds). Since in this work we are aiming for low round complexity, it would be beneficial to have the probability of unsuccessful abort to be significantly smaller than $1/2$. To achieve this, we will use a more redundant encoding. This encoding is more "dense" than the original one and thus guarantees that most strings can be decoded.

Definition 3.2 (Dense encoding of subsets) *For every integers $\ell \leq n$ let F be the mapping from Theorem 3.1. Given an integer $m \geq \lceil \log \binom{n}{\ell} \rceil$ we set $t_m = \lfloor 2^m / \binom{n}{\ell} \rfloor$. Define the mapping $F_m : \binom{[n]}{\ell} \times [t_m] \to \{0,1\}^m$ as $F_m(S, i) = (i-1)\binom{n}{\ell} + F(S)$ (every subset S is mapped to t_m different m bit strings).*

We now have the following Lemma (proof omitted).

Lemma 3.3 *For every $\ell \leq n$ and $m \geq \lceil \log \binom{n}{\ell} \rceil$, the encoding F_m is a one-to-one mapping. Furthermore: (1) F_m and F_m^{-1} are computable in time $\mathrm{poly}(n, \log m)$ and space $O(\log \binom{n}{\ell}) + \log m$. (2) Let D be the image of F_m (D contains all m bit strings that are legal encodings of subsets), then $\frac{|D|}{2^m} > 1 - \binom{n}{\ell}/2^m$.*

Min-entropy and Extractors. Min-entropy is a variant of Shannon's entropy that measures information on the *worst case*.

Definition 3.4 (Min-entropy) *For a distribution X over a probability space Ω the min-entropy of X is defined by: $H_\infty(X) = \min_{x \in \Omega} \log(1/\Pr[X = x])$. We say that X is a k-source if $H_\infty(X) \geq k$.*

Definition 3.5 (Statistical distance) *Two distributions P and Q over Ω are ϵ-close (also denoted $P \stackrel{\epsilon}{\equiv} Q$) if for every $A \subseteq \Omega$, $|\Pr_{x \leftarrow P}(A) - \Pr_{x \leftarrow Q}(A)| \leq \epsilon$.*

An extractor is a function that "extracts" randomness from arbitrary distributions which "contain" sufficient (min)-entropy[NZ96].

Definition 3.6 (Strong extractor) *A function* $\text{Ext} : \{0,1\}^{n_E} \times \{0,1\}^{d_E} \to \{0,1\}^{m_E}$ *is a* (k_E, ϵ_E)*-strong extractor if for every* k_E*-source* X *over* $\{0,1\}^{n_E}$ *the distribution* $(\text{Ext}(X,Y), Y)$ *where* Y *is uniform over* $\{0,1\}^{d_E}$ *is* ϵ_E*-close to* (U_{m_E}, Y) *where* U_{m_E} *is uniform over* $\{0,1\}^{m_E}$.

We remark that a *regular* (non-strong) extractor is defined in a similar way, replacing the random variable $(\text{Ext}(X,Y), Y)$ by $\text{Ext}(X,Y)$.

Averaging Samplers and Min-Entropy Samplers. A fundamental lemma by Nisan and Zuckerman [NZ96] asserts that given a δv-source X on $\{0,1\}^v$, with high probability over choosing $T \subseteq [v]$ of size t, X_T is roughly a δt-source.

In [CCM98] this lemma is used to assert that if a bounded storage adversary has memory bound νv for $\nu \approx 1 - \delta$ then for a random T he "remembers at most νt bits about X_T". This approach is also used in [Vad03] which constructs private key encryption in the bounded storage model. As shown in [RSW00, Vad03] the lemma does not require a uniformly chosen subset. It is sufficient that T is chosen using a "good averaging sampler"[7](such samplers have been a subject of a line of studies starting with [BR94], see survey of [Gol97]).

Definition 3.7 (Averaging sampler) *A function* $\text{Samp} : [L] \to [v]^t$ *is a* (μ, θ, γ)*-averaging sampler if for every function* $f : [v] \to [0,1]$ *with average value* $\frac{1}{v} \sum_i f(i) \geq \mu$,

$$\Pr_{p \in [L]} \left[\frac{1}{t} \sum_{1 \leq i \leq t} f(\text{Samp}(p)_i) < \mu - \theta \right] \leq \gamma$$

The function Samp *is said to have* distinct samples *if for every* $p \in [L]$, *the* t *outputs of* $\text{Samp}(p)$ *are distinct.*

A *min-entropy sampler* has the property that for most choices of p, the variable $X_{\text{Samp}(p)}$ is close to having high min-entropy. As shown in [Vad03], every averaging sampler yields a min-entropy sampler.

Definition 3.8 (Min-entropy sampler) *A function* $\text{Samp} : [L] \to [v]^t$ *with distinct samples is an* $(\delta, \delta', \phi, \epsilon)$*-min-entropy sampler if for every* δv*-source* X *over* $\{0,1\}^v$ *there is a set* $G \subseteq [L]$ *of density* $1 - \phi$ *such that for every* $p \in G$ *the distribution* $X_{\text{Samp}(p)}$ *is* ϵ*-close to a* $\delta' t$*-source.*

Lemma 3.9 ([Vad03] restated) *Let* $\text{Samp} : [L] \to [v]^t$ *be a* (μ, θ, γ)*-averaging sampler with distinct samples for* $\mu = (\delta - 2\tau)/\log(1/\tau)$ *and* $\theta = \tau/\log(1/\tau)$. *Then there is a constant* $c > 0$ *such that for every* $0 < \alpha < 1$, Samp *is a* $(\delta, \delta - 3\tau, (\gamma + 2^{-c\tau v})^{1-\alpha}, (\gamma + 2^{-c\tau v})^{\alpha})$*-min-entropy sampler.*

---

[7] We remark that most constructions of averaging samplers do not depend on μ and work for every $0 \leq \mu \leq 1$.

4   Oblivious Transfer in the Bounded Storage Model

We now turn to formally define oblivious transfer in the bounded storage model. The following definitions characterize malicious strategies for Alice and Bob. Note that in the definitions below the malicious strategies are asymmetric. We restrict malicious strategies for Bob to have bounded storage while no bounds are placed on malicious strategies for Alice. Clearly, if a protocol is secure against unbounded strategies for Alice, it is also secure against bounded strategies. Thus, the security defined here is even stronger than that explained in the introduction.

Definition 4.1 (Malicious Strategy for Alice) *A (malicious) strategy A^* for Alice is an unbounded interactive machine with inputs $\mathcal{R} \in \{0,1\}^N$ and $s_0, s_1 \in \{0,1\}^u$. That is, A^* receives $\mathcal{R}$ and s_0, s_1 and interacts with B, in each stage, it may compute the next message as any function of its inputs, its randomness and the messages it received thus far. The view of A^* when interacting with B that holds input c (denoted $\text{view}_{A^*}^{\langle A^*, B \rangle}(s_0, s_1; c)$) consists of its local output.* [8]

The following definition captures a bounded storage strategy with storage bound K. Loosely speaking, the only restriction made on a bounded storage strategy B^* is that it has some *memory function* $g^* : \{0,1\}^N \to \{0,1\}^K$ and its actions depend on $\mathcal{R}$ only through $g^*(\mathcal{R})$. This formally captures that B^* remembers only K bits about $\mathcal{R}$.

Definition 4.2 (Bounded storage strategy for Bob) *A bounded storage strategy B^* for Bob with memory bound K is a pair $(g^*, \widehat{B}^*)$ where:*

  - *$g^* : \{0,1\} \times \{0,1\}^N \to \{0,1\}^K$ is an arbitrary (not necessarily efficiently computable) function with input c and $\mathcal{R}$.*
  - *$\widehat{B}^*$ is an unbounded interactive machine with inputs $c \in \{0,1\}$ and $b^* \in \{0,1\}^K$.*

The behavior described by a strategy B^* with input c is the following: When given the string $\mathcal{R} \in \{0,1\}^N$, B^* computes $b^* = g^*(c, R)$. B^* then interacts with A using the interactive machine $\widehat{B}^*$ receiving inputs c and b^*. The view of B^* with input c when interacting with A with inputs s_0, s_1 (denoted $\text{view}_{B^*}^{\langle A, B^* \rangle}(s_0, s_1; c)$) is defined as the view of $\widehat{B}^*$ when interacting with A.

We now turn to the definition of oblivious transfer in the bounded storage model. The security of Bob asks that for any malicious strategy for Alice, its view is identically distributed whether Bob inputs $c = 0$ or $c = 1$. The definition of Alice's security is a bit more complex because one of her secrets is passed to Bob. For this definition, we partition *every* protocol that implements OT into two stages. The first stage called the *Setup Stage* and includes the transmission of the long string $\mathcal{R}$ and all additional messages sent by Alice and Bob until the point where Alice first makes use of her input s_0, s_1. The remaining steps in the protocol are called the *Transfer Stage*. Next define consistent pairs of secrets.

---

[8] The view of A may be thought of as also containing the party's randomness, inputs and outputs, as well as the messages received from B. This more intuitive "view" is possible since w.l.o.g. the malicious party may copy this view to his output.

Definition 4.3 *Two pairs* $\bar{s} = (s_0, s_1)$ *and* $\bar{s}' = (s_0', s_1')$ *are c-consistent if* $s_c = s_c'$.

The security of Alice asks that following the setup stage (which does not depend on the secrets), there is an index C (possibly a random variable which depends on $\mathcal{R}$ and the messages sent by the two parties in the setup stage) such that Bob's view is (close to) identically distributed for every two C-consistent pairs. In other words, Bob's view is (almost) independent of one of the secrets (defined by $1 - C$). We next present the actual definition.

Definition 4.4 (Oblivious Transfer) *A protocol* $\langle A, B \rangle$ *is said to implement* $(1-\epsilon)$-**oblivious transfer** (OT) *if it is a protocol in which Alice inputs two (secrets)* $s_0, s_1 \in \{0,1\}^u$, *Bob inputs a choice bit* $c \in \{0,1\}$, *and that satisfies:*

Functionality : *If Alice and Bob follow the protocol then for any* s_0, s_1 *and* c,
1. *The protocol does not abort with probability* $1 - \epsilon$.
2. *If the protocol ends then Bob outputs* s_c, *whereas Alice outputs nothing.*

Security for Bob*: The view of any strategy* A^* *is independent of* c. *Namely, for every* s_0, s_1:

$$\left\{ \mathrm{view}_{A^*}^{\langle A^*, B \rangle}(s_0, s_1; c) \mid c = 0 \right\} \equiv \left\{ \mathrm{view}_{A^*}^{\langle A^*, B \rangle}(s_0, s_1; c) \mid c = 1 \right\}$$

(K, ϵ)-**Security for Alice***: for every bounded storage strategy* B^* *for Bob with memory bound* K *and input* c *there is a random variable* C *defined by the end of the setup stage such that for every two pairs* $\bar{s}$ *and* $\bar{s}'$ *that are* C-*consistent:*

$$\left\{ \mathrm{view}_{B^*}^{\langle A, B^* \rangle}(\bar{s}; c) \right\} \stackrel{\epsilon}{\equiv} \left\{ \mathrm{view}_{B^*}^{\langle A, B^* \rangle}(\bar{s}'; c) \right\}$$

If Bob is semi-honest then $C = c$,[9] however, a dishonest receiver can always choose to ignore c and play with an input c' which depends on $\mathcal{R}$ and the messages in the setup stage. Thus, letting C depend on $\mathcal{R}$ and the messages in the setup stage is unavoidable. We remark that the definition would be meaningless if C was allowed to depend on the secrets s_0, s_1, and this is the reason we require a partitioning of a protocol into a setup stage and transfer stage. We stress that the security achieved in this definition is *information theoretic*.

Remark 4.1. We mention that it does not immediately follow that all the "standard" applications of OT can be performed in the bounded storage model (this is also the case for the previous protocols in this model [CCM98,Din01]). Nevertheless, we now explain how this protocol can be used as a sub-protocol to perform other cryptographic tasks. For this we note that the above definition implies security by a *simulation argument* (although the simulator is not necessarily efficient).[10] Thus, for example, our OT protocol can be used as in the

---

[9] A semi-honest receiver is one that follows the protocol but *remembers more than required about* $\mathcal{R}$ and attempts to use this information to learn both secrets.

[10] Loosely speaking, the simulation paradigm requires that any attack of a malicious party can be simulated in an ideal setting where the parties interact only through a trusted party. This insures that the protocol is as secure as an interaction in the ideal setting.

construction of Kilian [Kil88], to give a protocol for secure two-party computation in the bounded storage model. The security achieved guarantees that an unbounded party learns nothing about the input of the other party. We stress that typically one requires that the simulators should run with essentially the same efficiency as the attack being simulated, and that this provides a stronger notion of security.

We now give a sketch of the simulator for the receiver's strategy B^*. The simulator plays the roles of both B^* and A in the protocol up to the transfer stage. At this point the simulator computes the random variable C and calls the trusted party asking for secret C. It continues by simulating A with inputs s_C as received from the trusted party and a random s_{1-C}. By the definition this turns out to be a valid simulation, however, computing C is not necessarily efficient and therefore the simulation is unbounded.

5   Interactive Hashing

One of the main tools we use in this paper is the interactive hashing protocol. While useful in the bounded storage model, it is important to note that interactive hashing is not necessarily related to this model. As a matter of fact, the definitions and protocols given here achieve security against all powerful adversaries with no storage bounds at all.

5.1   Preliminaries: Permutations and Hash Functions

Definition 5.1 (2^k-to-1 Hash Functions) *A hash function* $h : \{0,1\}^m \to \{0,1\}^{m-k}$ *is* 2^k-to-1 *if for every output of h there are exactly* 2^k *pre-images. That is,* $|h^{-1}(z)\}| = 2^k$ *for every* $z \in \{0,1\}^{m-k}$.

One simple method of constructing a 2^k-to-1 hash function is to take a permutation on m-bit strings and omit the last k bits of its output. Clearly every output of the resulting function can be extended to 2^k different strings and therefore has 2^k pre-images. Examples of useful permutations follow.

Almost t-wise Independent Permutations. In our discussion we would like to use a random permutation on m bit strings. However, a description of such a permutation would be exponentially long since there are $(2^m)!$ such permutations. The solution is to use a permutation that falls short of being truly random but still has enough randomness to it. Specifically we want to efficiently sample a permutation π out of a small space of permutations such that when looking at π applied on any t points in $\{0,1\}^m$ then π behaves like a truly random permutation. Such a space is called a t-wise independent permutation space.

Unlike in the case of functions, where there are extremely randomness efficient constructions of t-wise independent functions, we are unaware of such constructions for permutations. Instead we further relax our demands and ask the construction to be *almost* t-wise independent, that is, the distribution induced by the permutation π on any t points is statistically close to the distribution induced on these points by a truly random permutation. Formally:

Definition 5.2 *An η-almost t-wise independent permutation space is a proce-dure that takes as input a seed of l bits and outputs a description of an efficiently computable permutation in S_{2^m}.[11] A uniformly chosen seed induces a distribu-tion $\Pi_{t,\eta}$ on permutations such that for any t strings $x_1, \ldots x_t \in \{0,1\}^m$:*

$$\{\pi(x_1), \ldots \pi(x_t)\}_{\pi \xleftarrow{r} \Pi_{t,\eta}} \overset{\eta}{\equiv} \{\pi(x_1), \ldots \pi(x_t)\}_{\pi \xleftarrow{r} S_{2^m}}$$

We use the construction presented by Gowers in [**?**].

Theorem 5.3 ([Gow96]) *There exists an η-almost t-wise independent permu-tation space $\Pi_{t,\eta}$ with $t = m$, $\eta = \left(\frac{1}{2^m}\right)^t$ and seed length $l = m^C$ for some con-stant C. Furthermore, $\Pi_{t,\eta}$ runs in time and space polynomial in the seed length.*

We note that the main Theorem of Gowers requires some special properties from the value of m. However, this is only needed to improve parameters, and the weaker results presented in the middle of the paper (Lemma 3) are satisfactory and put no limitation on the value of m. The constant in the exponent of the above Theorem is around $C = 10$, which is high but acceptable.

Other constructions of almost t-wise independent permutations were discus-sed in [NR99] and other references therein.

Pairwise Independent Permutations. A widely used tool is a pairwise in-dependent permutation of strings of m bits. This is simply a 2-wise independent permutation as defined above (i.e., a 0-almost 2-wise independent permutation).

The construction that we use identifies $\{0,1\}^m$ with the field $GF(2^m)$. A per-mutation is sampled by randomly choosing two elements $a, b \in GF(2^m)$ with the restriction that $a \neq 0$. The permutation is then defined by $g_{a,b}(x) = ax + b$ (where all operations are in the field). Generating a pairwise independent permutation therefore requires $2m$ random bits.

Note: To construct a pairwise independent 2-to-1 hash function simply take a pairwise independent permutation and omit the last bit of its output.

5.2   Definition: Interactive Hashing

Interactive hashing is a protocol between Alice with no input and Bob with an input string. At the end of the protocol Alice and Bob should agree on two strings: One should be Bob's input and intuitively the other should be random. Moreover, Alice should not be able to distinguish which of the two is Bob's input and which is the random string.

Definition 5.4 (Interactive Hashing) *A protocol $\langle A, B \rangle$ is called an inter-active hashing protocol if it is an efficient protocol between Alice with no input and Bob with input string $W \in \{0,1\}^m$. At the end of the protocol both Alice and Bob output a (succinct representation of a) 2-to-1 function $h : \{0,1\}^m \rightarrow$*

---

[11] S_{2^m} denotes the family of all permutations on m bit strings

$\{0,1\}^{m-1}$ and two values $W_0, W_1 \in \{0,1\}^m$ (in lexicographic order) so that $h(W_0) = h(W_1) = h(W)$.

Let $d \in \{0,1\}$ be such that $W_d = W$. Furthermore, if the distribution of the string W_{1-d} over the randomness of the two parties is η-close to uniform, then the protocol is called η-uniform interactive hashing (or simply uniform interactive hashing if $\eta = 0$).

Definition 5.5 (Security of Interactive Hashing) An interactive hashing protocol is **secure for B** if for every unbounded deterministic strategy A^*, and every W, if h, W_0, W_1 are the outputs of the protocol between an honest Bob with input W and A^*. Then

$$\left\{ \text{view}_{A^*}^{\langle A^*, B\rangle}(W) \mid W = W_0 \right\} \equiv \left\{ \text{view}_{A^*}^{\langle A^*, B\rangle}(W) \mid W = W_1 \right\}$$

An interactive hashing protocol is (s, ρ)-**secure for A** if for every $S \subseteq \{0,1\}^m$ of size at most 2^s and every unbounded strategy B^*, if W_0, W_1 are the outputs of the protocol, then:

$$\Pr[W_0, W_1 \in S] < \rho$$

where the probability is taken over the coin tosses of A and B^*.

An interactive hashing protocol is (s, ρ)-**secure** if it is secure for B and (s, ρ)-secure for A.

Remark 5.1. The definition above does not deal with the case that dishonest players abort before the end of the execution. Intuitively, such a definition is sufficient for our purposes since in our OT protocol, the interactive hashing is used before the players send any message that depends on their secrets, and thus their secrets are not compromised.

5.3   Partial Result: A Two Message Interactive Hashing

We start by showing that when the bad set S is small enough then the following naïve protocol is sufficiently good. In this 2 message protocol called 2M-IH, Alice sends a random 2-to-1 hash function $h : \{0,1\}^m \rightarrow \{0,1\}^{m-1}$ and Bob replies with $z = h(W)$.

Claim 5.6 For all u, the 2M-IH protocol is a $(s, 2^{-(m-2s+1)})$-secure uniform interactive hashing.

Proof: The 2M-IH is clearly an interactive hashing protocol, and since h is pairwise independent, then it is also uniform (W_{1-d} is uniformly distributed). The 2M-IH is also secure for B since all that Bob sends to Alice is $h(W)$, which is the exact same view whether Bob has input $W = W_1$ or $W = W_0$. On the other hand, since h is a pairwise independent hash function, then the probability over the choice of h for any two strings W_0, W_1 to be mapped to a certain cell $z \in \{0,1\}^{m-1}$ is perfectly random, that is:

$$\Pr_h[h(W_0) = h(W_1) = z] = 2 \cdot \frac{1}{2^m} \cdot \frac{1}{2^m - 1}$$

Denote $X_z = 1$ if both strings mapped to cell z are from the set S and $X_z = 0$ otherwise. Then:

$$\Pr_h[X_z = 1] \leq \binom{2^s}{2} \Pr_h[h(W_0) = h(W_1) = z] \leq \frac{2^s}{2^m} \cdot \frac{2^s - 1}{2^m - 1} \leq \frac{2^{2s}}{2^{2m}}$$

Denote by X the number of cells z such that both values mapped into z are from the set S, then:

$$E(X) = E\left(\sum_z X_z\right) = \sum_z E\left(X_z\right) \leq 2^{m-1} \cdot \frac{2^{2s}}{2^{2m}} \leq 2^{-(m-2s+1)}$$

The protocol is insecure only if Bob finds a cell z with two bad values, that is only if $X \geq 1$. But using Markov's inequality we have that $\Pr[X \geq 1] \leq E(x) \leq 2^{-(m-2s+1)}$. Thus this protocol is $(s, 2^{-(m-2s+1)})$-secure for Alice. ∎

5.4   A Four Message Protocol for Interactive Hashing

The two message protocol is useful when the bad set S is very small. However, if S is large (for example, if $|S| = 2^s$ and $s = \gamma m$ for any constant γ) then this protocol does not suffice. While the interactive hashing protocol of [NOVY98] takes m round of communication to overcome this, the following protocol achieves this using an interaction of just four messages.

Theorem 5.7 *For all s, the 4M-IH protocol is an $(s, 2^{-(m-s+O(\log m))})$-secure η-uniform interactive hashing protocol for $\eta = \left(\frac{1}{2^{s-\log m}}\right)^m < 2^{-m}$.*

Proof: We start by noting that the protocol is efficient for both parties due to the efficiency of the permutations used. Furthermore, they can run in small space. This is an η-uniform interactive hashing protocol since h is η close to pairwise independent and therefore the distribution of W_{1-d} is η close to uniform.

The 4M-IH protocol is secure for B since no matter what strategy A^* Alice uses, the messages that Bob sends are identical whether his input is $W = W_0$ or $W = W_1$ (recall that $h(W_0) = h(W_1)$).

This protocol has two stages of question and answer (4 messages), and in order to prove the security for A we view each of these two parts separately. In the first part, all strings $W \in \{0,1\}^m$ are divided by π' into 2^v cells (according to the value of $\pi'(W)$). Our goal is to show that no cell $z' \in \{0,1\}^v$ has too many strings from the bad set S mapped to it. The second part of the protocol can then be viewed as implementing the 2M-IH protocol on strings in the cell z', yielding the security of the combined protocol (the portion of bad strings in the cell z' is reduced to less than a square root of the strings in the cell). We start by bounding the probability that a specific set of t strings are mapped by π' to the same cell z.

4M-IH (4 Message Interactive Hashing)

Common Input: Parameters m and s.
    Let $v = s - \log m$.
    A family Π of η-almost t-wise independent permutations $\pi : \{0,1\}^m \to \{0,1\}^m$
        Take $t = m$ and $\eta = \left(\frac{1}{2^v}\right)^t$.
    A family G of 2-wise independent 2-1 hash functions $g \colon \{0,1\}^{m-v} \to \{0,1\}^{m-v-1}$
    A family H (induced by Π, G) of 2-1 hash functions $h : \{0,1\}^m \to \{0,1\}^{m-1}$
    defined as:

$$h(x) \stackrel{\text{def}}{=} \pi(x)_1, \ldots, \pi(x)_v, g\left(\pi(x)_{v+1} \ldots, \pi(x)_m\right)$$

    where $\pi(x)_i$ denotes the ith bit of $\pi(x)$.
Input of Alice: $\perp$.
Input of Bob: $W \in \{0,1\}^m$.
  – **Alice:** Choose $\pi \xleftarrow{r} \Pi$. Send π to Bob.
  – **Bob:** Compute $z_1, \ldots z_m = \pi(W)$. Send $\pi'(W) = z_1, \ldots, z_v$ to Alice (let π'
     denote π when truncated to its first v bits).
  – **Alice:** Choose $g \xleftarrow{r} G$. Send g to Bob.
  – **Bob:** Send $g(z_{v+1}, \ldots, z_m)$ to Alice.
  – **Alice and Bob:** Output W_0, W_1 s.t. $h(W_0) = h(W_1) = h(W)$.

Fig. 3. The four message protocol for interactive hashing.

Claim 5.8 *For every $z \in \{0,1\}^v$ and all $x_1, \ldots, x_t \in \{0,1\}^m$ we have that:*

$$\rho = \Pr_{\pi \in \Pi}[\pi'(x_1) = \pi'(x_2) = \ldots = \pi'(x_t) = z] \leq \left(\frac{1}{2^v}\right)^t + \eta$$

Proof: Suppose that π was a t-wise independent function (and not permutation), then for every $x_i \in \{0,1\}^m$ we have that the probability that $\pi'(x_i) = z$ is exactly $\frac{1}{2^v}$ and the probability that this is the case for t different values is exactly $\left(\frac{1}{2^v}\right)^t$. But since π is a permutation, this probability is smaller since for every i we have $\Pr[\pi'(x_i) = z | \pi'(x_1) = \pi'(x_2) = \ldots \pi'(x_{i-1}) = z] \leq \frac{1}{2^v}$. But π is actually an almost t-wise independent permutation, the probability on t elements may deviate by be up to η from the truly random permutation and therefore $\rho \leq \left(\frac{1}{2^v}\right)^t + \eta$ ∎

Let us focus on a specific cell $z \in \{0,1\}^v$. For every set of t elements $x_1, \ldots, x_t \in S$ denote the $Y_z^\pi(x_1, \ldots, x_t)$ the indicator if all x_i is mapped to z or not. That is:

$$Y_z^\pi(x_1, \ldots, x_t) = \begin{cases} 1 & \pi'(x_1) = \pi'(x_2) = \ldots = \pi'(x_t) = z \\ 0 & \text{otherwise} \end{cases}$$

Let Y_z^π denote the number of strings from S mapped to cell z by π'. Let $E = \frac{2^s}{2^v}$, which is the expected number of strings from S in each cell, if they were divided uniformly at random. We claim that with high probability, Y_z^π does not deviate much from E.

Lemma 5.9 *For all $z \in \{0,1\}^v$,*

$$\Pr_{\pi \in \Pi}\left[Y_z^\pi \geq 4E\right] \leq 2^{-(t-1)}$$

Proof: Consider the table of all possible $Y_z^\pi(x_1, \ldots, x_t)$, where each row stands for a specific set $x_1, \ldots, x_t$ and each column stands for a choice of π. By Claim 5.8, the fraction of ones in each row and hence the fraction of ones in the whole table is at most $\left(\frac{1}{2^v}\right)^t + \eta$. On the other hand, for each π such that $Y_z^\pi \geq 4E$ there are at least $\binom{4E}{t}$ sets of t elements for which $Y_z^\pi(x_1, \ldots, x_t) = 1$, therefore the fraction of ones is at least $\Pr_{\pi \in \Pi}[Y_z^\pi \geq 4E] \cdot \binom{4E}{t}/\binom{2^s}{t}$. Therefore we get that:

$$\Pr_{\pi \in \Pi}\left[Y_z^\pi \geq 4E\right] \leq \frac{\binom{2^s}{t}}{\binom{4E}{t}}\left(\left(\frac{1}{2^v}\right)^t + \eta\right)$$

Recall that $\eta = \left(\frac{1}{2^v}\right)^t$ and using the fact that $\binom{a}{c}/\binom{b}{c} \leq \left(\frac{a}{b-c+1}\right)^c$ we get:

$$\Pr_{\pi \in \Pi}\left[Y_z^\pi \geq 4E\right] \leq \left(\frac{2^s}{4E-t+1}\right)^t \cdot 2 \cdot \left(\frac{1}{2^v}\right)^t$$

We take $t + 1 \leq 2E$ and recall that $E = \frac{2^s}{2^v}$:

$$\Pr_{\pi \in \Pi}\left[Y_z^\pi \geq 4E\right] \leq 2 \cdot \left(\frac{2^s}{2E2^v}\right)^t$$

$$\leq 2 \cdot \left(\frac{2^s}{2\frac{2^s}{2^v}2^v}\right)^t = 2 \cdot 2^{-t}$$

This completes the proof of Lemma 5.9. ∎

As a corollary of Lemma 5.9 we get that with high probability there is no cell that contains a large number of bad elements. Applying a union bound gives:

$$\Pr_{\pi \in \Pi}\left[\exists z \text{ s.t. } Y_z^\pi \geq 4E\right] \leq 2^{-(t-1-v)}$$

Recall that $t = m$ and $v = s - \log m$ so the probability of error here is $2^{-(m-s)+\log m-1}$.

Assuming that indeed for all cells z we have $Y_z^\pi < 4E$ then the second part of the protocol is actually running the 2M-IH on the strings in a specific cell z'. This cell contains all the possible extensions of z' into an m bit string. Therefore, the 2M-IH is run on strings of length $m' = m - v$. There are no more than $2^{s'} = 4 \cdot 2^{s-v}$ strings that belong to the bad set S. According to Claim 5.6 the second part of the protocol is an $(s', 2^{-(m'-2s'+1)})$-interactive hashing protocol. The probability that Bob can choose a cell with two string from the bad set is therefore $2^{-(m'-2s'+1)} = 2^{-(m-v-2(s-v+2)+1)} = 2^{-(m-s)+\log m+3}$. Combined with the probability that there exist a z with $Y_z^\pi \geq 4E$ we get that the probability that any strategy B^* that Bob plays succeeds in choosing both W_0 and W_1 in the set S is at most $2^{-(m-s+O(\log m))}$. ∎

6   The Oblivious Transfer Protocol

Our BS-OT protocol is presented in figure 4. The protocol relies on three ingredients: An extractor, a min-entropy sampler, and an interactive hashing protocol. The precise requirements from the ingredients are presented in figure 5.

Input of Alice: Secret bits $s_0, s_1 \in \{0,1\}^u$.
Input of Bob: Choice bit $c \in \{0,1\}$.
Setup Stage:
    Subsets Stage: Alice and Bob store subsets of the string $\mathcal{R} \in \{0,1\}^N$.
        – **Alice:** Choose $P \xleftarrow{r} L_A$. Compute $A \subset [N]$ of size n by $A = \mathrm{Samp}_A(P)$ and store the bits $\mathcal{R}_A$.
        – **Bob:** Choose random $B \subset [N]$ of size n and store the bits $\mathcal{R}_B$.
        – **Alice:** Send A to Bob by sending P.
        – **Bob:** Determine $C = A \cap B$. If $|C| < \ell$ abort. If $|C| > \ell$, randomly truncate it to be of size ℓ.
        – **Bob:** Compute h_m as in Definition 3.2. Choose $Q \xleftarrow{r} [h_m]$ and compute $W = F_m(C, Q)$.*
    Interactive Hashing Stage: Interactively hash W.
        – **Bob:** Input W into the interactive hashing protocol.
        – **Alice and Bob:** Interactively obtain h and W_0, W_1 s.t. $h(W_0) = h(W_1) = h(W)$. Compute the subsets C_0, C_1 encoded by W_0, W_1. If W_0 or W_1 isn't a valid encoding then abort.
Choice Stage:
        – **Bob:** Let $d \in \{0,1\}$ be such that $W_d = W$. Send $e = c \oplus d$.
        – **Alice:** For $i \in \{0,1\}$ send $Y_i \xleftarrow{r} \{0,1\}^{d_E}$.
Transfer Stage:
        – **Alice:** Set $X_0 = \mathcal{R}_{C_0}$ and $X_1 = \mathcal{R}_{C_1}$.
        – **Alice:** Send "encrypted" values of s_0 and s_1: For $i \in \{0,1\}$, Send $Z_i = s_{i \oplus e} \oplus E(X_i, Y_i)$.
        – **Bob:** Compute $X = \mathcal{R}_C$. Bob's output is given by $\mathrm{Ext}(X, Y_{c \oplus e}) \oplus Z_{c \oplus e}$

---

* The range of F_m is $[n]$ and not $A = \mathrm{Samp}_A(P)$. For simplicity, we treat C as a subset of A.

Fig. 4. Protocol BS-OT for 1-2 OT in the bounded storage model.

In our suggested implementation of BS-OT we choose Samp_A to be the sampler from [Vad03], Ext to be an extractor from [RRV99] and use the $4M - IH$ interactive hashing protocol from the previous section. The precise choices of parameters for these ingredients appear in Section 8. These choices meet the requirements of figure 5 with $\epsilon = 2^{-\Omega(\ell)}$. The main theorem of this paper asserts that this implementation of BS-OT is a constant round protocol for oblivious transfer in the bounded storage model.

At first reading, the reader may safely ignore the sampler and assume that the set A is chosen uniformly at random. That is assume that Samp_A is the identity mapping on $\binom{[N]}{n}$.[12]

---

[12] Using different samplers allows choosing a "random" set A which has a shorter description. Specifically, using the sampler from Section 8 reduces the description size of A from $\log \binom{N}{n} = \Theta(n \log n)$ to $O(\ell)$.

Parameters:
- N - the length of the long random string $\mathcal{R}$.
- n - the number of bits honest players remember about $\mathcal{R}$.
- u - the length of the secrets.
- $\ell = n^2/2N$ - the size of the intersection set.
- ν - the dishonest receiver remembers at most νN bits about $\mathcal{R}$.
- ϵ - the error of the protocol. We can only achieve $\epsilon \geq 2^{-c\delta_A'\ell/\log(1/\delta_A')}$ where δ_A' is defined below and $c > 0$ is some constant which may depend on the constant c_{IH} defined below. We therefore require that ϵ satisfy this condition.

Ingredients:
- A $(\delta_A, \delta_A', \phi_A, \epsilon_A)$-min-entropy sampler $\mathrm{Samp}_A : [L_A] \to [N]^n$ with:
  - $\delta_A \leq (1 - \nu)/2$.
  - $\delta_A' = \delta_A/8$.
  - $\phi_A \leq \epsilon/20$.
  - $\epsilon_A \leq \epsilon/20$.
  - L_A determines the length of the first message sent by Alice.
- A (k_E, ϵ_E)-strong extractor $\mathrm{Ext} : \{0,1\}^{n_E} \times \{0,1\}^{d_E} \to \{0,1\}^{m_E}$ with:
  - $n_E = \ell$
  - $d_E \leq \delta_A'\ell/12$
  - $m_E = u \leq \delta_A'\ell/12$.
  - $k_E \geq \delta_A'\ell/6$.
  - $\epsilon_E \leq (\epsilon/20)^2$.
- An (s, ρ)-secure (2^{-m})-uniform interactive hashing protocol for strings of length $m = 10\ell \log n$ with:
  - $s \leq m - c_{IH}\delta_A'\ell/\log \delta_A' + 1$ ($c_{IH} > 0$ is a constant chosen in the proof).
  - $\rho \leq \epsilon/20$.*

---

* Note that ρ depends on c_{IH} and this is why we allow the constant c in the requirement on ϵ to depend on c_{IH}. The order of quantifiers is as follows: There is some constant $c_{IH} > 0$ chosen in the proof. The constant c depends on this constant.

Fig. 5. Ingredients and requirements for Protocol BS-OT.

Theorem 6.1 *There is a constant $\alpha > 0$ such that if N, n and ℓ satisfy $\log n \leq \ell \leq n^\alpha$ then for every constant $\nu < 1$ let protocol BS-OT use the ingredients described in Section 8. Protocol BS-OT is a $(1 - \epsilon)$-oblivious transfer protocol for $\epsilon = 2^{-\Omega(\ell)}$. Furthermore:*

- *The protocol has 5 messages.*
- *The strategies for Alice and Bob runs in time $poly(n)$ and space $k = O(n \log n)$.*
- *The protocol passes secrets of length $u = \Omega(\ell)$.*
- *The overall number of bits exchanged is $TC = O(\ell^{O(1)})$.*

The constants hidden in ϵ, s, u and TC above depend on ν.[13]

---

[13] Tracing this dependency gives that for $\delta = (1 - \nu)$: $\epsilon = 2^{-\Omega(\delta\ell/\log(1/\delta))}$, $s = m - O(\delta\ell/\log(1/\delta))$, and $u = \Omega(\delta\ell)$. This holds even when ν isn't a constant as long as $n \geq \ell/\delta^4$. That is, the Theorem holds even for $\nu \approx 1 - (\ell/n)^4$.

The results mentioned in the introduction can be obtained by choosing $n = N^{1/2+a}/\log N$ for some small constant $a > 0$. Note that if a is sufficiently small then the space of honest players satisfies $k = O(n \log n) = O(N^{1/2+a}) \leq O(K^{1/2+a})$, where the last inequality follows assuming $\nu > 1/2$ which we can assume w.l.o.g. As $\ell = n^2/2N$ we have that $\ell = n^{2a}/2\log N \geq k^a$ for large enough n, and we have that $\epsilon = 2^{-\Omega(\ell)} = 2^{-\Omega(k^a)}$.

7   The Functionality and Security of the OT Protocol

The proof of Theorem 6.1 follows from the combination of several lemmas stated below. The first Lemma asserts that protocol BS-OT indeed implements oblivious transfer.

Lemma 7.1 *For every choice of ingredients for BS-OT and every s_0, s_1, c, If Alice and Bob follow protocol BS-OT then*

- *With probability $1 - 2^{-\Omega(\ell)}$ the protocol does not abort.*
- *If the protocol does not abort then Bob's output is indeed s_c.*

Proof: We first show that with high probability $|A \cap B| \geq \ell$. This is because for every fixed A, as B is a random set the expected size of $A \cap B$ is $n^2/N \geq 2\ell$. A standard Lemma (see for example Corollary 3 in [Din01]) can be used to show that there exists a constant $0 < d < 1$ such that probability that $|A \cap B| < \ell$ is at most $2e^{-d\ell}$.

We now show that the probability that one of W_0, W_1 is not a valid encoding of a subset is small. W_d was chosen by Bob and is certainly a valid encoding. By the definition of Interactive Hashing, the other string W_{1-d} is η-close to uniformly distributed in $\{0,1\}^m$, for $\eta < 2^{-m}$. By Lemma 3.3 the probability that a random string $W \in \{0,1\}^m$ is not a valid encoding is at most $\binom{n}{\ell}2^{-m} \leq 2^{\ell \log n - m} \leq 2^{-\ell-1}$ as $m = 10\ell \log n$. It follows that the probability of abort is bounded by $2^{-m} + 2^{-\ell-1} \leq 2^{-\ell}$.

To see that whenever the protocol does not abort Bob indeed outputs s_c, we observe that $X = \mathcal{R}_C$ is known to Bob (since $C = A \cap B \subseteq B$ and Bob has stored all the bits $\mathcal{R}_B$). In particular, Bob is always able to compute $E(X, Y_{c \oplus e})$ and subsequently use it in order to "decrypt" the value $Z_{c \oplus e}$. By the definition of the protocol we then have:

$$E(X, Y_{c \oplus e}) \oplus Z_{c \oplus e} = E(X, Y_d) \oplus (s_c \oplus E(X_d, Y_d))$$
$$= E(X, Y_d) \oplus (s_c \oplus E(X, Y_d)) \tag{1}$$
$$= s_c$$

where Eq. (1) follows from the fact that X_d equals $\mathcal{R}_C (= X)$, which in turns follows from the fact that $C_d = C$ (since $W_d = W$ and the encoding F_m is one-to-one). The lemma follows. ∎

Theorem 7.2 *For every choice of ingredients of BS-OT, the protocol is secure for Bob.*

Proof: We show that for any strategy A^*, the view of A^* is independent of the bit c. This is shown by the following argument: Fix the randomness of A^* and $\mathcal{R}$. We show a perfect bijection between possible pairs of B's randomness r_B and input c. That is, for each pair (r_B, c) that is consistent with the view V of A^*, there exists a unique pair $(r'_B, 1-c)$ such that r'_B and $1-c$ are consistent with the same view V. There are two possible options for a $V = \text{view}_{A^*}^{\langle A^*, B \rangle}$:

- The protocol aborts before the choice stage where Bob sends Alice the value $e = c \oplus d$. In such a case, the view V is totaly independent of c and we map every consistent r_B to itself ($r'_B = r_B$). Clearly r_B is consistent with both $c = 0$ and $c = 1$.
- V includes the message $e = c \oplus d$ sent by Bob. In such a case, suppose that (r_B, c) is consistent V. That is, r_B is the randomness that chooses the random set B so that $C = A \cap B$ is encoded by the string W_d. By the fact that the protocol did not abort, we are assured that also W_{1-d} encodes a legal set C'. Then we choose r'_B to be the randomness that chooses $B' = B \setminus C \cup C'$ and encodes C' by W_{1-d}. This perfectly defines $(r'_B, 1-c)$ that is consistent with the view V. Furthermore, $(r'_B, 1-c)$ is mapped by the same process back to (r_B, c), hence we get a perfect bijection.

Theorem 7.2 follows. ■

The following theorem (which is technically the most challenging theorem of this paper) guarantees Alice's security against bounded storage receivers. This theorem refers to a list of requirements on the parameters of the ingredients which appears in figure 5.

Theorem 7.3 For every $\nu < 1$ (not necessarily constant), if all the requirements in figure 5 are met then protocol BS-OT is $(\nu N, \epsilon)$-secure for Alice.

The proof of this theorem is long and technical and appears in the full version of this paper. Section 9 is dedicated to giving an outline of this proof.
As we show in section 8, Ext and Samp_A and 4M–IH satisfy all the requirements in figure 5 for $\epsilon = 2^{-\Omega(\ell)}$. Theorem 7.3 thus implies the following corollary.

Corollary 7.4 Let Ext, Samp_A and IH be chosen as in Theorem 6.1. Protocol BS-OT is $(\nu N, \epsilon)$-secure for Alice, for $\epsilon = 2^{-a\ell}$ where $a > 0$ is a constant that depends on ν.

Lemma 7.5 Let Ext, Samp_A and IH be chosen as in Theorem 6.1. The statements in the itemized list in Theorem 6.1 hold.

Proof: It is easy to verify that the protocol has 5 messages (not including the transmission of $\mathcal{R}$). By section 8 the extractor and sampler run in time polynomial in n and space $\ell^{O(1)} + O(n)$. Protocol 4M-IH runs in time and space polynomial in $m = 10\ell \log n$. Thus, both parties run in time polynomial in n. Both parties require space n to store $\mathcal{R}_A$ and $\mathcal{R}_B$ and space $m^{O(1)}$ to play 4M-IH. Alice's set A is chosen by a sampler with $\log L_A = O(\ell)$, thus it can be stored in space $O(\ell)$. Overall, Alice's space is bounded by $O(n) + poly(\ell)$. Bob's set B is a random set, and thus takes $O(n \log n)$ bits to store. We conclude that both players can run their strategies in space $O(n \log n) + poly(\ell)$ which is bounded by $O(n)$ for sufficiently small α as required. The protocol passes secrets of length m_E where $m_E = \Omega(\ell)$. Finally, the longest message sent in the protocol is the description of the permutation π in the interactive which is of length at most $\ell^{O(1)}$. $\blacksquare$

8   Choosing the Ingredients

We now turn to choose the ingredients for BS-OT to get the parameters guaranteed in Theorem 6.1. Given n, N, u, ν, we shoot for $\epsilon = 2^{-\Omega(\ell)}$. We need to show an extractor and sampler that satisfy the conditions specified in figure 5.

The extractor. In [RRV99] it was shown how to construct a (k_E, ϵ_E)-strong extractor, $Ext : \{0,1\}^\ell \times \{0,1\}^{d_E} \to \{0,1\}^u$, for every k_E, $u = k_E - 2\log(1/\epsilon_E) - O(1)$ and $d_E = c\log(1/\epsilon_E)$ for some constant c as long as $\log(1/\epsilon) > \log^4 \ell$.

Setting $k_E = \delta'_A \ell/6$, we can get $u = \delta'_A \ell/12$ for $d_E \le \delta'_A \ell/6$ and $\epsilon_E = 2^{-c'\delta'_A \ell}$ for some constant $c' > 0$ (which depends on c). This choice satisfies the requirements in figure 5. We note that the above extractor can be computed in time and space polynomial in ℓ.

The sampler. In [Vad03] it was shown how to construct a (μ, θ, γ)-averaging sampler Samp : $[L] \to [v]^t$ with distinct samples for every $\mu > \theta > 0$ and $\gamma > 0$ as long as $t \ge \Omega(\log(1/\gamma)/\theta^2)$. This sampler has $\log L \le \log(v/t) + \log(1/\gamma)(1/\theta)^{O(1)}$. By Lemma 3.9, for every δ, γ such that $\log(1/\gamma)/\delta^4 \le n$ this sampler yields a $(\delta, \delta/2, (\gamma + 2^{-\Omega(\delta n)})^{1/2}, (\gamma + 2^{-\Omega(\delta n)})^{1/2})$-min-entropy sampler $Samp_A : [L_A] \to [N]^n$. Setting $\gamma = 2^{-\ell}$ we have that as long as $n \ge \ell/\delta^4$ this sampler has $\phi = \epsilon = 2^{-\Omega(\delta \ell))}$, and $\log L_A \le \log n + \ell(1/\delta)^{O(1)}$.

Note that the condition $n \ge \ell/\delta^4$ is satisfied when ν is a constant (as in this case $\delta = \delta_A$ is also a constant).[14] We also note that the above sampler can be computed in time polynomial in n and space $O(n)$.

The interactive hashing protocol. We need to show that protocol 4M-IH satisfies the requirements of figure 5. It is required there that 4M-IH is $(s, 2^{-\Omega(\delta'_A \ell/\log \delta'_A)})$-secure for $s \le m - c_{IH}\delta'_A \ell/\log \delta'_A + 1$ where $c_{IH} > 0$ is some constant and $\delta'_A = \alpha(1 - \nu)$ for some $\alpha > 0$. By Theorem 5.7, we have that

$$\rho \le 2^{-(m-s+\log m)} \le 2^{-c_{IH}\delta'_A \ell/\log \delta'_A + O(\log m)} \le 2^{-\Omega(\delta'_A \ell/\log \delta'_A)}$$

as $m = 10\ell \log n$ and $\ell \ge \log n$. When ν is a constant, δ'_A is also a constant and we have that $\rho = 2^{-\Omega(\ell)}$ as required. We note that Protocol 4M-IH requires requires time and space polynomial in ℓ.

---

[14] We remark that we don't have to require that ν is a constant. Our protocol also works for $\nu = 1 - o(1)$ as long as the condition above ($n \ge \ell/\delta^4$) is satisfied.

9 Overview of Proof of Security for Alice

Theorem 7.3 regarding Alice's security is somewhat technical and involves many parameters. Due to lack of space, we will only give a sketch of the proof while ignoring the precise parameters.

Fix some bounded storage strategy B^* with storage bound νN for some $\nu < 1$, and an input c. We need to show that there exists a random variable C determined in the setup stage such that for every two pairs of secrets s, s' which are C-consistent the view of B^* is distributed roughly the same way no matter whether Alice's input is s or s'.

Recall that in the protocol, the secrets s_0, s_1 are only involved in the transfer stage where $z_i = Ext(X_i, Y_i) \oplus s_i$ for $i \in \{0, 1\}$. Our goal is to show that there exists a random variable I determined in the setup stage such that for every choice of secrets s_0, s_1, the string Z_I is close to uniformly distributed from B^*'s point of view. More precisely, for every $i \in \{0, 1\}$ we split Alice's messages into Z_i and all the rest of the messages which we denote by MSG_i. For every fixing of r of $\mathcal{R}$ and msg_i of MSG_i, B^*'s point of view on Z_i is captured by considering the distribution $Z_i' = (Z_i | g^*(\mathcal{R}) = g^*(r), MSG_i = msg_i)$. We show that for most fixings r and msg_I, the random variable Z_I' is close to uniformly distributed.

We now explain how we achieve this goal. It is instructive to first consider a simplified scenario in which B^* chooses to remember the content of $\mathcal{R}$ at νN indices. We call these indices "bad" indices, and the remaining $(1 - \nu)N$ indices "good" indices. Let $\delta = (1 - \nu)$. The proof proceeds as follows:

1. We note that B^* does not remember the δN good indices.
2. When Alice uses a sampler to choose A, with high probability she hits a large fraction (say $\delta n / 2$) of the good indices.
3. We have that the set A contains many good indices. If we were to choose a random subset of A with ℓ indices, then with high probability we will hit many (say $\delta \ell / 4$) good indices. Let S be the set of all such subsets which hit less indices. By the above argument S is a small set.
4. It follows that when Alice and Bob use interactive hashing to determine the subsets C_0 and C_1, at least one of the subsets is not in S. We define the random variable I to point to this subset. It follows that C_I contains many good indices.
5. We now consider $X_I = \mathcal{R}_{C_I}$ given MSG_I. As it contains many good indices, it has high min-entropy. It follows that with high probability over the choice of Y_I, $E(X_I, Y_I)$ is close to uniformly distributed even given MSG_I. Thus, Z_I is close to uniformly distributed as required.

We now sketch how to make this argument work when B^* is allowed to remember an arbitrary function $g^* : \{0, 1\}^N \to \{0, 1\}^{\nu N}$ of $\mathcal{R}$. Intuitively, the notion of "min-entropy" replaces that of "good bits" in this case.

1. It is easy to see that for most fixings r of $\mathcal{R}$, the random variable $(\mathcal{R} | g^*(\mathcal{R}) = g^*(r))$ has high min-entropy (say $\Omega(\delta N)$).
2. When Alice uses a min-entropy sampler for most fixings p of P she obtains a set A such that $(\mathcal{R}_A | g^*(\mathcal{R}) = g^*(r), P = p)$ has high min-entropy.

3. Choosing a random subset is a min-entropy sampler, and thus for most choices of a subset of C of size ℓ, $(\mathcal{R}_C|g^*(\mathcal{R}) = g^*(r), P = p)$ has high min-entropy.
4. As before it follows that following the interactive hashing with high probability there exists an I such that $(\mathcal{R}_{C_I}|g^*(\mathcal{R}) = g^*(r), P = p)$ has high min-entropy.
5. Here we have to be a little more careful than before. It is no longer the case that $\mathcal{R}_{C_0}$ and $\mathcal{R}_{C_1}$ are independent given the conditioning. Thus, it may be the case that Z_{1-I} gives information about $\mathcal{R}_{C_I}$. However, we set the parameters so that $\mathcal{R}_{C_I}$ has min-entropy much larger than the length of the pair (Z_{1-I}, Y_{1-I}). As a consequence we can argue that for most fixings z_{1-I} and y_{1-I}, $(\mathcal{R}_{C_I}|g^*(\mathcal{R}) = g^*(r), P = p, Z_{1-I} = z_{1-I}, Y_{1-I} = y_{1-I})$ has high min-entropy. Thus, running an extractor, with high probability over Y_I we obtain a distribution which is close to uniform given MSG_I just as before.

10   Conclusions and Open Problems

We have shown a 5-message protocol for oblivious transfer in the bounded storage model. As mentioned before, this protocol has some additional concrete improvements over previous work [CCM98,Din01].

Our protocol achieves k very close to $\sqrt{K} \approx \sqrt{N}$. In words, the space of the honest parties is about a square root of the space allowed for the malicious parties. It is not clear whether there exist protocols that allow $k = N^\delta$ for every constant $\delta > 0$. We remark that to achieve $\delta < 2$ it is required to break the "birthday paradox barrier". A typical first step of a bounded storage protocol instructs both parties to store random subsets of the $\mathcal{R}$. When $k << \sqrt{N}$ these sets are not likely to overlap. It seems that breaking this barrier requires introducing some new ideas. We mention that to the best of our knowledge, this barrier is also present in protocols for Key-Agreement in the bounded storage model [Mau93,CM97].

We give a new constant round protocol for interactive hashing. This protocol can replace the NOVY-protocol of [NOVY98] in our setting. A similar phenomena was observed also in the context of Zero-Knowledge. Damgård [Dam93] used the NOVY-protocol to give certain transformations of "honest verifier" Zero-Knowledge protocols into general Zero-Knowledge protocols. Later works [DGOW95, GSV98] replaced the NOVY-protocol with a constant round protocol. This raises the question whether the NOVY-protocol can be replaced by a constant round protocol for the application in [NOVY98]. That is, for constructing perfectly hiding bit commitment schemes from arbitrary one-way permutations. We remark that constant round perfectly hiding bit commitment schemes are known only using seemingly stronger assumptions [NY89,DPP93,GK96].

The NOVY-protocol achieves a stronger security for interactive hashing than the one defined here. This stronger security allows its use in the application of [NOVY98]. Loosely speaking, it is shown in [NOVY98] that their protocol is secure in the following sense: For every polynomial time malicious strategy B^* for Bob there is a polynomial time "simulator" $A_{B^*}(W')$ such that for most

$W' \in \{0,1\}^m$, the simulator can run B^* playing Alice's role and generate random transcripts in which one of the outputs is W'. (Intuitively, this is a stronger and *computational* form of the intuition that Bob does not "control" the two outputs.) Obtaining this property with fewer rounds seems hard. A very related open problem was raised in [DGW95] in the context of Zero-Knowledge.

Acknowledgements. We thank Yuval Ishai for bringing [CCM98] to our attention and Oded Goldreich for helpful discussions and for pointing out some relevant work. We are also grateful to Moni Naor for insights on the NOVY protocol. Thanks also to Claude Crépeau, Salil Vadhan and the reviewers for their helpful remarks.

References

[ADR02]   Y. Aumann, Y.Z. Ding, and M. O. Rabin. Everlasting security in the bounded storage model. *IEEE Transactions on Information Theory*, 48, 2002.

[AR99]   Y. Aumann and M. O. Rabin. Information theoretically secure communication in the limited storage space model. In *Advances in Crypology - CRYPTO '99*, volume 1666, pages 65–79, 1999.

[BBCS92]   C.H. Bennett, G. Brassard, C. Crépeau, and M.H. Skubiszewska. Practical quantum oblivious transfer protocols. In *Advances in Cryptology - CRYPTO '91, Lecture Notes in Computer Science*, volume 576, pages 351–366. Springer, 1992.

[BM89]   M. Bellare and S. Micali. Non-interactive oblivious transfer and applications. In *Advances in Cryptology - CRYPTO '89, Lecture Notes in Computer Science*, volume 435, pages 547–557. Springer, 1989.

[BR94]   M. Bellare and J. Rompel. Randomnessefficient oblivious sampling. In *35th IEEE Symposium on Foundations of Computer Science*, pages 276–287, 1994.

[CCM98]   C. Cachin, C. Crépeau, and J. Marcil. Oblivious transfer with a memorybound receiver. In *39th IEEE Symposium on Foundations of Computer Science*, pages 493–502, 1998.

[CK88]   C. Crépeau and J. Kilian. Achieving oblivious transfer using weakened security assumptions. In *29th IEEE Symposium on Foundations of Computer Science*, pages 42–52, 1988.

[CM97]   C. Cachin and U. Maurer. Unconditional security against memory-bound adversaries. In *Advances in Cryptology - CRYPTO '97*, pages 292–306, 1997.

[Cov73]   T.M. Cover. Enumerative source encoding. *IEEE Transaction on Information Theory*, 19(1):73–77, 1973.

[Cre87]   C. Crépeau. Equivalence between two avours of oblivious transfers. In *Advances in Cryptology - CRYPTO '87, Lecture Notes in Computer Science*, volume 293, pages 350–354. Springer-Verlag, 1987.

[Dam93]   I. Damgård. Interactive hashing can simplify zero-knowledge protocol design without computational assumptions. In *Advances in Cryptology - CRYPTO '93, Lecture Notes in Computer Science*, volume 773, pages 100–109. Springer, 1993.

[DGOW95] I. Damgård, O. Goldreich, T. Okamoto, and A. Wigderson. Honest verifier vs dishonest verifier in public cain zero-knowledge proofs. In *Advances
in Cryptology - CRYPTO '95, Lecture Notes in Computer Science*, volume
963, pages 325–338. Springer, 1995.

[DGW95]   I. Damgård, O. Goldreich, and A. Wigderson. Information theory versus
complexity theory: Another test case, 1995.

[Din01]   Y.Z. Ding. Oblivious transfer in the bounded storage model. In *Advances
in Cryptology - CRYPTO '01, Lecture Notes in Computer Science*, volume
2139, pages 155–170, Springer, 2001.

[DM02]   S. Dziembowski and U. Maurer. Tight security proofs for the boundedsto-
rage model. In *34th ACM Symposium on the Theory of Computing*, pages
341–350, 2002.

[DPP93]   I. Damgård, T. Pedersen, and B. Pfitzmann. On the existence of statistically hiding bit commitment schemes and fail-stop signatures. In *Advances
in Cryptology - CRYPTO '93, Lecture Notes in Computer Science*, volume
773, pages 250–265. Springer, 1993.

[DR02]   Y.Z. Ding and M.O. Rabin. Hyper-encryption and everlasting security. In
Annual Symposium on Theoretical Aspects of Computer Science (STACS),
pages 1–26, 2002.

[EGL85]   S. Even, O. Goldreich, and A. Lempel. A randomized protocol for signing
contracts. *Communications of the ACM*, 28(6):637–647, 1985.

[GK96]   O. Goldreich and A. Kahan. How to construct constant-round zeroknow-
ledge proof systems for np. *Journal of Cryptology*, 9(2):167–189, 1996.

[GKM+00] Y. Gertner, S. Kannan, T. Malkin, O. Reingold, and M. Viswanathan. The
relationship between public key encryption and oblivious transfer. In *41st
IEEE Symposium on Foundations of Computer Science*, pages 325–335,
2000.

[GMW87]   O. Goldreich, S. Micali, and A. Wigderson. How to play any mental game
- a completeness theorem for protocols with honest majority. In *19th ACM
Symposium on the Theory of Computing*, pages 218–229, 1987.

[Gol97]   O. Goldreich. A sample of samplers - a computational perspective on
sampling (survey). In *Electronic Colloquium on Computational Complexity (ECCC)(20)*, volume 4, 1997.

[Gol03]   O. Goldreich. Foundations of cryptography - volume 2. Working Draft,
available at www.wisdom.weizmann.ac.il/oded/foc-vol2.html, 2003.

[Gow96]   W.T. Gowers. An almost m-wise independent random permutation of the
cube. *Combinatorics, Probability and Computing*, 5:119–130, 1996.

[GSV98]   O. Goldreich, A. Sahai, and S. Vadhan. Honest-verifier statistical zerokno-
wledge equals general statistical zero-knowledge. In *30th ACM Symposium
on the Theory of Computing*, pages 399–408, 1998.

[HCR02]   Dowon Hong, Ku-Young Chang, and Heuisu Ryu. Efficient oblivious transfer in the bounded-storage model. In *Advances in Cryptology. ASIACRYPT
'02, Lecture Notes in Computer Science*, pages 143–159. Springer-Verlag,
December 2002.

[IR89]   R. Impagliazzo and S. Rudich. Limits on the provable consequences of one-
way permutations. In *21st ACM Symposium on the Theory of Computing*,
pages 44–61, 1989.

[Kil88]   J. Kilian. Founding cryptography on oblivious transfer. In *20th ACM Symposium on the Theory of Computing*, pages 20–31, 1988.

[Lu02]   C. Lu. Hyper-encryption against space-bounded adversaries from on-line strong extractors. In *Advances in Cryptology - CRYPTO '02*, volume 2442, pages 257–271. Springer, 2002.

[Mau92]   U. Maurer. Conditionally-perfect secrecy and a provably-secure randomized cipher. *Journal of Cryptology*, 5(1):53–66, 1992.

[Mau93]   U. Maurer. Secret key agreement by public discussion. *IEEE Transaction on Information Theory*, 39(3):733–742, 1993.

[Nis96]   N. Nisan. Extracting randomness: How and why, a survey. *IEEE Conference on Computational Complexity*, pages 44–58, 1996.

[NOVY98]   M. Naor, R. Ostrovsky, R. Venkatesan, and M. Yung. Perfect zero-knowledge arguments for np using any one-way permutation. *Journal of Cryptology*, 11(2):87–108, 1998. preliminary version in CRYPTO 92.

[NP01]   M. Naor and B. Pinkas. Efficient oblivious transfer protocols. *In SIAM Symposium on Discrete Algorithms (SODA 2001)*, pages 448–457, 2001.

[NR99]   M. Naor and O. Reingold. On the construction of pseudorandom permutations: Luby-rackoff revisited. *Journal of Cryptology*, 12(1):29–66, 1999.

[NY89]   M. Naor and M. Yung. Universal one-way hash functions and their cryptographic applications. In *21st ACM Symposium on the Theory of Computing*, pages 33–43, 1989.

[NZ96]   N. Nisan and D. Zuckerman. Randomness is linear in space. *JCSS*, 52(1):43–52, 1996.

[Rab81]   M.O. Rabin. How to exchange secrets by oblivious transfer. TR-81, Harvard, 1981.

[RRV99]   R. Raz, O. Reingold, and S. Vadhan. Error reduction for extractor. In *40th IEEE Symposium on Foundations of Computer Science*, pages 191–201, 1999.

[RSW00]   O. Reingold, R. Shaltiel, and A. Wigderson. Extracting randomness via repeated condensing. In *41st IEEE Symposium on Foundations of Computer Science*, pages 22–31, 2000.

[Sha02]   R. Shaltiel. Recent developments in explicit constructions of extractors. *Bulletin of the EATCS*, 77:67–95, 2002.

[Vad03]   S.P. Vadhan. On constructing locally computable extractors and cryptosystems in the bounded storage model. In *Advances in Cryptology - CRYPTO '03*. Springer, 2003.

[Yao86]   A.C. Yao. How to generate and exchange secrets. In *27th IEEE Symposium on Foundations of Computer Science*, pages 162–167, 1986.

Hierarchical Threshold Secret Sharing

Tamir Tassa

Division of Computer Science,
The Open University, Tel Aviv, Israel
and
Department of Computer Science,
Ben Gurion University, Beer Sheva, Israel
tamir_tassa@yahoo.com

Abstract. We consider the problem of threshold secret sharing in groups with hierarchical structure. In such settings, the secret is shared among a group of participants that is partitioned into levels. The access structure is then determined by a sequence of threshold requirements: a subset of participants is authorized if it has at least k_0 members from the highest level, as well as at least $k_1 > k_0$ members from the two highest levels and so forth. Such problems may occur in settings where the participants differ in their authority or level of confidence and the presence of higher level participants is imperative to allow the recovery of the common secret. Even though secret sharing in hierarchical groups has been studied extensively in the past, none of the existing solutions addresses the simple setting where, say, a bank transfer should be signed by three employees, at least one of whom *must* be a department manager. We present a perfect secret sharing scheme for this problem that, unlike most secret sharing schemes that are suitable for hierarchical structures, is ideal. As in Shamir's scheme, the secret is represented as the free co-efficient of some polynomial. The novelty of our scheme is the usage of polynomial derivatives in order to generate lesser shares for participants of lower levels. Consequently, our scheme uses Birkhoff interpolation, i.e., the construction of a polynomial according to an unstructured set of point and derivative values. A substantial part of our discussion is dedicated to the question of how to assign identities to the participants from the underlying finite field so that the resulting Birkhoff interpolation problem will be well posed. In the course of this discussion, we borrow some results from the theory of Birkhoff interpolation over $\mathbb{R}$ and import them to the context of finite fields.

1 Introduction

A (k, n)-threshold secret sharing is a method of sharing a secret among a given set of n participants, $\mathcal{U}$, such that every k of those participants ($k \leq n$) could recover the secret by pooling their shares together, while no subset of less than k participants can do so [4,15]. Generalized secret sharing refers to situations where the collection of permissible subsets of $\mathcal{U}$ is any collection $\Gamma \subset 2^{\mathcal{U}}$. Given such a collection, the corresponding generalized secret sharing is a method of

M. Naor (Ed.): TCC 2004, LNCS 2951, pp. 473–490, 2004.
© Springer-Verlag Berlin Heidelberg 2004

sharing a secret among the participants of $\mathcal{U}$ such that only subsets in Γ (that is referred to as *the access structure*) may recover the secret, while all other subsets cannot; this makes sense, of-course, only if the access structure is monotone in the sense that if $B \in \Gamma$ then any superset of B also belongs to Γ.

There are many real-life examples of threshold secret sharing. Typical examples include sharing a key to the central vault in a bank, the triggering mechanism for nuclear weapons, or key escrow. We would like to consider here a special kind of generalized secret sharing scenarios that is a natural extension of threshold secret sharing. In all of the above mentioned examples, it is natural to expect that the participants are not equal in their privileges or authorities. For example, in the bank scenario, the shares of the vault key may be distributed among bank employees, some of whom are tellers and some are department managers. The bank policy could require the presence of, say, 3 employees in opening the vault, but at least one of them must be a department manager. Or in key escrow, the dealer might demand that some escrow agents (say, family members) must be involved in any emergency access to his private files. Such settings call for special methods of secret sharing. To this end, we define hierarchical secret sharing as follows:

Definition 1. *Let $\mathcal{U}$ be a set of n participants and assume that $\mathcal{U}$ is composed of levels, i.e., $\mathcal{U} = \bigcup_{i=0}^{m} \mathcal{U}_i$ where $\mathcal{U}_i \cap \mathcal{U}_j = \emptyset$ for all $0 \leq i < j \leq m$. Let $\mathbf{k} = \{k_i\}_{i=0}^{m}$ be a monotonically increasing sequence of integers, $0 < k_0 < \cdots < k_m$. Then the $(\mathbf{k}, n)$–hierarchical threshold secret sharing problem is the problem of assigning each participant $u \in \mathcal{U}$ a share of a given secret S such that the access structure is*

$$\Gamma = \left\{ \mathcal{V} \subset \mathcal{U} : \left| \mathcal{V} \cap \left(\cup_{j=0}^{i} \mathcal{U}_j \right) \right| \geq k_i \quad \forall i \in \{0, 1, \ldots, m\} \right\} . \tag{1}$$

In other words, if $\sigma(u)$ stands for the share assigned to $u \in \mathcal{U}$, and for any $\mathcal{V} \subset \mathcal{U}$, $\sigma(\mathcal{V}) = \{\sigma(u) : u \in \mathcal{V}\}$, then

$$H(S|\sigma(\mathcal{V})) = 0 \quad \forall \mathcal{V} \in \Gamma \qquad \text{(accessibility)} \tag{2}$$

while

$$H(S|\sigma(\mathcal{V})) = H(S) \quad \forall \mathcal{V} \notin \Gamma \qquad \text{(perfect security)} . \tag{3}$$

The zero conditional entropy equality (2) should be understood in a constructive sense. Namely, if it holds then $\mathcal{V}$ may compute S.

There are few methods of solving this problem. The simplest way [18] is to generate m random and independent secrets S_i, $1 \leq i \leq m$, of the same size as S and define $S_0 = S \oplus S_1 \oplus \cdots \oplus S_m$. Then, for every $0 \leq i \leq m$, the secret S_i is distributed among all participants of $\cup_{j=0}^{i} \mathcal{U}_j$ using a $(k_i, \sum_{j=0}^{i} |\mathcal{U}_j|)$ threshold secret sharing scheme. The secret S may be recovered only if all S_i, $0 \leq i \leq m$, are recovered. As the recovery of S_i requires the presence of at least k_i participants from $\cup_{j=0}^{i} \mathcal{U}_j$, the access requirements are met by this solution. This scheme is perfect since if $\mathcal{V} \notin \Gamma$, it fails to satisfy at least one of the threshold conditions in (1) and, consequently, it is unable to learn a thing about the corresponding share S_i; such a deficiency implies (3). However, its information rate is $1/(m+1)$ since all members of $\mathcal{U}_0$ are assigned $m+1$ shares.

Another method is the monotone circuit construction due to Benaloh and Leichter [2]. Assume a monotone access structure Γ over a set of n participants. Let $C(x_1, \ldots, x_n)$ be a monotone circuit that recognizes the access structure (namely, $C(x_1, \ldots, x_n) = 1$ if and only if the subset of the variables that have a 1 value belongs to Γ). They then show how to build a perfect secret sharing scheme from the description of that circuit. However, for threshold access structures the resulting schemes are far from being ideal. Even for the simplest threshold problem of only one level (i.e., all participants are equal), an optimal circuit is of size $O(n \log n)$ [9], which implies an information rate of $O(1/\log n)$ for the corresponding secret sharing scheme.

Another construction is due to Brickell [5]. The main observation in his construction is the following: let $\mathbb{F}$ be a finite field such that $S \in \mathbb{F}$ and let $\mathbb{F}^d$ be the d-dimensional vector space over that field. Assume that there exists a function $\phi : \mathcal{U} \to \mathbb{F}^d$ with the property

$$(1, 0, \ldots, 0) \in \text{Span}\{\phi(u) : u \in \mathcal{V}\} \Leftrightarrow \mathcal{V} \in \Gamma . \tag{4}$$

Then the dealer selects random and independent values $a_i \in \mathbb{F}$, $2 \leq i \leq d$, and then

$$\sigma(u) = \phi(u) \cdot \mathbf{a} \quad \text{where} \quad \mathbf{a} = (S, a_2, \ldots, a_d) . \tag{5}$$

This is indeed a perfect secret sharing scheme, (2)+(3), and, as opposed to the previous construction of Benaloh and Leichter, it is ideal since every participant receives a share that is of the same size as the secret. Alas, finding a mapping ϕ that satisfies condition (4) is not simple. Given a specific access structure, it is usually a matter of trial and error until such ϕ is found.

In this paper, we present a simple solution for the hierarchical secret sharing problem that is both perfect and ideal. Our construction is, in fact, a realization of the general vector space construction of Brickell for the case of hierarchical threshold secret sharing. Our idea is based on *Birkhoff interpolation* (also known as *Hermite-Birkhoff* or *lacunary interpolation*). The basic threshold secret sharing of Shamir [15] was based upon Lagrange interpolation, namely, the construction of a polynomial of degree less than or equal to k from its values in $k + 1$ distinct points. There are two other types of interpolation that are encountered in numerical analysis. In such problems, one is given data of the form

$$\frac{d^j P}{dx^j}(x_i) := P^{(j)}(x_i) = c_{i,j} \qquad (k+1 \text{ equations}) \tag{6}$$

and seeks a polynomial of degree less than or equal to k that agrees with the given data (6). If for each i (namely, at each interpolation point) the sequence of the derivative orders j that are given by (6) is an unbroken sequence that starts at zero, $j = 0, \ldots, j_i$, then the problem falls under the framework of *Hermite interpolation*. In that case, the problem always admits a unique solution $P \in \mathbb{R}_k[x]$. The more general case is when the data is lacunary in the sense that, at some sample points, the sequence of orders of derivatives is either broken or does not start from $j = 0$. This case is referred to as *Birkhoff interpolation* and it differs radically from the more standard Hermite or Lagrange interpolation. In particular, Birkhoff interpolation problems may be ill posed in the sense that a solution may not exist or may not be unique.

In our method, like in Shamir's, the secret is the free coefficient of some polynomial $P(x) \in \mathbb{F}_{k-1}[x]$, where $\mathbb{F}$ is a large finite field and $k = k_m$ is the maximal threshold, i.e., the total number of participants that need to collaborate in order to reconstruct the secret. Each participant $u \in \mathcal{U}$ is given an identity in the field, denoted also u, and a share that equals $P^{(j)}(u)$ for some derivative order j that depends on the position of u in the hierarchy. The idea is that the more important participants (namely, participants who belong to levels with lower index) will get shares with lower derivative orders, since lower derivatives carry more information than higher derivatives. By choosing the derivative orders properly, this allocation of shares dictates the threshold access requirements (1). As a consequence, when an authorized subset collaborates and attempts to recover the secret, they need to solve a Birkhoff interpolation problem. Hence, a great part of our analysis is devoted to the question of how to assign participants with identities in the field so that the Birkhoff interpolation problems that are associated with the authorized subsets would be well posed.

Organization of the paper. In Section 2 we review the basic terminology and results from the theory of Birkhoff interpolation [12]. We present those results in the context of the reals, $\mathbb{R}$, which is the natural context in numerical analysis. However, as $\mathbb{R}$ is not the field of choice in cryptography, one should be very careful when borrowing results from such a theory and migrating them to the context of finite fields. The algebraic statements usually travel well and survive the migration; the analytic ones, however, might not. Part of our analysis later on will be dedicated to those issues. Section 3 is devoted to our scheme. After presenting the scheme, we discuss in Section 3.1 conditions for accessibility, (2), and perfect security, (3). Then, we proceed to examine strategies for allocating participant identities in the underlying finite field so that accessibility and perfect security are achieved. In Section 3.2 we consider the strategy of random allocation of participant identities and prove that such a strategy guarantees that both (2) and (3) hold with almost certainty. In Section 3.3 we consider a simple monotone allocation of participant identities. Borrowing an interesting result from the theory of Birkhoff interpolation, we prove that such an allocation is guaranteed to provide both accessibility and perfect security, (2)+(3), provided that the prime order of the field is sufficiently large with respect to n (number of participants) and k_m (minimal number of participants in an authorized subset), Theorem 4.

Related work. The problem of secret sharing in hierarchical (or *multilevel*) structures, was studied before under different assumptions, e.g. [3,5,6,7,16,17]. Already Shamir, in his seminal work [15], has recognized that in some settings it would be desired to grant different capabilities to different participants according to their level of authority. He suggested to accomplish that by giving the participants of the more capable levels a greater number of shares. More precisely, if $\mathcal{U}$ has an hierarchical structure as in Definition 1, the participants in $\mathcal{U}_i$, $0 \le i \le m$, get w_i shares of the form $(u, P(u))$, $u \in \mathbb{F}$, where $w_0 > w_1 > \cdots > w_m$. This way, the number of participants from a higher level that would be required in order to reconstruct the secret would be smaller than the number of participants from a lower level that would need to cooperate towards that end.

Simmons [16], and later Brickell [5], considered a similar, yet slightly more rigid setting. Assume a scenario where an electronic fund transfer (up to some maximum amount) may be authorized by any two vice presidents of a bank, or, alternatively, by any three senior tellers. A natural requirement in such a scenario is that also a mixed group of one vice president and two senior tellers could recover the private key that is necessary to sign and authorize such a transfer. Motivated by this example, Simmons studied a general hierarchical threshold secret sharing problem that agrees with the problem in Definition 1 with one difference: while we require in (1) a *conjunction* of threshold conditions, Simmons studied the problem with a *disjunction* of the threshold conditions. Namely, in his version of the problem,

$$\Gamma = \left\{ \mathcal{V} \subset \mathcal{U} : \exists i \in \{0, 1, \ldots, m\} \text{ for which } \left| \mathcal{V} \cap \left(\cup_{j=0}^{i} \mathcal{U}_j \right) \right| \geq k_i \right\} . \quad (7)$$

His solution to that version is based on a geometric construction that was presented by Blakley [4]. Assume that the secret S is d-dimensional (typically $d = 1$; however, Simmon's construction may easily deal with the simultaneous sharing of $d > 1$ secrets as well). Then the construction is embedded in $\mathbb{F}^r$, where $\mathbb{F}$ is a large finite field and $r = k_m + d - 1$. Simmons suggests to construct a chain of affine subspaces $\mathcal{W}_0 \subset \mathcal{W}_1 \subset \cdots \subset \mathcal{W}_m$ of dimensions $k_i - 1$, $0 \leq i \leq m$, together with a publicly known affine subspace $\mathcal{W}_S$ of dimension d, with the property that $\mathcal{W}_i \cap \mathcal{W}_S = \{S\}$ for all $0 \leq i \leq m$ (i.e., each $\mathcal{W}_i$ intersects $\mathcal{W}_S$ in a single point whose d coordinates in $\mathcal{W}_S$ are the d components of the secret S). Then, each participant from level $\mathcal{U}_i$ gets a point in $\mathcal{W}_i \setminus \mathcal{W}_{i-1}$, $0 \leq i \leq m$ ($\mathcal{W}_{-1} = \emptyset$), such that every k_i points from $\cup_{j=0}^{i} \mathcal{U}_j$ span the entire subspace $\mathcal{W}_i$. Hence, if a subset of participants $\mathcal{V}$ satisfies at least *one* of the threshold conditions, say, $\left| \mathcal{V} \cap \left(\cup_{j=0}^{i} \mathcal{U}_j \right) \right| \geq k_i$ for some i, $0 \leq i \leq m$, then the corresponding $\mathcal{W}_i$ may be constructed and intersected with $\mathcal{W}_S$ to yield the secret S.

Shamir's version of the hierarchical setting is slightly more relaxed than Simmons'. In the former, the number of participants that are required for recovery is determined by a *weighted average* of the thresholds that are associated with each of the levels that are represented in the subset of participants. In the latter, the necessary number of participants is the *highest* of the thresholds that are associated with the levels that are represented. However, it is natural to expect that more rigid conditions will be imposed in some scenarios. Namely, even though higher level (i.e., important) participants could be replaced by lower level ones, a minimal number of higher level participants would still need to be involved in any recovery of the secret. For example, the common practice of authorizing electronic fund transfers does call for the presence of at least one vice president or manager department. The above described solutions of Shamir and Simmons are incapable of imposing such restrictions since they allow the recovery of the secret for any subset of lower-level participants that is sufficiently large. This difference in the definition of the problem is manifested by the replacement of the existential quantifier $\exists$ in (7) with the universal quantifier $\forall$ in (1).

We note that none of the above mentioned explicit secret sharing schemes that are suitable for hierarchical structures (i.e., the first solution of splitting the secret to $m+1$ sub-secrets, Benaloh and Leichter's monotone circuit construction, Shamir's scheme and Simmons' scheme) is ideal. The scheme introduced herein is.

Padró and Sáez [13] studied the information rate of secret sharing schemes with a bipartite access structure. A bipartite access structure is one in which there are two levels of participants, $\mathcal{U} = \mathcal{U}_0 \cup \mathcal{U}_1$, and all participants in the same level play an equivalent role in the structure. They showed that the ideal bipartite access structures are exactly those that are vector space access structures, namely, are consistent with Brickell's construction [5]. Furthermore, they showed that all such ideal access structures are quasi-threshold in the sense that a subset $\mathcal{V} \subset \mathcal{U}$ is authorized if $|\mathcal{V}|$, $|\mathcal{V} \cap \mathcal{U}_0|$ and $|\mathcal{V} \cap \mathcal{U}_1|$ satisfy some threshold conditions [13, Theorem 5]. They characterized four types of quasi-threshold access structures, denoted Ω_i, $1 \leq i \leq 4$. It may be shown that when there are two levels, i.e., $m = 1$, our *conjunctive* problem, (1), is consistent with type Ω_2 or Ω_3, while Simmons' *disjunctive* problem, (7), agrees with Ω_1. What we show in this paper is that in the multi-partite case, the conjunctive threshold access structures are vector access structures and that Birkhoff interpolation yields an explicit construction.

2 Birkhoff Interpolation

Let $X = \{x_1, \ldots, x_k\}$ be a given set of points in $\mathbb{R}$, where $x_1 < x_2 < \cdots < x_k$, $E = (e_{i,j})_{i=1 \ j=0}^{k \ \ell}$ be a matrix with binary entries, $I(E) = \{(i,j) : e_{i,j} = 1\}$, $d = |I(E)|$, and $C = \{c_{i,j} : (i,j) \in I(E)\}$ be a set of d real values (we assume hereinafter that the right-most column in E is nonzero). Then the Birkhoff interpolation problem that corresponds to the triplet $\langle X, E, C \rangle$ is the problem of finding a polynomial $P(x) \in \mathbb{R}_{d-1}[x]$ that satisfies the d equalities

$$P^{(j)}(x_i) = c_{i,j} \quad , \quad (i,j) \in I(E) . \tag{8}$$

The matrix E is called the *interpolation matrix*.

Unlike Lagrange or Hermite interpolation that are unconditionally well-posed, the Birkhoff interpolation problem may not admit a unique solution. The pair $\langle X, E \rangle$ is called *regular* if the system (8) has a unique solution for any choice of C, and *singular* otherwise. The matrix E is called *regular* or *poised* if $\langle X, E \rangle$ is regular for all $X = \{x_1 < x_2 < \cdots < x_k\} \subset \mathbb{R}$.

The following lemma provides a simple necessary condition that E must satisfy, lest $\langle X, E \rangle$ would be singular for *all* X [14].

Lemma 1. *(Pólya's condition) A necessary condition that the interpolation matrix E must satisfy in order for the corresponding Birkhoff interpolation problem to be well posed is that*

$$|\{(i,j) \in I(E) \ : \ j \leq t\}| \geq t+1 \quad , \quad 0 \leq t \leq \ell . \tag{9}$$

Pólya's is a necessary condition. *Sufficient* conditions, on the other hand, are scarce. We continue to describe one such condition that will serve us later on in our application to secret sharing. To this end we define the following.

Definition 2. *A 1-sequence in the interpolation matrix E is a maximal run of consecutive 1s in a row of the matrix E. Namely, a triplet of the form (i, j_0, j_1) where $1 \leq i \leq k$, $0 \leq j_0 \leq j_1 \leq \ell$, such that $e_{i,j} = 1$ for all $j_0 \leq j \leq j_1$ while $e_{i,j_0-1} = e_{i,j_1+1} = 0$ (letting $e_{i,-1} = e_{i,\ell+1} = 0$). A 1-sequence (i, j_0, j_1) is called supported if E has 1s both to the northwest and southwest of the leading entry in the sequence, i.e., there exist $i_{nw} < i$, $i_{sw} > i$ and $j_{nw}, j_{sw} < j_0$ such that $e_{i_{nw},j_{nw}} = e_{i_{sw},j_{sw}} = 1$.*

The following theorem was first proved by K. Atkinson and A. Sharma [1].

Theorem 1. *Assume that $x_1 < x_2 < \cdots < x_k$. Then the interpolation problem (8) has a unique solution if the interpolation matrix E satisfies Pólya's condition and contains no supported 1-sequences of odd length.*

Lemma 1, being algebraic, is not restricted to the reals and applies over any field. Theorem 1, on the other hand, relies upon the existence of *order* in $\mathbb{R}$. Hence, as finite fields are not ordered, Theorem 1 does not apply to them. However, Theorem 1 may be of use over finite fields as well if we impose further restrictions on the set of points in X. This will be dealt with in Section 3.3.

3 An Ideal Hierarchical Secret Sharing Scheme

Consider the hierarchical secret sharing problem $(\mathbf{k}, n)$, $\mathbf{k} = \{k_i\}_{i=0}^{m}$, as defined in Definition 1. Let $\mathbb{F}$ be a finite field of large size, say $\mathbb{F}_q$ where q is a prime number. The size of the field is determined by the size of the secret S (for example, if S is an AES key then q should be at least 128 bits long). Let $k = k_m$ be the overall number of participants that are required for recovery of the secret. Then the dealer selects a random polynomial $P(x) \in \mathbb{F}_{k-1}[x]$, where

$$P(x) = \sum_{i=0}^{k-1} a_i x^i \quad \text{and} \quad a_0 = S , \qquad (10)$$

and then distributes shares to all participants $u \in \mathcal{U}$ in the following manner. First, each participant is identified with a field element, which we also denote by u (i.e., $\mathcal{U}$ may be viewed as a subset of the field $\mathbb{F}$). Then, each participant of the ith level in the hierarchy, $u \in \mathcal{U}_i$, $0 \leq i \leq m$, receives the share $P^{(k_{i-1})}(u)$, i.e., the (k_{i-1})th derivative of $P(x)$ at $x = u$, where $k_{-1} = 0$. This scheme is of-course ideal, as every participant receives a share that is a field element, just like the secret. Note that the Shamir secret sharing scheme [15] is a special case of our scheme since in that case all users belong to the same level (i.e., $\mathcal{U} = \mathcal{U}_0$) and, consequently, there are no derivatives and all users get shares of the form $P(u)$.

3.1   Conditions for Accessibility and Perfect Security

The main questions that arise with regard to the scheme are whether it complies with conditions (2) and (3). Let $\mathcal{V} = \{v_1, \ldots, v_{|\mathcal{V}|}\} \subset \mathcal{U}$ and assume that

$$
\begin{aligned}
&v_1, \ldots, v_{\ell_0} \in \mathcal{U}_0 \\
&v_{\ell_0+1}, \ldots, v_{\ell_1} \in \mathcal{U}_1 \\
&\quad\vdots \\
&v_{\ell_{m-1}+1}, \ldots, v_{\ell_m} \in \mathcal{U}_m
\end{aligned}
\qquad \text{where} \quad 0 \leq \ell_0 \leq \cdots \leq \ell_m = |\mathcal{V}| . \tag{11}
$$

$\mathcal{V}$ is authorized if and only if $\ell_i \geq k_i$ for all $0 \leq i \leq m$. Let $\mathbf{r} : \mathbb{F} \to \mathbb{F}^k$ be defined as $\mathbf{r}(x) = (1, x, x^2, \ldots, x^{k-1})$ and, for all $i \geq 0$, let $\mathbf{r}^{(i)}(x)$ denote the ith derivative of that vector. Using this notation, we observe that the share that is distributed to participants $u \in \mathcal{U}_i$ is $\sigma(u) = \mathbf{r}^{(k_i-1)}(u) \cdot \mathbf{a}$ where $\mathbf{a} = (a_0 = S, a_1, \ldots, a_{k-1})$ is the vector of coefficients of $P(x)$. Hence, when all participants of $\mathcal{V}$, (11), pool together their shares, the system that they need to solve in the unknown vector $\mathbf{a}$ is $M_{\mathcal{V}}\mathbf{a} = \boldsymbol{\sigma}$, where the coefficient matrix is (written by its rows),

$$
M_{\mathcal{V}} = \Big(\mathbf{r}(v_1), \ldots, \mathbf{r}(v_{\ell_0}) \; ; \; \mathbf{r}^{(k_0)}(v_{\ell_0+1}), \ldots, \mathbf{r}^{(k_0)}(v_{\ell_1}) \; ; \; \ldots \; ;
$$

$$
\mathbf{r}^{(k_{m-1})}(v_{\ell_{m-1}+1}), \ldots, \mathbf{r}^{(k_{m-1})}(v_{\ell_m}) \Big) , \tag{12}
$$

while

$$
\boldsymbol{\sigma} = (\sigma(v_1), \sigma(v_2), \ldots, \sigma(v_{\ell_m}))^T .
$$

In view of the discussion in Section 2, the matrix $M_{\mathcal{V}}$ is not always solvable even if $\mathcal{V} \in \Gamma$. Our first observation is as follows.

Proposition 1. *The Birkhoff interpolation problem that needs to be solved by an authorized subset satisfies Pólya's condition (9).*

Next, assume that $0 \in \mathcal{U}$ is a special phantom participant and that it belongs to the highest level $\mathcal{U}_0$. This assumption enables us to answer both questions of accessibility and perfect security by examining the regularity of certain matrices.

Theorem 2. *Assume that $0 \in \mathcal{U}_0$ and that for any minimal authorized subset $\mathcal{V} \in \Gamma$ (namely, $|\mathcal{V}| = k$), the corresponding square matrix $M_{\mathcal{V}}$, (12), is regular, i.e., $\det M_{\mathcal{V}} \neq 0$ in $\mathbb{F}$. Then conditions (2) (accessibility) and (3) (perfect security) hold.*

Proof. Let $\mathcal{V}$ be a "genuine" authorized subset, namely $\mathcal{V} \in \Gamma$ and $0 \notin \mathcal{V}$. If $\mathcal{V}$ is minimal, $|\mathcal{V}| = k$, then $M_{\mathcal{V}}$ is square and regular; therefore, $\mathcal{V}$ may recover the polynomial $P(x)$ and, consequently, the secret S. If $\mathcal{V}$ is not minimal, $|\mathcal{V}| > k$, there exists a subset $\mathcal{V}_0 \subset \mathcal{V}$ of size $|\mathcal{V}_0| = k$ that is authorized. Since all $|\mathcal{V}|$ equations in the linear system of equations $M_{\mathcal{V}}\mathbf{a} = \boldsymbol{\sigma}$ are consistent and since, by assumption, the sub-matrix $M_{\mathcal{V}_0}$ is regular, then $M_{\mathcal{V}}\mathbf{a} = \boldsymbol{\sigma}$ has a unique solution $\mathbf{a}$, the first component of which is the secret S. Therefore, the assumptions of the theorem imply accessibility.

Next, we prove that those assumptions also imply the perfect security of the scheme. Let $\mathcal{V} \in 2^{\mathcal{U}\setminus\{0\}} \setminus \Gamma$ be an unauthorized subset and assume that $\mathcal{V}$ is as in (11). We aim at showing that even if all participants in $\mathcal{V}$ pool their shares together, they cannot reveal a thing about the secret S. Every unauthorized subset may be completed into an authorized subset (though not necessarily minimal) by adding to it at most k participants. Without loss of generality, we may assume that $\mathcal{V}$ is missing only one participant in order to become authorized. Therefore, if we add to $\mathcal{V}$ the phantom participant 0 we get an authorized subset, $\mathcal{V}_1 = \{0\} \cup \mathcal{V} \in \Gamma$, since 0 belongs to the highest level $\mathcal{U}_0$.

Let us assume first that $|\mathcal{V}| = k - 1$. Then $|\mathcal{V}_1| = k$ and, consequently, $M_{\mathcal{V}_1}$ is square and regular. Therefore, the row in $M_{\mathcal{V}_1}$ that corresponds to the user 0 is independent of the rows that correspond to the original $k - 1$ members of $\mathcal{V}$, i.e.,

$$\mathbf{r}(0) = (1, 0, \ldots, 0) \notin \text{row-space}(M_{\mathcal{V}}) \ .$$

Hence, the value of the secret S is completely independent of the shares of $\mathcal{V}$.

Next, assume that $|\mathcal{V}| > k - 1$. Assume that the single participant that $\mathcal{V}$ is missing in order to become authorized is missing at the jth level for some $0 \leq j \leq m$; i.e., using the notations of (11),

$$\ell_i \geq k_i \quad 0 \leq i \leq j-1 \quad , \quad \ell_j = k_j - 1 \quad \text{and} \quad \ell_i \geq k_i - 1 \quad j+1 \leq i \leq m \ . \tag{13}$$

Since $|\mathcal{V}| = \ell_m > k - 1$, we conclude that $\ell_m - \ell_j > k - k_j$. All $\ell_m - \ell_j$ rows in $M_{\mathcal{V}}$ that correspond to the participants of $\mathcal{V}$ from levels $\mathcal{U}_{j+1}$ through $\mathcal{U}_m$ have at least k_j leading zeros, since they all correspond to derivatives of order k_j or higher. Therefore, those rows belong to a subspace of $\mathbb{F}^k$ of dimension $k - k_j$. Hence, we may extract from among them $k - k_j$ rows that still span the same subspace as the original $\ell_m - \ell_j$ rows. Let $\mathcal{W}$ denote the subset of $\mathcal{V}$ that corresponds to the $(\ell_m - \ell_j) - (k - k_j)$ redundant rows from among the last $\ell_m - \ell_j$ rows in $M_{\mathcal{V}}$; let $\mathcal{V}_0 = \mathcal{V} \setminus \mathcal{W}$. By (13),

$$|\mathcal{V}_0| = |\mathcal{V}| - |\mathcal{W}| = \ell_m - [(\ell_m - \ell_j) - (k - k_j)] = \ell_j + k - k_j = k - 1 \ .$$

Clearly, the removal from $\mathcal{V}$ of the participants in $\mathcal{W}$ cannot create new deficiencies, whence, $\mathcal{V}_0$, like $\mathcal{V}$, also lacks only a single participant at the jth level in order to become authorized. Hence, we may apply to it our previous arguments and conclude that

$$\mathbf{r}(0) = (1, 0, \ldots, 0) \notin \text{row-space}(M_{\mathcal{V}_0}) \ .$$

But since

$$\text{row-space}(M_{\mathcal{V}_0}) = \text{row-space}(M_{\mathcal{V}}) \ ,$$

we arrive at the sought-after conclusion that

$$\mathbf{r}(0) = (1, 0, \ldots, 0) \notin \text{row-space}(M_{\mathcal{V}}) \ ,$$

which implies perfect security.

3.2 Random Allocation of Participant Identities

The first strategy of allocating participant identities that we consider is the random one. Namely, recalling that $|\mathcal{U}| = n$ and $|\mathbb{F}| = q$, the random strategy is such that

$$\mathrm{Prob}(\mathcal{U} = \mathcal{W}) = \frac{1}{\binom{q-1}{n}} \qquad \forall\, \mathcal{W} \subset \mathbb{F} \setminus \{0\} \ , \ |\mathcal{W}| = n \ . \tag{14}$$

Theorem 3. *Assume a random allocation of participant identities, (14). Let $\mathcal{V}$ be a randomly selected subset from $2^{\mathcal{U}}$. Then if $\mathcal{V} \in \Gamma$*

$$\mathrm{Prob}\left(H(S|\sigma(\mathcal{V})) = 0\right) \geq 1 - \varepsilon \ , \tag{15}$$

while otherwise

$$\mathrm{Prob}\left(H(S|\sigma(\mathcal{V})) = H(S)\right) \geq 1 - \varepsilon \ , \tag{16}$$

where

$$\varepsilon = \frac{(k-2)(k-1)}{2(q-k)} \ . \tag{17}$$

Proof. Let $\mathcal{V} \in \Gamma$ be an authorized subset, not necessarily minimal. In view of Theorem 2 there exists a minimal authorized subset $\mathcal{V}_0$ (i.e., $|\mathcal{V}_0| = k$) such that if $\det M_{\mathcal{V}_0} \neq 0$, $\mathcal{V}$ may recover S. On the other hand, we saw in Theorem 2 that if $0 \in \mathcal{U}_0$ and $\mathcal{V} \notin \Gamma$ is an unauthorized subset, there exists a minimal authorized subset $\mathcal{V}_0$ such that $\det M_{\mathcal{V}_0} \neq 0$ implies that $\mathcal{V}$ cannot learn any information about S.

Hence, in order to prove both statements of the theorem, (15) and (16), it suffices to assume that $0 \in \mathcal{U}_0$ and then show that if $\mathcal{V} \in \Gamma$ is a *minimal* authorized subset, $M_{\mathcal{V}}$ has a nonzero determinant in probability at least $1 - \varepsilon$.

To that end, let $\mathcal{V}$ be such a subset and assume that its participants are ordered according to their position in the hierarchy, (11). We proceed to show that

$$\mathrm{Prob}\left(\det(M_{\mathcal{V}}) = 0\right) \leq \frac{(k-2)(k-1)}{2(q-k)} \ . \tag{18}$$

Noting that (18) clearly holds when $k = 1, 2$, we continue by induction on k. There are two cases to consider:

1. The last row in $M_{\mathcal{V}}$ is $\mathbf{r}^{(h)}(v_k)$ where $h < k-1$ (this happens if $k_{m-1} < k_m - 1$ or if $\mathcal{V} \cap \mathcal{U}_m = \emptyset$).
2. The last row in $M_{\mathcal{V}}$ is $\mathbf{r}^{(k-1)}(v_k)$ (this happens when $k_{m-1} = k_m - 1$ and $\mathcal{V} \cap \mathcal{U}_m \neq \emptyset$; in that case v_k is the only participant in $\mathcal{V} \cap \mathcal{U}_m$).

We begin by handling the first case. Let $\mathbf{v} = (v_1, \ldots, v_{k-1})$ and $(\mathbf{v}, v_k) = (v_1, \ldots, v_k)$. Let $\mu_{k-1} = \mu_{k-1}(\mathbf{v})$ denote the determinant of the $(k-1) \times (k-1)$ minor of $M_{\mathcal{V}}$ that is obtained by removing the last row and last column in $M_{\mathcal{V}}$. Then

$$\det(M_{\mathcal{V}}) = \sum_{i=0}^{k-2-h} c_i v_k^i + \frac{(k-1)!}{(k-1-h)!} \cdot \mu_{k-1} \cdot v_k^{k-1-h} \ , \tag{19}$$

for some constants c_i that depend on $\mathbf{v}$. Let Ω denote the collection of all $\mathbf{v} \in \mathbb{F}^{k-1}$ for which $\mu_{k-1} = \mu_{k-1}(\mathbf{v}) = 0$. Then

$\text{Prob}(\det(M_{\mathcal{V}}) = 0) =$

$$= \sum_{\mathbf{v} \in \mathbb{F}^{k-1} \setminus \Omega} \text{Prob}(\det(M_{\mathcal{V}}) = 0 | \mathbf{v}) \cdot \text{Prob}(\mathbf{v}) + \sum_{\mathbf{v} \in \Omega} \text{Prob}(\det(M_{\mathcal{V}}) = 0 | \mathbf{v}) \cdot \text{Prob}(\mathbf{v}) .$$

(20)

If $\mathbf{v} \in \mathbb{F}^{k-1} \setminus \Omega$ then $\det(M_{\mathcal{V}})$ is a polynomial of degree $k - 1 - h$ in v_k, (19). Hence, there are at most $k - 1 - h$ values of v_k for which $\det(M_{\mathcal{V}}) = 0$. This implies that

$$\text{Prob}(\det(M_{\mathcal{V}}) = 0 | \mathbf{v}) \leq \frac{k - 1 - h}{(q - 1) - (k - 1)} \qquad \forall \mathbf{v} \in \mathbb{F}^{k-1} \setminus \Omega \qquad (21)$$

(recall that the participant identities are distinct and are randomly selected from $\mathbb{F} \setminus \{0\}$). Note that h could take any value between 0 and $k - 2$. However, if $h = 0$ it means that all participants in $\mathcal{V}$ belong to the highest level, so that $M_{\mathcal{V}}$ is a Vandermonde matrix. In that case, the matrix is invertible and, consequently, $\text{Prob}(\det(M_{\mathcal{V}}) = 0) = 0$. Therefore, the worst case in (21) is when $h = 1$. Hence, we rewrite (21) as follows:

$$\text{Prob}(\det(M_{\mathcal{V}}) = 0 | \mathbf{v}) \leq \frac{k - 2}{q - k} \qquad \forall \mathbf{v} \in \mathbb{F}^{k-1} \setminus \Omega . \qquad (22)$$

If $\mathbf{v} \in \Omega$ then the degree of $\det(M_{\mathcal{V}})$ as a polynomial in v_k is less than $k - 1 - h$. The problem is that it may completely vanish and then $\det(M_{\mathcal{V}})$ would be zero for all values of v_k. However, as $\mathbf{v}$ is a vector of dimension $k - 1$, we may invoke the induction assumption (i.e., (18) for $k - 1$) and conclude that

$$\text{Prob}(\mathbf{v} \in \Omega) \leq \frac{(k - 3)(k - 2)}{2(q - k + 1)} . \qquad (23)$$

Finally, combining (20), (22) and (23) we may prove (18) in this case:

$$\text{Prob}(\det(M_{\mathcal{V}}) = 0) \leq \frac{k - 2}{q - k} + \frac{(k - 3)(k - 2)}{2(q - k + 1)} \leq \frac{(k - 2)(k - 1)}{2(q - k)} .$$

In the second case, $\det(M_{\mathcal{V}})$ does not depend on v_k as the last row in the matrix in this case is $(0, \ldots, 0, (k-1)!)$. Hence, we may solve for a_{k-1} and reduce the system to a system in only $(k-1)$ unknowns, $\{a_i\}_{i=0}^{k-2}$. Consequently, we may apply induction in order to conclude that

$$\text{Prob}(\det(M_{\mathcal{V}}) = 0) \leq \frac{(k - 3)(k - 2)}{2(q - k + 1)} < \frac{(k - 2)(k - 1)}{2(q - k)} .$$

The proof is thus complete.

Theorem 3 implies that if k, the number of overall participants that are required in an authorized subset, is a small number, the failure probability is $\Theta(1/q)$ and therefore negligible, as it is equivalent to the probability of simply guessing the secret.

Corollary 1. *Assume a random allocation of participant identities, (14). Then the probability that the resulting scheme has accessibility, (2), for all authorized subsets and and perfect security, (3), for all unauthorized subsets is at least $1 - \binom{n+1}{k} \cdot \varepsilon$, where ε is as in (17).*

The random allocation is therefore a safe bet. Since usually n and k are not too large, the dealer may adopt this strategy and be certain in a high probability that both requirements – accessibility, and perfect security – will be satisfied.

3.3 Monotone Allocation of Participant Identities

Here, we present a simple allocation method that guarantees both accessibility, (2), and perfect security, (3), if the size of the underling field, q, is sufficiently large.

For every $0 \leq i \leq m$ we define $n_i = |\bigcup_{j=0}^{i} \mathcal{U}_i|$ and let $n_{-1} = 0$. The simpler version of our method associates all $n_i - n_{i-1}$ members of $\mathcal{U}_i$ with the identities $[n_{i-1}+1, n_i] \subset \mathbb{F}$. The more flexible version of this method leaves gaps between the $m + 1$ intervals of identities, in order to allow new participants to be added to any level while still maintaining the monotonic principle,

$$u \in \mathcal{U}_i \ , \ v \in \mathcal{U}_j \ , \ i < j \Rightarrow u < v \ , \tag{24}$$

where the inequality is in the usual sense between integers in the interval $[0, q-1]$.

In Lemma 2 and Theorem 4 we prove that this method guarantees accessibility and perfect security, (2)+(3), provided that the size of the underlying field, q, is sufficiently large with respect to the parameters of the problem. In Lemma 2 we prove our basic lower bound on q that guarantees these two conditions. Then, in Theorem 4, we use the bound of Lemma 2 and carry out a more delicate analysis that yields a better bound.

Lemma 2. *Let $(\mathbf{k}, n)$ be a hierarchical secret sharing problem. Assume that the participants in $\mathcal{U}$ were assigned identities in $\mathbb{F}$ in a monotone manner, namely, in concert with condition (24), and let $N = \max \mathcal{U}$. Finally, assume that*

$$2^{-k} \cdot (k + 1)^{(k+1)/2} \cdot N^{(k-1)k/2} < q = |\mathbb{F}| \ , \tag{25}$$

(where $k = k_m$ is the minimal size of an authorized subset). Then our hierarchical secret sharing scheme satisfies conditions (2) and (3).

Proof. In view of Theorem 2, it suffices to prove that if $\mathcal{V} \in \Gamma$ is a minimal authorized subset, that may include the phantom participant $u = 0$, then the corresponding square matrix $M_\mathcal{V}$, (12), is regular. Without loss of generality we assume that the participant identities in $\mathcal{V}$ are given by (11) (with $\ell_m = k$) and that they are ordered in the usual sense in $\mathbb{R}$, $v_1 < v_2 < \cdots < v_k$. First, we prove that

$$\det M_\mathcal{V} \neq 0 \quad \text{in } \mathbb{R} \ . \tag{26}$$

Then, invoking (25), we shall prove that

$$|\det M_\mathcal{V}| < q \qquad \text{in } \mathbb{R} . \tag{27}$$

Combining (26) and (27) we conclude that $\det M_\mathcal{V} \neq 0$ in $\mathbb{F} = \mathbb{Z}_q$, as required.

In order to prove (26), we observe that the interpolation matrix E that corresponds to the Birkhoff interpolation problem with which the participants in $\mathcal{V}$ are faced, has an echelon form. Indeed, all rows have exactly one entry that equals 1, and the position of the 1 is monotonically non-decreasing as we go down the rows of E: in the first ℓ_0 rows we encounter the 1 in column $j = 0$, in the next $\ell_1 - \ell_0$ rows the 1 appears in column $j = \ell_0$ and so forth. Hence, the matrix E has no supported 1-sequences in the sense of Definition 2. Recalling Proposition 1, we infer that the conditions of Theorem 1 are satisfied. Therefore, the corresponding Birkhoff interpolation problem is well-posed over $\mathbb{R}$, (26).

In order to bound the determinant of $M_\mathcal{V}$, we invoke Hadamard's maximal determinant theorem [8, problem 523]. According to that theorem, if A is a $k \times k$ real matrix, and

$$|A_{i,j}| \leq 1 \quad , \quad 0 \leq i, j \leq k - 1 , \tag{28}$$

then

$$|\det(A)| \leq 2^{-k} \cdot (k+1)^{(k+1)/2} . \tag{29}$$

Let A be the matrix that is obtained from $M_\mathcal{V}$ if we divide its jth column by N^j, $0 \leq j \leq k - 1$. Since that matrix A satisfies condition (28), we conclude, in view of (29) and (25), that $M_\mathcal{V}$ satisfies (27). That completes the proof.

Theorem 4. *Under the conditions of Lemma 2, the hierarchical secret sharing scheme satisfies conditions (2) and (3) provided that*

$$\alpha(k)N^{(k-1)(k-2)/2} < q = |\mathbb{F}| \quad \text{where} \quad \alpha(k) := 2^{-k+2} \cdot (k-1)^{(k-1)/2} \cdot (k-1)! . \tag{30}$$

Proof. Assume that $\mathcal{V} \in \Gamma$ is as in (11), and assume that it has k participants whose identities are ordered in the usual sense in $\mathbb{R}$, $v_1 < v_2 < \cdots < v_k$. Let d_i, $1 \leq i \leq k$, be the order of derivative of the share that v_i got. Namely, in view of (11) and (12), $d_i = 0$ for $1 \leq i \leq \ell_0$, $d_i = k_0$ for $\ell_0 + 1 \leq i \leq \ell_1$, and so forth. We refer to $\mathbf{d} = (d_1, \ldots, d_k)$ as the *type* of the interpolation problem that needs to be solved by the participants of $\mathcal{V}$ since it characterizes the form of the coefficient matrix $M_\mathcal{V}$, (12). Finally, let t be the largest integer such that $d_i = i - 1$ for all $1 \leq i \leq t$. We note that t is well defined and $t \geq 1$ since always $d_1 = 0$ (i.e., $\mathcal{V}$ must always include at least one participant of the highest level $\mathcal{U}_0$).

Let $\mathcal{P}$ denote the problem of recovering P from the shares of $\{v_i\}_{1 \leq i \leq k}$. We claim that $\mathcal{P}$ may be decomposed into two independent problems that may be solved in succession:

- Problem $\mathcal{P}_1$. Recovering $P^{(t-1)}$ (namely, the coefficients a_i, $t - 1 \leq i \leq k - 1$, see (10)) from the shares of v_i, $t \leq i \leq k$.

– Problem $\mathcal{P}_2$. Recovering a_{i-1} from the share of v_i, for $i = t - 1, \ldots, 1$.

Indeed, the equations that correspond to the $k-t+1$ last participants – $\{v_i\}_{t \leq i \leq k}$ – involve only the $k - t + 1$ coefficients $\{a_i\}_{t-1 \leq i \leq k-1}$ (note that if $t = 1$, $\mathcal{P}_1$ coincides with the original problem $\mathcal{P}$ and then $\mathcal{P}_2$ is rendered void). Hence, we may first concentrate on solving the (possibly reduced) interpolation problem $\mathcal{P}_1$. If that problem is solvable, we may proceed to problem $\mathcal{P}_2$. That problem is always solvable by the following simple procedure: for every i, $i = t-1, \ldots, 1$, we perform one integration and then, using the share of v_i, we recover the coefficient a_{i-1} of $\mathcal{P}$. Hence, we may concentrate on determining a sufficient condition for the solvability of $\mathcal{P}_1$. That condition will guarantee also the solvability of $\mathcal{P}$. (Note that $\mathcal{P}_1$ still satisfies Pólya's condition, Lemma 1.)

The dimension of the interpolation problem $\mathcal{P}_1$ is $k - t + 1$. Hence, since the left hand side in (30) is monotonically increasing in k, we may concentrate here on the worst case where $t = 1$ and the dimension of $\mathcal{P}_1$ is k (namely, $\mathcal{P}_1 = \mathcal{P}$). The main observation, that justifies this preliminary discussion and the decomposition of $\mathcal{P}$ into two sub-problems, is that in the type $\mathbf{d}$ of $\mathcal{P}_1$, $d_1 = d_2 = 0$. Indeed, $d_1 = 0$ and $d_2 \leq 1$ as enforced by Pólya's condition; moreover, $d_2 \neq 1$ for otherwise $t \geq 2$, as opposed to our assumption that $t = 1$. With this in mind, we define $s \geq 2$ to be the maximal integer for which $d_i = 0$ for all $1 \leq i \leq s$.

Next, we write down the system of linear equations that characterizes the interpolation problem $\mathcal{P}_1$. To that end, we prefer to look for the polynomial P in its Newton form with respect to $\{v_i\}_{1 \leq i \leq k}$ (as opposed to its standard representation (10)):

$$P(x) = \sum_{j=0}^{k-1} c_j \prod_{i=1}^{j} (x - v_i) . \tag{31}$$

Writing down the system of linear equations in the unknowns $\{c_j\}_{0 \leq j \leq k-1}$, we see that the corresponding coefficient matrix, $\hat{M} = \hat{M}_{\mathcal{V}}$, has a block triangular form,

$$\hat{M} = \begin{pmatrix} B_1 & 0 \\ B_2 & B_3 \end{pmatrix} \tag{32}$$

where the upper-left $s \times s$ block is given by

$$B_1 = \begin{pmatrix} 1 & 0 & 0 & 0 & \cdots & 0 \\ 1 & v_2 - v_1 & 0 & 0 & \cdots & 0 \\ 1 & v_3 - v_1 & \prod_{i=1}^{2}(v_3 - v_i) & 0 & \cdots & 0 \\ \vdots & \vdots & \vdots & \vdots & \vdots & \vdots \\ 1 & v_s - v_1 & \prod_{i=1}^{2}(v_s - v_i) & \prod_{i=1}^{3}(v_s - v_i) & \cdots & \prod_{i=1}^{s-1}(v_s - v_i) \end{pmatrix} \tag{33}$$

(we use the notation $\hat{M}$ in order to distinguish this matrix from $M = M_{\mathcal{V}}$, (12), that was the coefficient matrix in the linear system for the unknowns a_i in the standard representation of the interpolant $P(x)$, (10)). Invoking the same arguments as in Lemma 2, we conclude that

$$\det \hat{M} \neq 0 \quad \text{in } \mathbb{R} . \tag{34}$$

We need to show that

$$\det \hat{M} \neq 0 \quad \text{in } \mathbb{F} . \tag{35}$$

In order to prove (35), we first invoke (32) to conclude that

$$\det \hat{M} = \det B_1 \cdot \det B_3 . \tag{36}$$

As $N < q$, all terms on the diagonal of B_1, (33), are nonzero in $\mathbb{F}$, so that B_1 is invertible over $\mathbb{F}$. Therefore, by (36), we only need to show that

$$\det B_3 \neq 0 \quad \text{in } \mathbb{F} , \tag{37}$$

in order to prove (35). Since $\det B_3 \neq 0$ in $\mathbb{R}$, as implied by (34) and (36), this amounts to showing that

$$|\det B_3| < q \quad \text{in } \mathbb{R} . \tag{38}$$

In order to prove (38), we shall show that

$$|\hat{M}_{i,j}| \leq j \cdot N^{j-1} \quad \text{for all} \quad s+1 \leq i \leq k , \ s \leq j \leq k-1 \tag{39}$$

(note that the rows of $\hat{M}$ correspond to v_i, $1 \leq i \leq k$, while the columns of $\hat{M}$ correspond to the unknown coefficient c_j, $0 \leq j \leq k-1$). Then, we may proceed to prove (38) using Hadamard's inequality: let A be the matrix that is obtained from B_3 after dividing its jth column, $s \leq j \leq k-1$, by $j \cdot N^{j-1}$. Then according to (39), the normalized block A satisfies condition (28) of Hadamard's maximal determinant theorem. Hence, by (29),

$$|\det A| \leq 2^{-k+s} \cdot (k - s + 1)^{(k-s+1)/2} .$$

Consequently, since $s \geq 2$,

$$|\det B_3| = |\det A| \cdot \left(\prod_{j=s}^{k-1} j \cdot N^{j-1} \right) \leq 2^{-k+2} \cdot (k-1)^{(k-1)/2} \cdot (k-1)! \cdot N^{(k-1)(k-2)/2} .$$

$$\tag{40}$$

Inequalities (40) and (30) prove (38).

The only missing link is (39). In order to prove this inequality, we need to derive an expression for the derivatives of $P(x)$, (31). Let us introduce the notations

$$P_j(x) = \prod_{i=1}^{j} (x - v_i) \quad \text{and} \quad P_{j,h}(x) = \frac{d^h P_j(x)}{dx^h} \quad , \quad 0 \leq j \leq k-1 , \ h \geq 0 . \tag{41}$$

Then, since $P_{j,h} = 0$ for all $j < h$,

$$P^{(h)}(x) = \sum_{j=h}^{k-1} c_j P_{j,h}(x) \ . \tag{42}$$

The expression for $P_{j,h}(x)$ is given by

$$P_{j,h}(x) = \sum \left\{ \Pi_{(g_1,\ldots,g_h)}(x) \ : \ (g_1,\ldots,g_h) \in G(j,h) \right\} \ , \tag{43}$$

where $G(j,h)$ is the set of all $\frac{j!}{(j-h)!}$ ordered selections of h elements from $\{1,\ldots,j\}$ and

$$\Pi_{(g_1,\ldots,g_h)}(x) = \prod \left\{ (x - v_i) \ : \ i \in \{1,\ldots,j\} \setminus \{g_1,\ldots,g_h\} \right\} \ . \tag{44}$$

Setting $x = v_\ell$, for some $s + 1 \leq \ell \leq k$, in (42), we see that the ℓth row in $\hat{M}$ takes the form

$$(\hat{M}_{\ell,j})_{0 \leq j \leq k-1} = \left(0 \cdots 0 \ P_{h,h}(v_\ell) \cdots P_{k-1,h}(v_\ell) \right) \ , \tag{45}$$

where $h = d_\ell$ is the order of derivative of the share of v_ℓ. From (43),

$$|P_{j,h}(v_\ell)| \leq |G(j,h)| \cdot \max_{(g_1,\ldots,g_h)} |\Pi_{(g_1,\ldots,g_h)}(v_\ell)| \ .$$

Since, by (44), $|\Pi_{(g_1,\ldots,g_h)}(v_\ell)| \leq N^{j-h}$, we conclude that

$$|P_{j,h}(v_\ell)| \leq \frac{j!}{(j-h)!} \cdot N^{j-h} \ , \quad h \leq j \leq k-1 \ . \tag{46}$$

As the definition of s implies that $h \geq 1$ for all rows $s + 1 \leq \ell \leq k$, and since $j \leq k - 1 < N$, we infer by (46) and (45) that

$$|\hat{M}_{\ell,j}| \leq j \cdot N^{j-1} \ , \quad h \leq j \leq k-1 \ . \tag{47}$$

Since, by (45), the inequality in (47) holds trivially for columns $0 \leq j \leq h - 1$ as well, that proves (39). The proof of the theorem is thus complete.

Condition (30) is pretty sharp. It may be seen that the worst scenario is that in which $\mathbf{d} = (0, 0, 1, \ldots, 1)$ – namely, $k_0 = 1$ (the number of participants from $\mathcal{U}_0$ must be at least 1) and there are two participants from $\mathcal{U}_0$ while all the rest are from $\mathcal{U}_1$. In such cases, the (real) determinant of the block B_3 in the matrix of coefficients $\hat{M}$ is $\Theta(N^{(k-1)(k-2)/2})$, though the constant $\alpha(k)$ may be somewhat improved.

Table 1 includes for each value of k, $5 \leq k \leq 8$, the maximal value of N for which the original condition, (25), and the improved one, (30), still holds when the secret to be shared is an AES key (namely, q is of size 128 bits). The figures in the table demonstrate the exponential drop in the capacity of the scheme, N, when k increases. However, this should not be worrisome because n and k in any plausible real-life application are usually small. In the unlikely scenario of k and N so large that condition (30) fails to hold for any prime q of the size of the secret to be shared, we may always go back to the random allocation strategy that was described in the previous section.

Table 1. Values of k and N that satisfy conditions (25) and (30)

k	Condition (25)	Condition (30)
5	$N \leq 5497$	$N \leq 1234795$
6	$N \leq 296$	$N \leq 3637$
7	$N \leq 56$	$N \leq 200$
8	$N \leq 19$	$N \leq 38$

4 An Ideal Scheme for the Disjunctive Hierarchical Secret Sharing Problem

As described in the Introduction, Simmons [16] studied a closely related hierarchical secret sharing problem, where the conjunction of threshold conditions is replaced by a disjunction (compare (1) to (7)). His solution to the problem was not ideal. Using the ideal secret sharing scheme that we presented herein for the conjunctive version of the problem, we may get an ideal secret sharing scheme also for the disjunctive version.

Karchmer and Wigderson [11] introduced monotone span programs as a linear algebraic model of computation for computing monotone functions. A monotone span program (MSP hereinafter) is a quintuple $\mathcal{M} = (\mathbb{F}, M, \mathcal{U}, \phi, \mathbf{e})$ where $\mathbb{F}$ is a field, M is a matrix of dimensions $a \times b$ over $\mathbb{F}$, $\mathcal{U} = \{u_1, \ldots, u_n\}$ is a finite set, ϕ is a surjective function from $\{1, \ldots, a\}$ to $\mathcal{U}$, which is thought of as *labeling* of the rows of M, and $\mathbf{e}$ is some target row vector from $\mathbb{F}^b$. The MSP $\mathcal{M}$ realizes the monotone access structure $\Gamma \subset 2^{\mathcal{U}}$ when $\mathcal{V} \in \Gamma$ if and only if $\mathbf{e}$ is spanned by the rows of the matrix M whose labels belong to $\mathcal{V}$. The size of $\mathcal{M}$ is the a, the number of rows in M. Namely, in the terminology of secret sharing, the size of the MSP is the total number of shares that were distributed to all participants in $\mathcal{U}$. An MSP is ideal if $a = n$.

If Γ is a monotone access structure over $\mathcal{U}$, its dual is defined by $\Gamma^* = \{\mathcal{V} : \mathcal{V}^c \notin \Gamma\}$. It is easy to see that Γ^* is also monotone. In [10] it was shown that if $\mathcal{M} = (\mathbb{F}, M, \mathcal{U}, \phi, \mathbf{e})$ is a MSP that realizes a monotone access structure Γ, then there exists a MSP $\mathcal{M}^* = (\mathbb{F}, M^*, \mathcal{U}, \phi, \mathbf{e}^*)$ of the same size like $\mathcal{M}$ that realizes the dual access structure Γ^*. Hence, an access structure is ideal if and only if its dual is.

Returning to the disjunctive hierarchial access structure that was studied by Simmons, (7), we claim the following straightforward proposition.

Proposition 2. *Let* $\mathcal{U} = \bigcup_{i=0}^{m} \mathcal{U}_i$ *and* $\mathbf{k} = \{k_i\}_{i=0}^{m}$ *be as in Definition 1. Let* Γ *be the corresponding disjunctive access structure as defined in (7). Then* Γ^* *is the conjunctive access structure that is defined in Definition 1 with thresholds* $\mathbf{k}^* = \{k_i^*\}_{i=0}^{m}$ *where* $k_i^* = |\bigcup_{j=0}^{i} \mathcal{U}_j| - k_i + 1$, $0 \leq i \leq m$.

Since the conjunctive hierarchial access structure is ideal, at least over fields that are sufficiently large, we conclude the following.

Corollary 2. *The disjunctive access structure (7) is ideal.*

490   T. Tassa

Acknowledgement. The author thanks Amos Beimel and the anonymous referees for insightful comments on the manuscript.

References

1. Atkinson, K., Sharma, A.: A partial characterization of poised Hermite-Birkhoff interpolation problems. Siam Journal on Numerical Analysis **6** (1969) 230–235
2. Benaloh, J., Leichter, J.: Generalized secret sharing and monotone functions. Advances in Cryptology - CRYPTO 88, LNCS **403** (1990) 27–35
3. Beutelspacjer, A., Vedder, K.: Geometric structures as threshold schemes. In Cryptography and Coding, Clarendon Press (1989) 255–268
4. Blakley, G.R.: Safeguarding cryptographic keys. In Proceedings of the National Computer Conference, AFIPS **48** (1979) 313–317
5. Brickell, E.F.: Some ideal secret sharing schemes. Journal of Combinatorial Mathematics and Combinatorial Computing **9** (1989) 105–113
6. Charnes, C., Martin, K., Pieprzyk, J., Safavi-Naini, R.: Sharing secret information in hierarchical groups. Information and Communications Security, LNCS **1334** (1997) 81–86
7. Dawson, E., Donovan, D.: The breadth of Shamir's secret sharing scheme. Computers and Security **13** (1994) 69–78
8. Faddeev, D.K., Sominskii, I.S.: Problems in Higher Algebra, San Francisco, W. H. Freeman, 1965
9. Friedman, J.: Constructing $O(n \log n)$ size monotone formulae for the k-th elementary symmetric polynomial of n Boolean variables. IEEE Symposium on Foundations of Computer Science (1984) 506–515
10. Gál, A.: Combinatorial Methods in Boolean Function Complexity. Ph.D. thesis, University of Chicago, 1995
11. Karchmer, M., Wigderson, A.: On span programs. In 8th Annual Conference on Structure in Complexity Theory (SCTC'93), IEEE Computer Society Press (1993) 102–111
12. Lorentz, G.G., Jetter, K., Riemenschneider, S.D.: Birkhoff Interpolation. In Encyclopedia of Mathematics and its Applications **19** (1983), Addison-Wesley, Reading, Mass.
13. Padró, C., Sáez, G.: Secret sharing schemes with bipartite access structure. Advances in Cryptology - EUROCRYPT 98, LNCS **1403** (1998) 500–511
14. Schoenberg, I.J.: On Hermite-Birkhoff interpolation. Journal of Mathematical Analysis and Applications **16** (1966) 538–543
15. Shamir, A.: How to share a secret. Communications of the ACM **22** (1979) 612–613
16. Simmons, G.J.: How to (really) share a secret. Advances in Cryptology - CRYPTO 88, LNCS **403** (1990) 390–448
17. Simmons, G.J.: An introduction to shared secret and/or shared control schemes and their applications. In Contemporary Cryptology, The Science of Information Integrity, IEEE Press (1991) 441–497
18. Wool, A.: Private communication

On Compressing Encrypted Data without the Encryption Key*

Mark Johnson, David Wagner, and Kannan Ramchandran

Department of Electrical Engineering and Computer Sciences,
University of California, Berkeley, CA 94720, USA.
{mjohnson, kannanr}@eecs.berkeley.edu
daw@cs.berkeley.edu

Abstract. When it is desired to transmit redundant data over an insecure and bandwidth-constrained channel, it is customary to first compress the redundant data and then encrypt it for security reasons. In this paper, we investigate the novelty of reversing the order of these steps, i.e. first encrypting and then compressing. Although counter-intuitive, we show surprisingly that through the use of coding with side information principles, this reversal in order is indeed possible. In fact, for lossless compression, we show that the theoretical compression gain is unchanged by performing encryption before compression. We show that the cryptographic security of the reversed system is directly related to the strength of the key generator.

1 Introduction

Consider the problem of transmitting redundant data over an insecure, bandwidth-constrained communications channel. It is desirable to both compress and encrypt the data. The traditional way to do this is to first compress the data to strip it of its redundancy followed by an encryption of the compressed bitstream. In this paper, we investigate the novelty of reversing the order of these steps, i.e. first encrypting and then compressing, and the effect of that reversal on the compression efficiency and the cryptographic security.

We present a scheme, based on distributed source coding, that enables us to realize this reversal of operations. Our scheme allows us to compress a stationary, i.i.d. source that has been encrypted with a stream cipher (cf., [1]) to a rate close to the entropy rate of the source. Although the code that is used to compress the encrypted source is entirely different from the code that would be used to compress the original source, we can in fact compress the encrypted source to the same rate as we could have compressed the original source. We focus exclusively on this class of stationary, i.i.d. sources in this work. The existence of linear codes that achieve these compression gains can be proven in a non-constructive manner. Furthermore, recent results from distributed source coding

---

* This research was supported by the Fannie and John Hertz Foundation and by NSF under grants CCR-0093337, CCR-0325311, and CCR-0208883.

M. Naor (Ed.): TCC 2004, LNCS 2951, pp. 491–504, 2004.

can be applied to this problem to give constructions for codes that can compress any i.i.d. source that has been encrypted with a stream cipher. In general, these codes will have inefficient decoding algorithms, which limits their usefulness. However, for the case of binary i.i.d. sources, we present code constructions from the literature that support computationally efficient decoding and still achieve compression gains close to the information-theoretic bounds.

Our scheme requires that the decompression algorithm have access to the cryptographic key, but importantly, the compression algorithm does not receive the key. The compressor must know the entropy rate of the original source in order to select an appropriate code, but it does not use the encryption key. To be specific, the compressor only needs to know the entropy rate of the source, not the full distribution. Our scheme is statistical in nature, and there is the possibility that the output of the decoder will not match the original source. We show that for i.i.d. sources this probability of error decreases exponentially toward 0 as the blocklength of the code increases.

While we focus here on the theoretical feasibility of our claim, we have uncovered a few application scenarios of possible interest. In one scenario, the generator of the redundant data (the content author) has no incentive to compress the data as it is not interested in saving bandwidth that it does not own at the cost of unnecessary computational complexity. Nevertheless, the content generator is very interested in protecting the privacy of the content via encryption. This content is typically distributed to its client base by a content distribution unit which has great incentive to remove all redundancy from the content in order to maximize its network utilization. However, there is no trust between the content generator and the compressor, so the former will supply only encrypted data to the latter. Our scheme allows the compressing unit to compress the encrypted data at the same efficiency as if it was compressing the original, unencrypted data, even though the compressor does not have access to the key used in the encryption step.

The main contribution of this work is in the identification of the connection between the stated problem and distributed source coding, as well as an analysis of the compression efficiency and cryptographic security of our scheme. This paper is organized as follows. Section 2 gives some background information. The scheme for compressing encrypted data is presented in Section 3. The cryptographic security of the scheme is studied in Section 4. Related work is discussed in Section 5. Some conclusions and future work are described in Section 6.

2   Background

Before describing our solution to the problem of compressing encrypted data, we will briefly present some background information. First, we will discuss the principles of distributed compression that underpin our solution. Then we will cover some concepts from cryptography that will be used to quantify the strength of the encryption.

2.1   Distributed Source Coding

Distributed source coding considers the problem of separately compressing sources X and S that are correlated, where the two compressors cannot communicate with each other. The Slepian-Wolf theorem [2] gives the smallest rates required to losslessly communicate X and S to the decoder, when both X and S come from memoryless sources outputting an unending stream of i.i.d. values. The Slepian-Wolf theorem is a non-constructive result that states these smallest rates, but does not show how to construct codes that approach the minimum rates. For a practical code construction there will be a tradeoff between the blocklength and the probability or error, i.e. as the blocklength increases the probability of error can be made smaller. However, this theorem also does not provide any specific insight what the tradeoff is. Subsequent work by Csiszar [3], which we discuss in Theorem 1 in Section 3, has shown that linear codes can approach the bounds given by the Slepian-Wolf theorem.

An important special case of this problem, upon which we will focus, is when X needs to be sent to a decoder which has access to the correlated side-information S. For this special case, the Slepian-Wolf theorem asserts that the minimum rate required to transmit X is given by the conditional entropy (cf., [4]) of X given S, denoted by $H(X|S)$ bits/sample.

While the Slepian-Wolf theorem is non-constructive, there has been some recent work that provides practical code constructions to realize these distributed compression gains [5]. We will use an example to show the intuition behind these constructions.

We begin by looking at the problem where S is available at both the encoder and the decoder, as depicted in Figure 1. In our example, X and S are correlated, uniformly distributed binary strings of length 3. The correlation structure is such that their Hamming distance is at most 1, i.e. they differ in at most one of the three bit positions. For example, if X is 010, then S will equally likely be one of the four patterns {010,011,000,110}. The encoder forms the error pattern $e = X \oplus S$. Because X and S differ in at most one bit position, the error pattern e can take on only four possible values, namely {000,001,010,100}. These four values can be indexed with two bits. That index is transmitted to the decoder,

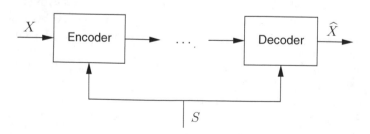

Fig. 1. A source coding with side information problem: The side information S is available at both the encoder and the decoder.

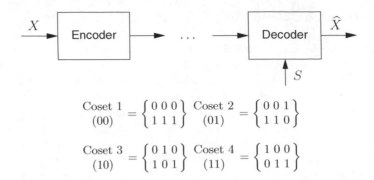

$$\text{Coset 1} \atop (00) = \left\{ \begin{matrix} 0\ 0\ 0 \\ 1\ 1\ 1 \end{matrix} \right\} \quad \text{Coset 2} \atop (01) = \left\{ \begin{matrix} 0\ 0\ 1 \\ 1\ 1\ 0 \end{matrix} \right\}$$

$$\text{Coset 3} \atop (10) = \left\{ \begin{matrix} 0\ 1\ 0 \\ 1\ 0\ 1 \end{matrix} \right\} \quad \text{Coset 4} \atop (11) = \left\{ \begin{matrix} 1\ 0\ 0 \\ 0\ 1\ 1 \end{matrix} \right\}$$

Fig. 2. A source coding with side information problem: X *and* S *are three bit binary sequences which differ by at most one bit.* S *is available only at the decoder. The encoder can compress* X *to two bits by sending the index of the coset in which* X *occurs.*

which looks up the error pattern corresponding to the index received from the encoder, and then computes $X = e \oplus S$.

Now, we consider the case in Figure 2 where S is available at the decoder, but not the encoder. Without S, the encoder cannot form the error pattern e. However, it is still possible for the encoder to compress X to two bits and for the decoder to reconstruct X without error. The reason behind this surprising fact is that there is no reason for the encoder to spend any bits to differentiate between $X = 000$ and $X = 111$. The Hamming distance of 3 between these two codewords is sufficiently large to enable the decoder to correctly decode X based on its access to S and the knowledge that S is within a Hamming distance of 1 from X. If the decoder knows X to be either $X = 000$ or $X = 111$, it can resolve this ambiguity by checking which of the two is closer in Hamming distance to S, and declare that codeword to be X. We observe that the set $\{000,111\}$ is a 3-bit repetition code with a Hamming distance of 3.

Likewise, in addition to the set $\{000,111\}$, we can consider the following 3 sets for X: $\{100,011\}$, $\{010,101\}$, and $\{001,110\}$. Each of these sets is composed of two codewords whose Hamming distance is 3. These sets are the cosets of the 3-bit repetition code. While we typically use the set $\{000,111\}$ as the 3-bit repetition code (0 is encoded as 000, and 1 as 111), it is clear that one could just as easily have used any of the other three cosets with the same performance. Also, these 4 sets cover the complete space of binary 3-tuples that X can assume. Thus, instead of describing X by its 3-bit value, all we need to do is to encode the coset in which X occurs. There are 4 cosets, so we need only 2 bits to index the cosets. We can compress X to 2 bits, just as in the case where S was available at both the encoder and decoder.

In practical situations, the correlation structure between X and S is often not as simple as in this example. For instance, X and S could be three-bit binary numbers such that the Hamming distance between X and S is equal to 0 or 1 with probability $1 - 10^{-6}$. If we compress X with the same code construction as above, then with probability $1 - 10^{-6}$ the Hamming distance between X and S will be at most 1 and $\hat{X}$ will be equal to X. However, with probability 10^{-6} the Hamming distance between X and S will be more than 1. In that case, $\hat{X}$ and X will be different, which means that the decoder has incorrectly decoded the message. The important point is that in these code constructions, unlike in standard source codes, there is a probability of error at the decoder.

In practice, we will use a much more complex channel code than the simple repetition code. The channel code is chosen based on the correlation structure between X and S, so as to minimize the probability of error. However, the encoding and decoding procedures are the same as in our three-bit example. The encoder finds the coset which contains X and transmits the index of this coset. The decoder finds the codeword in the coset denoted by the received index which is closest to S in the Hamming metric.

2.2   Security

We will express an arbitrary encryption scheme with the notation $c = E_k(m)$. Here, m is the plaintext, c is the ciphertext, and k is the key used by the algorithm.

We will quantify the security of an encryption scheme against chosen-plaintext attacks by means of the concept of left-or-right (LOR) security, which was introduced in [6]. The central feature of LOR security is an oracle which supplies responses to queries. A query consists of a pair of plaintexts, denoted by (x, y). The response of the oracle will be the encryption of one of the two plaintexts in the query. There are two types of oracles. A left oracle, which we denote by $\S_0$, will always return the encryption of the first plaintext in the query. The functionality of selecting the first plaintext is denoted by the function $\S_0$, where we define $\S_0(x, y) = x$. In contrast, the right oracle uses a selection function, written $\S_1$, which always returns its second argument: $\S_1(x, y) = y$. In either case, the result of the selection algorithm is encrypted using E_k. Consequently, the functionality of the left oracle can be expressed as $E_k \circ \S_0$, and the right oracle as $E_k \circ \S_1$.

In the left-or-right security model, one of the two types of oracles is chosen at random. An adversary, denoted by A, attempts to determine whether the oracle is a left oracle or a right oracle by making queries to it. Intuitively, if the encryption scheme is very weak then the adversary will be able to examine a ciphertext response and determine with high probability which of the two plaintexts in the query was encrypted. Conversely, for a very strong encryption scheme it is difficult to match plaintexts to the corresponding ciphertexts: the adversary cannot do much better than randomly picking one of the two plaintexts.

We use the superscript notation $A^{E_k \circ \S_0}$ to denote the output of the adversary after interacting with a left oracle, and $A^{E_k \circ \S_1}$ for its result after interacting with a right oracle. The output of the adversary will be 0 if the adversary decides that the oracle is a left oracle, and 1 if the adversary decides that it is a right oracle.

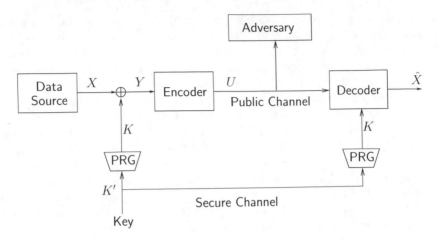

Fig. 3. Secure compression scheme: The data X is first encrypted with a stream cipher and then compressed. At the receiver, decoding and decryption are performed in a joint step. The eavesdropper sees U, but (as we show) cannot learn anything useful about X.

For left-or-right security, we require that:

$$|\Pr[A^{E_k \circ \S_1} = 1] - \Pr[A^{E_k \circ \S_0} = 1]| \le \varepsilon$$

In this equation, the probability is taken across the distribution of keys k and any randomness in the adversary. If this equation holds for all possible adversaries that run in time t and make q or fewer queries to the oracle, then we say that the encryption scheme E is (t, q, ε)-LOR-secure. One other cryptographic concept which we will use is the variational distance. This distance measures the dissimilarity between two probability distributions [1]. If D_1 and D_2 are two probability distributions, then the variational distance $V(D_1, D_2)$ between the two is defined as:

3 Secure Compression Scheme

Our scheme for compressing encrypted data is illustrated in Figure 3. The message is first encrypted with a binary stream cipher. The seed K' is used as the input to a pseudo-random generator (PRG), whose output is denoted by K. The message is encrypted by forming the bitwise binary sum $Y = X \oplus K$. Then, Y is compressed to obtain the result $U = C(Y)$, and U is transmitted to the recipient. The adversary is assumed to be able to eavesdrop on the ciphertext U.

---

[1] The variational distance is related, but not identical, to the K-L divergence (cf., [4]).

Throughout this work, we will assume that all sources are memoryless. In other words, we have a distribution D on some alphabet $\mathcal{X}$; the source outputs an unending sequence of i.i.d. random variables, each distributed according to D. If X denotes the sequence of outputs from such a source, we will sometimes write X_1, X_2, etc., for the first, second, etc., output from the source. Also, if X is such a source, we write X^n for the source that outputs a block of n items from X at a time. The first output of X^n is $(X_1, X_2, \ldots, X_n)$ (which is distributed according to $D \times \cdots \times D$); the second output of X^n is $(X_{n+1}, \ldots, X_{2n})$; and so on. The entropy rate of the source X is $H(D)$, or sometimes written just $H(X)$; consequently, the entropy rate of X^n is $n \cdot H(X)$.

Also, we assume that the seed has been transmitted to the decoder through a secure channel. By implementing an identical PRG, the decoder also has access to K. This reduces the problem of compressing encrypted data to the distributed source coding problem. Y and K are two correlated sources, because Y was generated via $Y = X \oplus K$. Our goal is to compress Y, using the fact that K is available at the decoder as side information. The Slepian-Wolf theorem asserts that Y can be compressed to a rate of $H(Y|K)$. Because $Y = X \oplus K$, it follows that $H(Y|K) = H(X)$. Hence, we can compress the encrypted source Y to a rate $H(X)$, which is the entropy rate of the original source X, conditioned on the fact that K is available at the decoder. In order to select a code to perform this compression, the encoder needs only to know $H(X)$, not the full distribution on X.

3.1   Theoretical Bounds on Compression Efficiency

Although the Slepian-Wolf theorem is non-constructive, the distributed source coding using syndromes (DISCUS) framework [5] provides a constructive method of achieving the coding gains promised by Slepian-Wolf through the use of linear codes. In order for the DISCUS encoder to select a code matched to the particular source, it only needs to know the entropy rate of the original source, not the full distribution. Csiszar showed in [3] that linear codes can achieve the bounds given by the Slepian-Wolf theorem as the block length of the code approaches ∞. Therefore, by restricting our attention to linear codes we do not reduce the compression gains that can be achieved. We present the following theorem, which is our statement of a more general theorem from Csiszar as applied to our specific problem.

Theorem 1 (Csiszar). *Let X and Y be memoryless sources with entropy $H(X)$ and $H(Y)$, respectively. Suppose that X and Y are correlated, in the following sense: we have a joint distribution function $f(x, y)$ which describes the distribution of (X_i, Y_i) for every i. Also, suppose that Y^n is side-information that is available perfectly at the decoder. Then, for every $\epsilon > 0$ and every blocklength n, there exists a linear code C_n for compressing the source X^n at an encoding rate of $n \cdot (H(X|Y) + \epsilon)$ such that the probability p_e of not being able to recover the source message correctly at the decoder is bounded above by: $p_e \leq \exp\{-n \cdot g(\epsilon) + o(n)\}$.*

The function $g(\cdot)$ depends on the distribution (X, Y), but not on n. Thus, Csiszar's work shows not only that the probability of error p_e can be made arbitrarily small for large blocklengths and rates greater than $H(X|Y)$, but also that p_e will decrease exponentially with the blocklength n for suitably chosen codes. Although this theorem proves the existence of linear codes that approach the Slepian-Wolf bounds, it makes no guarantees on the decoding complexity or uniformity of such codes. In general, the codes will require computationally inefficient decoding and nonuniform encoding.

Notice that Csiszar's result is also non-constructive, in that it proves only the existence of a linear code achieving these rates, but does not specify how to find such a linear code explicitly. Hence, this result is achieved in a non-uniform model of computation: the code might depend in a non-uniform way on ϵ, p, X, Y, f, and n; there is no guarantee that we can find a single compression algorithm that works for all n. These non-constructive aspects are unfortunate, but we do not know how to avoid them.

The advantage of using a linear code is in the computational complexity required to implement the encoder. The encoder divides the encrypted source Y into blocks of length n. Each block, which we will denote as Y_i^n, is then mapped to a value U_i in the set $\{0, 1\}^{nR}$, where R is the rate of the code. Hence, U_i can be represented by nR binary digits. This mapping is performed via a simple matrix multiplication, $U_i = H^T Y_i^n$, where H is a matrix of size nR by n that is referred to as a parity check matrix in the coding theory literature (cf., [7])[2]. The complexity of the compressor is quadratic in the block length, since the encoder compresses each block by performing a single matrix multiplication.

The parity check matrix used in the encoder corresponds to a particular code. This code in turn partitions the space of all n bit binary numbers into cosets, just as in the example in Section 2 where the repetition code partitioned the space of three-bit binary numbers into four cosets. The decoder finds the codeword in the coset indexed by U_i which is closest to the side information K_i^n in Hamming distance. This codeword is denoted by $\hat{Y}_i^n$. The decoder then computes its estimate of the original source X_i, which is $\hat{X}_i^n = \hat{Y}_i^n \oplus K_i^n$.

Unfortunately, the complexity of the decoder is not as easily quantified as the encoder, and is highly dependent on the particular code used. We don't know the best achievable time for decoding in Csiszar's result, but we suspect that it may be exponential in n. For instance, we could find the $\hat{Y}_i^n$ which is the maximum likelihood estimate of Y_i^n by exhaustive search through all of the codewords in the coset indexed by U_i, but the complexity of such a search would be exponential in n.

Also, the super-polynomial complexity of the decoder raises a correctness issue for compressing encrypted data: There is, in general, no guarantee that the decoder's error probability remains bounded by about p_e in Figure 3, since the PRG is not guaranteed to remain pseudorandom against distinguishers with

---

[2] This can be readily generalized to non-binary sources. The elements of U and H are then from the same field as X.

super-polynomial running time. However, it seems reasonable[3] to assume we can find a PRG whose security when used with κ-bit keys is $\exp\{\Omega(\kappa^\delta)\}$, for some constant $\delta > 0$. In this case, we can choose parameters so that the PRG provides security against all distinguishers running in time $|\mathcal{X}|^n$, say, and then we will obtain a polynomial-time encoder and a decoder whose error probability is bounded by not much more than p_e.

In summary: Csiszar's result assures us of the existence of linear codes that provably meet the Slepian-Wolf rate, if our sources are memoryless. The encoder runs in polynomial time, but the decoder is suspected to require exponential time. (Note that our security results do not make any assumptions about the running time of the decoder; thus, our security claims for stream cipher encryption followed by Csiszar-style encoding are fully proven, not heuristic.) Also, Csiszar's result is non-constructive. Consequently, though Csiszar's results suffice to show (in principle) that compression can be securely and efficiently performed after encryption, the scheme thus obtained is, in several respects, not very attractive in practice.

3.2   Efficient Code Constructions

For practical uses, we have candidate compression schemes that seem to behave much better. We outline next several such codes that seem to have reasonable encoding and decoding complexity (in particular, with polynomial running time) and that seem to come very close to the Slepian-Wolf bound. In each case, we have extensive empirical evidence that these schemes behave well, but no theoretically proven guarantees. In practice, one would probably use one of these schemes.

The topic of linear codes (without side information) has been heavily studied in the coding literature, and several schemes are known that have computationally efficient, sub-optimal decoding algorithms. Turbo codes [8] and low density parity check (LDPC) codes [9] are two well-known examples. A class of LDPC codes known as expander codes were presented in [10] that were proven to have a polynomial-time decoding and to remove a constant fraction of the errors in a received codeword. Empirical results have consistently shown that LDPC codes have even better decoding performance than the proven bounds.

Recently, a significant amount of work has focused on applying both LDPC codes [11,12] and turbo codes [13,14] to the problem of source coding with side information. The authors of [12] consider a problem where the Slepian-Wolf theorem gives a bound of 0.466 bits/sample on the rate of the encoder. They used an LDPC code with block length 10^5 to compress the binary source to a rate of 0.5 bits/sample and had a probability of error at the decoder that was less than 10^{-6}. These schemes are constructive, and they have computationally efficient encoding and decoding routines. Since we have shown that the problem of compressing encrypted data is an example of source coding with side information,

---

[3] The existence of such a PRG is not guaranteed by the existence of one-way functions with super-polynomial security, but the usual candidate constructions of PRG's all seem to achieve this security level.

we could obtain the same compression gains in our problem by using the same code. Thus, in practice, one would probably use one of these schemes.

Using these constructions, we can efficiently compress any i.i.d. binary source that has been encrypted with a binary stream cipher. In theory, the encrypted source can be compressed to the entropy rate of the original source. In practice, by using LDPC or turbo codes, we can compress the encrypted source to a rate very close to the theoretical limit with a low probability of error. Obviously, if X is a Bernoulli(0.5) binary source, then it has an entropy rate of 1 bit/sample and we cannot compress the encrypted source. For any i.i.d. binary source with redundancy, however, we can compress Y to a rate close to $H(X)$. The gap between the rate of the encoded data and $H(X)$ is limited only by the code used in the encoder and decoder. In theory, a non-binary i.i.d. source could also be compressed to $H(X)$. Constructing codes for non-binary sources is a problem that has not been studied thoroughly, but if such codes were constructed then they could be used in this problem.

Note that in real-time applications, the use of block codes could prove problematic. Because the compressor cannot produce any output until it obtains n plaintext symbols, these approaches might add latency to the cryptosystem. The amount of latency will depend on the block length required to achieve the desired compression rate.

3.3   Other Encryption Algorithms

Up to this point, we have considered only a stream cipher encryption scheme. In a more general case, we could imagine using any encryption method whatsoever. For a general encryption method, it is still theoretically possible to compress the encrypted source to the entropy rate of the original source. However, in this case Y and K will have a very complex, non-linear correlation structure, whereas with a stream cipher the correlation between Y and K was the linear relationship $Y = K \oplus X$. Because the correlation structure is now nonlinear, we can no longer leverage existing channel code constructions to construct distributed source codes. The source coding with side information problem becomes much more difficult with a nonlinear correlation structure, and is not well studied in the coding theory literature.

The anonymous reviewers have pointed out that, in some cases, it may be possible to adapt our techniques to other encryption algorithms. If E is a secure encryption algorithm, then $E'(X) = (E(K'), G(K') \oplus X)$ is also secure (where K' is a fresh session key, randomly chosen for each message to be encrypted), and the second component of $E'(X)$ could be compressed using our scheme.

4   Cryptographic Security

In this section, we provide an analysis of the cryptographic security of the encryption step of our system, and we give a proof of security under plausible assumptions. In brief, the intuition behind our analysis is as follows: First, no computationally bounded attacker who observes Y can learn anything interesting about X, if the pseudorandom generator (PRG) is secure. Second, because U is computable from Y in polynomial time, no computationally bounded attacker who observes U can learn anything useful about X. Since U is what is actually transmitted across the insecure link, this will demonstrate that the system is a secure encryption scheme.

We will study the cryptographic security of the system in two steps. First, we will look at the case where the keystream K has been replaced with a Bernoulli(0.5) random variable. Then, we will extend this analysis to the case where K is the output of a PRG. Our main results will be stated as two theorems.

We begin with the information-theoretic case, where K is truly random. If the keystream K is truly random, then the stream cipher becomes a one-time pad scheme, and security will follow easily. In particular, let K be a source providing an unending stream of i.i.d. values uniformly distributed on $\{0,1\}^k$, chosen anew for each message transmitted independently of everything else (and assumed to be synchronized with the receiver). Let $C : \{0,1\}^k \to \{0,1\}^*$ be a compression algorithm, and define the cryptosystem $E_K : \{0,1\}^k \to \{0,1\}^*$ by $E_K(X) = C(X \oplus K)$ (more precisely, $E_{K_i}(X_i) = C(X_i \oplus K_i)$).

Theorem 2. *When K is uniformly distributed, $E_K(X) = C(X \oplus K)$ is $(\infty, q, 0)$-LOR secure.*

Proof. Fix any x, x', and let K be uniform. The distribution $x \oplus K$ is identical to the distribution $x' \oplus K$, hence $C(x \oplus K)$ has exactly the same distribution as $C(x' \oplus K)$. This means that, no matter the distribution of the random variables X, X', $(E_K \circ \S_0)(X, X')$ will have the same distribution as $(E_K \circ \S_1)(X, X')$. Consequently,

$$| \Pr[A^{E_K \circ \S_1} = 1] - \Pr[A^{E_K \circ \S_0} = 1]| = 0$$

for all adversaries A that make at most one query to their oracle. So, when $q = 1$, the scheme is $(\infty, 1, 0)$-LOR secure. For $q > 1$, we can use a straightforward hybrid argument. Consider the following hybrids, representing how each of the q oracle queries will be answered:

hybrid 0: $E_{K_1} \circ \S_0, E_{K_2} \circ \S_0, \ldots, E_{K_n} \circ \S_0$
hybrid 1: $E_{K_1} \circ \S_1, E_{K_2} \circ \S_0, \ldots, E_{K_n} \circ \S_0$

$\vdots$

hybrid q: $E_{K_1} \circ \S_1, E_{K_2} \circ \S_1, \ldots, E_{K_n} \circ \S_1$

By the above argument, A's output when run with hybrid i has the same distribution as A's output when run with hybrid $i+1$ (here we use that the value of K is chosen anew for each oracle query, independently of everything else). After a simple induction on q, we see that E_K is $(\infty, q, 0)$-LOR secure. $\square$

Next, we consider the full scheme, where the keystream K is generated using a PRG. More specifically, let the secret key K' be distributed uniformly on $\{0,1\}^{k'}$, let $G : \{0,1\}^{k'} \to \{0,1\}^{kq}$ be a pseudorandom generator (PRG), and define

$K = G(K')$. As before, let $C : \{0,1\}^k \to \{0,1\}^*$ be a compression algorithm. This time, we will need to assume that the compression algorithm C runs in polynomial time. Finally, define the cryptosystem $E'_{K'} : \{0,1\}^k \to \{0,1\}^*$ by $E'_{K'}(X) = E_{G(K')}(X) = C(X \oplus G(K'))$; more precisely, $E'_{K'}(X_i) = C(X_i \oplus K_i)$, where $K = G(K')$. When this cryptosystem is used to encrypt multiple messages, we assume that we use consecutive outputs from the PRG, throwing away keystream bits after they are used. Of course, the encryptor must remember his place in the PRG output stream; hence, this is a stateful encryption scheme, and the sender and receiver must be synchronized. We now analyze the security of this cryptosystem.

Theorem 3. *Let $G : \{0,1\}^{k'} \to \{0,1\}^{kq}$ be a (t_1, ε)-secure pseudorandom generator, and assume that the running time of C is at most t_2. Then $E'_{K'}(X) = C(X \oplus G(K'))$ is $(t_1 - (t_2 + c)q, q, 2\varepsilon)$-LOR secure, for some small constant c.*

Proof. Let E_K denote the encryption scheme when used with truly random K, and $E_{G(K')}$ denote the scheme where the keystream K is generated as the output of the PRG, $K = G(K')$. By Theorem 2,

$$\Pr[A^{E_K \circ \S_1} = 1] = \Pr[A^{E_K \circ \S_0} = 1].$$

Next, we apply the triangle inequality:

$$|\Pr[A^{E_{G(K')} \circ \S_1} = 1] - \Pr[A^{E_{G(K')} \circ \S_0} = 1]|$$
$$\leq |\Pr[A^{E_{G(K')} \circ \S_1} = 1] - \Pr[A^{E_K \circ \S_1} = 1] + \Pr[A^{E_K \circ \S_0} = 1] - \Pr[A^{E_{G(K')} \circ \S_0} = 1]|$$
$$\leq |\Pr[A^{E_{G(K')} \circ \S_1} = 1] - \Pr[A^{E_K \circ \S_1} = 1]| + |\Pr[A^{E_{G(K')} \circ \S_0} = 1] - \Pr[A^{E_K \circ \S_0} = 1]|.$$

We will show that both terms on the right-hand side are small.

We can define an adversary B_i that attempts to distinguish between K and $G(K')$ as follows:

$$B_i(z) = A^{E_z \circ \S_i}.$$

B_i can be thought of as a program that mimics the behavior of the attacker A and responds to A's oracle queries by executing the basic cryptosystem with keystream z. If A runs in time $t_1 - t_2 q - cq$, and if C runs in time t_2, then B_i will run in time t_1, since the extra overhead (beyond that of C) for answering each of A's oracle queries is a small constant. Now, because the pseudorandom generator G is assumed to be (t_1, ε)-secure and because B_i runs in time at most t_1, it follows that B_i's advantage at breaking G is minimal:

$$|\Pr[B_i(G(K')) = 1] - \Pr[B_i(K) = 1]| \leq \varepsilon.$$

Substituting the definition of B_i into the previous equation, we see that

$$|\Pr[A^{E_{G(K')} \circ \S_i} = 1] - \Pr[A^{E_K \circ \S_i} = 1]| \leq \varepsilon.$$

This completes the proof. □

We see that the security of our encryption scheme is directly dependent on the security of the pseudo-random generator. If we believe that we are using a strong PRG, then the stream cipher encryption scheme will also be secure.

5   Related Work

A problem closely related to source coding with side information has been studied in the communication complexity literature (cf., [15, Exercise 4.55, p.64]). Suppose Alice holds a n-bit binary string X, and Bob holds S, chosen so that the Hamming distance between X and S is at most d. How many bits does it take for Alice to communicate X to Bob?

This problem has a well-known solution [16,17,18] [19, §6] [20, Example 4] [21, Remark 5.1]: Pick any linear error correcting code $\mathcal{E} \subseteq \{0,1\}^n$ that corrects up to d errors; write $X = C \oplus U$, where $C \in \mathcal{E}$ is a codeword and U is a syndrome, and send U to Bob; Bob can apply the decoding algorithm to $U \oplus S = C \oplus (X \oplus S)$ to obtain C, and then Bob can compute $X = C \oplus U$. Also, if X and S are drawn from correlated i.i.d. binary sources, then for all $\epsilon > 0$, the Hamming distance between X and S is at most $n \cdot (\Pr[X \neq S] + \epsilon)$, except with exponentially small probability, so this yields a source coding algorithm with exponentially small decoding error for the special case of i.i.d. binary sources.

As a result, one can build protocols for source coding with side information out of any high-rate linear error-correcting code. The best provable rates for explicit constructions can be found in [10,22].

6   Conclusions

In this work, we have examined the possibility of first encrypting a data stream and then compressing it, where the compressor does not have knowledge of the encryption key. The encrypted data can be compressed using distributed source coding principles, because the key will be available at the decoder. Our principal contribution is in the observation that the problem of compressing encrypted data is a special case of the source coding with side information problem. We have studied both the compression efficiency and the cryptographic security aspects of this problem. It is an interesting open problem to extend our work to encryption schemes beyond the stream cipher.

Acknowledgements. We thank the anonymous reviewers for many extremely helpful comments.

References

1. B. Schneier, *Applied Cryptography*. New York: Wiley, 1996.
2. D. K. Slepian and J. K. Wolf, "Noiseless Coding of Correlated Information Sources," *IEEE Transactions on Information Theory*, vol. 19, pp. 471–480, July 1973.
3. I. Csiszar, "Linear Codes for Sources and Source Networks: Error Exponents, Universal Coding," *IEEE Transactions on Information Theory*, vol. 28, pp. 585–592, July 1982.

4. T. M. Cover and J. A. Thomas, *Elements of Information Theory*. New York: Wiley, 1991.
5. S. S. Pradhan and K. Ramchandran, "Distributed Source Coding Using Syndromes (DISCUS): Design and Construction," in *Proceedings of the Data Compression Conference (DCC)*, (Snowbird, UT), March 1999.
6. M. Bellare, A. Desai, E. Jokipii, and P. Rogaway, "A Concrete Security Treatment of Symmetric Encryption: Analysis of the DES Modes of Operation," in *38th Symposium on Foundations of Computer Science*, (Miami Beach, FL), October 1997.
7. S. Wicker, *Error Control Systems for Digital Communication and Storage*. Englewood Cliffs, NJ: Prentice Hall, 1995.
8. C. Berrou, A. Glavieux, and P. Thitimajshima, "Near Shannon Limit Error-Correcting Coding and Decoding: Turbo-Codes," in *IEEE International Conference on Communications*, (Geneva, Switzerland), May 1993.
9. R. G. Gallager, *Low Density Parity Check Codes*. PhD thesis, MIT, Cambridge, MA, 1963.
10. M. Sipser and D. A. Spielman, "Expander codes," *IEEE Transactions on Information Theory*, vol. 42, pp. 1710–1722, November 1996.
11. D. Schonberg, K. Ramchandran, and S. S. Pradhan, "LDPC Codes Can Approach the Slepian Wolf Bound for General Binary Sources," in *40th Annual Allerton Conference*, October 2002.
12. A. D. Liveris, Z. Xiong, and C. N. Georghiades, "Compression of Binary Sources with Side Information Using Low-Density Parity-Check Codes," in *IEEE Communication Letters*, 2002.
13. J. Garcia-Frias and Y. Zhao, "Compression of Correlated Binary Sources Using Turbo Codes," in *IEEE Communication Letters*, October 2001.
14. A. Aaron and B. Girod, "Compression with Side Information Using Turbo Codes," in *IEEE Data Compression Conference*, April 2002.
15. E. Kushilevitz and N. Nisan, *Communication Complexity*. New York: Cambridge University Press, 1997.
16. H. Witsenhausen and A. D. Wyner, "Interframe coder for video signals," 1980. United States Patent Number 4,191,970.
17. A. E. Gamal and A. Orlitsky, "Interactive data compression," in *Proceedings 25th IEEE Symposium on Foundations of Computer Science*, pp. 100–108, October 1984.
18. A. Orlitsky, *Communication Issues in Distributed Computing*. PhD thesis, Stanford University, Electrical Engineering Department, 1986.
19. T. Feder, E. Kushilevitz, M. Naor, and N. Nisan, "Amortized communication complexity," *SIAM Journal on Computing*, vol. 24, no. 4, pp. 736–750, 1995.
20. A. Orlitsky, "Interactive communication of balanced distributions and of correlated files," *SIAM J. Discret. Math.*, vol. 6, pp. 548–564, November 1993.
21. G. Cormode, M. Paterson, S. C. Sahinalp, and U. Vishkin, "Communication complexity of document exchange," in *Proceedings of the 11th annual ACM-SIAM symposium on Discrete algorithms*, pp. 197–206, Society for Industrial and Applied Mathematics, 2000.
22. M. Capalbo, O. Reingold, S. Vadhan, and A. Wigderson, "Randomness conductors and constant-degree lossless expanders," in *Proceedings of the 34th annual ACM symposium on Theory of computing*, pp. 659–668, ACM Press, 2002.

On the Notion of Pseudo-Free Groups

Ronald L. Rivest

Computer Science and Artificial Intelligence Laboratory
Massachusetts Institute of Technology
Cambridge, MA 02139
rivest@mit.edu

Abstract. We explore the notion of a *pseudo-free group*, first introduced
by Hohenberger [Hoh03], and provide an alternative stronger definition.
We show that if $\mathbf{Z}_n^*$ is a pseudo-free abelian group (as we conjecture), then
$\mathbf{Z}_n^*$ also satisfies the Strong RSA Assumption [FO97,CS00,BP97]. Being a
"pseudo-free abelian group" may be the strongest natural cryptographic
assumption one can make about a group such as $\mathbf{Z}_n^*$. More generally, we
show that a pseudo-free group satisfies several standard cryptographic
assumptions, such as the difficulty of computing discrete logarithms.

1 Introduction

Cryptographic schemes often work with finite groups in such a way that the
security of the scheme depends upon an explicit complexity-theoretic assumption
about computational problems in that group.

For example, the RSA public-key cryptosystem [RSA78] works with the multiplicative group $\mathbf{Z}_n^*$, where n is the product of two large primes. The security
of RSA encryption depends upon the "RSA Assumption."

RSA Assumption: It is computationally infeasible for a probabilistic
polynomial-time adversary, given an integer n that is the product of
two sufficiently large randomly chosen primes, an integer $e > 1$ that is
relatively prime to $\phi(n)$, and an element a chosen randomly from $\mathbf{Z}_n^*$, to
compute the $x \in \mathbf{Z}_n^*$ such that

$$x^e = a \pmod{n}$$

with non-negligible probability.[1]

Similarly, the Cramer-Shoup cryptosystem and signature scheme [CS98,
CS99] depend upon the "Strong RSA Assumption," [FO97,BP97]. which allows
the adversary himself to choose an exponent $e > 1$.

---

[1] A function $f(k)$ is considered to be a negligible function of k if for all constants $c > 0$
and all sufficiently large k we have that $|f(k)| < 1/k^c$. In the RSA Assumption, the
phrase "non-negligible probability" is interpreted to mean a non-negligible function
of $\log(n)$.

M. Naor (Ed.): TCC 2004, LNCS 2951, pp. 505–521, 2004.
© Springer-Verlag Berlin Heidelberg 2004

Strong RSA Assumption: It is infeasible for a probabilistic polynomial-time adversary, given an integer n that is the product of two sufficiently large randomly chosen primes, and an element a chosen randomly from $\mathbf{Z}_n^*$, to compute an $x \in \mathbf{Z}_n^*$ and an integer $e > 1$ such that

$$x^e = a \pmod{n}$$

with non-negligible probability.

Assuming that $\mathbf{Z}_n^*$ is *pseudo-free* takes this progression one step further: the adversary may choose whatever equation he wishes and try to solve it, as long as the equation is "nontrivial"—unsatisfiable in the free group, with appropriate care for some details. The pseudo-free assumption is that the adversary will succeed with at most negligible probability. The assumption of pseudo-freeness may be made for any arbitrary finite group, such as an elliptic curve group or even a nonabelian group. We might call the assumption that $\mathbf{Z}_n^*$ is pseudo-free the *Super-Strong RSA Assumption*.

We explore the assumption that a group is *pseudo-free* or, more specifically, *pseudo-free abelian*, and show how it implies some of these other standard assumptions. Assuming that a finite group is pseudo-free thus appears to be quite a strong assumption.

Why formulate and study such a strong assumption? Doesn't this go against the traditional style of making only the minimal complexity-theoretic assumptions necessary for a cryptographic scheme or protocol? Perhaps, but we provide the following motivation and justifications.

- It seems quite plausible that $\mathbf{Z}_n^*$ (for n the product of two sufficiently large randomly chosen primes) is in fact pseudo-free.
- Making stronger assumptions may make proofs easier (this is especially useful for pedagogic purposes).
- It may turn out that the pseudo-freeness is not a "stronger" assumption after all—it may be implied by simpler assumptions, perhaps more standard ones.
- Reasoning in a free group can be quite simple and intuitive, so assuming pseudo-freeness allows one to capture "natural" security proofs in a plausible framework. (This was Hohenberger's [Hoh03] motivation.)

Section 2 provides some mathematical background, and then Section 3 develops the definition of a pseudo-free group. Section 4 studies some of the implications of assuming that a group is pseudo-free. Section 5 considers some variations and generalizations of the basic definition, and then Section 6 discusses further issues related to the notion of a pseudo-free group. Finally, Section 7 provides some conclusions and lists some open problems.

2   Mathematical Background

2.1   Mathematical Groups

We first restate the definition of a mathematical group.

Definition 1. *A group $G = (S, \circ)$ consists of a set S of elements, and a binary operator $\circ$ defined on S, such that:*

Closure: *For all elements $x, y \in S$, we have $x \circ y \in S$.*
Identity: *There is an element $1 \in S$ such that for all elements $x \in S$,*
$x \circ 1 = 1 \circ x = x$.
Associativity: *For all elements $x, y, z \in S$, $x \circ (y \circ z) = (x \circ y) \circ z$.*
Inverses: *For every element $x \in S$, there is an element $y \in S$ such that*
$x \circ y = y \circ x = 1$.

We use multiplicative notation: ab means $a \circ b$. The inverse of x is denoted x^{-1}. We let G also denote the set S. A group G is finite iff $|S|$ is finite. A group G is *abelian* if $\circ$ is commutative: for all $x, y \in G$, $xy = yx$. We use the usual exponent notation: a^e is the word $aaa \ldots a$ of length e, and a^{-e} is the corresponding inverse word $a^{-1} a^{-1} \ldots a^{-1}$ of length e.

2.2   Computational Groups

A mathematical group G has some representation $[G]$ when used in cryptography. We call such a representation $[G]$ a *computational group* implementing an underlying *mathematical group*. Many computational groups may implement the same mathematical group.

In a computational group $[G]$, each element $x \in G$ has one or more representations as a finite-length bit string $[x]$. We often omit brackets, understanding that each element has such representation(s). When G is finite, it is convenient to assume that there is a common bit-length N such that any representation of any element of G requires exactly N bits.

A computational group provides efficient (polynomial-time) algorithms for all of the following operations: [2]

Composition: Given (representations of) group elements x and y, compute (a representation of) $x \circ y$.
Identity: Compute (a representation of) the identity element 1.
Inverses: Given (a representation of) an element x, compute (a representation of) x^{-1}.
Equality Testing: Given (representations of) any two elements $x, y \in G$, determine if $x = y$.

---

[2] Hohenberger [Hoh03] studies a variant where inversion is not efficiently computable, at least by the adversary, and relates such groups to transitive signatures schemes.

Sampling: (Only if G is finite.) Return (a representation of) an element chosen uniformly at random from G, or in a manner that is indistinguishable from uniformly at random to a probabilistic polynomial-time (PPT) adversary. We denote such a procedure as $x \in_R G$.

As a running example: given n, the product of two large primes, anyone, including an adversary, can efficiently do all the group operations in $\mathbf{Z}_n^*$, using the usual representation of elements as residues modulo n.

2.3   Black Box Groups

The parties in a cryptographic protocol may access the group in a *black-box* manner, a notion introduced by Babai and Szemerédi [BS84] (see also Babai [Bab97], and see Boneh and Lipton [BL96] for extension of the black-box notion to fields).

Under the black-box assumption, each element of the computational group is a bit string of some common length N, and "black-box" subroutines are available for the group operations. [3]

The black-box assumption is that group operations may only be performed using the supplied implementations. Furthermore, the representation of group elements is "opaque": operations on them other than through the black-box routines are forbidden. [4]

It is natural to ask if there are black-box algorithms for various group-theoretic problems. The black-box assumption is reasonable for algorithm design; it amounts to a convention or a self-imposed restriction on what operations may be performed. To find an efficient algorithm under the black-box assumption is then a satisfying result; no unusual "tricks" are required.

For example, Tonelli and Shanks [BS96, Section 7.1] [Coh93, Section 1.5.1] give a probabilistic black-box algorithm for computing square roots in $\mathbf{Z}_p^*$; it finds the black-box representation $[x]$ of a value x satisfying

$$x^2 = a \pmod{p}$$

given the black-box representation $[a]$ of a (assumed to be a quadratic residue), and also given the prime p. Other algorithms for this problem, such as Cipolla's [BS96, Section 7.2], violate the black-box assumption for $\mathbf{Z}_p^*$ by utilizing both field operations available in $\mathbf{F}_p$.

If no efficient black-box algorithm can be found for a problem, then the black-box assumption may be too restrictive. For example, Shoup [Sho97] proves lower bounds for discrete logarithms and other problems in the black-box group model.

---

[3] For Babai [Bab97], these operations include all but sampling, as he studies the implementation of the sampling procedure itself.

[4] In some applications side information such as the size or structure of the underlying group, such as the fact that the group is cyclic, is known, even though the group's representation is otherwise "black-box;" we don't consider such side information here.

However, we are studying here not algorithmic efficiency, but cryptographic security. A typical adversary may willfully violate any black-box assumption: he may examine the bits of any representation or examine the code implementing any group operation.

Consider our running example: $\mathbf{Z}_n^*$. Here an adversary is given n, and code for composition (i.e., for multiplication modulo n). Nothing prevents him from examining this code or the bit-level representations of elements, or from using methods such as "index-calculus methods" [SS98] not allowed under a black-box assumption.

Therefore, we do not make black-box assumptions. [5] We assume that an adversary may use any available information and may use methods that depend upon representation or implementation details. The adversary has "non-black-box" access to the group implementation. Whether a group is pseudo-free may then depend on the details of its representation as a computational group; one should properly speak of whether a computational group is pseudo-free or not. In any case, for our purposes it will be relevant that an equation is satisifiable in a mathematical group if and only if it is satisfiable in any computational group representing it.

2.4   Free Groups

Free groups are infinite groups derivable from a given set of generators that have no non-trivial relationships.

Free groups are defined formally as follows. (See also Gutiérrez [Gut00], for example.) Let $A = \{a_1, a_2, \ldots, a_k\}$ be a nonempty set of distinct symbols, which are the *generators* of a free group. For each such symbol a_i, let a_i^{-1} be a new symbol representing the inverse of a_i. Let A^{-1} denote the set $\{a_i^{-1} \mid a_i \in A\}$, and let $A^{\pm 1}$ denote $A \cup A^{-1}$; $A^{\pm 1}$ is the *set of symbols* for the free group with set A of generators.

We let $F(A)$ denote the free group defined by the set A of generators. We may equivalently write $F(a_1, a_2, \ldots, a_k)$ when $A = \{a_1, a_2, \ldots, a_k\}$. Elements of this free group may be represented as words (sequences of symbols of this free group). As an example, the word

$$a_1 a_2^{-1} a_2 a_1^{-1} a_3^{-1} a_2$$

represents an element of $F(a_1, a_2, a_3, a_4)$.

A word may be simplified, or reduced, by repeatedly eliminating any two adjacent inverse symbols; the resulting word is equivalent to the original. Thus, the word in the above example is equivalent to $a_3^{-1} a_2$. A word that can not be reduced further is *reduced* or *in canonical form*.

The elements of a free group are thus words in canonical form. One could alternatively define the elements to be equivalence classes of words.

The operation $\circ$ for a free group is concatenation followed by simplification. For example, $a_1 a_2 \circ a_2^{-1} a_3 = a_1 a_2 a_2^{-1} a_3 = a_1 a_3$.

---

[5] One could easily develop a theory of black-box pseudo-free groups.

The identity for a free group is the empty word ϵ. Two words represent the same element of a free group if their reduced forms are the same. The inverse of a word is just the reverse of the word, with each symbol replaced by its inverse. The operator $\circ$ is closed and associative—for a proof see, for example, Lyndon and Schupp [LS77, Chapter I].

A free group on at least one generator is an infinite group, since there are an infinite number of distinct words in canonical form (e.g. $\{a^k\}$).

Since a free group is infinite, it is not possible to even approximately implement uniform sampling. However, it is easy to construct a computational group that implements a free group on a countable set of generators except for the uniform sampling requirement.

We note that if $A \subseteq B$, then $F(A)$ is a subgroup of $F(B)$.

2.5   Free Abelian Groups

A free abelian group $FA(a_1, a_2, \ldots, a_k)$ is defined similarly to ordinary free groups, except that the group is abelian. Thus, for any pair of symbols a and b, we may replace the sequence ab by the sequence ba and preserve equivalence.

Commutativity enables one to define the canonical form for a word in $FA(a_1, a_2, \ldots, a_l)$ to be a word of the form:

$$a_1^{e_1} a_2^{e_2} \ldots a_l^{e_l}$$

for some integers $e_1, e_2, \ldots, e_l$. It is well known that $FA(a_1, a_2, \ldots, a_l)$ is isomorphic to the l-fold direct sum $\mathbf{Z} \oplus \mathbf{Z} \oplus \cdots \oplus \mathbf{Z}$. We could represent an element $a_1^{e_1} a_2^{e_2} \ldots a_k^{e_l}$ of $FA(a_1, a_2, \ldots, a_l)$ by the vector $(e_1, e_2, \ldots, e_l)$, and implement $\circ$ with vector addition.

3   Pseudo-Free Groups

A cryptographic scheme may utilize a particular mathematical group G; all parties have access to a computational group $[G]$ representing G.

Intuitively, a group is *pseudo-free* if it is indistinguishable from a free group. A free group has no surprising or anomalous identities; the only truths are those implied by the axioms of group theory.

Thus, informally, we say that a finite group G is pseudo-free if a probabilistic polynomial-time adversary can not efficiently produce an equation E and a solution to E in G where E has no solution in the "corresponding free group." Of course, we need to define what we mean by "corresponding free group."

Assuming that a finite group such as $\mathbf{Z}_n^*$ is pseudo-free is thus a complexity-theoretic assumption, similar to but stronger than the RSA Assumption or the Strong RSA Assumption.

This assumption turns out to be very strong, as it implies several standard cryptographic assumptions (at least for $G = \mathbf{Z}_n^*$). Nonetheless, it seems a plausible assumption in some cases, and it may be useful for new applications. In any case, we find its formulation and elaboration interesting.

For example, in a free group (abelian or not), there is no solution to

$$x^2 = a \qquad (1)$$

where x is a variable ranging over group elements, and a is a generator of the free group, since for any value of x the reduced form of x^2 has even length. However, the corresponding equation in $\mathbf{Z}_n^*$,

$$x^2 = a \pmod{n} , \qquad (2)$$

has a solution if a is a square in $\mathbf{Z}_n^*$. A solution to such a corresponding equation "proves" that $\mathbf{Z}_n^*$ is different than the corresponding free group.

The adversary may not claim that G is distinguishable from a free group merely because G is obviously finite, for example, because the elements of G all have N-bit representations. We insist on a different kind of proof: the adversary must provide a solution to an equation in G whose "corresponding equation" in a free group has no solution.

3.1 Equations in Free Groups

Let H denote a free group, such as $F(a_1, a_2, \ldots, a_l)$ or $FA(a_1, a_2, \ldots, a_l)$.

Let $x_1, x_2, \ldots, x_m$ denote variables that may take values in H.

An equation in H takes the form

$$w_1 = w_2$$

where w_1 and w_2 are words formed from the symbols of H and from the variables $x_1, x_2, \ldots, x_m$. One can always put such equations in a "canonical form" of the form $w = 1$ for some word w.

As an example, in $F(a_1, a_2)$ the equation

$$a_1 x_1 = x_2 a_2^{-1} ,$$

has many solutions (x_1, x_2), such as (a_2^{-1}, a_1) or $(1, a_1 a_2)$.

Equations that have solutions in the free group are called *satisfiable*, others are called *unsatisfiable*.

Our definition of a pseudo-free group depends on being able to distinguish effectively between satisfiable and unsatisfiable equations in a free group.

Can one decide whether a given equation is satisfiable or not? Fortunately, one can. In 1982 Makanin [Mak82] showed that it is decidable whether or not an equation in the free group is satisfiable. More recently Gutiérrez [Gut00] has shown that this problem is decidable in PSPACE. For our use, these results are quite sufficient; the decision procedure need not be in polynomial-time.

When the free group is the abelian group $FA(a_1, a_2, \ldots, a_l)$ it is easy to determine whether a given equation is satisfiable: the equation can always be rewritten in the form:

$$x_1^{d_1} x_2^{d_2} \cdots x_m^{d_m} = a_1^{e_1} a_2^{e_2} \cdots a_l^{e_l}$$

for integers $d_1, d_2, \ldots, d_m, e_1, e_2, \ldots, e_l$. Such an equation is satisfiable iff for all i, $1 \leq i \leq l$, we have

$$\gcd(d_1, d_2, \ldots, d_m) \mid e_i . \tag{3}$$

One can prove that this statement holds for $l = 1$ and that such solutions can be combined for larger l.

An equation that is satisfiable in $F(A)$ is also satisfiable in $FA(A)$ (but not necessarily conversely). This is useful since it provides an easy way to prove that an equation is *unsatisfiable* in a free group: merely prove that it is unsatisfiable in the corresponding free abelian group.

3.2   The Correspondence

Given an equation that is unsatisfiable in a free group $F(A)$, what counts as a "corresponding equation" in a given group G?

We have to be a little careful, since there are trivial cases to avoid. For example, the previously mentioned quadratic equation:

$$x^2 = a ,$$

which is unsatisfiable in $F(a)$, may have "trivial" solutions in $\mathbf{Z}_n^*$, depending on how the element in $\mathbf{Z}_n^*$ corresponding to the generator a of the free group is selected. For example, if the adversary is allowed to specify that $a = 4$, then there is clearly the trivial solution $x = 2$.

We resolve this issue (following Hohenberger's thesis [Hoh03]) by requiring that when making the correspondence between interpreting the equation in the free group and interpreting it in G, *each of the generators a_i must correspond to an independently generated random element of G.*

The adversary thus has no control over the choice of elements in G that are to correspond to the generators in the free group.

Thus, for example, the adversary must take the square root of a randomly chosen element $a \in \mathbf{Z}_n^*$ in order to demonstrate an acceptable solution to the above equation, when G is the group $\mathbf{Z}_n^*$.

This requirement that generators in the free group correspond to randomly chosen elements of G fits naturally with common cryptographic usage where, for example, one party publishes randomly-chosen elements g and h such that finding the discrete logarithm of h base g is assumed to be hard. For the adversary, the randomly chosen elements g and h are the "generators" of the group he must attack.

Informally, an adversary succeeds in distinguishing G from a free group if he can produce:

- An equation E that is unsatisfiable in the free group, where this equation has variables $x_1, x_2, \ldots, x_m$ and generators $a_1, a_2, \ldots, a_l$.
- A sequence $\alpha_1, \ldots, \alpha_l$ of values produced as random samples from the group G, to use as values for the generators $a_1, a_2, \ldots, a_l$. (If the inverse symbols a_i^{-1} are used, then they are to be replaced by the inverses of the randomly chosen values.)

- Values for the variables x_1, x_2, ..., x_m that satisfy the equation produced in G.

This definition allows the adversary to choose the equation himself, as long as the equation is unsatisfiable in the free group. This generalizes the situation for the Strong RSA assumption, where the adversary may choose the exponent e.

For efficiency in describing his equation, the adversary may use "exponential expressions," such as $a((ax)^{531}x^{17})$, (see [Gut00, Section 2.2.1]), or even the mathematically equivalent but potentially more compact notation of algebraic straight-line programs, as proposed in Hohenberger [Hoh03].

The adversary need not produce a proof that the equation is unsatisfiable in a free group, since this can be verified directly using Makanin's or Gutiérrez's algorithm. (One could alternatively require the adversary to produce an equation whose unsatisfiability can be verified in polynomial time, or to produce a polynomial-size proof of unsatisfiability; we do not study such a restriction here, since the impact of assuming pseudo-freeness is to support the infeasibility for an adversary to solve the equation, not to support using the equation in a protocol.)

We make our definition more precise as follows.

Definition 2. *A family $\mathcal{G} = \{G_k : k \geq 0\}$ of finite computational groups is pseudo-free if:*

- *All operations in G_k can be performed in time polynomial in k.*
- *For every probabilistic polynomial-time adversary $\mathcal{A}$, for every polynomial $p(\cdot)$, if $\alpha_1, \alpha_2, \ldots, \alpha_{p(k)}$ are elements chosen uniformly and independently at random from G_k, then the probability*

$$Pr[\mathcal{A}(G_k, \alpha_1, \alpha_2, \ldots, \alpha_{p(k)}) = (E, \beta_1, \beta_2, \ldots, \beta_m)]$$

where $\mathcal{A}$ is given access to the routines implementing the group G_k as well as the elements $\alpha_1, \alpha_2, \ldots, \alpha_{p(k)}$, and where

$$E = E(x_1, x_2, \ldots, x_m; a_1, a_2, \ldots, a_{p(k)})$$

is an equation over the free group $F(a_1, a_2, \ldots, a_{p(k)})$ with variables x_1, x_2, ..., x_m such that E is unsatisfiable in $F(a_1, a_2, \ldots, a_{p(k)})$ but $E(\beta_1, \beta_2, \ldots, \beta_m; \alpha_1, \alpha_2, \ldots, \alpha_{p(k)})$ is true in G_k, is a negligible function of k.

This definition refers to a family of computational groups, but one may apply it to a family of mathematical groups with the understanding that the groups are implemented in some standard way as computational groups. One may also wish to specify whether the adversary has black-box access or non-black-box access to the group.

If the groups G_k are abelian, then we may also say that $\mathcal{G}$ is *pseudo-free abelian*, although we prefer just saying that $\mathcal{G}$ is pseudo-free when, as in the case $\mathcal{G} = \{\mathbf{Z}_n^*\}$, the groups are obviously abelian.

4   Pseudo-Freeness Implies Many Other Cryptographic Assumptions

If G is pseudo-free, then several standard complexity-theoretic assumptions follow. We look at the six fundamental problems studied by Lipschutz and Miller [LI71], and then examine other standard cryptographic assumptions, such as Diffie-Hellman.

Lipschutz and Miller [LI71] consider six fundamental problems: the *order problem* [solving $a^e = 1$ for e], the *power problem* (aka the discrete logarithm problem) [solving $a^e = b$ for e], the *root problem* (aka the RSA problem) [solving $x^e = a$ for x], the *proper power problem* (aka the strong RSA problem) [solving $x^e = a$ for x and $e > 1$], the *generalized power problem* [solving $a^e = b^f$ for nonzero e, f], and the *intersection problem for cyclic subgroups* [solving $a^e = b^f \neq 1$ for e, f]. They show these problems are independent: for each pair of problems there is a group such that one problem is solvable (i.e. satisfiability of the relevant equation is decidable) while the other problem is unsolvable. These problems, while studied with respect to their decidability, are familiar ones for the cryptographer; we explore their satisfiability in the free group, and consequent implications for pseudo-free groups.

4.1   Order Problem

The *order problem* in G is the following: given an element $a \in G$, to determine a positive integer e (if any exist) such that

$$a^e = 1 . \tag{4}$$

The least positive such value e is the *order* of the element a in the group G. In a free group all elements except the identity have infinite order, implying the following theorem.

Theorem 1. *In a pseudo-free group G, it is infeasible for an adversary to determine the order of a randomly chosen element a.*

4.2   Discrete Logarithm Problem

The *discrete logarithm problem* in G is: given elements a and b from G, to determine an integer e (if any exist) such that

$$a^e = b ; \tag{5}$$

the value e is a "discrete logarithm" of b, to the base a, in the group G.

This problem is often assumed to be hard, for specific groups G; in their classic paper [DH76b], for example, Diffie and Hellman assumed that this problem was hard in Z_p^* for large primes p. (See also [DH76a] for a slightly earlier usage.)

In $F(a, b)$ and $FA(a, b)$ equation (5) never holds, for any value of e. Since a and b are distinct generators, the two sides of the equation are variable-free constant expressions that can not be equal.

Theorem 2. *In a pseudo-free group, the discrete logarithm problem is infeasible for an adversary to solve, for randomly chosen values a and b.*

4.3   RSA Assumption

In the free group $F(a)$ or $FA(a)$ the equation

$$x^e = a \tag{6}$$

has no solution, for any fixed value of $e > 1$. (It has no solution in $FA(a)$, by our previous discussion of the condition of equation (3).)

Theorem 3. *In a pseudo-free group, the RSA assumption holds.*

4.4   Strong RSA Assumption

The Strong RSA Assumption, defined earlier, was introduced by Barić and Pfitz-mann [BP97] and also by Fijisaki and Okamoto [FO97].

The ability of an adversary to himself choose an exponent $e > 1$ does not affect the satisfiability of equation (6) in a free group.

Theorem 4. *In a pseudo-free group, the Strong RSA Assumption holds.*

Similar equations, such as

$$x^e = a^f \ ,$$

where the adversary is given a and must find x, e, and f such that $e > 1$ and $\gcd(e, f) = 1$, are also infeasible for the adversary to solve in pseudo-free groups; indeed this problem equivalent to solving the strong RSA problem since $\tilde{x}^e = a$ where $\tilde{x} = x^{f'} a^{e'}$ and $ee' + ff' = 1$ (see [CS99, Lemma 1]).

4.5   Generalized Power Problem

The generalized power problem is: given group elements a and b, to find nonzero integers e, f satisfying

$$a^e = b^f \ . \tag{7}$$

Theorem 5. *In a pseudo-free group, it is infeasible for an adversary to solve the generalized power problem.*

4.6   Intersection Problem for Cyclic Subgroups

The intersection problem for cyclic subgroups is: given group elements a and b. to find integers e, f such that

$$a^e = b^f \neq 1 \ . \tag{8}$$

Theorem 6. *In a pseudo-free group, it is infeasible for an adversary to solve the intersection problem for cyclic subgroups.*

4.7   Diffie-Hellman Assumption

Interestingly, the (computational) Diffie-Hellman problem seems not to fit within our formalism. It is a very interesting open problem whether the Diffie-Hellman assumption is implied by pseudo-freeness.

The Computational Diffie-Hellman problem (CDH) is the following: given a value g, and two values

$$a = g^e \tag{9}$$
$$b = g^f \ , \tag{10}$$

for large randomly chosen integers e and f, to compute

$$x = g^{ef} \ . \tag{11}$$

The CDH assumption is that an adversary will have a negligible chance of computing x, given a and b. The natural way of trying to show that the CDH assumption is implied by pseudo-freeness is via equations (9)–(11), where e and f are integer-valued variables, and x is a group element variable (see section 5). However, this argument fails because an adversary who violates CDH to compute x need not be able to find e and f (this is DLP). There doesn't seem to be any equation in variable x alone (i.e., without e, f) available to verify that an adversary has correctly computed x. In other words, the decisional Diffie-Hellman problem doesn't seem to be solvable by verifying an appropriate set of equations involving the single unknown x.

5   Generalizations

In this section we discuss some variations and generalizations on the basic notion of pseudo-freeness.

5.1   Multiple Equations

Mal'cev [Mal60] (see also [KM, Lemma 3 and Corollaries 2–3]) shows that for any finite set of equations in the free group, one can construct a single equation having exactly the same set of solutions. Thus, we may consider sets of simultaneous equations as equivalent to a single equation. The method is based on showing that the two equations $x = 1$, $y = 1$ are equivalent to the single equation $x^2 a x^2 a^{-1} = (y b y b^{-1})^2$.

For abelian groups, it is easy to determine if a set of equations is satisfiable; one may apply standard techniques for solving a set of simultaneous equations over the integers (see Artin [Art91, Section 12.4], for example).

These results allow us to permit the adversary to produce a set of simultaneous equations rather than just a single equation, without loss of generality.

5.2   Adversary Must Prove That Equation Is Unsatisfiable in the Free Group

One could require that the adversary provide a polynomial-time checkable proof that the equation he produces is indeed unsatisfiable in the corresponding free group. However, this restriction seems somewhat pointless, since the reason for assuming pseudo-freeness anyway is to conclude that finding an equation together with its solution should be infeasible.

5.3   Generation of α's

Instead of providing random α's to the adversary directly, one could allow the adversary to produce them himself, as long as they are guaranteed to be "random" in some way.

For example, the adversary might be allowed to use a hash function with range G to derive the relevant α. If the hash function is pseudorandom, or can be modeled as a random oracle [BR93], then its output could be considered as an acceptable α for purposes.

Similarly, if the output of h is an integer, then we may be able to accept $g^{h(x)}$ as an acceptable element α from G for our purposes. The essential criterion for sampling is that the adversary should have no control over the element chosen, and it should be reasonable to model the element chosen as being independently chosen (approximately) uniformly at random from G.

The values α supplied might also be constrained to ensure that a solution in G exists; we don't pursue this variant further here.

5.4   Generalized Exponential Expressions

In the most general form of exponential expressions, the exponents may themselves be integer-valued variables. Consider for example, the equation $(ax)^e b = x^f$ in $F(a, b)$ where x is a variable ranging over group elements and e, f are integer-valued variables. This equation is satisfiable, for example, with $x = b$, $e = 0$, $f = 1$. It is an open problem how to decide if such equations, containing both element-valued variables and integer-valued exponent variables, are satisfiable—see Problem 3 in Section 7.

We may nonetheless allow an adversary to use these general exponential expressions, with variable exponents, because it is still possible to verify that the adversary has "done the impossible." The adversary produces an equation E with variable exponents, and also a solution that satisfies E. If E is unsatisfiable, then so is the equation E' obtained by substituting into E the exponent values supplied in the adversary's solution. One can then verify that E' is unsatisfiable using Makanin's algorithm.

Hohenberger uses straight-line programs in her definition of "equation" or "identity", a natural further generalization of the exponential expressions, which could also be allowed here.

5.5   Adaptive Attacks and Side Information

It may be possible generalize the definition of pseudo-freeness here to handle adaptive attacks and other forms of "side information." How might the definition of pseudo-freeness change if side information, such as the order of the group, is known? Is there a reasonable way to do this? Similarly, how can the notion of pseudo-freeness be adapted to handle adaptive attacks, where the adversary may obtain a solution to an equation before having to provide a different solution (perhaps with new generators)?

6   Discussion

We compare our definition of a pseudo-free group with that given in Hohenberger's thesis. Her work is motivated by transitive signature schemes, and does introduce the critical correspondence between elements drawn from G at random and generators in the free group.

   However, Hohenberger doesn't use variables, which are necessary for setting up equations and showing how pseudo-freeness implies other cryptographic assumptions, and she doesn't address the decidability of determining which equations are satisfiable in a free group. Also, her definition requires that an adversary have only "black-box" access to G.

7   Conclusions and Open Problems

We have taken the definition of pseudo-free group introduced by Hohenberger [Hoh03], strengthened it, and shown how it implies a number of other well-known cryptographic assumptions. While stronger than many previous cryptographic number-theoretic assumptions, pseudo-freeness seems fairly natural, worthy of study in its own right, and quite plausible for commonly used groups.

   The study of pseudo-freeness yields some intriguing open problems and conjectures. We begin with our main conjecture.

Conjecture 1 (Super-Strong RSA Assumption). $\mathbf{Z}_n^*$ is pseudo-free.

   The next open problem is to relate the Diffie-Hellman assumption to pseudo-freeness.

Conjecture 2 (Diffie-Hellman holds for Pseudo-free groups). In a pseudo-free group, both the computational and decisional Diffie-Hellman assumptions hold.

   The following interesting problem, discussed briefly earlier, also appears to be open.

Conjecture 3. It is decidable whether a given equation (or set of equations) with constants is satisfiable over a free group, when the equation is written in exponential notation and may have integer-valued variables in the exponents.

Here is a (satisfiable) example of such an equation: $a((ab)^e y)^f b = x^2$ where x and y are variables (over the group), a and b are constants (group elements), and e and f are integer-valued variables. Some partial results are known [Lyn60, LI71,CE84]; the introduction to [CE84] gives a brief survey. This problem may also be open over semigroups.

Another open research direction is to explore ways of showing that a group G is not a free group, other than by demonstrating the solution to an equation that has no solution in a free group. For example, some statement of the elementary theory of free groups may be (say) false, but provably true in G. Kharlampovich and Myasnikov [KM98] have shown that the elementary theory of a free group is decidable, even if constants are allowed, a much more general result than determining whether a given equation is satisfiable in the free group.

The theory of pseudo-free groups might also be expanded to handle cases such as Z_p^*; this group is typically not pseudo-free, since the size of the group is presumably known in a typical implementation.

Finally, we note that we have only scratched the surface of the study of adaptive attacks against cryptographic schemes defined on pseudo-free groups; much work remains to be done here.

Acknowledgments. I'd like to thank Susan Hohenberger, Albert Meyer, Olga Kharlampovich, and an anonymous referee for helpful guidance and advice.

References

[Art91]   Michael Artin. *Algebra*. Prentice Hall, 1991.

[Bab97]   L. Babai. Randomization in group algorithms: conceptual questions. In L. Finkelstein and W. M. Kantor, editors, *Groups and Computation II. Proc. 1995 DIMACS Workshop*, volume 28 of *DIMACS Ser. in Discr. Math. and Theor. Comp. Sci.*, pages 1–16. AMS, 1997.

[BL96]   Dan Boneh and Richard J. Lipton. Algorithms for black-box fields and their application to cryptography. In Neal Koblitz, editor, *Advances in Cryptology—CRYPTO '96*, pages 283–297. Springer-Verlag, 1996. Lecture Notes in Computer Science No. 1109.

[BP97]   Niko Barić and Birgit Pfitzmann. Collision-free accumulators and fail-stop signature schemes without trees. In *Proc. EUROCRYPT '97*, volume 1233 of *Lecture Notes in Computer Science*, pages 480–494. Springer-Verlag, 1997.

[BR93]   Mihir Bellare and Phillip Rogaway. Random oracles are practical: A paradigm for designing efficient protocols. In *First ACM Conference on Computer and Communications Security*, pages 62–73, Fairfax, 1993. ACM.

[BS84]   L. Babai and E. Szemerédi. On the complexity of matrix group problems I. In *Proc. 25th IEEE FOCS*, pages 229–240, 1984.

[BS96]   Eric Bach and Jeffrey Shallit. *Algorithmic Number Theory; Volume I: Efficient Algorithms*. The MIT Press, 1996.

[CE84]   Leo P. Comerford, Jr. and Charles C. Edmunds. Quadratic parametric equations over free groups. In K. I. Appel, J. G. Ratcliffe, and P. E. Schupp, editors, *Contributions to Group Theory*, volume 33 of *Contemporary Mathematics*, pages 159–196. AMS, 1984.

[Coh93]   Henri Cohen. *A Course in Computational Algebraic Number Theory.* Springer, 1993.

[CS98]   Ronald Cramer and Victor Shoup. A practical public key cryptosystem provably secure against adaptive chosen ciphertext attack. In Hugo Krawczyk, editor, *Proceedings Crypto '98*, pages 13–25. Springer-Verlag, 1998. Lecture Notes in Computer Science No. 1462.

[CS99]   Ronald Cramer and Victor Shoup. Signature schemes based on the strong RSA assumption. In *Proceedings 6th ACM Conference on Computer and Communications Security*, pages 46–52. ACM, Nov 1999.

[CS00]   Ronald Cramer and Victor Shoup. Signature schemes based on the strong RSA assumption. *ACM Transactions on Information and System Security*, 3(3):161–185, 2000.

[DH76a]   W. Diffie and M. E. Hellman. Multiuser cryptographic techniques. In *Proc. AFIPS 1976 National Computer Conference*, pages 109–112, Montvale, N.J., 1976. AFIPS.

[DH76b]   W. Diffie and M. E. Hellman. New directions in cryptography. *IEEE Trans. Inform. Theory*, IT-22:644–654, November 1976.

[FO97]   Eiichiro Fujisaki and Tatsuaki Okamoto. Statistical zero knowledge protocols to prove modular polynomial relations. In Jr. Burton S. Kaliski, editor, *Proc. CRYPTO '97*, volume 1294 of *LNCS*, pages 16–30. Springer-Verlag, 1997.

[Gut00]   Claudio Gutiérrez. Satisfiability of equations in free groups is in PSPACE. In *Proc. 32nd ACM STOC*, pages 21–27. ACM Press, 2000.

[HMR03]   Susan Hohenberger, David Molnar, and Ronald L. Rivest. Special signatures need special algebra, May 2003. Submitted.

[Hoh03]   Susan Hohenberger. The cryptographic impact of groups with infeasible inversion. Master's thesis, EECS Dept., MIT, June 2003.

[KM]   Olga Kharlampovich and Alexei Myasnikov. Implicit function theorem over free groups. Available at www.math.mcgill.ca/olga/publications.html.

[KM98]   Olga Kharlampovich and Alexei Myasnikov. Tarski's problem about the elementary theory of free groups has a positive solution. *Electronic Research Announcements of the American Mathematical Society*, 4:101–108, December 14, 1998. S 1079-6762(98)00047-X.

[LI71]   Seymour Lipschutz and Charles F. Miller III. Groups with certain solvable and unsolvable decision problems. *Communications on Pure and Applied Mathematics*, XXIV:7–15, 1971.

[LS77]   Roger C. Lyndon and Paul E. Schupp. *Combinatorial Group Theory.* Springer, 1977.

[Lyn60]   R. C. Lyndon. Equations in free groups. *Trans. Amer. Math. Soc.*, 96:445–457, 1960.

[Mak82]   G. S. Makanin. Equations in a free group. *Izvestiya NA SSSR*, 46:1199–1273, 1982. English translation in Math USSR Izvestiya, 21 (1983), 483–546.

[Mal60]   A. I. Mal'cev. On some correspondence between rings and groups. *Math. Sbornik*, 50:257–266, 1960.

[MW99]   Ueli Maurer and Stefan Wolf. The relationship between breaking the Diffie-Hellman protocol and computing discrete logarithms. *SIAM Journal on Computing*, 28(5):1689–1721, 1999.

[MW00]   Ueli Maurer and Stefan Wolf. The Diffie-Hellman protocol. *Designs, Codes, and Cryptography*, 19:147–171, 2000.

[Raz84]   A. A. Razborov. On systems of equations in free groups. *Izvestiya AN SSSR*, 48:779–832 (In Russian), 1984. English translation in Math. USSR Izvestiya 25,1 (1985) 115–162.

[RSA78]   Ronald L. Rivest, Adi Shamir, and Leonard M. Adleman. A method for obtaining digital signatures and public-key cryptosystems. *Communications of the ACM*, 21(2):120–126, 1978.

[Sho97]   Victor Shoup. Lower bounds for discrete logarithms and related problems. In Walter Fumy, editor, *Proc. Eurocrypt '97*, volume 1233 of *Lecture Notes in Computer Science*, pages 256–266. Springer-Verlag, May 1997.

[SS98]   Joseph H. Silverman and Joe Suzuki. Elliptic curve discrete logarithms and the index calculus. In *Proc. Asiacrypt '98*, volume 1514 of *Lecture Notes in Computer Science*, pages 110–125. Springer-Verlag, 1998.

Author Index

Lecture Notes in Computer Science

For information about Vols. 1–2830

please contact your bookseller or Springer-Verlag

Vol. 2881: E. Horlait, T. Magedanz, R.H. Glitho (Eds.), Mobile Agents for Telecommunication Applications. Proceedings, 2003. IX, 297 pages. 2003.

Vol. 2880: H.L. Bodlaender (Eds.), Graph-Theoretic Concepts in Computer Science. XI, 386 pages. 2003.

Vol. 2879: R.E. Ellis, T.M. Peters (Eds.), Medical Image Computing and Computer-Assisted Intervention - MICCAI 2003. Proceedings, 2003. XXXIV, 1003 pages. 2003.

Vol. 2878: R.E. Ellis, T.M. Peters (Eds.), Medical Image Computing and Computer-Assisted Intervention - MICCAI 2003. Proceedings, 2003. XXXIII, 819 pages. 2003.

Vol. 2877: T. Böhme, G. Heyer, H. Unger (Eds.), Innovative Internet Community Systems. VIII, 263 pages. 2003.

Vol. 2876: M. Schroeder, G. Wagner (Eds.), Rules and Rule Markup Languages for the Semantic Web. Proceedings, 2003. VII, 173 pages. 2003.

Vol. 2875: E. Aarts, R. Collier, E.v. Loenen, B.d. Ruyter (Eds.), Ambient Intelligence. Proceedings, 2003. XI, 432 pages. 2003.

Vol. 2874: C. Priami (Eds.), Global Computing. XIX, 255 pages. 2003.

Vol. 2871: N. Zhong, Z.W. Raś, S. Tsumoto, E. Suzuki (Eds.), Foundations of Intelligent Systems. Proceedings, 2003. XV, 697 pages. 2003. (Subseries LNAI).

Vol. 2870: D. Fensel, K.P. Sycara, J. Mylopoulos (Eds.), The Semantic Web - ISWC 2003. Proceedings, 2003. XV, 931 pages. 2003.

Vol. 2869: A. Yazici, C. Şener (Eds.), Computer and Information Sciences - ISCIS 2003. Proceedings, 2003. XIX, 1110 pages. 2003.

Vol. 2868: P. Perner, R. Brause, H.-G. Holzhütter (Eds.), Medical Data Analysis. Proceedings, 2003. VIII, 127 pages. 2003.

Vol. 2866: J. Akiyama, M. Kano (Eds.), Discrete and Computational Geometry. VIII, 285 pages. 2003.

Vol. 2865: S. Pierre, M. Barbeau, E. Kranakis (Eds.), Ad-Hoc, Mobile, and Wireless Networks. Proceedings, 2003. X, 293 pages. 2003.

Vol. 2864: A.K. Dey, A. Schmidt, J.F. McCarthy (Eds.), UbiComp 2003: Ubiquitous Computing. Proceedings, 2003. XVII, 368 pages. 2003.

Vol. 2863: P. Stevens, J. Whittle, G. Booch (Eds.), "UML" 2003 - The Unified Modeling Language. Proceedings, 2003. XIV, 415 pages. 2003.

Vol. 2860: D. Geist, E. Tronci (Eds.), Correct Hardware Design and Verification Methods. Proceedings, 2003. XII, 426 pages. 2003.

Vol. 2859: B. Apolloni, M. Marinaro, R. Tagliaferri (Eds.), Neural Nets. X, 376 pages. 2003.

Vol. 2857: M.A. Nascimento, E.S. de Moura, A.L. Oliveira (Eds.), String Processing and Information Retrieval. Proceedings, 2003. XI, 379 pages. 2003.

Vol. 2856: M. Smirnov (Eds.), Quality of Future Internet Services. IX, 293 pages. 2003.

Vol. 2855: R. Alur, I. Lee (Eds.), Embedded Software. Proceedings, 2003. X, 373 pages. 2003.

Vol. 2854: J. Hoffmann, Utilizing Problem Structure in Planing. XIII, 251 pages. 2003. (Subseries LNAI).

Vol. 2853: M. Jeckle, L.-J. Zhang (Eds.), Web Services - ICWS-Europe 2003. VIII, 227 pages. 2003.

Vol. 2852: F.S. de Boer, M.M. Bonsangue, S. Graf, W.-P. de Roever (Eds.), Formal Methods for Components and Objects. VIII, 509 pages. 2003.

Vol. 2851: C. Boyd, W. Mao (Eds.), Information Security. Proceedings, 2003. XI, 453 pages. 2003.

Vol. 2849: N. García, L. Salgado, J.M. Martínez (Eds.), Visual Content Processing and Representation. Proceedings, 2003. XII, 352 pages. 2003.

Vol. 2848: F.E. Fich (Eds.), Distributed Computing. Proceedings, 2003. X, 367 pages. 2003.

Vol. 2847: R.d. Lemos, T.S. Weber, J.B. Camargo Jr. (Eds.), Dependable Computing. Proceedings, 2003. XIV, 371 pages. 2003.

Vol. 2846: J. Zhou, M. Yung, Y. Han (Eds.), Applied Cryptography and Network Security. Proceedings, 2003. XI, 436 pages. 2003.

Vol. 2845: B. Christianson, B. Crispo, J.A. Malcolm, M. Roe (Eds.), Security Protocols. VIII, 243 pages. 2004.

Vol. 2844: J.A. Jorge, N. Jardim Nunes, J. Falcão e Cunha (Eds.), Interactive Systems. Design, Specification, and Verification. XIII, 429 pages. 2003.

Vol. 2843: G. Grieser, Y. Tanaka, A. Yamamoto (Eds.), Discovery Science. Proceedings, 2003. XII, 504 pages. 2003. (Subseries LNAI).

Vol. 2842: R. Gavaldá, K.P. Jantke, E. Takimoto (Eds.), Algorithmic Learning Theory. Proceedings, 2003. XI, 313 pages. 2003. (Subseries LNAI).

Vol. 2841: C. Blundo, C. Laneve (Eds.), Theoretical Computer Science. Proceedings, 2003. XI, 397 pages. 2003.

Vol. 2840: J. Dongarra, D. Laforenza, S. Orlando (Eds.), Recent Advances in Parallel Virtual Machine and Message Passing Interface. Proceedings, 2003. XVIII, 693 pages. 2003.

Vol. 2839: A. Marshall, N. Agoulmine (Eds.), Management of Multimedia Networks and Services. Proceedings, 2003. XIV, 532 pages. 2003.

Vol. 2838: N. Lavrač, D. Gamberger, L. Todorovski, H. Blockeel (Eds.), Knowledge Discovery in Databases: PKDD 2003. Proceedings, 2003. XVI, 508 pages. 2003. (Subseries LNAI).

Vol. 2837: N. Lavrač, D. Gamberger, L. Todorovski, H. Blockeel (Eds.), Machine Learning: ECML 2003. Proceedings, 2003. XVI, 504 pages. 2003. (Subseries LNAI).

Vol. 2836: S. Qing, D. Gollmann, J. Zhou (Eds.), Information and Communications Security. Proceedings, 2003. XI, 416 pages. 2003.

Vol. 2835: T. Horváth, A. Yamamoto (Eds.), Inductive Logic Programming. Proceedings, 2003. X, 401 pages. 2003. (Subseries LNAI).

Vol. 2834: X. Zhou, M. Xu, S. Jähnichen, J. Cao (Eds.), Advanced Parallel Processing Technologies. Proceedings, 2003. XIV, 679 pages. 2003.

Vol. 2833: F. Rossi (Eds.), Principles and Practice of Constraint Programming – CP 2003. Proceedings, 2003. XIX, 1005 pages. 2003.

Vol. 2832: G.D. Battista, U. Zwick (Eds.), Algorithms - ESA 2003. Proceedings, 2003. XIV, 790 pages. 2003.